Emerging Trends, Global Perspectives, and Systemic Transformation in AI

Viktor Wang
California State University, San Bernardino, USA

IGI Global
Scientific Publishing
Publishing Tomorrow's Research Today

Vice President of Editorial	Melissa Wagner
Director of Acquisitions	Mikaela Felty
Director of Book Development	Jocelynn Hessler
Production Manager	Mike Brehm
Cover Design	Jose Rosado

Published in the United States of America by
IGI Global Scientific Publishing
701 East Chocolate Avenue
Hershey, PA, 17033, USA
Tel: 717-533-8845
Fax: 717-533-7115
Website: https://www.igi-global.com E-mail: cust@igi-global.com

Library of Congress Cataloging-in-Publication Data

Names: Wang, Viktor editor
Title: Emerging trends, global perspectives, and systemic transformation in AI / edited by: Viktor Wang.
Description: Hershey, PA : IGI Global Scientific Publishing, [2026] | Includes bibliographical references. | Summary: "This book explores global case studies, institutional change, and system-wide adoption of AI tools across learning environments"-- Provided by publisher.
Identifiers: LCCN 2025026913 (print) | LCCN 2025026914 (ebook) | ISBN 9798337351025 hardcover | ISBN 9798337351032 paperback | ISBN 9798337351049 ebook
Subjects: LCSH: Artificial intelligence--Educational applications | Education--Data processing | Computer-assisted instruction
Classification: LCC LB1028.43 .E4476 2026 (print) | LCC LB1028.43 (ebook)
LC record available at https://lccn.loc.gov/2025026913
LC ebook record available at https://lccn.loc.gov/2025026914

British Cataloguing in Publication Data
A Cataloguing in Publication record for this book is available from the British Library.

Table of Contents

Detailed Table of Contents

formative assessments, supported by data analytics, ensures personalized learning. Integrating SCL with technology creates inclusive, flexible learning environments that prepare students for 21st-century challenges.

In this paper, curriculum enhancement and methods of evaluation for students through the application of artificial intelligence (AI) is discussed. It starts by describing the history of educational technology, the developments made and trends observed in modern learning environment. AI is discussed as applied to curricula, with a focus on the role of embedment in establishing individual learning trajectories. Examples of institutions that have implemented AI to support curation and learners' assessment are illustrated with enhanced learning interests and outcomes. The paper also highlights issues such as ethical implication, data privacy, and organizational AI skepticism. Last but not the least its focus on way forward for these challenges and captured the essence of the collective responsibilities of educators, policy makers and technology developers to unleash the true beauty of the AI in education.

This chapter investigates the profound influence of Artificial Intelligence (AI) on education, highlighting its role in transforming teaching strategies, student engagement, and personalized learning. It explores various AI-driven technologies, including machine learning, natural language processing (NLP), intelligent tutoring systems, and predictive analytics, which are reshaping the educational landscape. By enabling adaptive learning, personalized instruction, and improved accessibility, AI has the potential to make education more efficient and inclusive. However, the chapter also addresses key challenges, such as data privacy, algorithmic bias, and the digital divide, emphasizing the need for ethical and responsible AI implementation. Aimed at educators, policymakers, and researchers, this chapter provides a comprehensive analysis of AI's impact on modern education and the critical considerations for its integration.

This chapter will explore the role of artificial intelligence (AI) in data-driven decision-making within educational settings, highlighting how AI can enhance the process of collecting, analyzing, and interpreting vast amounts of data to inform strategic choices. By leveraging AI-powered tools, educators and administrators can gain deeper insights into student performance, engagement, attendance, and other critical metrics, enabling more informed, timely, and personalized decisions. The chapter will examine the benefits of AI in improving educational outcomes, such as identifying at-risk students, optimizing resource allocation, and supporting evidence-based policy development. Additionally, it will address the challenges and ethical considerations associated with using AI for decision-making, including data privacy, algorithmic bias, and the need for transparency and accountability.

This chapter will explore the potential of artificial intelligence (AI) to streamline and automate administrative tasks in educational settings, enhancing operational efficiency and allowing educators to focus more on teaching and student engagement. It will examine the types of administrative functions that can be automated, such as grading, scheduling, data management, and communication, and how AI technologies can reduce the time and effort required for these tasks. The chapter will also discuss the benefits of automation in improving accuracy, consistency, and decision-making processes within educational institutions. Additionally, it will address the challenges of implementing AI solutions, including concerns about data privacy, the need for adequate training, and the potential for resistance to change. Through case studies and examples, this chapter will demonstrate how AI can transform administrative operations, ultimately contributing to a more efficient, effective, and student-centered educational environment.

This chapter examines the transformative role of AI-powered tutoring systems in redefining student support through personalized, scalable, and adaptive learning experiences. The discussion highlights their capacity to identify knowledge gaps,

Foreword

Higher education is entering an era defined not only by digital transformation, but by the challenge of ensuring that innovation serves institutional integrity, data-informed practice, and learner success. This book, edited by Dr. Viktor Wang, arrives at a critical juncture—one in which artificial intelligence (AI) is no longer theoretical, but fully embedded in our educational ecosystems.

My experience in educational statistics and university leadership has shown me that effective change depends not just on adopting new technologies, but on grounding those technologies in evidence, ethics, and systemic insight. Dr. Wang's work embodies this balance. His volume does not chase trends; it carefully curates global voices and emerging frameworks that allow educators and administrators to make informed, strategic decisions in AI adoption and implementation.

This book stands apart in its clarity, breadth, and commitment to real-world application. From adaptive learning systems to policy implications and workforce readiness, the chapters push beyond abstraction. They ask the questions institutions must now confront: How do we ensure equity in algorithmic design? What does AI literacy look like across disciplines? How can universities harness data responsibly while preserving student trust?

Dr. Wang has brought together a global network of contributors—researchers, practitioners, and visionaries—who challenge the status quo and offer concrete steps for academic leadership. Their insights reinforce a fundamental truth: AI must enhance—not replace—human decision-making. It must support—not displace—the values of transparency, collaboration, and lifelong learning.

I commend this book to my colleagues across the higher education landscape. This volume provides both the theoretical foundation and practical tools necessary for rethinking instruction, improving student support systems, and aligning innovation with mission. In doing so, it will help shape a future in which AI serves education—not the other way around.

Sean W. Mulvenon

University of Nevada, Las Vegas, USA

Preface

INTRODUCTION

The idea for this book, *Emerging Trends, Global Perspectives, and Systemic Transformation in AI*, emerged from the convergence of two lifelong passions: my dedication to advancing adult, career, and higher education, and my deep curiosity about the potential of artificial intelligence to reshape the ways we teach, learn, and lead. As an educator, researcher, and mentor with more than two decades of global academic engagement, I have had the privilege of witnessing—and contributing to—many waves of educational reform. Yet none has been as rapid, as disruptive, or as full of possibility as the current era of AI innovation.

My academic foundation is rooted in one of the most influential departments in the history of adult education—the Department of Vocational and Adult Education at the University of Arkansas, where I earned both my doctoral degree in education and a master's degree in educational technology. This is the same department where the late Dr. Malcolm Knowles, the father of andragogy, taught until his passing in 1997. It is a profound honor to have graduated from a department so deeply connected to the origins of adult learning theory. I have proudly carried Dr. Knowles' torch of andragogical leadership forward, guiding research across disciplines and continents, and advancing his legacy through my own teaching, writing, and mentorship.

To date, I have published over 240 refereed works, including approximately 80 volumes of scholarly books. My publications are held in the libraries of leading universities such as Stanford, New York University, and Princeton, a testament to their relevance and scholarly impact. I have had the privilege of publishing articles and book chapters authored by some of the most respected figures in the field of education, including Dr. Stephen Brookfield. Furthermore, my *Encyclopedia of Strategic Leadership and Management* drew contributions from over 300 scholars worldwide, reflecting a truly global conversation around leadership and learning in a changing world.

I also take great pride in my long-standing relationship with Dr. John A. Henschke, one of Malcolm Knowles' own doctoral students and a towering figure in his own right. Dr. Henschke has been both a mentor and a friend, and it is with deep gratitude that I acknowledge his contribution of a foreword to this volume. His lifelong dedication to andragogical principles and international education has deeply shaped my thinking and my work.

The inspiration for this work also draws from a career in teaching that spans continents. I have had the distinct honor of teaching in both China and across many states in the United States, including California, Florida, Arizona, and Montana. My classrooms have included doctoral candidates, educational leaders, adult learners, and pre-service teachers—all eager to make sense of the complexities of learning in the 21st century. Across all these settings, a common thread emerged: the desire to understand how technology, when guided by values and vision, can support deeper, more inclusive learning experiences.

This book is the result of ongoing conversations with colleagues, students, institutional leaders, and policymakers from around the world. It is built upon decades of work in instructional leadership, curriculum development, and the integration of andragogical principles in both physical and virtual learning environments. Over time, I began to realize that while AI was gaining traction in the fields of industry, healthcare, and business, its application in education was often misunderstood, oversimplified, or siloed. There was—and still is—a need for thoughtful, ethical, and strategically guided exploration of what AI can actually do to support and uplift teaching and learning.

My intent with this book is not to celebrate technology for its own sake. Rather, it is to invite educators, leaders, and learners into a dialogue about how AI can be used to advance the values we hold most dear: access, inclusion, equity, adaptability, and lifelong learning. I firmly believe that AI tools, when integrated intentionally and reflectively, can serve as catalysts for educational transformation—not only enhancing instructional efficiency, but also deepening human connection and creativity in ways that support the full spectrum of learning.

ORGANIZATION OF THE BOOK

The book is organized into several volumes, each focused on a specific aspect of AI in education—from practical tools and case studies to theoretical frameworks and future-facing models of leadership. The contributors to this work represent a wide range of disciplines and global perspectives. Together, we aim to highlight both the promise and the limitations of AI, always with the understanding that technology must serve human development—not replace it.

Chapter 1: Evaluation of Artificial Intelligence Applications for Foreign Language Learning in the Context of Skills, Gamification, and Interaction

In this opening chapter, we explore the dynamic interplay between artificial intelligence, gamification, and foreign language acquisition. The authors critically examine 29 AI-powered applications, focusing on their effectiveness across core language skills—speaking, listening, reading, and writing—and their support for various forms of learner interaction. Particularly noteworthy is the strong emphasis on speaking and listening, with over 60% of applications demonstrating high performance in these areas. However, the chapter also points to a relative underperformance in writing support and limited engagement in teacher-learner and peer-to-peer interaction. Through a detailed analysis of tools like Gliglish, eigo.ai, Rosetta Stone, and Babbel, this chapter calls for more balanced and inclusive AI designs, advocating for enhanced feedback mechanisms and deeper gamified engagement strategies.

Chapter 2: Innovative Approaches to Revolutionize Student-Centered Learning in the 21st Century

This chapter presents a compelling case for revolutionizing Student-Centered Learning (SCL) by integrating forward-thinking pedagogical approaches with cutting-edge technologies. From competency-based and experiential learning to the strategic use of AI, virtual reality, and adaptive platforms, the authors illustrate how 21st-century learners benefit from personalized, active engagement. While the transformative potential is clear, the chapter also identifies critical obstacles, including infrastructure disparities and the need for professional development. Emphasizing institutional support and data-informed formative assessment, this chapter champions a learner-centric paradigm shift that prepares students for a rapidly evolving world.

Chapter 3: AI in Education: Shaping Curriculum and Student Assessment

Focusing on the integration of artificial intelligence into curriculum development and student assessment, this chapter traces the trajectory of educational technology and its current manifestations in learning environments. Through real-world examples, the authors illustrate how AI enables personalized learning pathways and enhances academic outcomes. Yet, this advancement is not without ethical and practical concerns—data privacy, institutional resistance, and the need for transparent governance remain pressing issues. Ultimately, the chapter envisions a collaborative path forward, where educators, policymakers, and developers unite to responsibly harness AI's transformative power in education.

Chapter 4: Transforming Education: The Role of AI Tools in Shaping Personalized and Inclusive Learning

This chapter offers a comprehensive overview of how AI technologies are reshaping educational experiences to be more personalized, accessible, and inclusive. Highlighting innovations such as machine learning algorithms, natural language processing, and intelligent tutoring systems, the authors discuss how these tools enhance instructional delivery and student engagement. Alongside these benefits, the chapter tackles significant challenges, including algorithmic bias, digital inequality, and privacy concerns. The authors call for responsible implementation, urging stakeholders to adopt ethical frameworks and equitable policies as AI continues to redefine the future of learning.

Chapter 5: AI and Arts Education: Creative Possibilities

In this thought-provoking chapter, the intersection of artificial intelligence and arts education is explored with a focus on creative enrichment and pedagogical innovation. By revisiting the historical roots of arts instruction and juxtaposing them with AI's capabilities, the authors illustrate how machine learning, generative design, and interactive technologies can expand the horizons of music, visual arts, and performance. Through detailed case studies, the chapter underscores AI's role not as a replacement for creativity but as a powerful collaborator, fostering novel artistic expressions and dynamic learning environments.

Chapter 6: Personalized Learning Through AI: The Power of Tailored Education

Chapter 6 delves into the heart of AI's promise for education—personalization. The authors examine how AI applications can deliver instruction that aligns with each learner's pace, style, and goals. Machine learning algorithms provide predictive insights that inform targeted interventions and adaptive content delivery. As institutions seek to move beyond standardized instruction, this chapter makes a compelling case for tailored education strategies that drive engagement and improve learner outcomes. It also highlights the broader implications for curriculum design and learning and development (L&D) practices in both academic and corporate settings.

Chapter 7: Revolutionizing Fashion Education with Integrating AI and 3D Design for a Sustainable Future

This chapter presents a groundbreaking look at the convergence of AI, 3D design, and fashion education, emphasizing the sector's shift toward sustainability and innovation. By leveraging virtual prototyping and intelligent design tools, students are empowered to create and iterate without physical waste, significantly reducing environmental impact. The chapter explores how AI supports trend forecasting, circular economy models, and efficient production systems, preparing future designers to navigate a tech-driven, eco-conscious industry. Through this lens, fashion education becomes a catalyst for broader societal change and interdisciplinary learning.

Chapter 8: Revolutionizing Vocational Education: Harnessing Transformational AI Tools for Enhanced Learning and Skill Development

This chapter takes readers to the forefront of vocational education reform, where artificial intelligence is enabling a paradigm shift in how practical skills are developed and applied. By integrating adaptive learning platforms, AI-driven simulations, and intelligent career guidance systems, vocational training becomes more personalized, efficient, and aligned with real-world industry needs. The authors examine both the promise and the pitfalls of these technologies, including the challenges of accessibility, data ethics, and the importance of human oversight. The chapter presents AI not merely as a tool, but as a transformative force that can reimagine vocational education for a future-ready workforce.

Chapter 9: AI for Data-Driven Decision Making in Education

In this data-rich era, education systems are turning to artificial intelligence to support smarter, evidence-based decision-making. This chapter explores how AI technologies empower educators and administrators to collect, interpret, and act on vast quantities of student and institutional data. From predicting at-risk students to guiding policy development and optimizing resource use, AI is positioned as a critical ally in educational leadership. Yet, the authors also stress the importance of ethical guardrails—transparency, fairness, and data privacy must underpin these data-driven advancements to ensure trust and accountability in AI-assisted decision-making.

Chapter 10: Automating Administrative Tasks with AI Efficiency in Education

Here, the focus shifts to the often-overlooked but essential dimension of education: administration. This chapter explores how AI streamlines repetitive tasks like grading, scheduling, data handling, and communication, thereby enhancing operational efficiency and enabling educators to devote more time to teaching. Through case studies and practical examples, the authors show how automation not only increases accuracy but also transforms the management of educational institutions. While the benefits are substantial, the chapter also highlights implementation barriers—ranging from training needs to cultural resistance—calling for thoughtful strategies to integrate AI solutions responsibly and effectively.

Chapter 11: AI-Powered Tutoring: Enhancing Student Support

This chapter delves into the growing influence of AI-powered tutoring systems, which are redefining student support with adaptive, individualized learning pathways. By identifying knowledge gaps, accommodating different paces, and offering real-time feedback, these systems enhance academic outcomes and promote learner autonomy. However, the authors do not shy away from ethical concerns, emphasizing the need for human oversight, inclusive design, and data protection. This balanced exploration encourages a future where AI tutors serve not as replacements, but as partners in a holistic educational ecosystem.

Chapter 12: Professors in Transition: The Impact of Commodification and AI on Higher Education

The landscape of higher education is shifting, and this chapter critically examines the dual pressures of marketization and technological disruption on the academic profession. As AI tools reshape how knowledge is disseminated and learning is assessed, the traditional role of professors as scholars and public intellectuals is being challenged. The chapter explores how universities' increasing reliance on AI for administrative and instructional purposes reflects broader neoliberal trends, raising urgent questions about academic labor, autonomy, and the soul of higher education. It offers a clarion call to rethink the professoriate's role in defending the university's mission as a space for critical inquiry and societal advancement.

Chapter 13: AI for Formative and Summative Assessment: A Balanced Approach

In this chapter, readers are invited to explore the complex terrain of AI-enhanced assessment. The authors present a compelling case for how AI can improve formative practices through real-time feedback and personalized support, while also making summative evaluations more efficient and consistent. Yet, with these benefits come new responsibilities: safeguarding against bias, ensuring transparency, and preserving the human connection in student assessment. The chapter calls for a balanced approach, integrating AI as a complement to educator expertise in order to advance fair, ethical, and impactful evaluation strategies.

Chapter 14: Artificial Intelligence in Education: Supporting Diverse Learning Styles and Addressing Ethical Considerations

Closing this section, the final chapter focuses on AI's capacity to honor learner diversity while reinforcing ethical educational practice. Drawing from established pedagogical theories, the authors explore how AI-driven tools can support multiple learning styles and promote inclusive, student-centered teaching. Intelligent systems capable of adapting to learners' preferences and needs hold promise for increasing accessibility and engagement. However, this chapter also emphasizes the importance of aligning AI integration with Universal Design for Learning principles and global ethical standards. It affirms the enduring value of human guidance in education, advocating for thoughtful partnerships between technology and pedagogy.

CONCLUSION

It is no coincidence that this work includes contributions from educators and thought leaders across continents. We are in a moment of global transformation, and our responses must be equally global. AI is not a trend—it is an inflection point. And the choices we make now, as educators and institutions, will determine whether we amplify opportunity or exacerbate inequality. This book is a humble offering in service of the former.

I would like to express my deepest gratitude to my co-authors, contributors, reviewers, and institutional partners who have supported this project. Your insights and commitment have shaped every chapter. I also want to thank the students and doctoral candidates I've mentored over the years—you continue to inspire me with your questions, your resilience, and your determination to make education more inclusive and more effective for future generations.

I also wish to extend my heartfelt appreciation to IGI Global, the publisher of this volume, for their enduring commitment to scholarly excellence and their support in bringing this multi-volume work to fruition. Their dedication to disseminating transformative research in education and leadership has been instrumental throughout this process.

Special thanks are also due to the many reviewers whose critical feedback helped refine the clarity, depth, and coherence of the chapters included. Your thoughtful engagement enriched the work in ways too numerous to count.

To the global network of contributors who lent their voices, perspectives, and expertise—thank you. Your diverse insights and dedication to educational advancement have shaped this book into a truly international and collaborative effort.

Finally, I wish to express deep gratitude to the university libraries around the world—including Stanford University, New York University, and Princeton University—that continue to catalog and share my work. Your support ensures that knowledge remains accessible, visible, and impactful for future generations of learners and researchers.

To the readers: whether you are a faculty member rethinking your curriculum, a dean or provost leading systemic change, a policymaker designing new frameworks, or a student exploring the frontiers of digital learning—I hope you find in these pages not only knowledge, but encouragement. This is your invitation to engage, to question, and to lead. The future of education is not just about digital tools or predictive algorithms—it's about the people who wield them with wisdom and care.

In closing, I offer this book as both a scholarly resource and a starting point for transformation. May it spark ideas, challenge assumptions, and serve as a guide for all who believe in the power of education to shape a better, more equitable world—onelearner, one classroom, one innovation at a time.

This book, *Emerging Trends, Global Perspectives, and Systemic Transformation in AI,* explores global case studies, institutional change, and system-wide adoption of AI tools across learning environments. As the concluding volume, it invites readers to look outward—toward international collaborations, emergent innovations, and the broader educational ecosystems being reshaped by ethical AI integration.

Viktor Wang

California State University, San Bernardino, USA

Chapter 1
Evaluation of Artificial Intelligence Applications for Foreign Language Learning in the Context of Skills, Gamification, and Interaction

Serap Sisman-Ugur
https://orcid.org/0000-0002-4211-1396
Anadolu University, Turkey

İlke Altun
Namık Kemal Ortaokulu, Turkey

Süheyla Ander
Anadolu University, Turkey

Güzin Başdemir
https://orcid.org/0009-0005-7282-1371
Anadolu University, Turkey

ABSTRACT

This study examines the role of AI and gamification in foreign language learning, analyzing 29 AI-driven applications based on their support for speaking, listening, reading, and writing, as well as interaction types. Findings show that speaking and listening are the most supported skills (over 60% rated "high"), while writing

DOI: 10.4018/979-8-3373-5102-5.ch001

receives less emphasis. Gamification enhances engagement, particularly in learner-content and learner-interface interactions, but lacks sufficient teacher-learner and learner-learner engagement. Notable applications like Gliglish and eigo.ai perform well across all skills using multimodal AI, while Rosetta Stone and Babbel provide comprehensive interaction frameworks. The study highlights the need for balanced interaction strategies, recommending improved AI-driven feedback for writing, expanded gamification, and further research on long-term learning impacts.

INTRODUCTION

Artificial intelligence (AI) applications, emerging and evolving with technological advancements, are now integral to various professional fields and everyday activities. From academic tools like online courses and videos to banking, transportation, and entertainment systems, AI has become a transformative force in modern life (Komalavalli et al., 2020). In educational contexts, particularly in foreign language education, AI has opened new avenues for independent and interactive learning by offering personalized learning experiences, adaptive feedback, and real-time interaction (Huang et al., 2022). However, AI tools vary in their capabilities; some rely on predictive AI models that use rule-based algorithms, while others employ generative AI models that enable real-time, context-aware interaction (IBM, 2024).

Among AI-based technologies, chatbots powered by natural language processing (NLP) systems have become particularly effective tools in language education. AI-driven chatbots simulate human communication through text or voice-based interactions (Shevat, 2017) and continuously refine their responses through learning-based interaction (Haristiani, 2019). These features make AI chatbots highly valuable in foreign language education, where authentic dialogue, contextual learning, and real-time feedback are critical components of skill development.

The purpose of this study is to evaluate AI-supported language learning applications in terms of their effectiveness in improving language skills, fostering interaction, and utilizing gamification strategies. By systematically analyzing 29 widely-used AI-powered applications, this research aims to identify their strengths and limitations in facilitating speaking, listening, reading, and writing skills, as well as their capacity to support different types of learner interactions and engagement mechanisms.The concept of AI traces back to the mid-20th century, with milestones such as Turing's (1950) exploration of machine thinking and the Dartmouth Conference in 1956 that laid the foundation for AI research. Over time, AI applications like Eliza, Parry, and more recently, A.L.I.C.E have advanced human-machine interaction capabilities, forming the basis for modern educational tools (Belda-Medina and Ferrer, 2022). These developments have particularly influenced language education, where AI applications offer authentic dialogs and opportunities for practice anytime and anywhere, independent of the teacher (Tyen et al, 2022).

Despite their growing prevalence, research on AI tools' specific impact on core language skills—reading, writing, listening, and speaking—remains limited. Moreover, the interaction types facilitated by these applications, as conceptualized in Moore's Interaction Framework (student-content, student-teacher, and student-student), are yet to be fully explored. This study addresses these gaps by examining the top 50 most-used AI-powered language learning applications, evaluating their contributions to core language skills and interaction dynamics.

Artificial Intelligence Applications in Foreign Language Learning

Effective communication in a foreign language is a fundamental skill in today's interconnected world, where cross-cultural interactions and multilingual competence are increasingly valued. To achieve this, learners must develop four essential language skills: listening, reading, speaking, and writing. These skills form the backbone of language acquisition, and neglecting any one of them can lead to communicative deficiencies. As such, language teaching aims to foster balanced development across all four skills. AI applications have emerged as a powerful tool in language education, offering adaptive learning environments that cater to individual learner needs and pace (Imran et al., 2023). Traditional language instruction often faces challenges in ensuring balanced skill development, and AI-powered applications address this by providing personalized learning paths and real-time feedback, optimizing engagement and learning outcomes.

Research on AI-assisted language learning suggests that predictive AI tools, such as Duolingo and Babbel, primarily support structured language acquisition by tracking learners' progress and adjusting lesson difficulty accordingly (Jeon, 2021). These applications employ statistical models and pre-defined rules to optimize learning paths (Unite.ai, 2024). However, their ability to provide real-time, personalized feedback remains limited.

While predictive AI relies on structured, rule-based models for optimizing learning paths (Jeon, 2021), generative AI facilitates interactive, real-time engagement by producing human-like responses (Huang et al., 2022). Applications such as ChatGPT-based platforms and Gliglish leverage large language models (LLMs) to generate natural language responses, enhancing real-time interaction and enabling dynamic learning experiences. These applications engage users in meaningful conversations and provide immediate corrective feedback, fostering a more immersive language learning environment. Nevertheless, concerns regarding their accuracy and contextual understanding persist (Öztürk, 2023).

While AI tools provide personalized and adaptive language instruction, sustaining learner engagement remains a crucial challenge. To address this, gamification strategies have been widely integrated into AI-driven language learning platforms. Research indicates that gamification elements, such as points, badges, and leaderboards, enhance motivation and learning retention (Özdemir & Karaca, 2023). However, these features are not consistently implemented across all AI applications, leading to variability in learner engagement.

Supporting Language Skills

Traditional language teaching methods often face challenges, such as limited resources and linguistic barriers, that hinder the effective teaching of language skills. AI-based technological applications have mitigated these barriers, making foreign language education more efficient and accessible. For instance, studies comparing AI-based teaching tools with traditional methods have found that students using AI tools show greater improvement in language skills (Huang et al, 2022). AI technologies, such as speaking recognition and machine learning, are particularly promising for their ability to provide immediate, personalized feedback (De la Vall & Atraya, 2023; Jeon, 2021).

Listening and speaking skills benefit significantly from AI-powered systems that enable real-time interaction and error correction. Similarly, writing skills improve through AI tools that provide iterative feedback, allowing learners to refine their output (Abdullayeva & Musayeva, 2023; Liu et al., 2021). Reading skills, though less discussed, also gain from AI's capacity to tailor content difficulty to individual learner levels.

Chatbots represent a significant advancement in AI-driven language learning. These systems simulate human-like interactions, enabling learners to practice the target language in a stress-free environment. Studies have shown that chatbots reduce language anxiety, provide effective feedback, and allow learners to repeat activities as needed (Fryer & Carpenter, 2006; Haristani, 2019). For example, Shawar (2017) found that students enjoy using chatbots due to their multimodal capabilities and the novelty they bring to language practice.

In the digital era, language learning has transitioned from traditional classroom settings to technology-based platforms. Gamification, a pedagogical approach incorporating game design elements such as points, badges, leaderboards, and challenges, has gained traction in foreign language education. Research indicates that gamification enhances learner engagement and fosters intrinsic motivation by transforming learning into a more enjoyable experience (Deterding et al., 2011).

Gamification applications in language learning are diverse, ranging from mobile apps to online platforms. Popular tools such as Duolingo and Memrise leverage gamified elements to teach vocabulary, grammar, and pronunciation. Key benefits include:

1. **Increased Motivation**: Gamification transforms repetitive tasks like vocabulary drills into engaging challenges.
2. **Immediate Feedback**: Points and badges provide instant gratification, reinforcing learning outcomes.
3. **Active Engagement**: Leaderboards and social competition encourage learners to actively participate and progress.

However, the effectiveness of gamification depends on its alignment with pedagogical goals. Overemphasis on rewards can shift focus from meaningful learning to superficial task completion (Sailer et al., 2017).

Interaction in Applications

The rise of online and distance education, particularly through AI-based platforms, has underscored the relevance of Moore's interaction theories in educational technology. Moore (1973) introduced the transactional distance theory, emphasizing that the "distance" in education is not merely geographic but also psychological and pedagogical. Transactional distance is shaped by three factors: dialogue, structure, and autonomy. Dialogue refers to the two-way communication between the learner and the instructor; structure pertains to course design elements that address individual learner needs; and autonomy reflects the learner's control over their educational goals and methods (Moore, 1983 and 1993).

Moore (1989) identified three primary interaction types—learner-teacher, learner-content, and learner-learner interactions—fundamental to effective language acquisition. With technological advancements, Hillman et al. (1994) introduced a fourth category: learner-interface interaction, which is particularly relevant in AI-based learning environments

AI-enabled tools offer diverse opportunities for enhancing interactions in language learning. These tools include applications like Duolingo, Busuu, Grammarly, Write & Improve, and Google Translate, which provide tailored feedback, adaptive content, and multimodal learning experiences (Hockly, 2023). For instance, Duolingo, with over 100 million users globally in 2018, has revolutionized language learning through gamification and adaptive algorithms (Kannan et al., 2018; Underwood, 2017).

Each tool facilitates unique interaction types:

- **Student-Content Interaction**: Duolingo and Babbel provide learners with structured lessons and quizzes to engage with content.
- **Student-Teacher Interaction**: Tools like Grammarly offer AI-based feedback, mimicking the role of an instructor.
- **Student-Student Interaction**: Applications such as Quizlet promote collaborative learning through shared resources and group activities.
- **Learner-Interface Interaction**: AI tools like Write & Improve and Google Translate exemplify interactions where learners directly engage with technological systems to enhance skills.

Despite their widespread use, limited research exists on how these tools align with Moore's interaction framework in addressing transactional distance and supporting language skill development.

Research Gap and Objectives

While the literature underscores AI's potential in enhancing individual language skills, limited attention has been given to how these applications facilitate interaction types, as outlined in Moore's Interaction Framework. This study aims to bridge this gap by analyzing AI-powered language learning applications' contributions to interaction dynamics and skill development.

Existing studies have explored the role of mobile applications in language learning (Şenel et al., 2019; Tılıç, 2016; Yaman, 2016; Yıldırım, 2012). However, research on AI-powered language learning applications remains sparse, particularly in the context of interaction types and skill development. This study seeks to address these gaps by examining:

1. What modes of interaction (student-teacher, student-content, student-student, learner-interface) are facilitated by AI applications in language learning?
2. How do these applications contribute to the development of specific language skills (listening, reading, speaking, writing)?
3. How do AI applications address transactional distance in language learning environments?
4. Which interaction types are more supported in applications involving gamification?
5. Which skills are supported more in applications that include gamification?

METHOD

This study aims to evaluate artificial intelligence applications used in foreign language learning in terms of their contributions to language skills and interaction types. The research adopts a qualitative descriptive design to provide a detailed understanding of these applications. This approach was chosen to explore the specific features, outcomes, and interaction types of AI tools without aiming for generalization to a broader population. Descriptive studies are generally used to describe the sample with descriptive statistics such as mean and percentage, but these studies are not used to make inferences about the population (Grimes & Schulz, 2002).

Data Collection

The data collection process consisted of the following steps:

Selection of Applications

- AI Integration; applications utilizing AI for language learning.
- A search was conducted using the keywords "artificial intelligence language teaching," "artificial intelligence language learning," and "widely used artificial intelligence applications."
- The Statista list of the top 50 widely used AI applications (accessed March 4, 2024) was used to cross-check and identify relevant tools. This process was completed by March 7, 2024.
- Applications specifically designed for foreign language learning were shortlisted.
- Popularity; minimum 1 million downloads or significant citation in academic research.
- Availability in 2024 with the latest version analyzed.

Evaluation Criteria

The applications were assessed based on four key dimensions:

- Language Skills Support: Evaluated on a three-level scale (Low, Medium, High) for speaking, listening, reading, and writing skills.
- Interaction Types: Based on Moore's Interaction Model (1989): Learner-content, learner-instructor, learner-learner, and learner-interface interactions.
- Gamification Elements: Presence of motivational features such as rewards, challenges, and progress tracking.

- Technical Features: Comparison of free vs. premium versions, usability, and targeted user demographics.

Categorization

- To evaluate the features, outcomes, and interaction types of the applications, three categories with 15 distinct features were identified:

1. Language Learning Skills: Reading, writing, speaking, and listening.
2. Application Features: Subject expression, use of case studies, target age groups, supported languages, usage fees, compatible mobile operating systems, and target languages.
3. Interaction Types: Based on Moore's transactional distance theory (1989) and Hillman et al.'s learner-interface interaction (1994), interactions were classified as:
    - Learner-Learner
    - Learner-Learner/Artificial Intelligence
    - Learner-Content
    - Learner-Interface

Expert Evaluation Process

The assessment was conducted by five experts:

- Three linguists with over 10 years of experience in language education.
- Two educational technology specialists with expertise in AI-driven learning platforms.

The evaluators independently tested each application's free and premium versions for two weeks, followed by a cross-validation session to ensure scoring consistency.

Data Analysis

The analysis involved a detailed evaluation of the applications in terms of the opportunities they provided, the outcomes they achieved, and the interaction types they facilitated. The following steps were followed:

Skill Evaluation

- Each application was rated as "low," "medium," or "high" based on its contribution to language learning skills (reading, writing, speaking, listening).
- These ratings were assigned by field experts with 5, 15, and 18 years of experience in foreign language teaching.

Interaction Type Evaluation

- Interaction types were assessed by distance education experts with 16 and 22 years of experience.
- Ratings were informed by the interaction categories described above.

Application features were analyzed and categorized by the same experts, focusing on their relevance to language learning objectives. To ensure consistency, the evaluations were cross-checked among experts, and discrepancies were resolved through discussion. The findings were synthesized and interpreted by the researchers, integrating insights from the evaluations into the study's narrative.

Limitations

This study is limited by its reliance on publicly available data about the selected applications. Additionally, the subjective nature of expert evaluations introduces potential biases, which were mitigated through cross-checking and collaborative discussions.

FINDINGS AND INTERPRETATIONS

This study analyzed 29 AI-powered language learning applications to evaluate their contributions to language skills (reading, writing, speaking, and listening) and interaction types. A summary of the findings is presented in Tables 1 and 2, highlighting the features and interaction modes of the applications.

The 29 artificial intelligence applications used for language learning and their general information are given in Table 1.

Table 1. Introductory information about the examined foreign language learning applications

No	Name	Informations
1	Duolingo	Duolingo uses artificial intelligence (AI) technology to personalize the language learning process. AI monitors the user's progress and adapts lessons according to their learning needs. For example, if a user is unable to pronounce a word correctly, Duolingo offers them the opportunity to practice more. It also uses language recognition technology to analyze the user's speaking to encourage correct pronunciation. The app's language translation feature helps users understand text and speaking in the target language, and AI also contributes to language content development by creating interactive games and exercises.
2	Rosetta Stone	Rosetta Stone's artificial intelligence (AI) technology is used in many areas, including personalized learning, language recognition and language translation. AI provides a personalized learning experience by tracking users' progress and adapting lessons according to their learning needs.
3	aiLango	The platform can provide 'medium' level support in reading, listening and writing skills and 'high' level support in speaking skills. Users can chat with their AI friends in the language of their choice. AI profiles can be asked questions and receive instant answers. aiLango facilitates language learning with features such as lectures and case studies.
4	Memrise	The application's artificial intelligence technology is used to create a personalized learning experience, allowing users to learn grammar more easily by giving the learned language through expressions used in daily life.
5	Mondly	Mondly uses artificial intelligence (AI) technology in areas such as personalized learning, language recognition, language translation and language content creation. AI provides a personalized learning experience by tracking the user's progress and adapting lessons according to their learning needs. It also analyzes the user's speaking to encourage correct pronunciation and plays a video to show the correct pronunciation when a user mispronounces a word. If a user does not know the meaning of a new word, Mondly provides a translation. AI can also be used to create interactive games and exercises to help users learn new words and phrases.
6	Tutor Lily	Tutor Lily is a language learning platform suitable for users aged 7 and up. It supports 19 different languages. The app supports various language skills such as speaking, listening, reading and writing. Users can practice in a natural speaking environment, read level-appropriate texts and assess their level with comprehension questions. They can also listen to podcasts, follow conversations and assess their comprehension level. Tutor Lily also offers the opportunity to receive feedback on written materials and helps to make the learning process more effective with personalized lesson plans. While the app provides free access to basic features, there is also a paid version that offers more advanced features.
7	Lola Speak	Lola Speak is a language learning platform suitable for users aged 13 and above. It supports 20 different languages. The platform focuses on improving speaking skills and pronunciation. Users can access basic features for free, while more advanced features are available with the premium version. Lola Speak offers an effective and accessible option for language learners to improve their communication skills.
8	Cake	Cake is a language learning platform suitable for users aged 13 and above. It offers support in 2 different languages. The platform provides a high level of speaking skill development support. It offers moderate support for listening, writing and reading skills. Cake facilitates language learning by providing a variety of teaching materials including lectures and case studies. It is available on iOS and Android platforms. Cake is available on the website and offers both a free trial and a more detailed paid option.
9	Busuu	Busuu is an AI-powered language learning app designed to help users aged 13 and up learn a new language. The app supports more than 120 languages. Busuu's AI technology allows users to practice vocabulary, grammar and pronunciation, and personalizes the language learning process, providing lessons that match the user's learning style and speed. Users can also practice pronunciation through audio exercises and receive feedback.

continued on following page

Table 1. Continued

No	Name	Informations
10	Babel	Babbel is an AI-powered language learning app that makes it easy for users aged 13 and above to learn a new language. The app includes 14 languages. It supports effective language learning in vocabulary, grammar and pronunciation. Babbel's artificial intelligence features make the learning process more effective by personalizing the users' learning process by providing lessons through realistic dialogues and colloquial expressions. The application analyzes users' responses and learning progress, allowing for more intensive practice in this area. Babbel helps language learning by making the language learning process more interactive and personalized.
11	Elsa Speak	Elsa Speak is a language learning app suitable for users aged 7 and above. It only offers support in English. The app is good at improving elements of speaking such as correct pronunciation, intonation. The platform provides free access to all its features and is helpful and beneficial for users to improve their speaking and listening skills.
12	Langeek	Langeek is a language learning platform suitable for users aged 13 and above. It supports 18 different languages. For users who want to learn English, the platform offers activities to help users improve their vocabulary and better understand grammar topics. Langeek helps users effectively improve their language skills with a variety of educational materials and activities that facilitate language learning. Langeek offers free access to basic features, while more advanced features are available with a premium account.
13	SpeakingCoach.io	SpeakingCoach.io is a language learning platform suitable for users aged 7 and above. It offers support in 10 different languages. This platform focuses specifically on improving elements of speaking such as correct pronunciation, intonation and stress. SpeakingCoach.io offers users the opportunity to improve their fluency. The platform provides free access to basic features, while more advanced features are available with a premium account. It can only be accessed via the web.
14	Reverso	Reverso is a translation and language learning platform suitable for users aged 13 and above, with support for 15 different languages. In addition to providing text translations, the platform helps users improve their written communication with grammar and spell-checking tools. Available for free, Reverso is ideal for multilingual translation and grammar correction.
15	Lingodeer	Lingodeer is an interactive and comprehensive language learning platform for users aged 7 and above. The platform uses artificial intelligence (AI) technologies to benefit students in various learning areas such as grammar rules, vocabulary, listening and speaking practice. Listening and speaking practice is supported by AI. The use of AI makes the language learning process more effective and personalized.
16	TalkPal	TalkPal allows users to practice speaking in real-life scenarios, get feedback on their pronunciation, and ask grammar and vocabulary questions. It is a language learning app suitable for users aged 13 and above. It supports 57 different languages. While the app provides free access to basic features, more advanced features are available in a premium version. With these features, TalkPal offers an effective and flexible solution for users who want to learn languages.
17	ReadLang	Readlang is a language learning platform suitable for users aged 13 and above. It offers support in many different languages. The platform focuses on improving reading skills. It provides comprehensive vocabulary learning support. Readlang translates words from texts and adds them to the learning list. This platform for vocabulary development helps users learn new words quickly, making the language learning process more effective and efficient. Available on iOS and Android platforms and accessible via the website.
18	Voscreen	Voscreen is a language learning platform suitable for users aged 7 and up. It offers support in various languages. The platform focuses on the development of listening and comprehension skills by supporting English language learning, especially with audio-visual materials. Voscreen uses clips from movies, TV series and other video content to encourage realistic and everyday language use. It is available on both iOS and Android platforms and can also be accessed via the website. Voscreen has a free version and a paid version that offers more features.

continued on following page

Table 1. Continued

No	Name	Informations
19	Falou	Falou is a language learning platform suitable for users aged 7 and up. It supports 22 different languages. The platform offers activities to improve various language skills such as interactive speaking practice, listening materials, reading comprehension activities and analyzing texts. It provides feedback by identifying users' spelling mistakes, grammatical errors and lack of expression. There are free and paid options. With these features, Falou is ideal for users who want to improve their language skills in various languages.
20	Gliglish	Gliglish is a language learning platform suitable for users aged 7 and above. It supports 36 different languages. The platform specifically focuses on improving elements of speaking such as correct pronunciation, intonation and stress. Gliglish is an ideal platform for users to speak more fluently and accurately. The app also supports various language skills such as listening, reading and writing. The app offers free access to basic features, but advanced features are available for a fee. It can only be accessed via the web.
21	Eigo.ai	Eigo.ai is a language learning tool suitable for users aged 7 and above. It offers support in the English language. The platform offers a variety of texts and activities to develop different language skills such as reading activities, listening activities, speaking activities and pronunciation improvement. The ability to receive feedback on written materials is also available in beta. Eigo.ai provides free access to basic features. There is also a paid version that offers more advanced features. Eigo.ai offers an effective and accessible solution for users who want to learn English.
22	DeepL.io	DeepL.io is a language learning platform suitable for users aged 7 and above. It allows users to improve their vocabulary, learn sentence structures and rules, and correct grammar mistakes. With DeepL.io, basic features can be accessed for free. Advanced features are available for a fee. It supports 30 different languages. This platform offers an effective and accessible solution for users who want to learn languages.
23	TinyWow	TinyWow is a language learning tool suitable for users aged 7 and up. It offers support in English. The platform is specifically designed to improve writing skills. All of its features are accessible free of charge, allowing users to effectively improve their English writing skills.
24	LangoTalk	Langotalk is a language learning platform suitable for users aged 7 and above. It supports 19 different languages. The platform offers activities to improve various language skills such as interactive speaking practice, listening materials, reading comprehension activities and analyzing texts. It provides feedback by identifying users' spelling mistakes, grammatical errors and lack of expression. While Langotalk provides free access to basic features, more advanced features are available through a premium option. With these features, Langotalk is effective for users who want to improve their language skills in various languages.
25	Tutor AI	TutorAI is a language learning platform suitable for users aged 13 and above. It offers support in English. The platform offers various reading comprehension activities to assess users' reading skills. TutorAI provides free access to basic features and charges for more advanced features. This platform is particularly suitable for users who want to improve their English reading skills. It can only be accessed via the web.
26	Univerbal	Univerbal is suitable for users aged 13 and above. language learning platform. It supports 22 different languages. The platform is focused on teaching real-life sentence structures, improving oral expression skills through similar scenarios and actively using new vocabulary. Univerbal offers a learning environment where users can practice their language skills in real- world scenarios. The platform provides free access to basic features and charges for more advanced features. With these features, Univerbal is suitable for users who want to learn languages in a variety of languages.

continued on following page

Table 1. Continued

No	Name	Informations
27	italki	italki is an online platform that brings language learners and teachers together. It has teachers in more than 130 languages. The platform personalizes the language learning process by offering one-to-one or group lessons to users over the age of 18 or to their children under their control. italki's use of artificial intelligence plays an important role, especially in the tutor matching process. AI helps users find the most suitable tutor based on their learning goals and preferences. The platform is paid.
28	Ewa	Ewa is a language learning platform suitable for users aged 7 and above. It offers support in various languages. The platform focuses on the development of listening and reading skills by supporting English language learning, especially with audio-visual materials. Ewa encourages realistic and everyday language use by using clips taken from video content. It is available on both iOS and Android platforms. Ewa offers free and premium paid options.
29	Preply	Preply is a language learning platform suitable for users aged 7 and above. It is a platform where users can take one-to-one online lessons with teachers specialized in various subjects. On Preply, users can take lessons in language learning, academic subjects, music, art, sports and many more. On Preply, teachers usually provide information about their language skills, experience and areas of specialization, and students can make their choices based on this information. The platform offers a variety of filtering and evaluation options to facilitate the course-taking process for students. There is a fee.

When Table 1 is analyzed, it can be said that one of the prominent features of the applications is that they offer free access to many options while providing this opportunity to users who want to learn a language at the age of 7 and above who can read and write today. The platforms generally offer a learning experience for more than 1 language. Platforms have been created where speaking, writing, listening and reading skills can be developed with a wide variety of tools, and activities have been organized for the acquisition of all these skills down to the finest details. For example, in speaking skills, Duolingo, Memrise, Mondly, Lola Speak, Elsa Speak, SpeakingCoach.io, Eigo.ai and Gliglish provide feedback and activities for improvement such as correction and repetition in order for the learner to improve in details such as pronunciation and intonation in speaking activities. Kushmar et al. (2022) stated that artificial intelligence significantly improves the quality of language learning by adapting to the individual characteristics, goals and objectives of each learner. In this study, Duolingo, Rosetta Stone, Memrise, Mondly, Busuu, Babbel, Lingodeer and italki were found to offer a personalized learning experience to foreign language learners in line with their goals and performance with the support of artificial intelligence. The common feature of all the apps is that there are both free versions and paid versions that are more detailed and have more features. When the audience of the apps was analyzed, it was found that 16 apps served users aged 7 and above, 12 apps served users aged 13 and above, and one of the apps was an app that could only be used by those aged 18 and above and could offer lessons to children of all ages under the control of these people. When the general structure of the applications is analyzed, it is seen that 26 of them use artificial intelligence as a supporting element and 3 applications offer education with artificial intelligence support. This situation can be interpreted as that the applications prefer artificial intelligence to personalize the services they offer according to the needs of the users. In a study conducted to determine artificial intelligence-based interactions in foreign language teaching software in the context of human-computer interaction, it was concluded that such applications should be supported with audio and visual elements and recognition engines and algorithms should be developed to identify audio input (Alyaz, 2003). It is thought that the reasons why the applications examined in this study offer content for audiences who have completed the physical development of the language and why their use in the role of instructor is currently low are due to the development needs stated by Alyaz (2003).

In addition, it is seen in Table 1 that 2 of the applications examined offered games. Although there are many studies in the literature on the use of games in foreign language learning, there are also studies indicating that the use of games improves especially reading and listening skills (Kazu et al., 2022).

In the analysis of the data related to the question "Which types of transmission are used in presenting information in artificial intelligence applications that can be used in foreign language learning?", these applications were categorized and evaluated according to their features such as subject expression, case study, age groups, supported languages, usage fee, available mobile operating systems and target languages. The findings are given in Table 2.

Table 2. Characteristics of the transfers in the foreign language learning applications analyzed

No	Application	Gamification	Subject Description	Case Example	Age Groups	Supported Language	Mobile Operating Systems
1	Duolingo	Yes	Yes	Yes	7+	41 different languages	ios/android
2	Rosetta Stone	Yes	Yes	Yes	13+	24 different languages	ios/android
3	aiLango	None	Yes	Yes	13+	40 different languages	ios/android
4	Memrise	Yes	Yes	Yes	7+	10 different languages	ios/android
5	Mondly	Yes	Yes	Yes	7+	33 different languages	ios/android
6	Tutor Lily	None	Yes	Yes	7+	19 different languages	ios/android
7	Lola Speak	Yes	None	None	13+	20 different languages	ios/android

continued on following page

Table 2. Continued

No	Application	Gamification	Subject Description	Case Example	Age Groups	Supported Language	Mobile Operating Systems
8	Cake	Yes	Yes	Yes	13+	2 different languages	ios/android
9	Busuu	Yes	Yes	Yes	13+	14 different languages	ios/android
10	Babel	Yes	Yes	Yes	13+	13 different languages	ios/android
11	Elsa Speak	Yes	Yes	Yes	7+	9 different languages	ios/android
12	Langeek	None	Yes	Yes	13+	18 different languages	ios/android
13	SpeakingCoach.io	None	None	None	7+	8 different languages	web
14	Reverso	None	Yes	None	13+	5 different languages	ios/android
15	Lingodeer	Yes	Yes	Yes	7+	12 different languages	ios/android
16	TalkPal	None	Yes	Yes	13+	57 different languages	ios/android
17	ReadLang	None	None	None	13+	61 different languages	ios/android
18	Voscreen	Yes	None	None	7+	21 different languages	ios/android
19	Falou	Yes	None	Yes	7+	20 different languages	ios/android
20	Gliglish	None	None	None	7+	36 different languages	web
21	Eigo.ai	None	None	Yes	7+	2 different languages	web
22	DeepL.io	None	None	None	7+	18 different languages	ios/android
23	TinyWow	None	None	None	7+	unspecified	web
24	LangoTalk	None	None	Yes	7+	19 different languages	ios/adroid
25	Tutor AI	None	None	None	13+	unspecified	web
26	Univerbal	Yes	None	Yes	13+	unspecified	ios/android
27	italki	Yes	Yes	None	7+	150 different languages	ios/android
28	Ewa	Yes	None	None	7+	42 different languages	ios/android
29	Preply	Yes	None	None	7+	10 different languages	ios/android

When Table 2 is examined, it was found that 15 of the applications were conveyed through lectures, while 14 were not conveyed through lectures. While case studies were used in 17 of the interventions, 12 of the interventions did not use case studies. In addition, when the findings are analyzed, it is seen that the delivery method used to present the content is not related to characteristics such as age or the number of languages supported. It is seen that 5 of the analyzed applications are open on the web and 24 of them are open to be accessed from devices with iOS and Android operating systems. This shows that users mostly use these applications from mobile devices. In the light of these findings, it can be concluded that these applications, which provide services to lifelong learners, are structured for these devices to provide a learning experience independent of time and space. 16 applications used gamification, while 13 applications did not. The development and use of games and/or gamification elements for lifelong learning processes is an application in order to reinforce learning and provide learning with fun (Büyük et al., 2018). In the light of this information, it can be said that using gamification in artificial intelligence applications to be developed for language learning will bring positive results. In Table 3, the levels of the foreign language learning applications analyzed in terms of providing acquisition of skills.

Table 3. Characteristics of the transfers in the foreign language learning applications analyzed

No	Application	Gamification	Subject Description	Case Example	Age Groups
1	DUOLINGO	high	high	middle	high
2	ROSETTA STONE	high	high	middle	high
3	aiLango	high	middle	middle	middle
4	MEMRISE	high	high	middle	middle
5	MONDLY	high	middle	middle	middle
6	Tutor Lily	middle	middle	middle	middle
7	LOLA SPEAK	high	high	low	low
8	CAKE	high	middle	middle	middle
9	BUSUU	high	middle	middle	middle
10	BABBEL	middle	middle	middle	middle
11	ELSA	high	high	middle	middle
12	LANGEEK	middle	middle	high	high
13	Speaking Coach.io	high	middle	middle	high
14	REVERSO	low	low	high	high
15	LINGODEER	middle	middle	middle	middle

continued on following page

Table 3. Continued

No	Application	Gamification	Subject Description	Case Example	Age Groups
16	TALK PAL	middle	middle	middle	middle
17	READLANG	low	low	low	high
18	VOSCREEN	low	high	low	high
19	FALOU	high	high	middle	middle
20	gliglish	high	high	high	high
21	eigo.ai	high	high	high	high
22	deepL.ai	high	high	high	low
23	tinywow	low	low	high	middle
24	langotalk	high	high	middle	middle
25	tutorAI	low	low	low	high
26	univerbal (former quazel)	high	middle	middle	middle
27	italki	high	high	middle	middle
28	ewa	low	high	low	high
29	preply	high	high	middle	middle

Applications are highly focused on speaking and listening, with 60% of the applications rated as "high" in these skills. This suggests an emphasis on oral communication, likely supported by AI-driven speaking recognition and feedback technologies (e.g., Duolingo, Elsa, and gliglish). Reading is moderately supported, while writing remains the least prioritized skill. Only a few applications, such as gliglish and eigo.ai, deliver high performance in writing. Gliglish and eigo.ai excel in supporting all four skills at a high level, reflecting their advanced use of multimodal AI technologies. Tools like Reverso and tinywow focus heavily on specific skills (e.g., writing and reading), catering to niche learning needs.

Most applications rated writing as "middle" or "low." Advanced natural language processing (NLP) could enhance this area by offering real-time, context-sensitive feedback. Tools focusing solely on oral skills (e.g., Lola Speak, Falou) could incorporate structured activities for reading and writing to deliver a holistic language learning experience.

Experts recommend diversifying learning paths to ensure equal emphasis on all four skills. A balance between guided learning (e.g., tutorAI) and self-paced learning (e.g., Duolingo) can enhance outcomes. Applications like Mondly and Rosetta Stone effectively leverage AI for personalized learning, which could be expanded to support writing and advanced reading comprehension.

As a result of this analysis, the most powerful acquisition of the artificial intelligence language learning applications examined within the scope of this study came to the fore as speaking skill. This was followed by reading and listening skills, and finally writing skills.

Kushmar et al. (2022) stated that artificial intelligence significantly improves the quality of language learning by adapting to the individual characteristics, goals and objectives of each student. In parallel to this, the evaluations of Duolingo, Rosetta Stone, Memrise, Mondly, Mondly, Busuu, Babbel, Lingodeer and italki, which are personalized among the applications examined in the study, were also examined and it was stated that none of them provided low gains in a skill, mostly high and then medium gains.

Applications are classified as "strong performers" based on the following criteria:

- High Performance Across All Skills: Applications that provide "High" support for all four language skills.
- Focused Expertise: Applications excelling in specific skill areas, such as speaking or writing, while maintaining balanced support for others.
- Balanced Distribution: Applications demonstrating consistent "Middle" or "High" support across multiple skills.

The findings of their evaluations in the context of the third question of the research, "Which interaction types are used in artificial intelligence applications that can be used in foreign language learning?" are given in Table 4.

Table 4. The interaction types of the foreign language learning applications

No	Application	Learner-learner	Learner-Teacher	Learner-Content	Learner-interface
1	Duolingo	None	None	Yes	Yes
2	Rosetta Stone	Yes	human	Yes	Yes
3	aiLango	None	AI	Yes	Yes
4	Memrise	None	Human and AI	Yes	None
5	Mondly	None	Yes	Yes	Yes
6	Tutor Lily	None	AI	None	None
7	Lola Speak	None	AI	Yes	Yes
8	Cake	None	AI	Yes	Yes
9	Busuu	None	AI	Yes	Yes
10	Babel	Yes	AI	Yes	Yes
11	Elsa Speak	None	AI	None	Yes

continued on following page

Table 4. Continued

No	Application	Learner-learner	Learner-Teacher	Learner-Content	Learner-interface
12	Langeek	None	AI	None	None
13	SpeakingCoach.io	None	AI	None	None
14	Reverso	None	AI	None	None
15	Lingodeer	None	None	Yes	Yes
16	TalkPal	None	AI	Yes	Yes
17	ReadLang	None	None	Yes	Yes
18	Voscreen	None	None	Yes	Yes
19	Falou	None	AI	None	None
20	Gliglish	None	AI	None	Yes
21	Eigo.ai	None	None	Yes	Yes
22	DeepL.io	None	None	Yes	None
23	TinyWow	None	None	Yes	None
24	LangoTalk	None	AI	Yes	Yes
25	Tutor AI	None	None	Yes	None
26	Univerbal	None	AI	Yes	Yes
27	italki	None	human	Yes	None
28	Ewa	None	AI	Yes	Yes
29	Preply	None	human	Yes	Yes

When Table 4 is analyzed, it is seen that there is no learner-learner interaction in 27 of the applications. This situation suggests that individuals who want to learn a language by logging in from a mobile device do not feel the need to communicate with other learners in the first place in the learning process or that application producers do not offer this service based on the risks that may occur if learners communicate. The table also shows that while providing learner-teacher interaction, the applications intensively provide services with artificial intelligence chat bots. AI chatbots provide feedback to the user while chatting with them to improve their speaking or writing skills. In the literature, it is seen that the positive results of this use are predominant, especially in the results of studies on language learning realized with the use of ChatGPT as a chat bot (Çıldır, 2023; Çınar Yağcı et al., 2023; Zileli, 2023). Written or voice communications with AI chatbots for different languages will enrich the data used by the bot and enable it to develop further. In this way, it can be said that artificial intelligence chat bots will quickly assume the role of instructor completely and provide the development of 4 language skills in the context of learner-teacher interaction. When the learner-content interactions of the applications are analyzed, it is seen that 22 applications provide this interaction and 7 do not. This situation shows that the applications are structured in a way to provide learning especially with the content they offer. In individual-centered learning, the learner's ability to choose the type of content that will address his/her own learning needs contributes to the permanence of learning (Tosun et al., 2009). According to Uğur and Okur (2016), in learner-interface interaction, features such as user-friendly menu design, online registration, status information, evaluation statuses, scores, keyword search feature, site maps, online problem diagnosis, database queries are discussed. According to the table, 11 applications do not provide learner-interface interaction, while 19 applications provide learner-interface interaction. Considering the online registration criterion, it can be said that all applications provide learner-interface interaction. This shows that developing technologies increase the use of interfaces day by day, so it can be said that learner-interface interaction will be more and more important when developing such applications.

The learner-learner interaction type is rare among the applications, with only Rosetta Stone and Babbel supporting it. This highlights a significant gap in peer collaboration opportunities within AI-driven language learning platforms.

The integration of learner-teacher interaction, whether via real teachers (e.g., Rosetta Stone, Preply) or artificial intelligence (e.g., Busuu, Duolingo), is more common. Applications like Memrise combine real-person and AI-driven teacher interaction, offering a hybrid experience.

Almost all applications provide robust learner-content interaction, reinforcing the importance of well-structured content in language learning. Applications like Duolingo and eigo.ai excel in this area by offering gamified, dynamic content.

Many applications prioritize interface interaction, leveraging advanced AI features. Tools like Lola Speak and Mondly demonstrate strong interface interaction, enhancing usability and personalized learning experiences.

Figure 1 shows the percentage distribution of interaction types.

Figure 1. Percentage distribution of interaction types

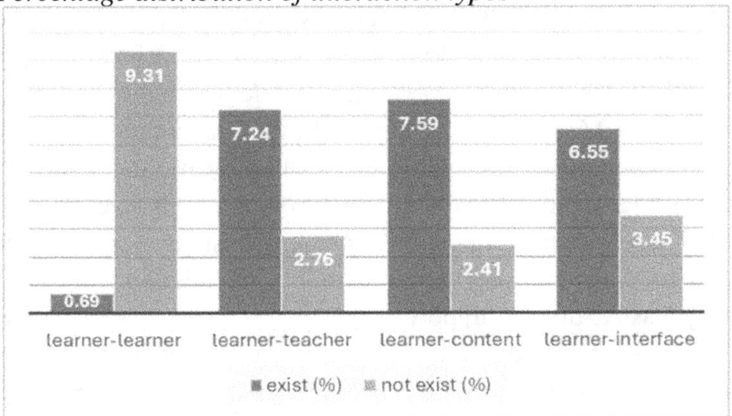

When the percentage distribution of the interaction types in the applications was analysed, it was observed that learner-content (7.59%) and learner-teacher (7.24%) were the most frequently presented interaction types in the applications. On the other hand, learner-learner interaction type is present only 0.69% of the time. Learner-interface interaction type shows a strong presence with 6.55%. These findings reveal that content and teacher-student interactions play an important role in language learning processes, but inter-user interactions are limited.

Figure 2 shows the percentage distribution of language skills.

Figure 2. Percentage distribution of language skills

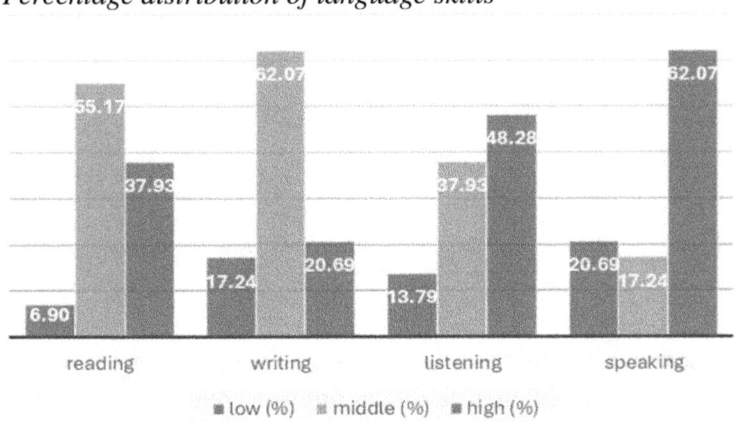

Analyzing the percentage distribution of language skills by proficiency levels reveals a clear prioritization of speaking and listening skills in AI-assisted language learning applications. Speaking skills receive the highest level of support, with 62.07% of applications categorized as "high," while writing skills are the least prioritized, with only 20.69% receiving high support. Listening follows as the second most frequently supported skill, with 48.28% of applications providing high-level assistance. Reading, in comparison, is supported at a high level in 37.93% of the applications. These findings indicate a strong emphasis on verbal communication skills (speaking and listening), whereas textual skills (reading and writing) receive comparatively less AI-driven support.

Additionally, AI-powered speech recognition tools have been found to provide accurate and immediate feedback on pronunciation and fluency, making them particularly effective for oral language development. However, the study highlights a notable limitation in AI-generated corrective feedback for writing skills, particularly in free versions of these applications. This suggests that while AI excels in facilitating spoken language practice, its capabilities in written language support remain relatively underdeveloped. Figure 1 shows applications that offer all four basic language skills according to their levels.

Figure 3. Apps that offer all four language skills by level

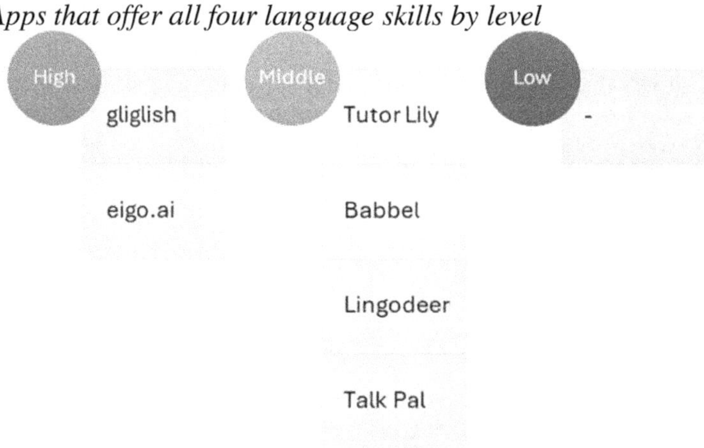

The analyses revealed that Gliglish and eigo.ai applications supported the four basic language skills (speaking, listening, writing and reading) at a high level. These applications strengthen individuals' learning processes with artificial intelligence-based feedback and interaction tools. For example, Gliglish focuses on speaking skills, while eigo.ai offers materials to support reading and writing skills. This emphasises the contribution of artificial intelligence technology to individualised learning processes (Huang et al., 2022; Kim et al., 2022). Tutor Lily, Babbel, LingoDeer and TalkPal applications support the four basic skills at a middle level. These applications offer a balanced approach with structured lessons and limited AI integration, but they do not have a high impact on skill development levels (Jeon, Lee & Choe, 2022). For example, Babbel focuses on grammar and vocabulary, while TalkPal offers personalised speaking practice.

AI-powered language learning applications exhibit varying levels of interaction support. Learner-content and learner-interface interactions are strongly facilitated by most applications, allowing users to engage with interactive materials and adaptive learning systems. However, learner-instructor and learner-learner interactions remain insufficiently supported, limiting opportunities for direct feedback from educators or collaborative learning among peers.

Among the analyzed applications, Rosetta Stone and Babbel stood out by offering a comprehensive interaction framework encompassing all four interaction types (learner-learner, learner-instructor, learner-content, and learner-interface). Rosetta Stone enhances real-time engagement by allowing learners to interact with human instructors, offering a structured approach to teacher-led learning. In contrast, Babbel provides a balanced interaction model, integrating AI-driven instructional content with teacher-supported guidance, ensuring a blended learning experience (Fryer & Carpenter, 2019; Loewen et al., 2020).

The fact that these applications offer four interaction types together allows them to address the different learning needs of users by providing diversity in learning processes. For example, in learner-content interaction, Rosetta Stone draws attention with powerful visual and audio materials, while in learner-teacher interaction, Babbel uses real-time feedback mechanisms (Thinh et al., 2020).

Gamification has been widely integrated into AI-driven language learning applications to enhance learner engagement. Research highlights that elements such as points, badges, and leaderboards play a crucial role in maintaining motivation and retention (Özdemir & Karaca, 2023).

Analysis of the 29 applications examined in this study reveals that gamification is particularly effective in fostering learner-content and learner-interface interactions. Applications incorporating gamification tend to structure learning experiences around interactive content delivery and adaptive user interfaces, providing a more dynamic and engaging learning process. Conversely, applications without gamification rely more heavily on traditional teacher-student interactions, which often result in lower levels of engagement in learner-content and learner-interface interactions.

When evaluating the impact of gamification on language skills, findings indicate that applications utilizing gamification demonstrate higher performance in speaking and listening skills. Notably, speaking and listening skills are supported at the highest level in gamified applications, whereas reading and writing skills receive moderate levels of support. In contrast, non-gamified applications exhibit lower performance across all language skills, particularly in productive skills like speaking and writing.

These results suggest that gamification serves as an effective tool for improving oral proficiency and engagement in AI-based language learning environments. However, to ensure a more balanced development across all language skills, future applications should expand gamification features to better support reading and writing while maintaining pedagogically sound instructional strategies.

CONCLUSION

This study offers a comprehensive evaluation of AI-powered language learning applications, focusing on their contributions to the four fundamental language skills and the interaction types defined by Moore's framework. The findings reveal a distinct pattern: while speaking and listening skills are well supported, reading and writing skills remain comparatively underdeveloped. This imbalance echoes prior research emphasizing AI's natural affinity for oral skill development due to advancements in speech recognition and generative dialogue systems (Huang et al., 2022; De la Vall & Atraya, 2023).

One major limitation identified is the insufficient support for writing skills across most applications. Developing AI models capable of offering nuanced, context-sensitive feedback on writing is technically challenging (Liu et al., 2021). Moreover, the risks associated with inaccurate or contextually inappropriate generative outputs further discourage developers from prioritizing writing tasks (Öztürk, 2023). This finding highlights a critical research gap: while AI excels at mimicking conversational speech patterns, it still struggles with the complex cognitive demands of written communication, such as argument structure, coherence, and critical thinking.

Another significant finding is the dominance of learner-content and learner-interface interactions, whereas learner-learner and learner-teacher interactions are notably scarce. While the emphasis on content-driven and interface-mediated learning aligns with trends in personalized education (Komalavalli et al., 2020; Hillman et al., 1994), the neglect of social and instructional interactions raises concerns. Language learning is inherently social, relying heavily on authentic communication, negotiation of meaning, and cultural immersion (Bandura, 1986; Moore, 1989). The limited opportunities for peer collaboration and instructor guidance may undermine the depth of learning and the development of pragmatic competence.

The analysis also shows that gamification is a powerful driver of engagement, but its benefits are unevenly distributed across skills. Consistent with Özdemir & Karaca (2023) and Deterding et al. (2011), the study confirms that gamification significantly enhances motivation and learner retention. However, current gamification strategies disproportionately favor speaking and listening tasks, often neglecting reading and writing. This misalignment suggests that while gamification has successfully transformed language learning into a more interactive experience, its full pedagogical potential remains underutilized.

From a broader perspective, while AI-based applications demonstrate remarkable progress in delivering personalized, accessible learning experiences, they often lack pedagogical depth. Hockly (2023) critiques the prevailing techno-optimism in AI-based education, warning that without a strong pedagogical foundation, technological innovations risk becoming superficial enhancements rather than transformative tools. The findings of this study reinforce this caution: most applications focus on optimizing user engagement and progress tracking but pay less attention to fostering critical thinking, intercultural competence, and metacognitive skills — all essential for true language proficiency.

Importantly, this study also underscores the growing need for hybrid instructional models that combine AI-driven personalization with human instructor guidance. Applications like Rosetta Stone and Babbel, which integrate human interaction alongside AI support, offer promising models for balancing automation and pedagogy. Future developments could benefit from incorporating live virtual classrooms, AI-human co-teaching strategies, and adaptive feedback loops that combine machine-generated suggestions with human validation.

Given the global and diverse nature of language learners, another critical issue is inclusivity. While many applications support major world languages, minority and less commonly taught languages remain underserved. Expanding AI language models to cover diverse linguistic communities would not only promote equity but also help preserve endangered languages, aligning AI development with broader social justice goals.

Finally, this study highlights key directions for future research. Longitudinal studies are needed to assess the sustained impacts of AI-assisted learning on language proficiency and learner autonomy. Comparative studies exploring age-specific interaction patterns could reveal how different demographics engage with AI tools and benefit from various interaction types. Moreover, research should examine how gamification elements can be redesigned to support not just motivation, but also deeper cognitive engagement, particularly in reading and writing domains.

In conclusion, AI-powered language learning applications hold great potential for transforming language education through personalized, flexible, and engaging learning environments. However, achieving a balanced, socially rich, and pedagogically grounded approach requires deliberate design choices that go beyond technological novelty. By addressing current limitations in writing support, social interaction, pedagogical depth, and linguistic inclusivity, future AI applications can play a pivotal role in fostering comprehensive and meaningful language learning experiences for diverse global audiences.

RESULTS AND RECOMMENDATIONS

This study examined 29 AI-powered language learning applications in terms of their contributions to the four core language skills (speaking, listening, reading, and writing) and their support for different interaction types based on Moore's interaction framework.

The findings revealed several key patterns:

- Skill Emphasis: Speaking and listening skills were the most supported, with 62.07% and 48.28% of applications rated as "high," respectively. Reading skills were moderately supported (37.93% at a high level), whereas writing skills received the least high-level support (only 20.69%).
- Interaction Types: Learner-content (7.59%) and learner-teacher (7.24%) interactions were the most common interaction types. Learner-interface interaction was moderately represented (6.55%), while learner-learner interaction was notably rare (only 0.69%).
- Gamification: Applications incorporating gamification demonstrated higher levels of learner engagement, particularly in supporting speaking and listening skills. However, gamification strategies often lacked effective integration with reading and writing activities.
- Holistic Applications: Gliglish and eigo.ai were the only applications that provided high-level support across all four language skills, highlighting the importance of multimodal and adaptive AI technologies.
- Overall, the analysis indicates that AI-driven applications prioritize oral communication development but fall short in offering balanced skill enhancement and peer collaboration opportunities.
- Based on the findings, several recommendations can be proposed for developers, educators, and future researchers:
- Enhancing Writing and Reading Support: Developers should prioritize the integration of advanced natural language processing (NLP) technologies to provide context-sensitive, real-time feedback for writing tasks and personalized reading pathways. Structured writing challenges and interactive reading modules should be incorporated within gamification frameworks.
- Fostering Learner-Learner Interaction: Future applications should embed social learning features such as real-time discussion forums, collaborative

projects, and peer assessment activities to foster meaningful learner-learner interaction and authentic communication practice.

- Balancing Gamification Strategies: Gamification elements should be carefully aligned with pedagogical goals. In addition to motivating speaking and listening practice, game-based tasks for reading comprehension and creative writing could ensure a more holistic language learning experience.
- Personalization and Adaptivity: Applications should continue to leverage AI's ability to personalize learning paths but also expand adaptive features across all skill areas, ensuring balanced language development for diverse learner profiles.
- Hybrid Interaction Models: Combining AI-driven feedback with human instructor guidance through hybrid models (e.g., AI-human co-teaching, live virtual tutoring) can enhance instructional quality and address the current gap in learner-teacher interactions.
- Inclusivity and Diversity: Future AI language applications should extend language support beyond English and major global languages, ensuring inclusivity for minority languages and diverse learner populations.
- Longitudinal Evaluation: Researchers should conduct longitudinal studies to assess the long-term effects of AI-driven language learning interventions on learner outcomes, motivation, and skill retention across different demographics.

Implementing these targeted improvements will enable developers and educators to build holistic, adaptive, and inclusive AI-based language learning ecosystems. By emphasizing personalization, enhancing social engagement, and embracing diversity, future AI technologies can redefine language education for diverse global communities.

REFERENCES

Abdullayeva, M., & Musayeva, Z. M. (2023). The impact of chat Gpt on students' writing skills: An exploration of AI-assisted writing tools. *Int. Conf. Educ. Res. Innov.*, *4*, 61–66.

Alyaz, Y. (2003). Yabancı il öğretim yazılımlarında yapay zekaya dayalı etkileşim. *Dil Dergisi*, (121), 22–35.

Bandura, A. (1986). Social foundations of thought and action. *Englewood Cliffs*, NJ, 1986(23-28), 2.

Belda-Medina, J., & Calvo-Ferrer, J. R. (2022). Using chatbots as AI conversational partners in language learning. *Applied Sciences (Basel, Switzerland)*, *12*(17), 8427.

Büyük, K., Uğur, S., Saykılı, A., & Şahin, V. (2018). Using games with gamification elements in open and distance learning: Sorukiip application example. *Journal of Open Education Applications and Research*, *4*(2), 211–234.

Çıldır, M. (2023). Collaborating with ChatGPT: An exploratory study on german language teaching. *Journal of German Language and Culture Studies*, *5*(2).

Çınar Yağcı, Ş., & Aydın Yıldız, T. (2023). Is ChatGPT a reliable artificial intelligence chat buddy of a foreign language learner? *RumeliDE Journal of Language and Literature Studies*, (37), 1315–1333. DOI: 10.29000/rumelide.1407539

De la Vall, R. R. F., & Araya, F. G. (2023). Exploring the benefits and challenges of AI-language learning tools. *International Journal of Social Sciences and Humanities Invention*, *10*(01), 7569–7576.

Deterding, S., Dixon, D., Khaled, R., & Nacke, L. (2011, September). From game design elements to gamefulness: defining" gamification". In *Proceedings of the 15th international academic MindTrek conference: Envisioning future media environments* (pp. 9-15).

Fryer, L., & Carpenter, R. (2006). Bots as anguage learning tools. *Language Learning & Technology*, *10*(3), 8–14.

Grimes, D. A., & Schulz, K. F. (2002). Descriptive studies: What they can and cannot do. *Lancet*, *359*(9301), 145–149. PMID: 11809274

Haristiani, N. (2019, November). Artificial Intelligence (AI) chatbot as language learning medium: An inquiry. [). IOP Publishing.]. *Journal of Physics: Conference Series*, *1387*(1), 012020.

Hillman, D. C. A., Willis, D. J., & Gunawardena, C. N. (1994). Learner-interface interaction in distance education: An extension of contemporary models and strategies for practitioners. *American Journal of Distance Education*, *8*(2), 30–42.

Hockly, N. (2023). Artificial intelligence in English language teaching: The good, the bad and the ugly. *RELC Journal*, *54*(2), 445–451.

Huang, W., Hew, K. F., & Fryer, L. K. (2022). Chatbots for language learning-are they really useful? A systematic review of chatbot-supported language learning. *Journal of Computer Assisted Learning*, *38*(1), 237–257.

Imran, M. C., Amaliah, N., Syam, N. I., Room, F., & Sage, M. S. D. (2023). The Feasibility of Artificial Intelligences (AI) In Speaking Skill: Lecturers' Perceptions. *IJOLEH: International Journal of Education and Humanities*, 2(2), 135–144.

Jeon, J. (2021). Exploring AI chatbot affordances in the EFL classroom: Young learners' experiences and perspectives. *Computer Assisted Language Learning*, 1–26.

Jeon, J., Lee, S., & Choe, H. (2022). Enhancing EFL pre-service teachers' affordance noticing and utilizing with the Synthesis of Qualitative Evidence strategies: An exploratory study of a customizable virtual environment platform. *Computers & Education*, *190*, 104620.

Kannan, J., & Munday, P. (2018). New trends in second language learning and teaching through the lens of ICT, networked learning, and artificial intelligence. In Fernández Juncal, C., & Hernández Muñoz, N. (Eds.), *Vías de transformación en la enseñanza de lenguas con mediación tecnológica. Círculo de Lingüística Aplicada a la Comunicación, 76, 13-30.*, DOI: 10.5209/CLAC.62495

Kazu, I. Y., Kazu, H., & Kuvvetli, M. (2022). Evaluation of language skill areas in digital game-based foreign language learning. *SSD Journal*, *7*(29), 117–127.

Kim, H. Y., Lampertico, P., Nam, J. Y., Lee, H. C., Kim, S. U., Sinn, D. H., & Lee, J. H. (2022). An artificial intelligence model to predict hepatocellular carcinoma risk in Korean and Caucasian patients with chronic hepatitis B. *Journal of Hepatology*, *76*(2), 311–318. PMID: 34606915

Komalavalli, K., Hemalatha, R., & Dhanalakshmi, S. (2020). A survey of artificial intelligence in smart phones and its applications among the students of higher education in and around chennai city. *Shanlax International Journal of Education*, *8*(3), 89–95.

Kushmar, L. V., Vornachev, A. O., Korobova, I. O., & Kaida, N. O. (2022). Artificial intelligence in language learning: What are we afraid of. *Arab World English Journal (AWEJ). Special Issue on CALL*, (8), 262–273.

Liu, C., Hou, J., Tu, Y. F., Wang, Y., & Hwang, G. J. (2021). Incorporating a reflective thinking promoting mechanism into artificial intelligence-supported English writing environments. *Interactive Learning Environments, 31*, 3340–3359. DOI: 10.1080/10494820.2021.1927115

Loewen, S., Isbell, D. R., & Sporn, Z. (2020). The effectiveness of app-based language instruction for developing receptive linguistic knowledge and oral communicative ability. *Foreign Language Annals, 53*(2), 209–233.

Moore, M. (1973). Toward a theory of independent learning and teaching. *The Journal of Higher Education, 44*, 661–679.

Moore, M. G. (1983). The individual adult learner. In Tight, M. (Ed.), *Adult Learning and Education* (pp. 153–168). Croom Helm.

Moore, M. G. (1989). Editorial: Three types of interaction. *American Journal of Distance Education, 3*(2), 1–6.

Moore, M. G. (1993). Theory of transactional distance. In Keegan, D. (Ed.), *Theoretical principle of distance education* (pp. 22–38). Routledge.

Sailer, M., Hense, J. U., Mayr, S. K., & Mandl, H. (2017). How gamification motivates: An experimental study of the effects of specific game design elements on psychological need satisfaction. *Computers in Human Behavior, 69*, 371–380.

Şenel, S., Şenel, H., & Günaydın, S. (2019). Herkes için mobil öğrenme: Mobil uygulamaların evrensel tasarım ilkelerine göre incelenmesi. *Ankara Üniversitesi Eğitim Bilimleri Fakültesi Özel Eğitim Dergisi, 20*(1), 73–92.

Shevat, A. (2017). Designing bots: Creating conversational experiences. " O'Reilly Media, Inc.". Shawar, B. A. (2017). Integrating CALL systems with chatbots as conversational partners. *Computación y Sistemas, 21*(4), 615–626.

Thinh, N. T., Hai, N. D. X., & Tho, T. P. (2020). The influential role of robot in second language classes based on artificial intelligence. *International Journal of Mechanical Engineering and Robotics Research, 9*(9), 1306–1311.

Tılıç, G. (2016). Yabancı dil öğreniminde kullanılan etkileşimli mobil uygulamalar: Duolingo örneği. *Journal of Research in Education and Teaching, 5*, 34.

Tosun, N., Özgür, H., & Şahin, İ. (2009, October). Student-content interaction in e-learning environments. *In 3rd International Computer&Instructional Technologies Symposium* (pp. 327- 331).

Turing, A. (1950). Computing machinery and intelligence. *Mind, 49*(236), 433–460.

Tyen, G., Brenchley, M., Caines, A., & Buttery, P. (2022). Towards an open-domain chatbot for language practice. In *Proceedings of the 17th Workshop on Innovative Use of NLP For Building Educational Applivations* (pp. 234-249), Association for Computational Linguistics.

Uğur, S., & Okur, M. R. (2016). The use of interactive video in open and distance learning. *Journal of Open Education Applications and Research*, *2*(4), 104–126.

Underwood, J. (2017). Exploring AI language assistants with primary EFL students. *CALL in a climate of change: adapting to turbulent global conditions–short papers from EUROCALL, 2017*, 317-321. https://doi.org/DOI: 10.14705/rpnet.2017.eurocall2017.733

Yaman, I. (2016). The potential benefits of podcasts for language learning. *Journal of educational and instructional studies in the world, 6*(1), 60-66.

Yıldırım, Ö. (2012). A Study on a Group of Indian English as a Second Language Learners' Perceptions of Autonomous Learning. *Turkish Online Journal of Qualitative Inquiry, 3*(2).

Zileli, E. N. (2023). ChatGPT Example in Turkish learning as a foreign language. *International Karamanoğlu Mehmetbey Journal of Educational Research*, *5*(1), 42–51. DOI: 10.47770/ukmead.1296013

Chapter 2
Innovative Approaches to Revolutionize Student-Centered Learning in the 21st Century

Fahad A. Salendab
https://orcid.org/0000-0003-4459-443X
Sultan Kudarat State University, Philippines

Kendatu L. Tago
Sultan Kudarat State University, Philippines

ABSTRACT

Student-Centered Learning (SCL) fosters autonomy, critical thinking, and engagement through active learning. This chapter explores innovative pedagogies like competency-based education, experiential learning, collaborative learning, and gamification, alongside emerging technologies such as artificial intelligence, virtual and augmented reality, and adaptive learning platforms. While these enhance learning experiences, challenges like teacher readiness, digital infrastructure gaps, and assessment limitations remain. Institutional support is crucial for sustaining SCL through resources and professional development. Shifting to competency-based and formative assessments, supported by data analytics, ensures personalized learning. Integrating SCL with technology creates inclusive, flexible learning environments that prepare students for 21st-century challenges.

DOI: 10.4018/979-8-3373-5102-5.ch002

INTRODUCTION

Meeting diverse students' needs and supporting their academic success is not easy. Educators must endure paradigm shifts and innovation to deliver effective instruction and develop critical thinking, problem-solving, and collaborative skills among students (Salendab, 2023; Salendab & Dapitan, 2021). Nowadays, conventional teaching approaches, manifested by lectures, are frequently replaced by student-centered learning (SCL) to assist students in achieving better academic performance. SCL is a teaching approach that provides opportunities for students to actively participate in various classroom activities conducted by the teacher and learn effectively using digital tools (Hardiyanti et al., 2023; Khoury, 2022)

Teachers must revolutionize students' learning experiences using competency-based education, gamification, and experiential learning to raise their academic performance (Duterte, 2024; Mula-Falcon et al., 2022). Teachers can also incorporate artificial intelligence, virtual and augmented reality, and adaptive learning platforms to stimulate and captivate students' interest, making learning more interesting and enjoyable (Brightwood et al., 2024; Khaldi et al., 2023; Bajaj, 2024; Zulkhaeriyah et al., 2024). These resources can provide real-time feedback for classroom-based assessments.

However, incorporating SCL posed significant challenges for students and teachers (Borhan et al., 2020; Chaudhary, 2024). Some of these challenges compromise the effective use of SCL, such as using alternative assessment tools, teacher readiness, and access to digital infrastructure (Chang-Tik, 2022; Borhan et al., 2020; Chaudray, 2024) Teacher-made tests are inadequate in capturing the necessary competencies that the SCL offers. Innovative assessment models can provide a comprehensive assessment system like formative, project-based evaluation, and self and peer assessment (Nazim et al., 2024; Ma et al., 2023; Malik et al., 2024).

Looking into best practices, new trends, and the role of institutional support in creating a sustainable learning environment are crucial as the educational system works to implement student-centered learning. This chapter examines the principles, benefits, and challenges of implementing a student-centered learning approach. It also discusses how innovative pedagogies, technological integration, and efficient assessment frameworks facilitate the SCL's effectiveness. This chapter offers insightful information for educators, policymakers, and researchers looking to improve students' academic performance and engagement in the digital era by looking at the practical implementations of such innovative pedagogies.

DEFINING STUDENT-CENTERED LEARNING (SCL)

The idea that the student is at the center of the learning process is the foundation of student-centered learning. This idea is the foundation for every effort to use the SCL approach. Even though this puts the students at the center of the process, the teacher's position is still crucial, especially when no students are identical (Keller, 2018; Sasson et al., 2022). The instructor provides students with opportunities to learn independently and from one another and coaches them in the skills they need to do so effectively (Bozzi et al., 2021). SCL approach uses strategies like self-paced and cooperative learning and open-ended problems requiring critical or creative thinking that cannot be solved by just following text examples. SCL involves students in role plays and simulations, replacing the lecture method with active learning experiences (Jony, 2016). When used effectively, SCL can improve comprehension, motivation to learn, knowledge retention, and positive reaction to the contents of the subject. With this concept, lessons should draw based on their prior knowledge, relevance to their learning experiences, and active interaction with other students and with the teacher (Baysal et al., 2023; Wijnia et al., 2024; Wang, 2023).

Meanwhile, learning resources are syllabi-directed, and the traditional teaching approach typically focuses on knowledge transfer and information availability to meet curriculum standards (Degago & Kaino, 2015; Tang, 2023). However, SCL is an approach that places more emphasis on the student than the teacher, and it emphasizes collaboration, active engagement, and personalization to fit each learner's unique learning needs, interests, and cultural background (Al-Balushi et al., 2020). By allowing students to take charge of their educational path, this pedagogical framework increases engagement and encourages lifelong learning while fostering learner autonomy and independence (Kerimbayev et al., 2023). According to Khoury (2022), the SCL approach enhances learning outcomes, student motivation, and active engagement in online and distance learning setups. However, it is difficult to implement the SCL approach due to various challenges, such as lack of infrastructure, limited resources, and teacher readiness.

The SCL approach has garnered much attention. Existing research examines how teachers and students view student-centered learning in different contexts (Muganga & Ssenkusu, 2019); Khoury, 2022). For instance, a study was conducted to determine how teachers and students in Jordan viewed or assessed the use of the SCL approach in translator learning. Although there were teamwork and time management issues, the study indicated that teachers and students perceived the SCL approach well. Teachers believed this strategy's effectiveness depended on the student's maturity (Khoury, 2022). Another study investigated how teachers perceived the SCL approach in middle school summer service-learning programs, including their challenges, their insights regarding teachers' and students' roles in this approach, and the assistance they need (Dunbar & Yadav, 2022). Another study of attitudes among Afghan lecturers and education experts found positive attitudes toward SCL outcome-based learning. However, the lack of infrastructure, facilities, and equipment and the country's current teaching and learning policies hindered the implementation of SCL (Katawazai, 2021). Komatsu et al. (2021) investigated several aspects of this teaching approach, including creating a learning environment that centers the students and the challenges encountered in implementing this concept.

THE ROLE OF INNOVATION IN MODERN EDUCATION

In an era of rapid technological advancements and global shifts, it is clear that the traditional paradigms of education are no longer sufficient (Çelik & Baturay, 2024). Innovations in education are understood broadly as the introduction of a new (innovation), a change, and an improvement of the existing innovations in the field of education are all related to the implementation of advanced pedagogical experience (Dilobarkhon, 2019). Innovative pedagogies are vital in making the teaching-learning process interesting, engaging, and outcome-based. Integrating these innovations in teaching and learning can address instructional problems, develop students' learning experiences, address students' diverse needs, and prepare learners to become job-ready (Kilag, 2024). By incorporating advanced technologies, personalized learning strategies, and learner-centered approaches, education becomes more responsive to the diverse needs of students (Gupta, 2024).

Furthermore, the pandemic's worldwide transition to remote learning has brought attention to both the advantages and disadvantages of using technology. There are two sides to emerging technology in education; while it can be an excellent instrument for preserving educational continuity, it can also pose serious problems (Al-Rawi et al., 2025; Maisano et al., 2024; Samala et al., 2024). The study of Üzmez and Ulutaş (2024), which investigates student well-being during emergency remote instruction, makes this clear. Based on their findings, student well-being has not increased during this time, which may indicate that although technology is necessary, it can also increase psychological stress and make learning more difficult. As a result, while new technologies may appear revolutionary, how well they are incorporated into the teaching-learning process determines their effectiveness (Samala et al., 2024; Çelik, 2024). Cutting-edge technology-enabled learning experiences can improve learning outcomes by providing students with practical exercises when carefully planned, sensitively shaped, pedagogically designed, and applied authentically (El Hajj & Harb, 2023; Wagner & Liu, 2021). However, these technologies may be risky of becoming another fleeting trend, impressive in their novelty but lacking their actual instructional value, unless they are carefully integrated into classroom dynamic (Shehata et al., 2025; Dimitriadou & Lanitis, 2023; Bhat, 2023).

Moreover, innovation in modern education plays a pivotal role in realizing the goals of Education 5.0. As Education 5.0 aims to integrate advanced ICT technologies to enhance the learning experience and eliminate educational barriers, innovation becomes the driving force behind this transformation (Lantada, 2020). Teachers can design immersive and personalized learning environments that meet the needs of a wide range of students by utilizing digital tools like artificial intelligence (AI), virtual reality (VR), the Internet of Things (IoT), augmented reality (AR), and mixed reality applications (Ahmad et al., 2023).

KEY CHALLENGES AND BENEFITS OF STUDENT-CENTERED LEARNING

Student-centered learning (SCL) promotes active student participation and learning autonomy as a response to the traditional teaching approach characterized by the lecture method (Capone, 2022; Sánchez et al., 2025). However, this poses challenges. For instance, in the study of Borhan et al. (2020), teachers are aware of the benefits the SCL offers to the readiness of Malaysian secondary schools. However, the results showed that teacher-centered learning is the typical strategy used and that SCL is still in its early stages. To implement the SCL effectively, they introduced it gradually and systematically among teachers in secondary schools so that they would not be hesitant to implement the SCL. Another study conducted by Marinko et al. (2022) in European nations showed that teachers are somewhat familiar with SCL but lack directions, information, and understanding of how to apply and practice the SCL. The shift to the SLC approach suggests a need for the modernization of educational processes that involve the introduction of innovative pedagogies, such as using online and digital learning resources in the teacher's teaching methods. Some SCL activities include peer feedback, peer argumentation, gamification, and formative assessment (Latifi et al., 2023; Taghizadeh et al., 2022; Valero Haro et al., 2022). Therefore, it is important to understand the readiness of Kazakhstan's university teachers to implement SCL.

Chaudhary (2024) also reported challenges encountered by teachers in using SCL. She highlighted that technological changes, time management, teacher training, availability of resources, and issues are common problems in utilizing SCL. Diverse teaching styles are necessary for technological change. In the current scenario, technology is used in every field.

In education, teachers use gadgets and animations to develop retaining power. However, problems arise when technology changes quickly and teachers cannot adapt quickly (Mardiana, 2020). Proper training is required to meet the challenges and adopt the opportunities (Kaminskienė et al., 2022). Time management also causes a problem using SCL since the teacher and student must manage their time accordingly, requiring proper planning (Kumar, 2016; Nazim et al., 2024; Tang, 2023). Assessment and evaluation at the end of the teaching posed significant challenges since the conduct differed from the traditional method. It is not only the teacher who plans the activity but also the students with their peer groups who must manage the time limit in which it has to be completed (Sridharan et al., 2023; Chang-Tik, 2022).

Moreover, the availability of resources was very low, which prevented students from exploring more and only gaining theoretical knowledge, which does not give our future generation practical knowledge (Feroz et al., 2022; Total, 2023). However, in the modern style of teaching, every kind of resource is provided by schools with proper infrastructure. Due to fewer resources, the learning process becomes slow and does not help students to participate in activities actively. If the resources are correctly available, then the participation of the students becomes entrusting, and They become curious to learn new things (Akpen et al., 2024; Okongo et al., 2015).

BENEFITS OF STUDENT-CENTERED PEDAGOGY

Student-centered learning (SCL) is an educational approach that places students at the core of the learning process. It shifts the focus from the teacher delivering information to students actively participating in constructing their knowledge. This approach tailors learning experiences to meet the diverse needs, abilities, interests, and learning styles of students, promoting a deeper understanding of the subject matter (Richardson & Khawaja, 2025; Bhardwaj, 2025; Aytaç & Kula, 2020)

- Academic Benefit: SCL encourages active participation through discussions, problem-solving, and collaborative projects. This active engagement leads to better comprehension and long-term knowledge retention because students connect learning to real-world applications (Ruijuan et al., 2023). In addition, SCL allows students to develop their critical thinking and problem-solving skills by exploring various solutions to problems and participating in inquiry-based activities. Through SCL, students can personalize their learning, making them more motivated and participative in the teaching-learning process (Yaseen et al., 2025; Loyens et al., 2023; Harris, 2022).
- Social and Emotional Benefits: SCL enhances students' collaboration and communication skills by incorporating group work activities and peer feedback,

helping them develop teamwork and communication skills. Collaboration and communication skills are vital to succeed in their academic journey (Karadağ & Yalçın, 2023; Chang-Tik, 2022). A teacher who incorporates SCL in the teaching-learning process can build students' resilience and adaptability, which are crucial components of emotional intelligence (Holdsworth, 2019). Leadership skills are also vital to the student's holistic development. By using the SCL, students will be allowed to take leadership roles in group project activities, helping them practice decision-making, conflict resolution, and organizational skills (Vinokur et al., 2024; Wilhoit et al., 2016)

- Relevance to Real-World Application: SCL fosters 21st-century skills such as critical thinking, digital literacy, and collaboration, aligning students' competencies with modern workplace demands. It often includes experiential learning opportunities like internships, community projects, and case studies, allowing learners to apply theoretical knowledge in practical settings (O'Brien, 2015).
- Institutional and Societal Impact: When used by teachers, SCL can satisfy students' academic journey, resulting in better retention and graduation rates. SCL also offers students access to education regardless of their backgrounds so that no one will be left behind (Hyun et al., 2017; Feng et al., 2025). They will also be able to develop a modern mindset to navigate their academic journey effectively in the rapidly changing environment (Khalid et al., 2020; Tao et al., 2022).

THE ROLE OF ARTIFICIAL INTELLIGENCE AND MACHINE LEARNING IN PERSONALIZED LEARNING

Artificial intelligence and machine learning are revolutionary in personalized learning by personalizing learning experiences to fit each student's needs, preferences, and learning styles (Bayly-Castaneda et al., 2024; Lata, 2024).

Implementation of SCL can be effectively realized using artificial intelligence. AI can improve teachers' assessment practices (Brightwood et al., 2024; Perkins et al., 2024). These applications provide teachers with a package of instructional models and information and may give teachers feedback on their instructional efficacy. Meanwhile, AI-powered tools can assist students in identifying their strengths and weaknesses by assessing their peer's performance and providing feedback (Grenander et al., 2021; Ward et al., 2024). AI-powered tools can generate feedback on teachers' instructional competencies that would serve as the baseline information to modify their teaching strategies (Wisniewski et al., 2020; Gan & Liu, 2021).

Moreover, implementing personalized instruction can be further strengthened using AI tools like data analytics and adaptive algorithms (Deng et al., 2023; Sajja et al., 2023). Personalized learning driven by AI attracts the attention of various researchers in the field of education. They have researched the theoretical frameworks and the significance of AI in education, but there is not much empirical data that would support the relationship between AI use in enhancing students' engagement and academic performance (Ellikkal & Rajamohan, 2024; Bernacki et al., 2021). Data analysis of student performance and behavior involves the use of AI. Intelligent tutoring and computer-assisted learning (CAL) became popular as these systems can offer a broader range of individualized solutions since they can tailor interactions with each student (Zylich & Lan, 2021).

In SCL, evaluating students' performance may be practical using AI tools as these offer feedback to help students improve while studying. Zylich and Lan (2021) reported that the memory and skill-based intelligent tutoring system can optimize teaching strategies using students' historical performance. The intelligent system can review items to guarantee learning effects by imitating students' memory decay curve and skills mastery. These intelligent systems powered by AI may produce recommendations based on students' performance and instruct them to identify errors and advance their skills effectively (Choffin et al., 2019; Zhang et al., 2025). In addition, a data-driven feedback system aligns the learning process with each student's learning preferences and skills. This is how AI works when teachers utilize it as a teaching method. It also enhances student learning outcomes through personalized learning and real-time feedback (Silva et al., 2024).

INTEGRATION OF VIRTUAL AND AUGMENTED REALITY IN CLASSROOMS

Two of the most technological developments, augmented reality (AR) and virtual reality (VR), are crucial in enhancing the teaching-learning process and educational system as a whole (Familoni & Onyebuchi, 2024). AR and VR are innovative pedagogies offering gigantic opportunities to improve student learning outcomes (Tan et al., 2022). Combined, students can better engage with various learning resources aside from textbooks and lectures given by the teacher, allowing the lecture type to tailor content for different learning styles. The role of these digital tools is not to replace traditional teaching methods but to assist and provide meaningful digital experiences among students (Childs et al., 2023; Phakamach et al., 2022). Additionally, AR and VR can enhance teachers' professional development by bridging the gap between traditional classroom training and real-world experience (Belwalkar & Maki, 2023).

Furthermore, Sun et al. (2023) found that utilizing AR and VR as innovative pedagogy can enhance student learning and engagement. Alizadehsalehi et al. (2021) discovered that when students start to use AR and VR, they can be more interested, subsequently perform better in classroom activities, and exhibit higher levels of motivation (Alizadehsalehi et al., 2021) because AR and VR provide students significant digital experiences and allow them to explore, learn, and engage with their surroundings.

GAMIFICATION AND INTERACTIVE LEARNING PLATFORMS

One of the innovative pedagogies that could revolutionize student-centered learning is gamification. It improves students' motivation, participation, and academic performance by using game design elements such as leaderboards, badges, arguments, and tasks in classroom environments (Huang et al., 2023; Ritzhaupt et al., 2021). Gamification has gained the attention of various researchers and authors. For instance, Khaldi et al. (2023) reported that gamification could enhance students' engagement and interest, but the effectiveness of using this innovation depends on the design of activities and the teachers' learning environment. Zainuddin et al. (2020) affirmed the report of Khaldi et al. (2023) that gamification utilized in higher education can boost students' motivation and engagement, resulting in the improvement of students' academic performance Aguiar-Castillo et al. (2021) and Rincon-Flores et al. (2023).

Meanwhile, the interactive learning platform suggests that students can gain knowledge through intensive and real-world learning experiences (Abykanova et al., 2023). In order to attain the most significant results based on the harmonious assimilation of knowledge that is prized in today's society, students engage in a hyperactive social process where they produce "living" knowledge while adhering to the teacher's supervision (Akpan et al., 2020; Nithideechaiwarachok & Chano, 2024).

Interactive learning platforms like Google Classroom, Edmodo, Moodle, and Kahoot, discussion forums, and real-time feedback support various learning styles by offering interactive content such as videos, simulations, and interactive exercises, promoting more profound understanding and retention of knowledge (Bajaj, 2024; Zulkhaeriyah et al., 2024). When combined, gamification and interactive learning platforms can create dynamic learning experiences. Students can personalize their learning, making their lessons more meaningful and relevant (Ibisu, 2024; Tang & Hare, 2023).

EMERGING PEDAGOGICAL APPROACHES

- **Competency-Based Education (CBE)**: It is an innovative approach in higher education that organizes academic content or delivery according to competencies, what a student knows and can do, rather than following a more traditional scheme, such as by course (Sölch et al., 2023; Alt et al., 2023). CBE puts forth the theory that the majority of students will achieve competence in the specified content area as long as they are given the opportunity and freedom to progress at their own pace and their learning experiences are structured according to their interests and needs (Lee & Chang, 2024; Ponomarioviené et al., 2025). In CBE, all students try to gain the desired level of mastery. For some, this will take a short time, while others will need more time to do so. In addition, some students may have already acquired the knowledge and skills before starting their education. They may have achieved these competencies through their previous experiences (Vasquez et al., 2021).
- **Experiential Learning:** Applying experiential learning helps students build their skills and abilities and is a teaching strategy that aligns with the learning objectives that students are expected to meet (Morris & Bilich-Erich, 2017). It is a complex model of a dynamic view of learning based on a learning cycle driven by the resolution of the dual languages of action/reflection and experience/abstraction (Kolb & Kolb, 2017). The philosophy of ELT, according to Kolb, is that learning is a continuous process. He added that students who employ experiential learning apply the knowledge that they have learned in a real-life context (Bernardus et al., 2023; Kolb, 1984). Kolb (1984) introduced the four phases of Experiential Learning Theory (ELT). Such phase included the Concrete Experience (CE), where students actively engage in learning rather than passively absorbing the knowledge from the instructor (Herod, 2012; Kolb, 1984); Reflective Observation (RO), where students use the experience to acquire new knowledge or perspectives (Kolb et al., 1999); Abstract Conceptualization (AC) where students relate their ideas in classes or from textbooks; Active Experimentation(AE) where students utilized the newly acquired knowledge and abilities in the new workplace.
- **Collaborative Learning:** It is characterized by students working together to accomplish a shared learning objective and taking responsibility for one another's education (Chounta, 2020; Garcia et al., 2024). It is important to distinguish between "collaborative learning" and "cooperative learning." Cooperative learning is a model where learning activity is broken down into minor activities that partners can complete independently. Working together to solve a problem in an interactive, asynchronous manner is known as collaborative learning. The difference between the two is that collaborative

learning emphasizes the discussion of participating in tasks and believes that cognition must be adjusted through communication between students (Chounta, 2020; Garcia et al., 2024).

- **Flexible and Adaptive Learning Models:** Flexible and adaptive learning models have emerged as transformative approaches in modern education, addressing the diverse needs of learners in an ever-evolving academic landscape (Mulenga & Shilongo, 2024; Zhang & Galaup, 2023). These models prioritize personalized learning experiences by accommodating varying learning styles, paces, and preferences, fostering inclusivity and learner autonomy. With technological advancements and a growing emphasis on student-centered education, flexible and adaptive learning frameworks leverage digital tools, data analytics, and innovative pedagogies to optimize learning outcomes (Sajja et al., 2023; Abbes et al., 2024). By enabling real-time feedback and tailored instructional strategies, these models enhance student engagement and equip learners with the skills necessary to thrive in dynamic educational and professional environments (Song et al., 2024; Yaseen et al., 2025).
    - **Blended or Hybrid Learning Approaches**: Blended learning is a student-centered learning method that combines traditional face-to-face classrooms (synchronous learning activities) with e-learning activities (asynchronous learning activities) (Attard & Holmes, 2022). According to Bruggeman et al. (2021), in a pedagogically well-structured blended learning practice, teachers (1) prioritize teaching and education, (2) hold a student-centered pedagogical belief, (3) encourage change, (4) are receptive to experimentation, (5) can express their needs and concerns, 6) can critically reflect on themselves, and (7) integrate technology into learning processes. Depending on the goals and educational setting, blended learning's intrinsic flexibility permits a variety of implementations. Because of its versatility, it has been widely used in various educational contexts (Platonova, et.al 2022)

ASSESSMENT AND FEEDBACK IN STUDENT-CENTERED FRAMEWORK

Assessment and feedback fosters student-centered learning (Nazim et al., 2024; Ma et al., 2023). The traditional classroom assessment, which is characterized by the teacher-made test and standardized test, may not fully capture the students' diverse learning needs and potential. However, using the SCL approach, assessment and feedback practices can be enhanced and prioritized for continuous, personalized, and competency-based evaluation (Walton, 2023; Arora et al., 2023). Students' autonomy, motivation, and deeper understanding can be optimized using formative assessments, self-reflection, peer feedback, and technology-driven analytics (Surawarachet et al., 2023; Steinert et al., 2023).

Alternative assessment methods, as one of the features of the SCL approach, go beyond the traditional assessment method. These methods evaluate creativity, problem-solving, higher-order thinking, and practical knowledge application (Avdiu & Ahmedi, 2024; Yang et al., 2024). Assessment methods like portfolios, performance-based assessment, peer and self-evaluation, project-based evaluation, rubric-based evaluation, and reflective journals can enhance students' practical application of knowledge (Malik et al., 2024).

The portfolio assessment enables students to systematically collect historical information and gather records of their development and accomplishments (Fox, 2016). Students are also evaluated according to their skills to finish practical projects by using performance-based assessment and evaluate their self and peers' work based on the criteria provided by the teacher by utilizing self and peer evaluation (Adjei et al., 2023; Dutta et al., 2023). The ability of students to finish real-world projects serves as the basis for project-based assessment (Zhao et al., 2023). Students' work and performance will be evaluated in an organized manner by using a rubric-based assessment (Panadero et al., 2023). Reflective journals aimed to assess student's reflection on their learning experiences, fostering critical thinking and self-awareness (Luştrea et al., 2024).

LEVERAGING DATA ANALYTICS TO TRACK STUDENT PROGRESS

Data analytics helps teachers track students' performance, like grades, test results, and assignment completion while spotting trends in their learning successes and challenges (Lewis & Kuhfeld, 2024; Sajja et al., 2023). Predictive analytics aimed to determine at-risk students and provide early interventions to minimize dropout rates and academic failure. In addition, data-driven information can personalize students' learning by customizing the teaching strategies in order to meet the students' diverse needs (Gonzalez-Nucamendi et al., 2023). Teachers can modify student motivation by examining involvement in class discussions and online learning environments (Marquez et al., 2023). With the help of dashboards and reports that offer real-time feedback, teachers, parents, and students can decide to improve the overall educational system (Kulkarni & Gkountouna, 2021; Sajja et al., 2023).

DISCUSSION

The Student-Centered Learning (SCL) framework creates a lively and meaningful learning environment. Through SCL, students can actively interact with the learning materials, develop their critical thinking and problem-solving abilities, and customize their learning pathways. In contrast to traditional or conventional learning, SCL allows teachers to be facilitators of learning who provide students with the opportunity to learn actively through experiential and inquiry-based learning strategies. These strategies strongly emphasize independence, collaboration, and the acquisition of 21st-century skills.

SCL efficacy can be strengthened and enhanced by integrating technologies such as adaptable platforms, virtual and augmented reality (VR/AR), and artificial intelligence (AI) in teaching-learning. These modern technologies can effectively obtain experiential learning, personalized instruction, and real-time assessments and feedback. While VR and AR foster deeper engagement with complex topics or subjects, AI systems may assess students' performance and generate data as a baseline to customize teaching strategies. The digital gap and disparities in teacher readiness continue to be significant obstacles to implementing the SCL approach.

A significant shift in assessment practices is also necessary to effectively implement the SCL framework since standardized or traditional assessment methods frequently do not capture students' mastery and learning. Alternative assessment methods that provide ongoing, formative assessments that align with the SCL principles include portfolios, peer assessments, rubric-based tools, and reflective journals. Learning analytics can also scaffold teachers to locate the students' performance gaps, and teachers can make timely interventions based on these students' performance gaps.

Support from educational institutions is essential. These institutions must invest primarily in infrastructure, assessment innovation, and professional development to successfully implement the SCL framework. Teachers may find the implementation of SCL challenging without the support of the institution.

Finally, the principles of Education 5.0 resonate with SCL, emphasizing human-centered, technology-supported learning. This future-forward paradigm promotes inclusivity, adaptability, and innovation in teaching, preparing students for real-world challenges in a digital society.

CONCLUSION

Student-centered learning (SCL) has emerged as a transformative educational approach. It promotes autonomy, critical thinking, and active engagement and enhances academic performance and student motivation by shifting the focus from teacher-led instruction to learner-driven exploration.

Innovative pedagogies—such as competency-based education, experiential learning, and gamification—complement the SCL framework. When supported by technologies like AI, VR/AR, and adaptive platforms, these approaches foster personalized, immersive, and meaningful learning experiences. These technologies also facilitate data-informed teaching practices and continuous feedback, improving learning outcomes.

Despite these advancements, challenges persist. Infrastructure limitations, insufficient teacher training, and resistance to change can hinder the widespread adoption of SCL. Furthermore, conventional assessment practices must evolve to reflect the competencies and skills emphasized in SCL. Embracing alternative and formative assessments, supported by learning analytics, ensures student progress is accurately measured and supported.

Institutional commitment is critical to sustaining the SCL model. Schools and universities must prioritize digital infrastructure, professional development, and supportive policies to empower educators and learners.

Aligned with Education 5.0's goals, SCL underscores the importance of a human-centered, technologically enriched learning environment. By embracing this model, educational institutions can equip students with the skills, adaptability, and mindset needed to thrive in an ever-evolving world.

REFERENCES

Abbes, F., Bennani, S., & Maalel, A. (2024). Generative AI and gamification for personalized learning: *Literature review and future challenges. SN Computer Science*, *5*(8), 1–12. DOI: 10.1007/s42979-024-03491-z

Abykanova, B., Nugumanova, S., Yelezhanova, S., Kabylkhamit, Z., & Sabirova, Z. (2023). The use of interactive learning technology in institutions of higher learning. *International Journal of Environmental and Science Education*, *11*(18), 12528–12539.

Adjei, Y., Osei-Himah, V., Duku, P., & Siaw, W. N. (2023). The Impact of performance-based assessment strategies on pre-service teachers' self-efficacy and academic achievement in general physics. *Pedagogical Research*, *8*(4), em0168. Advance online publication. DOI: 10.29333/pr/13388

Aguiar-Castillo, L., Clavijo-Rodriguez, A., Hernández-López, L., De Saa-Pérez, P., & Pérez-Jiménez, R. (2021). Gamification and deep learning approaches in higher education. *Journal of Hospitality, Leisure, Sport and Tourism Education*, *29*, 100290. DOI: 10.1016/j.jhlste.2020.100290

Akpan, V. I., Igwe, U. A., Mpamah, I. B. I., & Okoro, C. O. (2020). Social constructivism: Implications on teaching and learning. *Brock Journal of Education*, *8*(8), 49–56.

Akpen, C. N., Asaolu, S., Atobatele, S., Okagbue, H., & Sampson, S. (2024). Impact of online learning on student's performance and engagement: A systematic review. *Discover Education*, *3*(1), 1–15. DOI: 10.1007/s44217-024-00253-0

Al-Balushi, S. M., Ambusaidi, A., Al-Balushi, K., Al-Hajri, F. H., & Al-Sinani, M. S. (2020). Student-centered and teacher-centered science classrooms as visualized by science teachers and their supervisors. *Teaching and Teacher Education*, *89*, 103014. DOI: 10.1016/j.tate.2019.103014

Al-Rawi, O. Y. M., Elfezzani, W., Edwar, M. E., Al-Rawi, B. O., & Rashed, A. N. (2025). Challenges and Recent Developments in Smart Education Post-COVID-19 Pandemic. Business Sustainability with Artificial Intelligence (AI). *Challenges and Opportunities*, *1*, 857–870. DOI: 10.1007/978-3-031-71526-6_77

Alizadehsalehi, S., Hadavi, A., & Huang, J. C. (2021). Assessment of AEC students' performance using BIM-into-VR. *Applied Sciences (Basel, Switzerland)*, *11*(7), 3225.

Alt, D., Naamati-Schneider, L., & Weishut, D. J. (2023). Competency-based learning and formative assessment feedback as precursors of college students' soft skills acquisition. *Studies in Higher Education, 48*(12), 1901–1917. DOI: 10.1080/03075079.2023.2217203

Arora, C., Tubino, L., Cain, A., Lee, K., & Malhotra, V. (2023, May). Persona-based assessment of software engineering student research projects: An experience report. *In 2023 IEEE/ACM 45th International Conference on Software Engineering: Software Engineering Education and Training (ICSE-SEET)* (pp. 198-209). IEEE. DOI: 10.48550/arXiv.2302.05618

Attard, C., & Holmes, K. (2022). An exploration of teacher and student perceptions of blended learning in four secondary mathematics classrooms. *Mathematics Education Research Journal, 34*(4), 719–740.

Avdiu, V., & Ahmedi, V. (2024). Alternative Assessment Strategies to Enhance Learning for Students with Special Needs. *Journal of Social Studies Education Research, 15*(5), 1–25.

Aytaç, T., & Kula, S. S. (2020). The effect of student-centered approaches on Students' creative thinking skills: A meta-analysis study. *International Journal of Contemporary Educational Research, 7*(2), 62–80. DOI: 10.33200/ijcer.723894

Bajaj, M. (2024). THE ROLE OF DIGITAL LEARNING PLATFORMS IN ENHANCING STUDENT ENGAGEMENT. *UNIFIED VISIONS, 1*. DOI: 10.70088/xq3gy756

Bayly-Castaneda, K., Ramirez-Montoya, M. S., & Morita-Alexander, A. (2024, August). Crafting personalized learning paths with AI for lifelong learning: a systematic literature review. *In Frontiers in Education* (Vol. 9, p. 1424386). Frontiers Media SA. DOI: 10.3389/feduc.2024.1424386

Baysal, Y. E., Mutlu, F., & Nacaroglu, O. (2023). The Effectiveness of Student-Centered Teaching Applications Used in Determining Motivation toward Science Learning: A Meta-Analysis Study. *International Journal of Psychology and Educational Studies, 10*(1), 1–21.

Belwalkar, B. B., & Maki, B. (2023). Role of Artificial Intelligence in Workforce Development. *American Institutes for Research*, 2023-11.

Bernacki, M. L., Greene, M. J., & Lobczowski, N. G. (2021). A systematic review of research on personalized learning: Personalized by whom, to what, how, and for what purpose (s)? *Educational Psychology Review, 33*(4), 1675–1715. DOI: 10.1007/s10648-021-09615-8

Bernardus, D., Murwani, F. D., Aji, I. D. K., Radianto, W. E. D., Padmawidjaja, L., Jatiperwira, S. Y., & Jacob, G. H. (2023). Do entrepreneurial characteristics moderate the relationship between experiential learning and entrepreneurial mindset? *Journal of Educational and Social Research, 13*(1), 106–122. DOI: 10.36941/jesr-2023-0010

Bhardwaj, V., Zhang, S., Tan, Y. Q., & Pandey, V. (2025, February). Redefining learning: Student-centered strategies for academic and personal growth. [). Frontiers Media SA.]. *Frontiers in Education, 10*, 1518602.

Bhat, R. A. (2023). The Impact of technology integration on student learning outcomes: A comparative study. *International Journal of Social Science, Educational, Economics* [IJSET]. *Agricultural Research & Technology: Open Access Journal, 2*(9), 592–596.

Borhan, M., Saleh, S., Li, A., & Ong, E. (2020). Readiness in Implementing Student-centred Learning (SCL): An Insight to Developing a Problem-based Learning (PBL), Module *Universal. The Journal of Educational Research, 8*(1), 119–126. http://www.hrpub.org. DOI: 10.13189/ujer.2020.080114

Bozzi, M., Raffaghelli, J. E., & Zani, M. (2021). Peer learning as a key component of an integrated teaching method: Overcoming the complexities of physics teaching in large size classes. *Education Sciences, 11*(2), 67. 11020067DOI: 10.3390/educsci

Brightwood, S., Olusegun, J., Oluwaseyi, J., & Temitope, O. M. (2024). INTELLIGENT ASSESSMENT SYSTEMS: USING AI FOR FORMATIVE AND SUMMATIVE EVALUATIONS.

Bruggeman, B., Tondeur, J., Struyven, K., Pynoo, B., Garone, A., & Vanslambrouck, S. (2021). Experts speaking: Crucial teacher attributes for implementing blended learning in higher education. *The Internet and Higher Education, 48*, 100772. DOI: 10.1016/j.iheduc.2020.100772

Capone, R. (2022). Blended learning and student-centered active learning environment: A case study with STEM undergraduate students. *Canadian Journal of Science, Mathematics and Technology Education = Revue Canadienne de l'Enseignement des Sciences, des Mathématiques et de la Technologie, 22*(1), 210–236. DOI: 10.1007/s42330-022-00195-5

Chang-Tik, C. (2022). Student Collaboration Through Assessment, Feedback, and Peer Instruction. In Chang-Tik, C., Kidman, G., & Tee, M. Y. (Eds.), *Collaborative Active Learning*. Palgrave Macmillan., DOI: 10.1007/978-981-19-4383-6_3

Chaudhary, S. (2024). Challenges in Student-Centered Learning. *International Journal for Research in Applied Science and Engineering Technology, 12*(7), 983–986. DOI: 10.22214/ijraset.2024.63702

Childs, E., Mohammad, F., Stevens, L., Burbelo, H., Awoke, A., Rewkowski, N., & Manocha, D. (2023). An overview of enhancing distance learning through emerging augmented and virtual reality technologies. *IEEE Transactions on Visualization and Computer Graphics*. PMID: 37037228

Choffin, B., Popineau, F., Bourda, Y., & Vie, J. J. (2019). DAS3H: Modeling student learning and forgetting for optimally scheduling distributed practice of skills. *arXiv preprint arXiv:1905.06873*. https://doi.org//arXiv.1905.06873DOI: 10.48550

Chounta, I. A. (2020). Collaborative learning and patterns of practice. In *Encyclopedia of Education and Information Technologies* (pp. 310–323). Springer International Publishing., DOI: 10.1007/978-3-030-10576-1_83

Degago, A. T., & Kaino, L. M. (2015). Towards student-centered conceptions of teaching: The case of four Ethiopian universities. *Teaching in Higher Education, 20*, 493–505. DOI: 10.1080/13562517.2015.1020779

Deng, Y., Ren, Z., Zhang, A., Lei, W., & Chua, T. S. (2023). Towards goal-oriented intelligent tutoring systems in online education. *arXiv preprint arXiv:2312.10053*. https://doi.org//arXiv.2312.10053DOI: 10.48550

Dilobarkhon, K. (2019). The importance of modern innovation in education. *European Journal of Research and Reflection in Educational Sciences Vol, 7*(12).

Dimitriadou, E., & Lanitis, A. (2023). A critical evaluation, challenges, and future perspectives of using artificial intelligence and emerging technologies in smart classrooms. *Smart Learn. Environ., 10*, 12. DOI: 10.1186/s40561-023-00231-3 PMID: 40478141

Dunbar, K., & Yadav, A. (2022). Shifting to student-centered learning: Influences of teaching a summer service learning program. *Teaching and Teacher Education, 110*, 103578. DOI: 10.1016/j.tate.2021.103578

Duterte, J. P. (2024). The Impact of Educational Gamification on Student Learning Outcomes. *International Journal of Research and Innovation in Social Science, 8*(10), 477–487. DOI: 10.47772/IJRISS.2024.8100040

Dutta, S., He, M., & Tsang, D. C. (2023). Reflection and peer assessment to promote self-directed learning in higher education. *Journal of Educational Research and Reviews, 11*(3), 35–46. DOI: 10.33495/jerrv11i3.23.111

El Hajj, M., & Harb, H. (2023). Rethinking Education: An In-Depth Examination of Modern Technologies and Pedagogic Recommendations. *IAFOR Journal of Education, 11*(2), 97–113.

Ellikkal, A., & Rajamohan, S. (2024). *AI-enabled personalized learning: empowering management students for improving engagement and academic performance.* Vilakshan-XIMB Journal of Management.

Familoni, B. T., & Onyebuchi, N. C. (2024). Augmented and virtual reality in our education: a review: analyzing the Impact, effectiveness, and future prospects of ar/vr tools in enhancing learning experiences. *International Journal of Applied Research in Social Sciences, 6*(4), 642–663. DOI: 10.51594/ijarss.v6i4.1043

Feng, L., Close, E. W., Luxford, C. J., Pierson, J. A., Olmstead, A., Shim, J., & Galloway, H. C. (2025). Transforming Undergraduate STEM Education: The Learning Assistant Model and Student Retention and Graduation Rates. *Research in Higher Education, 66*(1), 1–26.

Feroz, H. M. B., Zulfiqar, S., Noor, S., & Huo, C. (2022). Examining multiple engagements and their Impact on students' knowledge acquisition: The moderating role of information overload. *Journal of Applied Research in Higher Education, 14*(1), 366–393. DOI: 10.1108/JARHE-11-2020-0422

Fox, J. (2016). Using Portfolios for Assessment/Alternative Assessment. In Shohamy, E., Or, I., & May, S. (Eds.), *Language Testing and Assessment. Encyclopedia of Language and Education.* Springer., DOI: 10.1007/978-3-319-02326-7_9-1

Gan, Z., An, Z., & Liu, F. (2021). Teacher feedback practices, student feedback motivation, and feedback behavior: How are they associated with learning outcomes? *Frontiers in Psychology, 12*, 697045. DOI: 10.3389/fpsyg.2021.697045 PMID: 34234729

Garcia, R., Treude, C., & Valentine, A. (2024, March). Application of Collaborative Learning Paradigms within Software Engineering Education: A Systematic Mapping Study. *In Proceedings of the 55th ACM Technical Symposium on Computer Science Education* V. 1 (pp. 366-372).DOI: 10.1145/3626252.3630780

Gonzalez-Nucamendi, A., Noguez, J., Neri, L., Robledo-Rella, V., & García-Castelán, R. M. G. (2023, October). Predictive analytics study to determine undergraduate students at risk of dropout. *In Frontiers in Education (Vol. 8*, p. 1244686). Frontiers Media SA. DOI: 10.3389/feduc.2023.1244686

Grenander, M., Belfer, R., Kochmar, E., Serban, I. V., St-Hilaire, F., & Cheung, J. C. (2021, May). Deep discourse analysis for generating personalized feedback in intelligent tutor systems. *In Proceedings of the AAAI Conference on Artificial Intelligence* (Vol. 35, No. 17, pp. 15534-15544). DOI: 10.48550/arXiv.2103.07785

Gupta, Y. (2024). Innovation In Education: Traditional To Modern. [IJCRT]. *International Journal of Creative Research Thoughts.*, *12*(1), d792–d796.

Hardiyanti, E., Fitriani, V., & Ashari, W. (2023). The Influence of Digital Tools on Student Engagement and Academic Outcomes Across Educational Levels. *Education Journal*, *1*(2), 59–68.

Harris, D. (2022). Promoting Critical Thinking Skills through Inquiry-Based Learning. *Frontiers of Educational Review*, *4*(1), 28. DOI: 10.69610/j.fer.20220413

Herod, L. (2012). "Adult learning: from theory to practice," available at: http://en.copian.ca/library/learning/adult_learning/adult_learning.pdf

Holdsworth, S., Turner, M., & Scott-Young, C. M. (2019). Developing the resilient learner: A resilience framework for universities. In *Transformations in Tertiary Education: The Scholarship of Engagement at RMIT University* (pp. 27–42). Springer Singapore., DOI: 10.1007/978-981-13-9957-2_3

Huang, A. Y., Lu, O. H., & Yang, S. J. (2023). Effects of Artificial Intelligence—Enabled personalized recommendations on learners' learning engagement, motivation, and outcomes in a flipped classroom. *Computers & Education*, *194*, 104684. DOI: 10.1016/j.compedu.2022.104684

Hyun, J., Ediger, R., & Lee, D. (2017). Students' Satisfaction with Their Learning Process in Active Learning and Traditional Classrooms. *International Journal on Teaching and Learning in Higher Education*, *29*(1), 108–118.

Ibisu, A. E. (2024). Development of a gamification model for personalized e-learning. *arXiv preprint arXiv:2404.15301*.https://doi.org//arXiv.2404.15301DOI: 10.48550

Jony, M. S. (2016). Student-Centered Instruction for Interactive and Effective Teaching Learning: Perceptions of Teachers in Bangladesh. *Online Submission*, *3*(3), 172–178.

Kaminskienė, L., Järvelä, S., & Lehtinen, E. (2022). How does technology challenge teacher education? *International Journal of Educational Technology in Higher Education*, *19*(1), 64. DOI: 10.1186/s41239-022-00375-1 PMID: 36591440

Karadağ, Y., & Yalçın, S. (2023). The Impact of peer feedback on collaborative problem-solving skills in the online environment. *International Journal of Assessment Tools in Education, 10*(3), 563–579. DOI: 10.21449/ijate.1290901

Katawazai, R. (2021). Implementing outcome-based education and student-centered learning in Afghan public universities: The current practices and challenges. *Heliyon, 7*(5), e07076. DOI: 10.1016/j.heliyon.2021.e07076 PMID: 34095574

Kerimbayev, N., Umirzakova, Z., Shadiev, R., & Jotsov, V. (2023). A student-centered approach using modern technologies in distance learning: A systematic review of the literature. *Smart Learning Environments, 10*(1), 61. DOI: 10.1186/s40561-023-00280-8

Khaldi, A., Bouzidi, R., & Nader, F. (2023). Gamification of e-learning in higher education: A systematic literature review. *Smart Learning Environments, 10*(1), 10. PMID: 40478066

Khalid, M., Bashir, S., & Amin, H. (2020). Relationship between Self-Directed Learning (SDL) and Academic Achievement of University Students: A Case of Online Distance Learning and Traditional Universities. *Bulletin of Education and Research, 42*(2), 131–148.

Khoury, O. (2022). Perceptions of student-centered learning in online translator training: Findings from Jordan. *Heliyon, 8*(6), e09644. DOI: 10.1016/j.heliyon.2022.e09644 PMID: 35756111

Kilag, O. K. (2024). Innovative Practices for 21st Century Education: The Future of Education Through Technology and Inclusivity. *International Multidisciplinary Journal of Research for Innovation, Sustainability, and Excellence (IMJRISE), 1*(12), 91-99. https://risejournals.org/index.php/imjrise/article/view/883

Kolb, A. Y., & Kolb, D. A. (2017). Experiential Learning Theory as a Guide for Experiential Educators in Higher Education. *Experiential Learning & Teaching in Higher Education, 1*(1), 1-38. Available at: https://nsuworks.nova.edu/elthe/vol1/iss1/7

Kolb, D. (1984). *Experiential Learning Theory: Experience as a Source of Learning and Development*. Prentice-Hall.

Kolb, D., Boyatzis, R. E., & Mainemelis, C. (1999). "Experiential learning theory: previous research and new directions", available at: http://learningfromexperience.com/media/2010/08/experiential- learning-theory.pdf.

Komatsu, H., Rappleye, J., & Silova, I. (2021). Student-centered learning and sustainability: Solution or problem? *Comparative Education Review*, *65*(1), 6–33. DOI: 10.1086/711829

Kulkarni, A., & Gkountouna, O. (2021). Demonstrating REACT: A real-time educational AI-powered classroom tool. *arXiv preprint arXiv:2108.07693.* https://doi.org//arXiv.2108.07693DOI: 10.48550

Kumar, M. K. (2016). Challenges of implementing student-centered strategies in classrooms. *International Research Journal of Engineering and Technology*, *3*(2), 1224–1227.

Lantada, A. D. (2020). Engineering education 5.0: Continuously evolving engineering education.

Lata, P. (2024). Beyond Algorithms: Humanizing Artificial Intelligence for Personalized and Adaptive Learning. *International Journal of Innovative Research in Engineering and Management, 11*(5), 10-55524. Available at *SSRN*: https://ssrn.com/abstract=4987208

Latifi, S., Noroozi, O., & Talaee, E. (2023). Worked example or scripting? Fostering students' online argumentative peer feedback, essay writing and learning. *Interactive Learning Environments*, *31*(2), 655–669. DOI: 10.1080/10494820.2020.1799032

Lee, D. C., & Chang, C. Y. (2024). Evaluating self-directed learning competencies in digital learning environments: A meta-analysis. *Education and Information Technologies*, 1–22. DOI: 10.1007/s10639-024-13083-2

Lewis, K., & Kuhfeld, M. (2024). *Recovery Still Elusive: 2023-24 Student Achievement Highlights Persistent Achievement Gaps and a Long Road Ahead. Brief.* NWEA.

Loyens, S. M., Van Meerten, J. E., Schaap, L., & Wijnia, L. (2023). Situating higher-order, critical, and critical-analytic thinking in problem-and project-based learning environments: A systematic review. *Educational Psychology Review*, *35*(2), 39. DOI: 10.1007/s10648-023-09757-x

Luştrea, A., Dincă, M., Berge, T., Oniţiu, A., Thomassen, M., Craşovan, M., & Lucheş, D. (2024). The Digital Reflective Journal: A Self-Assessment Tool for Higher Education Students. In *Digital Assessment in Higher Education: Navigating and Researching Challenges and Opportunities* (pp. 259–283). Springer Nature Singapore., Singapore., DOI: 10.1007/978-981-97-6136-4_12

Ma, T., Li, Y., Yuan, H., Li, F., Yang, S., Zhan, Y., & Mu, D. (2023). Reflection on the teaching of student-centered formative assessment in medical curricula: An investigation from the perspective of medical students. *BMC Medical Education, 23*(1), 141. DOI: 10.1186/s12909-023-04110-w PMID: 36864421

Maisano, D. A., Carrera, G., Mastrogiacomo, L., & Franceschini, F. (2024). Remote STEM education in the post-pandemic period: Challenges from the perspective of students and faculty. *International Journal of Educational Technology in Higher Education, 21*(1), 64. DOI: 10.1186/s41239-024-00497-8

Malik, Z., Munir, A., & Lestari, L. A. (2024). Integrating Alternative Assessment with Differentiated Instruction: Insights from a University-Level Setting. *Loquen: English Studies Journal, 17*(2), 65–77.

Mardiana, H. (2020). Lecturers' adaptability to technological change and its Impact on the teaching process. [Jurnal Pendidikan Indonesia]. *JPI, 9*(2), 275–289.

Marinko, I., Baužienė, Z., Daniels, N., Gołębiowski, A., Hughes, J., Kairienė, V., Knyviene, I., Krawczak, M., Maj, G. P., Marcinkiewicz-Marszałek, K., Marinko, J., Perkumienė, D., & Rees, A. (2022). Empowering teachers for a student-centered approach. Retrieved from https://ec.europa.eu/programmes/erasmus-plus/project-result-content/c55c65b9-7799-482e-b941cfe94b3f3924/2%20SCL%20RESEARCH%20IN%20ENGLISH.pdf

Márquez, J., Lazcano, L., Bada, C., & Arroyo-Barrigüete, J. L. (2023). Class participation and feedback as enablers of student academic performance. *SAGE Open, 13*(2), 21582440231177298. DOI: 10.1177/21582440231177298

Morris, E. M., & Bilich-Eric, L. (2017). A framework to support experiential learning and psychological flexibility in supervision: SHAPE. *Australian Psychologist, 52*(2), 104–113. DOI: 10.1111/ap.12267

Muganga, L., & Ssenkusu, P. (2019). Teacher-centered vs. student-centered: An examination of student teachers' perceptions about pedagogical practices at Uganda's Makerere University. *Cultural and Pedagogical Inquiry, 11*(2), 16–40.

Mula-Falcón, J., Moya-Roselo, I., & Ruiz-Ariza, A. (2022). The active methodology of gamification to improve motivation and academic performance in an educational context: A meta-analysis. *Review of European Studies, 14*, 32. DOI: 10.5539/res.v14n2p32

Mulenga, R., & Shilongo, H. (2024). Hybrid and Blended Learning Models: Innovations, Challenges and Future Directions in Education. *Acta Pedagogia Asiana, 4*(1), 1–13. DOI: 10.53623/apga.v4i1.495

Nazim, M., Alzubi, A. A. F., & Fakih, A. (2024). Teachers' employment for student-centered pedagogy and assessment practices in the EFL classroom from students' perspective. [IJEMST]. *International Journal of Education in Mathematics, Science, and Technology*, *12*(3), 605–620. DOI: 10.46328/ijemst.4089

Nithideechaiwarachok, B., & Chano, J. (2024). Socio-Cultural and Social Constructivist Theories and Its Application in EFL Classroom for Thai Pre-Service Teachers: A Review for Further Research. *International Journal of Language Education*, *8*(3), 564–572. DOI: 10.26858/ijole.v8i3.66499

O'Brien, W. D., Persinger, R., & Sahami, H. (2015). Integrating student-centered learning to promote critical thinking skills in the 21st-century classroom: A collaborative action research study thesis.

Okongo, R. B., Ngao, G., Rop, N. K., & Nyongesa, W. J. (2015). Effect of availability of teaching and learning resources on the implementation of inclusive education in pre-school centers in Nyamira North Sub-County, Nyamira County, Kenya. *Journal of Education and Practice*, *6*(35), 132–141.

Panadero, E., Jonsson, A., Pinedo, L., & Fernández-Castilla, B. (2023). Effects of rubrics on academic performance, self-regulated learning, and self-efficacy: A meta-analytic review. *Educational Psychology Review*, *35*(4), 113. DOI: 10.1007/s10648-023-09823-4

Perkins, M., Furze, L., Roe, J., & MacVaugh, J. (2024). The Artificial Intelligence Assessment Scale (AIAS): A framework for ethical integration of generative AI in educational assessment. *Journal of University Teaching & Learning Practice*, *21*(6), 49–66. DOI: 10.53761/q3azde36

Phakamach, P., Senarith, P., & Wachirawongpaisarn, S. (2022). The metaverse in education: The future of immersive teaching & learning. *RICE Journal of Creative Entrepreneurship and Management* www. ricejournal. net, *3*(2), 75-88.

Platonova, R. I., Orekhovskaya, N. A., Dautova, S. B., Martynenko, E. V., Kryukova, N. I., & Demir, S. (2022, July). Blended learning in higher education: Diversifying models and practical recommendations for researchers. *In Frontiers in education* (Vol. 7, p. 957199). Frontiers Media SA. https://doi.org/DOI: 10.3389/feduc.2022.957199

Ponomarioviené, J., Jakavonytė-Staškuvienė, D., & Torterat, F. (2025). Implementing Competency-Based Education Through the Personalized Monitoring of Primary Students' Progress and Assessment. *Education Sciences*, *15*(2), 252. DOI: 10.3390/educsci15020252

Richardson, J. W., & Khawaja, S. (2025, February). Meta-synthesis of school leadership competencies to support learner-centered, personalized education. *In Frontiers in Education* (Vol. 10, p. 1537055). Frontiers Media SA. https://doi.org/ DOI: 10.3389/feduc.2025.1537055

Rincon-Flores, E. G., Santos-Guevara, B. N., Martinez-Cardiel, L., Rodriguez-Rodriguez, N. K., Quintana-Cruz, H. A., & Matsuura-Sonoda, A. (2023). Gamit! Icing on the Cake for Mathematics Gamification. *Sustainability*, *15*(3), 2334. DOI: 10.3390/su15032334

Ritzhaupt, A. D., Huang, R., Sommer, M., Zhu, J., Stephen, A., Valle, N., & Li, J. (2021). A meta-analysis on the influence of gamification in formal educational settings on affective and behavioral outcomes. *Educational Technology Research and Development*, *69*(5), 2493–2522. DOI: 10.1007/s11423-021-10036-1

Ruijuan, L., Srikhoa, S., & Jantharajit, N. (2023). Blending of Collaborative and Active Learning Instructional Methods to Improve Academic Performance and Self-Motivation of Vocational Students. *Asian journal of education and training, 9*(4), 130-135. DOI: 10.20448/edu.v9i4.5211

Sajja, R., Sermet, Y., Cwiertny, D., & Demir, I. (2023). Integrating AI and learning analytics for data-driven pedagogical decisions and personalized interventions in education. *arXiv preprint arXiv:2312.09548*.https://doi.org//arXiv.2312.09548DOI: 10.48550

Salendab, F. A. (2023). Proposed Instructional Scheme in the New Normal Education: Basis for Pedagogical Strategies/Practices. *Psychology and Education: A Multidisciplinary Journal, 6*(8), 1-1.

Salendab, F. A., & Dapitan, Y. C. (2021). Performance of Private Higher Education Institutions and the School Heads' Supervision in South Central Mindanao. *Psychology and Education*, *58*(3), 3980–3997.

Samala, A. D., Rawas, S., Criollo-C, S., Bojic, L., Prasetya, F., Ranuharja, F., & Marta, R. (2024). Emerging technologies for global education: A comprehensive exploration of trends, innovations, challenges, and future horizons. *SN Computer Science*, *5*(8), 1–24. DOI: 10.1007/s42979-024-03538-1

Sánchez-López, M., Violero-Mellado, J., Martínez-Vizcaíno, V., Laukkanen, A., Sääkslahti, A., & Visier-Alfonso, M. E. (2025). Impact and Perceptions of Active Learning Classrooms on reducing sedentary behavior and improving physical and mental Health and Academic indicators in children and Adolescents: A scoping Review. *PLoS One*, *20*(2), e0317973. DOI: 10.1371/journal.pone.0317973 PMID: 39908255

Sasson, I., Yehuda, I., & Miedijensky, S. (2022). Innovative learning spaces: Class management and universal design for learning. *Learning Environments Research*, *25*(3), 725–739. DOI: 10.1007/s10984-021-09393-8

Shehata, B., Tlili, A., Huang, R., Hodges, C. B., & Kanwar, A. (2025). Implications and Challenges of Technology Adoption in Education: A 20-Year Analysis of Horizon Reports. *TechTrends*, *69*(1), 162–175. DOI: 10.1007/s11528-024-01027-z

Silva, R., Farias, C., & Mesquita, I. (2024). "It is Good to Have a Voice": What Do Students Think about the Impact of a Flexible Curricular Implementation of Student-Centered Pedagogies on Their Own Learning Experiences? *Education Sciences*, *14*(10), 1074. DOI: 10.3390/educsci14101074

Sölch, M., Aberle, M., & Krusche, S. (2023). Integrating competency-based education in interactive learning systems. *arXiv preprint arXiv:2309.12343*. https://doi.org//arXiv.2309.12343DOI: 10.48550

Song, C., Shin, S.-Y., & Shin, K.-S. (2024). Implementing the Dynamic Feedback-Driven Learning Optimization Framework: A Machine Learning Approach to Personalize Educational Pathways. *Applied Sciences (Basel, Switzerland)*, *14*(2), 916. DOI: 10.3390/app14020916

Sridharan, B., McKay, J., & Boud, D. (2023). The four pillars of peer assessment for collaborative teamwork in higher education. In *The Power of Peer Learning: Fostering Students' Learning Processes and Outcomes* (pp. 3–24). Springer International Publishing., DOI: 10.1007/978-3-031-29411-2_1

Steinert, S., Avila, K. E., Ruzika, S., Kuhn, J., & Küchemann, S. (2023). Harnessing large language models to enhance self-regulated learning via formative feedback. *arXiv preprint arXiv:2311.13984*. DOI: 10.1186/s40561-024-00354-1

Sun, J. C. Y., Ye, S. L., Yu, S. J., & Chiu, T. K. (2023). Effects of wearable hybrid AR/VR learning material on high school students' situational interest, engagement, and learning performance: The case of a physics laboratory learning environment. *Journal of Science Education and Technology*, *32*(1), 1–12.

Suraworachet, W., Zhou, Q., & Cukurova, M. (2023). The Impact of combining human and analytics feedback on students' engagement with and performance in reflective writing tasks. *International Journal of Educational Technology in Higher Education*, *20*(1), 1–24. DOI: 10.48550/arXiv.2211.08222

Tan, Y., Xu, W., Li, S., & Chen, K. (2022). Augmented and virtual reality (AR/VR) for education and training in the AEC industry: A systematic review of research and applications. *Buildings (Basel, Switzerland)*, *12*(10), 1529.

Tang, K. H. D. (2023). Student-centered Approach in Teaching and Learning: What Does It Really Mean? *Acta Pedagogia Asiana*, *2*(2), 72–83. DOI: 10.53623/apga.v2i2.218

Tang, Y., & Hare, R. (2023). Combining gamification and intelligent tutoring systems in a serious game for engineering education. *arXiv preprint arXiv:2305.16568*. https://doi.org//arXiv.2305.16568DOI: 10.48550

Tao, W., Zhao, D., Yue, H., Horton, I., Tian, X., Xu, Z., & Sun, H. J. (2022). The influence of growth mindset on the mental health and life events of college students. *Frontiers in Psychology*, *13*, 821206. DOI: 10.3389/fpsyg.2022.821206 PMID: 35496212

Üzmez, A., & Kavakli Ulutaş, N. (2024). An inquiry on the psychological well-being of the university students during emergency remote teaching: Application of the EMPATHICS model. *Smart Learning Environments*, *11*(1), 17. DOI: 10.1186/s40561-024-00302-z

Valero Haro, A., Noroozi, O., Biemans, H. J. A., & Mulder, M. (2022). Argumentation Competence: Students' argumentation knowledge, behavior, attitude, and relationships with domain-specific knowledge acquisition. *Journal of Constructivist Psychology*, *35*(1), 123–145. DOI: 10.1080/10720537.2020.1734995

Vasquez, J. A., Marcotte, K., & Gruppen, L. D. (2021). The parallel evolution of competency-based education in medical and higher education. *The Journal of Competency-Based Education*, *6*(2), e1234. DOI: 10.1002/cbe2.1234

Vinokur, E., Yomtovian, A., Marom, M. S., Itzchakov, G., & Baron, L. (2024). Social-based learning and leadership in school: Conflict management training for holistic, relational conflict resolution. *Frontiers in Social Psychology*, *2*, 1412968. DOI: 10.3389/frsps.2024.1412968

Wagner, C., & Liu, L. (2021). Creating immersive learning experiences: A pedagogical design perspective. In *Creative and collaborative learning through immersion: Interdisciplinary and international perspectives* (pp. 71–87). Springer International Publishing., DOI: 10.1007/978-3-030-72216-6_5

Walton, D. (2023). Personalized cognitive tutoring using davinci-003 API for adaptive question generation and assessment. *arXiv preprint arXiv:2304.02772*. https://doi.org//arXiv.2304.02772DOI: 10.48550

Wang, L. (2023). The Impact of student-centered learning on academic motivation and achievement: A comparative research between traditional instruction and student-centered approach. *Journal of Education. Humanities and Social Sciences, 22*, 346–353.

Ward, B., Bhati, D., Neha, F., & Guercio, A. (2024). Analyzing the Impact of AI Tools on Student Study Habits and Academic Performance. *arXiv preprint arXiv:2412.02166*. https://doi.org//arXiv.2412.02166DOI: 10.48550

Wijnia, L., Noordzij, G., Arends, L. R., Rikers, R. M., & Loyens, S. M. (2024). The effects of problem-based, project-based, and case-based learning on students' motivation: A meta-analysis. *Educational Psychology Review, 36*(1), 29. DOI: 10.1007/s10648-024-09864-3

Wilhoit, G. E. N. E., Pittenger, L. I. N. D. A., & Rickabaugh, J. (2016). *Leadership for learning: What is leadership's role in supporting success for every student?* Center for Innovation in Education.

Wisniewski, B., Zierer, K., & Hattie, J. (2020). The power of feedback revisited: A meta-analysis of educational feedback research. *Frontiers in Psychology, 10*, 487662. DOI: 10.3389/fpsyg.2019.03087 PMID: 32038429

Yang, T., Zhang, Q., Sun, Z., & Hou, Y. (2024). Automatic assessment of divergent thinking in Chinese language with TransDis: A transformer-based language model approach. *Behavior Research Methods, 56*(6), 5798–5819. DOI: 10.3758/s13428-023-02313-z PMID: 38129737

Yaseen, H., Mohammad, A. S., Ashal, N., Abusaimeh, H., Ali, A., & Sharabati, A.-A. A. (2025). The Impact of Adaptive Learning Technologies, Personalized Feedback, and Interactive AI Tools on Student Engagement: The Moderating Role of Digital Literacy. *Sustainability, 17*(3), 1133. DOI: 10.3390/su17031133

Zainuddin, Z., Chu, S. K. W., Shujahat, M., & Perera, C. J. (2020). The Impact of gamification on learning and instruction: A systematic review of empirical evidence. *Educational Research Review, 30*, 100326. DOI: 10.1016/j.edurev.2020.100326

Zhang, Y. F., Li, H., Song, D., Sun, L., Xu, T., & Wen, Q. (2025). From Correctness to Comprehension: AI Agents for Personalized Error Diagnosis in Education. *arXiv preprint arXiv:2502.13789*. https://doi.org//arXiv.2502.13789DOI: 10.48550

Zhang a, H., & Galaup ab, M. (2023). Reflection on the construction and Impact of an adaptive learning ecosystem. *Revue internationale des technologies en pédagogie universitaire, 20*(2), 125-138. DOI: 10.18162/ritpu-2023-v20n2-10

Zhao, L., Zhao, B., & Li, C. (2023). Alignment analysis of teaching–learning-assessment within the classroom: How teachers implement project-based learning under the curriculum standards. *Disciplinary and Interdisciplinary Science Education Research*, *5*(1), 13. DOI: 10.1186/s43031-023-00078-1

Zylich, B., & Lan, A. (2021, April). Linguistic skill modeling for second language acquisition. *In LAK21: 11th International Learning Analytics and Knowledge Conference* (pp. 141-150).

Chapter 3
AI in Education:
Shaping Curriculum and Student Assessment

Sandip Dey
https://orcid.org/0000-0002-1005-3304
Sukanta Mahavidyalaya, India

ABSTRACT

In this paper, curriculum enhancement and methods of evaluation for students through the application of artificial intelligence (AI) is discussed. It starts by describing the history of educational technology, the developments made and trends observed in modern learning environment. AI is discussed as applied to curricula, with a focus on the role of embedment in establishing individual learning trajectories. Examples of institutions that have implemented AI to support curation and learners' assessment are illustrated with enhanced learning interests and outcomes. The paper also highlights issues such as ethical implication, data privacy, and organizational AI skepticism. Last but not the least its focus on way forward for these challenges and captured the essence of the collective responsibilities of educators, policy makers and technology developers to unleash the true beauty of the AI in education.

INTRODUCTION

In the process of education today there are several difficulties. Nonetheless, conventional classroom instruction approaches have been found to be inadequate to address students' needs. It is a fact that classrooms are diversifying, teachers require having more forms to support every learner (Sandhu, 1994). Artificial Intelligence has gradually entered the field of education. It can also make deliveries of learning activities to students more distinct (Cope et al., 2021). As an example, AI can

DOI: 10.4018/979-8-3373-5102-5.ch003

differentiate between lessons according to a learner's accomplishment to let the student learn as per his/her abilities (Garcia, et al., 2024). AI is also transforming the ways the performance of students is being evaluated. Actual knowledge may not be revealed due to the often-low raw scores received by students on traditional tests. In this way, AI can generate better evaluations through a gendered analysis of various kinds of students' work (Swiecki, 2022). On the same note, Miller (2024) observes that AI has the capacity to enhance teaching and learning processes through a more customized learner approach and enhancing the assessment processes. Education is a very sensitive sector that should be adapted to the growth of technology to prepare future generations.

Curriculum in any Educational system or system of instruction is very important. They depict what students are expected to get and the way they receive the information (Tyler, 2021). The two aims of curriculum design are that it caters for the needs of various learners, and it equips them for the future tasks (Chimbunde, 2024). They should be content and skills that are relevant today (Tang, et. al., 2020). Equally important is the aspect of student assessment. From here, it assists teachers in establishing how effectively the learners are grasping (Mendez, et. al., 2014). A student's progress and any learning gaps that require that the teachers spend more time explaining can be determined with assessments. With the help of curriculum design as the concept that helps to create lessons and tests, student assessment makes receiving education efficient and useful. They assist in establishing the culture within which learning occurs to achieve growth (Miller, 2024). As education grows, is incorporating AI into these areas beneficial for better personalization within the education process (Cope et al., 2021). If successfully implemented, the afore described combination can contribute to preparation of the students for the future which is rapidly evolving.

At the same time, it is worth mentioning that AI technologies are altering education in numerous ways. One important type that should be highlighted is the adaptive learning systems. These systems suggest changes in terms of lesson delivery depending on the progress that the student has made (Tang, et. al., 2020). They assist students in learning at their own rate, and tutors can always intervene to offer additional help (Mendez, et. al, 2014). Another AI-relevant technology is intelligent tutoring systems. Such programs involve communication with a student as well as providing him/her with instructions and evaluations, which are characteristic for a tutor (Garcia, et al., 2024). They can assist in lessons where learning content involves numbers such as math and language (Swiecki, 2022). Another application is AI's integration into the assessment tools. These tools are used in the analysis of student work to give extend information that favors or disadvantages the students (Miller, 2024). It also assists the teachers to know how to better their teaching practices. Two last key technologies that largely influence the educational chatbots are as follows A. Natural Language Processing. These chatbots respond to queries students may have and assist them when the lecturer is not available because of class time (Cope et al., 2021). All in all, it is indicated that AI technologies can increase new possibilities of individualizing the learning process and assessment in education. Thesis statement on the transformative potential of AI in education.

AI continues to prove that it has the potential to change the education sector in a very big way. First, it can make learning more individualized as far as each student is concerned. When lessons are modified to the learner, it enables a student to learn at his or her own pace, this has been made possible using artificial intelligence (Tang, et. al., 2020). Second, through bidirectional knowledge flow, AI improves the curriculum. In terms of research uses, it gives information that enhances the coherence and usability of educational content (Mendez, et. al., 2014). From the insights obtained from the study teachers can devise more meaningful lessons that will be more engaging to the learners (Miller, 2024). Third, artificial intelligence enhances the evaluation of student's performance. It can take a broad approach to many submitted student works and provide a better understanding of their capabilities (Kim, et. al., 2022). This aids the teachers in giving extra attention where it is required most (Swiecki, 2022).

THE EVOLUTION OF EDUCATION TECHNOLOGY

Historical Context of Educational Technology

In this case there is an evolution of education technology. According to Cuban (1986), at the beginning of the twentieth century technology in classrooms included instruments such as film and radio. In the 1960s technological inventions such as television and the use of audio visuals boosted learning (Selwyn, N., & Facer, K., 2014). Technologies of today's contact such as use of computers in schools had prevailed by the beginning of 1980s. They included the provision of new approaches to learning and teaching (Jonassen, 1996). What the internet did was revolutionize everything in the 1990s. It gave a right to immense information and source. This led to the starting development of online learning, which allows students to be flexible (Moore & Kearsley, 2012). Stakeholders presented technology of mobile devices and educational apps in the 21st century. These tools enhanced learning by making it more creative, individualistic, and enjoyable (Santosh & Cai, 2016). This is a reality that the facet of artificial intelligence (AI) is already present in education. He said that technology supports developments of curriculum and effective evaluation of students too (Luckin., 2018). Thus, it is possible to try and predict the possible future development of the role of technology in education. To the extent that it enables us to relate the current with future development, it is important to comprehend such history.

Significant Milestones in the Integration of Technology in Education

The integration of technology in education has reached significant stages in the past. The following is a brief overview of the major accomplishments in the diffusion of technology in educational settings. They used the method of using film in classrooms in 1920. This supported the practice of other graphic approach to teaching/learning (Cuban, 1986). Computers were first brought to schools in the 1960s; nevertheless, these were limited to actual office uses (Jones & Brannigan, 2000).

In regards to increase in adoption of technology in the classroom the American society was Pioneer in the 1980s with the introduction of personal computers. This was helpful in enabling students to interact with software for learning (Selwyn, N., & Facer, K., 2014). I have noticed that the decade of 1990 was the one in which internet played a significant role as to education. It was used for research and communications when schools turned to it for these purposes (Moore & Kearsley, 2012).

The early 21st century introduced e-learning and online course. This have enabled students to have access to education they never did before (Santosh & Cai, 2016). The use of mobile devices was discovered by the end of the decade and thus there was an emergence of education applications (Luckin., 2018).

In the modern world, AI is essential in the process of providing personalization of learning, as well as for evaluating the outcome of the process. These highlights reflected the developmental history of technological advances in education as well as put on display the milestones that still mark current technological advancements.

Transition From Traditional Methods to Digital Learning Environments

As with any transformative area, education has not been left behind when adapting to adopting technology learning environments. In the past, teachers relied on instructions or storytelling and books. Teachers taught through lectures and note taking which the students were able to do (Cuban, 1986). This method restricted participation and involvement from the visitors.

Late in the 20th century, computers started being used in the classroom. They offer the opportunity to present content in a new form and engaged students (Jonassen, 1996). In the 1990s, the emergence of technology in explicit form of the internet enabled students to obtain resources from the internet. This increased their learning access and availability of learning to new areas (Moore & Kearsley, 2012).

In the 2000, there are online learning platforms available for learners. These platforms provided courses that the students could undertake on flexible or open credit arrangements. This flexibility altered perception concerning learning (Santosh & Cai, 2016). Today even such useful forms as interactive programs and applications provide an effective learning process. AI takes education to another level by allowing the system to deliver material based on a student's learning ability (Luckin & Holmes, 2016). It has also shifted competition and made education convenient and engaging as students learn in their preferred modes.

Current Trends in Educational Technology, Including AI Tools and Platforms

Information and learning technology are rapidly developing. One of the main emerging trends is the AI tools usage. AI enhances differentiation because tutors can present content in a form most suitable for students (Luckin & Holmes, 2016). This will enable enhanced learning delivery to students since tutors get to understand individual differences as well as students get to learn what impacts them positively.

Some trends we can thus speak of are a growing trend of online and blended learning. Ever increasing, schools provide learners with classes that include both face-to-face teaching and computer aided instruction. This approach is flexible and easily accessible to students according to Moore and Kearsley in their publication of 2012. Mobile learning is also on the rise. Students and mobile learners rely on the use of smartphone and tablets in any environment to run apps for learning (Santosh & Cai, 2016). These tools make learning fun and they incorporate the use of state - of - the art tools.

Further, data analytics is emerging as a factor. Jonassen (1996) has indicated that teachers utilize data that are used to monitor students' progress and facilitate decision making about instruction. Lastly, applications including Google Classroom allow students create group projects and work with fellow learners they do not know face-to-face from different locations conveniently.

Few popular AI Tool and their usages is presented in Table 1.

Table 1. Popular AI tools in education society and their usages

AI Tool	Use in Education Society	Example
Machine Learning	Strengthens learning content	Making exercise specific based on performance
Natural Language Processing	Comprehends student questions and language	Helps student to write, check their language proficiency
Computer Vision	Determines the reaction on the visual content	Identifies the handwritten assignments
Predictive Analytics	Student performance forecast	Drawing the teacher's attention to low performing students
Chatbots	Helps in answering questions, providing immediate feedback	Help in answering questions and providing guidance to study directions

IMPLEMENTATION OF ARTIFICIAL INTELLIGENCE IN CURRICULUM DESIGN

Importance of Curriculum Design

Role of Curriculum in Attaining Educational Goals

Curriculum plays an important role of facilitating the achievement of education goals and objectives. They state what students are expected to know at the end of a certain lesson and enables teachers to organize lessons (Tyler, 1949). An implementation of an efficient curriculum ensures that all areas are provided. In addition, learning should be systematic as well as organized. Curricula can also be designed to develop skills that are correlated to critical thinking and problem solving. By including various activities, students perform tasks by analyzing information and knowledge application in everyday life situations (Bloom, 1956). That helps them to prepare for the future.

In addition, setting is constructed in such a way that is is possible to be flexible when designing and implementing a nationwide curriculum. This is particularly true in the context of students with a learning disability and coming from dissimilar backgrounds (Tomlinson, 2001). The other aspect it has become almost impossible to teach without the use of technology is the integration of technology into lesson plans. This also gets the students involved and at the same time assists in nurturing the digital literacy of students (Luckin., 2018).

Finally, the form of the assessment ensures continuity within the curriculum in a way that can help monitor the student progress. It enables teacher to modify the teaching strategies and check the learning outcomes as a way of meeting the learning objective as postulated by Black and Wiliam (1998). In sum, the curriculum has significant functions and purposes to lead the result of education and form the learners for future.

Principles of Effective Curriculum Design

The principles that are used to inform curriculum design are as follows. First and foremost, there must be a clear and decisive vision and mission. In the curriculum, there should be clear objectives and learning achievements in order that the students understand the expectations that the system has placed on them (Tyler, 1949).

Second, it should help make the conversation meaningful for both people. The content should in fact relate to the lives and careers of students. By doing this they keep them absorbing and motivated to learn (Tomlinson, 2001).

Third, there is equality. The curriculum should contain variations according to the type and requirements of the learners. This means that every student can gain and achieve in education (Gardner, 1983).

Fourth, flexibility is vital. The good curriculum should be compatible with updated information, technologies, and society changes. This can be even more pressing in the current context of the increasing speed of experiences (Luckin, 2018).

Last but not the least; there is always a need to conduct an assessment that will continue indefinitely. Formal or informal evaluations enable the determination of the performance of students, and these ways instructional processes. This makes it possible to fine – tune to enhance learning impacts (Black & Wiliam, 1998).

AI-Powered Curriculum Development

How AI Analyzes Educational Data

AI has importance in analyzing the educational data. It is a rather logical type of application, which process enormous amount of information with the help of algorithms. This assists the teachers in evaluating the students' performance as well as assessing learning behavior (Luckin & Holmes, 2016).

First, AI gathers information from different sources which are tests, assignments, and the record of their attendance. It then can arrange all this information for the purpose of identifying patterns. For example, with the help of AI one can determine subjects that are hardest for students (Siemens, 2013).

AI can also help to make learning experiences highly individualistic. From this information it offers individualized learning resources and activities that can be used to address each student's learning needs. This assists in enhancing interaction as well as accomplishment (Baker & Inventado, 2014).

Thirdly, the AI is capable of forecasting program performance in the future. Using historical information, it can predict which students will require additional complimentary or corrective strategy (Ferguson, 2012). This approach enables teachers to act before the student fails and find means for the latter's success.

Last but not the least, AI gives information on the teaching ideas to be employed. This way, an assessment of student outcomes enables teachers to track which interventions are likely to prove successful (Luckin & Holmes, 2016). In general, AI realigns and optimizes the utilization of educational data to enhance learning processes.

Examples of AI Tools Used for Curriculum Design

Of the curriculum application areas, AI applications are most seen in the context of adaptive learning. These systems provide content adaptation of the learning material based on the subject's learning curve and difficulty level by student. A well-known one is an example of the DreamBox Learning company. It provides math lessons that change based on the action of the child and presents each learner with a learning plan (DreamBox, 2023).

Another example of this layer is Smart Sparrow. This platform provides the paraphrasing of education where the educator can design a course that reacts to the learners. It is used in determining which teaching contents the students are weak in and modify them (Smart Sparrow, 2023).

Another valued AI resource is a Knewton. It uses the information acquired from students' engagement to offer them suitable suggestions to access learning materials (Knewton, 2023). This helps teachers in obtaining the context needed to implement part-to-whole instructional strategies that would suit individual needs.

Also, using AI for tracking students' performance, some platforms are identified as Khan academy. They offer assignments that the child needs to solve as well as videos that teaches what the child needs to know (Khan Academy, 2023).

Such AI tools are also useful in facilitating proactively the curriculum development process and enhancing the students' experience and retention.

Benefits of Personalized Learning Paths Shaped by AI

The setting of tailored learning paths using Artificial intelligence has been of great advantage. First, they address unique learning needs of every student. AI interprets the data on the students to determine the areas of strength and areas of difficulty.

This can be described as an advantage as different children are taught in a way that accommodates their learning rate (Luckin & Holmes, 2016).

Second, most students are more involved with unique learning processes or tracks designed for them. Indeed, students can feel more in charge when they learn at their own tutoring speed. It can result into increased student engagement with the content being provided (Baker & Inventado, 2014).

Third, these paths can bring benefit for learners and enhance quality of the learning process. In this way, AI prevents any crucial topic that a student faces difficulties within from being left out. Ferguson (2012) suggested that this type of concentrating can support students to get better scores and allow them to understand the materials that are being taught in class.

Fourth, it shows that developing personalized learning paths increases independence. Students are empowered to take responsibility of what they learn. This is the development of positive attributes that include self- regulation and motivation.

Finally, teachers can receive Artificial Intelligence suggestions. They get good information on students' performance and are therefore able to address the methods they are using in teaching (Siemens, 2013).

CASE STUDIES OF AI IN CURRICULUM DESIGN

Examples of Renowned Institutions Applied AI in Curriculum Design

A lot of education institutions have already applied AI into their curriculum. Arizona State University (ASU) has made a tremendous success story in the development of signature undergraduate programs. Currently, ASU has introduced a new system called the Intelligent Adaptive Learning system on its online platform. This system uses individual performances in delivery of learning content and materials. For students, it allows them to redo the content they did not understand and receive further materials to learn which they may not grasp at first.

Another example can be liked to Carnegie Mellon University that employs the "Open Learning Initiative" (OLI). OLI offer online classes that incorporate features that allow for the analysis of interaction among students. It can set contents and difficulty to dynamically shift with real time data. Through implementation of this approach, Carnegie Mellon University (2023) has observed new enhanced students' performance and interest in certain areas of learning such as statistics and physics.

Also, the University of Illinois at Urbana-Champaign has integrated use of AI in the learning mechanism as a way of facing and adapting. Student's "Illinois Compass" system recommends courses and material to them. It assists students better in planning their academic careers (University of Illinois, 2023).

Also, at Georgia State University, AI is applied to the advising process. For instance, their "Pounce" chatbot helps students and answers their questions and assist them during course enlistment. These supports have been instrumental in enhancing the student retention levels as noted next – Georgia State University (2023).

The University of Southern California uses AI in its approach called "USC Hybrid Learning". This model integrates face-to-face learning with fully online learning and uses artificial intelligence for data processing. flexible support and feedback process is provided to each student that let them improves at their own pace (University of Southern California, 2023).

Analysis of Outcomes and Improvements in Student Engagement and Performance

Studies have indicated that incorporation of AI has boosted student interest, and performance in class. Several works suggest that further significant correlation between the assigned learning paths and students' interest and motivation. And when the content is personalized, students embrace that they are getting something that meets their needs (Luckin & Holmes, 2016).

For instance, a study done at Arizona State University showed that performances of students who adopted AI-based adaptive learning system outperformed those of students in normal classes. The personalized feedback availed to the learners made it easy for them to appreciate their errors, and engage in a rematch. This kind of support works to enhance confidence and perseverance which are so important to learning.

The Open Learning Initiative at Carnegie Mellon University also testified to better passing gradients in courses that employed devices that were intelligent. Those who engaged with the adaptive components learned more masters the areas such as statistic. This means to say that in addition to enhancing students' learning interest, the concept of AI is also capable of improving students' performance (Carnegie Mellon University, 2023).

In addition, AI-based advising at Georgia State University made massive jumps in student retention rates. Pounce the AI chatbot would offer timely help and information to students and helped keep students on track. Therefore, the university observed a positive transition into more students walking away with their degrees.

Furthermore, research has pointed to the effect and discovered that students' level of engagement may lead to higher levels of student participation in class activities and free discourses. This leads to a richer learning environment where students also do not feel neglected and unheard (Baker, & Inventado, 2014).

Collectively, AI instruments enhance the learning process by enhancing student attendance and their accomplishments with customized, timely assistance and appropriate feedback. These enhancements indicate that when AI is implemented into education learners can gain better learning outcomes.

Challenges Faced and Lessons Learned from These Implementations

This paper shall present the several challenges that have occurred while applying AI in education Even though applying AI in education has some advantages, the following issues have been realized. A significant problem is the protection of data. This means that irrespective of the amount of data collected about students, institutions should ensure that such data is safe and used appropriately (Luckin & Holmes, 2016). There are issues concerning data gathering and handling which make organization reluctant to adopt AI tools.

The other problem is that one often must seek a teacher to train him on how to use certain features. Teachers can only embrace the AI tools if they know how they can benefit the learning processes. Teacher himself or herself facing with technology pressure and often not fully utilize AI (Baker & Inventado, 2014). Thus, rich, and sufficient professional development is critical to the success of the plan at hand.

Also, AI tends to be introduced in combination with other existing systems, and its integration can be quite problematic. One challenge, for example, some institutions experience technical problems when they would like to integrate the new AI tools CBTs with the legacy Learning Management Systems (LMS) LMS (Carnegie Mellon University, 2023). This can slow down implementation and the process of tumbling be rousing the frustration of the implementors or righteousness bearers.

Last but not the least interestingly, AI is a tool that assists in learning yet it is a sovereign known fact that can never be overemphasized that health education cannot be fully imparted without the human factor. Autonomy for the students can also mean that individualization of instruction can sometimes negate the significance of interpersonal relationships in students and teachers. Appropriate participation of an individual in technology usage and face-to-face communication is therefore essential, (Tomlinson, 2001). Such experience can inform the successful implementation endeavors in the future studies.

AI IN STUDENT ASSESSMENT

Importance of Assessment in Education

Several Types of Assessment: Formative, Summative, Diagnostic

AI improves formative, summative and diagnostic assessments by introducing flexibility and individual differences within the learners. The formative checkups, which are carried out during the learning process, are enriched with using the benefits of AI because it provides feedback instantly to the learners and trainers. For instance, teachers can use the feedback of the AI systems to understand the areas that require little understanding among students (Black & Wiliam, 1998). When it comes to AI, it can help a teacher edit lessons as students might be getting off track. Other benefits of the AI-driven formative assessments include, student self-control learning as the AI leads the learners towards the necessary resource (Baker & Inventado, 2014).

Assessment that occurs at the end of a unit or course, has been used in the past to gauge overall learning. In addition, due to its analytical experience, AI helps make summative assessment valid and significant by identifying trends and patterns of students' performance. AI uses other measures as contrasted with test scores such as the rate of completion of projects and the level of participation. This provides a better picture of students' performance as well (Harlen, 2007). As such, AI can draw out skills and competencies more than rote knowledge (Shute, 2011).

For the formative assessments, which are conducted at the onset of learning, AI determines strengths, and weaknesses of a student. By taking quintessential data from previous performance, AI tools can set up learning maps for each learner, in such a way that early intervention strategies also flow actionable paths; that are more appropriate (Brookhart & Nitko, 2019). All this goes a long way in aiding the teachers to be able to do lesson plans in a way that is fair for all the students based on their levels of learning preparedness (Chen et al., 2020).

The Role of Assessment in Student Learning and Feedback

AI turn assessment into a powerful leverage in fostering student learning and providing feedback. In the traditional setup, assessments tell what a learner has grasped, but with the use of AI, the assessment can also guide how a learner learns in real-time. AI- Assessment steadily collects and processes data that comes from the students' practices enabling teachers to modify practice (Luckin, R. & Holmes,

W., 2016). Such a continuous feedback process gives students the chance to check strong and weak points at once and fosters students' activity (Shute, 2011).

Us through AI is frequently less time-consuming and more precise compared to conventional approaches, which enable the students to modify their learning techniques quickly. For instance, the AI system can identify patterns of students' mistakes and recommend appropriate tasks to enhance those skills in the case of assessment (Baker & Inventado, 2014). Such timely feedback enhances student performance on mistakes thus providing positive results on learning process (Brookhart & Nitko, 2019).

Additionally, AI-related formative assessments can select questions which are appropriate to the student's capability, providing both a manageable level of difficulty to encourage learners to stay focused and challenged (Chen et al., 2020). This makes it easier for students to learn rather than memorize, which in turn is good for their learning abilities than for end of semester tests.

AI-ENHANCED ASSESSMENT TOOLS USED

Overview of AI Technologies Used for Assessment

This kind of assessment utilizes Artificial Intelligence technologies including; Machine learning (ML), and Natural Language Processing (NLP). Machine learning works with the data received from students and seizures that the identification of patterns which will enable the teachers to understand the student better. Another capability of the ML algorithms is adaptive testing whereby questions given tend to vary depending on the student's choice (Baker & Inventado, 2014). Such dynamic assessment of the students is very effective in keeping the students active and at the same time gives a real picture of what they understand (Chen et al., 2020).

In the evaluative sense NLP may be used to help facilitate an AI to read out and grade an essay or any other open text response from a student. The opposite to paper grading and discussion is NLP that can quantify grammar, coherence, and content quality, giving more effective and uniform results than usual grading practices concerning suggested texts (Hirschberg & Manning, 2015). This technology also avails feedback on writing as students go through it with instructions given on the corrections they need to make (Luckin, R. & Holmes, W., 2016) .

Other AI tools like speech recognition intervene to assess spoken responses. This is mostly helpful in language acquisition since it considers pronunciation, fluency, and the usage of acquired vocabularies. By these technologies, one can design specific exercises; to help students achieve some skills they have difficulties with

(Litman et al., 2018). These developments prompt its protection so that, alongside efficiency, evaluations are relevant to the dynamic learning process.

Advantages of AI to Provide Real-Time Feedback and Personalized Assessments

Several benefits are postured to follow the adoption of AI especially in the provision of real time feedback and individual assessments that improves learning results. In the context of live tutoring, it is easy for students to see where they have gone wrong and to continue working through the problem without getting disgusted with the learning process (Shute, 2011). The instant feedback from such AI systems can only help with improvement since the students are told areas they struggled with directly.

AI also provides personalized feedback based on each student's performance because it can easily identify the rate and method that is best suited to the learning process for every student. For instance, machine learning to student performance to identify possible response patterns, and then modify the questions and offer each student a personalized pathway. This makes the program not too difficult frustrating the student or too easy to make the student lose interest in the program (Baker and Inventado, 2014). Also, different self-tests have less anxiety because students are not exposed to a normative approach that may not suit the mode they learn best (Chen et al., 2020).

AI also has the capability of handling large data means that teachers can have a clear picture of each student's progress and challenges. These provide teacher with information to be able to influence their teaching in accordance with the performance records of the learners thus enhancing the teaching process hence optimum (Luckin, R. & Holmes, W., 2016).

Also, specific comments give direction to every learner by pointing out what they did right and what they should change, which makes the students to work on character rather than being motivated by scores (Hattie & Timperley, 2007). AI's concurrent tracking of students' progress over a period also enhances the learning experience as it enhances long-term learning goals self-paced knowledge building. Few probable benefits of AI for teachers is presented in Table 2.

Table 2. Potential benefits of AI for teachers

Benefit	Description	Example
Less Grading Time	AI scores assignments fast	Saves time on grading essays
Improved Class Planning	AI suggests lesson plans on the basis of data	Acclimates plans to student needs
Early Warning System	AI recognizes struggling students	Helps teachers to interfere earlier
Real-Time Progress Tracking	Shows student progress promptly	Easier tracking of overall class performance
Access to Resources	AI curates extra learning materials	Recommends videos, articles for each topic

Comparison of Traditional Assessment Methods with AI-Driven Assessments

Conventional tests are normally in form of papers, quizzes or assignments that are marked by the instructors. These methods are universally known, and students and teachers have previously employed them (Cojorn, K., & Sonsupap, K., 2024) (Cojorn, K., & Sonsupap, K., 2024). Traditional grading is usually an arbitrary model of grading because teachers' opinions can differ (Cope et al., 2021). That is why some instructors may have some sort of prejudices or disparity when grading which is even more prevalent in large classes (Falasi, 2024). Also, teachers may spend much time on grading, and as a result, feedback to students may also take a while (Miller, 2024).

AI-based assessments on the other hand auto-generate algorithms such as, machine learning to analyze the student responses. Such systems may easily offer an option for automatically grading examinations or essays and provide feedback immediately (Cope et al., 2021). Such immediate feedback assists students and correct their work more efficiently than doing it on their own (Falasi, 2024). AI smart systems are also fair in decisions and results and produce comparable scores for each learner, thereby eliminating any chance of bias (Cojorn, K., & Sonsupap, K., 2024). Another is that assessment through AI means can develop a test considering the result of a student, in other words, an adaptive test (Miller, 2024).

But it is found that there are some limitations in its application. Additionally, AI-based facilities consider technological and internet connection facilities which are limited in access to students particularly those in the rural areas (Cope et al., 2021). They are often less reliant on technology, and therefore can be implemented in the classroom to teachers' benefit across all students (Miller, 2024). In addition, when AI is used in grading, it may lead to ignoring complex answers or creativity because it generally works with patterns and keywords (Falasi, 2024).

Therefore, Language Generation has its own benefits which may suit the intended use for the application better than the Method of Units. Traditional assessment methods can provide accurate and easily administered results, whereas AI-integrated tests provide faster, better-targeted, and more consistent results from the grading process (Cope et al., 2021). Perhaps moderating between the two might be the most effective approach in meeting all the learning types.

Comparison between Traditional and AI-Driven Assessment Methods is presented in Table 3.

Table 3. Comparison between traditional vs. AI-driven assessment methods

Category	Traditional Assessment	AI-Driven Assessment
Speed of Feedback	Usually, it takes days or even weeks	Often it is done immediately or within few minutes or hours
Personalization Level	Limited	High
Data Analysis Depth	Basic grading	Detailed performance insights
Adaptability to Student Needs	Standardized exams	Acclimates based on student responses
Frequency of Updates	Annual or occasional	Regular updates

CASE STUDIES OF AI IN STUDENT ASSESSMENT

Examples of Institutions Using AI for Assessment Purposes

Today, many institutions have integrated AI in student assessment. For instance, artificial intelligence software is utilized by the University of Sydney to mark written tasks. This software check essays for grammars, structures, and even their uniqueness and provides students with the feedback in a short time (Miller, 2024). This system becomes very useful to teachers, especially those with large learning groups and offers the students instant feedback that they can apply on (Miller, 2024).

Another use of AI tools at Stanford University is in assessments. Faculties in computer science use AI in grading coding exercising or homework. It also autonomously finds syntax errors in code and with suggestions allows students to correct mistakes and enhance their talent on the go (Paiva, et. al., 2022). The AI system also helps in minimizing grading blunders that is, all students are graded appropriately (Paiva, et. al., 2022). An artificial intelligence based chatbot 'Jill Watson' is employed in Georgia Institute of technology to help students and respond to questions in online courses. It is interactive and provides instant feedback and if a student does not understand a concept, they, (Goel & Joyner, 2017). This system enables the students to receive feedback on the assignment done anytime resulting to better learning experience (Goel & Joyner, 2017).

Finally, AI is implemented in language classes at Arizona State University. They also use AI software that transcribes what the students say, which assesses pronunciation, grammar, and fluency (Woo, 2021). This tool provides students with the first and second language written feedback that is fast and meticulous to enhance their writing skills.

Evaluation of Student Performance, Data Analysis, and Personalized Learning Outcomes

AI is enhancing how schools assess the performance of the students. From the quizzes, assignments, and the other learning activities that are set within the course, it can capture data for each of the students, to determine their areas of prowess as well as the areas where they require a lot of improvement in (González-Calatayud, et. al, 2021). This data is used to display trends in learning, for example, in which areas students may require more guidance (Vlasova, et. al., 2019). From this perspective, teachers can learn how students are coping and change the lessons to fit their learning pace (Shiva, 2024).

AI makes personalized learning less of a challenge. AI systems can recommend specific lessons or more practice sets based on data metrics using analysis which helps create more personalized learning (Xu, 2024). For instance, if a student has a weakness in mathematics, the AI is capable to recommend additional exercises to complete in that subject (González-Calatayud, et. al, 2021). When it comes to the academic life of a learner, this type of differentiation benefits helps the learner receive better results in Languages since he has been enlightened on areas that he has always found to be hard.

Another area is when AI can predict future performance. Being able to process complex student data themes, AI systems can identify students that may likely have difficulty with the forthcoming lessons (Shiva, 2024). It is due to this that a teacher can come in early warning and decide and availabilities to offer support after comprehending the book and facts of the class before the student drops even further behind. In addition, due to the AI, feedback can be also given in the form of more personal and easily assessed by the students rapidly with the possibility to correct the mistakes during the work process (Vlasova, et. al., 2019).

AI in student evaluation and data analysis leads to making learning as personal as possible. It offers information necessary for teachers to steer the learners in the right manner thus more favorable results for each learner.

Argument of Ethical Thoughts and Biases in AI Assessment Tools

The recent AI assessment tools raise ethical concerns that include issues to do with fairness and bias. AI systems learn from data and thus, if their data contains Bias, they too will exhibit bias (Sulaimon, 2023). For example, if some of the groups are missing in the data, the AI will give a wrong perception of other students especially those from that background (Omughelli et al., 2024). This could end up with wrong categorization of the students or wrong grading (Shiva, 2024).

This is the method that AI tools can affect students unequally due to bias. Language is also the principal downside of some AI systems because they sort language differently and non-native speakers suffer from that (Omughelli et al., 2024). Teachers must critically create and choose AI implementations so that they do not perpetuate bias or negatively affect any class population (Sulaimon, 2023).

Privacy is another ethical issue. Every human-being has a right to privacy. It should not be violated in any way, shape, or form. Machine learning predictions as part of AI evaluations employ student information in individual learning; this information is credible. Existing issues arise as to whether too much data should be compiled and how the acquisition of such data is handled (Vaza, et. al., 2024). To ensure appropriate use of data, 'students' data should be safeguarded to avoid misuse; the information gathered by the schools must well explain what data is gathered and why it is being gathered (Shiva, 2024). Few significant ethical concerns of AI in Education are presented in Table 4.

Table 4. Key ethical concerns of AI in education

Concern	Description	Possible Impact
Privacy	AI collects personal student data	Risk of unauthorized data access
Bias	AI may reflect biased training data	Unequal treatment in grading or resources
Lack of Transparency	AI's decisions can be hard to understand	Teachers may not trust or use AI tools
Accountability	AI may make wrong or unfair decisions	Hard to hold AI accountable in assessments
Consent	Students may not understand data usage	Leads to ethical and legal issues

CHALLENGES AND CONSIDERATIONS

Ethical Concerns

Privacy Issues Related to Data Collection and Usage

While using AI in delivering education there are various issues which rise in demand particularly privacy. AI systems also get a lot of data from students. This data can be personal information, academic performance, behavior patterns, etc (Vaza, et. al., 2024). This type of information gathering brings into fore how this information is managed and who get to have a hold on this info (Mehdaoui, 2024).

One main areas of concern is that the students may not be aware of the use of their data. The practices of many AI-based solutions often do not list their data acquisition processes transparently (González-Calatayud, et. al, 2021). Such opaqueness can cause discomfort to students and parents on account of privacy of their information. In the light of the present study, it is imperative that schools properly educate students on what data is compiled, the reasons for doing so, and the ways in which such data will be utilized moving forward (Omughelli et al., 2024).

The second potential problem is data protection. That is why if the data of the students is considered sensitive, then it can be easily compromised in case the data of the school is targeted by hackers and others. Cyber security means there is a risk of individuality theft or unlawful access to personal data (Attai, 2019). The school and other educational institutions are facing challenges of the high risk of their students' data being exposed to hackers (Vaza, et. al., 2024).

Also, there could be some cases of abuse of data as well. This data shared for educational use can be used in aspects that the students never consented to (Mehdaoui, 2024). Students' data must not be shared or utilized for any aim that is outside the scope of what the data was collected for (González-Calatayud, et. al, 2021).

To mitigate these risks it becomes necessary to address these concerns to safeguard students and increase the level of faith in AI.

Bias and Fairness in AI Algorithms

Automated systems involve application of artificial intelligence, with these serving objectives including enhancing assessments as well as designing of curricula. But such algorithms can be unfair most of the time. Bias refers to any unfair treatment of specific groups by artificial intelligence systems because of the data fed to them, or the structures developed in the system (Sulaimon, 2023). For example, if the training samples for an AI model are not diverse, the performance of the algorithm in evaluating all students will be questionable (Omughelli et al., 2024).

In equal measures this can lead to bias in grading and in equal measures eliminates the possibilities of some learners.

It is crucial that these computers are built to be fair. Education should be provided to all students at an equal level and the children equally should be provided equal opportunities (Shiva, 2024). If the AI tool does the evaluation of the students using a biased data set, then it ends up exaggerating the inequalities. For instance, it may be that student belonging to the minority group, will be less optimally served by an AI since their circumstances are not reflected in the training data (Attai, 2019). This prevents students and affects their confidence levels depending on what they have or have not been able to find.

Developers of AI algorithms are expected to use fair set of data that are equally balanced. Which in turn assist in developing systems that are capable to appraise and understand all students improved (Sulaimon, 2023). These algorithms need to be assessed continuously to detect if any bias found and change accordingly (Omughelli et al., 2024).

Also, the paper calls for transparency in the decisions made by algorithms. The general populace, teachers, and learners, we are still in the learning process, then they must understand how the AI assessment's function. Such transparency can go a long way in creating public trust into use of AI in education, as well as; guarantee proper usage of Application in education (Vaza, et. al., 2024). These issues therefore need to be appreciated by educators so that they can help all the learners in the most appropriate way.

Implementation Challenges

Technological Barriers and the Essential for Infrastructure

Technological options concern as AI finds its way more in education systems: There are some significant obstacles that are technological in nature. There is also limited resources sometimes especially in the rural areas (Vaza, et. al., 2024). As a result of such an implication, students are unable to harness the use of AI tools or even enroll for online courses since they must rely on the internet. This gap can further worsen the digital divide regarding students who do or do not have access to technology (Shiva, 2024).

A third challenge is the problems such as old computers and which are usually outdated in most schools. For example,, many educational universities and colleges try to implement AI technologies in their learning systems in outdated computing devices that might be incompatible. This constrains the adoption of sophisticated educational technologies within the organization to teachers and students.

Training for teachers is also important. Therefore, it is high time that educators learn how to incorporate the AI tools in their learning institutions (Cojorn, K., & Sonsupap, K., 2024). For this reason, lack of training for a teacher may make it hard for the teacher to incorporate AI into teaching. This leads to the underutilization of AI skills hence students denied the opportunity to be taught using the technique (Vlasova, et. al., 2019).

Also, there is an issue regarding the protection of information and security regarding data collected. Due to lack of strong security measures that is required when implementing AI tools in schools they may refuse to embrace this tool with a belief that this may lead to leakage of their data.

It could be mentioned that technological issues as well as the creation of the proper infrastructure is indispensable for achieving the goal of implementing AI in the field of education. They include; guaranteeing efficient internet connections; enhancing the technology used in teaching; offering staff development sessions for teachers; and incorporating secure data solutions in the class.

Resistance from Educators and Institutions Toward Adopting AI

Most of the educators and institutions that give a second thought to using the AI in education. The first cause for this resistance is obviously job insecurity. Students fear that AI may render their work unnecessary, or at least reduce their responsibilities in teaching (Alwaqdani, 2024). This fear can then result in rejection of new technologies, as educators may feel that AI enabled tools are capable of some aspects of teaching.

The other reason is the lack of knowledge regarding AI. Most the educators and students are not familiar with AI technologies, for which many of them do not feel at ease when using the technologies (Vaza, et. al., 2024). If teachers are not aware of how to incorporate its usage in their teaching methods, they can avoid its integration into their classroom (González-Calatayud, et. al, 2021). One such a complication is the lack of knowledge about how to adopt AI into the learning system.

Besides, there may be doubts about the role of AI in education or some doubts on the usefulness of AI in education. Some educators raise the argument that the use of AI can improve matters by increasing learning outcomes (Liando, N. V. F., & Tatipang, D. P., 2024). Such stakeholders may reason that conventional learning techniques are superior and consistent when compared to AI-enabled strategies (Vlasova, et. al., 2019).

Another is institutional one, as the information and other relevant data enter an organization, they meet with certain organizational. Structures which challenge or deny their reality. There may not be enough funds as well as school structure that would allow for the correct usage of AI systems (Cojorn, K., & Sonsupap, K.,

2024). The challenge here is that due to budgetary constraints, institutions unable to invest much in new technologies meaning that they cannot possibly implement AI (Alwaqdani, 2024).

Thus, educators' and institutions' reluctance to embrace AI we can state the following reasons – job loss, lack of knowledge, disbelief in the effectiveness of AI, and administrative barriers.

FUTURE DIRECTIONS AND SOLUTIONS

Thus, the future of education with AI appears quite bright but many things should be planned. First, more research is must to identify the effects of AI in classrooms. How AI influences learning can therefore inform the ways in which it can be enhanced (Kim, et. al., 2022). Research can also discover effective approaches toward the use of AI applications in learning and evaluation (Liando, N. V. F., & Tatipang, D. P., 2024).

Secondly, another component of learning is training for teachers. Teachers should understand how they can apply AI in teaching (González-Calatayud, et. al, 2021). Continual learning activities must involve an opportunity for teachers to practice and have the requisite tools for AI teaching (Alwaqdani, 2024). This will go a long way in making the educators to be at ease when using the AI in enhancing the students learning.

Thirdly, schools should put great emphasis on infrastructure. Internet stability, and recent technologies are essential conditions that can enable the proper functioning of the AI (Cojorn, K., & Sonsupap, K., 2024). Clients feel that schools should improve the use of IT technology so that every learner can benefit from artificial intelligence materials (Vaza, et. al., 2024).

This is also due to the reason that the various stakeholders involved in the project should work hand in hand. Due to the potential of different AI tools in education, educators, administrators, and AI developers need to find ways to develop such tools that will meet the needs of education (Liando, N. V. F., & Tatipang, D. P., 2024) . It can be advantageous in making sure that, as adopted and employed by teachers and students, AI interfaces are efficient.

Finally, corrupt issues are important to address. Specifically, it is crucial for schools to be confident that AI is equitable and private to students (Collinson, et. al, 2009). These AI algorithms work will assist in gaining the trust required among educators and students.

The future of practice of AI in education will best be served only through the call for research, for better teacher education programs, better infrastructure for technology and collaboration along with ethical practices at the same. If we strategist and implement these areas, it becomes possible to improve learning experiences and consequently the outcome of every student.

Strategies for Overcoming Challenges in AI Integration

That is why there are issues of integrating AI in education, but there are ways to address them. First, it means that schools should conduct teaching practices to train teachers. First, members of the educational community should realize potential benefits and, more importantly, limitations of practical application of AI tools (González-Calatayud, et. al, 2021). Teachers stand to benefit from the programs by gaining confidence as they go about their profession (Alwaqdani, 2024).

Second, institutions that will be involved in implementing this policy should enhance their infrastructure. Modern technology and reliable internet are prerequisites so that the AI tools could operate optimally (Cojorn, K., & Sonsupap, K., 2024). This way it is guarantee that every student will be able to use the AI resources once upgrades are made.

Third, schools need to pay our attention on data privacy and security aspects. The most notable recommendation is that clear policies about data use will go a long way in safeguarding students' information (Liando, N. V. F., & Tatipang, D. P., 2024). This increases trust from educators and students as they have a clear view of what is going on (Collinson, et. al, 2009).

Last but not the least stakeholders should collaborate. In this regard, educators, administrators, and AI developers must join hands to build tools that can address educational demand (Kim, et. al., 2022). It is due to this factor that collaboration happens to make certain that the AI solutions developed are applicable and efficient in the teaching processes for the tutors and learners.

Table 5. Challenges to AI adoption in schools

Challenge	Explanation	Example Impact
High Costs	AI tools are generally expensive	Limited adoption in underfunded schools
Lack of Technical Skills	Teachers need training to use AI	Delays in effective implementation
Resistance to Change	Some prefer traditional approaches	Fewer teachers willing to use AI
Infrastructure Needs	Necessitates internet and various modern devices	Challenges in rural or under-resourced areas
Data Security Concerns	Need to protect sensitive student information	Risk of data breaches if not secure

Returns of Continuing Education and Staff Development for Education

Teacher must continue their education and develop staff for them to effectively deliver their duties. These programs assist instructors in acquiring new knowledge and information with teaching technology with relation to AI (González-Calatayud, et. al, 2021). That means when teachers implement the knowledge of AI tools in courses, then students benefit from it (Alwaqdani, 2024).

Teacher training also helps in confidence enhancement owing to the financial commitment made in enhancing the profession. Teachers who have undergone through training can easily grab all the training they need and this will make them to be more prepared and satisfied with their parcels in school (Kim, et. al., 2022). This satisfaction can lead to lower turnover rates, which is good for students they will not have to deal with different professors and class (Liando, N. V. F., & Tatipang, D. P., 2024).

However, as one goes to the next level of learning or training, teachers are made to work together. Teachers can exchange with other teachers and this determines a good learning atmosphere (Cojorn, K., & Sonsupap, K., 2024). This kind of partnership can enrich the teaching and learning process for teachers, as well as for the students.

According to the research done it was evident that student performance improved where training was continuous. Collinson, et. al. has noted that if teachers are well trained, the students will do well in their tests (Collinson, et. al., 2009). Thus, it follows that the staff development and continuing education ensue to better teacher ratings, increased teacher assurance and staff cooperation, ideal learning, and increased achievement of students. Briefs summary about the paper is presented in Table 6.

Table 6. Briefs summary about the paper

Category	Key Information
Research Question	This paper seeks to answer the following questions; Firstly, what are the opportunities for AI in education curriculum design and student assessment? Secondly, what are the drawbacks of applying AI to education curriculum design and the assessment of students? Finally, what is the ethical implication of this approach to education curriculum design and the assessment of students?
Significance	This paper demonstrates how AI can help design optimized curriculum and assessment to cater for students' individual needs. Benefitting from and, at the same time, outlining managerially responsible strategies for addressing the presented opportunities and risks, it helps educators and policymakers deliberate about the proper ways of AI implementation for enhancing the efficiency and informativeness of educational processes.
The Evolution of Education Technology	Includes the history of integrating educational technology into classrooms, the foremost landmark dates of integration, and the shift from conventional to contemporary approaches to learning.
Current Trends in Educational Technology	Emphasizes on the increasing use of intelligent systems and technology tools, smart content, and services, intelligence and efficient methods of learning such as adaptive learning, big data, and analysis, and intelligent learning systems.
AI in Curriculum Design	Examines how artificial intelligence tools help in innovative curriculum development by working with educational data to build effective learning sequences and improve learner experiences.
Importance of Curriculum Design	Describes curriculum as means of attaining educational objectives and presents major concepts about how such objectives can be realized for students' benefit.
AI-Powered Curriculum Development	Touches upon the subject of data interpretation and its benefits for AI-based personalized curriculum design; it also lists some of the tools and advantages
AI in Student Assessment	Focuses on real time evaluation of assessments facilitated by AI, Personalized assessment, and the shift from measuring test/ exam related abilities only.
Types of Assessment	Explains formative, summative, and diagnostic practices of assessment with an exception towards how increase quality form support AI feedback and learning.
AI-Enhanced Assessment Tools	Provides information about AI technologies that are used during the assessment and highlights the difference from other forms of assessment.
Case Studies	Presents specific cases in terms of AI being employed in the design of learning curriculums and the assessment of students, demonstrated effects on interest and achievement.
Challenges and Considerations	Stipulates ethical and legal concerns in relation to AI, specifically, privacy, and bias challenges; Technological factors; and institutional factors that reject AI in education.
Future Directions and Solutions	Some recommendations include; staff development, planning, and bringing into practice ethically sound integration of AI in the educational systems.

CONCLUSION

In this chapter, we discussed one of the most promising adjuncts of the future education: artificial intelligence. In our conversation we walked through how AI can be deployed to enhance the creation of teaching material and assessment. According to the text, these two areas are essential for offering good education. The use of AI as part of business functions has positive effects that can be seen from practicing this technology in organizations, but it also brings problems that must be solved to advance this approach to its full potential.

First, we explained how exactly AI can improve the process of designing a curriculum. Here, AI has the potential of processing information concerning students learning behaviors. Including in their strengths and weaknesses. Thus, the teacher obtains the information to make different learning-teaching situations. The upshot of this is that the kind of lessons that will be taught can be designed in such a way that they can fit the requirement of any learner. For instance, using AI, a teacher can be able to give out feedback to students within no time. This enables them to see the progress they have made and make correction where required instantly.

Then, we considered AI-based evaluations in detail based on the findings presented in the earlier section. These assessments are also more efficient and accurate than conventional forms of evaluation. It may be done with ease using AI thereby establishing a correlation between student performance and several subjects. They can audit the learning in terms of patterns and or trends. In addition, it can eliminate bias in assessments to an extent. This results in a better evaluation of all students irrespective of the learning environment they come from.

Nevertheless, the following are some of the challenges that must be solved to achieve development in the integration of AI. The other major weakness is the fact that there is always a need for training for the teachers. AI utility should be learned by educators for its implementation in education. The ideal implementation of AI concepts in the classroom cannot be achieved without the adequate training. Hence, schools need to put more resources in professional development programs. This will assist teachers to have more confidence in the issue of AI technologies.

The fourth task is the need to have adequately developed infrastructure. This is especially the case since most schools in the society does not possess the facilities and technology like the internet that supports the use of artificial intelligence. This digital divide needs to be addressed to ensure that students at Georgian can get an appropriate resource in AI. Schools should strive at increasing the quality of the technological equipment they possess as well as guaranteeing strong internet connections.

As will be seen in the following section, ethical issues also form part of the debate as it concerns the incorporation of AI in learning. The protection of data and their security are the biggest concerns. School has the responsibility to safeguard and properly utilize student information. The effectiveness of recommendation algorithms also implies disclosing how these algorithms function to gain trust of educators, students, and parents. There should be clear cut measures to respond to these ethical questions.

As for the prospective the role of AI in education is quite perspective. Considering this then, the advancement of technology is likely to yield better and creative approaches to teaching and learning. This paper demonstrates that AI can be useful to educators in developing valuable and interesting education processes. Yet, for this potential to be fully realized, it is important that all the stakeholders in the value chain engage in partnerships.

Teachers, administrators, and technology designers and manufactures must collaborate. They should collaborate to achieve a proper optimization of using AI. Several agencies will be created to form a collaboration, which will in turn produce real tools for use by teachers and students. As a result, there is a need for policymakers to develop policies that will enable the increase of AI use in education. Technology and training program's funding is important. Schools require such resources to use and utilize AI optimally to enhance learning and education for every learner.

AI developers should always aim to work with or for educators and students. Applying teachers in planning the process can help guarantee that these tools are both effective and easy to use. The following approach can be used to develop options that may improve conceptual approaches to teaching and learning.

REFERENCES

Alwaqdani, M. (2024). Investigating teachers' perceptions of artificial intelligence tools in education: Potential and difficulties. *Education and Information Technologies*, 1–19.

Attai, L. (2019). *Protecting student data privacy: Classroom fundamentals*. Rowman & Littlefield.

Baker, R. S., & Inventado, P. S. (2014). Educational Data Mining and Learning Analytics. In Larusson, J. A., & White, B. (Eds.), *Learning Analytics: From Research to Practice* (pp. 61–75). Springer.

Black, P., & Wiliam, D. (1998). Assessment and Classroom Learning. *Assessment in Education: Principles, Policy & Practice*, *5*(1), 7–74.

Bloom, B. S. (1956). *Taxonomy of Educational Objectives, Handbook: The Cognitive Domain*. David McKay.

Brookhart, S. M., & Nitko, A. J. (2019). *Educational Assessment of Students*. Pearson.

. Carnegie Mellon University. (2023). [https://oli.cmu.edu/]Open Learning Initiative.

Chen, L., Chen, P., & Lin, Z. (2020). Artificial intelligence in education: A review. *IEEE Access : Practical Innovations, Open Solutions*, *8*, 75264–75278.

Chimbunde, P., & Moreeng, B. B. (2024). The Sustainability of Curriculum Reform and Implementation Through Teacher Participation. *Evidence from Social Studies Teachers*, *6*(1), 83–98.

Cojorn, K., & Sonsupap, K. (2024). A collaborative professional development and its impact on teachers' ability to foster higher-order thinking. [EduLearn]. *Journal of Education and Learning*, *18*(2), 561–569. DOI: 10.11591/edulearn.v18i2.21182

Collinson, V., Kozina, E., Lin, Y.-H. K., Ling, L., Matheson, I., Newcombe, L., & Zogla, I. (2009). Professional development for teachers: A world of change. *European Journal of Teacher Education*, *32*(1), 3–19.

Cope, B., Kalantzis, M., & Searsmith, D. (2021). Artificial intelligence for education: Knowledge and its assessment in AI-enabled learning ecologies. *Educational Philosophy and Theory*, *53*(12), 1229–1245.

Cuban, L. (1986). *Teachers and Machines: The Classroom Use of Technology Since 1920*. Teachers College Press. [ISBN: 9780807727928]

DreamBox Learning. (2023). [https://www.dreambox.com/] About DreamBox Learning.

Falasi, M. (2024). Innovative pedagogies: A comparative analysis of traditional and modern teaching methods. *Academy of Educational Leadership Journal*, *28*(1), 1–2.

Ferguson, R. (2012). Learning Analytics: Drivers, Developments and Challenges. *International Journal of Technology Enhanced Learning*, *4*(5-6), 304–317.

García, F. P., Cânovas, Ó., & Clemente, F. J. G. (2024). Exploring AI Techniques for Generalizable Teaching Practice Identification. *IEEE Access, PP*, (99), 1–1.

Gardner, H. (1983). *Frames of Mind: The Theory of Multiple Intelligences.,* Published by Basic Books, A Member of the Perseus Books Group.

Georgia State University. (2023). Pounce Chatbot. [https://news.gsu.edu/2022/03/21/classroom-chatbot-improves-student-performance-study-says/],

Goel, A. K., & Joyner, D. A. (2017). Using AI to teach AI: Lessons from an online AI class. *AI Magazine*, *38*(2), 48–59.

González-Calatayud, V., Prendes-Espinosa, P., & Roig-Vila, R. (2021). Artificial intelligence for student assessment: A systematic review. *Applied Sciences (Basel, Switzerland)*, *11*(12), 5467.

Harlen, W. (2007). *Assessment of Learning*. SAGE Publications.

Hattie, J., & Timperley, H. (2007). The Power of Feedback. *Review of Educational Research*, *77*(1), 81–112.

Hirschberg, J., & Manning, C. D. (2015). Advances in Natural Language Processing. *Science*, *349*(6245), 261–266. PMID: 26185244

Khan Academy. [https://www.khanacademy.org/about]. [Accessed on 10th November, 2024]

Kim, J., Lee, H., & Cho, Y. H. (2022). Learning design to support student-AI collaboration: Perspectives of leading teachers for AI in education. *Education and Information Technologies*, *27*(5), 6069–6104.

Liando, N. V. F., & Tatipang, D. P. (2024). *Enlightened Minds: Navigating The Nexus Of Artificial Intelligence And Educational Modernization*. Penerbit Tahta Media.

Litman, D., Strik, H., & Lim, G. S. (2018). Speech technologies and the assessment of second language speaking: Approaches, challenges, and opportunities. *Language Assessment Quarterly*, *15*(3), 294–309.

. Luckin, R. (2018). *Enhancing Learning and Teaching with Technology: What the Research Says*. UCL IOE Press. UCL Institute of Education, University of London, 20 Bedford Way, London WC1H 0AL.

. Luckin, R., & Holmes, W. (2016). Intelligence unleashed: An argument for AI in education.

Mehdaoui, A. (2024). Unveiling Barriers and Challenges of AI Technology Integration in Education: Assessing Teachers' Perceptions, Readiness and Anticipated Resistance. *Futurity Education*, *4*(4), 95–108.

Mendez, G., Ochoa, X., Chiluiza, K., & De Wever, B. (2014). Curricular design analysis: A data-driven perspective. *Journal of Learning Analytics*, *1*(3), 84–119.

Miller, W. (2024). Adapting to AI: Reimagining the Role of Assessment Professionals. Intersection: A Journal at the Intersection of Assessment and Learning, 5(4), 99-113.

Moore, M. G., & Kearsley, G. (2012). Distance Education: A Systems View of Online

Omughelli, D., Gordon, N., & Al Jaber, T. (2024). Fairness, Bias, and Ethics in AI: Exploring the Factors Affecting Student Performance. *Journal of International Communication*, *3*(2), 100–110.

Paiva, J. C., Leal, J. P., & Figueira, Á. (2022). Automated assessment in computer science education: A state-of-the-art review. [TOCE]. *ACM Transactions on Computing Education*, *22*(3), 1–40.

Sandhu, D. S. (1994). Cultural Diversity in Classrooms: What Teachers Need To Know.

Santos, L., & Cai, J. (2016). Curriculum and assessment. In *The second handbook of research on the Psychology of Mathematics Education* (pp. 151–185). Brill.

Selwyn, N., & Facer, K. (2014). The sociology of education and digital technology: Past, present and future. *Oxford Review of Education*, *40*(4), 482–496.

Shiva, K., Etikani, P., Bhaskar, V. V. S. R., Nuguri, S., & Dave, A. (2024). Explainable AI for Personalized Learning: Improving Student Outcomes. *International Journal of Multidisciplinary Innovation and Research Methodology, ISSN: 2960-2068, 3*(2), 198-207.

Shute, V. J. (2011). Stealth assessment in computer-based games to support learning. *Computer games and instruction, 55*(2), 503-524.

Siemens, G. (2013). Learning analytics: The emergence of a discipline. *The American Behavioral Scientist*, *57*(10), 1380–1400.

Smart Sparrow. (2023). [https://www.smartsparrow.com/] Adaptive Elearning Platform. [Accessed on 11th November, 2024].

Swiecki, Z., Khosravi, H., Chen, G., Martinez-Maldonado, R., Lodge, J. M., Milligan, S., Selwyn, L., & Gašević, D. (2022). Assessment in the age of artificial intelligence. *Computers and Education: Artificial Intelligence*, *3*, 100075.

Tang, Y., Liang, J., Hare, R., & Wang, F. Y. (2020). A personalized learning system for parallel intelligent education. *IEEE Transactions on Computational Social Systems*, *7*(2), 352–361.

Tomlinson, C. A. (2001). *How to Differentiate Instruction in Mixed-Ability Classrooms*. ASCD.

Tyler, R. (2021). *Basic Principles of Curriculum and Instruction*. University of Chicago Press.

University of Illinois. (2023). [https://online.illinois.edu/] Illinois Compass.

University of Southern California. (2023). [https://viterbigrad.usc.edu/] USC Hybrid Learning [Accessed on 11th November, 2024].

Vaza, R. N., Parmar, A. B., Mishra, P. S., Abdullah, I., & Velu, C. M. (2024). Security And Privacy Concerns In AI-Enabled Iot Educational Frameworks: An In-Depth Analysis. *Educational Administration: Theory and Practice*, *30*(4), 8436–8445.

Vlasova, E. Z., Avksentieva, E. Y., Goncharova, S. V., & Aksyutin, P. A. (2019). Artificial intelligence-The space for the new possibilities to train teachers. *Espacios*, *40*(9), 17.

Woo, L. J., & Choi, H. (2021). Systematic review for AI-based language learning tools. *Journal of Digital Contents Society*, *22*(11), 1783–1792.

Xu, Z. (2024). AI in education: Enhancing learning experiences and student outcomes. *Appl. Comput. Eng*, *51*, 104–111.

ADDITIONAL READING

Chen, X., Zou, D., Xie, H., Cheng, G., & Liu, C. (2022). Two decades of artificial intelligence in education. *Journal of Educational Technology & Society*, *25*(1), 28–47.

DeMonte, J. (2013). *High-Quality Professional Development for Teachers: Supporting Teacher Training to Improve Student Learning*. Center for American Progress.

Gouëdard, P., Pont, B., Hyttinen, S., & Huang, P. (2020). Curriculum reform: A literature review to support effective implementation.

Khan, M. (2023). *Ethics of Assessment in Higher Education–an Analysis of AI and Contemporary Teaching* (No. 11445). EasyChair.

Kotob, M. M., & Abadi, M. A. (2019). The influence of differentiated instruction on academic achievement of students in mixed ability classrooms. *International Linguistics Research*, *2*(2), 8–p8.

Luckin, R., & Holmes, W. (2016). Intelligence unleashed: An argument for AI in education.

Owan, V. J., Abang, K. B., Idika, D. O., Etta, E. O., & Bassey, B. A. (2023). Exploring the potential of artificial intelligence tools in educational measurement and assessment. *Eurasia Journal of Mathematics, Science and Technology Education*, *19*(8), em2307.

Rabiatu, M. M., & Abdullahi, S. S. (2024). Adopting artificial intelligence (AI) in education: Challenges and possibilities. *Asian Journal of Advanced Research and Reports, 18*(2), 106-111. Article no. AJARR.109484. ISSN: 2582-3248.

Wilson, B. G. (1996). Constructivist learning environments: Case studies in instructional design. *Educational Technology.*

Yean, A. S. (2014). Education for Sustainable Development in Malaysia's National Curriculum Reformation: A Theoretical Exploration. *Journal of International and Comparative Education (JICE)*, 199-212.

Chapter 4
Transforming Education: The Role of AI Tools in Shaping Personalized and Inclusive Learning

S. Deepa
https://orcid.org/0000-0001-7690-0839
SRM Institute of Science and Technology, India

Uma A. Mageswari
https://orcid.org/0000-0001-9750-2127
SRM Institute of Science and Technology, India

ABSTRACT

This chapter investigates the profound influence of Artificial Intelligence (AI) on education, highlighting its role in transforming teaching strategies, student engagement, and personalized learning. It explores various AI-driven technologies, including machine learning, natural language processing (NLP), intelligent tutoring systems, and predictive analytics, which are reshaping the educational landscape. By enabling adaptive learning, personalized instruction, and improved accessibility, AI has the potential to make education more efficient and inclusive. However, the chapter also addresses key challenges, such as data privacy, algorithmic bias, and the digital divide, emphasizing the need for ethical and responsible AI implementation. Aimed at educators, policymakers, and researchers, this chapter provides a comprehensive analysis of AI's impact on modern education and the critical considerations for its integration.

DOI: 10.4018/979-8-3373-5102-5.ch004

1. INTRODUCTION

Education is experiencing a profound revolution due to the hasty progressions in technology, and at the forefront of this transformation is AI. AI is reforming how knowledge is delivered, assessed, and experienced by students around the world. It has introduced new opportunities for personalization, efficiency, and accessibility in learning, enabling educators to provide more tailored and inclusive experiences for all learners.

Figure 1. AI in Education (https://www.bing.com/images/search?view=detailV2)

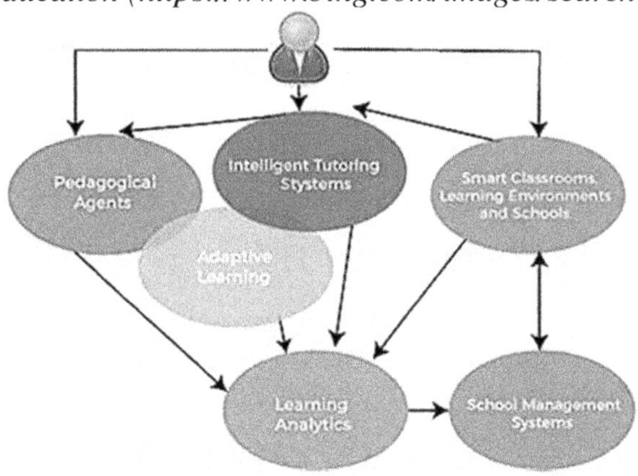

Figure 1 shows the various methods in for AI in education. Artificial Intelligence (AI) is rapidly transmuting the landscape of education, contributing advanced solutions that develop learning experiences, improve educational results, and streamline administrative tasks (L. Chen,2020). By harnessing AI skills, such as natural language processing, machine learning, and data analytics, education systems can provide personalized learning pathways, automate assessments, and support both scholars and educators in unprecedented ways. From AI-powered tutoring systems and adaptive learning platforms to smart learning management systems (LMS), AI is making education more accessible, efficient, and engaging. However, while the potential benefits are immense, the integration of AI in teaching also raises important questions about ethics, data privacy, and equity. As AI continues to evolve, its role in teaching is set to reshape the future of learning, offering chances for innovation and development across the global education system.

1.1. The Role of AI in Modern Education

AI's role in modern education can be seen as a catalyst for innovation, shaping not just in what way education is administered but also how pupils involve with content. The integration of AI into education is helping both teachers and students achieve better outcomes through automation, real-time data, and modified culture experiences. AI plays a essential role in modern education, revolutionizing how education is distributed and experienced (A. S. Najar,2014). It empowers educators with powerful tools to personalize instruction, adapt lessons to students' unique needs, and systematize tedious tasks, allowing teachers to focus more on engaging with students. AI technologies, such as intelligent tutoring systems, adaptive learning platforms, and AI chatbots, provide real-time, individualized support, helping students progress at their own pace and improving learning results.

Key areas where AI is influencing education include:

- **Automation of administrative tasks**: AI tools handle time-consuming tasks like scheduling, grading, and even responding to basic queries, allowing teachers to focus more on education.
- **Personalized learning paths**: AI allows the creation of individualized learning knowledges, adapting content to scholars' needs, pace, and progress. This leads to a more attractive and operative learning experience.
- **Enhanced feedback and assessment**: AI can provide instant feedback on exams and assignments offering students the opportunity to improve continuously.
- **Data-driven decision-making**: It provides valued insights into student performance, helping educators identify learning gaps, track progress, and make well-versed decisions about involvements.

1.2. Overview of AI Tools in Learning

AI tools in learning are transforming education by providing tailored, adaptive, and efficient experiences for students. These harness the power of technologies like natural language processing, machine learning, and predictive analytics to tailor educational content to individual needs, monitor progress in real-time, and offer instant feedback. Intelligent tutoring systems (ITS) pretend one-on-one tutoring, guiding students through lessons and offering personalized support (K. Holstein,2018).

By analysing big amounts of data, AI tools can generate more flexible, inclusive, and accessible learning environments, improving outcomes for varied learners and transforming traditional educational methods. These tools offer both teachers and students valuable resources to improve the overall learning experience, making education more, personalized, dynamic and accessible. AI tools in learning are transforming education by providing innovative solutions that enhance both teaching and learning experiences. These designed to cater to the varied needs of scholars and educators, making education more efficient, personalized, and engaging.

- **Adaptive Learning Platforms:** These AI-driven tools personalize content delivery based on individual students' progress, adjusting the difficulty of lessons and offering tailored resources to help students learn at their own pace.
- **AI-Powered Tutoring Systems:** Virtual teachers provide real-time assistance, explaining concepts and contributing full guidance, ensuring that students receive help whenever they need it, both inside and outside the classroom.
- **Intelligent LMS:** These automate administrative tasks, such as attendance tracking and grading, while also offering personalized learning pathways based on student performance data.
- **AI Chatbots & Virtual Assistants:** These tools offer instant support to students, answering questions, providing resources, and assisting with administrative tasks, making learning more interactive and accessible.
- **Speech-to-Text & Accessibility Tools:** AI technologies such as text-to-speech and speech recognition enhance accessibility for students with disabilities, converting spoken language into text and vice versa, while also providing real-time translations.
- **AI-Powered Valuation & Feedback Tools:** AI helps systematize the assessment process, offering instant response on assignments and exams, ensuring fair, unbiased evaluations, and helping students improve continuously.

2. AI TECHNOLOGIES IN EDUCATION

AI is redesigning education by introducing new tools and systems that improve learning outcomes, enhance teaching efficiency, and provide personalized educational experiences. AI technologies in education attach the power of algorithms and data to offer advanced capabilities in areas like learning customization, assessment, and feedback.

2.1. Machine Learning Algorithms

ML algorithms are at the heart of many AI tools in education, enabling them to personalize learning, automate processes, and improve student outcomes. Below are several machine learning algorithms commonly used in AI-powered educational tools, along with specific examples of how they are applied (B. M. McLaren,2015).

2.1.1 Linear Regression

Linear Regression is a foundational algorithm in machine learning, designed to predict a continuous dependent variable based on one or more independent variables. It operates under the assumption of a linear relationship between the input variables and the target output. The primary objective is to determine the optimal line that best represents the data by minimizing the error between the predicted values and the actual observations(B. M. McLaren,2017).

Key Concepts:

- **Dependent Variable (Y)**: The variable you're trying to predict (e.g., house prices, student grades and sales revenue).
- **Independent Variables (X)**: The features or inputs used to predict the dependent variable (e.g., hours studied, number of rooms, advertising budget).
- **Equation of the Line**: The equation is typically represented as:

$$Y = \beta 0 + \beta 1X1 + \beta 2X2 + ...+\beta nXn + \epsilon$$

  - $\beta 0$ is the intercept, where the line crosses the Y-axis.
  - $\beta 1,\beta 2,...,\beta n$ are the coefficients that represent the relationship between each independent variable and the dependent variable.
  - ϵ is the error term, accounting for difference between predicted and actual values.

Linear Regression Types:

1. **Simple Linear Regression**: Involves a single variable.

$$Y = \beta 0 + \beta 1X1 + \epsilon$$

2. **Multiple Linear Regression**: Includes multiple independent variables.

$$Y = \beta 0 + \beta 1X1 + \beta 2X2 + ...+\beta nXn + \epsilon$$

Figure 2. Linear Regression in Education (https://sl.bing.net/h6LEVV3ScqO)

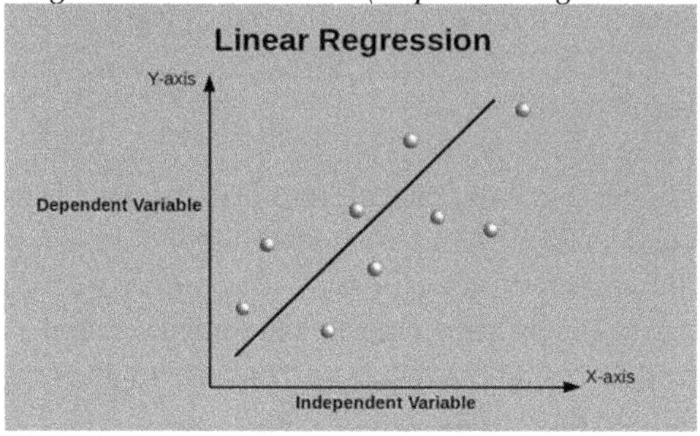

Figure 2 shows the linear regression model for AI in education.

Example Use Case in Education: Linear regression could be used to predict student performance (e.g., final exam marks) created on variables such as hours of study, and prior academic performance, attendance. After analysing this data, teachers can gain insights into which factors most influence academic success and provide targeted interventions.

2.1.2 Decision Trees & Random Forests for AI Tools in Education

DT and RF) are two of the most widely used machine learning algorithms in education AI tools. Both algorithms are used for predictive tasks like classifying student performance, detecting at-risk students, or recommending personalized learning paths. Here's how each of these works in the context of education:

Decision Trees

A DT is a simple, interpretable model which breaks down a decision-making process into a series of "yes" or "no" questions, based on the features of the dataset. The tree structure consists of nodes, branches, and leaves. The model splits the dataset into smaller subsets at each node based on feature values, continuing this process until it reaches a predefined condition, such as a maximum tree depth.

In the context of education, DT can be applied to forecast student activities or classify students based on their likelihood of success. For example, using features like attendance, assignment scores, and engagement, the Decision Tree might classify a student as "at risk" or "on track." Decision Trees are great for automated grading, as they can identify patterns in student answers and classify them accordingly, but they can also be used for personalized learning paths, adjusting the resources provided to students based on their predicted success.

Use Cases in Education

- Student Performance Prediction: Classifies students as "at risk" or "on track" based on attendance, assignments, and engagement.
- Automated Grading: Determines whether an answer is correct or incorrect based on patterns.
- Personalized Learning Paths: Suggests different learning materials based on student performance.

Example Predicting Student Performance: A Decision Tree might classify a student's likelihood of passing based on:

- Attendance (≥75% = "Good", <75% = "Poor")
- Assignment Scores (≥60% = "Pass", <60% = "Fail")
- Engagement (High, Medium, Low)

Random Forests

A Random Forest is an ensemble learning method that enhances prediction accuracy by combining multiple Decision Trees. Each tree is trained on a randomly selected subset of the data, introducing diversity and reducing overfitting—a common drawback of individual Decision Trees. The final prediction is determined by aggregating the outputs of all trees, resulting in improved generalization and better performance on unseen data.

Random Forests help in handling the complexity of these diverse data points and can provide more accurate predictions than a single Decision Tree.

Use Cases in Education

- Student Dropout Prediction: More accurate than a single Decision Tree, predicting at-risk students.
- Exam Score Forecasting: Predicts future grades based on past performance.
- Adaptive Learning Systems: Recommends personalized learning resources.

Example Predicting Student Dropout Risk: If a student has:

- Low attendance (35%)
- Poor assignment scores (40%)
- Low engagement in online courses

A single Decision Tree might wrongly predict that the student will pass. But a Random Forest, using multiple trees, would likely predict a higher dropout risk.

2.2. NLP in Education

NLP, a branch of AI, enables machines to understand, interpret, and respond to human language. In education, it is revolutionizing learning, teaching, and academic management. AI-powered tools leveraging NLP offer personalized learning experiences, automate administrative tasks, and improve accessibility for students with disabilities. Figure 3 illustrates NLP's role in AI-driven education.

Figure 3. Applications of NLP (https://sl.bing.net/ikPwuAT3xtY)

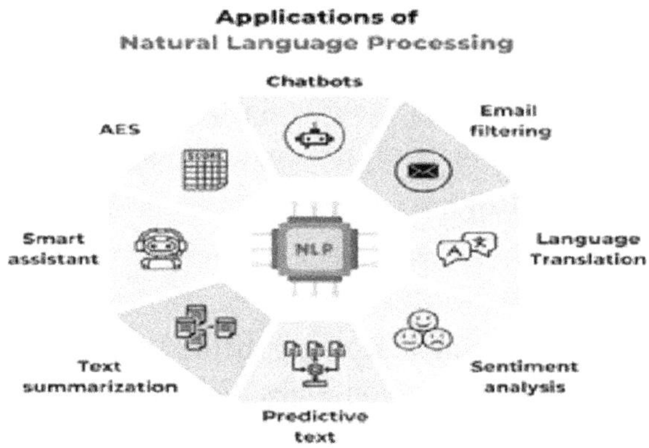

1. AI-Powered Chatbots & Virtual Tutors

NLP enables the growth of AI-driven virtual tutors and chatbots that can assist students 24/7. These AI tutors can response questions, provide descriptions, and even offer modified study recommendations based on student interactions. They help students reinforce concepts outside of class, reducing the need for one-on-one teacher intervention.

AI-powered virtual tutors and chatbots are transforming education by giving instant, 24/7 provision to students. These offer explanations, and guide learners through complex topics in real time. They personalize learning by adapting to each student's pace and needs, ensuring better understanding and retention. Virtual tutors enhance engagement through interactive conversations, making learning more dynamic and accessible. Additionally, they decrease the workload for educators by handling administrative tasks, routine queries and allowing teachers to focus on deeper instruction.

Example: AI chatbots like IBM Watson Tutor or Google's Dialogflow can answer students' queries, provide explanations, and suggest relevant learning resources.

2. Automated Essay Scoring & Feedback

NLP-based grading systems can analyse student essays, providing instant feedback on grammar, coherence, argument structure, and originality. These tools save teachers time and ensure consistent grading while helping students improve their writing skills. These tools analyse coherence, grammar, structure, and content relevance, offering thorough feedback for improvement. By providing personalized suggestions, they help students polish their inscription skills over time. AI-powered grading reduces the burden on educators, allowing them to focus on more complex teaching tasks. Additionally, these systems promote fair and unbiased evaluation, ensuring consistency across large-scale assessments.

Example: Tools like Grammarly, Turnitin, and ETS e-Rater use NLP to assess essays, detect plagiarism, and offer grammar/style suggestions.

3. Personalized Learning & Adaptive Education

NLP helps create modified learning experiences by analysing progress, preferences, and challenges. AI-driven platforms can suggest reading materials, quizzes, and exercises tailored to each student's learning style and pace. Personalized learning and adaptive education powered by AI tailor lessons to individual student needs, ensuring a customized learning experience. AI-driven platforms analyse student presentation and adjust content, pace, and difficulty levels in real time. This approach helps address learning gaps, providing extra support or advanced challenges based on student progress. Adaptive learning ensures greater engagement and retention, making education more effective and student-centric. By offering data-driven insights, AI empowers educators to refine teaching strategies for improved outcomes.

Example: Duolingo, an AI-powered language learning platform, uses NLP to adapt lesson difficulty based on student responses, making learning more effective.

4. Speech-to-Text & Accessibility Tools

For the students with infirmities, NLP-driven speech acknowledgment and text to speech applications improve accessibility. These tools support students with dyslexia, visual impairments to engage more effectively with learning materials. AI-powered speech-to-text and accessibility tools enhance education by converting spoken language into written text, aiding students with hearing impairments or learning disabilities. These tools provide real-time transcription, making lectures, discussions, and videos more accessible. They also support multilingual learners by offering instant translations and captions. AI-driven accessibility solutions, these tools help students with different learning needs engage more effectively.

By breaking down barriers, these technologies promote inclusivity and equivalent learning occasions for all students.

Example: Microsoft's Immersive Reader and Google's Live Transcribe provide real-time speech-to-text conversion, helping students with hearing impairments follow lessons.

5. Text Summarization & Content Recommendation

NLP can analyze textbooks, research papers, or online resources and generate summaries, making complex content easier for students to understand. Additionally, NLP-powered recommendation systems suggest relevant study materials based on student interests and performance. AI-powered text summarization and content recommendation tools help students and educators by condensing large amounts of information into concise, easy-to-understand summaries. These tools enhance comprehension by extracting key points from textbooks, research papers, or articles. AI-driven content recommendation systems suggest personalized learning materials, adapting to a student's interests, progress, and learning style. By saving time and improving focus, these technologies make studying more efficient. Additionally, they support lifelong learning by continuously recommending relevant resources based on evolving educational needs.

Example: AI-powered summarization tools like **SMMRY** and **Scholarcy** help students quickly grasp key concepts from lengthy academic articles.

6. Sentiment Analysis for Student Feedback

Educational institutions use NLP-based sentiment analysis to assess student feedback, identifying areas for improvement in teaching methods, course content, or campus policies. This allows for better decision-making and enhanced student satisfaction. AI-powered sentiment analysis helps educators analyze student feedback by identifying emotions, opinions, and concerns from surveys, reviews, or discussions. It detects patterns in student satisfaction, engagement, and learning challenges, providing valuable insights for improving teaching strategies. By categorizing responses as positive, negative, or neutral, sentiment analysis helps institutions make data-driven decisions to enhance the learning experience. This technology also enables early intervention, allowing educators to address student concerns proactively. Overall, AI-driven sentiment analysis fosters a more responsive and student-centric education system.

Example: Universities analyze student reviews, feedback forms, and online discussions to understand common concerns and improve the learning experience.

NLP Algorithms Used in Education

- **Transformer Models (BERT, GPT-4, T5)** – Power AI tutors, chatbots, and essay grading systems.
- **Named Entity Recognition (NER)** – Identifies key concepts in textbooks and research papers.
- **Latent Dirichlet Allocation (LDA)** – Extracts main topics from large text corpora (e.g., student forums, academic papers).
- **Word Embeddings (Word2Vec, GloVe, FastText)** – Enhances search functionality in e-learning platforms by improving keyword understanding.
- **Recurrent Neural Networks (RNNs) & Long Short-Term Memory (LSTM)** – Used in automated text summarization and speech recognition.

2.3. Intelligent Tutoring Systems (ITS) in Education

ITS are AI-powered instructive platforms that provide modified learning experiences by acclimatizing to students' needs in real time. These systems use ML, NLP, and cognitive science to simulate the role of a human tutor, offering customized lessons, real-time feedback, and targeted assessments. Unlike traditional learning environments where students follow a fixed curriculum, ITS dynamically regulates the difficulty and contented based on individual performance, ensuring a more effective and attractive learning process.

The key features of ITS is personalized learning paths, where the system analyzes student progress and tailors lessons accordingly. If a student scuffles with a specific concept, this model provides added explanations and exercises, while advanced learners can move on to more challenging topics. Additionally, ITS offers real-time feedback and assessment, instantly correcting mistakes and guiding students toward the correct understanding. Unlike traditional grading, where feedback may take days, ITS allows students to learn from their errors immediately, reinforcing concepts more effectively.

Another significant advantage of ITS is the integration of AI-powered virtual tutors that interact with students using NLP. These tutors can explain concepts, answer questions, and engage in step-by-step problem-solving, creating a more interactive and conversational learning experience. Platforms like Duolingo and Socratic by Google use AI-driven tutoring to provide instant explanations and personalized recommendations. Furthermore, adaptive assessments within ITS modify quiz difficulty based on student responses, ensuring that students are neither bored with easy questions nor discouraged by overly difficult ones.

To enhance engagement, many ITS platforms incorporate gamification elements such as badges, leaderboards, and rewards. By turning learning into a game-like experience, these systems boost student motivation and retention. Technologies behind ITS include machine learning algorithms, which predict student performance and optimize learning materials, and NLP, which powers chatbots, text summarization, and speech-to-text functionalities. Additionally, cognitive science principles are used to model student behavior, ensuring that the system adapts to different learning styles and attention spans.

ITS provides numerous benefits, such as 24/7 learning accessibility, reduced teacher workload, and early detection of struggling students, making education more efficient and inclusive. However, challenges remain, including the lack of emotional intelligence in AI tutors, potential biases in AI models, and accessibility issues for students without reliable internet or devices. The future of ITS will likely involve more human-like AI tutors, AR/VR for immersive learning, and advanced predictive analytics to better support students. As technology evolves, ITS will continue to transform education by creation learning more personalized, data-driven, and engaging (B. M. McLaren,2010).

2.4. Predictive Analytics and Data-Driven Decision Making

These decision-making are transforming the education sector by enabling institutions to informed, proactive choices based on historical and real time data. Predictive analytics involves using machine learning algorithms, statistical techniques, and big data analysis to forecast future student performance, dropout risks, and learning outcomes.

One of the most important applications of predictive analytics in education is early warning systems that detect students who may struggle academically or drop out. These systems analyze multiple data points, such as test scores, attendance records, and participation levels, to provide educators with actionable insights. For example, if a student's engagement in online learning platforms decreases significantly, predictive models can flag this as a potential risk, prompting teachers to offer additional support or counselling.

Data-driven decision-making also improves curriculum design and resource distribution by helping institutions identify which courses, teaching methods, and learning materials yield the best outcomes. By analyzing student performance across different subjects and instructional strategies, educators can optimize lesson plans to improve engagement and comprehension. Universities and schools can also use predictive models to forecast enrollment trends, allowing them to allocate resources efficiently, such as hiring faculty, managing classroom sizes, and planning infrastructure development.

Moreover, predictive analytics plays a vital role in adaptive assessments and AI-driven tutoring systems. By continuously analyzing student responses and learning behaviors, AI-powered platforms can adjust the difficulty level of quizzes, ensuring an optimal challenge level for each learner. This not only improves learning retention but also reduces frustration and disengagement. Additionally, employability and career guidance benefit from predictive models that assess student skills, interests, and industry trends to recommend appropriate career paths and training chances.

Despite its advantages, predictive analytics in education originates with challenges, including algorithmic biases, and data privacy concerns, the need for high-quality data. Ensuring ethical data collection and interpretation is crucial to avoid reinforcing educational inequalities or making inaccurate predictions. However, as technology advances, institutions are increasingly adopting AI-driven predictive analytics to create additional personalized, effective and efficient education systems. By leveraging data-driven decision-making, schools and universities can shift from reactive to proactive strategies, ultimately improving student success and institutional efficiency.

3. APPLICATIONS OF AI IN EDUCATION

AI is revolutionizing education by enhancing education experiences, improving efficiency, and personalizing instruction to encounter the needs of distinct students. AI-driven tools and technologies enable more dynamic and engaging learning environments, making education more accessible and effective. Some of the key applications of AI in education include personalized learning paths, adaptive learning systems, AI-assisted assessments and grading, and the integration of virtual and augmented reality in learning. Figure 4 shows the applications of AI in education.

Figure 4. Applications of AI in Education Sector (https://www.matellio.com/blog/application-of-ai-in-education/)

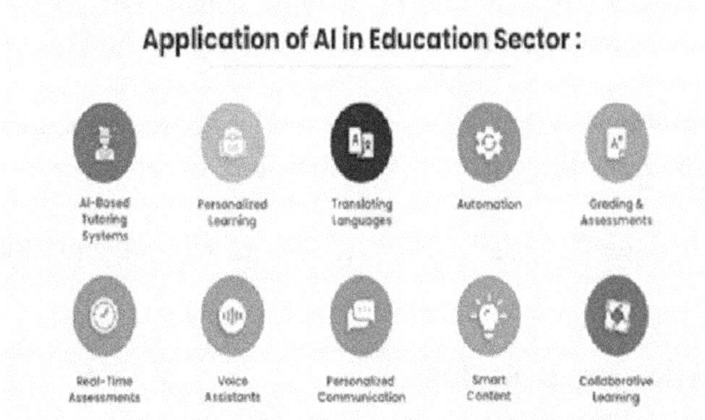

3.1. Personalized Learning Paths

AI to customize learning materials according to a student's learning style, areas of strength, and shortcomings. Through the analysis of student performance data, artificial intelligence (AI) systems make recommendations for personalized lesson plans, extra resources, and task difficulty adjustments to maximize learning.AI-powered personalized learning paths adapt educational content to each student's unique needs, pace, and learning style. By analyzing performance data, AI identifies strengths and weaknesses, recommending customized lessons and resources. This approach ensures targeted support, helping struggling students with extra practice while challenging advanced learners with more complex material. Personalized learning paths increase engagement and motivation, making education more effective and enjoyable. Ultimately, AI-driven customization enhances learning outcomes by providing a tailored, student-centric experience. This approach ensures that students receive the right level of challenge and support, reducing frustration and improving overall engagement. AI Tools for Personalized Learning Paths are

Adaptive Learning Platforms

These systems dynamically modify material based on student performance analysis. AI is used by adaptive learning systems to personalize course materials according to a student's performance, learning style, and speed. To make sure that students receive the right challenges or extra help when they need it, these systems continually evaluate data to modify the lesson's complexity. Adaptive learning improves understanding and engagement by offering individualized recommendations and real-time feedback. By assisting teachers in identifying learning gaps, these platforms enable focused interventions. All things considered, AI-powered adaptive learning guarantees a more effective, student-focused method of instruction.

- **Khan Academy:** Uses AI to suggest exercises based on student progress.
- **Dream Box Learning:** Adapts math lessons in real time based on student responses.
- **Smart Sparrow:** Provides interactive lessons that adjust to individual learning needs.

AI-Powered Tutoring Systems

These virtual tutors provide real-time feedback and explanations. AI-powered tutoring systems provide real-time, personalized support to students by adapting to their learning styles and needs. These intelligent systems use machine learning and natural language processing to explain concepts, answer questions, and offer step-by-step guidance. They ensure 24/7 availability, making education more accessible beyond traditional classroom hours. By analyzing student performance, AI tutors identify knowledge gaps and adjust lessons accordingly. This technology enhances self-paced learning and reduces the workload on educators while improving overall student outcomes.

- **Socratic by Google:** Uses AI to answer student questions via photo or text input.
- **Cognii:** An AI-based tutor for personalized learning with open-response questions.
- **Querium:** Helps students prepare for STEM exams with AI-driven feedback.

Intelligent Learning Management Systems (LMS)

AI-integrated LMS platforms enhance course delivery and learning paths. Intelligent Learning Management Systems (LMS) leverage AI to enhance educational experiences by personalizing content, automating administrative tasks, and providing data-driven insights. These systems track student progress, analyze learning patterns, and recommend tailored resources to improve outcomes. AI-powered LMS platforms enable adaptive learning, offering customized lessons and assessments based on individual performance. They also streamline course management for educators, automating grading, attendance tracking, and feedback generation. Overall, intelligent LMS platforms make learning more efficient, engaging, and accessible for both students and teachers.

- **Coursera & edX:** Use AI to recommend courses based on student preferences.
- **Blackboard Learn:** AI-driven analytics track student progress and suggest improvements.
- **Knewton Alta:** Customizes coursework based on student weaknesses.

AI Chatbots and Virtual Assistants

Chatbots with AI capabilities offer immediate assistance and direction. Artificial Intelligence chatbots and virtual assistants are essential to education because they provide instructors and students with round-the-clock assistance. These intelligent technologies can support students whenever they need it by providing study resources, answers to queries, and assignment guidance. AI chatbots also simplify administrative duties, such responding to frequently asked questions concerning timetables or course material, allowing teachers to concentrate on instruction. These systems use natural language processing to comprehend and react to student questions instantly, enhancing student engagement and offering individualized learning experiences. They can also aid with language acquisition and other subjects, providing individualized support and creating a more engaging learning atmosphere.

- **IBM Watson Tutor:** AI-based chatbot that answers academic queries.
- **Brainly:** A community-driven AI-powered education platform.
- **ChatGPT:** Can be used for answering questions and generating study materials.

3.2. Adaptive Learning Systems

Adaptive learning systems take personalization further by dynamically adjusting the curriculum in real time. These systems continuously monitor student progress and modify instructional materials accordingly. If a student struggles with a concept, the system provides additional explanations, practice exercises, or alternative learning formats. Conversely, if a student excels, they can move on to more advanced topics without unnecessary repetition. This method ensures efficient learning, catering to both struggling and advanced learners simultaneously. AI-powered platforms like Smart Sparrow and DreamBox Learning utilize adaptive learning models to improve comprehension and retention. Adaptive learning platform and tools follows:

- **DreamBox Learning:** Adaptive math platform for K-8 students.
- **McGraw-Hill ALEKS:** AI-powered adaptive learning for STEM subjects.
- **Knewton Alta:** Adjusts coursework dynamically based on student responses.
- **Smart Sparrow:** Provides real-time adaptive feedback in interactive lessons.
- **Socratic by Google:** AI-powered tutor that answers student questions via text or images.
- **Cognii:** AI-based virtual tutor that supports open-ended learning.
- **Querium:** Provides personalized tutoring for STEM subjects and test preparation.
- **Coursera & edX:** AI-driven course recommendations based on learning history.
- **Moodle with IntelliBoard:** Provides adaptive learning analytics.
- **Blackboard Learn:** Uses AI to track student engagement and suggest improvements.
- **Gradescope:** AI-assisted grading and feedback for written assignments.
- **Century Tech:** AI-driven assessments that personalize study plans.
- **Carnegie Learning MATHia:** AI-based math assessment and tutoring system.

- **Duolingo:** AI-powered language learning that adjusts difficulty based on performance.
- **Prodigy:** Adaptive math game for K-8 students.
- **Knowre Math:** AI-driven gamified math learning tool.

3.3. AI-Assisted Assessments and Grading

By automating tasks like grading multiple-choice exams, reviewing essays, and giving immediate feedback, AI-assisted evaluations and grading simplify the evaluation process. Artificial intelligence (AI)-powered resources such as Turnitin and Gradescope evaluate student work for the amount of plagiarism grammar, and general organization while providing thorough comments to help students become better writers. AI is also capable of identifying frequent misunderstandings and suggesting focused treatments by analyzing trends in student replies. Teachers' burden is lessened by this automation, freeing them up to concentrate on giving pupils more significant help (B. M. McLaren,2015).

AI-assisted assessments and grading tools

- **Gradescope:** AI-assisted grading for multiple-choice, short-answer, and programming assignments.
- **Turnitin:** AI-powered plagiarism detection and writing assessment tool.
- **ExamSoft:** AI-enhanced exam creation, grading, and analytics platform.
- **Quillionz:** AI-powered tool that generates quizzes and assessments from text content.
- **SAGrader:** AI-based tool that evaluates essays and provides detailed feedback.
- **Ecree:** AI-driven real-time writing feedback platform.
- **Write and Improve by Cambridge:** AI-assisted writing analysis and feedback tool.
- **Century Tech:** AI-powered formative assessment and learning path recommendations.
- **Knewton Alta:** AI-driven adaptive assessment system.
- **Carnegie Learning MATHia:** AI-based math assessment and personalized tutoring tool.

3.4. Virtual and Augmented Reality in Learning

By producing enveloping, interactive experiences that make difficult subjects more approachable and understandable, virtual and augmented reality (VR/AR) improve education. Students can practice medical operations in a risk-free setting, perform virtual experiments in science, or visit historical locations thanks to augmented reality. By superimposing digital material on the physical environment, augmented reality (AR) enhances the participatory nature of disciplines like engineering, astronomy, and anatomy. By tailoring experiences according to student development and engagement, AI improves these technologies. AI and VR/AR are combined in products such Google Expeditions and the HoloLens from Microsoft to make learning in the traditional classroom more engaging and hands-on.

Tools for Virtual and Augmented Reality in Learning

- **Google Expeditions VR:** Allows students to take virtual field trips to historical sites, oceans, and outer space.
- **Engage VR:** A VR collaboration platform for virtual classrooms and corporate training.
- **Labster:** Provides immersive VR science labs for biology, chemistry, and physics.
- **VictoryXR:** Offers a library of VR classrooms, labs, and training simulations.
- **Unimersiv:** Provides VR educational content on history, space, and anatomy.
- **Merge Cube:** A handheld AR device that lets students interact with 3D models in subjects like science and math.
- **Google Lens & AR Search:** Enables students to scan objects and textbooks for interactive learning experiences.
- **QuiverVision:** AR coloring books that bring drawings to life.
- **Human Anatomy Atlas AR:** Allows students to explore 3D human anatomy in augmented reality.
- **Wonderscope:** AR storytelling app that makes reading more interactive for young learners

4. BENEFITS OF AI IN EDUCATION

Artificial Intelligence (AI) is transforming education by increasing accessibility, efficiency, and personalization of learning. AI improves both teaching and learning, as shown in smart classrooms, automated grading, and tutors. There are several advantages of using AI in education, which greatly enhances student learning and academic results. In the first place, it makes individualized learning possible by adjusting resources and information to meet the needs of each unique student, allowing them to study at their own speed and increasing engagement. Additionally, AI automates administrative duties like attendance and grading, freeing up teachers to engage with students and improve their teaching strategies. By offering accessible materials, dynamic learning environments, and real-time feedback, the incorporation of AI-powered technologies contributes to increased student motivation and engagement. By offering speech-to-text, translations tools, and personalized learning experiences for students with impairments, it encourages better accessibility and inclusion. AI may also aid in closing educational gaps by providing underprivileged areas with top-notch learning materials, opening up educational chances in areas with limited resources. Finally, by detecting learning gaps, proposing teaching techniques, and facilitating proactive interventions to enhance student results, AI's data-driven insights assist teachers. Figure 5 illustrates how AI is being used in education.

Figure 5. Benefits for AI in Education

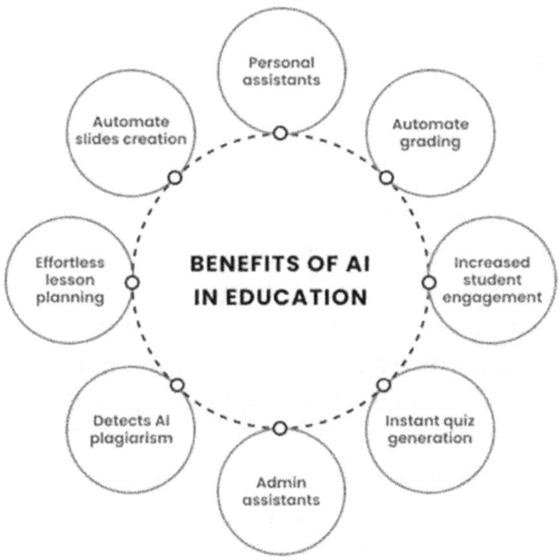

4.1. Enhancing Student Engagement and Motivation

Through the creation of immersive, customized, and interactive learning experiences, AI raises student motivation and engagement. Artificial intelligence (AI) is used by adaptive learning systems to customize courses to each student's speed, preventing them from becoming disinterested in repetitious material or feeling overly challenged. This level of personalization keeps students engaged and invested in their own learning. Furthermore, gamified learning experiences powered by AI integrate rewards, leaderboards, and challenges, making learning fun and motivating students to continue progressing. AI also powers virtual tutors and study assistants, offering real-time feedback and personalized guidance, which encourages self-directed learning. Additionally, the integration of Augmented Reality (AR) and Virtual Reality (VR) powered by AI provides hands-on, immersive experiences, allowing students to explore complex concepts through virtual simulations or field trips. This makes abstract ideas more tangible and engaging, keeping students actively involved. AI-driven tools, like chatbots, also provide instant support, answering questions and keeping students motivated by eliminating frustration with delays in feedback. When combined, these AI tools create a vibrant and stimulating learning environment that boosts student motivation and keeps them interested in and focused on their studies.

4.2. Improving Learning Outcomes

By offering individualized, data-driven, and adaptable learning experiences, artificial intelligence (AI) significantly contributes to better learning outcomes. Adaptive learning systems, which customize instructional materials to each student's unique requirements and make sure they are pushed without feeling overburdened, are one of the primary ways AI enhances results. A more focused and efficient learning route is made possible by these technologies, which continually assess students' progress and modify lessons in real time. Furthermore, AI-powered solutions—like intelligent tutoring systems—offer rapid, tailored feedback, assisting students in recognizing their areas of strength and weakness right away. Learning is reinforced and misunderstandings may be corrected more quickly thanks to this short feedback loop. Predictive analytics, which AI facilitates, aids teachers in monitoring performance patterns and identifying kids who may be at danger of falling behind, allowing for early interventions and individualized support. Additionally, AI can improve students' retention of knowledge by tailoring the educational process to their cognitive styles and developing interactive simulations that simplify and engage difficult ideas. Teachers may devote more time to teaching when AI takes care of administrative duties like data analysis and grading, which enhances learning results overall.

4.3. Supporting Teachers and Educators

Teachers and educators benefit greatly from AI's ability to simplify administrative duties, improve individualized training, and provide insights for wiser decision-making. Automatic grading systems that manage standard assessments, like essays and multiple-choice exams, are one of the main ways AI helps educators. This frees up instructors to concentrate on more intricate and imaginative facets of instruction. Additionally, AI provides instructors with insightful data that allow them to monitor student development, spot gaps in learning, and even forecast future performance, facilitating early interventions and individualized teaching methods. This enables educators to give pupils who most need it focused help.Furthermore, AI-powered virtual assistants and chatbots can respond to common student questions, freeing up teacher time and allowing for more individualized interactions with students. AI-driven content generation tools help educators create customized lessons, quizzes, and study materials quickly and efficiently, which is especially valuable for teachers managing large classes or multiple subjects. By handling the administrative and repetitive tasks, AI provides teachers with more time and resources to focus on creating engaging learning environments and developing meaningful relationships with their students, ultimately enhancing the educational experience for both teachers and learners.

4.4. Bridging Educational Gaps

AI is essential to closing educational disparities because it guarantees every student, regardless of socioeconomic background, geography, or learning style, fair access to high-quality education. AI can offer specialized educational experiences through personalized learning to satisfy students' various demands.For instance, AI-powered tools can adapt content to fit various learning styles, ensuring that struggling students receive the support they need, while advanced learners are appropriately challenged. In areas where there is a shortage of qualified teachers, AI-based virtual tutors and intelligent tutoring systems can offer 24/7 support, providing students with assistance that would otherwise be unavailable.

By providing real-time translation services, AI also aids in removing language barriers, enabling students from various cultural backgrounds or languages to attend education. Additionally, AI-powered assistive technologies that empower students with impairments and provide them with equitable possibilities for success include text-to-speech, speech-to-text, and personalized reading tools. Furthermore, AI-powered online learning systems give students in underprivileged or rural areas access to excellent educational materials, either at no cost or at a reduced cost, enabling them to study at their own speed without requiring physical infrastructure. AI is assisting in closing educational disparities by developing more flexible, inclusive, and effective learning environments that make education accessible to all learners, irrespective of their circumstances.

5. CHALLENGES AND LIMITATIONS

5.1. Data Privacy and Security Concerns

The effectiveness of AI systems depends on vast volumes of data, which raises questions around student confidentiality and security of sensitive data. Particularly when working with kids, the management of personal data may result in breaches, abuse, or exploitation. Building confidence and guaranteeing the safe application of AI within educational settings requires implementing strong security measures and adhering to data protection regulations, such as the GDPR.Concerns about data security and privacy pose serious obstacles to the use of AI in education. Large volumes of private student data, including academic records, behavioral data, and personal information, are frequently used by AI systems to enhance results and offer individualized learning experiences. This data may be abused or obtained by unauthorized persons in the absence of appropriate measures, resulting in privacy breaches. To guarantee the secure processing of student data, educational institutions must abide by data protection laws including FERPA, GDPR, and others. However, data anonymization is not always fully implemented, and AI tools may expose identifiable information if not properly secured. Third-party vendors used by schools can also be a source of concern, as they may not always follow strict privacy protocols, potentially putting student data at risk. Additionally, AI systems are vulnerable to cybersecurity threats, including data breaches and hacking attempts, which makes strong encryption, multi-factor authentication, and regular security audits essential. To address these issues, educational institutions must prioritize transparency by clearly explaining how student data is collected and used, ensuring that consent is obtained from students and parents. By establishing robust data protection practices and working with trusted vendors, educational institutions can leverage AI technologies while safeguarding students' privacy and security.

5.2. Algorithmic Bias and Fairness

Since AI systems have the potential to inadvertently reinforce or even magnify preexisting prejudices in the information they are trained on, computational bias and fairness are crucial issues when utilizing AI in education.These biases can lead to unfair treatment or outcomes for certain groups of students, impacting their learning experiences and academic performance. For example, an AI algorithm might unintentionally favor students from specific socioeconomic backgrounds, genders, or ethnicities, resulting in inequitable learning experiences. Ensuring fairness means developing AI models that are transparent, accountable, and inclusive, with constant evaluation and updates to eliminate biases. It is imperative that educators and developers make sure AI tools are made with equality in mind, providing equal possibilities for all students, regardless of their experience. In addition to ensuring that AI systems are equitable and just, addressing algorithmic bias increases technology trust and makes it possible for it to effectively serve a variety of educational groups.

Bias in Data

AI systems learn from data, and if the information used to train these systems contains inherent biases—such as racial, gender, or socio-economic bias—the AI may make decisions that disproportionately affect certain sets. For instance, an AI-powered admissions system trained on historical data may unintentionally favor students from certain demographic backgrounds, while disadvantaging others. This bias can lead to unequal opportunities in education, exacerbating existing inequalities.

Discrimination in Educational Outcomes

Biased algorithms run the danger of unjustly judging students when artificially intelligent machines are used to grade assignments, suggest courses, or assess student achievement. An AI system may not take into consideration the particular difficulties experienced by learners from underrepresented or underprivileged backgrounds, for instance, if it gets educated on data from a student body that is primarily male or rich. This might result in biased educational outcomes.

Lack of Transparency and Accountability

The decision-making processes of AI algorithms, especially those employed in education, are frequently perceived as "black boxes," indicating they are difficult to access or comprehend. It is challenging for parents, teachers, and students to spot potential biases or unequal practices in the system because of this lack of openness. Without transparency, AI tools could unintentionally discriminate against certain groups without anyone noticing or being able to challenge the decision-making process.

Reinforcement of Stereotypes

AI systems trained on historical data may also reinforce pre-existing stereotypes, such as gender biases or racial prejudices. For instance, if AI tools are used to recommend career paths to students based on their academic performance, they may perpetuate outdated ideas about which careers are suitable for certain genders or ethnic groups, further limiting opportunities for marginalized students.

Fairness in AI Design

Ensuring fairness in AI systems requires the development of algorithms that are not only accurate but also equitable for all students, regardless of their background.

This involves using diverse and representative datasets that account for the variety of students' experiences and ensuring that algorithms are regularly audited for bias. Moreover, involving a diverse group of educators, technologists, and ethicists in the design and deployment of AI tools is essential to address potential biases and promote fairness.

To address algorithmic bias and ensure fairness, AI systems in education must be designed with equity in mind. This can include steps like diverse dataset collection to reflect various student backgrounds, bias detection during the development and testing of algorithms, and continuous monitoring of AI tools to identify and correct any emerging biases. Additionally, increasing transparency by making AI decision-making processes more understandable and ensuring accountability can help prevent unintentional discrimination. Schools and educational institutions must also focus on ethical guidelines and policy frameworks that ensure AI technologies promote fairness and equal opportunity for all students.

5.3. The Digital Divide and Accessibility Issues

The broad use of AI in education is severely hampered by digital gap and accessibility concerns. The equipment and internet connectivity needed for AI-powered learning resources are not equally available to all pupils. Students in rural or economically disadvantaged areas may lack high-speed internet, computers, or smart devices, preventing them from fully benefiting from AI-driven educational resources. This creates a gap in learning opportunities, as students in wealthier areas with better access to technology are able to take full advantage of AI tools, while others are left behind. Furthermore, accessibility issues affect students with disabilities who may struggle to use AI tools that are not planned with their needs in mind. For example, students with visual impairments may find it difficult to engage with AI systems that rely heavily on visual interfaces, while those with hearing impairments may face challenges with audio-based tools. To bridge this divide, it is essential for educational institutions to ensure that AI technologies are inclusive and accessible, by providing assistive technologies, offering low-cost or subsidized devices to students in need, and working toward equitable internet access for all students. Only by addressing these disparities can AI in education fulfill its potential to provide equal learning opportunities to all students, regardless of their background or abilities.

6. ETHICAL CONSIDERATIONS

When incorporating AI into education, ethical considerations are essential since the technology brings up a number of significant issues including human agency, privacy, justice, and responsibility. Since AI systems frequently gather enormous volumes of academic and personal data, protecting the security and confidentiality of student data is one of the main ethical issues. In order to prevent misuse, schools must install robust safeguards and comply with data privacy legislation. The possibility of bias from algorithms is also a serious worry as AI systems may inadvertently give preference to some groups, producing discriminating results. AI technologies must be created with equity in mind, utilizing a variety of datasets and carrying out frequent audits in order to solve this. Since many AI systems operate as "black boxes," making it challenging to comprehend how choices are made, transparency is also crucial. To maintain responsibility and confidence, ethical AI has to be explicable. Additionally, human agency must be preserved in order for AI to help instructors rather than replace them and maintain the crucial role that teachers play in assisting and directing pupils. Since AI technologies must be made available to all students, even those from disadvantaged backgrounds and those with impairments, the digital gap and availability are also ethical issues. Lastly, worries regarding displacement of jobs and the impact of automation in education are raised by AI's effects on the workforce, especially teachers. AI and educators should work together to adopt AI ethically, making sure that technology complements and improves instruction rather than takes its place. AI may be applied in a way that advances justice, openness, and the welfare of students as well as educators by tackling these ethical issues.

6.1. Responsible AI Usage in Education

Responsible AI usage in education focuses on the ethical, transparent, and equitable implementation of AI technologies to ensure they enhance learning experiences without compromising students' rights or well-being. To achieve responsible AI use, several key principles must be adhered to.Firstly, privacy and data protection are paramount. AI systems must be designed to safeguard student data, adhering to strict privacy laws such as FERPA or GDPR. Educational institutions should prioritize data anonymization, limit access to sensitive information, and ensure transparency in how data is collected, stored, and used. Secondly, AI must be fair and unbiased. Developers should work to eliminate algorithmic bias by ensuring that AI systems are trained on diverse, representative datasets, reducing the risk of disadvantaging specific groups of students. Regular audits should be conducted to check for unintended biases and ensure that AI tools promote equal opportunities for all learners.

Transparency and accountability are also vital. AI systems should be designed to be explainable, meaning educators, students, and parents can understand how decisions are made. This transparency helps to build trust in AI tools, ensuring that stakeholders can question and challenge decisions when necessary.

6.2. Transparency and Accountability in AI Systems

Transparency and accountability in AI systems are crucial for ensuring that AI tools in education are trustworthy, fair, and ethical. As AI is increasingly used to make important decisions, such as grading, recommending courses, or providing personalized learning experiences, it's essential that the decision-making processes behind these systems are clear and understandable. AI systems should be designed with explainability in mind, allowing students, educators, and parents to understand how decisions are made, what data is used, and what algorithms influence outcomes. Along with transparency, there must be clear accountability for AI decisions.

Educators should remain at the center of decision-making, ensuring that AI supports, rather than replaces, their expertise. Additionally, there should be mechanisms in place for recourse if AI makes errors, allowing for corrections or appeals. Regular audits are necessary to ensure that AI systems remain accurate, unbiased, and effective over time, with transparent reporting to all stakeholders. Stakeholder engagement is also vital, with feedback loops that allow students, parents, and educators to provide input on AI's impact. Lastly, AI systems must comply with ethical standards and legal regulations, such as privacy laws like FERPA and GDPR, to protect student data and promote fairness and accessibility. By ensuring transparency and accountability, educational institutions can use AI in a way that fosters trust and benefits all students and educators, without compromising fairness or ethics.

6.3. The Role of AI in Equity and Inclusion

AI has a difficult and exciting role in promoting fairness and inclusion in education. Though they must be used cautiously to make sure they promote justice and do not worsen already-existing disparities, artificial intelligence (AI) technologies have the ability to close gaps and offer tailored learning experiences. By removing obstacles that certain students encounter because of their socioeconomic background, physical location, or disability, artificial intelligence (AI) can, when applied properly, contribute to the development of a more inclusive and equitable learning environment.

Personalized learning pathways that address each student's particular requirements are a crucial method AI may promote fairness. Students who need extra help, such those with learning difficulties or those who are falling behind in certain courses, may find this very helpful. AI-powered solutions may provide tailored interventions, suggest resources, and modify the learning speed to give every student the help they require to succeed.

AI can also help in identifying and addressing biases that might exist in traditional educational practices. For example, AI systems can be used to analyze grading patterns and highlight any potential biases in teacher assessments, such as unintentional favoritism toward certain genders or ethnic groups. By doing so, AI can help educators recognize and correct biased behaviors, promoting fairness and equal opportunity for all students (B. M. McLaren,2003).

7. INTERNATIONAL CASE STUDIES

Across the globe, countries are embracing AI to personalize learning and promote educational equity. These international case studies highlight how AI tools are being implemented in diverse contexts to meet learners' individual needs and bridge access gaps.

- **China – Scaling Personalization with Squirrel AI:** China's Squirrel AI is a pioneer in adaptive learning, offering real-time, personalized tutoring in subjects like math and science. By analyzing student performance data, the platform identifies knowledge gaps and tailors content to each learner. Used widely across urban and rural regions, Squirrel AI helps raise student performance, particularly among those previously struggling, demonstrating AI's ability to scale personalized learning.
- **United States – Blended Learning through Carnegie Learning:** In the U.S., Carnegie Learning blends AI software with teacher-led instruction. Its platform delivers customized math learning paths based on cognitive science, while giving teachers real-time analytics to guide classroom interventions. This model promotes equity by helping diverse learners master complex content at their own pace.
- **India – Reaching the Underserved with ConveGenius:** India's ConveGenius utilizes AI-powered chatbots on platforms like WhatsApp to deliver quizzes and educational content in regional languages. This innovative approach supports millions of students in low-income and rural areas, using familiar, low-

bandwidth technology to deliver personalized learning without the need for expensive devices or high-speed internet.

- **Kenya – SMS-Based AI Learning via M-Shule:** M-Shule in Kenya offers an SMS-based AI platform designed for primary education in communities with limited digital access. It personalizes math and literacy content through mobile messages and provides regular progress updates to parents and teachers. This approach empowers underserved learners and fosters a supportive learning ecosystem using basic technology.
- **Finland – Inclusive Support for Special Education:** Finland integrates AI tools into special education to support students with learning challenges such as dyslexia and ADHD. Through speech recognition, predictive text, and AI tutoring systems, students receive targeted support that enables them to thrive in inclusive classroom environments, reflecting Finland's commitment to equity and innovation.
- **Brazil – Bridging Gaps in Public Education with Geekie:** Brazil's Geekie platform provides AI-powered personalized learning to public school students, helping reduce educational inequality. It offers adaptive content and real-time diagnostics aligned with national curricula. Studies show improved student engagement and performance, especially in under-resourced schools.

8. FUTURE DIRECTIONS

The future directions of AI in education hold immense potential to revolutionize the learning experience, with advancements poised to enhance personalization, equity, and efficiency. As AI continues to evolve, it will enable even more personalized learning, with systems becoming adept at tailoring content to individual students' needs, preferences, and learning speeds.

8.1. AI in Lifelong Learning

AI in lifelong learning is transforming how individuals pursue continuous education and skill development throughout their lives. As the job market evolves and new technologies emerge, lifelong learning has become essential for staying relevant and competitive. AI plays a crucial role in this process by offering personalized, flexible, and efficient learning experiences tailored to individual needs, interests, and goals.

One of the most significant ways AI supports lifelong learning is through personalized learning pathways. AI-powered platforms can analyze a learner's current skills, identify gaps, and recommend customized courses or learning materials that align with their specific needs and career aspirations. This personalized approach helps learners focus on what matters most, ensuring they acquire the most relevant skills at their own pace. AI also allows for adaptive learning, meaning that the system can adjust in real-time to the learner's progress, providing additional support or challenges as needed.

AI-driven systems can also provide real-time feedback and assessment of progress, helping learners stay on track and understand areas that require improvement. This feedback is immediate, offering a more dynamic and responsive learning experience compared to traditional methods. Furthermore, AI-powered tools, such as intelligent tutoring systems, provide personalized assistance, guiding learners through complex topics or answering specific questions, simulating the support they would receive in a classroom setting (B. M. McLaren,2006).

8.2. The Future of AI in Global Education Systems

The future of AI in global education systems holds transformative potential, offering opportunities to revolutionize how education is delivered, accessed, and experienced across diverse regions and communities. As AI technology advances, it promises to create more inclusive, efficient, and personalized learning environments, addressing both global challenges and individual learning needs(R. S. Baker, 2021). Here are key areas where AI will play a pivotal role in reshaping the global education landscape:

1. Personalization at Scale

AI will enable hyper-personalized learning for students around the world, providing tailored educational experiences that address individual needs, learning styles, and paces. This is especially crucial in diverse classrooms where students come from different backgrounds, have varying levels of prior knowledge, and learn in distinct ways. With AI tools, each student can have a personalized learning path, receiving content and feedback that suits their unique requirements. These personalized experiences could be scaled globally, ensuring that quality education reaches students regardless of their geographic location.

2. Overcoming Geographic and Socio-Economic Barriers

AI has the potential to address global inequalities in education by providing affordable, scalable, and accessible learning solutions to underserved regions. In remote areas where there may be a lack of physical schools, teachers, or resources, AI-powered platforms can deliver high-quality education through digital learning tools, virtual classrooms, and intelligent tutoring systems. Furthermore, AI's ability to break down language barriers through translation and real-time support can ensure that education is more inclusive for non-native speakers, expanding access to global educational content.

3. Teacher Support and Professional Development

AI will not replace educators but will serve as a powerful tool for supporting teachers and enhancing their effectiveness. AI can automate administrative tasks, such as grading and attendance, allowing teachers to focus more on teaching and student engagement. It can also serve as a resource for professional development, providing teachers with real-time feedback on their teaching styles, recommending pedagogical strategies, and offering access to online training and skill-building courses. By improving the capacity of educators globally, AI can help raise the standard of teaching, particularly in regions with teacher shortages.

4. Predictive Analytics for Educational Improvement

AI can harness the power of predictive analytics to identify trends, spot at-risk students, and anticipate educational needs on a global scale. By analyzing student performance data, AI can provide actionable insights into how to improve learning outcomes, tailor interventions, and allocate resources more effectively. On a larger scale, governments and educational bodies can use AI-driven data to make informed decisions about curriculum design, teacher training, and infrastructure development, leading to evidence-based improvements in education systems worldwide.

5. AI as a Catalyst for Innovation

The use of AI in education will stimulate innovation in teaching and learning methodologies. AI can enable more dynamic, interactive learning environments, including virtual and augmented reality experiences, where students can engage with immersive content that enhances understanding and retention. AI's ability to simulate real-world scenarios and provide hands-on experiences in a virtual space could be particularly beneficial for disciplines such as science, medicine, engineering, and the arts. The future of education will see more creative and diverse learning experiences as AI-powered tools foster innovative approaches to curriculum design and student engagement.

8.3. Innovations in AI-Driven Educational Tools

AI-powered educational technologies are quickly changing the face of education by providing creative answers that improve teaching methods and the learning process. Important developments include adaptive educational platforms that change courses in real-time to the learner's progress and automated tutoring systems that offer tailored instruction based on each student's needs and speed. Additionally, AI-powered grading and assessment tools streamline administrative tasks, providing more accurate, objective evaluations while offering detailed feedback. Personalized learning assistants, such as AI-powered chatbots, support students 24/7 by answering questions and providing reminders, ensuring continuous engagement. AI is also revolutionizing language learning, with tools like Duolingo using speech recognition to improve pronunciation and grammar. The combination of AI with VR/AR creates immersive, hands-on learning environments, helping students experience complex concepts through real-life simulations. Moreover, learning analytics powered by AI analyze student data, predicting performance and enabling proactive interventions. AI is also making significant strides in special education, offering tailored solutions for students with learning disabilities and helping them engage with content more effectively. Finally, AI's predictive analytics assist institutions by forecasting student outcomes and identifying at-risk learners, allowing for timely intervention. Collectively, these innovations are creating more personalized, accessible, and efficient educational experiences, breaking down barriers and fostering a more inclusive learning environment.

9. CONCLUSION

In conclusion, artificial intelligence has the ability to completely transform education by increasing the efficiency, accessibility, and personalization of learning. AI is revolutionizing education with breakthroughs like AI-driven tests, adaptive learning platforms, intelligent tutoring systems, and immersive VR/AR experiences. By automating administrative activities and supplying data-driven insights, these solutions are relieving instructors of some of their workload while simultaneously improving the learning experience for students by providing personalized material, real-time feedback, and ongoing assistance.

9.1. Summary of Key Findings

AI education is bringing about revolutionary changes in a number of areas of the educational process. It makes learning more efficient and interesting by enabling individualized learning, which adjusts tests and content to each student's requirements. By automating administrative duties like grading and giving real-time feedback, AI also improves productivity and frees up teachers to concentrate more on instruction.By providing affordable and scalable solutions, AI helps overcome geographic and socio-economic barriers, making quality education accessible to underserved regions and breaking down language barriers. The technology fosters greater student engagement through interactive tools such as intelligent tutoring systems, and it supports teachers by offering data-driven insights and professional development recommendations.

9.2. The Future of AI in Education: A Vision for Change

The future of AI in education presents transformative possibilities, reshaping how learning is experienced and taught. AI will enhance personalized and adaptive learning, tailoring educational content and assessments to individual student needs and progress, ensuring that each learner receives the support and challenge required for success. It will foster lifelong learning, enabling individuals to continually acquire new skills and knowledge through AI-driven recommendations and microlearning platforms. AI's potential to bridge global educational gaps is significant, offering scalable solutions and breaking down language barriers to make education more accessible worldwide. Teachers will be empowered, not replaced, as AI automates administrative tasks, provides data-driven insights into student performance, and offers personalized professional development, allowing educators to focus more on student engagement. The integration of immersive technologies like AR and VR with AI will create interactive, hands-on learning experiences, making education more engaging and experiential. Data-driven insights will guide educational improvements, helping institutions refine curricula and teaching strategies for better outcomes. To ensure AI's benefits are equitable, ethical AI systems will be essential, focusing on transparency, fairness, and accessibility for all students. AI will also foster global collaboration by connecting students across borders and cultures, encouraging a diverse exchange of ideas. As AI prepares students for the future of work, it will help align education with the skills required by emerging industries, while continuously evolving through innovation to enhance educational practices. Overall, the future of AI in education promises to be more personalized, inclusive, and dynamic, creating a learning environment that supports the needs of all learners and educators.

REFERENCES

Baker, R. S., McLaren, B. M., Hutt, S., Richey, J. E., Rowe, E., Almeda, M. V., & Andres, J. M. A. (2021, June). Towards sharing student models across learning systems. In *International conference on artificial intelligence in education* (pp. 60-65). Cham: Springer International Publishing.

Chen, L., Chen, P., & Lin, Z. (2020). *Artificial Intelligence in Education: A Review* (Vol. 8). IEEE Access. [Online], DOI: 10.1109/ACCESS.2020.2988510

Holstein, K., McLaren, B. M., & Aleven, V. (2018). Student learning benefits of a mixed-reality teacher awareness tool in AI-enhanced classrooms. In Artificial Intelligence in Education: 19th International Conference, AIED 2018, London, UK, June 27–30, 2018 [Springer International Publishing.]. *Proceedings*, *19*(Part I), 154–168.

McLaren, B. M. (2003). Extensionally Defining Principles and Cases in Ethics: An AI Model. *Artificial Intelligence*, *150*(1–2), 145–181.

McLaren, B. M. (2006). Computational Models of Ethical Reasoning: Challenges, Initial Steps, and Future Directions. *IEEE Intelligent Systems*, *21*(4), 29–37.

McLaren, B. M., Adams, D. M., & Mayer, R. E. (2015). Delayed Learning Effects with Erroneous Examples: A Study of Learning Decimals with a Web-Based Tutor. *International Journal of Artificial Intelligence in Education*, *25*(4), 520–542.

McLaren, B. M., Adams, D. M., Mayer, R. E., & Forlizzi, J. (2017). A Computer-Based Game That Promotes Mathematics Learning More Than a Conventional Approach. *International Journal of Game-Based Learning*, *7*(1), 36–56.

McLaren, B. M., Scheuer, O., & Mikšátko, J. (2010). Supporting Collaborative Learning and E-Discussions Using Artificial Intelligence Techniques. *International Journal of Artificial Intelligence in Education*, *20*(1), 1–46.

McLaren, B. M., van Gog, T., Ganoe, C., Yaron, D., & Karabinos, M. (2015). Worked examples are more efficient for learning than high-assistance instructional software. In Artificial Intelligence in Education: 17th International Conference, AIED 2015, Madrid, Spain, June 22-26, 2015. [Springer International Publishing.]. *Proceedings*, *17*, 710–713.

Najar, A. S., Mitrovic, A., & McLaren, B. M. (2014). Adaptive support versus alternating worked examples and tutored problems: which leads to better learning? In User Modeling, Adaptation, and Personalization: 22nd International Conference, UMAP 2014, Aalborg, Denmark, July 7-11, 2014. [Springer International Publishing.]. *Proceedings*, *22*, 171–182.

Chapter 5
AI and Arts Education: Creative Possibilities

Goh Ying Yingsoon
https://orcid.org/0000-0002-6654-2887
Universiti Teknologi MARA, Malaysia

Wei Rukuan
https://orcid.org/0009-0000-1685-8691
Teesside University, UK

Tie Xiaoyao
Qilu University of Technology, China

Nurul Ain Chua Binti Abdullah
https://orcid.org/0000-0003-2915-1577
University Terengganu Malaysia, Malaysia

Nurul Ajleaa Abdul Rahman
Universiti Teknologi MARA, Malaysia

Zhang Suyan
https://orcid.org/0009-0003-4518-1650
Shandong Jianzhu University, China

ABSTRACT

This chapter delves into the burgeoning intersection of Artificial Intelligence (AI) and arts education, unveiling a realm of creative possibilities that are reshaping traditional learning paradigms. As AI continues to revolutionize various sectors, its potential to transform and enhance creative learning experiences in the arts becomes increasingly evident. The introduction provides a snapshot of AI's broad impact and sets the stage for a focused exploration of its applications in arts education. The narrative unfolds with a historical perspective on the evolution of arts education, highlighting the limitations of conventional methods and the pressing need for innovation. It then transitions into the role of AI as a creative partner, supported by case studies from music, visual arts, and performing arts, illustrating the symbiotic relationship between human creativity and AI augmentation.

DOI: 10.4018/979-8-3373-5102-5.ch005

MISSION AND FOCUS OF THE CHAPTER

The mission of this chapter, "AI and Arts Education: Creative Possibilities," is to explore the transformative potential of AI tools in reshaping arts education. It aims to address the key issues of accessibility, innovation, and personalization in artistic learning and creation. The chapter delves into questions such as: How can AI enhance traditional arts education methods? What are the ethical considerations of integrating AI in creative processes? And how can these tools be leveraged to make arts education more inclusive and diverse?

By examining cutting-edge AI applications, from virtual art assistants to intelligent tutoring systems, the chapter seeks to bridge the gap between technology and the arts. It aligns with the book's overarching goal of highlighting the impact of AI on various sectors, emphasizing the educational domain's evolution through technological advancements.

The relevance to the target audience, including educators, artists, technologists, and students, lies in its practical insights and visionary perspectives on the future of arts education. The chapter's potential impact on the field is substantial, as it advocates for a paradigm shift in how arts are taught and experienced, fostering a new era of creativity and collaboration. Ultimately, it aims to inspire and guide the integration of AI in arts education, thereby enriching the creative landscape and expanding the boundaries of artistic expression.

KEY THEMES AND CONCERNS

Introduction

The integration of Artificial Intelligence (AI) into arts education represents a paradigm shift, offering unprecedented opportunities for creativity, accessibility, and innovation. This chapter delves into the transformative potential of AI tools in arts education, exploring how they can enhance learning experiences, foster artistic expression, and address key educational challenges. The significance of this topic lies in its potential to reshape the future of arts education, making it more inclusive, personalized, and technologically advanced.

Main Arguments

1. Enhanced Creativity and Expression: AI tools can augment human creativity, providing new avenues for artistic expression and exploration.

2. Accessibility and Inclusivity: AI can make arts education more accessible to diverse populations, including those with disabilities and those in remote areas.
3. Personalized Learning: AI enables personalized learning experiences, adapting to individual student needs and preferences.
4. Pedagogical Innovation: AI prompts a reevaluation of traditional teaching methods, encouraging more interactive and collaborative learning environments.

Supporting Evidence

Data and Case Studies

1) Creative AI Tools: Case studies of AI-powered software like Adobe Sensei, which assists in graphic design, and AIVA (Artificial Intelligence Virtual Artist), which composes music, demonstrate how AI can enhance creative processes.
2) Accessibility Initiatives: Projects like Google's AI for Accessibility, which includes tools for visual storytelling and music composition for people with disabilities, showcase AI's role in making arts education more inclusive.
3) Personalized Learning Platforms: Platforms such as Kadenze, which use AI to tailor art and music courses to individual learning styles, provide evidence of AI's impact on personalized education.
4) Pedagogical Innovations: Examples from schools and universities that have integrated AI into their arts curricula, such as the use of AI in dance choreography and virtual reality in art history classes, illustrate new pedagogical approaches.

Theoretical Frameworks

1) Constructivist Learning Theory: This theory posits that learners construct knowledge through experiences. AI tools can provide immersive, interactive experiences that align with this theory.
2) Social Cognitive Theory: AI can facilitate collaborative learning environments, supporting the idea that learning is a social process influenced by observation and interaction.
3) Technological Determinism: This perspective suggests that technology shapes society and education. AI's integration into arts education is a testament to this influence.

Practical Implications

1) Educational Institutions: Schools and universities can adopt AI tools to create more engaging, personalized arts education programs. For instance, AI-driven virtual studios can offer students real-time feedback and guidance.
2) Professional Development: Educators can benefit from training in AI tools, enhancing their ability to integrate these technologies into their teaching practices.
3) Policy and Curriculum Development: Policymakers can consider the inclusion of AI in arts education curricula, ensuring that students are prepared for a technology-driven future.
4) Industry Collaboration: Partnerships between educational institutions and tech companies can foster the development of innovative AI tools tailored to arts education needs.

Future Directions

1) Ethical Considerations: As AI becomes more prevalent, addressing ethical issues such as copyright, authenticity, and the role of the artist will be crucial.
2) Technological Advancements: Emerging technologies like AI-driven virtual reality and augmented reality hold promise for even more immersive arts education experiences.
3) Research and Development: Continued research is needed to understand the long-term impacts of AI on artistic development and education.
4) Global Collaboration: International collaboration can promote the sharing of best practices and innovations in AI and arts education.

Conclusion

This chapter highlights the transformative potential of AI in arts education, emphasizing its role in enhancing creativity, accessibility, and personalized learning. By examining case studies, theoretical frameworks, and practical implications, we underscore the importance of integrating AI into arts education curricula. The insights presented contribute to the book's mission of exploring the intersection of technology and education, and they invite further exploration into the ethical, technological, and collaborative future of AI in arts education. Ultimately, this chapter advocates for a forward-thinking approach to arts education, one that embraces the creative possibilities offered by AI while addressing the key themes and concerns that accompany such innovation.

INTRODUCTION

Artificial intelligence (AI) is rapidly transforming various sectors, from healthcare and finance to manufacturing and transportation, by automating tasks, improving efficiency, and driving innovation. Within this wave of technological advancement, the arts education sector stands to gain significantly. AI has the potential to revolutionize how creative skills are taught and learned, offering personalized feedback, generating novel artistic content, and fostering interactive learning environments. This exploration delves into the transformative power of AI in arts education, examining how it can enhance creative learning experiences for students of all ages and backgrounds. (Sáez-Velasco et al., 2024).

Brief Overview of AI's Impact On Various Sectors

Artificial intelligence (AI) is rapidly transforming industries across the board. In healthcare, AI algorithms are assisting with disease diagnosis, drug discovery, and personalized treatment plans. In finance, AI-powered systems are used for fraud detection, risk assessment, and algorithmic trading. Manufacturing is becoming increasingly automated with AI-driven robots and predictive maintenance. Even sectors like transportation are being revolutionized by self-driving vehicles and optimized logistics. AI's ability to analyze massive datasets, identify patterns, and make predictions is driving efficiency, innovation, and decision-making in ways previously unimaginable.

Beyond these prominent examples, AI's influence extends to various other fields. In retail, AI personalizes shopping experiences and optimizes inventory management. The energy sector utilizes AI for smart grids and renewable energy forecasting. Agriculture benefits from AI-powered precision farming and crop monitoring. Even creative industries like art, music, and writing are being impacted by AI tools that assist with content generation and artistic exploration. As AI technology continues to evolve, its impact on diverse sectors is only expected to grow, reshaping how we live and work. (Dwivedi et al., 2021).

Introduction to AI's Potential in Arts Education

Artificial intelligence (AI) has the potential to revolutionize arts education in profound ways. Imagine a drawing program that can analyze a student's brushstrokes and provide personalized feedback on technique, or a music composition tool that can generate melodies in response to a student's input, fostering creative exploration. AI can also help students understand art history and theory by analyzing artworks and providing contextual information. Furthermore, AI-powered virtual reality environments can create immersive art experiences, allowing students to explore different artistic styles and techniques in an engaging and interactive manner. By automating repetitive tasks, AI can free up educators' time to focus on individualized instruction and mentorship, fostering deeper creative learning experiences for students. (Torres Carceller, 2024).

AI's potential in arts education is vast and varied. Imagine a music education program that uses AI to analyze a student's playing and provide real-time feedback on pitch, rhythm, and tempo, or a visual arts application that can generate different artistic styles based on a student's initial sketches, encouraging experimentation and exploration. AI-powered tools could also create personalized learning pathways, tailoring exercises and projects to individual student's needs and skill levels. For art history, AI could analyze vast databases of artworks, allowing students to explore connections between different periods, styles, and artists in an interactive way. Furthermore, AI-driven virtual reality experiences could immerse students in famous artworks or historical artistic movements, providing a deeper understanding and appreciation of art. These are just a few examples of how AI can transform arts education, making it more engaging, personalized, and effective. (Hutson, 2024).

Exploring How AI Can Transform and Enhance Creative Learning Experiences

AI has the potential to transform creative learning experiences by offering personalized and adaptive learning pathways. Imagine a student learning to play the piano. AI could analyze their playing in real-time, identifying areas where they struggle with rhythm, fingering, or dynamics, and then generate customized exercises to address those specific weaknesses. This personalized feedback, delivered instantly, can accelerate learning and boost student motivation. Beyond skill development, AI can also foster creative exploration. AI-powered tools can generate variations on musical themes, suggest different color palettes for a painting, or even help students brainstorm ideas for a story, acting as a creative partner and expanding the possibilities for artistic expression. By automating tedious tasks like transcribing music or organizing images, AI can also free up students' time to focus on the more creative aspects of their art. (Fortino, 2023).

Furthermore, AI can enhance creative learning by providing access to vast amounts of information and resources. Students could use AI to explore different artistic styles, learn about the lives and works of famous artists, or even analyze the composition of master paintings. AI-powered virtual museums and galleries can offer immersive experiences, allowing students to explore art from different cultures and historical periods without leaving the classroom. By providing personalized feedback, fostering creative exploration, and democratizing access to information,

AI can empower students to develop their artistic talents and cultivate a deeper appreciation for the arts.

THE EVOLUTION OF ARTS EDUCATION

Having explored the burgeoning creative possibilities unlocked by the integration of AI in arts education, let's now turn our attention to the historical trajectory and development of arts education itself. Traditional arts education methods, while valuable, often face challenges such as limited resources, large class sizes, and a focus on rote memorization rather than creative exploration. These constraints can hinder students' ability to develop their individual artistic voices and fully engage with the creative process. There's a growing need for innovation in arts education to address these challenges and cultivate a new generation of creative thinkers and artists. Emerging technologies, including AI, virtual reality, and augmented reality, offer exciting possibilities for transforming arts education by providing personalized learning experiences, access to vast resources, and opportunities for interactive engagement with art forms.

Traditional Methods and Challenges of Arts Education

Traditional methods in arts education often rely on direct instruction, where teachers demonstrate techniques and students replicate them. This can involve lectures on art history, demonstrations of painting or sculpting techniques, or rote learning of musical scales. While these methods provide a foundation in artistic skills and knowledge, they can also present several challenges (refer Table 1). (Freedman & Hernández-Hernández, 2024).

Table 1. Challenges of arts education

Number	Challenge	Elaboration
1	Limited Individualization	Traditional classrooms often have large student-to-teacher ratios, making it difficult to provide personalized feedback and instruction tailored to each student's unique learning style and pace. This can lead to some students feeling left behind or unchallenged.
2	Emphasis on Product over Process	In some traditional settings, there's a strong focus on the final artistic product rather than the creative process itself. This can discourage experimentation and risk-taking, as students may fear making mistakes.
3	Lack of Engagement	Traditional lecture-based approaches can sometimes be passive, leading to a lack of student engagement and motivation. Students may struggle to connect with the material or find it relevant to their own interests.

continued on following page

Table 1. Continued

Number	Challenge	Elaboration
4	Limited Access to Resources	Many schools face budget constraints, which can limit access to art supplies, equipment, and technology. This can restrict students' ability to explore different art forms and experiment with various media.
5	Assessment Challenges	Assessing artistic creativity can be subjective and challenging. Traditional methods often rely on grading finished products, which may not fully capture the student's creative thinking, problem-solving skills, and artistic growth.

The Need for Innovation in Arts Education

The traditional model of arts education, often constrained by limited resources and a focus on rote learning, struggles to fully nurture the creative potential of today's students. In a rapidly changing world that demands innovation and adaptability, fostering creativity is no longer a luxury but a necessity. Students need opportunities to explore different art forms, experiment with new technologies, and develop their own unique artistic voices. Innovation in arts education is crucial for equipping students with the skills and mindset they need to thrive in the 21st century, including critical thinking, problem-solving, collaboration, and communication. By embracing new approaches and technologies, arts education can become more engaging, relevant, and impactful, preparing students not just for careers in the arts but also for success in any field that values creativity and innovation. (Rocky Mountain College of Art + Design, 2024).

Furthermore, innovation in arts education is essential for making the arts more accessible and inclusive. Traditional arts education often caters to a specific demographic, leaving many students behind. Emerging technologies like AI and virtual reality have the potential to democratize access to arts education by offering personalized learning experiences, removing geographical barriers, and catering to diverse learning styles. By embracing innovation, arts education can reach a wider audience and empower students from all backgrounds to explore their creative potential. This inclusivity is not only beneficial for individual students but also enriches society as a whole by fostering a more diverse and vibrant artistic landscape. (Jiang, 2023).

Emerging Technologies and Their Influence on Arts Education

Emerging technologies are poised to reshape arts education in exciting ways. Here are some key examples (refer Table 2). (Usca et al., 2024).

Table 2. Emerging technologies and their influence on arts education

Number	Technology	Elaboration
1	Artificial Intelligence (AI) tools	AI tools can personalize learning by analyzing student work and providing tailored feedback. It can also generate creative content, assist with brainstorming, and offer new ways to explore art history and theory.
2	Virtual Reality (VR)	VR can create immersive art experiences, allowing students to step inside famous paintings, explore different artistic styles, and even sculpt in a virtual environment. This can deepen engagement and understanding of art.
3	Augmented Reality (AR)	AR can overlay digital information onto the real world, enhancing art experiences. For example, students could use an AR app to point their phone at a painting in a museum and get instant information about the artist, the historical context, and the techniques used.
4	3D Printing	3D printing allows students to create physical objects from digital designs. This opens up new possibilities for sculpture, design, and other art forms, fostering hands-on learning and creative problem-solving.
5	Digital Art Tools	Software like Procreate, Adobe Photoshop, and Blender offer powerful tools for digital painting, animation, 3D modeling, and graphic design. These tools empower students to explore new mediums and develop digital literacy skills.
6	Interactive Whiteboards and Tablets	These technologies facilitate collaborative learning, allowing students to share their work, provide feedback to each other, and engage in interactive lessons.

These emerging technologies have the potential to make arts education more engaging, personalized, and accessible. They can also help students develop valuable skills for the 21st century, including creativity, critical thinking, problem-solving, and digital literacy.

AI AS A CREATIVE PARTNER

Considering the evolution of arts education, we can now delve into the exciting prospect of AI functioning not merely as a tool, but as a genuine creative partner in artistic endeavors. AI is increasingly being recognized not just as a tool, but as a creative partner in the arts. AI algorithms can augment human creativity by generating novel ideas, suggesting variations on existing themes, and even helping artists overcome creative blocks. For example, AI models can compose music in various styles, generate unique visual art pieces, or even choreograph dance movements. Case studies have shown AI's successful application in these fields. In music, AI has been used to compose original pieces, assist composers in exploring new musical ideas, and even create personalized music experiences for listeners. In visual arts, AI tools like DALL-E and Midjourney are enabling artists to generate stunning images from text descriptions, opening up new avenues for artistic expression. In performing arts, AI is being used to analyze movement data and generate new dance sequences, providing choreographers with fresh inspiration. The benefits of this AI collaboration are numerous, including expanded creative possibilities, accelerated artistic workflows, and the potential for artists to push the boundaries of their respective fields. (Alagar, 2024).

AI's Role in Augmenting Human Creativity for Arts Education

AI is not intended to replace human creativity in arts education but rather to augment and enhance it. Imagine a student struggling with writer's block. An AI tool could suggest different plot lines, character ideas, or even generate sample text in various styles, providing a springboard for the student's own writing. Or consider a music student experimenting with different melodies. AI could analyze their compositions, identify potential areas for improvement, and even suggest harmonic variations, helping the student explore new musical possibilities. In visual arts, AI tools can generate diverse textures, patterns, and color palettes, inspiring students to experiment with different visual elements and develop their own unique artistic style. By acting as a creative partner, AI can help students overcome creative obstacles, explore new ideas, and push the boundaries of their artistic expression. (Crabtree-Ireland, 2025).

Furthermore, AI can augment human creativity by democratizing access to artistic tools and knowledge. Students who may not have access to traditional art supplies or expert instruction can utilize AI-powered tools to explore different art forms and develop their skills. AI can provide personalized feedback, generate customized exercises, and even simulate the experience of working with different media, making arts education more accessible and inclusive. By removing barriers to entry and providing personalized support, AI can empower students from all backgrounds to unleash their creative potential and discover their artistic voices. This collaborative approach, where AI acts as a tool for exploration and inspiration, can foster a new generation of creative thinkers and artists. (Pitta, 2023).

Case Studies of AI in Music, Visual Arts, and Performing Arts

These case studies demonstrate the diverse applications of AI in the arts, showcasing its potential to augment human creativity, inspire new artistic forms, and transform the way art is created and experienced. (refer Table 3).

Table 3. Case studies of AI in music, visual arts, and performing arts

Music		
1	AIVA (Artificial Intelligence Virtual Artist) Karpov, 2020	This AI composer has created original classical music used in films, advertising, and games. AIVA demonstrates AI's ability to compose complex and emotionally resonant music.
2	Amper Music Bonini & Magaudda, 2023	This platform allows users to create custom music for videos, games, and other media. Users can specify the mood, genre, and length of the music, and AI generates unique compositions tailored to their needs.
3	Jukebox (OpenAI) Jeon & Kim, 2021	This AI model can generate original music with lyrics in various genres. It can even mimic the style of specific artists, showcasing AI's potential for creative expression in music.
Visual Arts		
1	DALL-E 2 (OpenAI) Ramdhani & Susanti, 2024	This AI model can generate realistic and creative images from natural language descriptions. It allows artists to explore new visual concepts and create unique artwork by simply describing their ideas in words.
2	Midjourney Tsidylo & Sena, 2023	This AI art generator creates images from text prompts, allowing users to quickly visualize and experiment with different artistic styles and compositions. It has been used by artists to create stunning visuals for various projects.
3	Deep Dream Generator Wylder, 2022	This tool uses AI to transform images into dreamlike and surreal artworks. It allows users to explore the intersection of art and artificial intelligence, creating visually captivating and thought-provoking pieces.
Performing Arts		
1	AI-generated choreography Liu & Sra, 2024	Researchers have used AI to analyze movement data and generate new dance sequences. This can provide choreographers with fresh inspiration and help them explore new possibilities in dance.
2	AI-powered stage design Kocaballi, 2023	AI can be used to create dynamic and interactive stage designs that respond to the performers' movements and the music being played. This can enhance the audience experience and create a more immersive and engaging performance.
3	AI-assisted scriptwriting Yaseen, 2023	AI tools can help playwrights and screenwriters brainstorm ideas, develop characters, and even generate dialogue. This can speed up the writing process and help artists explore new narrative possibilities.

Benefits of AI Collaboration in Artistic Expression in Arts Education

AI collaboration in artistic expression offers numerous benefits within arts education. Firstly, it democratizes access to creative tools and resources. Students who may lack access to traditional art supplies or specialized instruction can leverage AI-powered platforms to explore various art forms, from music composition to digital painting. AI can provide personalized guidance, offering tailored feedback and suggesting exercises based on individual student progress. This personalized learning experience can foster a deeper understanding of artistic principles and techniques, regardless of prior experience or background. Moreover, AI can spark creative exploration by generating novel ideas, suggesting variations on existing themes, and even helping students overcome creative blocks. This collaborative partnership empowers students to experiment more freely, take creative risks, and discover their unique artistic voices. (PRO EDU, 2024).

Secondly, AI collaboration can enhance the learning process by fostering critical thinking and problem-solving skills. Students working with AI tools are not simply passive consumers of technology; they are actively engaged in shaping the creative output. They learn to evaluate AI-generated content, make informed decisions about its application, and refine their own artistic vision in response to the AI's suggestions. This iterative process of creation and reflection strengthens their critical thinking abilities and cultivates a deeper understanding of the artistic process. Furthermore, AI collaboration can expose students to cutting-edge technologies and prepare them for a future where AI is increasingly integrated into creative industries. By embracing AI as a creative partner, arts education can equip students with the skills and knowledge they need to thrive in the digital age.

TRANSFORMATIONAL AI TOOLS IN ARTS EDUCATION

Overview of AI Tools Specifically Designed for Arts Education

Building upon the understanding of AI as a creative partner, let's now examine the specific transformational AI tools that are reshaping the landscape of arts education. A growing number of AI tools are being developed specifically for arts education, catering to various disciplines and skill levels. These tools range from AI-powered music composition software that can generate melodies and harmonies based on student input to visual art applications that can analyze brushstrokes and provide real-time feedback on technique. Some platforms offer AI-driven virtual reality experiences that immerse students in famous artworks or allow them to sculpt in a virtual environment. Others focus on personalized learning, using AI to assess student progress and tailor exercises to individual needs. These AI tools are designed not to replace human instructors but rather to augment their capabilities, providing personalized support, fostering creative exploration, and making arts education more engaging and accessible for all students.

AI-Driven Music Composition Tools

AI-driven music composition tools are revolutionizing the way music is created and learned. These tools leverage artificial intelligence algorithms to assist with various aspects of the compositional process, from generating melodies and harmonies to creating entire musical arrangements. (refer Table 4). (Li, 2025).

Table 4. AI-driven music composition tools

Number	Tool	Elaboration
1	Melody and Harmony Generation	AI can analyze vast datasets of existing music to learn patterns and structures, allowing it to generate original melodies and harmonies in various styles. Users can often specify parameters like genre, mood, and tempo, and the AI will create musical content that aligns with those preferences. This can be a valuable tool for songwriters looking for inspiration or composers exploring new musical ideas.
2	Accompaniment and Arrangement	Some AI tools can generate accompaniments for existing melodies, creating harmonies, chord progressions, and rhythmic backing. Others can arrange compositions for different instruments, automatically creating parts for strings, brass, or other ensembles. This can be particularly helpful for composers who may not have expertise in orchestration or arrangement.
3	Personalized Music Learning	AI-powered music education platforms can analyze a student's playing or compositions and provide personalized feedback on pitch, rhythm, timing, and other musical elements. These platforms can also generate custom exercises and lessons tailored to the student's individual needs and progress.
4	Creative Exploration	AI tools can be used to experiment with different musical styles and ideas. Users can input a simple melody or chord progression, and the AI can generate variations, suggesting new directions for the composition. This can be a powerful tool for sparking creativity and discovering new musical possibilities.
5	Accessibility	AI music tools can make music composition more accessible to individuals who may not have formal musical training. By providing assistance with melody generation, harmony creation, and arrangement, these tools can empower aspiring musicians to express their creative ideas, regardless of their background.

It's important to note that AI is not meant to replace human composers. Rather, it serves as a powerful tool that can augment human creativity, streamline the compositional process, and make music creation more accessible to a wider audience.

Virtual Reality and Immersive Art Experiences

Virtual reality (VR) is transforming how we experience and interact with art, creating immersive experiences that blur the lines between the physical and digital worlds. (Kim & Lee, 2022). (refer Table 5).

Table 5. Virtual reality and immersive art experiences

Number	Experience	Elaboration
Stepping into the Artwork		
1	Virtual Museums and Galleries	VR allows the visitors to explore world-renowned museums and galleries from the comfort of the visitors' home. The visitors can walk through the halls of the Louvre, examine masterpieces up close, and even interact with virtual guides who provide information about the art and its history.
2	Experiencing Art in Context	VR can recreate historical settings, allowing the visitors to experience art in its original context. Imagine stepping into a Renaissance workshop to see how a painting was created or exploring an ancient Egyptian tomb filled with hieroglyphics.
3	Immersive Storytelling	VR can be used to create interactive narratives that combine art, storytelling, and gaming elements. The visitors might find the themselves immersed in a virtual world where the visitors have to solve puzzles, interact with characters, and make choices that affect the story's outcome, all while being surrounded by stunning visuals and soundscapes.
Creating Art in VR		
1	3D Painting and Sculpting	VR tools like Tilt Brush and Medium allow artists to create 3D art in a virtual environment. The visitors can paint with light, sculpt with virtual clay, and experiment with different textures and materials, all without the limitations of the physical world.
2	Interactive Installations	VR can be used to create interactive art installations that respond to the visitors' movements and gestures. The visitors might find the themselves controlling a virtual orchestra with the visitors' hands or manipulating virtual objects to create dynamic sculptures.
Benefits of VR in Arts Education		
1	Enhanced Engagement	VR experiences can be more engaging and memorable than traditional art education methods. By immersing students in a virtual world, VR can capture their attention and make learning more interactive and fun.
2	Accessibility	VR can make art more accessible to students who may have physical limitations or who live in areas with limited access to museums and galleries.
3	Creative Exploration	VR provides a safe and experimental space for students to explore different art forms and techniques. They can experiment with different media, make mistakes, and learn from them without fear of damaging materials or wasting resources.

VR is still a relatively new technology, but its potential for transforming arts education is immense. As VR technology continues to evolve, we can expect even more innovative and immersive art experiences to emerge, opening up new possibilities for creativity, learning, and artistic expression.

AI-Powered Art Analysis and Critique Platforms

AI-powered art analysis and critique platforms are emerging as valuable tools for both artists and art enthusiasts. These platforms leverage artificial intelligence to analyze artworks, provide insights into their composition, style, and meaning, and even generate critiques. (Cerruti & Valeri, 2022). (refer Table 6).

Table 6. AI-powered art analysis and critique platforms

Image Recognition and Analysis		
1	AI algorithms can be trained to recognize different artistic styles, techniques, and subjects within an artwork. They can analyze elements like color palettes, brushstrokes, composition, and use of light to identify patterns and characteristics.	
2	These platforms can provide information about the artwork's historical context, the artist's biography, and the potential influences on their work. This can help viewers gain a deeper understanding and appreciation of the art.	
Critique Generation		
1	Some AI platforms can generate critiques of artworks, offering insights into their strengths and weaknesses. These critiques might focus on technical aspects, such as the artist's use of perspective or color harmony, or on more conceptual elements, such as the artwork's emotional impact or its social commentary.	
2	While AI-generated critiques may not replace human expertise, they can offer a fresh perspective and help viewers consider different interpretations of the artwork.	
Personalized Learning		
1	AI-powered platforms can be used in educational settings to provide students with personalized feedback on their own artwork. The AI can analyze their work and suggest areas for improvement, helping students develop their skills and refine their artistic vision.	
2	These platforms can also be used to teach art history and theory, providing students with interactive tools to explore different artistic movements and analyze famous artworks.	
Benefits of AI in Art Analysis and Critique		
1	Objectivity	AI can provide a more objective analysis of artwork, reducing the influence of personal biases and preferences.
2	Accessibility	AI-powered platforms can make art analysis and critique more accessible to a wider audience, regardless of their background or expertise.
3	Efficiency	AI can analyze large datasets of artworks quickly and efficiently, providing insights that would be difficult or time-consuming for humans to obtain.
4	Personalization	AI can personalize the learning experience, tailoring feedback and suggestions to individual students' needs and progress.

While AI is still evolving in its ability to understand and interpret art, these platforms have the potential to revolutionize the way we engage with and learn about art. They can provide valuable tools for artists, educators, and art enthusiasts alike, fostering a deeper appreciation and understanding of the creative process.

Adaptive Learning Systems for Personalized Arts Education

Adaptive learning systems are revolutionizing arts education by providing personalized learning experiences tailored to each student's unique needs and progress. These systems leverage artificial intelligence to analyze student work, track their progress, and adjust the learning path accordingly. (Shao, 2024). (refer Table 7).

Table 7. Adaptive learning systems for personalized arts education

Personalized Learning Paths		
1	Adaptive learning systems can assess a student's current skill level and knowledge in a particular art form, such as painting, music, or creative writing. Based on this assessment, the system creates a personalized learning path that includes relevant exercises, lessons, and projects.	
2	As the student progresses, the system continuously monitors their performance and adjusts the learning path accordingly. If a student is struggling with a particular concept, the system may provide additional support or suggest alternative learning materials. If the student is excelling, the system may offer more challenging tasks to keep them engaged and motivated.	
Adaptive Feedback and Guidance		
1	Adaptive learning systems can provide personalized feedback on student work, highlighting strengths and weaknesses. The AI can analyze aspects like technique, composition, creativity, and originality, offering specific suggestions for improvement.	
2	The system can also provide guidance and support throughout the creative process. For example, in a music composition tool, the AI might suggest different harmonies or rhythmic variations based on the student's melody. In a visual arts application, the AI could offer feedback on color balance or perspective.	
Dynamic Content Delivery		
1	Adaptive learning systems can deliver content in a variety of formats, including text, images, videos, and interactive simulations. The system can choose the most appropriate format based on the student's learning style and the specific concept being taught.	
2	The system can also adjust the difficulty level of the content based on the student's progress. If a student is struggling with a particular concept, the system may provide simpler explanations or examples. If the student is excelling, the system may offer more advanced materials.	
Benefits of Adaptive Learning in Arts Education		
1	Personalized Learning	Adaptive learning systems cater to each student's unique needs, learning style, and pace, maximizing their learning potential.
2	Increased Engagement	By providing relevant and challenging tasks, adaptive learning systems can keep students engaged and motivated.
3	Improved Learning Outcomes	Personalized feedback and guidance can help students develop their skills and improve their artistic abilities.
4	Accessibility	Adaptive learning systems can make arts education more accessible to students with diverse learning needs and backgrounds.

Adaptive learning systems are still evolving, but they have the potential to transform arts education by providing personalized, engaging, and effective learning experiences for all students.

ENHANCING LEARNING AND TEACHING

Having explored the transformative potential of specific AI tools in arts education, it's crucial to consider their impact on the fundamental aspects of learning and teaching. These innovative technologies offer unprecedented opportunities to enhance both the student experience and pedagogical approaches within the arts.

AI's Impact on Pedagogical Approaches in Arts Education

AI is beginning to significantly impact pedagogical approaches in arts education, shifting the focus from traditional lecture-based instruction to more personalized and interactive learning experiences. AI-powered tools can facilitate differentiated instruction by tailoring content and feedback to individual student needs and skill levels. Educators can leverage AI to automate administrative tasks, freeing up more time for individualized mentorship and creative guidance. AI also fosters a more student-centered learning environment by empowering students to explore artistic concepts and techniques at their own pace and through personalized pathways. Furthermore, AI can facilitate new forms of creative expression and collaboration, as students and teachers alike utilize AI tools as partners in the artistic process. (Erişti & Freedman, 2024).

Personalized Learning Paths and AI Tutors

Personalized learning paths, powered by AI, are transforming the educational landscape, particularly within the arts. Instead of a one-size-fits-all approach, AI algorithms analyze each student's strengths, weaknesses, learning style, and pace to create a unique learning journey. In arts education, this could mean tailoring exercises in painting, music, or creative writing to address specific skill gaps or foster individual talents. The AI might recommend specific resources, suggest relevant projects, or even adjust the difficulty level of assignments based on the student's progress. This personalized approach maximizes engagement and accelerates learning by ensuring that students are always challenged appropriately and receiving the support they need to succeed. It allows them to focus on areas where they need the most improvement while also nurturing their unique artistic strengths. (Robert, 2024a,b).

AI tutors are emerging as valuable partners in personalized arts education. These AI-powered systems can provide individualized feedback on student work, offering specific suggestions for improvement. For example, an AI tutor might analyze a student's painting and provide feedback on composition, color mixing, or brushwork. In music, an AI tutor could assess a student's playing and offer guidance on rhythm, intonation, or technique. Beyond feedback, AI tutors can also provide personalized instruction, answering student questions, explaining complex concepts, and even demonstrating techniques. By offering individualized support and guidance, AI tutors can free up educators' time to focus on more complex tasks, such as mentoring students and fostering their creative development. This combination of personalized learning paths and AI tutors creates a dynamic and supportive learning environment that empowers students to reach their full artistic potential. (Robert, 2024a,b).

AI in Assessing and Providing Feedback on Student Work

AI is revolutionizing the assessment of student work in arts education by providing more objective, detailed, and efficient evaluations. AI algorithms can analyze various aspects of student creations, from technical skills like brushstrokes in painting or fingering in music to more subjective elements like composition, creativity, and originality. For example, an AI could assess a student's musical performance by analyzing pitch accuracy, rhythm, and dynamics, providing a comprehensive evaluation that goes beyond simple subjective impressions. In visual arts, AI could analyze a student's artwork, identifying strengths and weaknesses in areas like perspective, color theory, and composition. This automated assessment process not only saves educators valuable time but also provides students with more consistent and data-driven feedback on their work. (González-Calatayud et al., 2021).

Beyond assessment, AI is also transforming how feedback is provided to students. AI-powered systems can generate personalized feedback tailored to each student's specific needs and progress. Instead of generic comments, AI can offer specific suggestions for improvement, pointing out areas where the student excels and identifying areas where they could focus their efforts. For instance, an AI might provide feedback on a student's creative writing, suggesting ways to strengthen character development, improve pacing, or enhance the overall narrative arc. This personalized feedback is more actionable and effective than generic comments, empowering students to understand their strengths and weaknesses and make targeted improvements. Furthermore, AI can provide feedback in real-time, allowing students to learn from their mistakes immediately and iterate on their work more effectively. This combination of objective assessment and personalized feedback creates a powerful learning loop that accelerates student progress and fosters creative growth. (Hooda et al., 2022).

Teacher Support and Professional Development Through AI in Arts Education

AI offers significant support for arts educators, streamlining administrative tasks and freeing up valuable time for personalized instruction and creative mentorship. AI-powered tools can automate tasks such as grading routine assignments, organizing student portfolios, and even generating personalized learning plans. This allows teachers to dedicate more time to working directly with students, providing individualized feedback, and fostering creative exploration. Furthermore, AI can assist teachers in identifying students who may be struggling or excelling, enabling them to provide targeted interventions and support. By automating time-consuming tasks and providing data-driven insights, AI empowers teachers to focus on what they do best: inspiring and nurturing the creative potential of their students. (Tomaskinova & Tomaskin, 2024).

Beyond direct support, AI also plays a crucial role in professional development for arts educators. AI-powered platforms can offer personalized recommendations for professional learning resources, connecting teachers with relevant articles, workshops, and online courses. These platforms can also facilitate peer-to-peer learning by connecting teachers with colleagues who have expertise in specific areas. AI can even provide teachers with data-driven insights into their own teaching practices, helping them identify areas for improvement and refine their pedagogical approaches. By providing access to personalized learning resources and fostering collaboration among educators, AI empowers teachers to stay up-to-date with the latest trends in arts education and continuously improve their skills. (Zhao et al., 2021).

ETHICAL CONSIDERATIONS AND CHALLENGES IN USING AI FOR ARTS EDUCATION

As we consider the significant enhancements AI brings to learning and teaching in the arts, it's equally important to address the inherent ethical considerations and potential challenges that arise with its implementation. Navigating these complexities thoughtfully will be crucial for responsible and equitable integration of AI in this field.

Addressing Ethical Issues in Using AI in Arts Education

The integration of AI in arts education, while offering numerous benefits, also raises important ethical considerations that must be addressed proactively. One key concern is the potential for bias in AI algorithms. If the training data used to develop AI tools reflects existing societal biases, the AI may perpetuate or even amplify these biases in its assessments, feedback, and recommendations. This could lead to unequal opportunities for students from different backgrounds, reinforcing existing disparities in arts education. It's crucial to ensure that AI tools are developed using diverse and representative datasets, and that their outputs are carefully scrutinized for potential bias. Furthermore, transparency is essential. Educators and students should understand how AI tools work and how they are being used in the learning process. This transparency builds trust and allows for critical evaluation of the AI's role in arts education. (Pente et al., 2022).

Another ethical challenge lies in the potential impact of AI on human creativity and the role of the arts educator. There's a risk that over-reliance on AI tools could stifle students' own creative thinking and problem-solving skills. It's important to emphasize that AI should be used as a tool to augment, not replace, human creativity. Arts educators must play a crucial role in guiding students in the ethical use of AI, fostering critical thinking about its capabilities and limitations, and ensuring that AI serves to enhance rather than diminish human expression. Furthermore, the role of the arts educator must evolve alongside the introduction of AI. Teachers need professional development opportunities to learn how to effectively integrate AI into their teaching practices, understand its ethical implications, and adapt their pedagogical approaches to maximize the benefits of this technology while mitigating its risks.

Copyright and Ownership of AI-Generated Art

The issue of copyright and ownership of AI-generated art is a complex and evolving legal landscape. Traditional copyright law typically protects works created by human authors. However, when AI is involved in the creative process, the question of authorship becomes blurred. If an artist uses AI as a tool to generate an image based on their prompts, the artist's creative input and direction might be enough to claim copyright. However, if the AI generates the artwork with minimal human intervention, the question of who owns the copyright becomes more ambiguous. Some argue that the AI itself should be considered the author, while others suggest that the programmer or the user who provided the prompts should hold the copyright. These questions are still being debated in legal circles, and there is no clear consensus yet. (Škiljić, 2021).

The lack of clear legal frameworks surrounding AI-generated art creates uncertainty for artists, developers, and users. It's crucial to establish clear guidelines to protect the rights of all involved parties. One approach could be to consider AI as a tool, similar to a paintbrush or a camera. In this scenario, the artist who uses the AI to create the artwork would be considered the author and copyright holder, provided they made significant creative contributions. Another approach could be to create a new category of intellectual property specifically for AI-generated works, with rules governing ownership and usage rights. As AI technology continues to advance, it's essential to have open discussions about these issues and develop legal frameworks that are fair, balanced, and encourage innovation in the field of AI art. (Watiktinnakorn et al., 2023).

Ensuring Accessibility and Inclusivity in Using AI for Art Education

Ensuring accessibility and inclusivity in AI-driven arts education is paramount. AI tools have the potential to democratize access to arts education, but this potential can only be realized if careful consideration is given to the needs of diverse learners.

This includes ensuring that AI platforms and tools are compatible with assistive technologies used by students with disabilities, such as screen readers, alternative input devices, and closed captions. Furthermore, the design of AI-powered learning experiences should be inclusive, catering to different learning styles and preferences. This means providing options for visual, auditory, and kinesthetic learners, as well as offering content in multiple formats and languages. Addressing the digital divide is also crucial. Not all students have equal access to technology and reliable internet connectivity. Efforts must be made to bridge this gap by providing access to devices and internet resources, particularly for students from low-income backgrounds. (Davoodi, 2024).

Beyond technical accessibility, inclusivity in AI-driven arts education also requires attention to cultural sensitivity and representation. AI algorithms are trained on data, and if that data reflects existing societal biases, the AI may perpetuate or even amplify those biases in its outputs. This could lead to AI tools that favor certain artistic styles or perspectives while marginalizing others. It's crucial to curate diverse and representative datasets for training AI models and to critically evaluate the AI's outputs for potential bias. Furthermore, AI tools should be designed to be culturally responsive, recognizing and respecting the diverse artistic traditions and cultural backgrounds of all students. By prioritizing accessibility, inclusivity, and cultural sensitivity, we can harness the power of AI to create a more equitable and enriching arts education experience for all students. (Evangelidis et al., 2024).

The Role of Human Artists in an AI-Dominated Landscape

The rise of AI in art does not signal the obsolescence of human artists; rather, it marks a transformation in their role. In an AI-augmented landscape, human artists become curators, collaborators, and innovators, leveraging AI as a powerful tool to enhance their creative processes. Instead of fearing replacement, artists can embrace AI as a partner, using it to explore new artistic avenues, experiment with different styles, and push the boundaries of their chosen medium. Human artists will continue to bring their unique perspectives, emotions, and critical thinking to the creative process, guiding the AI's output and imbuing it with meaning and purpose. The focus shifts from technical execution, which AI can often handle, to conceptualization, artistic direction, and the communication of human experiences. (Qorbani 2020).

Furthermore, the human element in art will become even more valuable in an AI-dominated world. As AI generates increasingly sophisticated and technically perfect artworks, the imperfections, emotions, and unique perspectives that characterize human art will become more sought after. Human artists will be prized for their ability to connect with audiences on an emotional level, to tell stories that resonate with human experiences, and to offer unique interpretations of the world around us. The emphasis will shift from technical skill to creative vision, conceptual depth, and the ability to evoke emotional responses. In this new landscape, human artists will not only survive but thrive, finding new ways to express themselves and connect with audiences in a world where art is both human-made and AI-generated. (Wu et al., 2022).

FUTURE PROSPECTS

Having navigated the ethical considerations and challenges associated with AI in arts education, we can now turn our gaze towards the exciting future prospects that lie ahead. The continued evolution of AI promises even more profound and transformative possibilities for the realm of artistic learning and creation.

Predictions for the Future of AI in Arts Education

The future of AI in arts education promises a more personalized, engaging, and accessible learning experience for all students. We can anticipate AI tutors that provide real-time, tailored feedback on student artwork, fostering rapid skill development and creative exploration. AI-powered platforms will likely offer dynamic learning pathways, adapting content and challenges to suit individual student progress and learning styles. Imagine virtual reality experiences that immerse students in historical art movements or allow them to collaborate with AI on complex artistic projects. AI could also facilitate cross-cultural artistic exchange, connecting students from different backgrounds and enabling them to learn from diverse artistic traditions. As AI technology evolves, we can expect even more innovative applications to emerge, transforming how art is taught, learned, and experienced. (Renkema & Tursunbayeva, 2024).

Beyond the classroom, AI has the potential to democratize access to arts education on a global scale. AI-powered platforms could offer personalized art instruction to students in remote areas or those lacking access to traditional art programs. AI could also translate artistic resources and educational materials into multiple languages, breaking down language barriers and fostering a more inclusive and interconnected artistic community. Furthermore, AI could play a crucial role in preserving and promoting endangered art forms and cultural traditions by analyzing, documenting, and even recreating them through AI-powered tools. In the future, AI will not only enhance the learning process but also empower individuals from all backgrounds to explore their creative potential and contribute to the rich tapestry of human artistic expression. (Rona-Tas, 2020).

Potential Advancements and Their Implications of Using AI in Art Education

One potential advancement lies in the development of sophisticated AI models that can understand and respond to the nuances of artistic expression. Imagine AI that can not only analyze technical skill but also interpret the emotional intent and artistic vision behind a piece of work. This could lead to AI tutors that provide more insightful and nuanced feedback, going beyond technical corrections to offer guidance on how to better communicate ideas and emotions through art. Furthermore, AI could be used to create personalized art experiences tailored to individual student preferences and learning styles. Imagine an AI that curates virtual museum tours based on a student's interests or generates customized art projects that challenge them in specific areas. These advancements could foster a deeper appreciation for art and empower students to develop their own unique artistic voices. (Hutson & Cotroneo, 2023).

Another promising area of development is the integration of AI with other emerging technologies like virtual and augmented reality. Imagine students using AI-powered VR tools to sculpt in virtual clay, paint with light, or even collaborate with AI on the creation of immersive art installations. AI could also be used to create augmented reality experiences that overlay digital information onto real-world artworks, providing students with instant access to historical context, artistic techniques, and critical interpretations. These advancements could make art education more engaging, interactive, and accessible, opening up new possibilities for creative exploration and learning. However, these advancements also raise important questions about the role of human teachers and the potential for over-reliance on technology. It will be crucial to strike a balance between leveraging the power of AI and preserving the human element in arts education, ensuring that technology serves to enhance, not replace, the crucial role of teachers and mentors. (Swargiary, 2024).

CONCLUSION

Considering the vast potential and evolving landscape of AI in arts education, alongside its inherent ethical considerations, it is now time to draw together the key insights we have explored. Reflecting on these points will allow us to form a comprehensive understanding of AI's role in shaping the future of artistic learning and expression.

Final Thoughts on the Synergy Between AI and Arts Education

The synergy between AI and arts education holds immense potential for transforming the way we teach and learn art. AI is not a replacement for human creativity or educators but rather a powerful tool that can augment both, offering personalized learning experiences, fostering creative exploration, and democratizing access to artistic resources. By embracing AI responsibly and ethically, we can empower a new generation of artists and creative thinkers, equipping them with the skills and knowledge they need to thrive in a rapidly changing world. The future of arts education lies in finding the right balance between human intuition and artificial intelligence, creating a dynamic and enriching learning environment that nurtures both artistic talent and technological fluency. (Manu, 2024).

Call to Action for Educators and Stakeholders to Embrace AI's Creative Possibilities

The transformative potential of AI in arts education is undeniable, and it's time for educators and stakeholders to embrace its creative possibilities. We urge teachers, administrators, policymakers, and technology developers to actively explore and experiment with AI-powered tools and platforms. Let's collaborate to develop ethical guidelines and best practices for integrating AI into the arts curriculum. Let's invest in professional development opportunities for educators to learn how to effectively leverage AI in their classrooms. And most importantly, let's foster a culture of innovation and open-mindedness, encouraging students to explore the intersection of art and artificial intelligence, empowering them to become not just consumers of technology, but also creators and innovators in their own right. The future of arts education is here, and it's powered by the synergy of human creativity and artificial intelligence. Let's work together to unlock its full potential. (Flores-Viva & García-Peñalvo, 2023).

REFERENCES

Alagar, A. (2024, November 14). *How AI is transforming the creative process for artists.* IABAC. https://iabac.org/blog/how-ai-is-transforming-the-creative-process-for-artists

Bonini, T., & Magaudda, P. (2023). Artificial Intelligence: Where the Music of the Future Is Heading. In *Platformed! How Streaming, Algorithms and Artificial Intelligence are Shaping Music Cultures* (pp. 121–148). Springer Nature Switzerland.

Cerruti, C., & Valeri, A. (2022). *AI-Powered Platforms: automated transactions in digital marketplaces* (Doctoral dissertation, Dissertation, Master of Science in Business Administration, Università degli Studi di Roma" Tor Vergata" Department of Management and Law).

Crabtree-Ireland, D. (2025, January 21). *Labour leaders: Artificial intelligence must serve human creativity, not replace it.* World Economic Forum. https://www.weforum.org/stories/2025/01/artificial-intelligence-must-serve-human-creativity-not-replace-it/

Davoodi, A. (2024). EQUAL AI: A Framework for Enhancing Equity, Quality, Understanding and Accessibility in Liberal Arts through AI for Multilingual Learners. *Language, Technology, and Social Media, 2*(2), 178–203.

Dwivedi, Y. K., Hughes, L., Ismagilova, E., Aarts, G., Coombs, C., Crick, T., & Williams, M. D. (2021). Artificial Intelligence (AI): Multidisciplinary perspectives on emerging challenges, opportunities, and agenda for research, practice and policy. *International Journal of Information Management, 57,* 101994.

Erişti, S. D. B., & Freedman, K. (2024). Integrating Digital Technologies and AI in Art Education: Pedagogical Competencies and the Evolution of Digital Visual Culture. *Participatory Educational Research, 11*(Prof. Dr. H. Ferhan Odabaşı Gift Issue), 57-79.

Evangelidis, V., Theodoropoulou, H. G., Katsouros, V., & Kiourt, C. (2024). AI-Enabled Art Education: Unleashing Creative Potential and Exploring Co-Creation Frontiers. In *CSEDU (2)* (pp. 294-301).

Flores-Viva, J. M., & García-Peñalvo, F. J. (2023). Reflections on the Ethics, Potential, and Challenges of Artificial Intelligence in the Framework of Quality Education (SDG4). *Comunicar: Media Education Research Journal, 31*(74), 35–44.

Fortino, A. (2023, November 2). *Embracing creativity: How AI can enhance the creative process.* NYU School of Professional Studies. https://www.sps.nyu.edu/homepage/emerging-technologies-collaborative/blog/2023/embracing-creativity-how-ai-can-enhance-the-creative-process.html

Freedman, K., & Hernández-Hernández, F. (Eds.). (2024). *Curriculum, culture, and art education: Comparative perspectives.* Suny Press.

González-Calatayud, V., Prendes-Espinosa, P., & Roig-Vila, R. (2021). Artificial intelligence for student assessment: A systematic review. *Applied Sciences (Basel, Switzerland), 11*(12), 5467.

Hooda, M., Rana, C., Dahiya, O., Rizwan, A., & Hossain, M. S. (2022). Artificial intelligence for assessment and feedback to enhance student success in higher education. *Mathematical Problems in Engineering, 2022*(1), 5215722.

Hutson, J. (2024). Integrating art and AI: Evaluating the educational impact of AI tools in digital art history learning. *Faculty Scholarship, 578.* Lindenwood University. https://digitalcommons.lindenwood.edu/faculty-research-papers/578

Hutson, J., & Cotroneo, P. (2023). Generative AI tools in art education: Exploring prompt engineering and iterative processes for enhanced creativity. *Metaverse, 4*(1), 14.

Jeon, M. J., & Kim, J. (2021). A Study on the Production of Real-Time Algorithmic Composition System Using the VQ-VAE Algorithm of OpenAI Jukebox. *Journal of Digital Contents Society, 22*(3), 375–381.

Jiang, H. (2023). Research on Innovation and Reform Strategy of Fine Arts Education in Colleges and Universities. *Journal of Humanities, Arts and Social Science, 7*(4).

Karpov, N. (2020). *Artificial Intelligence for Music Composing: Future Scenario Analysis.* Can be accessed at https://urn.fi/URN:NBN:fi:amk-2020052012578

Kim, Y., & Lee, H. (2022). Falling in love with virtual reality art: A new perspective on 3D immersive virtual reality for future sustaining art consumption. *International Journal of Human-Computer Interaction, 38*(4), 371–382.

Kocaballi, A. B. (2023). *Conversational ai-powered design: Chatgpt as designer, user, and product.* arXiv preprint arXiv:2302.07406.

Li, S. (2025). The impact of AI-driven music production software on the economics of the music industry. *Information Development*, 02666669241312170.

Liu, Y., & Sra, M. (2024, July). DanceGen: Supporting Choreography Ideation and Prototyping with Generative AI. In *Proceedings of the 2024 ACM Designing Interactive Systems Conference* (pp. 920-938).

Manu, A. (2024). *Transcending Imagination: Artificial Intelligence and the Future of Creativity*. CRC Press.

Pente, P., Adams, C., & Yuen, C. (2022). Artificial Intelligence, ethics, and art education in a posthuman world. In *Global media arts education: Mapping global perspectives of media arts in education* (pp. 197–211). Springer International Publishing.

Pitta, J. P. (2023). AI in Art & Creativity. *The Spicerian*, *72*(2), 3–7.

PRO EDU. (2024, November 22). *Collaborating with AI: Co-creative processes in art revolutionize artistic expression*. PRO EDU. https://proedu.com/blogs/photoshop-skills/collaborating-with-ai-co-creative-processes-in-art-revolutionize-artistic-expression

Qorbani, M. (2020). *Humanity in the Age of AI: How to Thrive in a Post-Human World*. Bloomsberry.

Ramdhani, A. W. F., & Susanti, A. (2024). Pemanfaatan Teknologi Openai Dall-E 2 dalam Meningkatkan Kreativitas Desainer Grafis pada Komunitas Desain Grafis Indonesia. *Jurnal Bisnis Dan Komunikasi Digital*, *1*(2), 8–8.

Renkema, M., & Tursunbayeva, A. (2024). The future of work of academics in the age of Artificial Intelligence: State-of-the-art and a research roadmap. *Futures*, *163*, 103453.

Robert, A. (2024a). *Your ai tutor: Personalized learning paths and 24/7 support*. EasyC-hair. Sanal lise öğretmeni 3d—Google Play'de Uygulamalar.

Robert, A. (2024b). *Investigating the Effectiveness of AI Tutors in Developing Personalized Learning Paths for Students* (No. 13031). EasyChair.

Rocky Mountain College of Art + Design. (2024, December 23). *The future of art education: Exciting possibilities for teaching art with technology*. RMCAD. https://www.rmcad.edu/blog/the-future-of-art-education-exciting-possibilities-for-teaching-art-with-technology/

Rona-Tas, A. (2020). Predicting the future: Art and algorithms. *Socio-economic Review*, *18*(3), 893–911.

Sáez-Velasco, S., Alaguero-Rodríguez, M., Delgado-Benito, V., & Rodríguez-Cano, S. (2024). Analysing the Impact of Generative AI in Arts Education: A Cross-Disciplinary Perspective of Educators and Students in Higher Education. *Informatics (MDPI)*, *11*(2), 37. DOI: 10.3390/informatics11020037

Shao, J. (2024). *Personalized Learning for Art Major Students Based on Learner Characteristics*. [Doctoral dissertation, Chapman University]. Chapman University Digital Commons. https://doi.org/DOI: 10.36837/chapman.000560

Škiljić, A. (2021). When art meets technology or vice versa: Key challenges at the crossroads of AI-generated artworks and copyright law. *IIC-International Review of Intellectual Property and Competition Law*, *52*(10), 1338–1369.

Swargiary, K. (2024). *Exploring The Impact Of Artificial Intelligence On Visual Arts: Technological Advancements, Market Dynamics, Ethical Considerations, And Human Creativity*. GOOGLE.

Tomaskinova, J., & Tomaskin, J. (2024). UNLOCKING THE FUTURE OF EDUCATION: EMPOWERING EDUCATORS WITH AI BY OVERCOMING PROFESSIONAL DEVELOPMENT CHALLENGES. In *ICERI2024 Proceedings* (pp. 10633-10642). IATED.

Torres Carceller, A. (2024). The ARTificial revolution: Challenges for redefining art education. *Digital Education Review*, *45*, 84–90. DOI: 10.1344/der.2024.45.84-90

Tsidylo, I. M., & Sena, C. E. (2023). Artificial intelligence as a methodological innovation in the training of future designers: Midjourney tools. *Information Technologies and Learning Tools*, *97*(5), 203.

Usca, N., Samaniego, M., Yerbabuena, C., & Pérez, I. (2024). Arts and Humanities Education: A Systematic Review of Emerging Technologies and Their Contribution to Social Well-Being. *Social Sciences*, *13*(5), 269.

Watiktinnakorn, C., Seesai, J., & Kerdvibulvech, C. (2023). Blurring the lines: How AI is redefining artistic ownership and copyright. *Discover Artificial Intelligence*, *3*(1), 37.

Wu, Z., Li, Y., Ji, D., Wu, D., Shidujaman, M., Zhang, Y., & Zhang, C. (2022, December). Human-AI co-creation of art based on the personalization of collective memory. In 2022 *6th Asian Conference on Artificial Intelligence Technology (ACAIT)* (pp. 1-6). IEEE.

Wylder, J. (2022). *An Illustrated Guide to AI Prompt Mastery: for MidJourney, DALL-E, NightCafe, Deep Dream Generator, and More*. Baen Books.

Yaseen, M. (2023). Scriptwriting in the Age of AI: Revolutionizing Storytelling with Artificial Intelligence. [JMC]. *Journal of Media & Communication*, *4*(1).

Zhao, X., Guo, Z., & Liu, S. (2021). Exploring key competencies and professional development of music teachers in primary schools in the era of artificial intelligence. *Scientific Programming*, *2021*(1), 5097003.

ADDITIONAL READINGS

Fortino, A. (2023, November 2). *Embracing creativity: How AI can enhance the creative process*. NYU School of Professional Studies. https://www.sps.nyu.edu/homepage/emerging-technologies-collaborative/blog/2023/embracing-creativity-how-ai-can-enhance-the-creative-process.html

Hutson, J. (2024). Integrating art and AI: Evaluating the educational impact of AI tools in digital art history learning. *Faculty Scholarship, 578*. Lindenwood University. https://digitalcommons.lindenwood.edu/faculty-research-papers/578

Sáez-Velasco, S., Alaguero-Rodríguez, M., Delgado-Benito, V., & Rodríguez-Cano, S. (2024). Analysing the Impact of Generative AI in Arts Education: A Cross-Disciplinary Perspective of Educators and Students in Higher Education. *Informatics (MDPI)*, *11*(2), 37. DOI: 10.3390/informatics11020037

Torres Carceller, A. (2024). The ARTificial revolution: Challenges for redefining art education. *Digital Education Review*, *45*, 84–90. DOI: 10.1344/der.2024.45.84-90

KEY TERMS AND DEFINITIONS

Artificial Intelligence (AI): A broad field of computer science focused on creating machines capable of performing tasks that typically require human intelligence, such as learning, problem-solving, decision-making, and perception. In the context of arts education, AI can refer to algorithms and systems that analyze artwork, generate creative content, provide personalized feedback, and create interactive learning experiences.

Arts Education: Encompasses teaching and learning in various art forms, including visual arts (painting, drawing, sculpture), performing arts (music, dance, theater), literary arts (writing, poetry), and media arts (film, photography, digital art). Its goal is to foster creativity, critical thinking, aesthetic appreciation, and technical skills in students.

Creative Learning: An educational approach that emphasizes the development of students' creative thinking, problem-solving abilities, and innovative expression. It encourages exploration, experimentation, risk-taking, and the generation of original ideas. In arts education, creative learning involves fostering students' ability to imagine, invent, and communicate through artistic mediums.

Immersive Art: Art experiences that engage multiple senses and create a sense of presence for the viewer or participant. This can be achieved through various technologies like virtual reality (VR), augmented reality (AR), and interactive installations. Immersive art can transport viewers to different environments, allow them to interact with artworks in new ways, and deepen their understanding and appreciation of art.

Chapter 6
Personalized Learning Through AI:
The Power of Tailored Education

Indranil Mutsuddi
https://orcid.org/0000-0002-4202-8744
JIS University, India

ABSTRACT

AI-powered applications hold the potential to craft learning experiences that are tailored to the unique needs of each learner, boosting both engagement and performance. By embracing AI, educational institutions can move beyond the traditional one-size-fits-all model, providing personalized learning pathways that align with individual strengths, weaknesses, and interests. Furthermore, machine learning (ML) algorithms can analyze large volumes of academic data to predict learning behaviors, habits, and outcomes, allowing L&D professionals to design targeted learning solutions that address each learner's specific needs. With this in mind, this chapter aims to delve into the influence of AI-driven applications on enhancing the effectiveness of personalized learning.

INTRODUCTION

Personalized learning is an educational approach that tailors the learning experience to meet the individual needs, strengths, preferences, and goals of each student. It involves customizing the curriculum, pace, and teaching methods to align with the unique characteristics of every learner, ensuring that the educational journey is both effective and engaging. The U.S. Department of Education (U.S. Department of Education, 2016)defines personalized learning as an approach where the pace

DOI: 10.4018/979-8-3373-5102-5.ch006

and strategies of learning are adjusted to suit the specific needs of each student. This includes flexibility in learning goals, content, and delivery, making learning more adaptable and relevant to each student's interests and abilities. In a personalized learning environment, activities are designed to be meaningful and connect to students' personal interests, encouraging autonomy and self-directed learning.

Key components of personalized learning include relevance, interest-based engagement, and self-driven motivation (Walkington & Bernacki, 2020). These aspects highlight the importance of crafting learning experiences that resonate with students, fostering greater motivation and deeper understanding. Research in educational psychology suggests that when learning experiences are linked to students' interests, it can significantly boost both motivation and achievement (Bernacki & Walkington, 2018). According to other authors like (Bray & McClaskey, 2014), personalized learning empowers students to take an active role in their educational journey. They have the freedom to choose the content they explore, tailor their learning paths to their preferences, and decide how to demonstrate their knowledge and showcase their progress.

However, over the years there has been a paradigm shift in the realm of personalized learning perspectives with the implementation of sophisticated technologies like artificial intelligence (AI). AI is transforming education by customizing learning experiences to meet the unique needs of each student, surpassing traditional teaching methods once widely regarded as standard. By analyzing extensive data, AI personalizes instruction, enhancing engagement and boosting overall learning outcomes (Pratama et al., 2023). AI is reshaping personalized education by tailoring learning experiences to meet the individual needs of students, increasing engagement, and improving overall learning outcomes. Building on this introductory overview, this chapter explores the significant role and impact of AI in shaping personalized learning and the modern education system.

REVIEW OF LITERATURE

AI's impact goes beyond boosting productivity and automating tasks; it also affects areas like ethics, social structures, environmental sustainability, and corporate governance (Mutsuddi, 2024). Artificial Intelligence (AI) has had a profound impact on various industries, and its role in education, particularly in the realm of personalized learning, continues to grow. Personalized learning seeks to cater to the unique needs, learning styles, and abilities of each student, leading to more effective educational outcomes. AI-powered tools and technologies can revolutionize traditional education by delivering adaptive and tailored learning experiences that enhance student engagement, increase learning efficiency, and improve the overall quality of education (Garg et al., 2024). AI-powered tools tailor content to meet the individual needs of each student, providing adaptive tutoring and other technological advancements in education. AI-driven personalized learning enhances students' autonomy, competence, and relatedness, thereby boosting engagement. Autonomy, in particular, is a key factor closely associated with improved academic performance. The path analysis model confirms these connections, underscoring AI's crucial role in transforming educational experiences and intrinsically motivating students (Ellikkal & Rajamohan, 2024). The themes of theoretical foundations and practical applications of personalized learning, particularly in the context of AI-driven applications, can certainly offer rich insights into the evolving educational paradigm (*Personalized Learning With Generative AI*, 2025).

The use of artificial intelligence (AI) in higher education is reshaping how institutions design and enhance learning systems. As HEIs adopt AI, they are increasingly implementing adaptive learning strategies to foster more dynamic and personalized educational environments. By utilizing data from teaching and learning activities, these strategies customize educational experiences to meet each student's unique needs, strengths, and learning pace (Das et al., 2025). The adoption of artificial intelligence (AI) in higher education institutions, both at the macro and micro levels, involves the widespread implementation of technology selected for its ability to support personalized learning for students (Hardaker & Glenn, 2025a). The incorporation of AI in higher education holds the power to revolutionize teaching methods, enhancing every facet of the educational experience. By leveraging AI, institutions can develop personalized learning pathways for each student, adapting content and pacing to accommodate their unique strengths and challenges, including those with special needs or varying language abilities. This transformation not only improves learning outcomes but also enriches the overall student experience by providing individualized support and resources. AI technologies facilitate personalized instruction and learning, while generative AI enhances intuitive learning by tracking data (Hardaker & Glenn, 2025b). AI supports the personalization of curriculum design, creation of instructional materials, foundational learning assistance, self-reflection, student assessment, career guidance, student management, and administrative tasks. The list of AI tools and platforms is compiled by evaluating their features according to specific criteria: they must be free to use, offer functionalities for personalized learning, and be suitable for application in educational settings(*AI Tools and Platforms for Personalized Learning*, 2025).

AI, as it is currently understood, exists and is actively used today through complex algorithms that enable narrow machine intelligence, deep learning, transfer learning, and machine vision. By incorporating a learner's prior knowledge and personal disposition, AI-driven applications can support adaptive learning systems that effectively foster student skill development (Garg et al., 2024). AI has the potential to transform education by improving both teaching and learning. It offers numerous ways to support educators and students, including content creation through voice and video, task automation, and the delivery of personalized learning experiences via adaptive learning platforms (Delello et al., 2024). AI provides a powerful tool for enhancing personalized learning experiences. By analyzing student data and utilizing advanced algorithms, AI is reshaping education, offering customized learning paths designed to meet each student's unique needs. By recognizing individual learning preferences, AI can craft tailored educational journeys, accommodating a variety of learning styles. AI-driven applications are transforming learners' educational experiences through the use of data analytics and machine learning algorithms. These technologies help tailor instruction to meet the specific needs of each learner (Yekollu et al., 2024). This adaptability improves knowledge retention, deepens comprehension of complex topics, and delivers content that is specifically aligned with each student's learning process (Khine, 2024). These innovations encompass differentiated instruction, personalized exercises, and intelligent feedback systems. AI can improve the personalized learning experiences of students by implementing a robust online Learning Analytics (LA) framework (Klinck-van der Merwe & Goosen, 2024). However, some scholars have noted that research on the use of generative AI in flipped classrooms is limited, with many questions still needing exploration and validation through further studies. This gap is a crucial aspect of the ongoing need for personalized learning (Zhen & Yahaya, 2024). With the advent of AI, researchers must examine the fundamental changes needed in pedagogical approaches, curriculum design, assessment frameworks, and the thoughtful integration of technology within the context of modern higher education (Munna et al., 2024). The education sector is progressively adopting digital tools to enhance personalized learning and support equity. As universities extend their global reach and students become more interconnected, the integration of artificial intelligence (AI) in education has unlocked new opportunities. With AI poised to play a crucial role in the future of education, current research aims to evaluate faculty members' understanding of AI's potential applications and its adoption within academic settings (Rahiman & Kodikal, 2024).

OVERARCHING ROLE OF AI IN PERSONALIZED LEARNING

The rapid progress of artificial intelligence (AI) is revolutionizing many areas of our lives, including education. While these changes present both opportunities and challenges, traditional teaching methods are gradually being replaced by more targeted learning experiences. AI enables the analysis of extensive data to tailor teaching strategies to individual needs. AI is transforming education by personalizing learning experiences to suit each student, improving engagement, and enhancing overall learning outcomes.AI-powered personalized digital support strategies can effectively meet the needs of learners in online environments. By analyzing data and learning patterns, AI systems can pinpoint each student's strengths and weaknesses, offering tailored learning content, pacing, and feedback to enhance their educational experience. AI facilitates personalized learning by enabling students to learn at their own pace and access materials when it's most convenient for them. By analyzing individual learning patterns, AI can generate content tailored to each student's goals and past accomplishments. As AI becomes a key player in education, it allows educators to customize learning experiences that address the specific needs, preferences, and learning styles of each student. AI-driven platforms can create personalized learning paths for students, taking into account their goals, interests, and prior knowledge. By adjusting the curriculum and learning pace to suit each student's needs, AI ensures they face the right challenges and receive the necessary support, optimizing their learning outcomes.

Further, AI has the potential to transform educational administration by streamlining processes and reducing time spent on administrative tasks. Functions like grading, attendance tracking, and scheduling can be automated, giving educators more time to concentrate on teaching and engaging with students. Additionally, AI-powered analytics will offer valuable insights into student performance and engagement, making it easier to identify students at risk and implement timely interventions.

The following table (Table 1) illustrates the overarching role of AI for personalized learning.

Table 1. Overarching role of AI in personalized learning

AI for Personalized Learning	Features
Adaptive Learning	AI-powered adaptive learning platforms assess student data such as performance, strengths, weaknesses, and learning pace. With this data, the system designs personalized learning pathways, offering content, resources, and activities that are specifically aligned with each student's individual needs.
Focused Interventions	AI-powered educational tools help educators identify and support students with particular academic difficulties. By analyzing data on student performance and behavior, AI systems can detect areas where students might encounter challenges. Furthermore, these tools provide proactive assistance through practice exercises, remedial resources, or individualized tutoring to help overcome these obstacles.
Multisensory learning	AI technologies enhance multimodal learning by combining various formats, such as text, audio, video, and interactive features. This approach allows students to engage with content in ways that best match their learning preferences, fostering a more personalized and engaging educational experience

continued on following page

Table 1. Continued

AI for Personalized Learning	Features
AI-driven Predictive Analytics	AI enables educators to gather and analyze extensive student data, such as assessment results, engagement metrics, and behavioral trends. By extracting meaningful insights from this data, teachers can better understand each student and make informed decisions to personalize learning experiences. Additionally, AI utilizes predictive analytics to assess students' performance and forecast potential challenges. By evaluating past performance, engagement levels, environmental factors, and other relevant data, AI systems can anticipate future academic struggles and recommend targeted interventions for support.
Personalized Evaluation	AI can streamline the learner assessment process and deliver timely, personalized feedback to students. Intelligent grading systems can assess assignments, quizzes, and exams, allowing for quicker feedback. This enables students to pinpoint areas for improvement and receive tailored recommendations for further learning.
Cognitive Guidance & Tutoring	AI-driven cognitive tutoring systems have the ability to transform the way learners receive academic support. These systems allow students to participate in interactive problem-solving tasks that adjust based on their responses, mimicking a virtual tutoring experience. By offering real-time, individualized assistance, they deliver personalized, one-on-one guidance that caters to each student's unique needs. AI-powered tutoring systems offer personalized guidance and support to students. These systems evaluate students' understanding, pinpoint areas of struggle, and provide targeted explanations, feedback, and practice exercises. They adjust the learning material based on each student's progress, ensuring a tailored educational experience.
Effective Learning Content Delivery	AI can help create personalized educational content for each student, adapting to their learning progress and personality in real time. AI-powered learning systems can deliver content in various formats, such as videos, interactive simulations, or text-based materials, to suit individual preferences.
Ease of accessing customized learning content	AI has the potential to break down educational barriers, offering a personalized learning experience for students with diverse learning disabilities and needs. Through features like text-to-speech and natural language processing, AI can provide additional support for students with disabilities. By presenting education as an interactive dialogue between the system and the student, AI equips learners with tools that enhance their learning experience. Furthermore, AI's ability to adjust content based on specific accessibility requirements ensures that it can meet the needs of all students.
Personalized enquiry & studies	AI algorithms can process large volumes of data, such as a student's previous performance, interests, and goals, to offer personalized suggestions for educational resources, books, articles, videos, and other learning materials. This enables students to find content that aligns with their unique needs and preferences.
AI-chat bot driven learning	Students interact with an AI-powered chatbot to discover new concepts, hone their skills, and receive tailored feedback. Functioning as a virtual tutor, the chatbot answers questions, provides explanations, and adapts to each learner's individual needs in a conversational style.
Integrated Learning Approaches	AI technologies improve learning experiences by incorporating diverse formats like text, audio, video, and interactive elements. This approach allows students to engage with the material in ways that best suit their preferences, resulting in a more dynamic and personalized educational journey.

Source: Author

AI-ENABLED ADAPTIVE LEARNING

AI-driven adaptive learning represents a forward-thinking educational model where artificial intelligence tools continuously evaluate each learner's progress, strengths, and areas for improvement. The system dynamically adjusts content and pacing to meet individual needs, providing a tailored learning experience that accommodates each student's unique strengths, challenges, and preferences. Unlike traditional methods, which often adopt a one-size-fits-all approach, AI-powered systems use data and algorithms to monitor student progress and adapt lessons in real-time. This enables the system to present more challenging material when a student excels and offer additional support or review when difficulties arise.

Additionally, AI-driven adaptive learning provides a sophisticated assessment method, allowing educators to track progress in real-time, identify areas of struggle, and deliver personalized feedback. This ensures that learner progress at an optimal pace and receive the targeted support they need to succeed. Traditional educational models assume that all students learn in the same way and at the same rate, but this approach fails to account for individual learning styles and abilities. In contrast, AI-powered adaptive learning personalizes the experience, adjusting the learning journey to suit each student's specific needs, fostering better outcomes and increased engagement.

Moreover, AI and adaptive learning technologies include tools like gamification, interactive content, and virtual reality, which enhance student engagement by making learning more enjoyable and immersive. These features motivate students to actively participate, enriching their educational experience.

On the other hand, AI and adaptive learning also significantly improve faculty support. Educators, trainers, and researchers can use these technologies to monitor student progress, identify challenges, and offer personalized feedback. This not only streamlines assessment but also frees up valuable time for educators to focus on important tasks such as lesson planning, classroom management, and providing one-on-one support to students. As a result, AI-powered adaptive learning systems enhance both the student experience and the effectiveness of educators.

Case Illustration: RealizeIt

RealizeIt's adaptive learning platform offers a dynamic approach to personalized learning, creating customized learning paths for each individual. This self-adjusting system responds to the evolving abilities of each learner, continuously fine-tuning its performance for greater accuracy. By regularly assessing a learner's knowledge and skills, the platform tailors the learning journey to meet their specific needs, allowing educators to adjust their strategies and approach to effectively reach learning goals. Figure 1 illustrates the adaptive learning perspective of RealizeIt.

For faculty and trainers, the platform provides valuable insights through big data, highlighting what students know and where gaps remain. This empowers educators to personalize training efforts, ensuring each learner receives the support necessary to reach their full potential.

Figure 1. Adaptive learning system of Realizeit (https://www.gettingsmart.com/2015/03/27/realizeit-can-make-your-program-adaptive/)

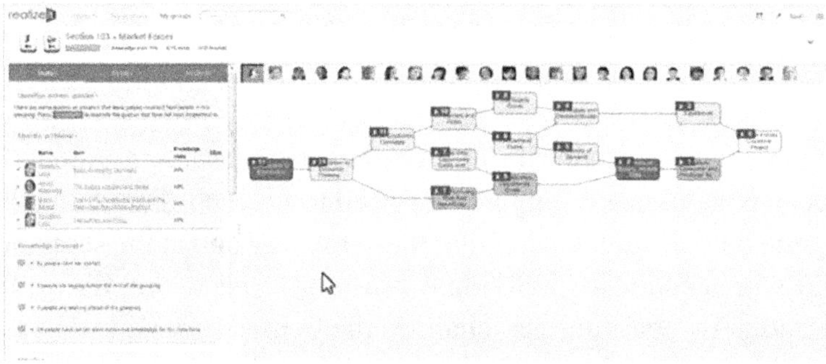

RealizeIt's adaptive learning platform generates a probability distribution for each content module, indicating the likelihood of a student's knowledge (ranging from 0-100%). It guides students through the material based on these probabilities, delivering targeted learning at the right moment. The system also collects data from each student's interactions, providing instructors with insights into course performance and the effectiveness of the content. On the other hand, educational leaders can shift from a one-size-fits-all training model to a more refined, personalized approach, optimizing learning experiences for greater impact. Academic content creators can also design more relevant, engaging, and effective educational experiences that cater to the diverse needs of learners, ultimately helping them succeed through a meaningful and interactive learning process. Additionally, the Student and Educator dashboards in RealizeIt allow tracking of learner competencies and their progress in completing the material, using real-time data from learning analytics. A key feature of RealizeIt is that it is a cloud-based platform, offering both mobile and browser-based experiences for users.

AI-ENABLED PREDICTIVE ANALYTICS FOR PERSONALIZED LEARNING

Predictive analytics leverages historical data and statistical algorithms to forecast future trends, providing valuable insights that support informed decision-making. As a subset of advanced analytics, predictive analytics uses data, statistical techniques, and machine learning to predict future outcomes based on past information. In education, it can be applied to forecast student performance, identify at-risk students, enhance curriculum development, and optimize administrative operations.

AI plays a vital role in predictive analytics by enabling the processing and analysis of large datasets, uncovering hidden patterns that may be overlooked by traditional methods. Machine learning (ML), a branch of AI, further strengthens predictive analytics by allowing systems to learn from data, recognize patterns, and make decisions with minimal human oversight. Machine learning algorithms refine their parameters according to the patterns they identify in the data, continuously enhancing the accuracy of their predictions. The selection of the algorithm is crucial, as it directly influences the precision of the predictive insights. For instance, machine learning algorithms can analyze a student's academic history to predict future performance, allowing educators to adapt their teaching strategies to better meet each student's needs.

Steps involved in Predictive Analytics: AI enabled predictive analytics follows the following steps, namely:

Data Processing: In the education sector, a vast amount of diverse academic and administrative data is collected, ranging from student performance metrics to various interactions within the system, such as attendance records, engagement levels, and even administrative details. This data is crucial for understanding patterns, making informed decisions, and improving educational outcomes. However, before this data can be effectively analyzed or used in predictive models, it undergoes a critical preparation phase. This phase includes data cleaning, which involves identifying and rectifying errors or inconsistencies such as missing values, duplicates, or incorrect entries that could distort the analysis. Additionally, preprocessing steps are undertaken to structure and organize the data in a way that is suitable for modeling, such as normalizing values, converting categorical data into numerical formats, or creating relevant features. Proper preparation ensures that the data is accurate, reliable, and ready for analysis, laying a solid foundation for generating meaningful insights and achieving the desired outcomes.

Data Model Development: Once the data has been properly prepared, the next critical step is to develop a predictive model, where artificial intelligence (AI), and more specifically machine learning (ML), plays a pivotal role in transforming raw data into actionable insights. During this phase, the model is trained on historical data, allowing it to learn and identify underlying patterns, trends, and relationships that may not be immediately apparent. By exposing the model to a large set of data points, it begins to understand how different variables interact and how they influence outcomes. The selection of the appropriate machine learning algorithm is a key decision in this process, as it directly impacts the model's ability to learn effectively. There are a variety of algorithms to choose from, ranging from simple techniques like linear regression, which assumes a straightforward relationship between variables, to more sophisticated methods such as neural networks, which are capable of learning complex, non-linear relationships in large datasets. The choice of algorithm depends on the problem at hand, the complexity of the data, and the level of accuracy required. This step is crucial in ensuring the model's capacity to make reliable predictions and generate valuable insights.

Data Validation: Once the predictive model is developed, it becomes crucial to evaluate its performance by assessing its reliability, validity, and effectiveness. This is typically done by testing the model on a separate dataset that it has not been exposed to during its training phase. By doing so, data validation provides insight into how well the model can generalize and apply the patterns and insights it has learned to new, unseen data. This step is essential to ensure that the model is not simply overfitting to the training data but can instead make accurate predictions across a variety of scenarios, thereby demonstrating its true potential and robustness in real-world applications.

Real Time Prediction: Once the data is validated, the predictive model is deployed to generate real-time predictions. This process involves continuously analyzing a student's data, enabling the system to predict future performance based on their current progress, past behavior, and learning patterns. By identifying a student's strengths and weaknesses, the AI system can proactively adjust their learning path, ensuring that the content, pace, and level of difficulty are personalized to meet their unique needs. This dynamic approach fosters a more tailored and engaging learning experience. Additionally, AI can assess academic data to identify students who may be at risk of falling behind. Early detection of these students allows for targeted interventions, such as personalized tutoring, additional resources, or modified learning strategies, to address their challenges. These proactive measures not only help students stay on track but also improve overall retention rates and academic success, ensuring that each learner receives the support they need to thrive.

AI is increasingly shaping the academic sector, transforming not only how learning is delivered but also how educational institutions operate. This rapid advancement underscores the need for education systems to evolve in order to prepare students for an AI-driven future. In particular, there is a growing emphasis on skills like data analytics, problem-solving, and strategic decision-making, which are becoming essential in an AI-dominated job market. As AI continues to infiltrate various sectors, the educational system must adapt to meet students' expectations for more personalized, flexible learning experiences. The integration of AI in personalized learning (PL) and teaching support is already showing tangible benefits, helping to enhance academic performance by tailoring content to individual learning styles and needs, while also enabling teachers to focus on higher-level, more impactful tasks. However, these technological advancements also highlight the irreplaceable role of human educators, who are essential for fostering critical thinking, emotional intelligence, and the nuanced understanding that technology alone cannot provide. This perspective aligns with broader discussions about AI's role in education, emphasizing the importance of balancing cutting-edge innovation with the invaluable human touch that nurtures creativity, empathy, and ethical reasoning.

AI-ENABLED CHATBOTS FOR PERSONALIZED LEARNING

AI-driven chatbots for personalized learning are sophisticated digital tools that utilize AI tools to engage learners in dynamic, conversational interactions. These chatbots are engineered to deliver customized learning experiences by recognizing and adapting to the unique learning needs, preferences, and progression of each student. Functioning similarly to a personal tutor, they offer individualized content, instant feedback, and continuous guidance, empowering students to learn at their own pace and in the style that best suits them. Through AI, these chatbots are able to evolve in real-time, tailoring their responses to ensure students receive the most appropriate and impactful learning resources exactly when they need them.

With the rise of chatbots powered by Generative AI technologies like ChatGPT, their role in education has become increasingly linked to the transformative potential of personalized learning (PL). These sophisticated AI systems are capable of tailoring learning experiences to meet the specific needs of each student, providing customized support that boosts engagement and enhances academic outcomes. As these chatbots become more embedded in educational settings, they are seen as essential tools for creating individualized learning journeys that adapt to each student's unique strengths, challenges, and learning preferences. This shift towards AI-driven personalization is poised to reshape traditional education, making learning more accessible, inclusive, and effective for students with diverse backgrounds and abilities. ChatGPT's proficiency in processing and generating language-driven content makes it an excellent resource for crafting personalized learning materials and experiences. Whether it's providing customized feedback or offering tailored study resources, ChatGPT has the potential to greatly enrich each student's educational journey.

Functions of AI-Enabled Chatbots for Personalized Learning

a) *Effective Learning Experiences*: AI-powered chatbots can serve as personalized tutors, providing students with instant explanations, clarifications, and additional resources tailored to their specific inquiries and learning pace. By analyzing student responses and monitoring progress, these chatbots can create adaptive learning paths that ensure content complexity and teaching methods are aligned with each student's current knowledge and capabilities. Through engaging, interactive conversations, they foster a more dynamic and participatory learning environment. Furthermore, AI chatbots can replicate real-world situations or discussions, making abstract concepts more tangible and easier to understand. With their advanced language processing skills, these chatbots also help enhance students' language proficiency and communication abilities.

b) *Academic Content Design & Delivery:* L&D managers and educators can enhance the design and delivery of educational programs by strategically integrating AI chatbots into the curriculum. These chatbots can be utilized in various ways, from reinforcing essential concepts as supplementary tools to being embedded as core elements of course content. In advanced applications, AI chatbots can become key components of the learning process, supporting teaching through interactive modules, quizzes, and assessments. They can also be valuable in project-based learning settings, offering real-time assistance, resources, and feedback to guide students through their projects, ultimately enriching the overall learning experience.

c) *Benchmarking Best Learning Practices*: Use of AI-chatbots can also allow learners and especially educators to bring in the best practices used by state of the art institutions as overarching benchmarks which could further enhance the quality of learning experiences for students.

d) *Real Time Feedback & Doubt Clearance:* Learner queries and doubts on lessons can also be cleared by AI-Chatbots on a real time basis with ready made solutions and clues on problem solving and case study analysis. Chatbots may provide additional research clues to learners which may excite them to have further probing leading to fruitful learning.

e) *Virtual Teaching Assistant:* AI chatbots can deliver immediate support by answering inquiries, clarifying concepts, and offering supplementary materials. Additionally, they can function as virtual teaching assistants, aiding instructors in numerous tasks.

f) *24/7 Learning Support*: AI chatbots provide learners with the flexibility to learn whenever and wherever they choose. Whether it's getting help with homework outside of school hours or revisiting content over the weekend, the chatbot is always accessible. This on-demand learning model encourages self-reliance and allows for personalized, self-paced progress.

g) *Engaging Interactions*: Interactive chatbots make the learning experience more engaging for students. By turning quizzes into games, providing helpful hints during problem-solving, or sparking lively conversations, chatbots maintain student motivation and focus. This approach moves beyond passive learning, fostering greater involvement and active participation.

h) *Customized Learning Solutions*: A key advantage of AI chatbots is their ability to personalize the learning experience for each student. By analyzing a student's strengths and areas for improvement, the chatbot can suggest tailored activities, lessons, or exercises that match their skill level. This approach ensures students progress at their own pace, advancing only after they've fully grasped a concept, leading to a deeper and more effective learning journey

Intelligent Tutoring Assistant: AI-driven tutoring assistants utilize sophisticated algorithms to deliver personalized, real-time feedback to students. As learners interact with educational materials, the AI evaluates their responses, pinpoints challenges, and customizes explanations to improve understanding. This tailored approach addresses knowledge gaps and adjusts the pace of learning to meet individual needs. By offering instant support and adapting to various learning styles, these systems help students better grasp difficult concepts. The ongoing engagement with AI cultivates a dynamic and interactive learning atmosphere, enhancing student confidence and boosting academic achievement

AI-ENABLED COGNITIVE GUIDANCE FOR PERSONALIZED LEARNING

By leveraging artificial intelligence to evaluate a learner's cognitive strengths and weaknesses, educators can adapt the learning experience in real time. This enables personalized content, feedback, and customized learning pathways that cater to each student's unique needs and learning preferences. AI thus acts as a personalized cognitive guide, supporting learners throughout their educational journey. It also gives faculty the ability to offer tailored feedback, helping students recognize their strengths and pinpoint areas for improvement.

Cognitive AI systems are designed to mirror human intelligence—they understand, learn, and interact in ways that resemble human behavior. While all cognitive AI systems are AI-driven, not every AI system is cognitive in nature. These systems adjust how information is presented to accommodate the cognitive challenges learners face, especially in complex educational settings. The "Adaptive Cognitive Fit" (ACF) framework specifically explores how AI-enhanced representations and information elements influence human performance in learning environments.

When educators use AI-driven tools like chatbots, they gain valuable insights into students' cognitive processes, such as their ability to think critically, ask meaningful questions, and engage in reflective thought. However, one key element is often overlooked: the connection between AI-driven interactions and the development of higher-order thinking skills, especially in problem-solving contexts. By focusing on how students engage with AI to solve complex problems, educators can better understand how these interactions nurture essential cognitive skills, vital both in academics and real-world situations.

When an AI system collaborates with a human, it sets in motion a dynamic, evolving feedback loop that grows more effective over time. In this partnership, the AI serves as a data-driven advisor, offering insights, suggestions, and analyses that help guide decision-making. The human then processes this input, integrating it into their thinking or using it to take action. These decisions and actions produce new data, which is fed back into the AI system. This allows the AI to learn from the human's choices, adapt its recommendations, and refine its models based on the updated information. As the AI absorbs this new data, it becomes increasingly attuned to the user's unique needs, preferences, and behavior patterns. Over time, it enhances its ability to provide more accurate, context-aware support. In turn, the human benefits from more tailored insights and can make more informed decisions, leading to more effective problem-solving. This ongoing exchange of feedback strengthens both the AI and the human. The AI transforms from a simple tool into an active participant in the cognitive process, continuously learning from the user and improving its assistance. Likewise, the human gains the power to make data-driven decisions that improve problem-solving efficiency. Together, the human and AI form a unified cognitive team, where both parties complement and enhance each other's capabilities. As this iterative process continues, the partnership between the user and the AI becomes more fluid and collaborative, fostering deeper cognitive engagement. Both can tackle increasingly complex challenges with a refined set of strategies and insights. With every interaction, their ability to innovate, solve problems, and adapt to new situations sharpens, making the decision-making or learning process more adaptive and effective. Over time, this dynamic feedback loop not only improves immediate outcomes but also accelerates the development of advanced cognitive skills in the learner, preparing them to handle future challenges more independently and with greater confidence.

GAMIFICATION & PERSONALIZED LEARNING

Gamification is a powerful strategy for helping learners achieve their educational goals. By incorporating game-like features, it has the potential to transform traditional learning environments into vibrant, interactive, and motivating experiences, fully immersing students in their educational journey. In education, gamification integrates elements like rewards, levels, points, badges, and leaderboards to reinforce learning objectives, tapping into both intrinsic and extrinsic motivation. Within Learning Management Systems (LMS), gamification is rapidly gaining popularity as an innovative trend that makes learning more engaging and interactive, fostering greater student motivation and participation.

A crucial factor in the success of gamification in education is personalization. Tailoring the gamified experience to the individual needs and preferences of each learner can significantly boost engagement and motivation. Personalized gamification empowers students to take charge of their learning, allowing them to progress at their own pace and focus on areas that interest them or require more attention. This learner-centered approach fosters a sense of control, encouraging deeper and more meaningful participation.

One of the major benefits of personalized gamification is its ability to create customized learning paths that target each student's unique challenges, offering focused recommendations for further practice. By identifying individual needs, educators can guide students toward relevant resources and activities that enhance their knowledge and skills. Additionally, personalized gamification allows students to set their own goals and receive tailored feedback, helping them track progress and gain insights into their strengths and areas for improvement. As the learning experience adapts to each student's needs, personalized gamification greatly enhances the overall effectiveness of education.

In gamified learning, artificial intelligence (AI) plays a vital role in creating personalized experiences by adjusting content to meet each learner's needs. AI adapts the difficulty level, provides real-time feedback, and suggests relevant materials based on individual performance. This dynamic approach not only increases engagement and motivation but also brings a game-like feel to the learning process, keeping students actively involved. A key advantage of AI-powered gamification is its ability to offer real-time, adaptive learning experiences. As students engage with the gamified platform, AI continuously analyzes their performance, identifying areas where they excel or face challenges. Based on this data, AI can adjust task difficulty, provide targeted hints, or recommend new learning paths. This responsive and evolving approach not only keeps learners motivated but also enhances their overall satisfaction, improving retention and fostering long-term commitment to the learning process. Table 2 illustrates the outcomes of AI-driven Gamification in Personalized Learning.

Table 2. Outcomes of AI-driven gamification in Personalized Learning (PL)

Outcomes of AI-driven Gamification in PL	Features
Enhanced Learner Involvement	AI-powered personalized gamification captivates learners' attention and promotes active involvement, resulting in greater engagement throughout the learning experience.
Effectives Learning Outcomes through feedback	By providing real-time personalized feedback and tailored learning plans, learners can concentrate on areas for improvement, fostering a deeper understanding and better retention of knowledge and practical skills.
Learner Behaviour Analysis	As learners engage with the gamified platform, AI systems can assess their performance and behavior, pinpointing areas of success and areas of struggle. Based on this analysis, the AI can modify the difficulty of tasks, offer tailored hints, or recommend alternative learning paths. This adaptive approach enhances learning and keeps users motivated and engaged.
Needs of diverse learners	Personalized gamification acknowledges and adapts to various learning styles, allowing educators to effectively address the unique needs of diverse learners.
Learner Motivation	AI-driven personalized gamification, by focusing on learners' unique needs and interests, fosters intrinsic motivation, transforming the learning experience into a more enjoyable and fulfilling journey.
Inclusive education	AI enabled gamification tools can be customized to meet the unique needs of students with disabilities, promoting a more inclusive learning environment. With features like speech-to-text, text-to-speech, and adjustable interfaces, these tools enable students with varying abilities to interact with content more easily and effectively

Source: Author

Case Illustration: Course Hero

Course Hero strives to connect higher education institutions with the professional world. Its gamification features are central to this, awarding achievement badges for actions like logging in on weekends, uploading materials, and completing courses. This online learning platform provides students and educators with access to a wide range of educational resources, including syllabi, problem sets, flashcards, class notes, tutoring services, and much more. Although a sitewide leaderboard is available, the platform lacks opportunities for student interaction or community building. Its key strengths are the comprehensive study resources, round-the-clock homework assistance, textbook solutions, in-depth explanations, and expert tutoring.

AI-DRIVEN MULTISENSORY LEARNING

AI-driven multisensory learning experiences are highly effective because they enable educators to deliver tailored, impactful learning solutions. With intuitive AI tools, teachers can easily create and customize resources that seamlessly integrate into their lesson plans, fostering engaging, personalized learning experiences that meet the diverse needs of their students. By incorporating sight, sound, and touch, AI-powered multisensory learning enhances both comprehension and retention. This approach represents a significant advancement in AI, as it allows machines to process and interpret information across multiple sensory channels, including text, speech, images, and videos. Unlike traditional AI, which relies on a single sensory modality, multisensory AI combines inputs from various senses, offering a richer, more nuanced understanding of content and enabling more contextually relevant responses. AI tools also create personalized content, interactive simulations, and accessible features like text-to-speech. An excellent example of this is QuizCat AI, which transforms conventional study materials into dynamic learning tools, such as interactive quizzes for active recall, flashcards for quick revision, and podcasts for auditory learners.

Multisensory AI systems harness advanced Natural Language Understanding (NLU) capabilities, allowing them to interpret and respond to human language in various forms, including both written text and spoken words. This fosters more natural and intuitive interactions between users and AI systems. Additionally, Visual AI plays a crucial role in multisensory AI, enabling machines to process and make sense of visual information, such as images and videos. This capability empowers AI systems to recognize objects, scenes, and gestures, unlocking new possibilities in applications like computer vision, augmented reality, and more. A core feature of multisensory AI is multimodal fusion, where data from different sensory channels are integrated to form a cohesive understanding of the environment. By combining inputs from text, speech, and vision, multisensory AI systems improve their ability to interpret user queries and contextual details, leading to more accurate and contextually relevant responses.

It can be mentioned here that, AI-powered multisensory learning has the potential to transform personalized education by assessing a learner's unique strengths and challenges across various sensory channels, such as visual, auditory, and kinesthetic. This enables the creation of adaptive learning experiences that cater to each individual's preferred learning style, ensuring a more tailored and engaging educational journey for every student. By leveraging this approach, AI can craft personalized learning pathways that evolve based on how each learner processes and absorbs information most effectively.

AI-DRIVEN LEARNING MANAGEMENT SYSTEM

An AI-powered Learning Management System (LMS) utilizes artificial intelligence and machine learning to enhance and streamline digital learning environments. These AI-driven platforms can tailor learning paths, automate administrative tasks, and provide personalized course recommendations. A key feature of such systems is adaptive learning, where AI algorithms adjust the learning experience to meet the individual needs of each student, often through skill-based suggestions that guide their progression. Additionally, AI-driven LMS platforms automate repetitive tasks and workflows, freeing up time for Learning and Development (L&D) teams to focus on more strategic, human-centered activities. By analyzing a learner's past interactions, AI-powered systems also offer personalized course recommendations, much like recommendation algorithms, creating a more customized and engaging learning journey.

The essential features of AI-Driven LMS include those of (Table 3):

Table 3. Essential features of AI-driven LMS

Features of AI-driven LMS	Details
Smart Course Creation	With an AI-powered LMS, faculty can drastically reduce course creation time to just minutes! This applies to every aspect of course development, including research, structure, and design, all through a few simple steps. The system also allows educators to build more engaging courses by adding interactive elements such as animations, buttons, narration, quizzes, videos, and real-time assessments. Additionally, the AI-powered LMS enhances content curation by sourcing materials from various open platforms, giving students seamless access to valuable resources.
Personalized Upskilling	AI-powered LMS applications also serve as an effective solution for learner upskilling, making them ideal for helping enterprise organizations address their complex training and development needs. These platforms enable educators to deliver personalized learning paths at scale, ensuring learners remain engaged and motivated as they advance in their roles.
Admin Task Automation	AI-driven LMS streamlines content management, tracks learner progress, and manages grades, leading to substantial time and cost savings. AI-integrated LMS personalizes learning by analyzing data, behavior, performance, preferences, and goals. This approach caters to diverse learner needs, offers real-time feedback and adjustments, and provides detailed analytics to enhance the efficiency of learning management.
Personalized Content Delivery	AI-powered LMS can adjust and refine learning paths in real-time according to each learner's progress. Additionally, they personalize content to align with the learner's individual style and pace. AI-powered LMS also engages learners through interactive experiences, encouraging active participation.
Adaptive Learning Experience	AI-powered LMS creates a tailored, supportive learning environment that aligns with the unique needs of each learner.

continued on following page

Table 3. Continued

Features of AI-driven LMS	Details
Adaptive Evaluation	This feature of AI-powered LMS delivers personalized assessments using advanced technologies such as speech recognition. Unlike traditional evaluations, it adapts to each learner's pace and performance, taking into account individual strengths and weaknesses in real time.
Personalized Learning paths	AI-integrated LMS personalizes the learning experience by analyzing data, behavior, performance, preferences, and goals. This approach allows it to cater to a wide range of learner needs, offering real-time feedback and adjustments while providing in-depth analytics to optimize learning management and efficiency.
Intelligent Gamification	Gamification turns monotonous learning sessions into dynamic and enjoyable experiences by adding elements like animation, storytelling, and friendly competition. Meanwhile, an AI-powered LMS enhances the course creation process by automatically generating quizzes that align with course content, boosting knowledge retention and increasing learner engagement. This AI-driven feature enables course creators to quickly design and refine quizzes with minimal effort, streamlining development and saving valuable time
Knowledge Repository	AI-powered LMS can integrate research, subject expertise, and the latest information into a unified knowledge library, bridging knowledge gaps by combining self-created courses with external resources.
Intelligent Recommendations	This feature of AI-powered LMS provides personalized content recommendations based on each learner's strengths, preferences, and areas for improvement. By leveraging Intelligent Recommendations, the LMS further enhances growth opportunities by analyzing learner data to suggest new content that matches their interests, as well as popular courses that are likely to keep them engaged.
Data Analytics & Reporting	AI-powered teaching technologies offer precise and comprehensive data tracking for both educators and learners. It is worth mentioning that, AI-driven LMS platforms deliver actionable insights, such as identifying students who may be struggling, assessing the effectiveness of content, and optimizing its delivery for better outcomes.

Source: Author

CHALLENGES FACED BY AI-DRIVEN APPLICATIONS FOR FACILITATING PERSONALIZED LEARNING

The increasing adoption of Artificial Intelligence (AI) technology in educational settings, particularly in personalized learning environments, has gained significant attention. While the implementation of AI-driven applications in education may appear straightforward, academic institutions are likely to face various challenges, such as:

- **Data Privacy & Security**: A key challenge in implementing AI in academic settings is ensuring the privacy and security of student data. AI systems typically require the collection and analysis of large amounts of sensitive information, such as personal, academic, and behavioral data. While AI-driven personalized learning can be highly effective, it raises significant privacy and security concerns. Protecting student data from unauthorized access and breaches is essential. To mitigate these risks, educational institutions must establish robust data protection protocols and comply with privacy regulations to ensure the security of student information.

- **Ethical Considerations:** AI-powered tutoring systems, while promising in their ability to personalize learning, could unintentionally favor certain groups of students over others due to the biases present in the data they are trained on. If the training data is not diverse or representative of all student demographics, these systems may give preferential treatment to certain groups, exacerbating existing inequalities in education. For instance, students from underrepresented backgrounds or those with unique learning needs might not receive the same level of support, leading to further disparities in educational outcomes. In addition to algorithmic bias, there are several other significant ethical concerns. One such concern is algorithmic discrimination, where AI systems unintentionally treat students unfairly based on race, gender, socioeconomic status, or other factors. This could result in unequal access to learning resources, opportunities, or even assessments, perpetuating systemic inequality. Lack of transparency in AI decision-making processes is also a critical ethical challenge. Often, these systems operate as "black boxes," meaning the reasoning behind their recommendations or actions may not be clear to educators or students. This lack of clarity can make it difficult to trust the AI's decisions and could limit the ability to hold the system accountable for errors or unfair practices. Reduced autonomy is another concern, as students may become overly reliant on AI systems for guidance, which could impact their ability to think critically or make independent decisions. Furthermore, AI could potentially facilitate academic misconduct, such as cheating, if students find ways to exploit the system's vulnerabilities for personal gain.
- **Issues related to accessibility:** Although AI has the potential to improve access to education, it also carries the risk of widening existing inequalities. AI-driven personalized learning depends on reliable internet and digital devices, which may not be accessible to all students. To maximize the benefits of AI in education, it's crucial for schools and policymakers to tackle the digital divide and ensure every student, regardless of socioeconomic background, has the opportunity to benefit from these technologies.
- **Faculty Training:** The effective use of AI in online education relies on educators' willingness to embrace and become proficient with AI tools. Teachers require adequate training and support to successfully integrate AI-driven per-

sonalized learning into their classrooms. Furthermore, there may be resistance to these technologies, driven by concerns over job displacement or a perceived loss of control in the teaching process.

- **Infrastructure issues:** Academic institutions might also face the challenge of lack of infrastructure especially in terms of Information Technology infrastructure and resource scarcity to facilitate effective implementation of AI tools in learning and development.
- **Skill Development Perspective:** As AI and automation continue to shape the workforce, it's essential for education systems to prepare students with the skills required for the future. This means focusing not only on technical abilities to work with AI but also on soft skills like critical thinking and creativity—areas where AI still falls short.
- **Attitude of Educators:** Educators may also show their reluctance to integrate an all AI-driven academic delivery system. Lack of willingness to accept change can also pose to be a major behavioral challenge for ensuring smooth implementation of AI-driven technologies in the education sector.

ROAD AHEAD: FUTURE OF AI-ENABLED APPLICATIONS IN PERSONALIZED LEARNING

The rapid advancement of technology presents exciting opportunities for personalized learning. With AI, data analytics, and immersive digital tools progressing at a fast pace, the way we customize education to suit individual needs is set to undergo significant transformation. Let's delve into some potential developments that could shape the future of personalized learning, offering even more dynamic and flexible experiences for learners. As reported by Maximizemarketresearch, the global market for artificial intelligence in education was valued at $4.17 billion in 2023 and is expected to expand at a compound annual growth rate (CAGR) of 43.8%, reaching approximately $53.02 billion (Patel, 2025). This substantial growth highlights the increasing adoption of AI solutions in education, driven by the growing demand to improve learning outcomes, boost efficiency, and address the evolving needs of both students and educators.

AI is revolutionizing personalized education by transforming how students engage with learning. As technology advances, AI will increasingly shape the development of tailored learning paths that address each student's unique needs, strengths, and preferences. Through adaptive learning platforms, AI-driven tutoring, and data-informed insights, education is becoming more flexible and inclusive, empowering every student to reach their full potential. The future of education will be defined by intelligent systems that allow students to learn at their own pace and in the most effective ways for them.

Generative AI, such as ChatGPT, is also reshaping the traditionally time-consuming process of curriculum development. By analyzing vast amounts of educational content—including textbooks, lesson plans, quizzes, and assessments—AI uses deep learning algorithms to evaluate key elements like content depth, difficulty, teaching methods, and assessment formats. The result is the creation of personalized curricula tailored to individual learning needs, offering customized educational experiences.

Additionally, Augmented Reality (AR) and Virtual Reality (VR) are transforming how we interact with information, making learning more immersive and interactive. AR enhances the real world with digital overlays, while VR fully immerses users in simulated environments. These technologies break down complex concepts by providing interactive, visual learning experiences that simplify understanding. Whether it's virtually dissecting a frog, exploring historical events, or traveling through space, the integration of AR, VR, and AI creates engaging educational experiences that improve comprehension and retention.

Balancing Innovations in AI Technology and Human Resource Development

Advanced AI applications hold enormous potential to transform conventional Learning & Development (L&D) perspectives, but realizing this potential requires a willingness to embrace change and invest in student, trainee as well a faculty skill development. By finding the right balance between cutting-edge technology and Human resource Development interventions, AI-powered L&D can become a cornerstone of organizational as well as institutional success. The future of academics and L&D isn't solely about integrating new technology; it's about creating a learning environment that empowers learners develop their potential in ways that enhance both their personal fulfilment as well as contribute effectively towards the institution's success.

Understanding the Needs & Expectations of Students

As AI technology continues to advance, it is expected to become more proficient at meeting the diverse and complex needs of students. Beyond simply customizing academic content, future AI systems could play a key role in identifying and addressing the emotional and psychological states of learners. These systems could be designed to detect signs of stress, anxiety, or disengagement, offering timely support or interventions to help students manage their well-being. This could lead to a more holistic approach to education, where AI not only aids in academic achievement but also supports students' mental and emotional growth. By monitoring patterns in behavior, mood, and engagement, AI could provide valuable insights for educators and counsellors, enabling them to deliver more comprehensive care. In this way, AI could evolve into a powerful tool for both academic learning and creating a supportive, nurturing environment that addresses students' emotional and psychological needs, helping them thrive both inside and outside the classroom.

It's important to note that Emotion AI, a specialized branch of artificial intelligence, has the ability to identify, simulate, and even respond to human emotions. Using advanced technologies such as pattern recognition, machine learning algorithms, natural language processing, neural networks, and facial recognition software, Emotion AI analyzes real-world data—such as facial expressions, speech patterns, vocal tone variations, and physiological signals—to offer deeper insights into emotional states and mental health. These capabilities could help students better understand and manage their emotions during learning activities, promoting emotional self-regulation and fostering positive feelings that enhance learning outcomes. Emotion AI's ability to detect and respond to emotions has the potential to motivate students, making them more engaged and effective in their studies.

New AI-Driven Innovations in Learning & Development

Smart Text Books: One of the key innovations in AI-driven education is the smart textbook, which refers to digital textbooks in e-book format. Unlike traditional paper books, these electronic versions offer interactive and engaging features that enhance the learning experience. AI textbooks will incorporate formative assessments, including comprehension questions, with the collected data not being used for grading. Instead, the information will be analyzed to better understand each student's learning style and provide tailored, AI-powered support.

Immersive Learning Experiences: The future of integration of AI in modern education goes beyond personalization and automation; it's about enriching the learning experience through immersive technologies. AI-powered simulations and virtual reality (VR) environments allow students to engage with complex concepts in a more interactive and captivating way. These technologies offer a level of depth and engagement that traditional methods can't provide, making education both enjoyable and impactful.

Hyper-personalized Learning Opportunities: Advanced AI platforms allow educators and organizations to create highly personalized learning experiences that adapt to each learner's specific role, skills, and career objectives. By analyzing individual data, these platforms deliver customized training modules, keeping students/trainees engaged and motivated in their professional growth.

Evolving Role of the Stakeholders Associated with Education Sector

AI is constantly advancing and becoming more accessible. Educational institutions, policymakers, and educators must thoughtfully evaluate how AI is implemented in education. It is essential to integrate AI into learning environments in a way that is both effective and responsible, while also addressing the challenges it presents. Figure 2 illustrates the evolving role of the various stakeholders associated with the Education Sector.

Figure 2. Evolving role of the stakeholders associated with education sector (Author)

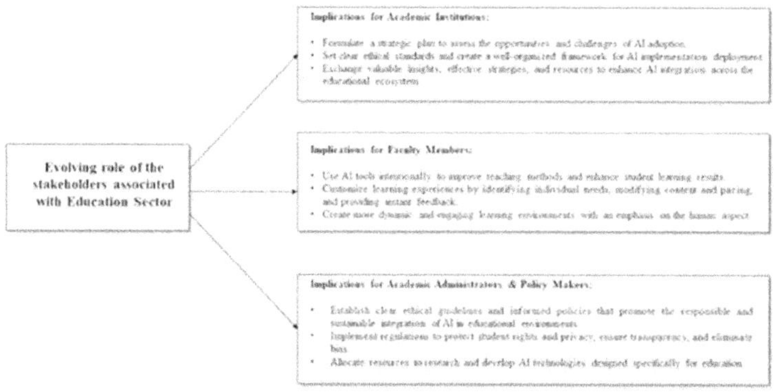

(a) ***Implications for Academic Institutions*:** Integrating AI-based applications into traditional academic settings requires institutions to develop a comprehensive strategic plan that identifies, explores, and leverages opportunities for AI adoption within established learning and development systems. This involves assessing existing gaps in academic processes and determining areas where AI-driven solutions can enhance and improve Learning Management Systems (LMS), content development, academic delivery, student support, and self-learning platforms for students, researchers, and educators. Additionally, the integration of AI into academic systems would require an evaluation of the effectiveness of personalized learning outcomes, supported by evidence-based data.

(b) ***Implications for Faculty Members:*** Integrating AI into traditional academic settings and fostering personalized learning through AI will present additional challenges for faculty members, student mentors, and institutional leaders. This will require providing hands-on training to manage AI-driven applications effectively, as well as becoming familiar with the operational and administrative aspects of utilizing analytical data for strategic decision-making to support student development and learning. Additionally, with the introduction of AI-powered tools, faculty will take on greater responsibility for monitoring customized content and learning delivery, ensuring quality checks at key stages of the student learning process. As the transition from traditional methods to AI-driven operations unfolds, faculty must also create a supportive and engaging learning environment at the institutional level. Moreover, they will need to stay vigilant in monitoring system upgrades and maintenance, collaborating closely with the AI technical team to ensure smooth operations. In the AI era, faculty members not only need to learn to leverage the vast amounts of data generated by AI platforms so as to make informed, strategic decisions. This data literacy would allow them to enhance learning programs, pinpoint skills gaps, and anticipate future learning needs. Additionally, with AI managing much of the tactical work, faculty can shift their focus to aligning learning initiatives with bigger institutional development and working closely with leadership to shape strategic goals.

(c) ***Implications for Academic Administrators and Policy Makers:*** Academic administrators and policymakers must develop clear policy frameworks for integrating AI into traditional academic environments and supporting personalized learning. These policies should be effectively communicated to all stakeholders to engage students and faculty in fostering a productive learning and development atmosphere. Additionally, they need to establish regulations that protect student rights and privacy, ensure transparency, and prevent bias. Moreover, administrators face the challenge of allocating funds and investing in research and development projects that will advance AI integration in the academic system to the next level.

Opportunities for Global Collaborative Learning

Emerging AI technologies are paving the way for enhanced global collaboration between students and educators. AI-driven online platforms are breaking down borders by connecting learners from various regions, providing them with opportunities to exchange ideas and collaborate on projects. This cross-cultural interaction enriches students' perspectives and cultivates a deeper understanding of global issues, which is essential for navigating an increasingly interconnected world. In addition to fostering cultural exchange, AI's ability to overcome language and geographic barriers allows for more seamless communication, making global collaboration more accessible than ever before. By creating opportunities for students to engage with peers from different backgrounds, AI helps equip them with the skills needed for a globalized job market. This integration of AI not only supports diverse learning experiences but also contributes to the creation of a truly unified global classroom that transcends traditional limitations.

CONCLUSION

Through a detailed literature review, this book chapter explores the transformative potential of AI-driven technologies in reshaping personalized learning. It delves into the significant ways AI applications are enhancing modern education by offering tailored learning experiences, automating administrative tasks, and creating immersive learning environments. Additionally, AI provides valuable predictive insights that help improve educational outcomes. However, the chapter also examines the challenges that may hinder the widespread implementation of AI in education, such as ethical concerns and the need for robust data privacy measures to maintain trust and integrity.

Looking forward, the chapter offers a positive perspective on the future of AI in education, emphasizing the opportunities it presents for educators, policymakers, and administrators. By embracing AI advancements, institutions can develop strategic plans to create more effective, engaging, and inclusive learning environments. These plans hold the potential to address the limitations of traditional education systems, ultimately paving the way for overcoming current challenges and preparing for success in a rapidly evolving digital and AI-driven world

REFERENCES

Bernacki, M. L., & Walkington, C. (2018). The role of situational interest in personalized learning. *Journal of Educational Psychology, 110*(6), 864–881. DOI: 10.1037/edu0000250

Bray, B., & McClaskey, K. (2014). *Make learning personal: The what, who, wow, where, and why* (1st ed., Vol. 1). Corwin Press.

Das, S., Mutsuddi, I., & Ray, N. (2025). *Artificial Intelligence in Adaptive Education.*, DOI: 10.4018/979-8-3693-8227-1.ch002

Delello, J. A., Watters, J. B., & Garcia-Lopez, A. (2024). *Artificial Intelligence in Education.*, DOI: 10.4018/979-8-3693-3003-6.ch001

Ellikkal, A., & Rajamohan, S. (2024). AI-enabled personalized learning: Empowering management students for improving engagement and academic performance. *Vilakshan - XIMB. Journal of Management.* DOI: 10.1108/XJM-02-2024-0023

Garg, A., Babu, B. V., & Balas, V. E. (2024). *Advances in Technological Innovations in Higher Education.* CRC Press., DOI: 10.1201/9781003376699

Hardaker, G., & Glenn, L. E. (2025a). Artificial intelligence for personalized learning: A systematic literature review. *The International Journal of Information and Learning Technology, 42*(1), 1–14. DOI: 10.1108/IJILT-07-2024-0160

Hardaker, G., & Glenn, L. E. (2025b). Artificial intelligence for personalized learning: a systematic literature review. *The International Journal of Information and Learning Technology.* https://doi.org/DOI: 10.1108/IJILT-07-2024-0160

Khine, M. S. (2024). Personalized Learning with AI, Eye-Tracking Studies and Precision Education. In *Artificial Intelligence in Education* (pp. 161–340). Springer Nature Singapore., DOI: 10.1007/978-981-97-9350-1_2

Klinck-van der Merwe, R., & Goosen, L. (2024). *Artificial Intelligence Algorithms as a Precursor for Personalized Learning and Education.*, DOI: 10.4018/979-8-3693-4252-7.ch009

Munna, A. S., Alharahsheh, H., Ferrazza, A., & Pius, A. (Eds.). (2024). *Transforming Education for Personalized Learning.* IGI Global., DOI: 10.4018/979-8-3693-0868-4

Mutsuddi, I. (2024). *Ethical Considerations in the Intersection of AI and Environmental Science.*, DOI: 10.4018/979-8-3693-6336-2.ch011

Patel, S. (2025). 21 Ways AI in Education is Reshaping the Industry. https://vlinkinfo.com/blog/ai-in-education-industry/

Pratama, M. P., Sampelolo, R., & Lura, H. (2023). Revolutionizing education: harnessing the power of artificial intelligence for personalized learning. Klasikal: Journal of education, language teaching and science, 5(2), 350-357.

Rahiman, H. U., & Kodikal, R. (2024). Revolutionizing education: Artificial intelligence empowered learning in higher education. *Cogent Education, 11*(1). Advance online publication. DOI: 10.1080/2331186X.2023.2293431

U.S. Department of Education. (2016). *Future Ready Learning: Reimagining the Role of Technology in Education.* Http://Tech.Ed.Gov/Files/2015/12/NETP16.Pdf

Walkington, C., & Bernacki, M. L. (2020). Appraising research on personalized learning: Definitions, theoretical alignment, advancements, and future directions. *Journal of Research on Technology in Education, 52*(3), 235–252. DOI: 10.1080/15391523.2020.1747757

Yekollu, R. K., Bhimraj Ghuge, T., Sunil Biradar, S., Haldikar, S. V., & Farook Mohideen Abdul Kader, O. (2024). *AI-Driven Personalized Learning Paths: Enhancing Education Through Adaptive Systems* (pp. 507–517). DOI: 10.1007/978-981-97-3191-6_38

Zhen, H., & Yahaya, W. A. J. W. (2024). *Use of Generative AI Tools to Facilitate Personalized Learning in the Flipped Classroom.*, DOI: 10.4018/979-8-3693-1351-0.ch016

Chapter 7
Revolutionizing Fashion Education With Integrating AI and 3D Design for a Sustainable Future

Nikita Singh
https://orcid.org/0000-0001-5493-4640
Lovely Professional University, India

Jyoti Rani
https://orcid.org/0000-0002-5577-7808
Lovely Professional University, India

ABSTRACT

By encouraging sustainability, fostering creativity, and providing aspiring designers with state-of-the-art resources, the incorporation of AI-driven 3D design into fashion school is revolutionizing the sector. Through virtual prototyping, these technologies allow students to design, test, and improve clothing without the need for physical materials, reducing waste and carbon footprints. Additionally, AI improves circular fashion, supply chain optimization, and trend forecasting, promoting moral and effective manufacturing techniques. This method equips students to handle the demands of a quickly changing, technologically advanced, and environmentally conscious fashion business by democratizing access to design tools and promoting interdisciplinary learning.

DOI: 10.4018/979-8-3373-5102-5.ch007

INTRODUCTION

Everything that is old has now become new again; there has been unprecedented pressure on the fashion industry to adopt measures of sustainability with climate issues bubbling away to the surface. Schools understand the potential of this shift because they can include up-and-coming technologies, such as AI-powered 3D models into the curriculum. In this chapter we will expand on why this integration matters, how it is organic to the future of fashion design and production. The fashion industry has started to embrace "sustainable fashion," the term for a more eco- and socially responsible path to fashion. It outlines many ways we can mitigate some of the damage from clothing producing and consuming (Sehnem et al, 2024).

ROLE OF AI AND 3D DESIGN IN REDUCING WASTE AND CARBON EMISSIONS

By mining vast amounts of data, A.I. can predict trends in fashion, helping companies create collections that align with consumer preferences while also limiting waste and overproduction. By examining materials and design patterns, AI systems can help to optimize resource use and significantly reduce waste in the production process. The production of multiple design alternatives by AI using initial constraints is commonly described as "generative design" (Casciani & D'Itria, 2024).

Share This Article 3D printing, also known as additive manufacturing, uses only the material necessary to create an object, eliminating excess waste compared to traditional subtractive manufacturing processes, which cut away material from a larger block. Because AI can help predict and model the lifecycle of a product, designers can create items that are not only efficient to resources but also easier to dispose of or repurpose when their useful lives are nearing an end. Some businesses, using artificial intelligence (AI) to analyze customer behavior and preferences, are able to decrease overproduction and the resulting waste by producing only what is necessary (Saad Alotaibi et al., 2024).

Textile manufacturing is very thirsty. Producing cotton, a frequently worn fabric, uses a lot of water. A pair of jeans can consume as much as 10,000 liters of water to manufacture. It's not just about water use, however. Another major cause of the ecosystem destruction is dying. The dyes contain harmful chemicals that are toxic to water and aquatic organisms. Fashion has not historically been especially ecologically sound. During the manufacturing cycles, especially so with synthetic materials, a high amount of greenhouse gasses is released. Would you believe that fashion accounts for 10% of the planet's entire carbon footprint — more than both international travel and shipping combined? (Casciani & D'Itria, 2024)

These problems began before the emergence of fast fashion, though they have only gotten worse. This is referred to as the "fast fashion cycle," the ability of fashion brands to rapidly design and manufacture inexpensive, stylish clothing. This cyclical overproduction creates mass waste in fashion. These garments, created with poor quality ephemeral materials, are quickly discarded and end up in landfills or incinerators, damaging the climate (Ridler, 2020).

ADOPTION OF CIRCULAR FASHION PRINCIPLES IN EDUCATIONAL PROJECTS

These can both relate to students through course materials and instructional pedagogy. Focusing on recycling, material reuse, and waste reduction, this approach allows students to understand the life cycle of fashion items (Ridler, 2020). Through projects such as upcycling clothes or creating with sustainable materials, students hone their critical thinking skills around consumption and its environmental impact. Moreover, establishing partnerships with local businesses and organizations can provide real-world applications and insight into sustainable practices in the garment industry (Sánchez-López et al., 2021).

Technological Empowerment in Creativity

Technological empowerment in creativity refers to the process of using digital tools and platforms to automate and enhance the creative process. This can relate to writing, graphics or music production software that helps individuals more rapidly experiment and iterate on their ideas. The future of fashion designing is closely associated with technology (Alotaibi at el, 2024). To prepare their students with the skills required to take advantage of these innovations during the design process, design schools have begun to integrate digital design technologies such as 3D modelling and virtual reality into their academic programs. As e-commerce increases, future fashion designers will need to know about retail technologies more than ever. Analysing tactics, data analytics and customer behaviour in digital contexts (Casciani & D'Itria, 2024), students are made ready for this shifting retail environment. It uses artificial intelligence, which has enabled it to code and analyse millions of data points on social networks, consumer behaviour and even climates. This diminishes mass production and the designer's "Don't care attitude" by helping designers create clothing that consumers would want to wear in everyday life. The amount of clothing going to landfills will go down because AI will create and deliver garments that are forecast to have the highest chance of being needed or wanted, delivering the latest fashions. Fabric wastage, which was common when fabrics were cut for stitching, has been eliminated. AI systems might analyse fabric patterns, for example, when cutting clothing and make recommendations for how to avoid fabric waste. This produces a win-win scenario, as it decreases the amount of material used in product manufacturing, resulting in cost efficiency (Bruno & Canina, 2019).

Virtual Prototyping Tools in Fashion

Virtual prototyping can be significantly less expensive and less time-consuming than traditional prototyping methods, which often require multiple physical samples. It also allows for greater creativity and exploration, because designers can quickly iterate on their ideas, without being hampered by physical materials. These tools can also improve teamwork, as design teams can share and review designs online. In conclusion, Virtual Prototype tools are changing the game for fashion reducing waste, allowing more creative methods of clothing creation, and speeding up the creation process (Bruno & Canina,2020). The 3D technology being implemented in the business is revolutionizing the fashion designers' design processes, and when developing basic shirts and types in the fashion industry (Papahristou & Bilalis, 2017). Using sophisticated software suites or tools like Adobe tools, designers can build MTM patterns that accurately reflect the unique characteristics of each body form. Besides, this feature allows designers to conduct fitting according to animated models (Sánchez-López et al., 2021). In using these immersive virtual fittings, designers can see as it happens how clothing works on different fit models and other elements. Expert users say that technology enhances collaboration and creativity, reducing the demand for physical samples and accelerating the design process. They needed to adopt custom-made 3D solutions, so fashion companies could innovate their products (Cugini, 2008).

Breaking Down Traditional Barriers with a Creative Digital Approach

Digital platforms have enabled an ever-expanding reach to information and services that were out of them before, due to social, economic or geographic constraints. For instance, online education provides students from diverse backgrounds with high-quality content and experienced instructors regardless of location (Volino et al, 2005). Digital tools also facilitate real-time collaboration and networking — fostering diversity and creativity across disciplines. Designers and brands are increasingly utilising digital technologies to engage with customers, display their collections and share their brand narratives in innovative ways (Vishwakarma et al, 2024). A further example of digital fashion is the production of virtual clothing and accessories that only exist in digital environments, such as social media or video games. Since this process gets rid of the waste associated with physical production, it allows for more experimentation and sustainability. One of the most significant impacts of 3D digital fashion is its ability to streamline the production process. Traditional fashion design is wasteful, using real physical prototyping and revisions which create materials waste. Designers no longer need physical samples because they can design and see clothing in a virtual environment. This reduces the environmental impact, increasing the design process at the same time (Papahristou & Bilalis, 2017).

LEVERAGING AI FOR TREND FORECASTING AND CONSUMER BEHAVIOR ANALYSIS

Leveraging AI for trend forecasting refers to applying machine learning algorithms to large datasets to analyse them and identify patterns that could indicate future trends. These algorithms can aggregate data on a multitude of factors — market reports, social media activity, behavioural data, historical data to yield insights. But methods such as natural language processing and predictive analytics enables artificial intelligence (AI) to identify correlations and anomalies that human analysts might overlook. Ultimately, this enables companies to anticipate market changes, enhance the strategy and make decisions based on data (Okeleke et al,2024) By analysing data from various sources, such as social media, online purchases, and reviews, artificial intelligence (AI) systems can detect patterns and trends of tastes, engagement, and buying habits. This data can help businesses enhance customer experiences, streamline offerings, and tailor marketing campaigns. Predictive analytics, in addition, allows businesses to stay one step ahead of industry trends and make informed decisions by predicting the future behaviour of customers (Alabi, 2024).

FASHION DESIGN TOOLS AND SOFTWARE IN EDUCATION

Today, fashion design is accompanied by designs for digital graphics, pattern making, 3D modeling and more, which can also be included in the tools. Programs like Adobe Illustrator and Photoshop are, very often, used to create technical and fashion sketches. Specialist software such as CLO 3D, helps students visualize clothing in a virtual environment and assists with their understanding of drape and fit (McQuillan, 2020). Educational institutions often integrate these tools in curricula to prepare students for the industry. By utilizing these technologies, students are able to gain a more comprehensive skill set that includes both traditional methods and digital competencies. In addition, the access to these resources may promote innovation and invention as it would give students more freedom to explore their varied ideas and testing (Dai, 2011) This, coupled with the need for a level of cooperation that is essential to utilize both fashion design software and tools more integrated into the classroom, is imperative in providing aspiring fashion designers with the skills they need to succeed in a competitive market (Kazlacheva et al, 2018). TUKAcad provides pattern drafters and graders, which are crucial for the production of apparel. In the field of education, online tutorials and resources for these tools can enhance learning by allowing students to better grasp complex concepts. Incorporating these resources into the curriculum helps students be more skilled for the workforce, where tech-savvy is becoming increasingly important. Overall, the combination of modern software and traditional techniques provide aspiring fashion designers with the tools required to be successful (Faerm, 2014).

Role of Fashion Designing Colleges

It also plays a critical role for elite fashion design schools. Industrial experienced faculties having join hand faculty mentorship and insight into real-life applications of such creative ventures, has paved way to overlog the gap between business sector and academia. This forms an ideal environment for learning with modern facilities. It is also important that students at design schools with well-stocked studios, digital labs, and ingenious libraries have everything they need to develop their ideas freely (Kohli, 2024). My style of teaching 2030 is the reason why entrepreneurial fashion design schools exist. Encouraging students to explore entrepreneurship through starting their own companies or consultancy assignments, or embarking on creative fashion ventures rather than the average professional path. The contemporary fashion education is largely geared towards nurturing students to be resilient and dynamic attuning to the changing tides. This will allow students to become current in industry developments, rapidly progress to a new norm, and help foster a mindset which will enable them to thrive in a field as fluid and dynamic (Rizzi & Vandi, 2023).

Benefits of AI and 3D Fashion in Fashion Education

Fashion schools should strive not to produce a new generation of students with no idea how the tools they use work when they ever pop their hoods. These skills don't need to be computer scientist level, but the ability to access the various types of skills and knowledge available in the digital space to complement traditional ones offered in fashion schools over the decades — fashion design, patternmaking, textiles, sewing and garment construction, draping, illustration, marketing, and merchandising — will probably come in handy. These graduates will be able to use AI but also understand its limitations (Kwon et al, 2017)

A third advantage of students possessing a solid understanding of AI concepts is their ability to troubleshoot issues as they happen. Fashion companies are already being forced to begin hiring people from outside the sector to interface with the APIs that link to these opaque-trained, cloud-based huge models. This leaves the customer at the mercy of the software supplier, who may have more pressing matters than answering your question (Ermer, 2018). Another difficult aspect for fashion schools is the fact that the best AI (according to the available general capabilities) is currently held by a small number of companies. This creates a desire to simply use their products and build educational programs around them (Yezhova et al, 2018). The title would be owned (or will be owned more fairly soon) by the company behind the popular open image generator Stable Diffusion, whose Chief Executive abandoned ship and who saw just how destructive in terms of cost training and running large models can be versus the low revenue they can mine users for, but no company better represents the difficulties in competing with some of the largest and richest tech companies in the world (less so the Open Source community's heroic efforts) than this one.

OpenAI's global head of alliances and partnerships has a point — students in that context should probably be trained to use whatever tools look like they will be the "de facto" AI tools there, since they appear to be monopolizing a world where both content licensing agreements (which ensures they will always get fresh access to training data from significant publishers and the like) and more recently, resale relationships with management consultants that "allow more penetration into industry verticals." Moreover, when a solution attains this level of institutional adoption and entrenchment, it may even make it a practical necessity for people to learn (Baeza & Jushchyshyn 2024). The emerging fashion talents are largely not being taught the tools they will require post-degree in a hyper-competitive market, where their competition now includes not only their peers, but artificial intelligence trained to either vastly improve their efficiency or one day obsolesce them, although some universities and colleges are doing exemplary work in providing their students with broad AI education (Noia et al, 2024).

Transformative Learning theories of AI in Fashion Education

Kolb's experiential learning cycle, which prioritizes active experimentation, abstract conceptualization, reflective observation, and concrete experience, is in line with the incorporation of AI and 3D design in fashion school. Using a learning-by-doing methodology, students participate in interactive digital prototyping, revising designs in response to real-time AI input. This strengthens students' technical ability and problem-solving abilities in sustainable fashion design by bridging theory and practice (Akella, 2010). Traditional business hierarchies are being challenged by the move to digital fashion education, which encourages student agency and critical involvement. By incorporating AI-driven sustainability analysis and virtual prototyping, students are encouraged to question fast fashion's environmental impact and explore ethical alternatives (Drakou et al., 2024).

Fashion Design Software Tools Used in 3D Fashion Education

The evolution of 3D in the fashion industry led to the development of dedicated CAD software that meets the specific needs of the industry. Below are some of the most frequently utilized tools in the industry:

Marvelous Designer: This software is renowned as one of the best 3D clothing design programs as it allows designers to get an unparalleled level of realism. Using its fabric analyzer, which simulates the qualities of a range of materials, designers can choose exactly those that best suit their vision before making samples.

CLO 3D: Leaving empty space for information about your perfromances or events? CLO 3D is software built with pattern makers in mind, offering tools for creating custom-fitted clothing and seeing how it fits on animated models. CLO 3D is great for technical designers who want precision when creating digital patterns and assembling garments.

Romans CAD: Popular with pattern makers and technical designers, Romans CAD is very helpful for large clothing companies who require precision as it shows accurate adjustments and changes in complex garments.

Adobe Illustrator: Adobe Illustrator is an essential tool for creating flat sketches and realistic texturing using Substance 3D. Whereas Adobe Substance provides realistic 3D textures which help designers generate ultrarealistic graphics for virtual prototyping, Adobe Illustrator is widely used for sketching.

As 3D fashion design becomes increasingly embedded in the business, appropriate education and training become critical. And, given this new necessity, many fashion schools and institutions now offer specialized courses and programs in 3D fashion design, equipping students with the skills they need to thrive in this pioneering field. From basic 3D modeling to high-end digital prototyping, these courses provide a comprehensive education. Online workshops and tutorials also provide designers with excellent learning opportunities taught by professionals in the field and help them stay updated with emerging trends and technologies. Investing in continuous education can help designers to be ahead of the curve and leverage 3D fashion design to the very best in order to create novel clothing (Kohli, 2024).

GLOBAL COLLABORATION AND INTERDISCIPLINARY LEARNING

As design schools begin to include fields such as technology, sustainability and business in their curricula, fashion education has become increasingly interdisciplinary over the years, offering students a deep dive into all areas of it. Interdisciplinary Learning in Fashion with AI and 3D Design Interdisciplinary learning in fashion with AI and 3D design consists of the incorporation of different academic subjects like technology, art, and design that enhance the quality of the fashion industry (Marku, 2023). By combining together 3D design methods and artificial intelligence, this approach creates a jolt of energy and speed in the fashion design workflow. 3D design allows clothing prototypes and images to be created quickly but artificial intelligence (AI) can analyze trends, predict customer preferences and optimize supply chains. This can help fashion designers create better and more sustainable production methods. Ai can help create designs that target audiences would like, and 3D printing can save waste and allow for customisation (de Medeiros, 2023). This interdisciplinary method promotes cooperation between designers, developers, and marketers, resulting in more innovative and practical fashion solutions.

The design of virtual fashion shows is an example of multidisciplinary fashion education that clouds AI and 3D design. In this environment, fashion designers buy collaboration with 3D artists and AI experts to create digital clothing that can be worn in an immersive environment. AI systems can analyze consumer preferences and current fashion trends, helping designers create pieces that will resonate with their target audience. After ideation, the designs are made into realistic design digital prototypes of the clothing using 3D design software. This way you do not need physical materials and can test it out and iterate quickly. AI-powered elements like personalized styling suggestions for the viewer based on their interests can then be integrated into the virtual fashion show. Not only does this method reduce the amount of waste associated with traditional fashion shows, but it also opens new pathways for experimentation and creativity within the industry. Integrating the three disciplines provides a solid understanding of how fashion design, technology, and data analysis interrelate and influence each other (Zhaoyan, & Renli 2011).

Fashion education often incorporates technology, art, psychology, and sustainability, which has also helped designers create more innovative and socially aware clothing. Fashion Designers can be one step ahead of the era by using AI for predicting future fashions through processing huge amount of datas to get the information on customers trends and preferences. Notably, rapid prototyping through 3D design technology allows for designers to create and prototype multiple versions of a garment, significantly reducing the time to produce compared to traditional methods (Ermer, 2018). Artificial intelligence and 3D design could make the fashion industry more sustainable by reducing waste. Designers can view and edit designs digitally ahead of using any real-world materials. Some fashion brands are using AI to create customized shopping experiences to enhance consumer satisfaction and engagement. Those experiences include algorithms that suggest designs based on personalized user data. AI and 3D modeling powered virtual fitting rooms allow customers to try on clothing for themselves. This drastically reduces return rates and improves the online purchasing experience. Using a technique known as generative design, whereby algorithms create unique patterns and styles based on specific parameters, the fashion world will examine the edges of originality and innovation. Curriculums combining technology, business, environmental studies of the system within the fashion sector is becoming common in fashion education in order to equip students with the complexity of the modern format of fashion. AI's ability to forecast demand and adjust inventory can also help leave a smaller environmental footprint by limiting overproduction. The partnership between computer scientists and fashion designers has given rise to smart textiles: fabrics that merge fashion and technology in ways that had never been conceived before. These textiles can change their color or texture through external stimuli (Lee, 2021).

Scalability Across Educational Contexts

Digital prototyping and AI-powered simulations can be used in product design and engineering to promote hands-on learning. Fashion-related 3D modeling software can be modified for use in biomedical engineering, architecture, and industrial design, allowing for experiential, project-based learning in a virtual environment (Lee, 2022). Virtual reality (VR) studios and AI-enhanced digital art tools have the potential to revolutionize visual arts education by giving students access to real-time generative design support. This promotes creative agency and democratizes access to sophisticated design tools, which is consistent with critical pedagogy (Faculty of Computing and Information Technology, King Abdulaziz University, Jeddah, Saudi Arabia et al., 2024). Digital fabrication, vehicle design, and interior design can all benefit from virtual prototyping, which lowers material waste and makes skill development more affordable. Training programs can be tailored using AI-powered adaptive learning systems, guaranteeing that students effectively acquire industry-relevant skills (Andrisano et al., 2012).

SUSTAINABILITY BEYOND DESIGN

This monstrous act includes the Whole Life Cycle Analysis which focuses on the interdependency between the product, the environment, society and economy throughout that product's entire lifecycle. Sustainability, therefore, must take a holistic view not only of the design of environmentally friendly products, but also of responsibly sourcing the resources, using processes in production that minimize waste and emissions and providing sustainable end-of-life options for products (Rissanen, 2017). It also stresses the need for collaboration among various stakeholders, including designers, producers, customers, and legislators, in order to achieve comprehensive sustainability objectives. Ultimately, the thought encourages a holistic, pluralistic approach to sustainability, and cheer for strategies that foster socio-ecological justice and system over the long-term instead of narrowly emphasizing the pragmatic or aesthetic features of design (Casciani & D'Itria (2024). It involves processing large sets of data with advanced algorithms and machine learning techniques to enhance efficiency and decision-making. By analyzing historical sales data, market trends, and external factors, AI can forecast demand, allowing companies to optimize inventory levels and avoid stockouts or overstock situations. AI also enhances logistics by optimizing delivery schedules and routes, which cuts costs and boosts customer satisfaction. AI is also capable of identifying potential supply chain disruptions enabling proactive risk mitigation and streamlined operations (Bruno & Canina 2020).

FUTURE OF SUSTAINABLE FASHION EDUCATION WITH AI AND 3D DESIGN

User-friendly interfaces of CAD software simplify the complex design process of a project. Marvelous Designer, for one, allows users to design realistic-looking digital clothes that can be modified in real time. Its fabric analyzer mimics the properties of different fabrics, from the stiffness of denim to the drape of silk. This level of fidelity is imperative as fashion designers need a clear visualization of how their clothing aligns with their vision before they begin production (Avădanei et al, 2021). It also includes video guidance and tutorials, helping both new and experienced designers to adopt digital design methods. Programs like Adobe Illustrator for flat designs and Substance 3D for realistic texturing have made it possible for designers to see lifelike renditions of their clothes without making a single sample. This technology is making the most sense regionally, especially in the early stages of design, as it allows for many more tests and iterations of fashion concepts (Manzo et al, 2024). One of the most remarkable advantages is sustainable 3D fashion. Traditional prototype techniques generate a large amount of waste through the use of dyes, wasted samples, and fabric scraps. Virtual prototyping minimizes physical material needs until the end design stage, allowing fashion designers to create digital clothes.

Digital sampling reduces waste by up to 35%, according to industry estimates. This strike is quite in step with the industry's push for eco-friendly production practices and sustainability. Using less physical samples can help fashion brands cut down on waste, water usage and their carbon footprint. This switch not only aids the environment, but also bolsters the fashion industry with eco-conscious consumers (Bertola & Colombi 2021). Integrating 3D fashion design into production workflows also speeds up the overall pace of production. A single article of clothing might go through several fits, adjustments and adaptations, each one requiring a new prototype. On the fashion industry 3D allows designers to create clothing, customized for the tastes and body of individual customers, saving the time it takes to reach and complete the end product, in addition 3D, allows quickly make changes digitally (Agarwal, 2018). Another tool offered in CAD fashion design software, is the ability to work with custom-fitted patterns which are easy to adapt to different body types, allowing them to cater to a wider array of customers. This level of customization enables brands to create new lines faster and more frequently, matching fossilized fashion trends. Also, the brands can respond better to customer feedback due to this agility since design changes can be made in real-time without delay in the development cycle (Faerm, 2012).

Shopping people can use (AR)-powered virtual fitting sessions using smartphone apps to view garments on digital models or the shoppers themselves. This technology is very beneficial for e-commerce platforms as it provides a more immersive experience to consumers. Allowing customers to visualize how clothing will drape on their own bodies may lead to lower return rates, increased consumer happiness and stronger brand affinity for brands. Fashion companies also can have virtual clothing models in their marketing, where the product is shown moving or on animated models that show how a garment reacts in real time to various body types and actions. This interactive methodology will attract modern customers looking for more personalized and engaging purchasing processes (Mohiuddin et al, 2024). 3D fashion design is also being transformed by prototyping and realistic visualizations. Using advanced 3D software, designers can make stunningly realistic digital prototypes, allowing them to visualize and test their ideas long before they make physical samples. This digital-first approach significantly shortens the need for costly and time-consuming changes by enabling designers to find potential issues early in the design process. Moreover, designers can explore different textiles, colours and textures in 3D prototyping, providing them with a comprehensive understanding of how their products will both look and feel. This capability not only enhances the creative process, but also ensures the result aligns with the designer's vision, leading to more sophisticated and commercially viable garments (Conlon & Gallery, 2024).

Demand of Learning AI and 3D Fashion in Education

Mass-market fashion shops as well as creative directors of high-end labels can apply generative AI to find different types of unstructured data in real time, instead of relying only on market analysis and trend reports to guide designs for the coming season's collection. For example, generative AI can rapidly aggregate and synthesize sentiment data from social media video clips or model trends across a range of consumer data sources (Jeon et al, 2021). Designers could play around with a wide range of aesthetics and appearances by inputting sketches and other styles they want, from textiles and colors to patterns, into a generative AI-based platform that automatically produces a variety of patterns. A team may then develop new products according to these results, imbuing each appearance with the distinctive style of a fashion house. That enables innovative, limited-edition product drops, which, in the future, could take the form of joint ventures between two companies. Generative AI-powered facial recognition technology could enable products like spectacles to be customized for every user by mapping the topography of the face and sizing to the personal preferences of the user (McQuillan, 2020).

The scenario became reality after a group of fashion designers from the Laboratory for Artificial Intelligence in Design (AiDLab) in Hong Kong staged a fashion show in December 2022 featuring designs aided by generative AI. 3. Fashion designers have already begun harnessing the power of generative AI to come up with fresh ideas, test hundreds of design variations without the need to create expensive samples and dramatically accelerate their workflows, sharing tools from tech companies such as Cala, Designovel and Fashable. (Generative AI also presents marketers with an opportunity to discover new product combinations, which could reduce costs of lab testing for the cosmetics industry.) Previous AI chats are already a clear step down from today's generative-AI-powered chats, which use better natural-language processing to understand and converse with humans. There is (not yet) a perfect generative-AI chatbot for businesses, though; existing chatbots and other text-generating programs still make errors that can incur major customer-service disasters. However, this technology might enable customer service practices to outsource complex queries in the long term, such as by enabling chatbots to provide customized inquiries to provide multilingual responses (Marku, 2023).

Career Opportunities with AI and 3D Fashion

Fashion technology jobs combine advanced technologies such as blockchain technology, 3D design, augmented reality, and artificial intelligence (AI) with traditional fashion practices. These technologies enable revolutionizing design processes, improving sustainability, enhancing customer experiences and creating new positions that were not previously in existence. The growing relationship between fashion and technology creates high demand for people with both technical know-how and a deep understanding of the fashion industry (Bertola & Colombi, 2021)

Digital Fashion Designer

As some of the fashion world shifts online, so too does the role of a fashion designer. Now, digital fashion designers create 3D clothing, digital fashion lines, and even NFT-based virtual clothing through programs such as Blender, Marvelous Designer, and CLO 3D and work directly with fashion brands to create virtual prototypes that save waste and eliminate the need for physical samples. As virtual fashion shows and augmented reality try-ons become more popular, digital designers are taking on a more critical role in the fashion tech ecosystem (Särmäkari, 2023).

Fashion Technologist

A fashion technologist merges technology with the processes in fashion. They rely on wearable technology, smart textiles and sustainable production methods including 3D printing. Worse, fashion technologists explore emerging materials and seek to introduce them to mass production. Written by QS November 21, 2020, they have an essential role in transforming the fashion industry into a more digitalized, sustainable, and efficient one (Zhang & Lee 2020).

Fashion Tech E-commerce Specialist

Due to online buying, e-commerce specialists are more focused than ever. These people are responsible for managing online channels, enhancing customer experience and implementing search engine optimization techniques for increasing traffic to websites in fashion technology. Fashion e-commerce experts also manage the integration of technology such as AR product visualizations, AI-driven recommendations, and virtual fitting rooms to create engaging customer experiences that drive sales (Colombi & Casciani, 2021).

Virtual Stylist

A virtual stylist relies on technology to provide clients with digital experiences. Virtual stylists offer augmented reality (AR) and virtual reality (VR) to help buyers visualize how clothing will appear on them in a virtual space prior to moving forward with a transaction. This role can be advantageous for online retailers wanting to offer a more personalized buying experience. The need for virtual styling services will grow as adoption of virtual fitting rooms increases (Vartak at el, 2024).

Data Analyst (Fashion Technology)

Fashion companies have an ever-growing dependence on data. The fashion tech data analyst collects and analyzes massive amounts of data from social networks, e-commerce sites, and market trends. Companies can utilize this data to improve marketing strategies, optimize supply chains, and provide better-informed decisions for new product development. Data scientists are also required to work with tools such as Python, SQL, and machine learning techniques, therefore for anyone who seeks to thrive in this business knowledge of these tools is essential (Lee & Suh, 2024).

Fashion Blockchain Specialist

Blockchain technology is revolutionizing everything from NFT-based fashion goods, to supply chain management and product authenticity. A blockchain fashion technology specialist who is building decentralized solutions to track the origins of product implements, providing ethical sourcing, and establish digital ownership of fashion in the form of NFTs. The role requires an in-depth knowledge of blockchain networks, cryptography, and smart contracts (Terra, 2021).

Fashion Product Manager

A fashion product manager is critical to the end-to-end development through launch of fashion technology goods. Product managers oversee projects charged with adhering to both technical and artistic parameters, whether they be wearable technology or sustainable materials or A.I.-based fashion tools. Technical knowledge, communication, and leading staffs through multiple disciplines by a good product manager (D'Amico et al, 2013).

Lifelong Learning in AI-Driven Fashion Education

Students can participate in experiential learning cycles by experimenting with virtual prototyping, predictive analytics, and generative design thanks to AI-powered tools that promote self-directed learning. In line with the tenets of lifelong learning theory, learners can hone their abilities outside of the classroom thanks to digital platforms that offer real-time feedback and adaptive learning systems (Yildirim et al., 2023). Real-world problems are simulated by AI and digital fashion ecosystems, guaranteeing that students acquire future-proof skills that are useful in a variety of industries. By enabling students to take charge of their education and stay adaptable to changes in the industry's environment and technology, this is consistent with critical pedagogy. Traditional educational barriers are broken by AI-driven tailored learning environments that enable professionals and students to reskill and upskill at their own speed. Immersion virtual platforms, such as AR/VR prototype spaces and online fashion laboratories, offer options for ongoing learning that change in tandem with developments in the industry (Akram et al., 2022).

CONCLUSION

Integrating AI-driven 3D design into fashion school is one of the most radical but efficient approaches to being equipped for the transition being implemented by the fashion industry. By incorporating sustainable practices, fostering creativity, and leveraging advanced technologies, this methodology prepares students to be future-ready designers who thrive in a dynamic and environmentally sensitive market.

Technologies such as data-driven design analytics, virtual prototyping, and collaborative tools can help reduce carbon emissions and material waste, allowing students to adopt circular fashion concepts and grow sustainably. The cross-cutting nature of this pedagogical structure encourages international cooperation and burgeoning creativity, equipping graduates with the skill set necessary to thrive in a competitive and globalized field.

Moreover, AI applied in understanding consumer behaviour and predicting trends provides insights into market dynamics and ensures supply meets demand. What you wear, how you planned on wearing it, where you'd planned to wear it, and when and why you had planned to wear it all changed, and fashion education explores it all under the new definitions of technology, sustainability and design excellence, arming a new generation of designers on how to balance the acts of innovation and ethics, creativity and responsibility. It's a new future for fashion, at this turning point of sustainability and technology empowerment that will redefine industry-type standards.

The evolving intersection of sustainability, tech and fashion offers a bright future for the fashion industry. From comprehensive sustainability policies to advanced artificial intelligence and 3D design tools, the sector is transforming to embrace its ecological balance, productivity, and innovation. Sustainability is not just limited to product design; it also involves reducing waste, using ethically sourced materials, and working with stakeholders across the ecosystem to promote long-term social and environmental well-being.

At the same time technologies such as artificial intelligence (AI), 3D designs software, augmented reality are disrupting the design and production processes. These technologies facilitate faster, personalised, and more engaging interactions with customers and decreased waste and resources. The increasing consumer satisfaction, decrease in environmental impact, and increased efficiency from AR-powered virtual fittings, AI-driven demand forecasting, and virtual prototyping

Their growing understanding of the importance of AI and 3D fashion design shows more than ever the need to fuse new technology into all levels of fashion education. On the one hand, digital design platforms have provided designers with tools for realistic and accurate representations, and on the other, generating AI is providing designers with the ability to experiment with a range of concepts accelerating creative processes, improving innovation and sustainability.

As traditional roles are being redrawn by the convergence of fashion and technology, career options are expanding. New roles, such as these, are helping to usher in the fashion tech, sustainable, and customer-centric future of the industry. Such roles highlight the necessity for a blend of technical skills, design sense, and an understanding of the evolving world of fashion.

Discover the how a blend of innovation, technology, and sustainable practices are paving the way for the future of fashion. By embracing these innovations, the sector can respond to the needs of tech-savvy consumers, address environmental challenges, and open up revolutionary job opportunities. The shift to a more sustainable, effective, and inclusive fashion business is not only critical, but it also holds tremendous potential

REFERENCES

Agarwal, V. (2018). Sustainable fashion education in changing world scenario. *European Journal of Sustainable Development, 7*(1), 365–365.

Akella, D. (2010). Learning together: Kolb's experiential theory and its application. *Journal of Management & Organization, 16*(1), 100–112. DOI: 10.5172/jmo.16.1.100

Akram, S. V., Malik, P. K., Singh, R., Gehlot, A., Juyal, A., Ghafoor, K. Z., & Shrestha, S. (2022). Implementation of Digitalized Technologies for Fashion Industry 4.0: Opportunities and Challenges. *Scientific Programming, 2022*, 1–17. DOI: 10.1155/2022/7523246

Alabi, M. (2024). Data-Driven Product Strategy: Leveraging AI to Forecast Market Trends and Identify Emerging Opportunities.

Alotaibi, B. S., Shema, A. I., Ibrahim, A. U., Abuhussain, M. A., Abdulmalik, H., Dodo, Y. A., & Atakara, C. (2024). Assimilation of 3D printing, Artificial Intelligence (AI) and Internet of Things (IoT) for the construction of eco-friendly intelligent homes: An explorative review. *Heliyon*. PMID: 39286162

Andrisano, A. O., Leali, F., Pellicciari, M., Pini, F., & Vergnano, A. (2012). Hybrid Reconfigurable System design and optimization through virtual prototyping and digital manufacturing tools. [IJIDeM]. *International Journal on Interactive Design and Manufacturing, 6*(1), 17–27. DOI: 10.1007/s12008-011-0133-9

Avădanei, M., Blaga, M., & Kazlacheva, Z. (2021). Best Practices of Sustainable Product Development through 3D-Design and Visualization. In *International Symposium Technical Textiles-Present and Future* (pp. 227-235).

Baeza, C., & Jushchyshyn, N. (2024). BRIDGING THE GAP BETWEEN THE FASHION INDUSTRY AND DIGITAL MEDIA: AN INTERDISCIPLINARY COURSE ON ETHICS, SUSTAINABILITY, AND IMMERSIVE TECHNOLOGY. In ICERI2024 Proceedings (pp. 9762-9767). IATED.

Bertola, P., & Colombi, C. (2021). Reflecting on the future of fashion design education: New education models and emerging topics in fashion design. The Routledge companion to fashion studies, 90-98.

Bruno, C., & Canina, M. (2019). CREATIVITY 4.0. EMPOWERING CREATIVITY IN THE DIGITAL ERA. In *DS 95: Proceedings of the 21st International Conference on Engineering and Product Design Education (E&PDE 2019), University of Strathclyde, Glasgow. 12th-13th September 2019.*

Bruno, C., & Canina, M. (2020). Developing a Method for Understanding How to Empower Creativity Through Digital Technologies: The Case of AI. In *Advances in Creativity, Innovation, Entrepreneurship and Communication of Design: Proceedings of the AHFE 2020 Virtual Conferences on Creativity, Innovation and Entrepreneurship, and Human Factors in Communication of Design, July 16-20, 2020, USA* (pp. 113-120). Springer International Publishing.

Casciani, D., & D'Itria, E. (2024). Fostering Directions for Digital Technology Adoption in Sustainable and Circular Fashion: Toward the Circular Fashion-Tech Lab. *Systems*, *12*(6), 190.

Colombi, C., & Casciani, D. (2021). Fashion-Tech Alliance: Innovating professional digital competences and skills in the Fashion Industry. In INTED2021 Proceedings (pp. 7842-7852). IATED.

Conlon, J., & Gallery, C. (2024). Developing digital skills: A fashion business masterclass in virtual 3D prototyping with Style3D. *International Journal of Fashion Design, Technology and Education*, *17*(1), 76–85.

Cugini, U., Bordegoni, M., & Mana, R. (2008). The role of virtual prototyping and simulation in the fashion sector. [IJIDeM]. *International Journal on Interactive Design and Manufacturing*, *2*, 33–38.

D'Amico, S., Giustiniano, L., Nenni, M. E., & Pirolo, L. (2013). Product Lifecycle Management as a tool to create value in the fashion system. *International Journal of Engineering Business Management*, *5*, 33.

Dai, L. (2011, July). The 3D digital technology of fashion design. In 2011 international symposium on computer science and society (pp. 178-180). IEEE.

Drakou, A., Papachristou, E., Tarnanidis, T., & Bilalis, N. (2024). Transforming Fashion Education: The Impact of AI-Driven 3D Design on Learning, Creativity, and Sustainability. *Proceedings of the 13th Hellenic Conference on Artificial Intelligence*, 1–6. https://doi.org/DOI: 10.1145/3688671.3688794

Ermer, C. (2018). Implementing sustainable thinking and acting into design-and textile education—A holistic and interdisciplinary learning model. Trends in Textile Engineering, 1(2).

Faculty of Computing and Information Technology. King Abdulaziz University, Jeddah, Saudi Arabia, Alshahrani, K., & Jameel Qureshi, R. (2024). Review the Prospects and Obstacles of AIEnhanced Learning Environments: The Role ofChatGPT in Education. *International Journal of Modern Education and Computer Science, 16*(4), 71–86. https://doi.org/DOI: 10.5815/ijmecs.2024.04.06

Faerm, S. (2012). Towards a future pedagogy: The evolution of fashion design education. *International Journal of Humanities and Social Science*, *2*(23), 210–219.

Faerm, S. (2014). From classroom to design room: The transitional experience of the fashion design graduate. *Cuadernos del Centro de Estudios en Diseño y Comunicación. Ensayos*, (48), 129–152.

Jeon, Y., Jin, S., Shih, P. C., & Han, K. (2021, May). FashionQ: an ai-driven creativity support tool for facilitating ideation in fashion design. In *Proceedings of the 2021 CHI Conference on Human Factors in Computing Systems* (pp. 1-18).

Kazlacheva, Z., Stoykova, V., Georgieva, K., & Ilieva, J. (2018, December). Application of innovative technologies in fashion design education. [). IOP Publishing.]. *IOP Conference Series. Materials Science and Engineering*, *459*(1), 012080.

Kohli, J. K. (2024). Impact of Artificial Intelligence on Fashion Education for Future Jobs. *Higher Education for the Future*, 23476311241284860.

Kwon, Y. M., Lee, Y. A., & Kim, S. J. (2017). Case study on 3D printing education in fashion design coursework. *Fashion and Textiles*, *4*, 1–20.

Lee, J. (2022). Toward Sustainable Fashion Product Development: The use of 3D Virtual Prototyping Technologies in the Synchronous Remote Learning Classroom. *Journal of Educational Technology Systems*, *51*(2), 215–235. DOI: 10.1177/00472395221132305

Lee, N., & Suh, S. (2024). How Does Digital Technology Inspire Global Fashion Design Trends? Big Data Analysis on Design Elements. *Applied Sciences (Basel, Switzerland)*, *14*(13), 5693.

Lee, Y. K. (2021). Transformation of the innovative and sustainable supply chain with upcoming real-time fashion systems. *Sustainability*, *13*(3), 1081.

Manzo, D. S. H., Jiang, Y., Elyan, E., & Isaacs, J. (2024). Artificial Intelligence-Based Conversational Agents Used for Sustainable Fashion: Systematic Literature Review. *International Journal of Human-Computer Interaction*, 1–13.

Marku, E. (2023). *AI-Artifcial Intelligence and the Growth of the Creative Potential of Designers in the Fashion Industry*. INTERDISCIPLINARY JOURNAL OF ARCHITECTURE AND BUILT ENVIRONMENT.

McQuillan, H. (2020). Digital 3D design as a tool for augmenting zero-waste fashion design practice. *International Journal of Fashion Design, Technology and Education*, *13*(1), 89–100.

Mohiuddin Babu, M., Akter, S., Rahman, M., Billah, M. M., & Hack-Polay, D. (2024). The role of artificial intelligence in shaping the future of Agile fashion industry. *Production Planning and Control*, *35*(15), 2084–2098.

Noia, E., Silvia, P. B., Mazzucotelli Salice, S., Carini, L., & Angeles, B. P. M. (2024). Digital, international, interdisciplinary learning: enhancing competences and changing mindsets about sustainability in fashion and food. Ciencias sociales en abierto, 1-14.

Okeleke, P. A., Ajiga, D., Folorunsho, S. O., & Ezeigweneme, C. (2024). Predictive analytics for market trends using AI: A study in consumer behavior. *International Journal of Engineering Research Updates*, *7*(1), 36–49.

Papahristou, E., & Bilalis, N. (2017). 3D virtual prototyping traces new avenues for fashion design and product development: A qualitative study. *Journal of Textile Science & Engineering*, *7*(2), 1–6.

Ridler, S. J. (2020). The designer perspective: Opportunities and Obstacles toward circular fashion.

Rissanen, T. (2017). Possibility in fashion design education—A manifesto. *Utopian Studies*, *28*(3), 528–546.

Rizzi, G., & Vandi, A. (2023). ARTIFICIAL INTELLIGENCE IN FASHION DESIGN EDUCATION: REDEFINING CREATIVE PROCESSES TOWARDS DESIGNER-AI CO-CREATION. In ICERI2023 Proceedings (pp. 3905-3912). IATED.

Sánchez-López, I., Bonilla-del-Río, M., & Soares, I. D. O. (2021). Digital Creativity to Transform Learning: Empowerment from a Com-Educational Approach. *Comunicar: Media Education Research Journal*, *29*(69), 105–114.

Särmäkari, N. (2023). Digital 3D fashion designers: Cases of atacac and the fabricant. *Fashion Theory*, *27*(1), 85–114.

Sehnem, S., Troiani, L., Lara, A. C., Guerreiro Crizel, M., Carvalho, L., & Rodrigues, V. P. (2024). Sustainable fashion: Challenges and barriers for advancing the circular economy. *Environment, Development and Sustainability*, *26*(2), 4097–4118.

Terra, A. C. W. (2021). Blockchain as a tool to improving work condition in the fashion supply chain. *Master's dissertation, COPPEAD Graduate School of Business, Universidade Federal do Rio de Janeiro.*

Vartak, A., Khot, A., Rane, S., Naik, P., & Mundye, G. (2024, May). Virtual Stylist Using IOT. In *2024 3rd International Conference on Artificial Intelligence For Internet of Things (AIIoT)* (pp. 1-4). IEEE.

Vishwakarma, A., Mehrotra, D., Agrahari, R., Kharub, M., Gupta, S., & Jagtap, S. (2024). Breaking barriers: paving the path to sustainable fashion–insights for a greener apparel and textile sector. *Journal of Advances in Management Research.*

Volino, P., Cordier, F., & Magnenat-Thalmann, N. (2005). From early virtual garment simulation to interactive fashion design. *Computer Aided Design*, *37*(6), 593–608.

Yezhova, O., Pashkevich, K., & Manoilenko, N. V. (2018). Comparative analysis of foreign models of fashion education. Revista Românească pentru Educaţie Multidimensională.

Yildirim, Y., Camci, F., & Aygar, E. (2023). Advancing Self-Directed Learning Through Artificial Intelligence. In Mncube, D. W., & Maphalala, M. C. (Eds.), (pp. 146–157). Advances in Higher Education and Professional Development. IGI Global., DOI: 10.4018/978-1-6684-6772-5.ch009

Zhang, H., & Lee, Y. (2020). Variations and types of high-tech fashion. *Journal of the Korea Fashion and Costume Design Association*, *22*(2), 117–136.

Zhaoyan, & Renli. (2011). Interdisciplinary Education Model of Fashion Marketing and E-Commerce. In Communication Systems and Information Technology: Selected Papers from the 2011 International Conference on Electric and Electronics (EEIC 2011) in Nanchang, China on June 20-22, 2011, Volume 4 (pp. 789-793). Springer Berlin Heidelberg.

Chapter 8
Revolutionizing Vocational Education: Harnessing Transformational AI Tools for Enhanced Learning and Skill Development

Liu Wenpang
https://orcid.org/0009-0009-1542-4870
Liaocheng Infant Normal School, China

Goh Ying Yingsoon
https://orcid.org/0000-0002-6654-2887
Universiti Teknologi MARA, Malaysia

Nurul Ajleaa Binti Abdul Rahman
Universiti Teknologi MARA, Malaysia

Nurul Ain Chua Binti Abdullah
https://orcid.org/0000-0003-2915-1577
University Terengganu Malaysia, Malaysia

Zhang Suyan
https://orcid.org/0009-0003-4518-1650
Shandong Jianzhu University, China

Chen Yiming
Shenzhen University, China

Tie Xiaoyao
Qilu Institute of Technology, China

ABSTRACT

The integration of transformational AI tools into vocational education is reshaping how skills are taught, learned, and applied in real-world contexts. This chapter explores the transformative potential of artificial intelligence in vocational training, focusing on its ability to personalize learning experiences, enhance skill acquisition, and bridge the gap between education and industry demands. By examining cutting-edge AI applications such as adaptive learning platforms, intelligent tutoring systems, virtual reality simulations, and AI-driven career guidance tools, this

DOI: 10.4018/979-8-3373-5102-5.ch008

chapter highlights how these technologies are fostering more engaging, efficient, and equitable vocational education. Additionally, it addresses the challenges and ethical considerations of implementing AI in this domain, including issues of accessibility, data privacy, and the need for human-AI collaboration. Ultimately, this chapter underscores the critical role of AI in creating a future-ready vocational education system that empowers individuals to thrive in a rapidly changing world.

MISSION AND FOCUS OF THE CHAPTER

The mission of this chapter is to explore the transformative potential of artificial intelligence (AI) in revolutionizing vocational education, with a focus on enhancing learning outcomes and skill development for a rapidly evolving workforce. Vocational education, which bridges the gap between academic knowledge and practical skills, faces challenges such as outdated curricula, limited access to personalized learning, and insufficient alignment with industry needs. This chapter addresses these issues by examining how AI-driven tools—such as adaptive learning platforms, virtual reality (VR) simulations, and intelligent tutoring systems—can create more engaging, efficient, and scalable vocational training programs.

This chapter challenges readers to envision a future where AI not only enhances vocational education but also redefines the roles of learners, educators, and industries, emphasizing a human-centered approach. By exploring the practical implications—such as personalized learning pathways, ethical considerations, and industry alignment—it urges stakeholders to critically assess how AI can address real-world challenges while fostering equity and inclusivity in education.

KEY THEMES AND CONCERNS

Vocational education plays a critical role in equipping individuals with the practical skills and knowledge needed to thrive in the workforce. However, traditional vocational training systems often struggle to keep pace with the rapid advancements in technology and shifting industry demands. This chapter explores how transformational AI tools can address these challenges, revolutionizing vocational education by making it more personalized, accessible, and aligned with the needs of the modern economy. The significance of this topic lies in its potential to bridge the global skills gap, enhance employability, and foster inclusive economic growth. By leveraging

AI, vocational education can transition from a one-size-fits-all model to a dynamic, learner-centric approach that prepares individuals for the jobs of tomorrow.

For instance, in healthcare, AI-powered simulations and diagnostic tools enable vocational students to practice complex procedures in risk-free environments, addressing the critical need for skilled professionals while reducing training costs. However, over-reliance on AI in construction training, such as automated machinery operation, may inadvertently widen socio-economic gaps if access to advanced technology remains uneven, raising ethical concerns about equitable skill development.

INTRODUCTION

Revolutionizing vocational education is essential in the modern economy, where skilled workers are in high demand. Traditional vocational training systems face numerous challenges, including outdated curricula, limited access to resources, and one-size-fits-all teaching methods. The integration of transformational AI tools offers a promising solution to these issues by providing personalized learning experiences, real-time feedback, and immersive simulations. This chapter aims to explore the potential of AI in enhancing vocational education, outline the objectives of this transformative approach, and present a structured overview of how AI can be harnessed to develop advanced skills and promote lifelong learning.

The rapid evolution of Industries driven by AI and automation has created an urgent demand for a workforce equipped with advanced technical and adaptive skills, making the transformation of vocational education not just beneficial but essential. AI offers a lifeline by enabling real-time skill alignment with industry needs, ensuring learners are prepared for jobs that are evolving faster than traditional curricula can adapt.

The Importance of Vocational Education in the Modern Economy

Vocational education stands as a cornerstone in the modern economy, providing a bridge between classroom learning and practical, job-ready skills that are crucial for addressing industry demands, fostering innovation, and ensuring economic resilience. By harnessing transformational AI tools, vocational training can be revolutionized to deliver personalized, immersive learning experiences that not only accelerate skill acquisition but also adapt to the evolving landscape of the workforce, thereby empowering students with the expertise and adaptability needed to thrive in their chosen fields and contribute meaningfully to society. (Kovalchuk et al., 2022).

AI ensures vocational training remains relevant by aligning curricula with the demands of the gig economy and automation, such as through adaptive learning platforms that teach in-demand skills like data analysis and machine learning, as seen in partnerships between universities and tech companies like Amazon and Deloitte. For instance, AI-driven tools like Khanmigo provide personalized tutoring and real-time feedback, preparing students for dynamic labor markets while addressing skill gaps in industries like healthcare and logistics (ETS, 2023).

Challenges in Traditional Vocational Training Systems

Traditional vocational training systems face significant challenges that hinder their effectiveness in preparing individuals for the modern workforce. These challenges include outdated equipment and facilities that do not reflect current industry standards, a lack of flexibility in course offerings that fails to accommodate diverse learning styles and schedules, limited access to hands-on training opportunities due to resource constraints, and a disconnect between educational content and the evolving demands of the job market, leading to a skills gap that leaves graduates ill-prepared for contemporary employment. (Köhler, & Drummer, 2018).

Outdated facilities in vocational education often leave students ill-prepared for modern workplaces, as seen in cases where learners trained on obsolete machinery struggle to adapt to advanced technologies used in industries like manufacturing and construction. The one-size-fits-all model further exacerbates disparities, failing to address the diverse needs of learners—such as those with disabilities or from low-income backgrounds—highlighting the urgent need for AI-driven personalized learning solutions that can bridge these gaps effectively.

The Role of AI in Addressing These Challenges

AI plays a pivotal role in addressing the challenges of vocational education by offering adaptive learning platforms that tailor instruction to individual student needs, simulating real-world scenarios through virtual and augmented reality, and providing data-driven insights for curriculum development and skill gap analysis. This integration of AI not only enhances the efficiency and effectiveness of vocational training but also democratizes access to quality education, ensuring that learners from diverse backgrounds can acquire in-demand skills and remain competitive in the rapidly transforming job market. (Ejjami, 2024; Çela et al., 2025; Liow, 2025; Thakur et al., 2025).

Adaptive learning platforms aim to address systemic inequities by providing personalized, scalable solutions that cater to diverse learning paces and styles, yet their effectiveness is often limited by unequal access to digital infrastructure, particularly in underfunded schools and rural areas. While VR and AR simulations offer immersive, hands-on training, their high costs and technical requirements make them inaccessible to many underfunded vocational programs, exacerbating existing disparities in educational quality. Barriers to AI adoption, such as the financial burden of implementation, the need for extensive educator training, and resistance to change from traditional teaching methods, further hinder the equitable integration of AI in vocational education.

Chapter Objectives and Structure

This chapter is structured to delve into the transformative potential of AI in vocational education, with the objective of outlining how AI can create personalized learning pathways, immersive experiences, and align training with industry needs. We will present case studies and evidence to support these claims, explore practical applications for various stakeholders including educational institutions, corporations, policymakers, and the global workforce, and address the ethical considerations and challenges that arise with AI integration. The final section will look to the future, discussing emerging trends and potential directions for the continued evolution of vocational education through AI.

Policymakers can create supportive frameworks by investing in digital infrastructure, establishing ethical guidelines for AI use, and fostering partnerships between educational institutions and tech companies to ensure equitable access to AI tools. Educators can leverage AI to enhance teaching by using adaptive platforms to personalize learning while maintaining the human element through mentorship and critical thinking exercises, ensuring technology complements rather than replaces traditional pedagogy.

THE TRANSFORMATIVE POTENTIAL OF AI IN VOCATIONAL EDUCATION

The transformative potential of AI in vocational education is realized through the creation of personalized learning pathways with adaptive learning systems and customized skill development plans, immersive learning experiences via VR and AR simulations and gamification, and a seamless alignment with industry needs through predictive analytics for skill demand forecasting and AI-facilitated industry-academia collaboration. This comprehensive integration of AI tools not only elevates the quality and relevance of vocational training but also empowers learners with the agility and proficiency required to succeed in their careers.

Educators can maintain their critical role by using AI as a supplementary tool to enhance personalized learning while focusing on fostering creativity, critical thinking, and ethical awareness through interactive discussions, project-based learning, and real-world problem-solving activities. By integrating AI-driven insights with human mentorship, educators can create a balanced approach that leverages technology to support, rather than overshadow, the development of essential human skills.

Personalized Learning Pathways

Personalized learning pathways are revolutionized by adaptive learning systems that dynamically adjust to a student's pace and performance, ensuring that each learner receives education tailored to their unique needs and strengths. Complementing this, customized skill development plans are crafted to map out individual career trajectories, providing a structured yet flexible approach to mastering vocational skills, thereby enhancing the overall educational experience and preparing students for specific industry roles. (Yekollu et al., 2024; Zhou, & Zhou, 2024).

Adaptive learning has been shown to improve retention rates by tailoring content to individual learning paces, as seen in programs like Squirrel AI, which reported a 30% increase in student performance, while also enhancing job placement by aligning skills with industry demands (Yekollu et al., 2024; Zhou, & Zhou, 2024). However, challenges such as maintaining the flexibility of customized skill development plans and ensuring their relevance in fast-evolving industries highlight the need for continuous updates and collaboration between educators and industry leaders.

Adaptive Learning Systems

Adaptive learning systems in vocational education are sophisticated platforms designed to modify the learning experience in real-time based on a student's interactions, performance, and learning preferences. These systems utilize advanced algorithms to analyze data and adjust the curriculum, providing resources, and support that cater to each learner's individual progress and needs. By doing so, adaptive learning systems enhance the efficiency and effectiveness of vocational training, ensuring that students acquire the necessary skills and knowledge at their own pace, which is essential for success in a diverse range of trades and professions.

Adaptive learning systems in vocational education can be seen in various examples that tailor the educational experience to the individual needs of students (Zhao et al., 2024) (refer Table 1).

Table 1 Adaptive learning systems in vocational education

Number	Type	Elaboration
1	Automotive Technician Training	An adaptive learning platform might assess a student's proficiency in engine repair and, based on their performance, suggest more advanced modules on electronic fuel injection systems or provide additional practice on basic engine components.
2	Culinary Arts Programs	In a culinary school, an adaptive learning system could track a student's knife skills and adjust the curriculum to focus more on different cutting techniques if needed, or move on to more complex tasks like sauce preparation if the student demonstrates mastery.
3	Healthcare Vocational Courses	For students training to be medical assistants, the system could monitor their understanding of patient intake procedures and adapt the content to focus on areas where the student is struggling, such as taking vital signs or updating patient records.
4	Information Technology Certifications	Adaptive learning software might analyze a student's progress in network configuration and automatically offer more challenging exercises on network security if the student excels, or provide additional support and resources on network troubleshooting if they encounter difficulties.
5	Welding and Metal Fabrication	An adaptive learning tool could assess a student's welding technique and suggest personalized training modules that focus on improving their bead consistency or provide more advanced training on different welding positions and materials once a certain level of proficiency is achieved.

These examples illustrate how adaptive learning systems can dynamically adjust the educational content and delivery to meet the unique learning paths of vocational students, optimizing their training experience and readiness for the workforce.

Customized Skill Development Plans

Customized skill development plans in vocational education are tailored to the individual strengths, weaknesses, and career aspirations of each student. These plans are crafted to ensure that learners acquire the specific competencies needed for their chosen trades (AI4VET4AI, n.d.; Shen et al., 2024). Examples are shown in Table 2.

Table 2. Customized skill development plans in vocational education

Number	Plan	Elaboration
1	Electrical Apprenticeship Programs	A customized plan might start with foundational courses in electrical theory and safety, then progress to hands-on training in residential wiring. As the apprentice demonstrates proficiency, the plan could evolve to include more complex commercial and industrial installations, as well as specialized areas like solar panel installation or smart home technology, based on the apprentice's interests and career goals.
2	Hairdressing and Cosmetology Schools	Students could begin with a broad range of styling techniques, but as they identify their strengths and preferences, their plan might focus on areas such as coloring, extensions, or cutting-edge styling methods. The plan could also incorporate business management courses for those aiming to open their own salons.
3	Construction Trades Education	A student interested in becoming a carpenter might start with basic woodworking and framing, with their plan evolving to include advanced cabinetry, fine finishing, or even architectural millwork, depending on their progress and career objectives.
4	Automotive Training Centers	A customized skill development plan might involve initial training in engine maintenance and repair, with subsequent modules that could range from specializing in diesel engines to focusing on electric vehicle technology, depending on the student's performance and the industry's demand.
5	Hospitality and Tourism Vocational Schools	A student's plan might begin with foundational courses in customer service and front desk operations, with the option to specialize in areas like event planning, culinary arts, or hotel management as they advance, aligning with their career aspirations within the hospitality sector.

These plans are dynamic, with regular assessments and feedback loops to ensure that the training remains relevant and effective, helping students to not only acquire the necessary skills but also to develop a personalized career path within their vocational field.

Immersive Learning Experiences

Revolutionizing vocational education through the integration of transformational AI tools, immersive learning experiences are at the forefront of enhanced learning and skill development; virtual reality (VR) and augmented reality (AR) simulations create realistic training environments that replicate real-world scenarios, allowing students to practice and refine their skills in a safe and controlled atmosphere, while gamification in skill training transforms monotonous tasks into engaging challenges, fostering a competitive and motivating atmosphere that drives students to excel and master their crafts.

While VR and AR offer immersive training experiences, they often fail to account for cultural differences, such as varying workplace norms or language barriers, which can limit their effectiveness in global vocational training programs. Gamification, though effective in boosting short-term engagement, risks losing its impact over time if not paired with meaningful content and real-world relevance, highlighting the need for a balanced approach that sustains long-term motivation.

Virtual Reality (VR) and Augmented Reality (AR) Simulations

Virtual Reality (VR) and Augmented Reality (AR) technologies have become increasingly important tools in vocational education. They offer a range of benefits that enhance the learning experience, provide realistic training scenarios, and improve skill acquisition. Here's how VR and AR can be applied in vocational education (Long et al., 2024; Chiang et al., 2021) (refer Table 3).

Table 3. Benefits of VR and AR in vocational education

Number	Benefit	Elaboration
1	Safe and Controlled Training Environment	Students can practice in a virtual environment without the risks associated with real-world training.
2	Realistic Scenarios	Simulations can closely mimic real-life situations, providing students with practical experience.
3	Cost-Effective	VR and AR can reduce the costs associated with materials, equipment, and travel.
4	Accessibility	Students can access training from anywhere, making education more flexible.
5	Personalized Learning	The technology can adapt to the pace and learning style of individual students.
6	Tracking and Assessment	Educators can monitor student progress and provide feedback based on the virtual interactions.

In the realm of vocational education, the integration of Virtual Reality (VR) and Augmented Reality (AR) has significantly enhanced training across various sectors. For instance, in healthcare, VR is used to simulate surgeries and emergency scenarios, while AR overlays anatomical details onto the physical world for medical students. In engineering and manufacturing, VR allows for the practice of operating intricate machinery, complemented by AR's real-time guidance for maintenance. Automotive and aviation industries benefit from VR simulations of driving and flying, with AR aiding in the repair of vehicles by superimposing digital data onto the physical parts. Construction and trades utilize VR for safety and design training, and AR for overlaying blueprints on worksites. Culinary arts students can engage in VR kitchen simulations and receive AR cooking instructions, while those in hospitality and tourism can experience VR-based hotel management training and AR-enhanced travel information. (refer Table 4). (Leong et al., 2023).

Table 4. Applications of VR and AR in vocational education

Number	Aspect	Examples
1	Healthcare Training	- VR: Simulate surgeries, patient interactions, and emergency response scenarios. - AR: Overlay anatomical information onto a real-world view for medical students.
2	Engineering and Manufacturing	- VR: Practice operating complex machinery or assembly line work. - AR: Provide real-time instructions and guides for maintenance and repair tasks.
3	Automotive and Aviation	- VR: Simulate driving, flying, and vehicle repair tasks. - AR: Assist technicians with maintenance and repair by overlaying digital information onto physical objects.
4	Construction and Trades	- VR: Train in construction site safety, architecture design, and building processes. - AR: Overlay blueprints and project data onto the actual worksite for better visualization and planning.
5	Culinary Arts	- VR: Simulate kitchen environments and cooking processes. - - AR: Provide step-by-step cooking instructions and visualizations of techniques.
6	Hospitality and Tourism	- VR: Train in hotel management, customer service, and tourist guiding in virtual environments. - - AR: Enhance travel experiences with historical and cultural information overlays.

To effectively implement VR and AR in vocational education, a systematic approach is essential, beginning with a needs assessment to pinpoint the skills best suited for simulation training. This is followed by the careful selection of appropriate technology that aligns with educational objectives and financial constraints. Content development then takes center stage, with the creation or acquisition of customized VR and AR simulations that complement the curriculum. Educators must be trained to adeptly use these tools, after which pilot programs can be launched to test the simulations with a select group of students. Feedback and iteration are crucial steps to refine the simulations based on user input. Finally, the integration of VR and AR into the regular curriculum allows for a comprehensive assessment of their impact on learning outcomes. (refer Table 5). (Mimbus, n.d.).

Table 5. Implementation steps

Number	Step	Elaboration
1	Needs Assessment	Identify the vocational skills that would benefit most from VR and AR training.
2	Technology Selection	Choose the right hardware and software that fit the educational goals and budget.
3	Content Development	Create or purchase high-quality VR and AR simulations tailored to the curriculum.
4	Training for Educators	Ensure that educators are proficient in using the technology and can integrate it into their teaching.
5	Pilot Programs	Test the simulations with a small group of students before full-scale implementation.
6	Feedback and Iteration	Collect feedback from students and educators to refine the simulations.
7	Integration	Incorporate VR and AR into the regular curriculum and assess its impact on learning outcomes.

The adoption of VR and AR in vocational education faces several challenges, including the high cost of high-quality equipment, which can be a barrier for many educational institutions. Additionally, technical issues such as glitches can interfere with the learning process, potentially undermining the value of the technology. The quality of the content is also a critical factor, as subpar simulations may fail to provide an effective learning experience. Furthermore, there may be resistance to adoption from both educators and students, who might be hesitant to embrace these new technological tools in traditional educational settings. (refer Table 6). (Kablitz et al., 2023).

Table 6. Challenges

Number	Aspect of challenge	Elaboration
1	Cost	High-quality VR and AR equipment can be expensive.
2	Technical Issues	Glitches and technical problems can disrupt the learning experience.
3	Content Quality	The effectiveness of the simulations depends on the quality of the content.
4	Adoption	There may be resistance from educators and students to adopt new technologies.

In summary, VR and AR simulations can revolutionize vocational education by providing immersive, interactive, and practical training experiences. As the technology continues to evolve, it is likely to play an even more significant role in preparing students for the demands of the modern workforce.

Gamification in Skill Training

Gamification in skill training for vocational education involves the integration of game design elements and principles into the learning process to enhance engagement, motivation, and retention among students. By incorporating features such as points, levels, challenges, and rewards, gamification transforms routine training exercises into interactive and competitive activities that mimic the excitement and focus typically found in games. This approach can significantly improve the effectiveness of vocational education (refer Table 7). (Rosunally, 2024).

Table 7. Gamification in skill training for vocational education

Number	Gain	Elaboration
1	Increasing Engagement	Gamification makes learning more enjoyable and absorbing, which can lead to higher levels of participation and focus from students.
2	Fostering Competition	Friendly competition among students can drive them to excel and improve their skills, as they strive to achieve higher scores or complete tasks faster than their peers.
3	Providing Immediate Feedback	Games often offer immediate feedback, allowing students to understand their progress and correct mistakes in real-time, which is crucial for skill development.
4	Encouraging Mastery	Gamification can break down complex skills into manageable levels or missions, encouraging students to master each step before moving on.
5	Promoting Collaboration	Many gamified training programs include team-based challenges, which can teach students the importance of collaboration and teamwork in a vocational setting.
6	Facilitating Learning Transfer	The interactive and practical nature of gamified training can help students apply their skills more easily to real-world scenarios.

However, it is important to ensure that gamification is aligned with the educational goals and that it does not overshadow the serious nature of vocational training. When implemented thoughtfully, gamification can be a powerful tool in preparing students for the demands of their future careers.

Alignment with Industry Needs

To ensure vocational education remains aligned with industry needs, predictive analytics for skill demand forecasting is employed to anticipate future job market trends, allowing educational institutions to tailor their curricula accordingly. Additionally, industry-academia collaboration is enhanced through the use of AI, which facilitates the exchange of knowledge, resources, and expertise, bridging the gap between classroom learning and industry practices to better prepare students for the evolving workforce.

Predictive Analytics for Skill Demand Forecasting

Predictive analytics for skill demand forecasting in vocational education utilizes advanced algorithms and data analysis to project future job market trends, enabling educational institutions to proactively adjust their training programs and curricula. By identifying emerging skills and sectors with high employment potential, vocational schools can ensure their students are equipped with the relevant competencies needed to succeed in a rapidly changing labor market, thereby enhancing employment outcomes and meeting industry demands. (Sghir et al., 2023). (refer Table 8).

Table 8. Applications in vocational education

Number	Area	Elaboration
1	Curriculum Design	Predictive analytics can inform the development of AI-focused courses by identifying the most in-demand skills. This ensures that students are equipped with relevant competencies for the job market.
2	Resource Allocation	Institutions can use predictive insights to allocate resources effectively, such as investing in AI labs or hiring specialized instructors.
3	Student Success Prediction	By analyzing student performance data, predictive models can identify at-risk students and recommend interventions to improve outcomes.

Industry-Academia Collaboration Through AI

Industry-academia collaboration through AI in vocational education leverages intelligent systems to foster seamless partnerships between educational institutions and industry leaders. This collaboration facilitates the exchange of real-time data, insights, and best practices, allowing vocational programs to align their training with industry standards and technological advancements. As a result, students benefit from up-to-date skills development that is directly relevant to current and future job market requirements, enhancing their employability and the overall effectiveness of vocational education. (Chen & Zhang, 2022, refer Table 9)

Table 9. Industry-academia collaboration through AI in vocational education

Number	Aspect	Elaboration
1	Role of AI in Industry-Academia Collaboration	AI technologies, such as machine learning, natural language processing, and predictive analytics, are being used to enhance collaboration between vocational institutions and industries. These technologies enable the analysis of industry trends, skill demands, and workforce requirements, allowing educational institutions to align their curricula with real-world needs. For example, AI-driven platforms can predict future skill demands and recommend curriculum adjustments to ensure students are equipped with relevant competencies.
2	Practical Applications	Curriculum Development: AI helps identify gaps in existing curricula by analyzing industry data and student performance. This ensures that vocational training programs are up-to-date and aligned with industry standards. Skill Demand Forecasting: Predictive analytics powered by AI can forecast emerging skill requirements, enabling institutions to proactively design courses that meet future industry demands. Work-Integrated Learning: AI facilitates the creation of virtual internships and simulations, allowing students to gain hands-on experience in a controlled environment. This bridges the gap between academic learning and practical application.
3	Case Study: Industry-Academia Collaboration in China	In China, the integration of AI into vocational education has been a key focus under the "Industry-Education Integration" framework. For instance, Beijing Union University has implemented AI-driven platforms to analyze industry trends and adjust its vocational training programs accordingly. This approach has significantly improved the employability of graduates by ensuring they possess the skills demanded by the job market.
4	Challenges and Future Directions	While AI-enhanced IAC offers numerous benefits, challenges such as data privacy, technological infrastructure, and the need for skilled personnel must be addressed. Future research should focus on developing robust frameworks for AI-driven collaboration and exploring the long-term impact of these technologies on vocational education outcomes

CASE STUDIES AND EVIDENCE OF AI IN VOCATIONAL EDUCATION IN CHINA

The integration of AI in vocational education in China has demonstrated significant potential to enhance learning outcomes, improve practical skills, and address the evolving needs of the job market. However, overcoming challenges related to technology, privacy, and teacher training will be essential for realizing the full benefits of AI in this field. (refer Table 10).

Table 10. Case studies and evidence of AI in vocational education in China

Number	Aspect	Elaboration
1	Application of AI in Vocational Training (Shen et al., 2024)	AI technologies, such as virtual reality (VR), augmented reality (AR), natural language processing (NLP), and speech recognition, are being integrated into vocational education to provide immersive and personalized learning experiences. For instance, VR and AR technologies enable students to simulate real work scenarios, enhancing their practical skills and ability to handle complex situations. NLP and speech recognition facilitate interactive learning by providing real-time feedback and answering student queries, thereby improving learning outcomes.
2	Generative AI in Vocational Education (Xie et al., 2024)	Generative AI has shown significant potential in transforming vocational education by creating personalized learning plans and adaptive teaching methods. A study highlights that generative AI can analyze the skill requirements of various vocational disciplines and provide tailored training approaches, such as AI general education and AI-embedded education. This has led to improved alignment between vocational training and industry needs.
3	Digital Transformation in Vocational Colleges (China National Academy of Educational Sciences, 2024)	Wuhan University of Technology has implemented a data-driven digital transformation strategy in vocational education. This initiative focuses on four key areas: work philosophy, governance methods, education and teaching, and comprehensive evaluation. By leveraging AI and big data, the university has enhanced the quality and efficiency of vocational training, providing a model for other institutions.
4	Challenges and Countermeasures (Zhou et al., 2024)	Despite the advancements, the integration of AI in vocational education faces challenges such as data privacy concerns, technological limitations, and the need for teacher training. To address these issues, measures such as transforming educational concepts, enhancing teachers' technical capabilities, and strengthening data privacy protection have been proposed.
5	Impact of New ICTs on Vocational Education (Cai & Qian, 2021)	New ICTs, including AI, have revolutionized vocational education by enabling cost-effective and high-quality online education services. A case study of Wuxi Vocational Institute of Commerce demonstrates how ICT-driven innovations have improved accessibility and affordability of vocational training, particularly for students in remote areas.
6	Future Trends and Investment (Deloitte, n.d.)	The AI-enabled education sector in China is experiencing rapid growth, with significant investments in intelligent adaptive education platforms. Companies like VIPKID and Squirrel AI are leading the way by developing innovative solutions that cater to diverse learning needs. This trend is expected to continue, with a focus on refining human-machine interaction models and expanding into tier-two and tier-three cities.
7	Policy and Regulatory Framework (Zhou et al., 2024; Deloitte, n.d.)	The Chinese government has been proactive in promoting AI in education through policies and regulations. However, there is a need for clearer guidelines to ensure ethical use of AI and equitable distribution of educational resources. This will be crucial for the sustainable development of AI-based vocational education.

PRACTICAL APPLICATIONS AND IMPLICATIONS

Revolutionizing vocational education through the integration of transformational AI tools holds significant implications across various sectors: for educational institutions, it means an opportunity to design more personalized and adaptive curricula that cater to the diverse learning styles and needs of students, thereby improving outcomes and preparing them for the dynamic job market; for corporate training and upskilling, AI can facilitate more efficient and effective training programs tailored to the specific demands of evolving industries, ensuring that employees remain competitive and skilled; policymakers and governments can leverage these technologies to align educational policies with future labor market requirements, fostering a skilled workforce that drives economic growth and innovation; and on a global scale, AI-driven vocational education can democratize access to quality training, narrowing the skills gap and promoting inclusive workforce development across borders.

For Educational Institutions

For educational institutions, the adoption of transformational AI tools represents a pivotal shift in vocational education, enabling the creation of immersive and interactive learning environments that can simulate real-world scenarios and enhance practical skill acquisition. These institutions can now offer personalized learning paths that adapt to each student's progress and learning preferences, ensuring that educational content is both relevant and engaging. Furthermore, AI can assist educators in identifying knowledge gaps and areas for improvement, allowing for more targeted instruction and support, which ultimately leads to higher retention rates and improved job readiness among graduates. (Shen et al., 2024, refer Table 11).

Table 11. Practical applications and implications for educational institutions on AI in vocational education

Number	Aspect	Elaboration
1	Personalized Learning and Adaptive Systems	AI enables the creation of personalized learning pathways by analyzing student data and tailoring content to individual needs. Adaptive learning systems adjust the difficulty of tasks in real-time, ensuring students are neither overwhelmed nor under-challenged. This approach enhances engagement and improves learning outcomes by addressing the unique strengths and weaknesses of each student.
2	Immersive Training with VR and AR	Virtual reality (VR) and augmented reality (AR) technologies, powered by AI, provide immersive training environments that simulate real-world scenarios. For example, vocational students can practice operating machinery or performing medical procedures in a risk-free virtual setting. This not only enhances practical skills but also builds confidence in handling complex situations.
3	Predictive Analytics for Student Success	AI-driven predictive analytics helps institutions identify at-risk students by analyzing performance data. Early interventions, such as targeted support or additional resources, can be implemented to improve retention rates and ensure student success. This proactive approach is particularly valuable in vocational education, where practical skills are critical.
4	Streamlined Administrative Processes	AI automates routine administrative tasks, such as admissions, grading, and scheduling, allowing institutions to allocate more resources to teaching and learning. For instance, AI tools can process applications, generate feedback, and optimize class schedules based on student enrollment and instructor availability.
5	Industry-Academia Collaboration	AI facilitates collaboration between educational institutions and industries by analyzing labor market trends and skill demands. This ensures that vocational training programs remain relevant and aligned with industry needs, improving the employability of graduates.

For Corporate Training and Upskilling

For corporate training and upskilling, the integration of transformational AI tools revolutionizes the approach to employee development by providing scalable, on-demand learning experiences tailored to the specific needs of the organization and its workforce. These AI-driven platforms can efficiently assess individual skill levels, identify training gaps, and deliver customized programs that accelerate skill acquisition and retention, ensuring that employees remain competitive in a rapidly evolving market. By leveraging AI for continuous learning, companies can also foster a culture of innovation, improve operational efficiency, and effectively adapt to industry disruptions, ultimately leading to a more agile and skilled workforce. (Observer, 2024, refer Table 12).

Table 12. Corporate training and upskilling for AI in vocational education

Number	Aspects	Elaboration
1	Personalized Learning Paths	AI enables the creation of personalized learning experiences by analyzing individual employee data, such as learning pace, strengths, and weaknesses. This tailored approach ensures that training programs are relevant and effective, addressing specific skill gaps and enhancing employee engagement. For example, AI-powered platforms can generate adaptive learning paths that adjust in real-time based on the learner's progress, providing additional resources or advanced materials as needed.
2	Skill Gap Identification and Targeted Training	AI tools can analyze workforce data to identify skill gaps and recommend targeted training programs. This data-driven approach ensures that employees acquire the skills needed to meet organizational goals. For instance, AI can predict future skill demands and design training modules to prepare employees for emerging roles, such as data analysts transitioning to AI-driven insights architects.
4	Immersive and Interactive Learning	AI-powered technologies, such as virtual reality (VR) and augmented reality (AR), are being used to create immersive training environments. These tools simulate real-world scenarios, allowing employees to practice skills in a safe and controlled setting. This is particularly beneficial for industries requiring hands-on training, such as healthcare and manufacturing.
5	Ethical and Responsible AI Use	As AI becomes more integrated into corporate training, it is essential to address ethical considerations, such as data privacy and bias. Training programs must include modules on responsible AI use, ensuring that employees understand how to leverage AI tools ethically and effectively.

For Policymakers and Governments

For policymakers and governments, the incorporation of transformational AI tools in vocational education presents a strategic opportunity to align training programs with national economic priorities and labor market demands. By investing in AI-enhanced vocational education, policymakers can facilitate the seamless transition of learners into the workforce, reduce unemployment rates, and stimulate economic growth. Additionally, these tools can inform data-driven policy decisions, ensuring that educational initiatives are not only responsive to current industry needs but also capable of anticipating future skill requirements, thereby fostering a sustainable and resilient workforce that can adapt to the challenges of the 21st century. (European Commission, 2021, refer Table 13).

Table 13. For policymakers and governments on AI in vocational education

Number	Aspects	Elaboration
1	Policy Frameworks for Ethical AI Implementation	Policymakers must establish robust frameworks to ensure the ethical use of AI in vocational education. This includes addressing issues such as data privacy, algorithmic transparency, and equity. For instance, UNESCO's guidance emphasizes the importance of ethical principles like accountability, responsibility, and transparency (ART principles) in AI systems to safeguard student rights and ensure fair access to educational resources.
2	Bridging the Gap Between Research and Practice	There is a need to bridge the gap between AI research and its practical application in vocational education. Policymakers should facilitate collaborations between researchers, educators, and industry stakeholders to develop AI-driven solutions that align with real-world skill demands. Workshops and initiatives, such as those proposed by the Center for Integrative Research on Computer and Learning Sciences (CIRCLS), can help identify global challenges and opportunities for AI in education.
3	Investment in AI Infrastructure and Training	Governments should invest in AI infrastructure and provide training for educators to effectively integrate AI into vocational education. This includes funding for AI labs, digital tools, and professional development programs. For example, the European Union's Erasmus+ program has supported projects like "Taccle AI," which focuses on improving the skills of vocational teachers in the age of AI.
4	Adaptive and Iterative Policy Development	AI technologies evolve rapidly, requiring adaptive and iterative policy frameworks. Policymakers should adopt flexible approaches that allow for continuous updates based on emerging trends and feedback from stakeholders. The TeachAI Policy Tracker provides foundational policy ideas and resources to help policymakers craft responsible AI policies for education.
5	Global Collaboration and Knowledge Sharing	Policymakers should promote global collaboration and knowledge sharing to address the challenges of AI in vocational education. International partnerships, such as those facilitated by UNESCO, can help develop standardized guidelines and best practices for AI implementation in education.

For Global Workforce Development

For global workforce development, the integration of transformational AI tools in vocational education represents a pivotal advancement, enabling a more skilled and adaptable labor force across the world. These AI-driven learning solutions can transcend geographical boundaries, offering standardized and accessible training to individuals in both developed and developing countries. As a result, global workforce development can benefit from a more equitable distribution of opportunities, reduced skill mismatches, and enhanced cross-cultural competencies, ultimately leading to a more interconnected and productive global economy. (Grit Daily, 2025, refer Table 14).

Table 14. For global workforce development in AI for vocational education

Number	Aspects	Elaboration
1	Addressing Job Displacement and Creating New Opportunities	AI is transforming the global workforce by automating traditional jobs while simultaneously creating new roles. For instance, while AI is expected to displace 85 million jobs by 2025, it will also create 97 million new jobs, many of which will require advanced technical and AI-related skills. This shift underscores the importance of vocational education in equipping workers with the skills needed to thrive in an AI-driven economy.
2	Upskilling and Reskilling the Workforce	Vocational education programs are increasingly incorporating AI to provide upskilling and reskilling opportunities. For example, AI-powered platforms offer personalized learning paths, enabling workers to acquire new skills efficiently. This is particularly critical for industries undergoing rapid technological changes, such as manufacturing, healthcare, and logistics.
3	Global Collaboration and Knowledge Sharing	AI is facilitating global collaboration in vocational education by enabling the sharing of best practices and resources across borders. For instance, international partnerships and online platforms are leveraging AI to deliver training programs that address global skill gaps. This approach ensures that vocational education remains relevant and accessible to diverse populations.
4	Immersive Learning with AI Technologies	AI-driven technologies, such as virtual reality (VR) and augmented reality (AR), are revolutionizing vocational training by providing immersive, hands-on learning experiences. These tools simulate real-world scenarios, allowing learners to practice skills in a safe and controlled environment. This is particularly beneficial for high-risk industries, such as construction and healthcare.
5	Ethical and Inclusive Workforce Development	As AI becomes more integrated into vocational education, it is essential to address ethical considerations, such as data privacy and bias. Policymakers and educators must ensure that AI-driven training programs are inclusive and accessible to all, regardless of socioeconomic background or geographic location.

ETHICAL CONSIDERATIONS AND CHALLENGES

Revolutionizing vocational education through the integration of transformational AI tools promises to enhance learning and skill development, yet this technological leap necessitates careful navigation of ethical considerations and challenges. Data privacy and security are paramount, requiring robust safeguards to protect sensitive student information; algorithmic bias and fairness demand continuous scrutiny to prevent discrimination and ensure equitable outcomes; and the necessity of equitable access to AI tools underscores the importance of inclusive educational policies to avoid exacerbating existing socio-economic disparities.

Data Privacy and Security

In the realm of vocational education, the integration of AI tools necessitates stringent measures to protect data privacy and security. With the collection and analysis of vast amounts of personal and performance data, educational institutions must implement advanced encryption, secure storage protocols, and access controls to prevent unauthorized use or breaches. Transparency in data handling practices and compliance with regulatory frameworks such as GDPR or FERPA are crucial to maintain the trust of students and stakeholders, ensuring that sensitive information is not misused and that the integrity of the educational process is upheld. (Tejeswar, n.d.,; Huris, 2024, refer Table 15).

Table 15. GDPR and FERPA in AI use for vocational education

Number	Aspects	Elaboration
1	Key Principles of GDPR and FERPA	GDPR: This EU regulation emphasizes transparency, data minimization, and user consent. It requires that personal data, including student information, be collected and processed only for specific, legitimate purposes. GDPR also grants individuals the right to access, rectify, and erase their data, which is crucial for vocational education platforms using AI to personalize learning experiences. FERPA: A U.S. law, FERPA protects the privacy of student education records. It restricts the disclosure of personally identifiable information (PII) without consent and ensures that students and parents have access to their records. AI tools in vocational education must comply with FERPA by securing student data and limiting its use to authorized purposes.
2	Challenges in AI Implementation	Data Privacy Risks: AI systems in vocational education often collect and process large amounts of sensitive data, such as academic performance, behavioral patterns, and personal identifiers. Ensuring compliance with GDPR and FERPA requires robust data protection measures, including encryption, access controls, and regular audits. Ethical Concerns: AI algorithms can inadvertently introduce biases, leading to unfair outcomes for students. Both GDPR and FERPA emphasize fairness and accountability, requiring institutions to audit AI systems for bias and ensure equitable treatment of all learners.
3	Practical Applications and Compliance Strategies	Data Minimization: Vocational education platforms should collect only the data necessary for AI functionality, adhering to GDPR's principle of data minimization. For example, AI tools can anonymize or pseudonymize data to protect student identities while still enabling personalized learning. Transparency and Consent: Under GDPR, institutions must obtain explicit consent from students or their guardians before collecting or processing data. FERPA similarly requires written consent for sharing student records with third parties, including AI vendors. Security Measures: Implementing end-to-end encryption (E2EE) and multi-factor authentication (MFA) can help secure student data, ensuring compliance with both GDPR and FERPA.
4	Future Directions	Adaptive Policies: As AI technologies evolve, vocational education institutions must adopt adaptive policies to address emerging privacy challenges. This includes staying updated on regulatory changes and integrating privacy-by-design principles into AI development. Global Collaboration: Institutions operating across borders must navigate the complexities of both GDPR and FERPA. Collaborative frameworks and standardized guidelines can help streamline compliance and ensure consistent data protection practices.

Algorithmic Bias and Fairness

Revolutionizing vocational education with transformational AI tools promises to enhance learning and skill development by personalizing curricula, simulating real-world scenarios, and providing immediate feedback, yet it also introduces the critical challenge of algorithmic bias and fairness. Ensuring that these AI systems are designed and implemented with ethical guidelines and rigorous testing is essential to prevent discrimination and promote equitable outcomes, allowing all students to benefit from the advanced educational opportunities irrespective of their background. (China et al., 2024; Baker & Hawn, 2022, refer Table 16).

Table 16. Algorithmic bias and fairness in AI use of vocational education

Number	Aspects	Elaboration
1	Understanding Algorithmic Bias in Vocational Education	Algorithmic bias occurs when AI systems produce unfair or discriminatory outcomes due to flaws in the data, algorithms, or their implementation. In vocational education, this can manifest in various ways, such as biased predictions of student performance, unfair allocation of resources, or discriminatory recommendations for career paths. For example, AI-driven systems may disproportionately flag students from marginalized groups as "at-risk" based on biased historical data, leading to unfair interventions or stigmatisation.
2	Common Forms of Bias in AI Systems	Data-Related Bias: AI systems trained on datasets that reflect historical inequalities or underrepresentation can perpetuate these biases. For instance, if a dataset predominantly includes data from certain demographic groups, the AI may perform poorly for underrepresented groups. Algorithmic Bias: The design of algorithms can introduce bias, especially when sensitive attributes like race, gender, or socioeconomic status are correlated with other features in the data. User-Interaction Bias: The way AI tools are implemented and used in vocational education can also introduce bias. For example, educators may over-rely on AI recommendations without critically evaluating their fairness.
3	Impact of Bias on Vocational Education	Algorithmic bias in vocational education can exacerbate existing inequalities by: Reinforcing Stereotypes: AI systems may recommend career paths based on biased data, steering students toward or away from certain fields based on their demographic background. Limiting Opportunities: Biased predictions of student performance can lead to missed opportunities for students from marginalized groups, such as being excluded from advanced training programs. Creating Self-Fulfilling Prophecies: If AI systems consistently flag certain groups as "at-risk," educators may treat these students differently, reinforcing negative outcomes.
4	Strategies for Mitigating Bias	To address algorithmic bias in vocational education, stakeholders can adopt the following strategies: Diverse and Representative Data: Ensure that training datasets are inclusive and representative of all student populations to reduce data-related bias. Fairness-Aware Algorithms: Develop and implement algorithms that explicitly account for fairness, such as those that minimize disparities in outcomes across demographic groups. Continuous Monitoring and Auditing: Regularly evaluate AI systems for bias and update them to address any identified issues. Collaborative Efforts: Foster collaboration between educators, developers, and policymakers to create ethical guidelines and standards for AI use in vocational education.
5	Ethical and Policy Considerations	Ensuring fairness in AI systems requires a commitment to ethical principles and robust policy frameworks. For example, the EU AI Act mandates bias audits for high-risk AI applications, including those used in education. However, practical implementation remains a challenge, highlighting the need for clear guidelines and accountability measures.

Ensuring Equitable Access to AI Tools

Revolutionizing vocational education means leveraging transformational AI tools to create a dynamic and personalized learning environment that accelerates skill development and job readiness. By ensuring equitable access to these AI-driven resources, we democratize opportunity, allowing learners from diverse backgrounds to benefit from advanced simulations, adaptive learning pathways, and real-time feedback, thereby bridging the gap between education and industry demands while fostering a more inclusive and proficient workforce. (Zaman, 2023; OnlineEducation, 2024, refer Table 17).

Table 17. Ensuring equitable access to AI tools for vocational education

Number	Aspects	Elaboration
1	Addressing the Digital Divide	The digital divide remains a significant barrier to equitable access to AI tools in vocational education. Marginalized communities often lack the necessary infrastructure, such as high-speed internet and digital devices, to fully utilize AI-driven learning platforms. For example, rural areas in developing countries face challenges in accessing reliable connectivity, which limits their ability to participate in digital learning environments.
2	Strategies for Equitable Access	Infrastructure Investment: Governments and educational institutions must prioritize investments in digital infrastructure, particularly in underserved regions. This includes expanding broadband access and providing affordable or free digital devices to students. Inclusive Design: AI tools should be designed with inclusivity in mind, ensuring they are accessible to learners with disabilities and those from diverse cultural and linguistic backgrounds. For instance, AI platforms can incorporate features like speech-to-text, auto-captioning, and multilingual support to cater to a wider audience. Subsidized Programs: Offering subsidized or free access to AI-driven vocational training programs can help level the playing field for low-income students. Public-private partnerships can play a key role in funding these initiatives.

FUTURE DIRECTIONS AND EMERGING TRENDS

Revolutionizing vocational education through the integration of transformational AI tools is a pivotal step toward equipping learners with the skills necessary for the modern workforce. As AI continues to evolve, its potential applications in vocational education are vast, promising to enhance learning outcomes, personalize education, and bridge the gap between education and industry demands. Here are some future directions and emerging trends in this field (refer Table 18). (Collegenp, 2025; Ravaglia, 2024; World of TVET, 2024).

Table 18. Future directions and emerging trends

Personalized Learning Pathways		
1	Adaptive Learning Systems	AI can tailor educational content to the individual learning styles, paces, and prior knowledge of students, ensuring that each learner receives a personalized educational experience.
2	Intelligent Tutoring Systems (ITS)	These systems can provide one-on-one tutoring, adjusting their teaching strategies based on the learner's responses and progress.
Immersive Learning Environments		
1	Virtual Reality (VR) and Augmented Reality (AR	These technologies can simulate real-world vocational scenarios, allowing learners to practice skills in a safe and controlled environment.
2	Mixed Reality (MR)	MR can blend physical and digital worlds, enabling hands-on training in situations that would be impractical or dangerous in real life.
Enhanced Assessment and Feedback		
1	Automated Grading	AI can assess complex tasks and provide instant feedback, allowing learners to improve their skills more efficiently.
2	Skill Profiling	AI can analyze a learner's performance across various tasks to identify strengths and areas for improvement, informing future learning paths.
Integration with Industry 4.0		
1	Robotics and Automation	Vocational education will increasingly incorporate training on how to work alongside robots and automated systems.
2	Data Analytics	Teaching learners how to interpret and utilize big data will become essential as industries become more data-driven.
Accessibility and Inclusivity		
1	Language Translation and Captioning	AI can make vocational education more accessible to non-native speakers and those with hearing impairments.
2	Assistive Technologies	AI can help learners with disabilities by providing tools that adapt to their unique needs.
Emerging Trends		
AI-Driven Curriculum Development		
1	Real-Time Updates	AI can continuously update curricula based on the latest industry standards and technological advancements.
2	Predictive Analytics	AI can predict future job market trends, guiding educators in developing courses that align with future employment needs.
3	AI-Driven Personalized Learning Systems	AI is revolutionizing vocational education by enabling personalized learning experiences. Adaptive learning platforms use AI to analyze student performance and tailor content to individual needs, ensuring that no student is left behind. This approach enhances engagement, motivation, and retention, making learning more effective and efficient.

continued on following page

Table 18. Continued

4	AI-Powered Career Guidance and Skill Forecasting	AI is being used to analyze labor market data and predict future skill demands, helping vocational institutions design curricula that align with industry needs. AI-driven career guidance systems provide personalized recommendations based on students' skills and interests, ensuring they are well-prepared for the job market
5	AI Agents and Autonomous Systems	AI agents are expected to play a significant role in vocational education by automating administrative tasks, providing personalized tutoring, and enhancing student-teacher interactions. These agents will act as virtual assistants, helping students navigate complex tasks and providing real-time feedback.
Collaborative Learning Platforms		
1	Global Classrooms	AI can facilitate international collaboration, allowing vocational students to learn from and work with peers and experts worldwide.
2	Peer Learning Networks	AI can help to create and manage peer-to-peer learning communities, enhancing the exchange of knowledge and skills.
Ethical and Social Implications		
1	Ethical AI Education	As AI becomes more prevalent, vocational education will need to include training on the ethical use of AI in various professions.
2	Social Skills Development	While AI can enhance technical skills, there will be a focus on the development of soft skills, which AI cannot replicate.
Lifelong Learning and Reskilling		
1	Microcredentials	AI can help design and deliver microcredentials that allow learners to quickly upskill or reskill in specific areas.
2	Just-in-Time Learning	AI platforms can provide on-demand training for specific tasks or skills as needed in the workplace.

In conclusion, the future of vocational education lies in the seamless integration of AI tools that not only enhance the learning experience but also ensure that learners are equipped with the most relevant and advanced skills for their chosen professions. As these trends continue to evolve, educators, policymakers, and industry leaders must collaborate to create a vocational education system that is adaptable, inclusive, and future-ready.

REFERENCES

AI4VET4AI. (n.d.). Transforming vocational training: The essential role of AI in employee skill development. https://www.ai4vet4ai.eu/news/transforming-vocational-training-the-essential-role-of-ai-in-employee-skill-development/

Baker, R. S., & Hawn, A. (2022). Algorithmic Bias in Education. *International Journal of Artificial Intelligence in Education, 32*, 1052–1092. DOI: 10.1007/s40593-021-00285-9

Cai, J., & Qian, X. (2021). Effect of New ICTs on Vocational Education in China: A Case Study of Wuxi Vocational Institute of Commerce. In Kosaka, M., Wu, J., Xing, K., & Zhang, S. (Eds.), *Business Innovation with New ICT in the Asia-Pacific: Case Studies*. Springer., DOI: 10.1007/978-981-15-7658-4_11

Çela, E., Vajjhala, N. R., Eappen, P., & Vedishchev, A. (2025). Artificial Intelligence in Vocational Education and Training. In Transforming Vocational Education and Training Using AI (pp. 1-16). IGI Global Scientific Publishing.

Chen, J., & Zhang, M. (2022). Exploration and research on industry-education integration of vocational education in AI era. *Advances in Vocational and Technical Education, 4*, 41–47. DOI: 10.23977/avte.2022.040306

Chiang, F.-K., Shang, X., & Qiao, L. (2021). Augmented reality in vocational training: A systematic review of research and applications. *Computers in Human Behavior, 129*, 107125. DOI: 10.1016/j.chb.2021.107125

China National Academy of Educational Sciences. (2024). Practical Cases of Smart Education in China: Data-Driven Curriculum and Research Innovation in Higher Education and Vocational Education. In *Report on China Smart Education 2023. Research in Chinese Education*. Springer., DOI: 10.1007/978-981-97-5090-0_5

Chinta, S. V., Wang, Z., Yin, Z., Hoang, N., Gonzalez, M., Quy, T. L., & Zhang, W. (2024). FairAIED: Navigating fairness, bias, and ethics in educational AI applications. arXiv preprint arXiv:2407.18745.

Collegenp. (2025). The future of vocational education: Emerging trends and technologies. https://www.collegenp.com/article/the-future-of-vocational-education-emerging-trends-and-technologies

Deloitte. (n.d.). Development of AI-based education in China. Retrieved January 18, 2025, from https://www2.deloitte.com/cn/en/pages/technology-media-and-telecommunications/articles/development-of-ai-based-education-in-china.htm

Ejjami, R. (2024). AI's impact on vocational training and employability: Innovation, challenges, and perspectives. [IJFMR]. *International Journal for Multidisciplinary Research*, *6*(4), 1–16.

ETS. (2023). Education and tech leaders come together to offer guidance on integrating AI safely into classrooms worldwide. https://www.ets.org/news/press-releases/education-and-tech-leaders-come-together-to-offer-guidance-on-integrating-ai-safely-into-classrooms-worldwide.html

European Commission. (2021). AI and education: Guidance for policymakers. https://school-education.ec.europa.eu/en/discover/publications/ai-and-education-guidance-policymakers

Grit Daily. (2025). The role of AI education in global workforce development. https://gritdaily.com/role-of-ai-education-in-global-workforce-development/

Hurix. (2024). Data privacy in education through FERPA and GDPR adherence. https://www.hurix.com/data-privacy-in-education-through-ferpa-and-gdpr-adherence/

Kablitz, D., Conrad, M., & Schumann, S. (2023). Immersive VR-based instruction in vocational schools: Effects on domain-specific knowledge and wellbeing of retail trainees. *Empirical Research in Vocational Education and Training*, *15*, 9. DOI: 10.1186/s40461-023-00148-8

Köhler, T., & Drummer, J. (2018). Recent technological challenges in (vocational) education. Vocational Teacher Education in Central Asia: Developing Skills and Facilitating Success, 3-14.

Kovalchuk, V., Maslich, S. V., Tkachenko, N., Shevchuk, S. S., & Shchypska, T. P. (2022). Vocational education in the context of modern problems and challenges. *Journal of Curriculum and Teaching*, *8*(11), 329–338.

Leong, W. Y., Leong, Y. Z., & Leong, W. S. (2023). Virtual reality in education: Case studies and applications. *IET International Conference on Engineering Technologies and Applications (ICETA 2023)*, 186–187. https://doi.org/DOI: 10.1049/icp.2023.3332

Liow, M. L. S. (2025). Artificial Intelligence Shaping the Future of Vocational Education and Training: Roles, Impacts, and Insights. In Transforming Vocational Education and Training Using AI (pp. 183-210). IGI Global Scientific Publishing.

Long, Y., Zhang, X., & Zeng, X. (2024). Application and effect analysis of virtual reality technology in vocational education practical training. *Education and Information Technologies*. DOI: 10.1007/s10639-024-13197-7

Mimbus. (n.d.). Enhancing education: VR use cases for vocational training. https://blog.mimbus.com/en/enhancing-education-vr-use-cases-for-vocational-training

Observer. (2024, September). How generative AI is transforming workforce development and corporate training.https://observer.com/2024/09/how-generative-ai-is-transforming-workforce-development-corporate-training/

OnlineEducation. (2024). Opportunities and guidelines for AI in education: Statistics.https://www.onlineeducation.com/features/opportunities-and-guidelines-for-ai-in-education-statistics

Ravaglia, R. (2024, December 26). AI agents will shape every aspect of education in 2025. Forbes. https://www.forbes.com/sites/rayravaglia/2024/12/26/ai-agents-will-shape-every-aspect-of-education-in-2025/

Rosunally, Y. Z. (2024). Harnessing generative AI for educational gamification: A framework and practical guide for educators. 2024 21st International Conference on Information Technology Based Higher Education and Training (ITHET), 1–8. DOI: 10.1109/ITHET61869.2024.10837655

Sghir, N., Adadi, A., & Lahmer, M. (2023). Recent advances in Predictive Learning Analytics: A decade systematic review (2012–2022). *Education and Information Technologies*, *28*, 8299–8333. DOI: 10.1007/s10639-022-11536-0 PMID: 36571084

Shen, Y., Liu, Q., Zhang, K., & Zou, R. (2024). The Application of Artificial Intelligence Technology in Vocational College Training. In Paas, F., Patnaik, S., & Wang, T. (Eds.), *Recent Trends in Educational Technology and Administration. EduTA 2023. Learning and Analytics in Intelligent Systems* (Vol. 38). Springer., DOI: 10.1007/978-3-031-60777-6_11

Tejeswar. (n.d.). Understanding GDPR and data privacy in AI educational tools. Medium. Retrieved January 18, 2025, from https://medium.com/@tejeswar_79802/understanding-gdpr-and-data-privacy-in-ai-educational-tools-6e576eaa6d16

Thakur, G. S. M., Banerjee, A., & Sarkar, P. (2025). AI in Vocational Education and Training: Technologies and Applications. In Transforming Vocational Education and Training Using AI (pp. 49-72). IGI Global Scientific Publishing.

World of TVET. (2024). TVET and AI. https://www.worldoftvet.com/blog/tvet-and-ai

Xie, H., Tao, L., & Xie, L. (2024, February 21). Research on prospective scope and approaches of artificial intelligence education in vocational college of China. In *Proceedings of the 3rd International Conference on Education, Language and Art (ICELA 2023)* (pp. 484–492). Atlantis Press. https://doi.org/DOI: 10.2991/978-2-38476-214-9_59

Yekollu, R. K., Bhimraj Ghuge, T., Sunil Biradar, S., Haldikar, S. V., & Farook Mohideen Abdul Kader, O. (2024). AI-Driven Personalized Learning Paths: Enhancing Education Through Adaptive Systems. In Asokan, R., Ruiz, D. P., & Piramuthu, S. (Eds.), *Smart Data Intelligence. ICSMDI 2024. Algorithms for Intelligent Systems.* Springer., DOI: 10.1007/978-981-97-3191-6_38

Zaman, B. U. (2023). Transforming education through AI, benefits, risks, and ethical considerations. Institute of Electrical and Electronics Engineers (IEEE). Retrieved from Institute of Electrical and Electronics Engineers (IEEE) website:DOI: 10.36227/techrxiv.24231583.v1

Zhao, S., Hai, G., & Ma, H. (2024). Adaptive learning systems: Exploring personalized paths in vocational education. *Curriculum Learning and Exploration*, *2*(2). Advance online publication. DOI: 10.18686/cle.v2i2.3720

Zhou, H., & Zhou, D. (2024). Transformation of vocational education based on generative artificial intelligence: Impact, opportunity, and countermeasures. *Proceedings of the 3rd International Conference on Internet Technology and Educational Informatization (ITEI 2023)*, November 24–26, 2023, Zhengzhou, China. EAI. https://doi.org/DOI: 10.4108/eai.24-11-2023.2343636

ADDITIONAL READINGS

Rosyadi, M. I., Kustiawan, I., Tetehfio, E. O., & Joshua, Q. (2023). The Role of AI In Vocational Education: A Systematic Literature Review. *Journal of Vocational Education Studies*, *6*(2), 244–263.

Suparyati, A., Widiastuti, I., Saputro, I. N., & Pambudi, N. A. (2023). The Role of Artificial Intelligence (AI) in Vocational Education. JIPTEK: Jurnal Ilmiah Pendidikan Teknik dan Kejuruan, 17(1).

Wu, X. (2021, April). Application of artificial intelligence in modern vocational education technology. [). IOP Publishing.]. *Journal of Physics: Conference Series*, *1881*(3), 032074.

Zhang, M., & Chen, J. (2022). Exploration and research on industry-education integration of vocational education in AI era. *Advances in Vocational and Technical Education*, *4*(3), 41–47.

KEY TERMS AND DEFINITIONS

AI in vocational education: AI in vocational education refers to the integration of artificial intelligence technologies into vocational and technical training programs to enhance the learning experience, personalize instruction, and improve outcomes for students preparing for specific trades, crafts, or careers.

Adaptive learning platforms: Adaptive learning platforms are educational technology systems that tailor the learning experience to the individual needs of each student. These platforms use algorithms to analyze a student's interactions, performance, and learning preferences to dynamically adjust the content, sequence, and presentation of educational material.

Intelligent tutoring systems (ITS): Intelligent tutoring systems are AI-based computer programs designed to simulate the one-on-one interaction of a human tutor. These systems provide personalized instruction, feedback, and guidance to learners, often in the form of questions, explanations, and hints, to help students master specific subjects or skills.

Virtual reality simulations: Virtual reality (VR) simulations are immersive experiences that replicate real-world environments or scenarios, allowing users to interact with the virtual environment as if they were in the actual situation. In vocational education, VR simulations are used to provide hands-on training and practice in a safe, controlled, and repeatable setting.

Skill development: Skill development refers to the process of acquiring and improving specific abilities, competencies, or proficiencies through training, practice, and experience. In vocational education, skill development is a core focus, aiming to prepare individuals with the practical abilities needed for employment in a particular trade or profession.

Workforce readiness: Workforce readiness, also known as employability, refers to the level of preparation and competence that individuals have to enter and succeed in the workforce. It encompasses a range of skills, including job-specific skills, foundational skills (like literacy and numeracy), and soft skills (such as communication, teamwork, and problem-solving). Workforce readiness is a critical goal of vocational education, ensuring that graduates are equipped to meet the demands of the job market.

Chapter 9
AI for Data-Driven Decision Making in Education

Dayna Lynn Mitchell
https://orcid.org/0009-0000-9385-7238
California State Polytechnic University, Pomona, USA

ABSTRACT

This chapter will explore the role of artificial intelligence (AI) in data-driven decision-making within educational settings, highlighting how AI can enhance the process of collecting, analyzing, and interpreting vast amounts of data to inform strategic choices. By leveraging AI-powered tools, educators and administrators can gain deeper insights into student performance, engagement, attendance, and other critical metrics, enabling more informed, timely, and personalized decisions. The chapter will examine the benefits of AI in improving educational outcomes, such as identifying at-risk students, optimizing resource allocation, and supporting evidence-based policy development. Additionally, it will address the challenges and ethical considerations associated with using AI for decision-making, including data privacy, algorithmic bias, and the need for transparency and accountability.

INTRODUCTION

The advent of artificial intelligence (AI) has brought about significant changes in various sectors, and education is no exception. In recent years, AI has emerged as a powerful tool for data-driven decision-making in educational settings, offering unprecedented opportunities for institutions to enhance the way they make decisions, allocate resources, and improve overall effectiveness (Alsbou & Alsaraireh, 2024;

DOI: 10.4018/979-8-3373-5102-5.ch009

Ashraf, 2024; Gade, 2021; Okokoyo & Nwachukwu, 2024). Traditional decision-making processes in education, often based on limited data or subjective judgment, are increasingly being supplemented—or even replaced—by AI-powered systems that can analyze vast amounts of data quickly and accurately. This shift is enabling educators, administrators, and policymakers to make more informed, precise, and timely decisions, ultimately benefiting students and enhancing educational outcomes.

AI's ability to process and analyze large volumes of data has the potential to revolutionize the way educational institutions operate (Ashraf, 2024). Traditionally, decision-making in education has been based on limited, often siloed data—test scores, attendance records, and anecdotal reports from teachers and staff. However, AI enables institutions to collect and analyze data from a wide range of sources, including student performance, engagement metrics, behavioral data, demographic information, and even external factors such as socio-economic background or community involvement. This holistic approach allows for a deeper understanding of student needs, enabling more personalized and targeted interventions that can significantly improve student outcomes (Alsbou & Alsaraireh, 2024).

One of the most compelling advantages of AI in education is its ability to provide real-time insights (Alsbou & Alsaraireh, 2024; Ashraf, 2024)). In traditional educational systems, decision-making can often be slow and reactive, with data collected at the end of a semester or academic year, leaving little room for timely interventions. AI, on the other hand, can process data in real-time, allowing educators and administrators to make immediate adjustments to teaching strategies, learning environments, and resource allocation. For example, if a student is struggling with a particular concept, AI-powered systems can flag this in real-time, enabling teachers to provide timely support and personalized instruction (Kavitha et al., 2025). Similarly, if a school is experiencing a drop in attendance or engagement, AI can identify the underlying causes and suggest corrective measures, preventing issues from escalating.

The chapter will explore the different types of data that AI can process and analyze, including both quantitative and qualitative data. Quantitative data, such as test scores, grades, and attendance records, has long been used in educational decision-making, but AI can now enhance this data by incorporating more complex variables. For instance, AI can analyze patterns in student performance over time, identifying trends that may not be immediately apparent to educators (Alsbou & Alsaraireh, 2024). It can also integrate data from various sources, such as learning management systems (Alotaibi, N. S. (2024), online assessments, and student feedback, to provide a more comprehensive view of student progress. Qualitative data, such as teacher observations, student surveys, and classroom interactions, can also be processed by AI to offer a more holistic understanding of the learning experience. By combining both types of data, AI can provide a more nuanced and accurate picture of student needs, enabling more effective decision-making.

In addition to the types of data that AI can process, the chapter will examine the various tools and techniques used in AI-driven analysis. Machine learning algorithms, for example, are a core component of many AI systems used in education (Alotaibi, 2024; Alsbou & Alsaraireh, 2024). These algorithms can identify patterns in data, make predictions about future outcomes, and recommend actions based on these insights. For example, a machine learning algorithm could predict which students are at risk of failing a course based on their performance data, allowing teachers to intervene early and provide additional support. Similarly, AI can be used to optimize resource allocation by analyzing data on classroom utilization, teacher workloads, and student needs, ensuring that resources are distributed in the most effective way possible.

Another important aspect of AI-driven decision-making is its ability to support personalized learning (Alotaibi, 2024; Alsbou & Alsaraireh, 2024; Ashraf, 2024). AI can help educators tailor their teaching strategies to meet the unique needs of individual students, providing a more customized and engaging learning experience. By analyzing data on student strengths, weaknesses, and learning preferences, AI can recommend personalized learning paths that help students progress at their own pace. For example, AI-powered tutoring systems can adapt to a student's level of understanding, providing targeted exercises and feedback to help them master specific skills. This level of personalization is difficult to achieve with traditional teaching methods, which often rely on a one-size-fits-all approach. AI allows for greater flexibility and adaptability, ensuring that all students receive the support they need to succeed.

At the institutional level, AI can help educational administrators make more informed decisions about resource allocation (Alsbou & Alsaraireh, 2024; Ashraf, 2024), staffing, and curriculum development. By analyzing data on student enrollment, graduation rates, and course demand, AI can help schools optimize their offerings, ensuring that they provide the right courses at the right times to meet student needs. AI can also be used to forecast future trends, such as changes in student demographics or shifts in the job market, enabling institutions to proactively adjust their strategies and stay ahead of emerging challenges. This level of foresight and planning is essential for educational institutions that want to remain competitive and relevant in an increasingly complex and dynamic environment.

The impact of AI on decision-making processes extends beyond individual classrooms and schools to larger educational systems. At the policy level, AI can be used to analyze data from across entire school districts or even national education systems, identifying trends and making recommendations for policy changes (Alsbou & Alsaraireh, 2024). For example, AI can help policymakers assess the effectiveness of different educational programs, identify gaps in access to quality education, and recommend strategies for improving equity and inclusion. By providing data-driven insights, AI can support evidence-based policy development, ensuring that decisions are grounded in objective analysis rather than political agendas or personal biases.

However, the integration of AI into educational decision-making also raises important ethical considerations (Ashraf, 2024). One of the primary concerns is data privacy and security. With AI systems processing large amounts of sensitive student data, it is crucial that educational institutions implement robust data protection measures to safeguard student privacy (Alsbou & Alsaraireh, 2024). Additionally, there are concerns about algorithmic bias, as AI systems are only as good as the data they are trained on (Okokoyo & Nwachukwu, 2024). If the data used to train AI models is biased or incomplete, the resulting recommendations may perpetuate existing inequalities in the education system. Therefore, it is essential that AI systems are designed and implemented with fairness, transparency, and accountability in mind.

This chapter will also explore the challenges and limitations of AI in education. While AI has the potential to greatly enhance decision-making processes, it is not a panacea. The success of AI-driven decision-making depends on the quality of the data being used, the accuracy of the algorithms, and the ability of educators and administrators to interpret and act on the insights provided by AI systems. Additionally, there is a need for ongoing professional development to ensure that educators and administrators are equipped with the skills and knowledge needed to effectively use AI tools.

AI has the potential to transform decision-making in education by providing more accurate, timely, and personalized insights into student performance, resource allocation, and institutional effectiveness (Okokoyo & Nwachukwu, 2024). By leveraging AI to analyze vast amounts of data, educational institutions can make more informed decisions that enhance student outcomes and improve overall effectiveness. However, the integration of AI into educational decision-making requires careful planning, ethical considerations, and ongoing research to ensure that these technologies are used responsibly and effectively. The chapter will provide a comprehensive overview of the current state of AI in education and offer practical insights into how these technologies can be harnessed to improve decision-making at all levels of education.

INTRODUCTION TO DATA-DRIVEN DECISION MAKING IN EDUCATION:

Data-driven decision-making (DDDM) in education refers to the practice of using data to inform decisions that affect various aspects of the educational process (Gade, 2021). This data can come from a variety of sources, including student assessments, attendance records, behavioral data, and even feedback from students, teachers, and parents. The primary aim of DDDM is to make decisions that are more objective, evidence-based, and focused on improving educational outcomes (Ashraf, 2024). Over the years, the importance of DDDM in education has grown as educators, administrators, and policymakers have realized that relying solely on intuition, experience, or anecdotal evidence is not enough to address the increasingly complex challenges facing educational systems (Gade, 2021). As the education landscape becomes more diverse and data-rich, the ability to analyze and interpret this data has become crucial for improving student performance, optimizing resource allocation, and enhancing institutional effectiveness (Okokoyo & Nwachukwu, 2024).

The role of data in informing decisions within educational contexts has expanded significantly in recent years. In traditional education systems, decisions regarding curriculum design, student support, resource allocation, and institutional planning were often made based on limited data or subjective judgment. Teachers and administrators would rely on their experiences and observations, but without comprehensive data to back up their decisions, there was always a risk of bias or inefficiency. However, with the advent of technology, educational institutions now have access to vast amounts of data that can provide a more accurate picture of student performance, resource utilization, and institutional needs (Okokoyo & Nwachukwu, 2024). By analyzing this data, schools and universities can make more informed decisions that are grounded in evidence rather than assumptions.

One of the key areas where data-driven decision-making plays a critical role is in curriculum design (Alsbou & Alsaraireh, 2024). Curriculum decisions, such as which subjects to offer, how to structure lessons, and what teaching methods to use, are often based on the collective experience of educators and policymakers. However, these decisions can be further enhanced by data that provides insights into how students are performing in different subjects, which teaching methods are most effective, and where students are struggling. For example, data on student performance in mathematics across multiple grade levels can help educators identify common areas of difficulty and adjust the curriculum to address those challenges. Additionally, data can be used to assess the effectiveness of different teaching strategies, helping educators refine their approaches to better meet the needs of diverse learners (Alotaibi, 2024). This data-driven approach to curriculum design allows for a more targeted and responsive educational experience, ensuring that the curriculum is relevant and effective in promoting student success.

In addition to curriculum design, data is also instrumental in student support. Educational institutions are increasingly recognizing the importance of providing personalized support to students, especially those who are at risk of falling behind or facing challenges in their academic journey. By analyzing data on student performance (Okokoyo & Nwachukwu, 2024), attendance, behavior, and engagement, schools can identify students who may need additional support and intervene early to prevent academic failure. For example, AI systems can track patterns in student behavior, such as frequent absences or declining grades, and flag students who may be at risk of dropping out. This allows for timely interventions, such as offering tutoring, counseling, or other resources, before the student's situation worsens. Moreover, data can help educators tailor their support strategies to individual students, ensuring that interventions are personalized and effective (Alotaibi, 2024). By leveraging data in this way, educational institutions can provide more proactive and targeted support, ultimately improving student outcomes and reducing dropout rates.

Resource allocation is another critical area where data-driven decision-making can make a significant impact (Alsbou & Alsaraireh, 2024). Educational institutions often face budget constraints and must make difficult decisions about how to allocate resources, such as funding for teachers, textbooks, technology, and facilities. By analyzing data on student enrollment, class sizes, teacher workloads, and resource utilization, schools can make more informed decisions about where to allocate resources for maximum impact. For example, data on student enrollment trends can help administrators predict future demand for courses and allocate resources accordingly (Alsbou & Alsaraireh, 2024). Similarly, data on classroom utilization can help optimize the use of physical space, ensuring that classrooms are being used efficiently and that resources are not wasted. AI can also help identify areas where resources are being underutilized or misallocated, allowing institutions to make adjustments that improve efficiency and effectiveness. By using data to guide resource allocation, educational institutions can ensure that their resources are being used in the most effective way possible, ultimately improving the quality of education and student outcomes.

Institutional planning is another area where data-driven decision-making plays a vital role (Gaftandzhieva et al., 2023). Educational institutions must constantly adapt to changing demographics, shifts in the job market, and evolving educational standards. By analyzing data on student enrollment, graduation rates, and employment outcomes, institutions can make more informed decisions about their long-term strategies and goals. For example, data on the demand for specific skills or industries can help universities design programs that align with the needs of the job market, ensuring that graduates are well-prepared for the workforce. Similarly, data on student success rates and retention can help identify areas where the institution needs to improve, such as student support services, curriculum design, or teaching methods. AI can also help forecast future trends, such as changes in student demographics or emerging technological advancements, enabling institutions to plan proactively and stay ahead of the curve. By integrating data into institutional planning, educational institutions can make more strategic decisions that align with their long-term vision and goals.

While traditional data-driven decision-making has already had a significant impact on education, the integration of AI is poised to take this process to the next level. AI can enhance traditional DDDM by processing and analyzing large, complex datasets more efficiently and accurately than human decision-makers alone. One of the key advantages of AI in this context is its ability to handle vast amounts of data at high speeds. Traditional data analysis methods often struggle to keep up with the sheer volume of data generated by educational institutions, especially when it comes to real-time data analysis. AI, on the other hand, can process and analyze data in real-time, providing immediate insights that can inform decision-making on the fly. This allows educators and administrators to make more timely decisions, leading to quicker interventions and better outcomes for students.

AI also enhances the accuracy and reliability of data analysis. While human decision-makers are often limited by cognitive biases, AI systems are capable of analyzing data objectively and without bias (Alsbou & Alsaraireh, 2024). For example, AI can identify patterns in student performance data that may not be immediately apparent to human analysts, such as subtle correlations between attendance and academic achievement. By removing human bias from the decision-making process, AI ensures that decisions are based on data-driven insights rather than personal assumptions or subjective judgments. Additionally, AI can improve the consistency of decision-making by applying the same analysis methods across large datasets, reducing the risk of inconsistencies that can arise from human error.

Furthermore, AI can help uncover hidden insights in data that might otherwise go unnoticed. For example, AI systems can identify trends in student performance (Okokoyo & Nwachukwu, 2024) across different demographic groups, allowing educators to address issues of equity and inclusion more effectively. AI can also analyze data from a variety of sources, such as online assessments, student surveys, and classroom interactions, to provide a more comprehensive view of student needs. This holistic approach to data analysis allows educators to make more informed decisions that take into account a wide range of factors, ultimately leading to better educational outcomes.

Data-driven decision-making is an essential practice in modern education, and AI is set to play a transformative role in enhancing this process. By leveraging AI to process and analyze large, complex datasets, educational institutions can make more informed, accurate, and timely decisions that improve student outcomes, optimize resource allocation, and enhance institutional effectiveness. AI can also help uncover hidden insights in data, improve the accuracy and consistency of decision-making, and provide real-time feedback that enables educators to intervene early and support students more effectively. As AI continues to evolve, its potential to revolutionize data-driven decision-making in education will only grow, offering new opportunities to improve educational systems and outcomes at all levels.

Types of Data in Education

Educational decision-making is increasingly reliant on data to ensure that the decisions made are informed, evidence-based, and ultimately lead to better outcomes for students. The vast amounts of data generated within educational institutions offer valuable insights into various aspects of the educational process, and understanding how to effectively use this data is critical to improving both individual and institutional performance. This chapter will explore the types of data that are most critical to educational decision-making, the importance of both quantitative and qualitative data, and how artificial intelligence (AI) can integrate data from multiple sources to provide a comprehensive view of student performance (Okokoyo & Nwachukwu, 2024).

One of the most fundamental types of data in educational decision-making is academic performance data. This data is typically gathered through assessments, grades, and standardized tests, and it serves as a key indicator of student achievement and progress. Academic performance data can provide educators and administrators with a clear picture of where students are excelling and where they may need additional support. For instance, by analyzing test scores and grades, schools can identify trends in performance, such as subject areas where students consistently perform poorly, and develop targeted interventions to address these gaps. This type of data is essential for making decisions about curriculum design, instructional strategies (Alotaibi, 2024), and student support services. However, academic performance data alone is not always sufficient to capture the full range of factors that influence student success.

Attendance data is another critical piece of the puzzle in educational decision-making. Regular attendance is strongly correlated with academic success (Al Hazaa et al., 2021), and monitoring attendance patterns can provide early indicators of potential academic or behavioral challenges. For example, frequent absences may signal that a student is struggling academically or facing personal challenges that are affecting their ability to engage with school. By analyzing attendance data, schools can intervene early and provide support to students who may be at risk of falling behind. Attendance data can also be used to assess the effectiveness of school policies or programs aimed at improving student engagement and reducing absenteeism. AI can enhance the analysis of attendance data by identifying patterns that might not be immediately apparent to human analysts, such as correlations between attendance and academic performance, and offering predictive insights that can help schools take proactive steps to address attendance-related issues.

Behavioral data is another important type of information that can inform educational decision-making. Behavioral data encompasses a wide range of information, including disciplinary records, engagement in classroom activities, participation in extracurricular programs, and interactions with peers and teachers. This data can help educators identify students who may be struggling with social or emotional challenges, which could be affecting their academic performance. For example, a student who frequently disrupts class may be dealing with underlying issues such as anxiety, bullying, or difficulties at home. By analyzing behavioral data, schools can provide targeted interventions, such as counseling or social-emotional learning programs, to address these challenges and improve student outcomes (Martins et al., 2022). AI can assist in processing behavioral data by recognizing patterns and predicting potential behavioral issues, allowing educators to intervene before problems escalate.

Demographic data also plays a significant role in educational decision-making (Yağcı, 2022). Demographic information includes details such as age, gender, socioeconomic status, ethnicity, and language proficiency, among others. This data is crucial for understanding the diverse needs of students and ensuring that educational interventions are equitable and inclusive. For instance, demographic data can help schools identify achievement gaps between different groups of students, such as those from low-income backgrounds or English language learners and implement targeted strategies to address these disparities. AI can help analyze demographic data in combination with academic performance and behavioral data to uncover insights into how different student groups are performing and where additional resources or support may be needed.

Feedback from students, teachers, and parents is another valuable source of data that can inform decision-making in education. Student feedback can provide insights into their experiences, challenges, and perceptions of the learning environment, helping educators understand what is working well and where improvements are needed. Teacher feedback is equally important, as teachers are often the first to identify students who may be struggling or who require additional support. Parent feedback is also essential, as parents can provide valuable information about a student's home life, behavior, and any external factors that may be influencing their performance. Collecting and analyzing feedback from all stakeholders helps create a more holistic understanding of a student's needs and can inform decisions related to teaching methods, classroom environment, and school policies. AI can assist in analyzing feedback data by processing large volumes of qualitative data, such as open-ended survey responses, and identifying key themes and trends that may not be immediately apparent.

In educational decision-making, both quantitative and qualitative data are important. Quantitative data, such as test scores, attendance records, and disciplinary data, provides measurable, objective insights into student performance and behavior (Okokoyo & Nwachukwu, 2024). This type of data is useful for identifying trends, making comparisons, and evaluating the effectiveness of specific interventions or programs. However, quantitative data alone may not fully capture the complexity of a student's experience or the factors that contribute to their success or challenges. Qualitative data, on the other hand, provides a more nuanced view of a student's needs and experiences. Feedback from students, teachers, and parents, as well as observations of classroom interactions, can offer valuable insights into the emotional, social, and cognitive factors that influence learning. Both types of data are essential for making informed decisions that take into account the full range of factors affecting student outcomes.

AI can enhance traditional data-driven decision-making by integrating and analyzing data from multiple sources. Educational institutions generate vast amounts of data from various platforms and systems, including learning management systems (LMS), standardized test scores, classroom assessments, and student surveys. Each of these sources provides a piece of the puzzle, but when analyzed in isolation, they may not offer a complete or accurate picture of student performance (Okokoyo & Nwachukwu, 2024). AI has the ability to integrate data from these diverse sources, providing a more holistic view of student achievement and needs. For example, AI can combine data from LMS platforms, which track students' interactions with course materials, with data from standardized tests, which measure academic proficiency, to provide a more comprehensive assessment of a student's learning progress. By analyzing data from multiple sources, AI can uncover hidden patterns and correlations that might not be immediately apparent, allowing educators and administrators to make more informed decisions.

One of the key advantages of AI in this context is its ability to process and analyze large datasets at scale. Traditional methods of data analysis often struggle to keep up with the sheer volume of data generated by educational institutions, especially as the use of digital tools and platforms continues to grow. AI, on the other hand, can process vast amounts of data quickly and efficiently, providing real-time insights that can inform decision-making. For example, AI-powered analytics tools can analyze student performance data (Okokoyo & Nwachukwu, 2024) from assessments, classroom activities, and online interactions to identify students who may be at risk of falling behind and suggest targeted interventions. AI can also track the effectiveness of these interventions over time, helping educators refine their strategies and improve student outcomes (Alotaibi, 2024).

AI can also enhance the personalization of educational interventions by analyzing data from multiple sources to create individualized learning profiles for students. By combining data on academic performance, attendance, behavior, and feedback, AI can identify each student's unique strengths, weaknesses, and learning preferences. This allows educators to tailor their teaching strategies and interventions to meet the specific needs of each student, ensuring that all students receive the support they need to succeed (Alotaibi, 2024).

In conclusion, the use of data in educational decision-making is essential for improving student outcomes, optimizing resource allocation, and enhancing institutional effectiveness. By analyzing a wide range of data, including academic performance, attendance, behavioral data, demographic information, and feedback from students, teachers, and parents, educational institutions can make more informed and targeted decisions. AI has the potential to revolutionize this process by integrating data from multiple sources and providing real-time insights that inform decision-making at all levels of education. By leveraging AI to analyze large, complex datasets, educational institutions can make more accurate, timely, and personalized decisions that improve student performance and overall educational outcomes (Okokoyo & Nwachukwu, 2024).

AI Tools and Techniques for Data Analysis

Artificial intelligence (AI) is revolutionizing the way educational institutions process and analyze data. With the ability to handle vast amounts of information quickly and efficiently, AI is becoming an indispensable tool for educators, administrators, and researchers seeking to improve student outcomes, optimize resource allocation, and enhance institutional effectiveness. This section will explore various AI tools and technologies that facilitate data analysis in education, including machine learning algorithms, predictive analytics (Esomonu, 2025; Okokoyo & Nwachukwu, 2024;), natural language processing (NLP), and data mining. By leveraging these technologies, educational institutions can gain deeper insights into student behavior, academic performance, and overall institutional trends, ultimately leading to more informed and effective decision-making.

One of the most powerful AI tools in education is machine learning (ML), a subset of AI that allows computers to learn from data and make predictions or decisions without being explicitly programmed (Ashraf, 2024). Machine learning algorithms can be used to identify patterns in student behavior, predict academic success or failure, and recommend personalized learning interventions. For example, machine learning models can analyze data from a variety of sources, including assessments, attendance records, and classroom interactions, to identify students who are at risk of falling behind or failing. These models can then predict the likelihood of a student's success or failure based on historical data and other factors, allowing educators to intervene early and provide targeted support. Machine learning can also be used to personalize learning experiences by identifying the most effective teaching strategies for individual students based on their learning styles, preferences, and progress. By tailoring instruction to meet the specific needs of each student, machine learning can help improve student engagement, motivation, and academic achievement.

Predictive analytics is another powerful AI tool that is transforming educational data analysis (Ashraf, 2024; Esomonu, 2025; Okokoyo & Nwachukwu, 2024). Predictive analytics involves using historical data to forecast future outcomes, such as student achievement, retention, and dropout rates. By analyzing patterns in student performance, predictive models can identify students who are at risk of academic failure or dropping out and provide insights into the factors that contribute to these outcomes (Okokoyo & Nwachukwu, 2024). For example, predictive analytics can help educators identify students who may be struggling with specific subjects or skills and recommend targeted interventions, such as tutoring or additional support. Similarly, predictive analytics can help administrators forecast trends in student enrollment, retention, and graduation rates, allowing them to make more informed decisions about resource allocation and program development. By leveraging predictive analytics, educational institutions can take proactive measures to improve student outcomes and reduce the risk of academic failure or dropout.

Natural language processing (NLP) is another AI technology that is increasingly being used in education to analyze qualitative data, such as open-ended student responses, teacher feedback, and social media data. NLP is a branch of AI that focuses on enabling computers to understand, interpret, and generate human language (Ashraf, 2024). In education, NLP can be used to analyze student essays, surveys, and feedback forms to gain insights into student experiences, sentiments, and learning needs. For example, NLP algorithms can analyze student responses to open-ended questions to identify common themes or patterns in their feedback, providing educators with valuable information about student perceptions of the curriculum, teaching methods, and classroom environment. Similarly, NLP can be used to analyze teacher feedback to identify areas where students may be struggling or where instructional improvements are needed. NLP can also be applied to social media data, such as tweets or online discussion forums, to gauge student sentiment and engagement with the learning process. By analyzing this type of unstructured data, NLP can help educators gain a deeper understanding of student experiences and make data-driven decisions to improve teaching and learning.

Data mining is another key AI tool that is used to uncover hidden patterns and relationships within large datasets (Ashraf, 2024). In the context of education, data mining can be used to analyze a wide range of data, including academic performance, attendance, behavioral data, and demographic information, to identify trends and insights that might not be immediately apparent. For example, data mining can help educators identify factors that contribute to student success or failure, such as the impact of socioeconomic status, extracurricular involvement, or parental support. Data mining can also be used to identify correlations between different variables, such as the relationship between attendance and academic performance, or the impact of specific teaching methods on student outcomes. By uncovering these hidden patterns, data mining can provide educators and administrators with valuable insights that can inform decision-making and help improve student outcomes.

One of the key advantages of AI tools such as machine learning, predictive analytics, NLP, and data mining is their ability to process and analyze large volumes of data quickly and efficiently. Traditional methods of data analysis often struggle to keep up with the sheer volume of data generated by educational institutions, especially as the use of digital tools and platforms continues to grow. AI, on the other hand, can process vast amounts of data in real-time, providing educators and administrators with up-to-date insights that can inform decision-making. For example, machine learning algorithms can analyze data from learning management systems (LMS), assessments, and student surveys to identify students who may be at risk of falling behind and recommend personalized interventions. Predictive analytics can forecast trends in student achievement, retention, and dropout rates, allowing educators to take proactive measures to address potential issues before they become critical (Esomonu, 2025).

AI tools also enable more accurate and objective decision-making (Alsbou & Alsaraireh, 2024). Traditional methods of decision-making in education often rely on subjective judgments or anecdotal evidence, which can lead to inconsistencies and biases. AI, however, uses data-driven models to make predictions and recommendations based on objective criteria. This helps ensure that decisions are based on evidence rather than assumptions or personal biases. For example, predictive analytics can help identify students who are at risk of dropping out based on a wide range of factors, such as attendance, academic performance, and engagement, without relying on subjective judgments about the student's potential. Similarly, machine learning models can help personalize learning experiences based on objective data about a student's progress and learning style, ensuring that each student receives the support they need to succeed.

Another significant advantage of AI tools is their ability to continuously learn and improve over time. Machine learning models, in particular, can be trained on new data to refine their predictions and recommendations. As more data is collected, these models can become more accurate and effective at identifying patterns and making predictions. This ability to learn and adapt is particularly important in the context of education, where student needs and learning environments are constantly evolving. By using AI tools that can continuously improve, educational institutions can ensure that their decision-making processes remain up-to-date and responsive to changing circumstances.

AI tools and technologies such as machine learning, predictive analytics, natural language processing, and data mining are transforming the way educational institutions analyze and use data. These tools enable educators and administrators to gain deeper insights into student behavior, academic performance, and institutional trends, ultimately leading to more informed and effective decision-making. By leveraging AI to process and analyze large, complex datasets, educational institutions can improve student outcomes, optimize resource allocation, and enhance institutional effectiveness. As AI continues to evolve, its role in education will only become more significant, providing new opportunities for personalized learning, proactive interventions, and data-driven decision-making.

AI in Personalized Learning and Student Support

AI-driven data analysis is transforming the landscape of personalized learning by providing educators with tools to better understand individual students' strengths, weaknesses, and learning preferences (Ashraf, 2024). Traditional educational approaches often take a one-size-fits-all approach, but AI enables a more nuanced, data-driven understanding of each student's unique learning needs. By analyzing vast amounts of data, including academic performance, behavior, and engagement, AI systems can identify patterns that would be difficult for human educators to detect. This allows for a deeper understanding of how each student learns, what challenges they face, and how they can best be supported in their educational journey.

One of the most significant ways AI supports personalized learning is through adaptive learning platforms (Ashraf, 2024). These platforms use AI algorithms to adjust content, pacing, and learning activities based on real-time data about a student's progress and performance. For example, if a student is struggling with a particular concept, the system can provide additional resources or explanations to reinforce that concept before moving on to more advanced material. Conversely, if a student demonstrates proficiency in a subject, the system can accelerate their learning by offering more challenging content. Adaptive learning platforms use AI to continuously monitor student performance, ensuring that each student receives an individualized learning experience that is tailored to their current level of understanding and learning pace.

AI-driven data analysis also plays a critical role in identifying students at risk of falling behind or struggling academically (Latif, 2022). By analyzing patterns in data such as grades, attendance, participation, and behavior, AI systems can flag students who may need additional support. For instance, a student who consistently performs poorly on assessments or who has irregular attendance may be identified as at risk for academic failure or disengagement. AI systems can then recommend timely interventions, such as tutoring, counseling, or access to specialized resources, to help these students get back on track. By providing early identification of at-risk students, AI enables educators to intervene proactively, rather than waiting until students are already far behind or struggling with significant challenges.

The ability to provide personalized learning experiences and early interventions is particularly valuable in large, diverse classrooms where teachers may struggle to give individual attention to every student. AI-driven systems can provide teachers with actionable insights and recommendations that allow them to focus their time and efforts on the students who need the most support. For example, an AI-powered dashboard can display a student's progress in real-time, highlighting areas where they are excelling and areas where they may need additional help. This allows teachers to make data-informed decisions about how to allocate their time and resources more effectively.

Several case studies have demonstrated the successful application of AI-powered personalized learning systems in educational settings. One such example is DreamBox Learning, an adaptive learning platform for K-8 math education. DreamBox uses AI algorithms to personalize learning for each student, adjusting content in real-time based on their responses and progress. The system tracks student interactions with the platform and uses this data to provide targeted feedback, instructional adjustments, and recommendations for further learning. Research has shown that students who use DreamBox consistently outperform their peers in traditional classroom settings, demonstrating the effectiveness of AI-driven personalized learning in improving student achievement.

Another example is Knewton, an adaptive learning platform used in higher education to personalize course content for students. Knewton analyzes data from students' interactions with digital course materials and uses this data to predict which content will be most helpful for each student. By providing tailored content that aligns with individual learning needs, Knewton helps students stay engaged and improves their chances of success. Case studies of Knewton's use in universities have shown improvements in student retention and academic performance, highlighting the positive impact of AI on student engagement and achievement.

AI-driven personalized learning is also being applied in the context of special education, where individualized support is essential. For example, platforms like Squirrel AI use AI to provide personalized learning experiences for students with learning disabilities. The system adapts content based on each student's specific learning needs and provides real-time feedback, helping students with diverse learning styles succeed in a way that traditional classroom settings may not be able to accommodate. The ability of AI to provide tailored support for students with disabilities is a significant advancement in making education more inclusive and accessible.

AI-driven data analysis is playing a transformative role in personalized learning by helping educators better understand individual student needs and providing tailored educational experiences. Through adaptive learning platforms, AI can adjust content and pacing to meet the specific needs of each student, ensuring that they receive the appropriate level of challenge and support. AI's ability to identify at-risk students and recommend timely interventions enables educators to take proactive measures to improve student outcomes. Case studies of AI-powered personalized learning systems have demonstrated their effectiveness in improving student engagement, achievement, and retention, providing a compelling case for the continued integration of AI in education. As AI technologies continue to evolve, their potential to support personalized learning and enhance student success will only increase.

AI in Institutional Decision Making

AI can significantly assist educational leaders in making data-informed decisions regarding curriculum development, teaching strategies, and policy changes by providing insights derived from large datasets that would be otherwise challenging to analyze manually. Traditional methods of curriculum development and teaching strategy decisions often rely on historical data, anecdotal evidence, and teacher feedback, but AI allows for a more robust, data-driven approach. By analyzing student performance data, learning behaviors, and engagement metrics, AI can provide educational leaders with a clearer understanding of which teaching methods and curriculum designs are most effective for diverse student populations. For example, AI systems can identify patterns in student performance, highlighting areas where students struggle or excel, thus informing curriculum revisions that target these areas. In this way, AI can help educational leaders create more personalized, adaptive curricula that meet the needs of all learners, improving student outcomes and engagement (Okokoyo & Nwachukwu, 2024).

Additionally, AI can assist in refining teaching strategies by analyzing various teaching methods and their effectiveness across different student demographics. By processing data from classroom assessments, student feedback, and engagement levels, AI can recommend teaching strategies that are more likely to resonate with students based on their individual learning preferences and challenges. AI can also help in the development of professional development programs for teachers by identifying areas where educators may need additional training or support.

Through continuous analysis of teaching effectiveness, AI can inform decisions about pedagogical approaches, helping educational leaders foster a more dynamic and responsive learning environment.

Resource allocation is another critical area where AI can provide immense value to educational leaders (Ikwuanusi et al.,2022). By analyzing institutional data, AI can help administrators optimize staffing, facilities, and budgets to ensure that resources are used efficiently and effectively. AI tools can process vast amounts of data on student enrollment, course demand, teacher workloads, and facility usage to recommend optimal staffing levels, classroom assignments, and facility utilization. For instance, AI can predict which courses are likely to have the highest demand and suggest the appropriate number of teachers or classroom spaces needed to meet that demand. Similarly, AI can identify underutilized resources, such as classrooms or equipment, and suggest ways to repurpose or redistribute them to maximize their use. By making these recommendations, AI helps administrators ensure that resources are allocated in a way that aligns with the institution's priorities and goals, leading to more efficient operations and cost savings.

Furthermore, AI's potential in supporting long-term strategic planning is another area where it can have a transformative impact (Narne et al., 2024). By analyzing historical data and identifying trends, AI can help educational leaders forecast future enrollment trends, workforce requirements, and funding needs. For example, AI can analyze demographic data, economic trends, and regional population shifts to predict changes in student enrollment. This allows educational institutions to plan for future capacity needs, ensuring that staffing, facilities, and resources are scaled appropriately to meet growing or declining student populations. Similarly, AI can forecast workforce requirements by analyzing trends in job markets and industry needs, helping educational leaders align curriculum offerings with the skills and knowledge that will be in demand in the future. AI can also support financial planning by predicting funding needs based on enrollment trends, resource usage, and program effectiveness, allowing institutions to plan their budgets more accurately and allocate resources more strategically.

AI can also be used to assess the effectiveness of educational programs and interventions, providing educational leaders with the data they need to make evidence-based decisions for continuous improvement (Esomonu, 2025). Traditional methods of assessing program effectiveness often rely on surveys, standardized test scores, and qualitative feedback, which can be time-consuming and limited in scope. AI, on the other hand, can analyze data from a wide range of sources, including student performance, attendance, engagement, and feedback, to provide a more comprehensive and real-time assessment of program effectiveness. For example, AI can identify which programs or interventions are most successful in improving student outcomes, such as increased graduation rates, higher test scores, or improved engagement (Esomonu, 2025). By continuously monitoring and analyzing data, AI can provide educational leaders with timely insights into how programs are performing, enabling them to make adjustments and improvements as needed.

In addition to evaluating the effectiveness of existing programs, AI can also help educational leaders identify areas where new programs or interventions may be needed. By analyzing student performance data, AI can identify gaps in learning, such as areas where students consistently struggle or where certain groups of students are underperforming. This data-driven approach allows educational leaders to make more informed decisions about where to focus their efforts and resources, ensuring that interventions are targeted where they are most needed.

The use of AI in educational decision-making promotes a shift from reactive to proactive leadership. Instead of waiting for problems to arise, educational leaders can use AI to anticipate challenges and take action before they escalate. This proactive approach enables institutions to be more agile and responsive to changing needs, ultimately leading to better outcomes for students and more efficient use of resources. By integrating AI into the decision-making process, educational leaders can ensure that their institutions are not only addressing current challenges but also preparing for the future in a strategic, data-driven manner.

AI has the potential to revolutionize the way educational leaders make decisions about curriculum development, teaching strategies, resource allocation, and long-term strategic planning. By leveraging AI to process and analyze vast amounts of educational data, institutions can make more informed, accurate, and timely decisions that improve student outcomes, optimize resource use, and enhance institutional effectiveness. AI's ability to provide real-time insights into program effectiveness, forecast trends, and identify areas for improvement allows educational leaders to make evidence-based decisions that support continuous improvement and long-term success. As AI continues to evolve, its role in educational decision-making will only grow, offering even greater opportunities for innovation and improvement in the education sector.

ETHICAL CONSIDERATIONS AND CHALLENGES IN AI-DRIVEN DECISION MAKING

As educational institutions increasingly adopt AI to analyze sensitive student data and inform decision-making, ethical concerns related to data privacy, security, and consent become paramount. Student data, which often includes personally identifiable information (PII), academic performance, behavioral records, and other sensitive details, must be protected from unauthorized access and misuse. Institutions must ensure that AI systems adhere to strict privacy standards and regulations, such as the Family Educational Rights and Privacy Act (FERPA) in the U.S., to prevent breaches that could compromise students' privacy (Yang & Beil, 2024). Moreover, data collection and analysis should be transparent, with clear policies regarding how data is collected, stored, and used. Obtaining informed consent from students and their families is critical, as individuals should have a say in how their data is utilized. Institutions must provide clear explanations of the AI tools and their purpose, ensuring that students and parents understand how their data will be analyzed and the potential implications for their educational experience.

Another significant ethical concern is the potential for algorithmic bias in AI models (Okokoyo & Nwachukwu, 2024). Algorithms are designed to analyze and process data, but if the data used to train these models is biased, the AI systems may reinforce those biases, leading to unfair or discriminatory outcomes. For example, if an AI model is trained on historical data that reflects biased patterns, such as disparities in achievement between different demographic groups, the model may inadvertently perpetuate those biases when making decisions about students. This could result in certain groups being unfairly disadvantaged or overlooked, such as students of color, students with disabilities, or students from low-income backgrounds. To mitigate this risk, it is crucial that AI systems are designed to be fair, transparent, and accountable. Educational institutions must ensure that AI models are regularly audited and tested for bias, and that the data used to train these models is diverse, representative, and free from discriminatory patterns. Furthermore, AI systems should be built with mechanisms that allow for human oversight and intervention to correct any biased outcomes.

The integration of AI into educational decision-making also raises the challenge of balancing data-driven decision-making with the human elements of teaching and learning. While AI can provide valuable insights and streamline administrative tasks, it cannot replace the nuanced understanding and emotional intelligence that educators bring to their roles (Chan et al., 2024). Teachers and administrators play a vital role in understanding students' unique needs, providing personalized support, and fostering a positive learning environment. AI should be viewed as a tool to enhance, not replace, the educator's role. For instance, AI can assist in identifying students at risk of falling behind or suggest personalized learning interventions, but it is the educator's responsibility to interpret the AI's findings and make decisions that consider the broader context of the student's experience. A successful integration of AI in education requires a balance where technology complements human judgment, ensuring that the educational experience remains student-centered and responsive to individual needs.

To ensure that AI is used responsibly and ethically in educational decision-making, institutions must implement safeguards to protect students' rights and well-being (Sumbera, 2025). These safeguards should include robust data protection policies, transparent communication with stakeholders about AI usage, and mechanisms for accountability. Institutions should establish clear ethical guidelines for the development and deployment of AI tools, ensuring that they are aligned with the institution's mission and values. Additionally, AI systems should be subject to regular audits to assess their impact on student outcomes and to identify any unintended consequences, such as bias or discrimination. It is also essential that institutions provide training for educators, administrators, and staff on the ethical implications of AI, ensuring that they are equipped to make informed decisions about how to use AI responsibly. By prioritizing ethics in AI deployment, educational institutions can harness the power of AI while safeguarding students' rights and fostering an environment of trust and accountability (Borenstein & Howard, 2021).

CASE STUDIES OF AI IN DATA-DRIVEN DECISION MAKING IN EDUCATION

Several educational institutions have successfully implemented AI to support data-driven decision-making, demonstrating the transformative potential of AI in improving student outcomes and institutional effectiveness. One notable example is Georgia State University, which has leveraged predictive analytics to improve student retention rates. The university developed an AI system that analyzes student data, including academic performance, attendance, and demographic information, to predict which students are at risk of dropping out. This system alerts academic advisors and student support services, enabling them to intervene early with personalized support, such as tutoring, counseling, or financial aid assistance. As a result, Georgia State University has seen significant improvements in retention and graduation rates, particularly among underrepresented student populations.

Another example comes from the University of Arizona, which implemented an AI-powered learning analytics dashboard to help instructors and administrators monitor student progress in real time. The dashboard aggregates data from various sources, such as learning management systems, assessments, and student surveys, to provide a comprehensive view of student performance. This allows educators to identify struggling students early, adjust their teaching strategies, and provide targeted interventions. The dashboard has been particularly effective in helping instructors personalize their teaching approaches and improve student engagement, leading to higher levels of student satisfaction and academic success.

In the K-12 sector, several school districts have adopted AI-assisted grading systems to reduce the administrative burden on teachers and provide more timely feedback to students. For example, the Lee County School District in Florida implemented an AI grading system for multiple-choice and short-answer assessments.

The system analyzes student responses and provides instant feedback, allowing teachers to focus on more complex tasks, such as providing personalized instruction and fostering student engagement. This system has helped improve grading accuracy, reduce turnaround times, and free up teachers to spend more time on student-centered activities.

These case studies highlight several key lessons learned from the implementation of AI in educational decision-making. One of the primary challenges faced during implementation is the need for robust data infrastructure and integration. Many institutions struggle with collecting and organizing data from various sources, which can make it difficult to fully leverage AI's capabilities. Institutions must invest in data management systems that can handle large volumes of data and ensure that the data is accurate, consistent, and accessible. Another challenge is the need for staff training and buy-in. Educators and administrators may be hesitant to adopt AI tools due to concerns about their complexity or potential job displacement. Successful implementation requires clear communication about the benefits of AI and ongoing professional development to ensure that staff members are comfortable using these technologies.

Despite these challenges, the benefits of AI in data-driven decision-making are evident. Institutions that have successfully implemented AI have seen improvements in student outcomes, such as higher retention and graduation rates, as well as more efficient resource allocation. AI tools enable administrators to make more informed decisions about curriculum design, staffing, and budgeting, leading to better alignment of resources with institutional priorities. Additionally, AI can enhance the learning experience by providing personalized recommendations for students, helping them succeed academically and stay engaged in their education.

AI is being used in a variety of educational contexts, from K-12 schools to higher education institutions, with diverse applications in decision-making processes. In K-12 schools, AI is being used to support personalized learning, improve student engagement, and streamline administrative tasks. AI-powered learning platforms can adjust content and pacing based on individual student needs, while predictive analytics can help identify students at risk of falling behind (Okokoyo & Nwachukwu, 2024). In higher education, AI is being used for more complex decision-making, such as optimizing course scheduling (Okokoyo & Nwachukwu, 2024), improving student retention, and supporting institutional planning. AI tools can analyze large datasets to forecast enrollment trends, predict student performance, and assess the effectiveness of academic programs.

The successful implementation of AI in educational decision-making has led to significant improvements in student outcomes and institutional effectiveness. However, institutions must overcome challenges related to data integration, staff training, and ethical considerations to fully realize the potential of AI. The diverse applications of AI in K-12 and higher education highlight its versatility and promise, and as AI technologies continue to evolve, their role in education will only become more critical in shaping the future of learning.

THE FUTURE OF AI IN DATA-DRIVEN DECISION MAKING IN EDUCATION:

As artificial intelligence (AI) continues to evolve, its role in educational decision-making is expected to become more sophisticated and integrated with other emerging technologies, further transforming educational practices. In the near future, AI models will likely become more advanced, capable of processing and analyzing vast amounts of data with greater accuracy and efficiency. These models will not only be able to predict student outcomes but will also provide actionable insights that can be used to optimize every aspect of the educational experience, from curriculum design to resource allocation. For instance, AI could integrate with blockchain technology to create secure, immutable records of student performance and progress, enhancing transparency and trust in academic assessments. Similarly, the integration of AI with the Internet of Things (IoT) could enable real-time monitoring of student engagement and behavior, providing educators with instant feedback on classroom dynamics and allowing them to adjust teaching strategies accordingly.

The potential for AI to further transform educational practices is vast. AI-powered tools could assist in creating highly personalized learning environments, where content and pacing are dynamically adjusted based on each student's needs and preferences. AI could also facilitate more efficient and equitable resource distribution, ensuring that students and teachers have access to the materials and support they need when they need them. For instance, AI could help identify underutilized resources, such as classrooms or equipment, and suggest ways to optimize their use, reducing waste and improving efficiency. Additionally, AI could assist in streamlining administrative tasks, such as scheduling (Okokoyo & Nwachukwu, 2024), grading, and communication, freeing up more time for educators to focus on teaching and student engagement.

As AI becomes more integrated into educational decision-making, data literacy will become increasingly important for educators, administrators, and policymakers. In a data-driven educational landscape, the ability to interpret and make sense of complex datasets will be crucial for making informed decisions. Educators will need to understand how to use data to tailor their teaching strategies to meet the needs of individual students, while administrators will need to leverage data to optimize resource allocation and improve institutional effectiveness (Okokoyo & Nwachukwu, 2024). Policymakers will need to be able to assess the impact of educational policies based on data, ensuring that decisions are grounded in evidence and that resources are directed toward initiatives that will have the greatest impact on student outcomes. As such, data literacy will become a core competency for all stakeholders in the education system, enabling them to navigate the complexities of data-driven decision-making and ensure that AI tools are used responsibly and effectively.

One of the most exciting prospects of AI in education is its ability to enable more dynamic, real-time decision-making. With the growing availability of data and the increasing sophistication of AI models, educational institutions will be able to make decisions more quickly and with greater accuracy. For example, AI could help identify students who are struggling academically or socially and recommend interventions in real time, allowing educators to provide targeted support before issues escalate. Similarly, AI could assist administrators in making decisions about staffing, budgeting, and curriculum design based on real-time data about student needs, performance, and institutional priorities. This ability to make decisions in real time will allow educational institutions to be more responsive to changing student needs, external factors, and emerging trends, ensuring that they remain agile and adaptive in an increasingly complex and fast-paced educational landscape.

In conclusion, the future role of AI in educational decision-making holds immense promise. As AI models become more sophisticated and integrated with other emerging technologies, they will enable more personalized, efficient, and responsive educational practices. The growing importance of data literacy will empower educators, administrators, and policymakers to make informed decisions based on data, ensuring that AI is used responsibly and effectively. The evolving capabilities of AI will enable educational institutions to be more agile and responsive to the changing needs of students and the broader educational environment, ultimately improving student outcomes and institutional effectiveness.

CONCLUSION

The transformative potential of artificial intelligence (AI) in data-driven decision-making in education is vast and far-reaching. As educational institutions increasingly recognize the power of AI to process and analyze large volumes of data, they gain the ability to make more informed, accurate, and timely decisions that can enhance student outcomes, optimize resource allocation (Okokoyo & Nwachukwu, 2024), and improve institutional effectiveness. The chapter has explored how AI can enhance traditional decision-making processes, offering insights into how it can be applied to various aspects of education, from curriculum design and student support to institutional planning and policy development. By leveraging AI technologies, educational institutions can move beyond traditional methods of decision-making and embrace a more data-driven approach that is grounded in evidence and aimed at improving the educational experience for all stakeholders.

One of the key benefits of AI in educational decision-making is its ability to process vast amounts of data more efficiently and accurately than human decision-makers alone. AI systems can analyze complex datasets from multiple sources, such as student performance records, attendance data, behavioral data, and demographic information, to identify trends, patterns, and correlations that may not be immediately apparent. This ability to sift through large volumes of data enables educational institutions to make more precise decisions based on a holistic understanding of student needs and institutional priorities. For example, AI can help identify students who are at risk of falling behind academically, predict which interventions will be most effective, and recommend personalized learning strategies that can help them succeed. Similarly, AI can assist administrators in making data-driven decisions about resource allocation, staffing, and budgeting, ensuring that resources are directed where they are most needed to support student success (Okokoyo & Nwachukwu, 2024).

Despite the many advantages that AI offers, its successful integration into educational decision-making requires careful consideration of several important factors. First and foremost, ethical issues must be addressed to ensure that AI systems are used responsibly and fairly (Borenstein & Howard, 2021). The use of AI in education raises concerns related to data privacy, security, and consent, particularly when dealing with sensitive student information. It is essential that educational institutions establish robust safeguards to protect students' rights and ensure that their data is used in compliance with privacy regulations. Additionally, AI systems must be designed to be transparent and accountable, with clear guidelines for how data is collected, analyzed, and used in decision-making processes. Transparency and accountability are crucial for building trust among students, parents, educators, and administrators, as they ensure that AI systems are not only effective but also fair and equitable.

Another important consideration is the potential for algorithmic bias in AI models (Borenstein & Howard, 2021; Okokoyo & Nwachukwu, 2024). AI systems are only as good as the data they are trained on, and if the data used to train these systems contains biases, those biases can be reflected in the decisions made by AI models. For example, an AI system that is trained on historical data from a particular demographic group may inadvertently reinforce existing inequalities, such as disparities in educational outcomes based on race, socioeconomic status, or gender. To mitigate this risk, it is essential that AI systems be designed to be fair, inclusive, and free from bias. This requires careful attention to the data used to train AI models, as well as ongoing monitoring and evaluation to ensure that AI systems are not perpetuating harmful stereotypes or reinforcing inequities.

The integration of AI into educational decision-making also requires a shift in the way educators, administrators, and policymakers approach their roles. While AI can provide valuable insights and recommendations, it is important to remember that AI should complement, rather than replace, the human element of teaching and learning. Educators bring essential skills such as empathy, creativity, and judgment to the classroom—qualities that AI cannot replicate. Therefore, AI should be viewed as a tool that enhances the work of educators, not as a substitute for their expertise. By combining the power of AI with the human touch, educational institutions can create more personalized, efficient, and equitable learning environments that support the needs of all students.

Collaboration between educators, administrators, and technology developers is also critical to the successful integration of AI in educational decision-making. AI is not a one-size-fits-all solution, and its implementation will vary depending on the unique needs and priorities of each educational institution. Therefore, it is important that AI systems are developed in close collaboration with educators and administrators who understand the challenges and opportunities of the educational context. This collaborative approach will ensure that AI systems are designed to meet the specific needs of students and educators, while also aligning with the goals and values of the institution. Furthermore, ongoing professional development and training will be necessary to ensure that educators and administrators are equipped with the knowledge and skills to use AI tools effectively and responsibly.

The future of AI in education holds tremendous promise. As AI technologies continue to evolve, their capabilities will expand, enabling even more sophisticated and personalized learning experiences. AI systems will become increasingly adept at analyzing data in real time, providing educators with actionable insights that can inform their teaching strategies and improve student engagement. Moreover, AI's ability to predict student outcomes and recommend timely interventions will help educators identify and support students who may be at risk of falling behind, ensuring that no student is left behind. AI will also continue to play a pivotal role in optimizing institutional operations, helping administrators make data-driven decisions about resource allocation, staffing, and strategic planning (Okokoyo & Nwachukwu, 2024). In this way, AI will help educational institutions become more efficient, responsive, and student-centered.

However, for AI to reach its full potential in education, it is essential that its implementation is done thoughtfully and ethically. Educational institutions must take proactive steps to address the challenges and risks associated with AI, including issues related to data privacy, algorithmic bias, and the need for transparency and accountability By ensuring that AI systems are designed and implemented with these considerations in mind, educational institutions can create a more equitable and effective learning environment for all students. Furthermore, by embracing AI's capabilities, educational institutions can foster a culture of innovation and continuous improvement, where data-driven decision-making is at the heart of every aspect of the educational experience.

In conclusion, the integration of AI into educational decision-making represents a paradigm shift that has the potential to revolutionize the way we approach teaching, learning, and institutional management. By harnessing the power of AI to analyze data more effectively and make more informed decisions, educational institutions can improve student outcomes, optimize resources, and create more personalized and equitable learning environments. However, the successful implementation of AI requires careful consideration of ethical issues, transparency and collaboration between educators, administrators, and technology developers. With a thoughtful and responsible approach, AI can play a transformative role in shaping the future of education, ensuring that all students have access to the support and resources they need to succeed.

REFERENCES

Al Hazaa, K., Abdel-Salam, A. S. G., Ismail, R., Johnson, C., Al-Tameemi, R. A. N., Romanowski, M. H., & Elatawneh, A. (2021). The effects of attendance and high school GPA on student performance in first-year undergraduate courses. *Cogent Education, 8*(1), 1956857.

Alotaibi, N. S. (2024). The Impact of AI and LMS Integration on the Future of Higher Education: Opportunities, Challenges, and Strategies for Transformation. *Sustainability, 16*(23), 10357.

Alsbou, M. K. K., & Alsaraireh, R. E. A. I. (2024, April). Data-driven decision-making in education: leveraging AI for school improvement. In *2024 International Conference on Knowledge Engineering and Communication Systems (ICKECS)* (Vol. 1, pp. 1-6). IEEE.

Ashraf, S. R. (2024). The Role of Artificial Intelligence in Enhancing Managerial Decision-Making in Education. *International Journal of Advanced Social Sciences Research, 1*(1), 10–20.

Borenstein, J., & Howard, A. (2021). Emerging challenges in AI and the need for AI ethics education. *AI and Ethics, 1*(1), 61–65. PMID: 38624388

Chan, C. K. Y., & Tsi, L. H. (2024). Will generative AI replace teachers in higher education? A study of teacher and student perceptions. *Studies in Educational Evaluation, 83*, 101395.

Esomonu, N. P. M. (2025) Utilizing AI and Big Data for Predictive Insights on Institutional Performance and Student Success: A Data-Driven Approach to Quality Assurance. *AI and Ethics, Academic Integrity and the Future of Quality Assurance in Higher Education*, 29.

Gade, K. R. (2021). Data-driven decision making in a complex world. *Journal of Computational Innovation, 1*(1).

Gaftandzhieva, S., Hussain, S., Hilcenko, S., Doneva, R., & Boykova, K. (2023). Data-driven decision making in higher education institutions: State-of-play. *International Journal of Advanced Computer Science and Applications, 14*(6).

Ikwuanusi, U. F., Azubuike, C. H. I. M. A., Odionu, C. S., & Sule, A. K. (2022). Leveraging AI to address resource allocation challenges in academic and research libraries. *Iconic Research and Engineering Journals, 5*(10), 311.

Kavitha, R. K., Krupa, C. R., & Kaarthiekheyan, V. (2025). AI-Powered Digital Solutions for Smart Learning: Revolutionizing Education. In *Cybersecurity and Data Science Innovations for Sustainable Development of HEICC* (pp. 213-227). CRC Press.

Latif, G., Alghazo, R., Pilotti, M. A., & Brahim, G. B. (2022). Identifying "at-risk" students: An AI-based prediction approach. *International Journal of Computing and Digital Systems*, *11*(1).

Martins, J., Cunha, J., Lopes, S., Moreira, T., & Rosário, P. (2022). School engagement in elementary school: A systematic review of 35 years of research. *Educational Psychology Review*, *34*(2), 793–849.

Narne, S., Adedoja, T., Mohan, M., & Ayyalasomayajula, T. (2024). AI-Driven Decision Support Systems in Management: Enhancing Strategic Planning and Execution. *International Journal on Recent and Innovation Trends in Computing and Communication*, *12*(1), 268–276.

Okokoyo, I. E., Nwaham, C. O., & Nwachukwu, O. G. (2024). Leveraging artificial intelligence for enhanced administrators decision making in educational institutions: A comprehensive exploration of applications, challenges, and opportunities. *NIU Journal of Educational Research*, *10*(1), 63–72.

Sumbera, B. G. (2025). The Ethical Use of AI in Education. In *Integrating AI Into Pedagogical Education* (pp. 175–210). IGI Global Scientific Publishing.

Yağcı, M. (2022). Educational data mining: Prediction of students' academic performance using machine learning algorithms. *Smart Learning Environments*, *9*(1), 11.

Yang, E., & Beil, C. (2024). Ensuring data privacy in AI/ML implementation. *New Directions for Higher Education*, *2024*(207), 63–78.

Chapter 10
Automating Administrative Tasks With AI Efficiency in Education

Dayna Lynn Mitchell
https://orcid.org/0009-0000-9385-7238
California State Polytechnic University, Pomona, USA

ABSTRACT

This chapter will explore the potential of artificial intelligence (AI) to streamline and automate administrative tasks in educational settings, enhancing operational efficiency and allowing educators to focus more on teaching and student engagement. It will examine the types of administrative functions that can be automated, such as grading, scheduling, data management, and communication, and how AI technologies can reduce the time and effort required for these tasks. The chapter will also discuss the benefits of automation in improving accuracy, consistency, and decision-making processes within educational institutions. Additionally, it will address the challenges of implementing AI solutions, including concerns about data privacy, the need for adequate training, and the potential for resistance to change. Through case studies and examples, this chapter will demonstrate how AI can transform administrative operations, ultimately contributing to a more efficient, effective, and student-centered educational environment.

DOI: 10.4018/979-8-3373-5102-5.ch010

INTRODUCTION

In recent years, artificial intelligence (AI) has emerged as a transformative force in many sectors, including education. One of the most promising applications of AI in education is its potential to automate administrative tasks, which have long been a time-consuming and often burdensome aspect of educational institutions. From grading assignments to scheduling classes and managing student data, educators and administrative staff are often overwhelmed by the sheer volume of routine tasks that demand their attention. By harnessing AI to handle these tasks, institutions can not only streamline their operations but also create more time and space for teachers to focus on what they do best—engaging with students and facilitating learning.

This chapter will explore how AI can be applied to various administrative functions within educational settings, highlighting the potential for automation to enhance efficiency, reduce workload, and improve decision-making processes. One of the most well-known applications of AI in education is automated grading. For years, grading has been a time-intensive process for educators, particularly in subjects that require subjective assessments such as essays, projects, or written exams. AI-powered grading systems, however, have the potential to significantly reduce the time and effort required to grade these assignments (Kakungulu, 2024; Rutner & Scott, 2022). By using natural language processing (NLP) algorithms and machine learning models, AI can assess written content for grammar, coherence, relevance, and argumentation, providing instant feedback to students and reducing the administrative burden on teachers (Kakungulu, 2024; Poonpon, 2023). This allows educators to dedicate more time to providing personalized support and engaging with students in meaningful ways.

In addition to grading, AI can also be used to automate scheduling and resource management (Adams & Thompson, 2025; Igbokwe, 2023; Saaida, 2023). Scheduling is often a complex and tedious process that requires balancing multiple variables, such as teacher availability, student preferences, and room assignments. AI systems can optimize this process by analyzing historical data, identifying patterns, and generating the most efficient schedules for both students and faculty. This can save significant time for administrators and ensure that resources are allocated in the most effective manner. Similarly, AI can assist with resource management by tracking the availability and usage of materials, equipment, and facilities, allowing institutions to make more informed decisions about resource allocation and reduce waste.

Another area where AI can improve efficiency is in communication. Administrative staff often spend a considerable amount of time responding to emails, answering questions, and providing updates to students, parents, and faculty. AI-powered chatbots and virtual assistants can automate many of these communication tasks, providing instant responses to common inquiries and freeing up staff to focus on more complex issues (Goyal et al., 2023). For example, AI chatbots can answer questions about class schedules, deadlines, and exam dates, or even provide basic technical support for students experiencing difficulties with online learning platforms. By automating routine communication tasks, AI can enhance the overall experience for students and staff while improving response times and reducing the likelihood of errors.

The potential benefits of automating administrative tasks with AI extend beyond efficiency and timesaving (Saaida, 2023). One of the most significant advantages is the potential for increased accuracy and consistency. Human error is inevitable in any administrative process, whether it's in grading, scheduling, or data entry. AI systems, on the other hand, can be programmed to follow strict guidelines and protocols, ensuring that tasks are completed accurately and consistently every time. This can help reduce the risk of mistakes, such as misgrading assignments or double-booking classrooms, and improve the overall quality of administrative operations.

Moreover, AI has the ability to analyze large amounts of data quickly and identify patterns that may not be immediately apparent to human administrators (National Education Association, 2024). For example, AI can analyze student performance data to identify trends, such as which students are struggling in particular subjects or which teaching methods are most effective. This data-driven approach can help administrators make more informed decisions about resource allocation, curriculum development, and student support services. By leveraging AI to analyze and interpret data, educational institutions can improve their ability to respond to the needs of students and faculty, ultimately enhancing the overall educational experience.

Despite the many potential benefits of automating administrative tasks with AI, there are also significant challenges and ethical considerations that must be addressed. One of the most pressing concerns is data privacy (National Education Association, 2024). The use of AI in education often involves the collection and analysis of large amounts of sensitive student data, such as grades, personal information, and learning behaviors. It is essential that institutions implement robust data protection measures to ensure that this data is kept secure, and that students' privacy rights are respected. Institutions must also be transparent about how AI systems are used and what data is being collected, ensuring that students, parents, and faculty members are informed and comfortable with the technology.

Another challenge is the potential for algorithmic bias (Clauser, et. al., 2024; National Education Association, 2024). AI systems are only as good as the data in which they are trained, and if that data is biased, the AI system may produce biased outcomes. For example, if an AI grading system is trained primarily on data from a particular demographic group, it may not accurately assess the work of students from other backgrounds. Similarly, if an AI scheduling system is based on historical data that reflects existing inequalities, it may perpetuate those inequalities in future schedules (Saaida, 2023). To mitigate these risks, it is crucial that AI systems are trained on diverse, representative data sets and that their outcomes are regularly audited to ensure fairness and equity.

The implementation of AI in educational administration also raises questions about the role of human staff. While AI can automate many routine tasks, there will always be a need for human oversight and intervention (National Education Association, 2024). For example, while AI can grade assignments, it may not be able to fully understand the nuances of a student's work or provide the personalized feedback that a teacher can offer. Similarly, while AI can optimize schedules, it may not be able to account for the unique needs and preferences of individual students and faculty members. As such, educators and administrators will need to strike a balance between leveraging AI for efficiency and maintaining the human touch that is essential for creating a supportive and inclusive learning environment.

Additionally, there may be resistance to the adoption of AI-powered automation in educational settings. Some educators and administrators may be wary of relying too heavily on technology, fearing that it could replace jobs or undermine the personal connections that are central to the educational experience. Others may simply be hesitant to adopt new technologies due to a lack of familiarity or training. To address these concerns, it will be important for institutions to provide adequate training and support for staff, ensuring that they feel confident in using AI tools and understand their potential benefits (Goyal et al., 2023). It will also be crucial to involve educators and administrators in the decision-making process when implementing AI systems, ensuring that their perspectives and concerns are considered.

Looking ahead, the future of AI in educational administration holds great promise. As AI technologies continue to evolve, they will likely become even more sophisticated, capable of automating increasingly complex tasks and providing deeper insights into student performance and institutional operations. For example, AI could be used to predict student outcomes, identifying at-risk students before they fall behind and enabling early intervention. AI could also be used to personalize learning experiences for students, tailoring content and assessments to individual needs and preferences (Poonpon, 2023). As these technologies become more integrated into educational systems, they will not only enhance efficiency but also improve the quality of education and support services.

AI has the potential to revolutionize educational administration by automating routine tasks, improving efficiency, and providing data-driven insights that can enhance decision-making. By reducing the administrative burden on educators and staff, AI allows them to focus more on teaching and student engagement, ultimately improving the overall educational experience. However, the implementation of AI in education must be approached with care, addressing challenges such as data privacy, algorithmic bias, and the need for human oversight (Clauser et. al., 2024). As AI technologies continue to evolve, they will play an increasingly important role in shaping the future of education, and it is essential that educators, administrators, and policymakers work together to ensure that these technologies are used responsibly and ethically.

INTRODUCTION TO AI IN EDUCATIONAL ADMINISTRATION

Artificial Intelligence (AI) has become an integral part of various industries, and its role in education is expanding rapidly. In the context of education, AI refers to the use of advanced algorithms and machine learning techniques to automate tasks, improve decision-making, and enhance the overall educational experience. AI in education can be applied in a wide range of areas, from personalized learning experiences to administrative functions (Saaida, 2023). In particular, the growing role of AI in educational administration offers significant potential to streamline processes, reduce the workload of educators and staff, and ultimately improve the efficiency and effectiveness of educational institutions.

As educational institutions continue to grow in size and complexity, administrators face increasing demands to manage a wide range of tasks, from grading assignments to scheduling classes and managing resources. These administrative functions are critical to the day-to-day operations of schools, colleges, and universities, yet they are often time-consuming and prone to human error. AI has the potential to address many of these challenges by automating routine administrative tasks, allowing educators and staff to focus more on student engagement, teaching, and strategic decision-making (Saaida, 2023). By leveraging AI technologies, educational institutions can improve their administrative efficiency, reduce costs, and enhance the overall educational experience for students, teachers, and staff alike.

One of the most prominent areas where AI can have a significant impact is in grading (National Education Association, 2024). Grading is a fundamental administrative task in education, but it can be incredibly time-consuming, especially in subjects that require subjective assessments, such as essays, projects, and written exams. AI-powered grading systems use natural language processing (NLP) algorithms and machine learning models to assess written content based on factors such as grammar, coherence, structure, and relevance. These systems can provide instant feedback to students, allowing them to understand their mistakes and improve their work. By automating the grading process, educators can save valuable time that would otherwise be spent on manual grading, enabling them to focus on providing more personalized support to students and engaging in more meaningful interactions (Poonpon, 2023).

In addition to grading, AI can also be used to automate scheduling, which is another complex and time-consuming administrative task in educational settings (Adams & Thompson, 2025; Igbokwe, 2023; National Education Association, 2024). Scheduling involves balancing multiple variables, such as teacher availability, student preferences, classroom capacity, and course requirements. This process can be further complicated by changes in enrollment, cancellations, and other unforeseen circumstances. AI-powered scheduling systems can analyze historical data and identify patterns to optimize scheduling decisions (Saaida, 2023). By doing so, these systems can generate the most efficient and effective schedules for both students and faculty, ensuring that resources are allocated appropriately and that the educational experience is as smooth as possible. AI can also be used to automate the process of room assignments, ensuring that classrooms are used efficiently and that there are no conflicts in scheduling.

Another administrative function that can benefit from AI automation is communication (Igbokwe, 2023). Educational institutions often manage a large volume of communication, including emails, phone calls, and in-person inquiries from students, parents, and faculty. Responding to these inquiries can be time-consuming for administrative staff, especially when the questions are repetitive or straightforward. AI-powered chatbots and virtual assistants can automate many of these communication tasks, providing instant responses to common questions and allowing staff to focus on more complex issues. For example, AI chatbots can answer questions about class schedules, deadlines, exam dates, and general administrative procedures. These systems can also provide basic technical support, helping students navigate online learning platforms or troubleshoot common issues. By automating routine communication tasks, AI can improve the efficiency of administrative operations and enhance the overall experience for students and staff.

Resource management is another area where AI can significantly improve administrative efficiency (Igbokwe, 2023). Educational institutions must manage a wide range of resources, including classrooms, equipment, teaching materials, and personnel. AI can be used to track the availability and usage of these resources, ensuring that they are allocated in the most efficient way possible. For example, AI-powered systems can monitor the usage of classrooms and teaching materials, identifying patterns and making recommendations for how resources can be distributed more effectively. Similarly, AI can help with personnel management by analyzing data on teacher performance, workload, and availability to ensure that staffing levels are appropriate and that educators are not overburdened. By automating resource management, AI can help institutions reduce waste, optimize resource allocation, and ensure that resources are used in the most effective way possible.

One of the most significant benefits of AI in educational administration is its potential to improve efficiency, accuracy, and consistency in the completion of administrative tasks (Adams & Thompson, 2025; National Education Association, 2024). Human error is inevitable in any administrative process, whether it's in grading, scheduling, or data entry. AI systems, on the other hand, can be programmed to follow strict guidelines and protocols, ensuring that tasks are completed accurately and consistently every time. For example, AI-powered grading systems can assess assignments based on a set of predefined criteria, ensuring that grading is consistent and unbiased (Clauser et. al., 2024). Similarly, AI scheduling systems can optimize schedules based on a set of rules, ensuring that conflicts are minimized and that resources are allocated efficiently.

AI also has the ability to process large amounts of data quickly and identify patterns that may not be immediately apparent to human administrators. For example, AI can analyze student performance data to identify trends, such as which students are struggling in particular subjects or which teaching methods are most effective. By analyzing this data, AI systems can provide valuable insights that can help administrators make more informed decisions about resource allocation, curriculum development, and student support services. AI can also be used to predict student outcomes (National Education Association, 2024), such as identifying students who are at risk of falling behind or dropping out. By providing early warnings and insights, AI can help administrators intervene early and provide targeted support to students in need.

Another advantage of AI in administrative tasks is its ability to scale (Kakungulu, 2024). As educational institutions grow, the volume of administrative tasks increases, making it more difficult for human staff to keep up. AI systems, however, can handle large volumes of data and tasks without the need for additional resources. For example, AI-powered grading systems can grade thousands of assignments in a fraction of the time it would take a human educator. Similarly, AI scheduling systems can generate schedules for large numbers of students and faculty without becoming overwhelmed. This scalability makes AI an ideal solution for educational institutions that are experiencing growth or facing increasing demands for administrative support.

Furthermore, AI can help educational institutions provide a more personalized experience for students (National Education Association, 2024). By analyzing data on student performance, preferences, and learning styles, AI systems can provide insights that allow administrators to tailor the educational experience to the individual needs of each student. For example, AI can help identify students who may benefit from additional support, such as tutoring or counseling services. Similarly, AI can help administrators create personalized learning plans that cater to the specific needs and goals of each student (Saaida, 2023). By providing personalized support, AI can enhance student outcomes and ensure that all students have the opportunity to succeed.

AI has the potential to revolutionize administrative tasks in education by automating routine functions, improving efficiency, and providing valuable insights into student performance and institutional operations. From grading and scheduling to communication and resource management, AI can streamline processes and reduce the workload on educators and staff, allowing them to focus more on teaching and student engagement. The ability of AI to improve accuracy, consistency, and scalability makes it an invaluable tool for educational institutions, and its potential to provide personalized support to students further enhances its value. As AI continues to evolve, its role in educational administration will likely expand, creating even greater opportunities for improving the efficiency and effectiveness of educational systems (Poonpon, 2023).

AI in Grading and Assessment

Artificial Intelligence (AI) has revolutionized various sectors, and education is no exception. One of the most impactful applications of AI in education is the automation of grading (U.S. Department of Education, 2023). Grading is a critical yet time-consuming task for educators, especially in large classrooms or when dealing with complex assessments such as essays (Poonpon, 2023). AI's ability to automate grading for multiple-choice, short-answer, and even essay-based assessments can provide significant benefits to both students and educators. By leveraging AI technologies, educational institutions can streamline the grading process, reduce educator workload, and provide students with quick and accurate feedback that enhances their learning experience. In this section, we will explore how AI can automate grading across different types of assessments, the role of AI in formative assessments and continuous evaluation, and the impact of AI-powered grading systems on reducing workload and improving assessment accuracy.

Automating Grading for Multiple-Choice, Short-Answer, and Essay-based Assessments

Multiple-choice assessments are one of the most common forms of evaluation in educational settings. While relatively simple to grade manually, the grading process can still be time-consuming when dealing with large volumes of students. AI-powered grading systems can automate this process, instantly grading multiple-choice assessments with a high degree of accuracy (Clauser et al., 2024; U.S. Department of Education, 2023). These systems use algorithms to compare student responses to the correct answers and provide immediate feedback. AI can even be programmed to handle variations in question formats, such as true/false or matching questions, ensuring that the grading process remains consistent and efficient.

Short-answer assessments, which require students to provide brief written responses to questions, present a greater challenge for traditional grading methods. Unlike multiple-choice questions, short-answer responses require subjective judgment to assess the quality and accuracy of the student's answer. AI can address this challenge by using natural language processing (NLP) algorithms to analyze student responses (Poonpon, 2023). NLP algorithms are capable of understanding and interpreting human language, allowing AI to evaluate short-answer responses based on factors such as content relevance, clarity, grammar, and structure. This technology enables AI systems to provide accurate and consistent grading for short-answer assessments, reducing the need for manual intervention.

Essay-based assessments, which are often used to evaluate higher-order thinking skills, present an even more complex challenge for AI-powered grading systems. Essays require not only the evaluation of factual accuracy but also the assessment of argument structure, coherence, and writing quality. AI systems have made significant strides in this area by using advanced machine learning models and NLP techniques to analyze essays (Poonpon, 2023). These systems can evaluate various aspects of an essay, including grammar, spelling, sentence structure, argumentation, and overall coherence. AI can also compare essays to a large database of existing content to check for plagiarism, ensuring that students' work is original. While AI-powered essay grading is not yet perfect, it has shown promise in providing consistent, objective, and efficient grading for essay-based assessments (Clauser et. al., 2024).

The Role of AI in Formative Assessments and Continuous Evaluation

In addition to automating traditional assessments, AI can play a significant role in formative assessments and continuous evaluation (Kakungulu, 2024; Zhai & Nehm, 2023). Formative assessments are designed to monitor student learning throughout the course, providing ongoing feedback that can help students improve their performance. Unlike summative assessments, which are typically administered at the end of a unit or course, formative assessments are conducted regularly to track student progress and identify areas where students may need additional support.

AI can automate formative assessments by continuously tracking student performance in real time (Kakungulu, 2024; Zhai & Nehm, 2023). For example, AI-powered learning management systems (LMS) can monitor students' interactions with course materials, such as quizzes, assignments, and discussion boards, and assess their understanding of key concepts. By analyzing patterns in student behavior and performance, AI can identify students who are struggling with specific topics and provide personalized recommendations for improvement. AI can also offer instant feedback on student work, allowing students to make adjustments and improve their understanding before moving on to more complex material (Zhai & Nehm, 2023).

One of the key advantages of AI in formative assessments is its ability to provide continuous, real-time feedback (Kakungulu, 2024; U.S. Department of Education, 2023). Traditional assessment methods, such as quizzes and exams, are often limited in their ability to provide immediate feedback. Students may have to wait days or even weeks for their work to be graded, which can delay their learning process. AI-powered systems, on the other hand, can offer instant feedback, allowing students to understand their mistakes and make corrections on the spot. This immediate feedback fosters a growth mindset, as students can see their progress and take proactive steps to improve their learning.

AI can also provide detailed insights into individual student performance. By analyzing data on student interactions, AI systems can identify trends and patterns that may not be immediately apparent to educators. For example, AI can detect when a student consistently struggles with a particular concept or skill, even if they perform well in other areas. This data can be used to inform targeted interventions, such as personalized tutoring or additional resources, to help students overcome challenges and succeed in their studies (Strielkowski et al., 2025).

CASE STUDIES OF AI-POWERED GRADING SYSTEMS AND THEIR IMPACT

Several educational institutions and organizations have already implemented AI-powered grading systems with promising results. These systems have not only reduced the workload for educators but also improved the accuracy and consistency of assessments. Below are some case studies of AI-powered grading systems and their impact on educational settings.

1. **Turnitin's Gradescope**: Gradescope, developed by Turnitin, is an AI-powered grading platform that helps educators grade a wide range of assessments, including multiple-choice, short-answer, and essay-based questions. The system uses machine learning algorithms to analyze student responses and provide instant feedback. Gradescope has been implemented in various educational institutions, including universities and K-12 schools, to streamline the grading process. Educators have reported significant time savings, as the system automates much of the grading process and reduces the need for manual intervention. In addition to saving time, Gradescope has been praised for its ability to provide consistent

and objective grading, ensuring that students are evaluated fairly and accurately (Columbia Center for Teaching and Learning, 2020).

2. **Socrative**: Socrative is an AI-powered formative assessment tool that allows educators to create quizzes, polls, and other assessments to monitor student progress. The platform uses AI to analyze student responses in real time, providing immediate feedback and insights into student performance. Socrative is particularly useful for tracking student progress during class, as it enables educators to quickly identify areas where students may be struggling and adjust their teaching strategies accordingly. The system has been widely adopted in K-12 schools and higher education institutions, with educators reporting increased student engagement and improved learning outcomes (Dakka, 2015).
3. **AI in High-Stakes Testing**: High-stakes testing, such as standardized exams, is a common form of assessment in many educational systems. AI-powered grading systems have been implemented in some standardized testing environments to automate the grading of multiple-choice and short-answer questions. For example, the Educational Testing Service (ETS) has developed an AI-powered grading system called e-rater (Yakubu et al., 2024), which is used to assess written responses in standardized tests such as the GRE. e-rater uses natural language processing algorithms to evaluate essays based on grammar, sentence structure, and coherence. The system has been shown to provide consistent and accurate grading, reducing the potential for human error and bias in the assessment process.

Impact on Educator Workload and Assessment Accuracy

The implementation of AI-powered grading systems has had a significant impact on reducing educator workload and improving assessment accuracy. By automating the grading process, educators can save valuable time that would otherwise be spent on manual grading (Rutner & Scott, 2022). This time savings allows educators to focus more on providing personalized support to students, engaging in meaningful classroom interactions, and developing new teaching strategies. AI-powered grading systems also help to reduce the potential for grading inconsistencies and human error, ensuring that students are evaluated fairly and accurately (Kakungulu, 2024).

In addition to reducing workload, AI-powered grading systems have been shown to improve assessment accuracy. Traditional grading methods are often subject to human bias, especially when grading subjective assessments such as essays. AI systems, on the other hand, are programmed to follow strict grading criteria, ensuring that assessments are graded consistently and objectively. This consistency is particularly important in large classrooms or high-stakes testing environments, where grading discrepancies can have significant consequences for students.

AI-powered grading systems have the potential to transform the way educational institutions assess student performance. By automating the grading of multiple-choice, short-answer, and essay-based assessments, AI can provide quick, accurate, and consistent feedback to students. The role of AI in formative assessments and continuous evaluation allows for real-time tracking of student progress and personalized interventions. Case studies of AI-powered grading systems demonstrate their effectiveness in reducing educator workload, improving assessment accuracy, and enhancing the overall learning experience. As AI technology continues to evolve, its role in educational assessments will likely expand, offering even greater opportunities for improving the efficiency and effectiveness of grading and feedback processes (Kakungulu, 2024; U.S. Department of Education, 2023).

AI IN SCHEDULING AND RESOURCE MANAGEMENT

The integration of Artificial Intelligence (AI) into educational settings has significantly transformed various aspects of administration, including scheduling and resource management. One of the most notable applications of AI in education is its ability to optimize the scheduling of classes, meetings, and events (National Education Association, 2024). Traditional scheduling methods often rely on manual processes that can be time-consuming, prone to errors, and inefficient, especially in large institutions with complex timetables. AI offers a powerful solution by automating and optimizing scheduling processes, taking into account various factors such as teacher availability, room capacity, student preferences, and even external constraints such as holidays or special events. Through machine learning algorithms and advanced data analysis, AI can create optimized schedules that minimize conflicts and maximize efficiency, ensuring that both students and faculty members can make the most of their time and resources.

AI can analyze a wide range of variables to create schedules that are both effective and flexible. For example, when scheduling classes, AI can consider the availability of instructors, the size of classrooms, and the number of students enrolled in each course. By factoring in these elements, AI can assign the right courses to the right rooms and instructors, avoiding situations where a class is scheduled in a room that is too small or when an instructor is double-booked. Additionally, AI can account for student preferences, such as their preferred time slots for classes or their availability for extracurricular activities, ensuring that the schedule is not only efficient but also accommodating to students' needs. AI can even take into account historical data to predict optimal scheduling patterns, helping to avoid clashes with other popular courses or events that might otherwise lead to scheduling conflicts (Saaida, 2023).

In addition to optimizing class schedules, AI can also streamline the scheduling of meetings and events. Educational institutions often host numerous meetings, workshops, conferences, and other events that require careful coordination. AI can automate the process of scheduling these events by considering factors such as room availability, the schedules of key participants, and the duration of each event. This not only saves time but also ensures that events are scheduled in a way that minimizes conflicts with other institutional activities. AI can even suggest alternative time slots or locations if the initial proposed schedule is not feasible, ensuring that the institution's activities are organized efficiently and with minimal disruption to the academic calendar.

AI's role in optimizing scheduling extends beyond just classes and events; it also plays a critical role in managing resources such as textbooks, equipment, and facilities. Efficient resource management is essential for ensuring that educational institutions can operate smoothly, but it can be a complex task, particularly in large institutions with numerous courses and departments. AI can help manage these resources by tracking inventory levels, monitoring usage patterns, and predicting future demand. For example, AI can track the availability of textbooks for specific courses and automatically order new copies when inventory levels run low. It can also monitor the usage of equipment, such as computers, projectors, and laboratory tools, ensuring that resources are allocated efficiently and that there is no overuse or underuse of expensive or limited resources.

AI can also optimize the allocation of facilities, such as classrooms, meeting rooms, and study spaces (Saaida, 2023). By analyzing data on room usage patterns, AI can suggest optimal room assignments for classes and events, taking into account factors such as room capacity, equipment needs, and student preferences. For instance, if a particular classroom is frequently underutilized during certain times of the day, AI can suggest that classes be scheduled in that room to maximize its use. Similarly, AI can ensure that rooms with specialized equipment, such as computer labs or science laboratories, are reserved for courses that require those resources, preventing scheduling conflicts and ensuring that resources are used efficiently.

In addition to managing physical resources, AI can also help with the management of human resources, such as faculty members and administrative staff. AI can optimize the allocation of staff based on factors such as workload, availability, and expertise. For example, AI can ensure that faculty members are assigned to courses that align with their areas of expertise, taking into account their teaching schedules and availability. Similarly, AI can help administrative staff manage their workloads by automating routine tasks, such as scheduling meetings or responding to inquiries, allowing them to focus on more complex tasks that require human intervention.

AI's ability to manage complex timetables and resources is particularly valuable in large educational institutions where scheduling and resource allocation can become a logistical nightmare. Traditional scheduling methods often involve a great deal of manual input and are prone to errors, leading to conflicts, inefficiencies, and wasted resources. AI, on the other hand, can analyze vast amounts of data and generate optimal schedules and resource allocations in a fraction of the time it would take a human administrator. By minimizing scheduling conflicts and ensuring that resources are used efficiently, AI helps educational institutions save time, reduce costs, and improve overall operational efficiency.

One of the key benefits of AI in scheduling and resource management is its ability to handle complexity. In large institutions, there are often numerous variables to consider when creating schedules and allocating resources. For example, a university may need to schedule hundreds of classes across multiple campuses, taking into account factors such as room availability, instructor preferences, student enrollment numbers, and external factors such as public holidays or institutional events. AI can process all of these variables simultaneously, generating schedules that minimize conflicts and optimize resource usage. By automating this process, AI allows educational institutions to focus on more strategic tasks, such as improving teaching quality or enhancing student engagement, rather than spending time on logistical challenges (Saaida, 2023).

AI can also assist in identifying patterns and trends in scheduling and resource usage. By analyzing historical data, AI can identify recurring scheduling conflicts or inefficiencies and suggest improvements (Saaida, 2023). For example, if a particular room is consistently overbooked during certain times of the day, AI can suggest alternative room assignments or adjust the scheduling patterns to ensure that the room is used more efficiently. Similarly, AI can identify periods of low resource usage, such as times when classrooms or equipment are underutilized, and suggest ways to optimize their use. By identifying these patterns, AI helps educational institutions continuously improve their scheduling and resource management processes, leading to better outcomes for students, faculty, and staff.

Another advantage of AI in scheduling and resource management is its ability to adapt to changing circumstances. In educational settings, schedules and resource allocations are often subject to change due to unforeseen events, such as faculty absences, student enrollment fluctuations, or last-minute changes in event schedules. AI can quickly adapt to these changes by analyzing new data and adjusting schedules and resource allocations accordingly. For example, if a faculty member is unable to teach a class due to illness, AI can automatically reschedule the class or assign a substitute instructor. Similarly, if a student drops a course, AI can adjust the schedule to accommodate the change, ensuring that the student's needs are met without disrupting the overall schedule. This flexibility makes AI an invaluable tool for managing the dynamic and often unpredictable nature of educational environments.

Despite the many benefits of AI in scheduling and resource management, there are challenges associated with its implementation. One of the main challenges is the need for accurate and up-to-date data (Pedro et al., 2019). AI relies on data to make decisions, and if the data is incomplete, outdated, or inaccurate, the AI system may generate suboptimal schedules or resource allocations. Ensuring that data is collected and maintained accurately is essential for the success of AI-powered scheduling and resource management systems. Additionally, there may be resistance to AI adoption from faculty and staff who are accustomed to traditional methods of scheduling and resource management. Overcoming this resistance may require providing training and support to ensure that all stakeholders are comfortable using AI systems (Tariq, 2024).

In conclusion, AI has the potential to transform scheduling and resource management in educational settings by optimizing class schedules, managing resources efficiently, and minimizing conflicts. By automating these processes, AI allows educational institutions to save time, reduce costs, and improve operational efficiency. The ability of AI to handle complex timetables and adapt to changing circumstances makes it an invaluable tool for managing the dynamic nature of educational environments. However, successful implementation requires accurate data and buy-in from faculty and staff. As AI technology continues to evolve, its role in educational administration will only grow, offering new opportunities for improving the efficiency and effectiveness of scheduling and resource management.

AI IN COMMUNICATION AND STUDENT SUPPORT

The use of AI-powered chatbots and virtual assistants in educational settings has gained significant traction as institutions look for ways to streamline communication and enhance the overall student experience (National Education Association, 2024). These AI-driven tools have the potential to handle routine communication tasks, freeing up administrative staff to focus on more complex and personalized interactions (Strielkowski et al., 2025; Zhai & Nehm, 2023). One of the primary functions of AI-powered chatbots in education is answering frequently asked questions (FAQs). Educational institutions often receive a high volume of inquiries from students, parents, and staff, ranging from questions about school policies, admission requirements, and course schedules to inquiries about campus facilities and events. Traditionally, answering these questions has been a time-consuming process for administrative staff, requiring significant resources and leading to delays in response times. AI-powered chatbots can address this issue by providing instant, automated responses to common questions, ensuring that individuals receive the information they need quickly and accurately. By leveraging natural language processing (NLP) and machine learning algorithms, these chatbots can understand and respond to a wide range of queries, offering real-time assistance at any time of day, even outside of regular office hours (Kakungulu, 2024; Poonpon, 2023).

Beyond answering FAQs, AI-powered chatbots can also provide detailed information on school policies, procedures, and upcoming events. For example, a chatbot can provide students with information about registration deadlines, exam schedules, and graduation requirements. By automating the delivery of this information, AI helps to ensure that students, parents, and staff are always up-to-date on important dates and policies. This can significantly reduce the administrative burden on staff members who would otherwise be responsible for manually disseminating this information. Furthermore, AI-powered chatbots can be programmed to send proactive reminders to students about upcoming deadlines, such as application deadlines or payment due dates, helping to keep students on track and preventing missed opportunities.

In addition to answering questions and providing information, AI can also play a key role in assisting with enrollment processes (Saaida, 2023). Enrollment is often a complex and time-consuming task for both students and administrators, involving multiple steps such as course selection, document submission, and fee payment. AI-powered virtual assistants can guide students through each stage of the enrollment process, offering step-by-step instructions and reminders. For example, a virtual assistant could help students select courses based on their academic goals and prerequisites, provide information on available sections, and even assist with the submission of necessary documents. AI can also help students navigate the payment process, providing them with clear instructions on how to pay tuition fees, apply for financial aid, and complete any other necessary administrative tasks. By automating these processes, AI not only saves time for students and staff but also reduces the likelihood of errors or omissions, ensuring a smoother and more efficient enrollment experience.

AI's ability to automate administrative communication extends beyond answering questions and guiding students through processes; it can also enhance communication with parents and staff (Strielkowski et al., 2025). Parents are often involved in their children's education, and they frequently have questions about their child's progress, school events, and policies. AI-powered chatbots can provide parents with quick access to this information, reducing the need for them to contact school staff directly. For example, a parent may want to know when parent-teacher conferences are scheduled or inquire about their child's attendance or academic performance. Rather than waiting for a response from an administrative staff member, the parent can use the chatbot to receive the information they need instantly. This not only improves the efficiency of communication but also ensures that parents are consistently informed and engaged in their child's education.

For staff members, AI-powered chatbots can help with routine administrative tasks such as scheduling meetings, providing updates on institutional policies, and answering common HR-related questions. Staff members can use the chatbot to access information on benefits, payroll, and training opportunities, reducing the need for human resources staff to handle these inquiries. By automating routine communication tasks, AI allows staff to focus on more complex or sensitive issues that require human intervention. This can lead to improved staff satisfaction and productivity, as well as a more efficient and streamlined administrative process.

The potential for AI to improve response times and ensure consistency in messaging is one of its most valuable features. In traditional administrative settings, communication can often be delayed due to factors such as staff availability, workload, or time zone differences. AI-powered chatbots, on the other hand, are available 24/7 and can provide immediate responses to inquiries, ensuring that individuals receive timely assistance. Additionally, because AI chatbots are programmed to follow predefined scripts and guidelines, they ensure that messaging remains consistent across all communication channels. This reduces the risk of conflicting or inaccurate information being shared, which can occur when different staff members provide different responses to the same question. By maintaining consistency in messaging, AI-powered chatbots help to ensure that all stakeholders—students, parents, and staff—receive accurate and reliable information.

Another key benefit of AI in administrative communication is its potential to provide personalized support to students. Education is not just about academics; it is also about the overall well-being and development of students. Many students face challenges outside of the classroom, such as emotional or psychological struggles, that can affect their academic performance and overall experience. AI-powered virtual assistants can offer personalized support to students by providing them with resources, advice, and guidance tailored to their individual needs. For example, if a student is struggling with stress or anxiety, an AI-powered assistant could recommend stress management techniques or direct the student to counseling services. Similarly, if a student is having difficulty with a particular subject, the assistant could suggest study tips, tutoring services, or online resources to help the student improve. By providing this level of personalized support, AI can help students navigate both academic and personal challenges, contributing to their overall success and well-being.

AI can also provide emotional support by offering a non-judgmental space for students to express their concerns. While AI-powered virtual assistants are not a replacement for human counselors, they can provide students with an initial point of contact when they are feeling overwhelmed or unsure about where to turn. The anonymity and accessibility of AI-powered assistants can make students feel more comfortable discussing sensitive issues, such as mental health, without fear of stigma or judgment. In this way, AI can serve as a valuable tool for promoting student well-being and providing early intervention for those who may need additional support (Goyal et al., 2023).

The use of AI to automate administrative communication tasks in educational settings is transforming the way institutions interact with students, parents, and staff. By streamlining routine communication, improving response times, and ensuring consistency in messaging, AI-powered chatbots and virtual assistants are enhancing the overall efficiency of educational administration. Moreover, AI's ability to provide personalized support to students helps them navigate academic, administrative, and emotional challenges, contributing to their overall success and well-being. As AI technology continues to evolve, its role in educational communication will only expand, offering new opportunities for improving the student experience and optimizing administrative processes.

DATA ANALYSIS AND DECISION-MAKING

AI's ability to analyze large volumes of data related to student performance, attendance, and behavior is one of its most powerful features, offering educational institutions valuable insights that can drive decision-making and improve educational outcomes. Traditionally, administrators and educators have relied on manual methods to collect and analyze student data, which can be time-consuming, error-prone, and often insufficient for making informed decisions. With the advent of AI, however, this process has been transformed. AI systems can process vast amounts of data from multiple sources, including learning management systems (LMS), student information systems (SIS), attendance records, and behavioral tracking tools, providing a more comprehensive and accurate picture of student performance. By analyzing this data, AI can identify patterns and trends that might otherwise go unnoticed, offering actionable insights that can help educators and administrators make data-driven decisions (Saaida, 2023).

For example, AI can analyze student performance data across various assessments, identifying students who may be struggling in specific subjects or concepts (Igbokwe, 2023). By examining patterns in test scores, homework assignments, and participation (Rutner & Scott, 2022), AI can flag students who are at risk of falling behind and suggest targeted interventions. Similarly, AI can analyze attendance records to identify students who may be chronically absent or disengaged from school, allowing administrators to intervene early and provide the necessary support to improve attendance and academic performance. In addition to performance and attendance,

AI can also track behavioral data, such as disciplinary incidents, to identify trends that might indicate underlying issues, such as bullying, mental health concerns, or socio-economic factors that could be impacting a student's success. By providing a more holistic view of student data, AI allows educators and administrators to make more informed decisions that address the root causes of challenges, rather than just treating the symptoms.

AI's ability to support data-driven decision-making is a critical component of its potential to revolutionize education (National Education Association, 2024). In addition to identifying trends and patterns in student performance, AI can also predict future outcomes based on historical data (National Education Association, 2024). For example, AI can analyze past performance data to predict which students are most likely to succeed or struggle in future courses, helping educators tailor their teaching strategies and provide additional support where needed. Similarly, AI can predict graduation rates, college readiness, and other key outcomes, allowing administrators to make proactive decisions to improve student success. These predictive capabilities are particularly valuable for identifying students who may be at risk of dropping out or failing to meet academic benchmarks, enabling institutions to intervene early and provide the necessary resources and support to help them stay on track.

Moreover, AI can support the development of more effective educational policies by providing administrators with data-driven insights into the impact of existing policies and practices (U.S. Department of Education, 2023). For instance, AI can analyze the effectiveness of different teaching methods, curriculum changes, or school interventions by comparing student outcomes before and after the implementation of these changes. This allows administrators to assess whether specific policies are achieving their intended goals and make adjustments as needed. AI can also help identify gaps in policy or areas where additional resources or support may be required, ensuring that decisions are based on evidence rather than assumptions or anecdotal data. In this way, AI can play a key role in shaping the future of education by informing policy decisions that are more aligned with the needs of students and educators.

In addition to supporting data-driven decision-making in academic settings, AI can also play a significant role in improving institutional planning, budgeting, and resource allocation (Igbokwe, 2023). Educational institutions often face complex challenges related to the efficient use of resources, particularly in an environment of limited funding and increasing demands for services. AI can assist administrators in making more informed decisions about how to allocate resources, ensuring that they are used where they will have the greatest impact (Igbokwe, 2023). By analyzing data on student enrollment, course offerings, faculty workloads, and facility usage, AI can help institutions optimize their scheduling and staffing decisions. For example, AI can predict student demand for specific courses or programs, allowing institutions to adjust their course offerings and staffing levels accordingly. This can help institutions reduce inefficiencies, such as overstaffing or underutilization of facilities, and ensure that resources are being used in the most effective way possible.

AI can also assist with budgeting by analyzing historical spending patterns and identifying areas where costs can be reduced or resources can be reallocated. AI tools such as Cleo, Microsoft, and Chat GPT can be used to identify trends in spending on materials, supplies, or technology, highlighting areas where cost savings can be achieved without sacrificing quality. Similarly, AI can help institutions identify areas where additional funding may be needed, such as for student support services, professional development, or infrastructure improvements. By providing data-driven insights into financial planning, AI enables administrators to make more informed decisions about how to allocate resources and ensure the long-term sustainability of the institution.

Furthermore, AI's ability to analyze data from multiple sources allows for more accurate and effective long-term planning (Adams & Thompson, 2025). For example, AI can help institutions forecast future enrollment trends, predict staffing needs, and assess the long-term impact of policy changes. This enables institutions to plan more effectively for the future, ensuring that they are prepared to meet the evolving needs of students, staff, and the broader community. AI can also support the development of strategic plans by providing data-driven insights into the strengths and weaknesses of the institution, helping administrators set realistic goals and priorities for the future.

AI's role in data analysis extends beyond just academic performance and resource management; it can also support the development of more personalized learning experiences for students (Goyal et al., 2023; Igbokwe, 2023; Saaida, 2023). By analyzing data on individual student preferences, learning styles, and progress, AI can help educators tailor their teaching methods to better meet the needs of each student. For example, AI can recommend personalized learning materials, suggest adaptive learning paths, and provide real-time feedback to students based on their performance (Strielkowski, 2025). This level of personalization helps ensure that each student receives the support and resources they need to succeed, improving learning outcomes and overall student satisfaction.

In conclusion, AI's ability to analyze large volumes of data and provide actionable insights has the potential to transform educational administration. By supporting data-driven decision-making, identifying trends, predicting outcomes, and informing policy changes, AI enables administrators and educators to make more informed, proactive decisions that improve student success. Additionally, AI can play a key role in institutional planning, budgeting, and resource allocation, ensuring that resources are used efficiently and effectively. As AI technology continues to evolve, its ability to enhance educational administration and support personalized learning experiences will only continue to grow, offering new opportunities for improving the quality and accessibility of education.

BENEFITS OF AI AUTOMATION IN EDUCATIONAL ADMINISTRATION

The integration of AI into educational administrative tasks offers significant advantages in terms of efficiency and time savings for educators, administrators, and support staff (Igbokwe, 2023). By automating routine and time-consuming tasks such as grading, scheduling, attendance tracking, and resource management, AI frees up valuable time that can be redirected toward more strategic and student-centered activities (Saaida, 2023). Educators, for example, can focus more on teaching and interacting with students rather than spending hours on administrative duties. Administrators can devote their time to shaping policies, improving student outcomes, and managing long-term institutional goals, while support staff can focus on student services, counseling, and addressing specific needs. The overall result is a more efficient use of human resources, with each individual able to dedicate their time and expertise to the tasks that matter most. This shift allows for a more dynamic and student-focused educational environment, where staff can collaborate on initiatives that improve the quality of education and student experience.

Moreover, AI's ability to improve the accuracy and consistency of administrative processes is one of its most impactful benefits (Saaida, 2023). Human error is inevitable in any system, and administrative tasks are no exception. Whether it's inputting grades, managing schedules, or processing enrollment data, mistakes can occur, leading to inefficiencies and even negative consequences for students. AI, on the other hand, can handle these tasks with a high degree of precision, reducing the likelihood of errors and ensuring that administrative processes are executed consistently. For example, AI-driven grading systems can quickly and accurately assess student work, whether it's multiple-choice, short-answer, or essay-based assessments, without the biases that may affect human evaluators. Similarly, AI-powered scheduling tools can ensure that class times, room assignments, and teacher availability are optimized without the risk of double-booking or scheduling conflicts. The result is a smoother, more reliable administrative system that enhances the overall functioning of the institution.

AI also enhances communication and collaboration among staff, students, and parents, contributing to better organizational coordination (Adams & Thompson, 2025). In educational institutions, effective communication is crucial for fostering a supportive and cohesive learning environment. AI-powered chatbots and virtual assistants can handle routine inquiries from students, parents, and staff, providing immediate responses to common questions about policies, procedures, and academic requirements (Goyal et al., 2023). This reduces the administrative burden on staff and ensures that all parties receive timely and accurate information. Furthermore, AI can streamline communication between departments, ensuring that all relevant stakeholders are kept informed about important events, deadlines, and changes. For example, AI can automate the distribution of meeting reminders, event notifications, and policy updates, reducing the likelihood of miscommunication and ensuring that everyone is on the same page. This enhanced communication and coordination ultimately lead to a more organized and efficient institution, where staff, students, and parents can work together to support student success.

In addition to improving efficiency and communication, AI can also generate significant cost savings for educational institutions (Goyal et al., 2023). By automating administrative tasks, institutions can reduce the need for manual labor, cutting down on staffings. For example, AI-driven grading systems can replace the need for teaching assistants or staff members to manually grade assignments, saving both time and money. Similarly, AI-powered scheduling tools can help institutions optimize the use of classroom spaces and resources, reducing the need for additional facilities or staff to manage room assignments (Saaida, 2023). AI can also help identify areas where resources are being underutilized, allowing institutions to make more informed decisions about where to allocate funds. This optimization of resources leads to cost savings, which can be reinvested into areas that directly impact student learning, such as hiring additional teachers, expanding student support services, or improving classroom technology. As a result, AI not only improves the operational efficiency of educational institutions but also contributes to the overall financial health of the institution, allowing it to better serve its students and stakeholders.

In conclusion, the integration of AI into educational administration offers numerous benefits, including increased efficiency, improved accuracy, enhanced communication, and cost savings. By automating routine tasks, AI allows educators, administrators, and support staff to focus on more strategic, student-centered activities that directly contribute to student success. The reduction of human error and bias in administrative processes ensures that tasks are completed accurately and consistently, while AI-powered communication tools improve coordination among staff, students, and parents. Additionally, AI's ability to optimize resources and reduce administrative overhead leads to significant cost savings for educational institutions. As AI continues to evolve, its potential to transform educational administration will only grow, offering even more opportunities for institutions to operate more efficiently and effectively, ultimately benefiting students and the wider educational community.

CHALLENGES AND ETHICAL CONSIDERATIONS

Integrating AI into existing administrative systems in educational institutions presents several challenges, many of which stem from the need for staff training, infrastructure upgrades, and system compatibility (Strielkowski et al., 2025). First, the successful adoption of AI in educational administration requires a workforce that is adequately trained to understand, operate, and troubleshoot AI systems. Many educators and administrators may not have the technical expertise required to use these advanced tools effectively. As a result, institutions must invest in comprehensive training programs to equip staff with the necessary skills to integrate AI into their daily workflows. Without proper training, there is a risk that the implementation of AI will be met with resistance or underutilization, undermining its potential benefits. Additionally, AI systems often require significant infrastructure upgrades to function optimally. These upgrades may involve investing in new hardware, software, and network capabilities, which can be costly and time-consuming. Furthermore, AI systems must be compatible with existing administrative tools and platforms. If the new AI tools do not integrate smoothly with current systems, it can lead to inefficiencies, data silos, and disruptions in administrative operations. Overcoming these integration challenges requires careful planning, resource allocation, and collaboration between educational institutions and technology providers.

Ethical concerns are also a significant consideration when integrating AI into administrative tasks. One of the primary concerns is data privacy and security (Goyal et al., 2023). AI systems rely on large volumes of data to function effectively, and this data often includes sensitive student information, such as academic records, attendance, and behavioral data. The collection, storage, and use of this data must comply with strict privacy regulations, such as the Family Educational Rights and Privacy Act (FERPA) in the United States or the General Data Protection Regulation (GDPR) in Europe. Failure to protect this data from breaches or unauthorized access can lead to significant legal and reputational consequences for educational institutions. Additionally, AI systems can inadvertently reinforce biases in decision-making processes (Rutner & Scott, 2022; Strielkowski et al., 2025). Since AI algorithms are often trained on, they may replicate existing biases present in the data, such as racial, gender, or socioeconomic biases. This can result in unfair or discriminatory outcomes, particularly in areas such as grading, admissions, and resource allocation. To mitigate these risks, educational institutions must ensure that AI systems are designed with fairness and inclusivity in mind, regularly auditing algorithms to identify and address any biases that may emerge (Adams & Thompson, 2025; Clauser et. al., 2024; Rutner & Scott, 2022).

Another critical ethical consideration is the importance of transparency and accountability in AI systems. For AI to be trusted and accepted by educators, administrators, and students, it is essential that the decision-making processes behind AI systems are transparent (Strielkowski et al., 2025). This means that the logic behind AI algorithms and the data they rely on should be clearly explained and accessible to all stakeholders. Transparency helps build trust in AI systems and ensures that they are being used appropriately and ethically. In addition to transparency, accountability is also crucial. Educational institutions must establish clear lines of responsibility for the decisions made by AI systems, particularly when these decisions have a direct impact on students. For example, if an AI system makes a recommendation about student placement, grading, or disciplinary action, there should be a process in place for reviewing and challenging these decisions. This ensures that AI does not replace human judgment but rather complements it, allowing for a more balanced and equitable approach to decision-making. Ultimately, transparency and accountability are key to ensuring that AI in educational administration is used fairly and responsibly, fostering trust among all stakeholders and ensuring that the benefits of AI are realized without compromising ethical standards.

In conclusion, while the integration of AI into educational administration holds great promise, it also presents several challenges and ethical concerns. Overcoming the technical and logistical hurdles of integrating AI into existing systems requires investment in staff training, infrastructure upgrades, and ensuring compatibility with current tools. At the same time, ethical considerations related to data privacy, security, and algorithmic bias must be carefully addressed to ensure that AI systems are used responsibly and fairly (Clauser et. al., 2024). Finally, maintaining transparency and accountability in AI decision-making processes is essential to building trust and ensuring that AI serves as a positive force in education. By addressing these challenges, educational institutions can harness the power of AI to improve administrative efficiency while safeguarding the rights and interests of students and staff.

FUTURE DIRECTIONS FOR AI IN EDUCATIONAL ADMINISTRATION

The future of AI in education holds immense potential, particularly in the realm of automating complex administrative tasks. As AI technology continues to evolve, we can expect to see more advanced AI tools capable of handling higher-level administrative functions such as strategic planning and policy development. These tools could analyze large volumes of institutional data, identifying trends, forecasting future needs, and providing actionable insights that help guide decision-making (Igbokwe, 2023). For example, AI could assist in creating long-term academic strategies by predicting enrollment trends, budgetary needs, and the demand for specific programs or courses. By automating these tasks, educational institutions can ensure more informed, data-driven decisions that align with both short-term goals and long-term institutional growth.

In addition to handling more complex tasks, the future of AI in education will likely see systems that are more intuitive and adaptable. AI systems will become increasingly capable of learning from human feedback, allowing them to refine their processes over time and improve their accuracy and relevance. This adaptability could result in AI tools that better align with the unique needs of individual educational institutions, as they learn from the specific challenges and goals faced by each institution. For instance, AI systems could continually adjust their recommendations based on feedback from administrators, teachers, and students, optimizing processes like scheduling, resource allocation, and student support (Saaida, 2023). This dynamic learning ability would make AI tools not only more efficient but also more personalized, enhancing their overall effectiveness in supporting educational administration (Adams & Thompson, 2025).

Emerging technologies such as blockchain, machine learning, and natural language processing (NLP) are poised to further enhance AI's role in automating administrative tasks. Blockchain technology, for example, could be used to secure and verify educational records, making data management more transparent, accurate, and tamper-proof. Machine learning algorithms could improve the AI's ability to analyze complex data sets, offering more sophisticated insights into student performance, institutional needs, and resource allocation. NLP could enable AI systems to better understand and process human language, allowing for more seamless interactions with students, staff, and faculty through chatbots, virtual assistants, and automated communication tools. Together, these emerging technologies will allow AI to become even more integral to the administrative functions of educational institutions, streamlining processes, improving decision-making, and ultimately enhancing the overall educational experience (Kakungulu, 2024; Poonpon, 2023).

CONCLUSION

In conclusion, the transformative potential of AI in educational administration is immense, offering the possibility to significantly improve the efficiency and effectiveness of administrative processes. By automating routine tasks such as grading, scheduling, communication, and resource management, AI can free up valuable time for educators, administrators, and support staff, allowing them to focus on more strategic and student-centered initiatives. This shift can lead to more responsive and personalized learning environments, where the needs of both students and staff are better met. However, the successful integration of AI into educational systems requires thoughtful planning and consideration of various factors, including the ethical implications surrounding data privacy, security, and algorithmic bias (Clauser et. al., 2024; Igbokwe, 2023). It is crucial that AI technologies are deployed in a way that ensures fairness, transparency, and accountability in decision-making processes.

Moreover, while AI has the potential to greatly enhance administrative functions, it is essential to recognize that the human element of education must remain central. Educators and administrators play an irreplaceable role in fostering relationships, providing emotional support, and making nuanced decisions that AI cannot replicate. Therefore, a balanced approach is necessary—one that leverages the power of AI to streamline administrative tasks while maintaining the human touch that is so vital to the educational experience. The chapter will also emphasize the importance of ongoing research and collaboration between educators, technologists, and policymakers to ensure that AI is implemented responsibly and effectively. By adopting a holistic and ethical approach to AI integration, educational institutions can create environments that are not only more efficient but also more inclusive and equitable for all stakeholders involved.

REFERENCES

Adams, D., & Thompson, P. (2025). Transforming School Leadership with Artificial Intelligence: Applications, Implications, and Future Directions. *Leadership and Policy in Schools*, *24*(1), 77–89. DOI: 10.1080/15700763.2024.2411295

Clauser, B. E., Yaneva, V., Baldwin, P., An Ha, L., & Mee, J. (2024). Automated Scoring of Short-Answer Questions: A Progress Report. *Applied Measurement in Education*, *37*(3), 209–224. DOI: 10.1080/08957347.2024.2386945

Columbia Center for Teaching and Learning. (2020). Creating Assignments and Grading Online with Gradescope. Columbia University. https://ctl.columbia.edu/resources-and-technology/teaching-with-technology/teaching-online/gradescope/

Dakka, S. M. (2015, September). Using Socrative to enhance in-class student engagement and collaboration. *International Journal of Integrating Technology in Education*, *4*(3), 13–19.

Goyal, P., Minz, N. K., & Sha, A. (2023). *Chatbots and virtual assistants in education: Enhancing student support and engagement.*

Igbokwe, I. C. (2023). Application of artificial intelligence (AI) in educational management. *International Journal of Scientific and Research Publications*, *13*(3), 300.

Kakungulu, S. J. (2024). The role of artificial intelligence in educational assessment. [EEJSAR]. *Eurasian Experiment Journal of Scientific and Applied Research*, *5*(2), 44–47.

National Education Association. (2024, April). *Report of the NEA Task Force on Artificial Intelligence in Education.*

Pedro, F., Subosa, M., Rivas, A., & Valverde, P. (2019). Artificial intelligence in education: Challenges and opportunities for sustainable development.

Poonpon, K., Manorom, P., & Chansanam, W. (2023). Exploring effective methods for automated essay scoring of non-native speakers. *Contemporary Educational Technology*, *15*(4), ep475.

Rutner, S. M., & Scott, R. A. (2022). Use of artificial intelligence to grade student discussion boards: An exploratory study. *Information Systems Education Journal*, *20*(4), 4–13.

Saaida, M. B. E. (2023). AI-driven transformations in higher education: Opportunities and challenges. *International Journal of Educational Research and Studies*, *5*(1), 29–36.

Strielkowski, W., Grebennikova, V., Lisovskiy, A., Rakhimova, G., & Vasileva, T. (2025). AI-driven adaptive learning for sustainable educational transformation. *Sustainable Development*, *33*(2), 1921–1947. DOI: 10.1002/sd.3221

Tariq, U. (2024). Challenges in AI-Powered Educational Technologies: Teacher Perspectives and Resistance. *Journal of AI Integration in Education*, *1*(3), 1–10.

U.S. Department of Education, Office of Educational Technology. (2023). *Artificial intelligence and the future of teaching and learning: Insights and recommendations*. U.S. Department of Education.

Yakubu, M. A., Sain, Z. H., Lawal, U. S., & Budiman, S. A. (2024). Application of Artificial Intelligence [AI] for Automated Essay Grading in Nigerian Schools. [IJoEd]. *Indonesian Journal on Education*, *1*(2), 93–103.

Zhai, X., & Nehm, R. H. (2023). AI and formative assessment: The train has left the station. *Journal of Research in Science Teaching*, *60*(6), 1390–1398.

Chapter 11
AI-Powered Tutoring: Enhancing Student Support

Linda Marie Ellington
https://orcid.org/0000-0002-7697-056X
Southern New Hampshire University, USA

ABSTRACT

This chapter examines the transformative role of AI-powered tutoring systems in redefining student support through personalized, scalable, and adaptive learning experiences. The discussion highlights their capacity to identify knowledge gaps, foster self-paced learning, and enhance academic outcomes across diverse educational contexts. However, the chapter also critically addresses ethical challenges, including data privacy concerns, algorithmic bias, and the imperative of maintaining human oversight to preserve the relational aspects of education. Additionally, it explores issues of accessibility and equity, emphasizing the need to bridge technological divides that may exacerbate existing disparities. The chapter outlines future directions for responsible integration, advocating for collaborative frameworks among educators, policymakers, and technologists to ensure ethical deployment and equitable access. By balancing innovation with inclusivity, AI-powered tutoring systems hold promise for creating more adaptive, inclusive, and effective educational ecosystems.

INTRODUCTION

The advent of artificial intelligence (AI) has ushered in a transformative era in education, redefining traditional paradigms of teaching and learning. As educational systems worldwide grapple with global challenges such as scalability, personalized instruction, equitable access, and teacher shortages, AI-powered tutoring emerges as a pivotal innovation poised to address these pressing issues (Jain, 2025; Roshanaei et

DOI: 10.4018/979-8-3373-5102-5.ch011

al., 2023). These technologies can customize educational content based on individual student needs, fostering engagement and improving outcomes for disadvantaged learners (Supramaniam et al., 2024; Dumbuya, 2024).

Historically, education has relied on a one-size-fits-all model, often struggling to meet diverse learner needs. AI-powered tutoring systems, leveraging advancements in machine learning, natural language processing, and generative models like GPT-4, offer dynamic solutions by tailoring content to individual learning styles, pacing, and preferences. These systems transcend geographical and temporal barriers, providing 24/7 accessibility and real-time feedback, thus democratizing access to quality education.

The benefits of AI tutoring are manifold: from fostering self-paced learning and closing achievement gaps to enabling data-driven insights that inform instructional strategies (Shahvaroughi & Ghasmi, 2024). AI-powered analytics enable educators to gain deeper insights into student learning patterns and adapt instructional strategies accordingly (Farahani & Ghasmi, 2024).

For instance, adaptive learning platforms can identify knowledge gaps and adjust curricula dynamically, while AI chatbots offer instant academic support, enhancing student engagement and autonomy. AI-driven solutions can create customized learning paths, enhance access to educational resources, and support real-time communication, fostering inclusivity in higher education (Mitre & Zeneli, 2024). These technologies empower educators with data-driven insights to inform teaching practices and provide more effective, personalized instruction. AI's potential extends beyond accommodation, reimagining inclusive classrooms through microlearning environments that are inherently responsive to learners' differences (Safdar et al., 2024). Artificial intelligence techniques allow for the development of microlearning environments that are intrinsically inclusive and responsive to learners' differences.

Looking ahead, the convergence of AI with emerging technologies like virtual reality and predictive analytics promises immersive and proactive learning environments. Yet, the enduring value of human interaction in education underscores the need for a balanced approach, where AI tools augment pedagogical practices rather than supplant them. The weaving together theoretical insights and understanding its underlying methods, capabilities, and limitations, hopefully equips educators, policymakers, and technologists with the knowledge to harness AI's potential responsibly in teaching practices. AI technologies like intelligent tutoring systems and adaptive learning platforms can improve educational outcomes and transform teaching practices (Kazimova et al., 2025). This approach will help harness AI's potential to empower learners and prepare them for a rapidly evolving world (Yadav, 2024). While this approach will help harness AI's potential to empower learners and prepare them for a rapidly evolving world, it is essential to acknowledge several key limitations and challenges that must be addressed to ensure responsible and effective implementation.

LIMITATIONS AND CHALLENGES

Implementing AI tutoring systems presents a range of technical, ethical, pedagogical, and institutional challenges, which must be addressed to ensure their effectiveness and equitable adoption. They include data privacy and security concerns that arise as institutions collect vast amounts of student information (Abimbola et al., 2024). There are also risks of algorithmic bias and the potential reinforcement of inequalities, (Mimoudi, 2024; Alam et al., 2024). Ethical considerations, including the role of human oversight and the need for transparent practices, must be addressed. While AI shows promise in enhancing language learning and overall educational experiences, careful implementation is crucial to balance technological benefits with ethical concerns and the preservation of essential human elements in education. Table 1.0 identifies limitations and challenges:

Table 1. Limitations and challenges

Category	Challenges
Technical Limitations	*Natural Language Processing (NLP) Barriers*: AI systems may struggle to interpret complex student inputs, especially in nuanced or multilingual contexts, leading to misunderstandings or inadequate feedback. *Scalability and Infrastructure:* Deploying AI systems requires robust computational resources and reliable internet access, which may be unavailable in under-resourced schools or regions. *Adaptive Learning Accuracy:* Ensuring algorithms accurately diagnose knowledge gaps and adapt content to diverse learning styles remains technically complex.
Ethical Concerns	*Data Privacy and Security:* Collecting and storing sensitive student data raises risks of breaches or misuse, particularly for minors. Compliance with regulations (e.g., GDPR, COPPA) adds complexity. *Algorithmic Bias:* Biased training data or flawed model design can perpetuate inequities, disadvantaging marginalized student groups. *Transparency and Accountability:* "Black box" AI systems may lack explainability, making it difficult for educators to trust or audit their recommendations.
Pedagogical Challenges	*Over-Reliance on Automation:* Excessive dependence on AI may undermine critical thinking and creativity, as systems often prioritize standardized answers over exploratory learning. *Teacher-AI Collaboration:* Integrating AI tools without displacing educators requires redefining roles, ensuring teachers remain central to mentorship and emotional support. *Curriculum Alignment:* AI systems must stay updated with evolving educational standards and pedagogical practices, which demands continuous oversight.

continued on following page

Table 1. Continued

Category	Challenges
Equity and Access	*Digital Divide*: Students without access to devices or broadband are excluded, exacerbating educational inequalities. *Language and Cultural Barriers*: Systems trained on dominant languages or cultural contexts may fail to serve linguistically diverse or global student populations.
Human and Institutional Resistance	*Teacher Skepticism:* Educators may resist adoption due to fears of job displacement or distrust in AI's pedagogical value. *Training Gaps:* Teachers and administrators often lack the technical expertise to effectively implement or troubleshoot AI tools. *Institutional Bureaucracy*: Slow adoption processes, budget constraints, and policy misalignment can hinder deployment.
Long-Term Sustainability	*Costs:* Development, maintenance, and updates for AI systems are expensive, raising questions about long-term funding. *Evaluation of Efficacy:* Measuring long-term educational outcomes (e.g., critical thinking, retention) versus short-term metrics (e.g., test scores) remains challenging.
Regulatory and Social-Emotional Challenges	*Lack of Standardized Guidelines:* Absence of universal frameworks for ethical AI in education complicates compliance and quality assurance. *Social-Emotional Gaps:* AI systems cannot replicate human empathy, mentorship, or motivation, which are critical for holistic student development.

Educational AI demands united action from diverse experts. Success hinges on placing equity, transparency, and human needs at the center of all designs. Only then can AI tutoring fulfill its promise as a catalyst for truly inclusive learning transformation. The integration of artificial intelligence into educational systems represents both unprecedented opportunity and significant challenge. To harness AI tutoring as a force for positive change requires a deliberate, thoughtful approach involving multiple stakeholders. Daish et al. (2024) present a framework for incorporating multiple stakeholders' perspectives in designing Human-AI environments, aiming to establish a common dialogue between end-users and AI developers. Figaredo & Stoyanovich (2023) advocate for a "stakeholder-first" approach in responsible AI literacy initiatives, addressing the limitations of current AI education practices. They argue (p. 7) that this approach allows for tailoring content and methodologies to diverse audiences beyond the usual targets of AI literacy programs.

Human-centered approaches prioritize stakeholder needs, contextual understanding, and iterative methods to bridge gaps (Rodriguez et al., 2023; Holeman & Kane, 2019). This shift from technocentric to human-centered design is crucial for improving equity (Rodriguez et al., 2023). By focusing on human values, stakeholder participation, and contextual investigation, human-centered design offers a flexible yet disciplined approach to innovation that can lead to more equitable and successful adoption of new technologies.

Technologists alone cannot create optimal AI education systems. The most effective solutions emerge when developers work alongside:

- Educators who understand classroom dynamics and pedagogical best practices.
- Policymakers who can create supportive regulatory frameworks.
- Ethicists who identify potential harms and guide responsible implementation.
- Students and families whose lived experiences must inform design choices.

These collaborations bridge critical gaps in ensuring AI tools respond to actual needs rather than assumed ones. When this collaboration guides development and implementation, AI tutoring can help create educational systems that are more responsive, equitable, and effective for all learners.

Engagement and Sustained Interaction

Effective user engagement in AI tutoring systems requires an integrated approach that addresses technical capabilities, psychological needs, and ethical considerations. AI-driven interface design strategies can significantly improve student engagement in intelligent tutoring systems (Kim et al., 2020).

By thoughtfully implementing these strategies within a continuous improvement framework, AI tutoring systems can maintain the sustained engagement necessary for transformative learning experiences for fostering engagement, addressing technical implementation and human-centered design principles, such as the strategies and considerations identified in Table 2.0.

Table 2. Engagement strategies and considerations

Strategy Category	Key Approaches	Implementation Examples	Benefits
Personalization and Adaptivity	Dynamic Content Tailoring	Machine learning analysis of user behavior, preferences, and performance data to adjust content difficulty, pacing, and formats	Ensures content remains in learner's zone of proximal development
	Learning Pathways	Customizable goals and branching scenarios aligned with interests or career aspirations	Increases relevance and intrinsic motivation
	Predictive Analytics	Anticipation of disengagement and proactive intervention with nudges and alternative resources	Prevents dropout and maintains engagement momentum
Interactive and Immersive Experiences	Conversational AI	Chatbots and virtual tutors with natural language processing for human-like dialogue	Creates sense of social presence and immediate assistance

continued on following page

Table 2. Continued

Strategy Category	Key Approaches	Implementation Examples	Benefits
	Gamification	Integration of badges, leaderboards, progress bars, and achievement milestones	Activates reward systems and creates healthy competition
	Multimodal Interaction	Voice, gesture, or augmented reality interfaces for immersive learning environments	Enhances experiential learning through multiple senses
Real-Time Feedback and Scaffolding	Immediate Feedback	AI-powered correction of errors, explanation of misconceptions, and validation of correct answers	Reduces frustration and maintains learning momentum
	Growth-Oriented Messaging	Effort-focused feedback emphasizing improvement rather than static success/failure metrics	Promotes growth of mindset and resilience
	Scaffolded Support	Gradual reduction of hints as mastery increases, balancing challenge and skill	Maintains optimal "flow state" for engagement
Emotional and Motivational Support	Affective Computing	Emotion recognition via text, voice, or facial analysis to detect frustration or boredom	Enables responsive adjustment to emotional states
	Empathic Design	Encouraging language, milestone celebrations, and expressions of empathy	Creates emotional connection and psychological safety
	Social Learning	Peer interaction through discussion forums, group challenges, or collaborative problem-solving	Builds community and provides social motivation
User-Centered Design and Accessibility	Intuitive Interfaces	Clean, user-friendly designs that minimize cognitive load and technical barriers	Reduces extraneous processing and focuses attention on learning
	Cultural and Linguistic Relevance	Localized content, examples, and communication styles	Improves relatability and cultural resonance
	Accessibility Features	Compatibility with assistive technologies and multiple engagement modes	Ensures inclusivity and equitable access
Continuous Improvement and Transparency	Learner Agency	User-controlled goal setting, progress tracking, and system feedback mechanisms	Empowers learners and increases ownership
	Explainable AI	Transparent algorithmic decisions and recommendations	Builds trust and helps learners understand their learning path
	Iterative Updates	Regular refinement of AI models based on user feedback and pedagogical research	Keeps content and methodology current and effective

Strategy Category	Key Approaches	Implementation Examples	Benefits
Balancing Automation with Human Touch	Hybrid Models	AI-driven instruction combined with periodic human check-ins	Maintains relational connections while leveraging AI efficiency
	Teacher Empowerment	Educator dashboards for monitoring AI recommendations and appropriate intervention	Combines AI analytics with human expertise and judgment

The integration of AI-driven interface design strategies in intelligent tutoring systems faces several key challenges. Personalization algorithms must balance adaptability with consistent learning frameworks, often struggling to interpret nuanced emotional and cognitive student states from limited interaction data. Designers grapple with creating interfaces that feel responsive and intelligent while avoiding the uncanny effect that occurs when systems appear almost—but not quite—human in their interactions. Mishra et al., (2022) suggest that nearly human-like artificial entities can evoke discomfort or unease in observers. Owing to this, they posit that there needs to be a guiding principle in design and cross-modal technologies, such as virtual character design, video games, and animations, and to be aware of the challenges. Table 3.0 exhibits the challenges, description, and potential mitigation.

Table 3. Challenges and mitigation

Challenge	Description	Potential Mitigation
Over-Gamification	Excessive rewards may distract from intrinsic motivation or deep learning	Balance extrinsic rewards with intrinsic motivation strategies
Privacy Trade-offs	Personalization requires data collection, necessitating strict privacy safeguards	Implement transparent data policies and minimum necessary collection
Algorithmic Rigidity	Over-standardized pathways may stifle creativity or curiosity-driven exploration	Include open-ended exploration options and serendipitous discovery paths

Sustaining meaningful engagement in AI tutoring systems requires a delicate orchestration of technology and human understanding. At its core, effective engagement emerges from creating experiences that are simultaneously adaptive to learning patterns, empathetic to emotional states, and empowering for individual growth journeys. Research suggests that supporting students' feelings of competence, autonomy, and belonging can promote adaptive motivation and emotion (Linnenbrink-Garcia et al., 2016). Engagement mediates the relationship between self-efficacy and active learning, which in turn contributes to adaptive performance (Nandini et al., 2022). Papamitsiou et al., (2020) posit the importance of tailoring learning experiences to individual needs, monitoring engagement through various data sources, and implementing strategies to maintain and improve engagement for optimal learning outcomes.

The most successful AI tutoring environments respond dynamically to learners' evolving needs—adjusting not merely to performance metrics, but to subtle signals of curiosity, confusion, or breakthrough moments. This adaptivity extends beyond algorithmic content selection to encompass the entire learning experience, from pacing and presentation to challenge calibration and support scaffolding.

Authentic engagement, however, transcends technical responsiveness. It emerges from systems designed with genuine empathy—recognizing frustration before it leads to abandonment, celebrating achievements with appropriate enthusiasm, and acknowledging the unique learning identity each user brings to the interaction. These emotional dimensions of learning, once considered beyond the reach of artificial intelligence, now represent the frontier of engagement design. Xie (2020) states empathic designs need to be extended with two important considerations: learners' engagement and context in which engagement occurs. To address the shift to digital remote learning, empathic design can be applied to consider four types of engagement: 1) behavioral, 2) cognitive, (3) affective, and 4) social engagement. Additionally, the instructional design approach needs to address the three contextual features: 1) physical environment, 2) technological, and 3) social features in order to best support learners experience sin the shift to digital remote learning.

Table 4. AI features that support adult learning theory in practice

Theory	Key Proponent(s)	Core Principles	AI Features
Andragogy	Malcolm Knowles	Adults are self-directed, bring experience, are goal-oriented, and internally motivated.	Personalized learning paths. Adaptive assessments. AI-curated resources based on learner goals.
Transformative Learning	Jack Mezirow	Critical reflection on experiences leads to personal transformation.	AI-generated reflective prompts. Sentiment analysis of journal entries. Conversational AI for deep inquiry.
Experiential Learning	David Kolb	Learning through experience: doing, reflecting, thinking, and applying.	Virtual simulations and AR/ VR experiences. AI-powered feedback on performance. Scenario-based learning tools.
Self-Directed Learning	Tough, Knowles, Garrison	Learners take initiative in planning, executing, and evaluating their learning.	AI learning coaches or chatbots. Goal-tracking dashboards. Intelligent content recommendations.

Theory	Key Proponent(s)	Core Principles	AI Features
Constructivism	Piaget, Vygotsky	Learners build knowledge actively based on prior experience and social context.	Collaborative AI tools (e.g., co-authoring, discussion analysis). AI-supported peer learning platforms.
Situated Learning	Jean Lave, Etienne Wenger	Learning takes place in real-world, authentic contexts, and communities of practices.	AI-enables simulations of real environments. Recommendation of communities or networks. AI for role-based learning.

Perhaps most critically, engagement-focused AI tutoring systems must fundamentally empower learners. They accomplish this by fostering agency through meaningful choices, building self-efficacy through strategically structured challenges, and developing metacognitive skills that transfer beyond any single learning environment. This empowerment transforms learning from passive consumption to active co-creation, enhancing student engagement and learning outcomes. In higher education, active learning methodologies centered on constructivism theory empower learners, fostering confidence, competence, and problem-solving skills, emphasizing the potential to enhance engagement and outcomes (Sewagegn & Diale, 2019).

Exceptional AI tutoring systems integrate cutting-edge technology with motivational psychology and inclusive design principles. By incorporating self-determination theory, these systems can cater to diverse student needs, recognize cultural contexts, and improving academic engagement and motivation (Chen et al., 2023).

ENHANCING USER ENGAGEMENT

In today's rapidly evolving educational landscape, AI tutoring systems offer unprecedented opportunities for personalized learning experiences. However, these systems face a critical challenge: maintaining sustained user engagement over time. The most technically sophisticated AI tutor will fail if learners don't remain actively involved in the learning process. To enhance user engagement in AI tutoring systems, a combination of technological innovation, pedagogical insight, and user-centered design is essential. Studies have shown that AI-powered interface designs can significantly improve student engagement factors by up to 25.13% in intelligent tutoring systems (Kim et al., 2020). The integration of machine learning algorithms and user-centered design principles is crucial for developing effective AI-driven educational tools (Gupta & Gadikar, 2024).

By addressing cognitive, emotional, and social dimensions of the learning experience, developers can create AI tutoring environments that not only deliver content effectively but also motivate continued interaction. Below are actionable strategies organized across key dimensions:

Technological Approaches

- Implement adaptive learning algorithms that personalize content difficulty based on user performance.
- Develop natural language processing capabilities for conversational interactions.
- Integrate multimodal feedback systems (text, audio, visual).
- Create seamless cross-platform experiences across devices.
- Utilize data analytics to identify engagement patterns and optimize learning paths.

Pedagogical Strategies

- Structure content with spaced repetition principles to optimize knowledge retention.
- Design scenario-based learning that connects to real-world applications.
- Balance challenge and achievement to maintain flow state.
- Provide timely, specific feedback that guides improvement.

User Experience Considerations

- Prioritize intuitive interfaces with minimal cognitive load.
- Establish clear progression systems that visualize advancement.
- Offer customization options for learning preferences and goals.
- Create aesthetically pleasing environments that reduce digital fatigue.
- Design for accessibility across different learning needs.

Emotional and Social Elements

- Foster a growth mindset through encouraging messaging.
- Implement virtual rewards and recognition systems.
- Create opportunities for collaborative learning experiences.
- Develop AI personalities that build rapport through consistent interaction.

- Include features for reflection and metacognitive development.

Implementation Framework

- Begin with user research to identify specific engagement barriers.
- Prototype minimal viable features focused on core engagement needs.
- Collect continuous feedback through multiple channels.
- Iterate based on both quantitative metrics and qualitative insights.
- Balance innovation with usability in each development cycle.

Successful AI tutoring systems must go beyond content delivery to create truly engaging learning experiences. By integrating technological capabilities with evidence-based pedagogical approaches and human-centered design principles, developers can overcome the engagement challenges that have historically limited educational technology. The most effective systems will continuously evolve based on learner interaction data while maintaining focus on the fundamental goal: supporting meaningful learning journeys. As AI capabilities advance, there remains an essential human element to engagement—connecting with learners' intrinsic motivations, respecting their autonomy, and facilitating their growth. Ma (2018) introduces the concept of Human-Engaged AI, highlighting the synergy between humans and technology. Chiu et al. (2023) demonstrate that teacher support and student expertise significantly influence intrinsic motivation and competence when learning with AI chatbots. Cao et al. (2023) explore multi-role AI chatbots as pedagogical agents, designed to satisfy learners' psychological needs of competence, autonomy, and relatedness. Their study reveals the potential of AI-powered chatbots in enhancing engagement and motivation in computer science education. Markauskaite et al. (2022) advocate for rethinking the relationship between AI and human learning, emphasizing the need to develop capabilities that go beyond AI-centric views. The future of AI tutoring lies not just in smarter algorithms but in more empathetic, responsive, and personalized learning partnerships.

REAL-WORLD EXAMPLES OF SUCCESSFUL USER ENGAGEMENT IN AI-DRIVEN EDUCATIONAL PLATFORMS

The integration of artificial intelligence into educational platforms has transformed how students learn and interact with educational content. Leading companies like Duolingo, Khan Academy, and Coursera have leveraged AI to create highly engaging learning experiences that not only retain users but also significantly improve learning outcomes. These platforms employ sophisticated personalization algorithms that adapt to individual learning styles, implement elements that maintain motivation through reward systems, and utilize conversational AI to provide immediate feedback and support. By analyzing user behavior patterns, these successful platforms continuously refine their engagement strategies, creating educational experiences that feel both responsive and tailored to each learner's unique needs. Data-driven strategies, including personalization, and predictive analytics, can be employed to boost user engagement while prioritizing data privacy (Nwaimo et al., 2024). By leveraging user data and employing various analytical techniques, educational platforms can continuously refine their engagement strategies, creating tailored and responsive learning experiences that meet individual learner needs.

Analytical techniques and implementation of strategies do not exist in isolation. Rather, they function within a broader AI learning engagement ecosystem where multiple components work in concert to create a comprehensive educational environment. Understanding this ecosystem reveals how various technological, pedagogical, and human elements interact to maximize learning outcomes and sustain user engagement over time.

AI LEARNING ENGAGEMENT ECOSYSTEM

The most effective AI tutoring systems blend personalization, interactivity, and human-centric design to create experiences that feel less like studying and more like exploration, achievement, and growth. The personality of AI tutors plays a crucial role in student engagement and satisfaction, drawing inspiration from effective human tutors (Afzal et al., 2019). By seamlessly orchestrating human decision-making with AI capabilities, these systems can enhance student engagement and improve learning outcomes (Kokku et al., 2018).

At the center of the engaged learning hub is the core goal of AI-driven education platforms, as identified in Graph 1.0. Surrounding this hub are six key engagement strategies, each represented by a circle with example platforms:

1. *Balance Intrinsic & Extrinsic Motivation*: Features Duolingo with its streaks system and Khan Academy with its mastery approach, showing how the elements work alongside meaningful learning progress.
2. *Reduce Friction*: Showcases Codecademy's instant feedback system and Socratic's multimodal support that lower barriers to engagement.
3. *Social Proof & Collaboration*: Highlights Quizlet's leaderboards and Kahoot's team challenges that foster accountability through social dynamics.
4. *Align with Real-World Goals*: Illustrates how Coursera's certificates and LinkedIn Learning's career-relevant content drive long-term commitment.

5. *Emotional Design*: Demonstrates how MATHia's encouraging language and Prodigy's immersive storytelling make learning enjoyable.
6. *Personalized Adaptive Learning*: Showing how these strategies work together to create engaging educational experiences. The dashed lines connecting all elements emphasize the interconnected nature of these engagement approaches.

Figure 1. Engagement ecosystem

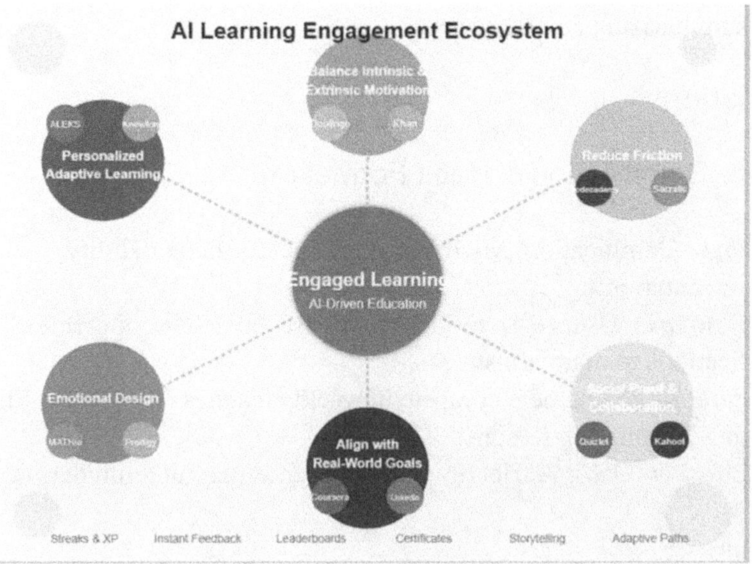

AI PIONEERS REDEFINING STUDENT ENGAGEMENT

In the rapidly evolving landscape of educational technology, organizations that effectively harness artificial intelligence to create engaging learning experiences are setting new standards for student success. The shift towards Education 4.0 and 5.0 emphasizes AI's role in creating dynamic, responsive systems that adapt to learners' progress in real-time (Rane et al., 2023). AI is also being implemented in various aspects of the student lifecycle, such as chatbots for student services, automated grading, and academic advising (Khare et al., 2018).

The following companies have successfully implemented user engagement strategies in AI-driven tutoring and educational platforms. These organizations have transformed traditional educational paradigms by developing systems that adapt to individual learning styles, maintain student motivation through personalized feedback loops, and create learning environments where students actively participate rather than passively consume content. By analyzing their strategies, successes, and even occasional missteps, we can extract valuable insights applicable across the educational technology sector. Each case demonstrates how thoughtful implementation of AI engagement strategies leads to measurable improvements in learning outcomes, retention rates, and student satisfaction—ultimately creating educational experiences that are both effective and deeply engaging.

Each example highlights the tactics used, outcomes, key lessons, challenges, and table 5.0 summarizing key takeaways.

Gamification

Duolingo: Gamification & Habit Formation

- Strategy: Gamification, Microlearning, Social Accountability.
- Implementation:
- *Daily Streaks*: Users earn rewards for consecutive days of practice, with push notifications to maintain streaks.
- *Leaderboards*: Learners compete in weekly leagues (e.g., Ruby, Emerald) by earning XP through lessons.
- *Owl Mascot (Duo):* A friendly character sends playful reminders (e.g., "Don't let Duo cry!").
- Results:
- Over 500 million downloads and 40 million monthly active users.
- 74% of users return after their first session, with streaks doubling retention rates.
- Key Lesson: Combining extrinsic rewards (badges) with intrinsic motivation (progress tracking) creates habitual engagement.
- Challenge: Balancing gamification to avoid distracting from learning outcomes

Prodigy Education: Game-Based Learning for K–12 Math

- Strategy: RPG-Style Gamification, Curriculum Alignment.
- Implementation:
- *Math Battles*: Students solve problems to cast spells and defeat monsters in a fantasy world.
- *In-Game Rewards*: Customizable avatars, pets, and gear incentivize practice.

- *Teacher Dashboard*: Educators align in-game content with classroom curricula.
- Results:
- Over 100 million registered users across 150+ countries.
- 83% of teachers report improved math scores among students.
- Key Lesson: Narrative-driven learning appeals to younger audiences while reinforcing academic standards.
- Challenge: Avoiding overstimulation with excessive game elements.

Math

Prodigy Math Game: RPG-Style Learning

- Strategy:
- *Math Battles*: Students solve problems to cast spells and defeat in-game characters.
- *Custom Avatars*: Personalization and in-game rewards (e.g., pets, gear) keep younger users engaged.
- Why It Works: Embeds curriculum-aligned math into a fantasy narrative, appealing to K–12 learners.

Carnegie Learning's MATHia: Real-Time Feedback

- Strategy:
- *Step-by-Step Hints*: AI tutor provides scaffolded guidance during problem-solving.
- *Error Analysis*: Flags misconceptions (e.g., "You forgot to carry the 1") instead of just marking answers wrong.
- Why It Works: Mimics human tutoring by addressing *how* students think, not just outcomes.

Carnegie Learning's MATHia: Real-Time Feedback

- Strategy:
- *Step-by-Step Hints*: AI tutor provides scaffolded guidance during problem-solving.
- *Error Analysis*: Flags misconceptions (e.g., "You forgot to carry the 1") instead of just marking answers wrong.
- Why It Works: Mimics human tutoring by addressing *how* students think, not just outcomes.

Coding

Codecademy: Interactive Coding Practice

- Strategy:
- *Instant Feedback*: Code is validated in real time, with hints for debugging errors.
- *Projects & Portfolios*: Learners build real apps/websites to showcase skills.
- *Streaks & Achievements*: Daily coding streaks unlock discounts or premium features.
- Why It Works: Balhands-on practice with career-relevant outcomes.

Personalized Learning

Coursera: Career-Aligned Learning & Credentials

- Strategy: Skill-Based Recommendations, Certifications.
- Implementation:
- *AI-Driven Skill Graphs*: Recommends courses based on job market trends (e.g., data science, UX design).
- *Professional Certificates*: Partnerships with Google, IBM, and Meta offer industry-recognized credentials.
- *Flexible Deadlines*: Self-paced courses with optional timelines reduce drop-out rates.
- Results:
- 113 million learners and 7,000+ institutional customers.
- 85% of learners report career benefits (e.g., promotions, new jobs).
- Key Lesson: Aligning education with tangible career outcomes drives long-term engagement.
- Challenge: Balancing free content with premium monetization.

Socratic by Google: Conversational AI & Visual Learning

- Strategy: Multimodal Interaction, Instant Feedback.
- Implementation:
- *Photo-Based Problem Solving*: Students snap pictures of homework, and AI provides step-by-step visual explanations.
- *Voice Queries*: NLP allows learners to ask questions conversationally (e.g., "Why does photosynthesis matter?").
- Results:

- Over 10 million downloads with a 4.8/5 app store rating.
- 92% of users report improved homework completion speed.
- Key Lesson: Reducing friction in accessing help increases trust in AI tools.
- Challenge: Ensuring accuracy across diverse subjects and question types.

Quizlet: Social Learning & Collaborative Tools

- Strategy: Peer Competition, User-Generated Content.
- Implementation:
- *Quizlet Live*: Teams compete to answer questions correctly in real time.
- *AI-Generated Study Sets*: Converts user-uploaded notes into flashcards and quizzes.
- *Spaced Repetition*: Schedules reviews based on forgetting curves.
- Results:
- 60 million monthly active users, with 90% of students reporting higher grades.
- Quizlet Live sessions increase class participation by 70%.
- Key Lesson: Social interaction transforms individual study into a communal experience.
- Challenge: Moderating low-quality user-generated content.

ELSA Speak: AI-Powered Pronunciation Coaching

- Strategy: Speech Recognition, Personalized Feedback.
- Implementation:
- *Pronunciation Scoring*: AI analyzes speech for accent, stress, and intonation errors.
- *Tailored Lessons*: Focuses on users' specific weaknesses (e.g., vowel sounds for Spanish speakers).
- Results:
- 40 million users across 130 countries, with a 4.7/5 app store rating.
- Learners improve pronunciation accuracy by 40% in 4 weeks.
- Key Lesson: Immediate, granular feedback builds confidence in skill development.
- Challenge: Addressing dialectal diversity in language learning.

Khan Academy: Mastery Learning + Personalization

- Strategy:

- *Mastery Challenges*: Students must achieve 100% on a skill to earn "mastery" badges.
- *Personalized Dashboards*: Visual progress meters show completion rates and recommend next steps.
- *Adaptive Practice*: AI adjusts question difficulty based on performance.
- Why It Works: Focuses on competency over speed, reducing anxiety and fostering a growth mindset.

Table 5. Summary of key insights behind successful edtech platforms

Insight	Example(s)	Key Takeaway
Gamification works, but context matters	Prodigy, Duolingo	Gamified elements should enhance the learning process, not distract from it.
Career relevance drives retention	Coursera	Learners stay engaged when content connects to real-world goals and careers.
Social dynamics enhance accountability	Quizlet, Duolingo	Peer competition and collaboration can drive motivation and consistency.
Lower friction, higher engagement	Socratic, ELSA Speak	Easy access and intuitive interfaces improve usage and sustained learning.
Balancing AI & Humanity	Khan Academy (educator dashboards)	AI should support and enhance human educators, not attempt to replace them.

These companies demonstrate that successful engagement hinges on understanding learners' emotional and practical needs, whether through fantasy RPGs (Prodigy), career credentials (Coursera), or conversational AI (Socratic). Learning science teaches us that the best strategies make learning feel relevant, rewarding, and effortless for students. While traditional educational environments have long sought to incorporate these principles, they often face practical constraints like limited resources, rigid curricula, and high student-to-teacher ratios. AI-powered tutoring enhances student learning outcomes through several targeted mechanisms that address the limitations of traditional educational models, creating personalized pathways that align with how our brains naturally acquire and retain knowledge. Personalized learning pathways have emerged as a promising approach to enhance student learning outcomes by tailoring educational experiences to individual needs and preferences (Amzil et al., 2023; Ferguson & Aitken, 2019). These pathways leverage advanced technologies and data analytics to customize content, assessments, and interventions, addressing the limitations of traditional one-size-fits-all models (Amzil et al., 2023).

LEARNING PATHWAYS

Learning pathways provide structured routes through educational content, allowing learners to progress at their own pace while ensuring they master necessary concepts along the way. Unlike rigid curriculums, pathways offer flexibility while maintaining clear direction, enabling personalized journeys tailored to individual goals, strengths, and learning styles. Whether in formal education, professional development, or self-directed learning, well-designed pathways guide learners through progressive skill development while allowing for exploration and discovery. Learning pathways facilitate the acquisition of knowledge, skills, and abilities through a progressive approach, aligning with constructivist theory (Reekie et al., 2023).

Below are key ways AI-powered tutoring specifically improves learning outcomes:

Personalized Learning Pathways

- *Adaptive Content Delivery*: AI systems analyze student performance in real time to adjust the difficulty, pace, and style of instruction. For example, if a student struggles with algebra, the system can provide additional practice problems, video tutorials, or alternative explanations until mastery is achieved.
- *Learning Style Alignment*: AI can identify whether a student learns better through visual, auditory, or kinesthetic methods and tailor content accordingly (e.g., interactive simulations for visual learners or podcasts for auditory learners).
- *Zone of Proximal Development (ZPD) Targeting*: By pinpointing the gap between what a student can do independently and what they can achieve with guidance, AI tutors scaffold instruction to keep learners in their optimal challenge zone, avoiding frustration or boredom.

Immediate, Actionable Feedback

- *Real-Time Corrections*: AI tutors provide instant feedback on assignments, quizzes, or problem-solving tasks. For instance, tools like MathGPT can detect calculation errors and explain step-by-step solutions, helping students correct misconceptions before they solidify.
- *Formative Assessment*: Continuous feedback loops allow students to iteratively improve their work. Writing assistants like **Grammarly** or AI essay graders highlight grammatical errors, structural weaknesses, and clarity issues, empowering students to refine drafts independently.

Scalable One-on-One Support

- *24/7 Accessibility*: AI chatbots (e.g., Khanmigo or Squirrel AI) offer round-the-clock academic assistance, answering questions, clarifying concepts, or guiding problem-solving outside classroom hours.
- *Support for Underserved Populations*: In schools with limited resources or overcrowded classrooms, AI tutors democratize access to high-quality instruction, ensuring students in rural or low-income areas receive the same level of support as their peers elsewhere.

Data-Driven Insights for Educators

- *Learning Analytics*: AI aggregates data on student performance, engagement, and knowledge gaps, generating dashboards that help teachers identify class-wide trends or individual struggles. For example, a teacher might use AI-generated reports to reteach a topic where 70% of students scored poorly.
- *Predictive Interventions*: Machine learning models predict at-risk students (e.g., those likely to fail a course) based on patterns in attendance, participation, or assignment completion, enabling early, targeted interventions.

Enhanced Engagement and Motivation

- *Gamification:* AI-powered platforms like **Duolingo** or **Quizlet** use game-like elements (badges, streaks, leaderboards) to motivate consistent practice and reward progress.
- *Personalized Recommendations*: AI curates resources (articles, videos, practice problems) aligned with a student's interests or career goals, fostering intrinsic motivation. For example, a student passionate about climate change might receive physics problems framed around renewable energy.

Reducing Achievement Gaps

- *Equity in Mastery Learning*: AI ensures all students achieve competency before advancing, unlike traditional models that move classes forward regardless of individual readiness. This is particularly impactful for students who need more time to grasp foundational concepts.
- *Language Support*: AI translation tools and multilingual tutors (e.g., Reverso or ELSA Speak) help non-native speakers access content in their primary language while improving proficiency in a secondary language.

Supporting Metacognition and Self-Regulation

- *Goal-Setting Tools*: AI tutors prompt students to set short- and long-term goals, track progress, and reflect on learning strategies. For example, an AI system might ask, "Did spaced repetition help you memorize vocabulary better than cramming?"
- *Study Habit Optimization*: By analyzing study patterns, AI can recommend optimal schedules (e.g., "Study calculus at 10 AM when focus is highest") or techniques (e.g., active recall vs. passive reading).

Continuous Assessment and Mastery

- *Low-Stakes Practice*: AI systems generate endless practice quizzes and simulations, allowing students to test knowledge without fear of penalties. This reduces test anxiety and encourages experimentation.
- *Mastery-Based Progression*: Students advance only after demonstrating proficiency, ensuring no critical gaps in understanding. Platforms like **ALEKS** (Assessment and Learning in Knowledge Spaces) use this approach effectively in STEM subjects.

Human-AI Collaboration

- *Teacher Empowerment*: AI handles repetitive tasks (grading, attendance, basic Q&A), freeing educators to focus on creative instruction, mentorship, and addressing complex student needs.
- *Hybrid Learning Models*: AI tutors complement human teachers by reinforcing lessons, providing extra practice, or offering alternative explanations. For example, a teacher might introduce a concept in class, while an AI tutor assigns follow-up exercises tailored to each student's grasp of the material.

Addressing Diverse Needs

- *Special Education Support*: AI tools assist students with disabilities through text-to-speech interfaces, customized pacing, or sensory-friendly content. For instance, apps like Microsoft Reading Coach use AI to support dyslexic learners with phonetic feedback.
- *Cultural Responsiveness*: AI can adapt examples, scenarios, and problem sets to reflect students' cultural backgrounds, making content more relatable and inclusive.

CHALLENGES AND CONSIDERATIONS

While AI-powered tutoring offers transformative benefits, its effectiveness depends on thoughtful implementation:

- *Ethical Design*: Guarding against algorithmic bias (e.g., racial or gender disparities in content recommendations) and ensuring data privacy.
- *Human Oversight*: AI should augment, not replace, with the emotional and social support provided by teachers.
- *Accessibility*: Bridging the digital divide to ensure all students have reliable internet access and devices.

AI-powered tutoring enhances learning outcomes by making education personalized, immediate, inclusive, and data-informed. When integrated ethically and equitably, these systems empower students to take ownership of their learning, enable teachers to act as facilitators of growth, and create pathways for lifelong success in an increasingly complex world. The future of education lies in the synergy between human educators and AI technologies, rather than choosing one over the other (Chan & Tsi, 2023). While AI can enhance teaching and learning through personalized feedback and real-time analytics, human teachers remain irreplaceable due to their unique qualities such as critical thinking, creativity, and emotional intelligence (Jantanukul, 2024). When educators leverage AI tools while maintaining their essential human connection with students, they create learning environments that address both individual needs and universal aspirations. The synergy between technological innovation and human guidance doesn't just empower students worldwide, it opens pathways through educational democratization that makes quality learning accessible regardless of location, socioeconomic status, or cultural background, while offering personalized experiences that honor each student's unique learning journey.

Empower Students Worldwide

AI-powered tutoring offers transformative potential for global education, presenting both opportunities and challenges. Educators need to acknowledge AI's potential and adapt to new perceptions of educational quality and workforce preparedness (Huong, 2024). AI-powered tutoring holds transformative potential for global education, offering both opportunities and challenges that need careful consideration

Opportunities

1. Language Support: Real-time translation and multilingual content can ridge language barriers, making education more inclusive.
2. Scalability: Can serve large populations, especially in regions with teacher shortages, by providing consistent quality education remotely.
3. Special Needs Support: Customizable tools (e.g., text-to-speech) offer tailored assistance for students with disabilities, promoting inclusivity.
4. Lifelong Learning: Facilitates continuous skill development aligned with evolving job markets, supporting adult education and professional growth.

Challenges

1. Digital Divide: Inequitable access to technology risks exacerbating global educational disparities. Solutions require infrastructure investment and public-private partnerships.
2. Bias and Fairness: AI systems must be rigorously tested to avoid perpetuating biases in data or content, ensuring cultural and contextual relevance.
3. Teacher Role Evolution: Educators may shift to mentoring roles, necessitating training and support to integrate AI tools effectively without diminishing human interaction,
4. Cultural Adaptation: Content must respect local contexts, languages, and values to ensure acceptance and effectiveness across diverse regions.

GLOBAL CASE STUDIES

While AI-powered tutoring represents a global phenomenon, its implementation varies across different regions, addressing unique educational challenges and opportunities. A few examples of AI tutoring initiatives from around the world identified in table below:

Table 6. Global edtech platforms

Region	Platform	Country	Key Features
Africa	Eneza Education	Kenya	- Mobile-based AI tutoring platform for rural/underserved communities - SMS, web, and app-based delivery - Multi-subject, local languages - 5M+ students served - Personalized learning & tracking - Ideal for limited infrastructure areas
	NumBots	Sub-Saharan Africa	- AI-powered math learning - Adaptive to student performance - Game-based learning - Supports low-resource educational environments
Asia	SQUIRREL AI	China	- Advanced adaptive AI learning - Personalized multi-subject tutoring - Machine learning for individual maps - Can outperform human tutors - Responds to high academic pressure
	BYJU'S	India	- Leading edtech with AI integration - Millions of users globally - Multi-language personalization - Adaptive content with ML - Video + interactive + feedback
Latin America	Geekie	Brazil	- AI-based platform to reduce education inequality - Personalized prep for national exams - Adaptive, multi-subject content
Middle East	ALEKS	United Arab Emirates	- Adaptive AI for math and science - Personalized learning paths - Supports diverse student backgrounds in international schools

These global examples demonstrate the transformative potential of AI-powered tutoring, and revolutionizing education across diverse cultural and economic contexts. Strategic collaboration among governments, educators, and technology developers is essential to harness AI's potential equitably, ensuring it builds bridges, rather than widenings global educational gaps.

While collaboration lays the foundation for equitable AI integration, it must be guided by strong ethical principles and clear regulatory policies. Without these guardrails, even well-intentioned collaborative efforts can drift from their intended goals or create unforeseen harms. Policy and ethical frameworks are crucial for ensuring responsible AI development and deployment. These frameworks should incorporate principles such as transparency, accountability, fairness, privacy, and security (Lottu et al., 2024). The United Nations emphasizes the need for ethical principles aligned with data governance, given the close relationship between AI and data (Hogenhout, 2021).

Governments worldwide are working to integrate AI into existing legal and ethical frameworks or develop new ones where necessary (Madhavan et al., 2020). Proposed frameworks suggest incorporating ethical considerations throughout the AI development lifecycle, from design to maintenance, recognizing AI systems as socio-technical artifacts with significant societal impact (Lottu et al., 2024).

POLICY AND ETHICAL FRAMEWORKS

The use of AI must be governed by robust ethical and policy frameworks that safeguard rights, promote fairness, and ensure no student is left behind. These frameworks serve as guardrails, ensuring that technological innovation does not outpace the moral and legal responsibilities owed to students, education, and global society as large. To address this, institutions need to develop comprehensive frameworks that consider pedagogical, governance, and operational dimensions (Chan, 2023). As the information society becomes more complex, policy approaches must evolve to include dynamic analytical frames, adaptive forms of policy, and reliance on ethics across all governance layers. By creating dynamic learning systems, policymakers can continuously improve governance and ensure that innovation aligns with moral and legal responsibilities (Bauer, 2022).

Protecting student data and privacy must be a top priority. AI tools often rely on large datasets, including sensitive personal information. Without strict data governance policies, there is a risk of misuse, breaches, or unintentional surveillance. Policies should reinforce transparency around what data is collected, how it is used, and who has access to it, with students and guardian given meaningful control over their information. Equally important is the need to address algorithmic bias. AI systems in education can perpetuate and exacerbate existing structural inequities and biases when trained on unrepresentative data and the biased algorithms can threaten students' learning experiences and support discriminatory practices (Matias & Zipitria, 2023; Madaio et al., 2021). Addressing these issues requires a multifaceted approach involving technical solutions, social justice considerations, and data governance measures (Leavy et al., 2020).

Recent research emphasizes the importance of embedding inclusivity and accessibility into AI design from the outset. Kinnula et al. (2021) propose collaborative efforts to define and conceptualize Accessible and Inclusive AI (AIAI), addressing algorithmic biases and limitations. AI's potential to enhance web accessibility for users with disabilities is highlighted by Hussain (2024), who explores its applications and benefits in improving user experiences. A systematic review by Chemnad & Othman (2024) reveals a predominant focus on AI-driven accessibility for visual impairments, identifying gaps in addressing other disabilities. They stress the need for adherence to accessibility standards and a comprehensive approach to digital accessibility. These studies collectively underscore

The integration of AI in education raises significant concerns, particularly regarding accountability and oversight. Multiple studies emphasize the need for robust regulatory frameworks to ensure responsible AI implementation in educational settings (Stevanović, 2024; Weber, 2020). The development of accountability structures is crucial, defining specific responsibilities for all stakeholders involved in AI implementation (Stevanović, 2024). Additionally, there is a call for preemptive measures to guarantee the responsible application of AI tools in world educational environments (Sywelem & El-Sayed Mahklouf, 2024).

The rise of AI presents a transformative opportunity to enhance global education, but only if approached with intentionality, collaboration, and care. Without robust policy frameworks and ethically grounded design, the very tools meant to empower learners could reinforce systemic biases, compromise privacy, and exclude marginalized communities.

Table 7. AI trends: Tools, risks, and solutions

Category	Tools/Technologies	Risks/Challenges	Solutions/Strategies
Ethical	Large Language Models (LLMs) Facial recognition Predictive analytics	Bias & discrimination Privacy invasion Misinformation Lack of transparency	Bias auditing tools Differential privacy Explainable AI (XAI) Ethics frameworks (e.g., IEEE, UNESCO)
Pedagogical	Adaptive learning systems Chatbots Automated grading	Over-reliance on automation Erosion of critical thinking Unequal access	Hybrid learning models Human-in-the loop design Digital equity initiatives
Technical	Neural networks Federated learning Generative models	Model opacity Data security Algorithmic brittleness	Interpretable ML methods Robustness testing Secure multi-party computation
Systemic	AI-powered platforms (e.g. surveillance, hiring) Algorithmic decision-making	Labor displacement Regulatory gaps Market monopolies	Policy and regulation Open-source alternatives Public education and upskilling

The table above highlights the interconnected nature of AI's evolving landscape, where technological innovation intersects with ethical responsibility, educational transformation, and systemic change. As AI continues to shape our societies, it is crucial to adopt a multidisciplinary approach hat balances risk with opportunities. By leverage appropriate tools, proactively addressing emerging risks, and implementing thoughtful solutions, stakeholders – from developers to policymakers-can guide AI development toward more equitable, transparent, and beneficial outcomes for all.

CONCLUSION

AI-powered tutoring systems represent a pivotal advancement in educational technology, offering significant potential to personalize and enhance learning experiences at scale. Their ability to adapt content, provide instant feedback, and support diverse learners positions them as valuable tools in addressing both individual and systemic educational challenges. Their effective and ethical implementation requires careful navigation of persistent concerns surround privacy, bias, and equitable access. Ensuring that these technologies supplement rather than supplant human educators is essential to preserving the relational and contextual richness of learning. As educational landscapes evolve, sustain collaboration among stakeholders will be critical to harnessing AI's capabilities responsibly and inclusively. When integrated thoughtfully, AI tutoring systems can serve as catalysts for more responsive, just, and learner-center education.

To realize the full promise of AI in education, stakeholders must embrace a shared vision that balances innovation with responsibility. This means centering human rights, inclusivity, transparency, and accountability in every decision—from the drafting of policies to the design of algorithms. By doing so, we can build an educational future where AI-powered tutoring not only enhances learning but does so in a way that is fair, ethical, and accessible to all.

REFERENCES

Afzal, S., Dempsey, B., D'Helon, C., Mukhi, N. K., Pribic, M., Sickler, A., Strong, P., Vanchiswar, M., & Wilde, L. (2019). The personality of AI systems in education: Experiences with the Watson Tutor, a one-on-one virtual tutoring system. *Childhood Education*, 95.

Alam, S., Kumar, M., Khursheed, S., Mahato, Z., Bashar, H. K., & Suman, A. (2024). Designing an AI driven intelligent tutorial system. *5th International Conference on Recent Trends in Computer Science and Technology (ICRTCST)*, 585-588.

Amzil, I., Aammou, S., & Tagdimi, Z. (2023). Enhance students' learning by providing personalized study pathways. *Conhecimento & Diversidade Journal, 15.*

Bauer, J. M. (2022). Toward new guardrails for the information society. *Telecommunications Policy.*

Cao, C.C., Ding, Z., Lin, J., & Hopfgartner, F. (2023). AI chatbots as multi-role pedagogical agents: Transforming engagement in CS education. *ArXiv, abs/2308.03992*

Chan, C. K. (2023). A comprehensive AI policy education framework for university teaching and learning. *International Journal of Educational Technology in Higher Education.*

Chan, C. K., & Tsi, L. H. (2023). The AI revolution in education: Will AI replace or assist teachers in higher education? *ArXiv, abs/2305.01185.* https://doi.org//arXiv.2305.01185DOI: 10.48550

Chemnad, K., & Othman, A. (2024). Digital accessibility in the era of artificial intelligence—Bibliometric analysis and systematic review. *Frontiers in Artificial Intelligence*, *7*. Advance online publication. DOI: 10.3389/frai.2024.1349668 PMID: 38435800

Chen, A., Liu, H., Li, K.-C., & Jia, J. (2023). For educational inclusiveness: Design and implementation of an intelligent tutoring system for student-athletes based on self-determination theory. *Sustainability*, *15*(20). Advance online publication. DOI: 10.3390/su152014709

Chiu, T. K., Moorhouse, B. L., Chai, C. S., & Ismailov, M. (2023). Teacher support and student motivation to learn with Artificial Intelligence (AI) based chatbot. *Interactive Learning Environments.*

Daish, P., Micallef, N., Lorenzo-Dus, N., Paiement, A., & Sahoo, D.R. (2024). Towards co-designing a continuous-learning human-AI interface: A case study in online grooming detection. *SYNERGY@AVI*.

Dumbuya, E. (2024). Personalized learning through artificial intelligence: Revolutionizing education. *International Journal of Science and Research Archive*.

Eden, C. A., Chisom, O. N., & Adeniyi, I. S. (2024). Integrating AI in education: Opportunities, challenges, and ethical considerations. *Magna Scientia Advanced Research and Reviews*, *10*(2). Advance online publication. DOI: 10.30574/msarr.2024.10.2.0039

Farahani, M. S., & Ghasmi, G. (2024). *Artificial intelligence in education: A comprehensive study*. Forum for Education Studies.

Ferguson, K., & Aitken, R. (2019). A large-scale project to develop personalized learning pathways at a university. *Online Journal of Distance Learning Administration*, 22.

Figaredo, D. D., & Stoyanovich, J. (2023). Responsible AI literacy: A stakeholder-first approach. *Big Data & Society*, •••, 1.

Gupta, R. K., & Gadikar, A. (2024). *Evaluating and enhancing user interaction in AI-driven educational tools: A comparative study of machine learning algorithms and design principles*. Computer Science, Engineering and Technology.

Hogenhout, L. (2021). A framework for ethical AI at the United Nations. *ArXiv, abs/2104.12547*.

Holeman, I., & Kane, D. (2020). Human-centered design for global health equity. *Information Technology for Development*, *26*(3). DOI: 10.1080/02681102.2019.1667289 PMID: 32982007

Huong, X. V. (2024). The implications of artificial intelligence for educational systems: Challenges, opportunities, and transformative potential. *The American Journal of Social Science and Education Innovations*, *6*(3). DOI: 10.37547/tajssei/Volume06Issue03-17

Hussain, S. A. (2024). The integration of artificial intelligence in web accessibility: Enhancing inclusivity. *International Journal for Research in Applied Science and Engineering Technology*, *12*(4).

Jain, N. (2025). AI as a catalyst for educational equity: Addressing global teacher shortages and learning disparities. *International Journal of Scientific Research in Computer Science*, *11*(1), 69–76. DOI: 10.32628/CSEIT25111200

Jantanukul, W. (2024). AI and human synergy: Utilizing AI to enhance teaching and learning. *Journal of Education and Learning Reviews.*

Kazimova, D., Tazhigulova, G., Shraimanova, G., Zatyneyko, A., & Sharzadin, A. (2025). Transforming university education with AI: A systematic review of technologies, applications, and implications. *International Journal of Engineering Pedagogy, 15*, 4–24.

Khare, K., Stewart, B., & Khare, A. (2018). *Artificial intelligence and the student experience: An institutional perspective*. IAFOR Journal of Education.

Kim, B., Suh, H., Heo, J., & Choi, Y. (2020). AI-driven interface design for intelligent tutoring system improves student engagement. *ArXiv, abs/2009.08976.*

Kinnula, M., Iivari, N., Sharma, S., Eden, G., Turunen, M., Achuthan, K., Nedungadi, P., Avellan, T., Thankachan, B., & Tulaskar, R. (2021). Researchers' toolbox for the future: Understanding and designing accessible and inclusive artificial intelligence (AIAI). *Proceedings of the 24th International Academic Mindtrek Conference.*

Kokku, R., Sundararajan, S. C., Dey, P., Sindhgatta, R., Nitta, S. V., & Sengupta, B. (2018). Augmenting classrooms with AI for personalized education. *2018 IEEE International Conference on Acoustics, Speech and Signal Processing (ICASSP).*

Leavy, S., O'Sullivan, B., & Siapera, E. (2020). Data, power and bias in artificial intelligence. *ArXiv, abs/2008.07341.*

Linnenbrink-Garcia; Patall, E.A., & Pekrun, R. (2016). Policy insights from the behavioral and brain sciences. *Sage (Atlanta, Ga.), 3*(2).

Lottu, O.A., Jacks, B. S., Aala, O. Ab., & Okafor, E.S. (2024). Towards a conceptual framework for ethical AI development in IT systems. *World Journal of Advanced Research and Reviews.*

Ma, X. (2018). Towards human-engaged AI. *Proceedings of the Twenty-Seventh International Joint Conference on Artificial Intelligence* (IJCAI-18).

Madaio, M.A., Blodgett, S., Mayfield, E., & Dixon-Rom'an, E. (2021). Confronting structural inequities in AI for education. *ArXiv, abs/2105.08847.*

Madhavan, R., Kerr, J. A., Corcos, A. R., & Isaacoff, B. (2020). Toward trustworthy and responsible artificial intelligence policy development. *IEEE Intelligent Systems,* •••, 35.

Markauskaite, L., Marrone, R.L., Poquet, O., Knight, S., Martínez-Maldonado, R., Howard, S., Tondeur, J., de Laat, M., Shum, S.B., Gašević, D., & Siemens, G. (2022). Rethinking the entwinement between artificial intelligence and human learning: What capabilities do learners need for a world with AI? *Computer and Education: Artificial Intelligence Journal, 3.*

Matias, A., & Zipitria, I. (2023). Promoting ethical uses in artificial intelligence applied to education. *International Conference on Intelligent Tutoring Systems.*

Mimoudi, A. (2024). AI, personalized education, and challenges. *International Conference on AI Research, 4*(1). https://doi.org/DOI: 10.34190/icair.4.1.3133

Mishra, N., Ramanathan, M., Tulsulkar, G., & Magnenat-Thalmann, N. (2022). Uncanny valley for interactive social agents: An experimental study. *Virtual Real. Intell. Hardw., 4.*

Mitre, X., & Zeneli, M. (2024). Using AI to improve accessibility and inclusivity in higher education for students with disabilities. *21st International Conference on Information Technology Based Higher Education and Training (ITHET).*

Nwaimo, C. S., Adegbola, A. E., & Adegbola, M. D. (2024). Data-driven strategies for enhancing user engagement in digital platforms. *International Journal of Management & Entrepreneurship Research, 6*(6). DOI: 10.51594/ijmer.v6i6.1170

Papamitsiou, Z. K., Pappas, I. O., Sharma, K., & Giannakos, M. N. (2020). Utilizing multimodal data through fsQCA to explain engagement in adaptive learning. *IEEE Transactions on Learning Technologies,* 13.

Rane, N. L., Choudhary, S. P., & Rane, J. (2023). Education 4.0 and 5.0: Integrating artificial intelligence (AI) for personalized and adaptive learning. *Social Science Research Network (*SSRN*) Electronic Journal.*

Reekie, M., de Bosch Kemper, N., Epp, S., Denison, J., Willson, M., & Moralejo, L. (2023). Learning pathways: Levelling, scaffolding & mapping curriculum. *Journal of Professional Nursing*, 46. PMID: 37188406

Rodriguez, N. M., Burleson, G., Linnes, J. C., & Sienko, K. H. (2023). Thinking beyond the device: An overview of human and equity-centered approaches for health technology design. *Annual Review of Biomedical Engineering.* DOI: 10.1146/annurev-bioeng-081922-024834 PMID: 37068765

Roshanaei, M., Olivares, H., & Lopez, R. R. (2023). Harnessing AI to foster equity in education: Opportunities, challenges, and emerging strategies. *Journal of Intelligent Learning Systems and Applications, 15*, 123–143. DOI: 10.4236/jilsa.2023.154009

Safdar, D. S., Kamran, D. F., & Anis, D. F. (2024). *Beyond accommodation artificial intelligence's role in reimagining inclusive classrooms*. Indus Journal of Social Sciences.

Sewagegn, A. A., & Diale, B. (2019). Empowering learners using active learning in higher education institutions. Manuel Brito, S. (Ed.). *Active Learning - Beyond the Future*. IntechOpen. https://doi.org/ DOI: 10.5772/intechopen.73460

Stevanović, K. (2024). Regulating artificial intelligence for higher education. *10th International Scientific Conference Technics, Informatic, and Education.*

Supramaniam, J. K., Baharudin, S. M., Halid, N. M., Abbas, M. S., Amin, M., Ghani, A., Affendy, K., Halim, A., & Nordin, M. N. (2024). Leveraging AI to bridge educational inequities: A global perspective. *Nanotechnology Perceptions.*

Sywelem, M. M., & Mahklouf, A. M. (2024). Ethical considerations in the integration of artificial intelligence in education. *Education and Information Technologies.*

Weber, A. S. (2020). Ethics concerns in artificial intelligence use in education. *14th International Technology, Education and Development Conference.*

Xie, K. (2020). Projecting learner engagement in remote contexts using empathic design. *Educational Technology Research and Development*, 69. PMID: 33223779

Yadav, D. S. (2024). *Navigating the landscape of AI integration in education: Opportunities, challenges, and ethical considerations for harnessing the potential of artificial intelligence*. BSSS Journal of Computer., DOI: 10.51767/jc1503

Chapter 12
Professors in Transition: The Impact of Commodification and AI on Higher Education

Linda Marie Ellington
https://orcid.org/0000-0002-7697-056X
Southern New Hampshire University, USA

ABSTRACT

This chapter explores professors' evolving role in the increasing commodification of higher education and the integration of artificial intelligence (AI) into academic environments. As universities adopt neoliberal policies and become more market-driven, professors are increasingly seen as service providers catering to student consumers rather than independent scholars and intellectual authorities. The rise of digital platforms, AI-driven learning tools, and open access to knowledge challenges the traditional gatekeeper role of professors, transforming how knowledge is created and disseminated. AI tools are often leveraged to optimize administrative processes and teaching outcomes. This chapter examines the implications of these changes for academic labor, intellectual autonomy, and the future of higher education, advocating for a reimagining of the professoriate as public intellectuals who can critically engage with AI and defend the university as a space for intellectual inquiry and the advancement of knowledge.

INTRODUCTION

The bedrock of higher education-academic freedom and shared governance faces ongoing challenges within the United States. Although not novel, recent incursions on tenure, academic freedom, and shared governance are alarming, as evidenced by legislative proposals and escalating corporate marketing encroach-

DOI: 10.4018/979-8-3373-5102-5.ch012

ments upon universities (Alibasic et al., 2024). In response, this chapter delves into the repercussions of higher education's shift toward a corporatized model period of transition where traditional academic values are at odds with emergent commercial imperatives. This shift is redefining professors' traditional functions and challenging their historical role as gatekeepers of knowledge within an increasingly digitized academic ecosystem (Lange, 2015).

Historically, professors were entrusted with transmitting knowledge and forming future minds that will improve the life in its complexity and aspects (Labidi & Barhoumi, 2023). In today's current academic landscape, the increasing commodification of education and the integration of AI tools disrupt this traditional paradigm. Recent research highlights the complex interplay of market logic, efficiency, and social missions in universities. Studies show that higher education institutions follow systematic scaling patterns, with different sectors leveraging economies of scale to address distinct priorities (Taylor et al., 2019). The growing need for affordable and accessible higher education is a major global challenge for the 21st century. There is a need to develop a deeper understanding of the functionality and taxonomy of universities and colleges and, in particular, how their various characteristics change with size. Scaling has been a powerful tool for revealing systematic regularities in systems across a range of topics from physics and biology to cities, and for understanding the underlying principles of their organization and growth (Taylor, et al., 2019) While market-driven approaches are seen as fostering efficiency and quality, concerns arise about their impact on educational equity and social stratification (Mann, 2015). There is significance in understanding the sociological consequences of education driven by corporate/private ethos. Public research universities, facing reduced state funding, increasingly adopt market-oriented strategies to generate revenue. Institutions could potentially blend some industry-oriented principles and behaviors to bolster social goals, as reflected in their newer resource-centered organizational discourses and strategies (Warshaw & Upton, 2020). This reflects a broader trend in contemporary universities, where three logics of practice - intellectual advancement, market pursuit, and social inclusion - coexist and shape institutional development. Despite potential conflicts, these principles are ultimately compatible, influencing how universities pursue knowledge, market opportunities, and greater inclusivity (Brint, 2018).

The integration of AI in education is transforming traditional paradigms, offering personalized learning experiences, and enhancing accessibility to knowledge (Ram & Bhandari, 2023). AI-driven technologies are revolutionizing teaching methods, curriculum design, and assessment practices, enabling educators to provide more interactive and engaging learning environments (Benitta et al., 2024). These tools facilitate adaptive learning pathways, real-time data analysis, and AI-enhanced virtual tutoring, promoting independent learning and data-informed decision-making (Silva

& Janes, 2020). The adoption of AI in higher education extends beyond classroom applications, impacting admissions, enrollment management, and student support services (Marmoah et al., 2024). While AI integration offers numerous benefits, it raises ethical concerns and challenges regarding privacy and the human-machine interface (Silva & Janes, 2020). Balancing AI capabilities with human-centric pedagogy and providing robust teacher training is crucial for effectively leveraging these technologies in education (Silva & Janes, 2020).

The growing influence of artificial intelligence (AI) in higher education has accelerated changes in teaching, learning, and administration. AI applications in higher education, such as profiling and prediction, assessment and evaluation, adaptive systems and personalization, and intelligent tutoring systems (Zawacki-Richter et al., 2019), are continuously enhancing learning outcomes. These technologies personalize experiences, augment faculty capabilities, and improve administrative efficiency (Rangavittal, 2024). AI-powered platforms enable instructors to perform administrative tasks more effectively and customize curriculum content to meet students' needs (Chen et al., 2020). However, the adoption of AI in education also presents challenges, including ethical considerations, data privacy concerns, and the need for infrastructure adjustments (Rangavittal, 2024). It is crucial that we, as educators, administrators, and policymakers, engage in ongoing exploration of AI's impact on higher education. As AI continues to evolve, its impact on the future nature of higher education remains a subject of our collective exploration and understanding (Popenici & Kerr, 2017). As a result, several neoliberal assumptions firmly rooted in conventional wisdom have contributed to a student-as-customer phenomenon, which is a cost driver (Mintz, 2021). This shift in perspective, bolstered by AI technologies, reinforces the idea of education as a market commodity rather than a public good, where the value of knowledge is increasingly tied to its monetary worth and accessibility through digital platforms.

THE PROFESSORIAL LANDSCAPE

Professors, with their capabilities, engagement, and critical awareness, are the backbone of universities. Their role is pivotal in the primary mission of universities—providing high-quality teaching and engaging in meaningful research (Altbach, 2015). It is their dedication that ensures the success of our academic institutions. Therefore, it is crucial to examine how professors can adapt to the dual transformation of corporatization and AI integration while maintaining their intellectual autonomy and commitment to advancing knowledge.

We know that the commodification of higher education is not a recent phenomenon. However, its impact has been increasingly felt in recent decades, particularly with the rise of neoliberal policies. Neoliberalism is a political and economic theory that emphasizes the value of free market competition. These policies have transformed the university into a business (Atalay, 2018). The turn toward a market-driven education model has not just altered but significantly shifted the very nature of academic work. Once seen as institutions dedicated to pursuing knowledge and cultivating critical thinking, universities are now more likely to be viewed as businesses that must generate revenue to remain competitive. In this environment, education is treated as a product, and students are seen as consumers who purchase this product in exchange for a degree expected to provide a return on investment through employment opportunities and economic mobility. Students who identify as consumers tend to perform worse academically than those intrinsically motivated by course content (Bunce, 2020). The long-term implications of these changes on higher education quality and student outcomes remain a subject of debate and research. Education is a metaphor operates in law to increase debt, reduce social mobility and degrade higher education itself (Kraiem, 2015).

The growing influence of artificial intelligence (AI) in higher education has accelerated these changes. AI technologies are being integrated into academic and administrative processes, from personalized learning platforms to automated grading systems, further emphasizing efficiency, scalability, and cost-effectiveness. While these advancements offer opportunities for innovation, they also raise significant concerns about the depersonalization of education, potential biases in AI systems, and the prioritization of profitability over the holistic development of students.

As a result, professors' roles have shifted from intellectual authorities to service providers in the marketplace. Professors are increasingly expected to cater to the demands of students, who are now viewed as customers with specific needs and expectations. This has led to a reevaluation of the professoriate's role, with professors under significant pressure to adapt to the changing landscape of higher education. This re-evaluation has led to a new philosophy of higher education has taken hold in institutions around the world. Its supporters disavow the pursuit of knowledge for its own sake and argue that the only knowledge worth pursuing is that with more or less immediate market value. Every other kind of learning is downgraded, its budget cut (Busch, 2017).

Professors are now expected to serve managerial interests rather than scholarly pursuits, focusing on measurable outcomes and economic value (Roberts, 2019). The emphasis on performativity and big data has further eroded support for traditional academic roles, particularly in the humanities. While these changes are not yet complete, they represent a significant threat to the traditional role of the professoriate and the university as a public institution dedicated to intellectual inquiry (Roberts, 2019).

The focus is now more on efficiency, performance metrics, and marketability, rather than on the pursuit of knowledge for its own sake. The growing integration of artificial intelligence (AI) into higher education has further compounded these challenges. It is crucial to approach this integration with a balanced perspective, considering both the benefits and the risks. AI-powered tools, such as learning analytics platforms and automated grading systems, reshape professors' responsibilities by streamlining tasks that were once central to their roles, such as assessment and personalized feedback. While these technologies can enhance efficiency and provide insights into student performance, they also risk reducing professors' autonomy and obscuring student evaluation processes, and shifting pedagogical decision-making to private entities (Zeide, 2017).

Artificial intelligence (AI) has played a crucial role in further democratizing knowledge. With AI-powered tools such as chatbots, virtual tutors, and intelligent search engines, learners can now receive instant answers, explanations, and recommendations that are uniquely tailored to their learning needs. This personalization makes learning more engaging and interesting. AI systems can analyze vast amounts of data from diverse sources and offer personalized learning experiences, enabling students to grasp complex concepts more effectively. This change has reduced reliance on traditional teaching methods and has enabled self-directed, lifelong learning. AI's role in education is not only limited to making knowledge more accessible but also to providing real-time feedback, optimizing learning paths, and supporting adaptive learning technologies that adjust to individual progress and performance. AI-power tools, such as learning analytics platforms and automated grading systems are redefining professors' responsibilities, allowing them to focus more on curriculum refinement and teaching quality improvement (Hamdi, 2024; Javvaji & Raghavulu, 2024). University teachers' perceptions of AI adoption vary, with some showing skepticism and concerns about fairness and responsibility (McGrath et al., 2023). Balancing AI with human instruction is crucial to maintaining meaningful interactions and fostering deeper understanding (Hamdi, 2024). Deposit challenges, AI has the potential to create more effective, inclusive, and forward-thinking educational environments (Javvaji & Raghavulu, 2024).

The Professor as Navigator

In this new environment, professors are increasingly seen not as intellectual authorities but as facilitators of learning. They are expected to guide students through acquiring knowledge, but they no longer hold exclusive control over the dissemination of information. Instead, students have become active participants in their education, using various digital and traditional resources to build their understanding of the world. The emergence of artificial intelligence (AI) further accelerates this shift by offering students an even broader array of tools to support their learning journey. AI-driven platforms, for example, allow students to access customized learning experiences where content is tailored to their specific needs, abilities, and learning preferences. AI can provide on-demand tutoring, automate repetitive tasks like grading, and even generate personalized study plans that help students track their progress. While this has the potential to empower students and promote greater autonomy in learning, it also raises important questions about the value of the professoriate and the role of traditional academic institutions in an age of digital learning. Once the sole arbiters of knowledge, professors integrate these technologies into their teaching practices while still maintaining a critical role in shaping the learning environment. However, students should be able to choose how to learn and be central to fostering the democratic culture of learning and teaching at a university (Macfarlane, 2016). AI plays a crucial role in this evolution, offering flexibility that allows students to take control of their educational experience and reshape how they engage with academic material. Ultimately, the growing integration of AI into education prompts a rethinking of the professor's role—not as the sole keeper of knowledge but as a mentor who helps students navigate an increasingly complex and tech-driven landscape.

As a result, several neoliberal assumptions firmly rooted in conventional wisdom have contributed to a student-as-customer phenomenon, which is a cost driver (Mintz, 2021). This shift in perspective, bolstered by AI technologies, reinforces the idea of education as a market commodity rather than a public good, where the value of knowledge is increasingly tied to its monetary worth and accessibility through digital platforms.

Professor's Role Re-Imagined

Much has been written about the changes in higher education administration, which is increasingly managed by professionals who treat the institution as businesses, focus on cost-benefits rather than a mission of scholarship and education, treating faculty as line workers with deans and department chairs as line managers, and consider students as customers (Burawoy, 2016). This process has taken a few decades to permeate most institutions, with various financial crises accelerating this shift. By reflecting on the growth of full-scale management systems in overseeing academic institutions, Kilkauer and Young (2021) combine academia and dementia to arrive at '*academentia.*' According to Kilkauer and Young, this new term refers to the outcome of a severe loss of touch with the scholarly reality of universities due to an environment shaped by the ideology of Managerialism and Neoliberalism.

This has led to reimagining the professoriate's role, as professors are now expected to align their work with the university's financial interests. In many cases, this has meant that professors are pressured to prioritize research likely to attract funding or have commercial applications rather than pursuing more abstract or theoretical research that may not have immediate financial returns. Similarly, teaching is increasingly focused on meeting the needs of students as consumers, with professors expected to design courses that are marketable, employable, and aligned with the job market. In this environment, the traditional academic values of intellectual autonomy, academic freedom, and the pursuit of knowledge for its own sake are often subordinated to the demands of the marketplace. The introduction of corporate management styles by academic administrators and boards of trustees, a consequent diminution of faculty participation in university governance, and the measurement of the value of a university education exclusively in economic terms augment the perception of higher education as a commodity (Scott, 2019).

In this context, the role of professors as intellectual leaders and scholars is being undermined as they are expected to demonstrate their value through metrics such as student satisfaction, research funding, and the employability of their graduates rather than through the depth and quality of their intellectual contributions. Faculty know their authority is weakened in the academic workplace and where, to varying degrees, their professional expertise and disciplines have lost respect and trust because of the defining issues – from enrollment-based funding to assessment and from curricular change to faculty hiring (Gumport, 2019). This has contributed to the rise of adjunct faculty, who are often paid lower wages, have fewer benefits, and face greater job insecurity than their tenure-track counterparts. The increasing reliance on adjunct faculty has further eroded the professional status of professors, as they are increasingly seen as temporary workers rather than permanent members of the academic community.

The commodification of higher education has significantly reshaped the relationship between professors and students. Traditionally, professors acted as mentors, guiding students through intellectual challenges and fostering critical thinking. Today, however, students are often viewed as customers purchasing a product, and professors are expected to deliver education tailored to meet those expectations. This change has created a more transactional dynamic, with students increasingly focused on securing a job rather than on the intellectual and personal growth that education once emphasized. As this transformation unfolds, the rise of artificial intelligence (AI) adds a new layer of complexity. AI's growing role in education—through tools like personalized learning platforms, automated grading systems, and career path prediction models—further shifts the professor-student relationship, making it even more centered on efficiency and outcomes. In job security and career preparation, the changes governments, universities, and organizations must address can be grouped into categories: globalization, technological advancements like AI, economic shifts, structural changes, and the redefinition of jobs and careers (Burns, 2020). AI, in particular, influences how skills are developed, measured, and applied in the workforce, challenging students and educators to adapt to a rapidly changing educational landscape.

Academic freedom thrives in an environment where scholars pursue knowledge without undue constraints. This freedom is essential for fostering innovation, critical thinking, and social progress. In a corporatized university setting, the emphasis on profitability and market alignment restricts this freedom, leading to a narrowed scope of research and teaching activities that align with commercial interests.

The Evolving Role of Professors in the Corporatization Market

According to Zadja (2020), the corporatization of higher education is underpinned by the ideology of neo-liberalism globally. Education has been affected in a way that concerns those who believe that higher education, rather than focusing on producing skilled workers for the global market, should concentrate on developing creative, critical thinkers engaged in work for the betterment of society (Zadja, 2020, p. xiii). Expanding economic rationality into the educational sector is one of the most ubiquitous dimensions of neo-liberalism and one of its most potent ideological tools, resulting in the commodification, commercialization, and marketization of education and knowledge. The rise of artificial intelligence (AI) further accelerates these trends as universities increasingly adopt AI-driven tools for teaching, administration, and research. While these technologies can enhance efficiency and personalization, they also reinforce the commodification of education, raising concerns about the role of professors as facilitators of critical thinking and whether AI might exacerbate the focus on producing market-ready graduates at the expense of fostering deeper societal engagement.

As knowledge becomes more accessible, higher education institutions are confronted with a transformative situation ingrained in the innovative business models. They must adapt if they are to endure throughout time as a crucial component of this transition and avoid disappearing from the scene (Alenezi, 2023). Digital transformation in higher education has introduced AI-driven technologies, reshaping how institutions operate and deliver education. Tools like AI-powered adaptive learning systems, intelligent tutoring platforms, and data analytics for student performance provide personalized, scalable, and efficient educational experiences. However, these advancements also present challenges, such as maintaining the human touch in education and ensuring the ethical use of AI. Institutions must strategically integrate

AI into their frameworks to remain relevant, balancing technological innovation with preserving core educational values.

Where do professors fit in this new marketplace? Like many business transformations enabled by the digital world, changes in education are partially fueled by a bottom-up dynamic. For higher education, students want to see new media reflected in the delivery of learning material on their chosen platforms. Educators need to anticipate change and reinvent themselves. This means stepping back and learning about opportunities to develop innovative approaches that rebuild the teaching practice in ways more suitable for the emerging world (McHaney, 2023). Faculty need to be interested in the conditions that facilitated industry logic, specifically, how it gained traction where their authority was weakened in the academic workplace and where, to varying degrees, their professional expertise and disciplines are perceived as no longer relevant to the marketplace demands (Gumport, 2019). Higher education faces spiraling funding declines that could decimate their reputations and capacities. Alongside financial concerns, there is unrelenting intensity – scrutiny from stakeholders demanding demonstrated accountability, distrust of higher education's leaders, changing demographics of students with divergent needs and aspirations, evolving technological opportunities and costs, and a devaluing of the liberal arts (Gumport, 2019, p.x). So, one wonders how intrepid academic leaders will engage in new and creative ways; how do they invent win-win scenarios to further higher education's legacy of service to all citizens and to preserve its centrality to society and the world?

A change in research priorities has significantly impacted professors' autonomy as independent scholars. Previously, professors were free to pursue research projects aligned with their intellectual interests and passions, regardless of their immediate financial returns. However, in the corporatized university, the pressure to secure funding, produce commercially viable results, and demonstrate tangible outcomes has led many professors to adapt their research agendas to the demands of the marketplace. This has led to the erosion of academic freedom, as professors are increasingly required to align their work with the financial interests of the university and its corporate partners. In some cases, this has led to the commercialization of knowledge itself, with universities and professors seeking to patent their research findings or develop products that can be sold to generate revenue. This trend has raised concerns about the potential for conflicts of interest, as the pursuit of knowledge may be driven more by financial considerations than by a commitment to advancing human understanding.

THE STUDENT LANDSCAPE

In this rapidly changing landscape, AI also has the potential to level the playing field for students from various backgrounds, regardless of location or financial resources. With tools powered by machine learning algorithms, people can learn at their own pace, gaining insights and expertise previously only accessible to those with formal education or specialized mentors. This transformation has shifted the focus of education from being a one-way transfer of knowledge from professor to student to a more interactive, learner-driven experience. Ultimately, combining digital platforms and AI reshapes how knowledge is shared and consumed, making education more inclusive, personalized, and efficient.

Artificial Intelligence has the potential to address educational inequities and promote inclusive learning environments. AI-driven personalized learning platforms can tailor content to individual student needs, enhancing engagement and performance for disadvantaged learners (Supramaniam et al., 2024; Roshanaei et al., 2023). However, challenges such as algorithmic bias, the digital divide, and the need for teacher training must be addressed (Supramaniam et al., 2024). While AI offers promising solutions, it is not a panacea for educational inequality; pre-existing social and economic disparities may exacerbate the digital divide (Bulathwela et al., 2024). To maximize AI's potential in education, stakeholders must prioritize inclusive design, equitable access, and collaborative efforts (Supramaniam et al., 2024; Bulathwela et al., 2024). Students view AI positively in educational settings but express concerns about potential drawbacks (Idroes et al., 2023). Ongoing research and policy development are crucial to ensure AI technologies contribute to a more equitable global educational landscape for students.

The digital age has democratized knowledge in previously unimaginable ways, but it has also raised questions about the value of traditional academic structures. With the proliferation of online courses, MOOCs (Massive Open Online Courses), Coursera, and other digital learning platforms, students can pursue education outside the traditional university setting. These platforms often offer education at a fraction of the cost of conventional university degrees, further contributing to the commodification of education. Collins and Halverson (2018) describe this as uncoupling schooling and learning. AI-powered platforms can now personalize learning, offering tailored content that adapts to students' needs and pace. For instance, AI-driven tutoring systems can assist students with real-time feedback, helping them progress through subjects at their own speed. These technologies not only enhance accessibility but also challenge traditional notions of authority in education. AI's ability to analyze vast amounts of data allows it to provide insights into student performance, making it easier to identify gaps in understanding and areas for improvement. This shift toward AI-enabled learning further diminishes the need for centralized educational institutions and reinforces learning as an individualize, self-directed process. The power dynamics of traditional education are being disrupted, and the traditional university model is being questioned as AI continues to reshape how knowledge is distributed and consumed.

MARKET-DRIVEN MODEL IN HIGHER EDUCATIONAL INSTITUTIONS

Neoliberalism, emphasizing market-driven principles, has transformed universities into businesses, where education is increasingly viewed as a commodity to be bought and sold. In this model, the traditional academic values of intellectual autonomy, academic freedom, and pursuing knowledge for its own sake are often subordinated to the market's demands. Universities are increasingly seen as businesses that must generate revenue to remain competitive. Research, teaching, and service are all evaluated based on their ability to attract funding, generate revenue, and meet the needs of students and other external stakeholders.

The neoliberal model has led to a redefinition of the professoriate, as professors are now viewed as employees incentivized to pursue research that aligns with the university's and external funders' financial interests. The redefinition has profound implications for the professoriate, as it challenges their professional identity and undermines their traditional role in the academic community. The focus on marketability and employability has led some professors to prioritize teaching that is more practical and job-oriented rather than focusing on intellectual exploration and critical inquiry. Research, too, is increasingly shaped by market considerations, with professors expected to produce work that is not only academically rigorous but also commercially viable. Commercialization is not a fully accepted norm; Halloway and Matthew found that established researchers continue to register an ambivalence toward commercialization practices (2019, p.264). Emerging researchers, in turn, are at times exposed to or note these signals of ambivalence. And yet those researchers who are aware of, or hold some complaint against, commercialization – whether established or emerging in their scientific careers– appear to accept its inevitability. In this way, even those who harbor reservations vis-à-vis the commercialization of academics tend to accept rather than question it.

Vican (2018) states that faculty members express a misalignment between their professional values and administrators' corporate logic. This incompatibility contributes to faculty dissatisfaction, much of which is centered around three themes: increasing managerial control, quantification of faculty performance using commensurable metrics, and the university's financial climate, where generating revenue is perceived to take priority over educational mission (Vican, 2018). Glerup et al.

wrote that professors articulated a pressure to demonstrate impact, which was often defined with the parameters of marketization and academic capitalism, and the fact that structures of academic capitalism might, to a large degree, structure or overtake the practices of responsibility in the teaching and researching practice (2017). "Faculty are resigned to the belief that to succeed, they should be knowledgeable and/or experienced with commercialization" (Halloway & Matthew, 2019, p. 268).

A critical thought affecting higher education can be posed as follows: Who owns teaching? Most might automatically answer that instructors do, but the honest answer is far from clear in the era of course designers, regimented mandatory syllabi, and now AI. The reality is that faculty have no leverage in the relatively new learning environment (Donoghue, 2018).

Characteristics in a Neoliberal Context

Neoliberalism is a political and/or economic ideology that emphasizes the efficiency of free markets, the significance of individual entrepreneurial freedom, and the reduction of government intervention in the economy. It advocates for policies such as deregulation, the privatization of state-owned enterprises, the reduction of public spending, free trade, and the promotion of economic growth led by the private sector and market forces. In neoliberalism, universities are characterized by key features that reflect the broader neoliberal ideology, which emphasizes market efficiency, individual responsibility, and a reduced role for the state in economic and social life. According to Gasser (2024. pp.2-3), key characteristics of higher education in a neoliberal context include:

1. Neoliberal policies encourage the privatization of some university services and the involvement of the private sector in funding and supporting research, leading to partnerships with corporations.
2. Marketisation of education as a commodity, with students being viewed as consumers purchasing a service.
3. Universities are increasingly held accountable through performance metrics such as graduation rates, employment outcomes, and student satisfaction surveys.
4. Commercialization of research.
5. Managerialism and corporate governance.
6. Increasing reliance on adjuncts, part-time faculty, and contract staff.
7. Policies can lead to the standardization of curricula and teaching practices, aiming for efficiency and scalability, which can reduce creativity and responsiveness to diverse student need.

8. The relationship between students and universities is increasingly framed as a consumer relationship, where students are seen as customers whose satisfaction is paramount.
9. Policies that encourage universities to recruit international students as a source of revenue from tuition fees, which often leads to competition for students from abroad, with universities tailoring programs and services to attract them.
10. The focus of higher education has moved from serving the public good to providing private benefits to individuals, potentially diminishing the role of universities as institutions that contribute to societal well-being, democratic citizenship, and social equity.

These ten characteristics reflect a broader influence of neoliberal ideology on higher education, leading to significant changes in how universities operate, how education is valued, and how academics and students engage with and relate to their institutions. Critics argue that these changes undermine the traditional mission of universities as centers of critical inquiry and public service, prioritizing economic efficiency and market-driven goals over intellectual and social ideals (Mintz, 2021; Gardner, 2024; Connell, 2019.).

A study conducted by Alibasic et al., 2024 delved into the problematic trajectory of modern higher education, spotlighting the rise of corporate practices within academic institutions, the swelling ranks of university administration, and the disproportionate weight given to student evaluations in assessing faculty. Their study examined the evolving landscape of academic freedom within the corporatized university model. They used the concept of liminality, which explores the transitional challenges faced by academia in balancing traditional scholarly values with emerging market-driven paradigms, arguing that the corporatization of universities represents a liminal phase, wherein the identity and purpose of academic institutions are in flux, significantly impacting the notion of academic freedom. The shift toward a consumer-oriented ethos endangers the foundational principles of higher education, risking substituting educational substance with the mere transaction of education services. This begs the question, does the complex relationship between market forces and educational values enhance or undermine the quality and purpose of higher education? The incursion of corporate governance models into higher education has posed significant challenges to the principle of academic freedom. The corporatization of universities often leads to a culture where economic values overshadow critical inquiry and intellectual freedom (Alibasic et al., 2024).

A Balanced Approach

The intersection of academic freedom and the corporatization of higher education presents a nuanced landscape. On the one hand, corporatization, with its focus on efficiency, marketability, and financial outcomes, potentially impinges on the principles of academic freedom. It shifts priorities away from open intellectual inquiry towards more market-driven objectives. A dismissal of corporatization ignores its potential benefits, such as increased resources for research, enhanced infrastructures, and broader global connections.

A balanced approach is necessary to ensure that academic freedom and corporatization coexist. According to Alibasic et al., 2024 the approach involves:

Hybrid models: Exploring hybrid models with academic and market-driven objectives and synergies. For example, the 'entrepreneurial university' model leverages corporatization to support academic endeavors without compromising core academic values. Stanford University, USA, is often cited as a successful example of the entrepreneurial university model. Stanford has fostered strong ties with Silicon Valley, encouraging innovation and entrepreneurship among its faculty and students. This model has led to numerous successful startups and technology companies while maintaining a solid commitment to academic excellence and freedom (Hollingsworth, 2023).

Governance and policy frameworks: Implementing governance structures and policies to protect academic freedom while acknowledging the realities of market forces, ensuring faculty representation in decision-making processes, and establishing clear policies that safeguard academic integrity. The University of Cincinnati, USA, offers one of the world's oldest and most successful cooperative education (co-op) programs. This model integrates classroom learning with practical work experience, allowing students to engage with industries relevant to their field of study. This approach enhances student learning experiences without compromising academic integrity.

Diverse funding sources: Encouraging universities to diversify their funding sources to reduce overreliance on market-driven revenue with a mix of public funding, private endowments, and partnerships that respect academic autonomy (Marginson, 2016). The University of Brighton, UK, implemented a successful community engagement model where academic work is closely aligned with community needs through partnerships with local organizations and faculty.

Alternative educational models: Alternative models like cooperative education, where universities are owned and operated by faculty and students, should be considered to align academic freedom with practical, community-oriented goals. The Georgia Institute of Technology, USA, established public-private partnerships to foster innovation while securing funding from diverse sources and supported research and educational initiatives to align with academic and industry goals, demonstrating a balance between corporatization and academic freedom.

Community engagement and social responsibility: Emphasizing the role of universities in serving the public good and engaging with local communities to bridge the gap between academic pursuits and societal needs, ensuring that corporatization does not overshadow the educational and social mission of higher education. The University of British Columbia (UBC), Canada, implemented sustainability and global engagement initiatives, emphasizing social responsibility and integrating academic excellence with a commitment to community service and global citizenship, reflecting a balanced approach to higher education (Lemoine et al., 2017).

THE PROFESSORIATE AS PUBLIC INTELLECTUALS

In response to the increasing corporatization and commodification of higher education, some scholars emphasize the value of public intellectual inquiry and the university's defense as a public institution. This vision contrasts sharply with the prevailing corporate model of universities, where professors are often reduced to service providers catering to the demands of students and the marketplace. Public intellectuals have historically played a vital role in shaping public discourse, challenging dominant ideologies, and advancing social justice. In higher education, professors can serve as public intellectuals by engaging with broader societal issues, advocating for the value of education as a public good, and upholding the principles of academic freedom and intellectual autonomy. The role of professors as public intellectuals in higher education is crucial for democracy and societal engagement. Giroux (2019) argues that academics should challenge neoliberalism by reinvigorating public scholarship and developing students' critical capacities.

The concept of the public intellectual is not a new one. Throughout history, professors and scholars have often engaged with the public, offering critical perspectives on social, political, and cultural issues. Public intellectuals are not confined to the ivory tower of academia; instead, they participate in public debates, contribute to policy discussions, and provide insights that help shape the direction of society. This tradition has been essential in holding power to account, challenging injustices, and promoting the public good. In the face of neoliberalism and the growing marketization of higher education, the role of the professor as a public intellectual is more important than ever. Professors can push back against the commodification of education by engaging in meaningful discussions about the purpose and value of higher education, advocating for policies that prioritize intellectual inquiry over profit, and working to maintain the university as a space for critical thought and social change. Osborne & Wilton (2017) examine professors' motivations for writing newspaper columns, highlighting their role as public intellectuals within their communities. Their work collectively underscores the significance of professors engaging with broader societal issues, advocating for education as a public good, and upholding academic freedom and intellectual autonomy in higher education.

Academic freedom is essential for the functioning of a university as a space for free thought and inquiry. Without it, professors may be deterred from exploring complex or unpopular topics, and students may be denied the opportunity to engage with a wide range of ideas. Public intellectuals contend that academic freedom must be protected at all costs, as it is the foundation upon which the university's social role is built. In this sense, professors are not merely service providers but custodians of intellectual autonomy, ensuring that the university remains a space where ideas can be freely exchanged and debated. Scholars argue that higher education should be considered a public-good benefiting society (Petrovic, 2024; Daviet, 2016). This perspective emphasizes education's role in promoting individual flourishing and collective well-being (Petrovic, 2024). Professors, as public intellectuals, can advocate for this vision of education by emphasizing its role in shaping democratic societies, promoting civic engagement, and addressing pressing social issues. They can challenge the notion that education is merely a stepping stone to employment and instead promote the idea that education is essential for developing informed, thoughtful, and engaged citizens.

In advocating for reimagining the professoriate's role, public intellectuals need to reclaim their role as scholars that can resist the force of corporatization and work that universities remain spaces for independent thought and intellectual engagement. They could use their expertise and platform to write op-eds, participate in public forums engage in activism that addresses issues such as the erosion of public institutions (Osborne & Wilton, 2017). Reimagining the professoriate's role as public intellectuals offers a powerful counter-narrative to the corporate model of higher education. By defending academic freedom, promoting intellectual autonomy, and advocating for the value of education as a public good, professors can reclaim their position as leaders in society, contributing to the advancement of knowledge and social justice. This vision challenges the commodification of knowledge and the reduction of education to a market-driven product, offering a path forward that prioritizes the public good over profit and intellectual inquiry over marketability. The role of professors as public intellectuals is essential to ensuring that universities remain spaces for critical thought, intellectual exploration, and the advancement of knowledge that serves the broader society.

CONCLUSION

The commodification of higher education and the rise of neoliberalism have fundamentally altered the role of the professoriate, transforming professors from independent scholars into service providers within a market-driven system. This shift directly results from the increasing corporatization of universities, where financial concerns often preceded scholarly pursuits. In this new environment, universities are treated as businesses, and professors are expected to meet the demands of a marketplace that prioritizes financial efficiency and job readiness over intellectual exploration and critical inquiry. The traditional role of professors as guardians of knowledge and intellectual autonomy is being undermined by a system that values profitability and consumer satisfaction more than the cultivation of critical thinking and independent thought.

Under neoliberalism, the focus of higher education has shifted away from pursuing knowledge for its own sake to a model that emphasizes vocational training and market-driven outcomes. As universities are expected to generate revenue and immediately produce employable graduates, professors are increasingly pressured to tailor their teaching and research to meet the demands of the job market. This shift has narrowed academic focus, with professors often asked to teach courses aligned with market trends or engage in research that has immediate commercial value. In many cases, this has resulted in a loss of intellectual autonomy, as professors are forced to prioritize subjects and methodologies that are financially lucrative rather than those that challenge dominant ideologies or push the boundaries of knowledge.

The role of professors as public intellectuals has become more important than ever. Public intellectuals have historically played a vital role in shaping public discourse, challenging dominant ideologies, and advocating for social justice. In the face of corporatization, professors can reclaim their role as public intellectuals by engaging with broader societal issues and advocating for the value of education as a public good. Rather than succumbing to market pressures, professors can use their platform and expertise to challenge the notion that education is merely a commodity to be bought and sold. By defending academic freedom and intellectual autonomy, professors can resist the forces that seek to transform universities into businesses and reaffirm their commitment to advancing knowledge.

At the heart of this reimagined role is the defense of the university as a space for intellectual inquiry and the pursuit of knowledge for its own sake. Public intellectuals contend that education should not be reduced to a tool for economic gain but should be viewed as a public good that benefits all of society. Pprofessors are responsible for engaging with issues central to the public interest, such as social inequality, climate change, and the erosion of democratic values. By participating in public debates, writing op-eds, and engaging in activism, professors can help shape public discourse and contribute to developing a more just and equitable society.

The challenge for the twenty-first-century professor is navigating the tension between the demands of the marketplace and the need to preserve the integrity of higher education as an institution of higher learning. Professors can balance the need to meet the expectations of students and administrators with the obligation to maintain intellectual autonomy and academic freedom. This requires a concerted effort to resist the pressures of corporatization and to advocate for a university system that prioritizes advancing knowledge, critical thinking, and the public good over financial gain. In doing so, professors can reaffirm their role as intellectual leaders and ensure that higher education remains a space for independent thought, social change, and the pursuit of knowledge for the benefit of society.

FUTURE DIRECTIONS AND PROFESSORIAL IMPLICATIONS

The future of higher education will be deeply influenced by the intersection of AI technologies and the commodification of learning. As these trends evolve, researchers, educators, and policymakers must work together to navigate the complex landscape they create, ensuring that higher education remains inclusive, ethical, and focused on the broader goals of personal and societal advancement.

The impact of AI and commodification on higher education will not be uniform globally. In some regions, AI may offer a way to address gaps in educational infrastructure, while in others, it could exacerbate educational divides. Future research should focus on how higher education institutions can adapt to a globalized environment. AI's ability to analyze vast amounts of data could revolutionize academic research and reshape how knowledge is produced and valued. Future directions could explore how AI influences research priorities, collaborations, and funding. Additionally, the potential for AI to automate aspects of research—such as literature reviews or data analysis—raises questions about the integrity and originality of academic work. Scholars must engage with these changes to maintain the integrity of knowledge production in a world where AI plays an ever-larger role.

Research is needed to understand how these shifts affect faculty job satisfaction, tenure processes, and quality of student-teacher relationships. Furthermore, attention must be given to AI's potential to exacerbate job insecurity issues, especially for adjunct professors. Research should investigate how AI's role in decision-making can perpetuate existing biases or lead to unintended consequences for marginalized groups in higher education.

Subscription-based or pay-per-course models might replace traditional degree structures, fragmenting education into skill-based learning experiences (Mateo-Berganza Díaz et al., 2022). One of the most significant changes is the emergence of skills-based, non-degree, alternative credentials as both complements and alternatives to traditional degrees. Several factors have combined to favor these shorter, less expensive, and more versatile ways to gain knowledge and skills for work. While this could enhance accessibility and flexibility, it may also deepen inequalities, as prestigious institutions continue to offer elite, high-cost education while lower-income students are pushed into standardized, corporate-led learning paths. Ultimately, education commodification may shift from holistic knowledge-building to career-centric, transactional learning, reinforcing education as a market-driven service rather than a public good.

REFERENCES

Alenezi, M. (2023). Digital Learning and Digital Institution in Higher Education. *Education in Science*, 13.

Alibasic, H., Atkinson, C. L., & Pelcher, J. (2024). The liminal state of academic freedom: Navigating corporatization in higher education. *Discover Education.*

Altbach, P. G. (2015). The deteriorating guru: The crisis of the professoriate. *International Higher Education.*

Atalay, S. (2018). When students become customers; The changing relationship between the student and the academic: A case study from social sciences in Turkey. *Journal of Higher Education and Science*, *8*(3), 512–521.

Badke, W. (2021). *Research strategies: Finding your way through the information fog*. iUniverse.

Benitta, G., Asha, H. J., & Josephine, J. A. (2024). An Integrated (Hybrid Based) Besuited Education System Design for the Better Models. *2024 4th International Conference on Advance Computing and Innovative Technologies in Engineering (ICACITE)*, 561-565.

Brint, S. F. (2018). *The Ends of Knowledge*. Two Cheers for Higher Education.

Bulathwela, S., Perez-Ortiz, M., Holloway, C., Cukurova, M., & Shawe-Taylor, J. (2024). Artificial Intelligence Alone Will Not Democratise Education: On Educational Inequality, Techno-Solutionism and Inclusive Tools. *Sustainability*. DOI: 10.3390/su16020781

Bunce, L. (2020). A degree of studying - students who treat education as a commodity perform worse than their intrinsically motivated peers. *Active Learning in Higher Education.*

Burawoy, M. (2016). The neoliberal university: Ascent of the spiralists. *Critical Sociology*, *42*(7/8), 941–942.

Burns, R. (2020). *The adult learner at work.* Routledge.

Busch, L. (2017). *Knowledge for Sale: The Neoliberal Takeover of Higher Education. Publication.* MIT Press.

Chen, L., Chen, P., & Lin, Z. (2020). Artificial Intelligence in Education: A Review. *IEEE Access : Practical Innovations, Open Solutions*, *8*, 75264–75278.

Collins, A., & Halverson, R. (2018). *Rethinking education in the age of technology: The digital revolution and school in America*. Teachers College Press.

Connell, R. (2019). *The good university: What universities actually do and why it's time for radical change*. Bloomsbury Publishing.

Daviet, B. (2016). Revisiting the Principle of Education as a Public Good. *United Nations Educational, Scientific and Cultural Organization (UNESCO), 17.*

Donoghue, F. (2018). *The Last Professors: The Corporate University and the Fate of the Humanities*. Fordham University Press.

Gardner, P. (2024). Loosening the straps on the neoliberal strait-jacket subjugating educational research. *Issues in Educational Research, 34*(1), xi–xiv.

Gasser, R.B. (2024). Neoliberalism in academia: Reflections from a parasitologist. *Gasser Parasites & Vectors, 17.*

Giroux, H. A. (2019). *Public Scholarship, Public Intellectuals, and the Role of Higher Education in a Time of Crisis*. The Oxford Handbook of Methods for Public Scholarship.

Glerup, C., Davies, S. R., & Horst, M. (2017). Nothing really responsible goes on here: Scientists' experience and practice responsibility. *Journal of Responsible Innovation, 4*(3), 319–336.

Gumport, P. J. (2019). *Academic fault lines: The rise of industry logic in public higher education*. Johns Hopkins University Press.

Hamdi, M. (2024). How AI is Transforming and Shaping the Future of Education. *2024 IEEE 28th International Conference on Intelligent Engineering Systems (INES)*, 000115-000116.

Hollingsworth, H. (2023). *Conservatives take aim at tenure for university professors*. AP NEWS. https://apnews.com/article/politics-colleges-and universities-florida-state-government-texas-education-4f0fe0c5c18ed227fabae3744e8ff51d.

Holloway, K., & Herder, M. (2019). A responsibility to commercialize? Tracing academic researchers' evolving engagement with the commercialization of biomedical research. *Journal of Responsible Innovation, 6*(3), 263–283.

Indroes, G.M., Noviandy, T.R., Maulana, A., Irvanizam, I., Jalil, Z., Lensoni, L., Lala, A., Abas, A., Tallei, T., & Idroes, R. (2023). Student Perspectives on the Role of Artificial Intelligence in Education: A Survey-Based Analysis. *Journal of Educational Management and Learning*. DOI: .DOI: 10.60084/jeml.v1i1.58

Javvaji, V. R., & Raghavulu, P. V. (2024). The Transformative Impact of Artificial Intelligence on Education. *International Journal for Multidisciplinary Research, 6*(4). Advance online publication. DOI: 10.36948/ijfmr.2024.v06i04.24987

Kilkauer T. & Young M. (2021). Academentia: the organization insanity of the modern university. *Counterpunch, 28.*

Kraiem, D. I. (2015). The Cost of Opportunity: Student Debt and Social Mobility. *Suffolk, 689.*

Labidi, L., & Barhoumi, W. (2023). *The Evolving Role of the University Professor Navigating the Past and the Present*. Information Sciences Letters.

Lange, J. (2015). Rise of the digitized public intellectual: Death of the professor in the network neutral internet age. *Interchange*, *46*, 95–112.

Lemoine, P., Jenkins, W., & Richardson, M. (2017). Global higher education: Development and implications. *J Educ Dev.*, *1*, 58. DOI: 10. 20849/ jed.v1i1.253

Mann, P. (2015). Market Logic in Higher Education: Rethinking with Sociological Imagination. *International Journal of Research in Finance and Marketing*, *5*, 1–7.

Marginson, S. (2016). *Higher education and the common good.* Melbourne University Publishing.

Marmoah, S., Murwaningsih, T., Nurhasanah, F., Saddhono, K., Sutomo, A. D., & Legowo, B. (2024). An Integration of AI and Traditional Methodology in the Education Field in Order to transform the trends. *2024 4th International Conference on Advance Computing and Innovative Technologies in Engineering (ICACITE)*, 884-889.

Mateo-Berganza Díaz, M. M., Lim, J. R., Cárdenas-Navia, I., & Elzey, K. (2022). *A World of Transformation: Moving from Degrees to Skills-Based Alternative Credentials*. IDB Publication.

McFarlane, B. (2016). *Freedom to learn.* Routledge.

McGrath, C., Cerratto P., T., Juth, N., & Palmgren, P.J. (2023). University teachers' perceptions of responsibility and artificial intelligence in higher education - An experimental philosophical study. *Computer Educational Artificial Intelligence, 4.*

McHaney, R. (2023). *The new digital shoreline*. Routledge.

Mintz, B. (2021). Neoliberalism and the crisis in higher education: The cost of ideology. *American Journal of Economics and Sociology*, *80*(1), 79–112.

Osborne, G., & Wilton, S. (2017). Professing in the Local Press: Professors and Public Responsibilities. *Journal of Community Engagement and Scholarship*, *10*(1), 67–80. DOI: 10.54656/VGBZ5148

Petrovic, J. E. (2024). Toward a non-economistic understanding of higher education as a public and private good for the public good. *Educational Philosophy and Theory*. Advance online publication. DOI: 10.1080/00131857.2024.2412755

Popenici, S. A., & Kerr, S. (2017). Exploring the impact of artificial intelligence on teaching and learning in higher education. *Research and Practice in Technology Enhanced Learning*. PMID: 30595727

Ram, D., & Bhandari (2023). CHATGPT and AI Tools: A Paradigm Shift in Education and Other Domains. *Pravaha.*

Rangavittal, B. P. (2024). Transforming Higher Education with Artificial Intelligence - Benefits, Challenges, and Future Directions. [IJSR]. *International Journal of Scientific Research.*

Robert, P. (2019). *Performativity, Big Data and Higher Education: The Death of the Professor?* Beijing International Review of Education.

Roshanaei, M., Olivares, H., & Lopez, R. R. (2023). Harnessing AI to Foster Equity in Education: Opportunities, Challenges, and Emerging Strategies. *Journal of Intelligent Learning Systems and Applications*, *15*, 123–143.

Scott, J. W. (2019). *Knowledge, power, and academic freedom*. Columbia University Press.

Silva, A. de O., & Janes, D. dos S. (2020). Exploring the role of artificial intelligence in education: A comprehensive perspective. *Review of Artificial Intelligence in Education*, *1*. Advance online publication. DOI: 10.37497/rev.artif.intell.education.v1i00.5

Supramaniam, J. K., Baharudin, S. M., Halid, N. M., Abbas, M. S., Amin, M., Ghani, A., Affendy, K., Halim, A., & Nordin, M. N. (2024). Leveraging AI To Bridge Educational Inequities: A Global Perspective. *Nanotechnology Perceptions*.

Taylor, R.C., Liang, X., Laubichler, M.D., West, G.B., Kempes, C.P., & Dumas, M. (2019). The Scalability, Efficiency and Complexity of Universities and Colleges: A New Lens for Assessing the Higher Educational System. *ArXiv, abs/1910.05470.*

Vican, S., Friedman, A., & Andreasen, R. (2019). Metrics, Money, and Managerialism: Faculty Experiences of Competing Logics in Higher Education. *The Journal of Higher Education*, *91*(1), 139–164.

Warshaw, J. B., & Upton, S. (2020). Hybrid logics in the resource strategies of US public research universities. *Journal of Further and Higher Education, 44*, 1289–1303.

Willis, J. E., & Strunk, V. A. (2015). *Ethical Responsibilities of Preserving Academicians in an Age of Mechanized Learning: Balancing the Demands of Educating at Capacity and Preserving Human Interactivity*. IGI Global.

Zajda, J. (Ed.). (2020). *Globalisation, ideology and neo-liberal higher education reforms*. Springer.

Zawacki-Richter, O., Marin, V. I., Bond, M., & Gouverneur, F. (2019). Systematic review of research on artificial intelligence applications in higher education – where are the educators? *International Journal of Educational Technology in Higher Education, 16*(39). DOI: 10.1186/s41239-019-0171-0

Zeide, E. (2017). The Structural Consequences of Big Data-Driven Education. *Big Data, 5*(2). DOI: 10.1089/big.2016.0061 PMID: 28632444

Chapter 13
AI for Formative and Summative Assessment:
A Balanced Approach

Ashley L. Dockens
https://orcid.org/0000-0002-9707-975X
Lamar University, USA

Kaye Shelton
https://orcid.org/0000-0001-5024-5629
Lamar University, USA

ABSTRACT

Artificial Intelligence (AI) is significantly reshaping educational assessment, offering useful tools to enhance both formative and summative practices. This chapter explores how AI can alter and improve assessment by providing personalized, real-time feedback and adaptive learning experiences for formative evaluation, while improving the efficiency, consistency, and scalability of summative assessments through automated grading and AI-driven rubrics. The integration of AI promises substantial benefits, including time-saving measures for educators, enhanced personalization, and data-driven insights. However, it also introduces critical challenges that necessitate a redesign of assessment practices. Ethical considerations such as algorithmic bias, the need for human oversight, data privacy, the importance of the teacher-student relationship, and equitable access must be carefully addressed. This chapter advocates for a balanced approach, emphasizing the synergistic potential of AI to augment human expertise and foster ethical, effective, and equitable assessment.

DOI: 10.4018/979-8-3373-5102-5.ch013

BRIEF GLOSSARY OF TERMS

To aid in your reading of this chapter, consider these key terms you will encounter.

- **Adaptive Learning Systems:** AI-powered educational platforms that dynamically adjust the presentation of content and learning pathways in real-time based on an individual student's performance and needs.
- **Algorithmic Bias:** Systematic and repeatable errors in an AI system that create unfair outcomes, such as disadvantaging certain groups of students, often stemming from biased training data or flawed algorithm design.
- **Artificial Intelligence (AI):** Technology that enables computer systems to perform tasks typically requiring human intelligence, such as learning, problem-solving, and decision-making, applied here to enhance educational assessment.
- **Automated Grading:** The use of AI systems, particularly Natural Language Processing, to evaluate and score student work, such as essays or short answers, based on predefined criteria.
- **Data Privacy:** The protection of sensitive student information collected and processed by AI assessment tools, ensuring confidentiality and compliance with ethical and legal standards.
- **Formative Assessment:** Ongoing assessment processes during instruction designed to monitor student learning and provide immediate, actionable feedback to improve teaching and learning.
- **Item Response Theory (IRT):** A psychometric model used in AI-powered adaptive testing to estimate a student's ability level based on their responses to assessment items of varying difficulty and characteristics.
- **Knowledge Tracing:** An AI technique that models a student's understanding of specific concepts over time by analyzing their interactions with learning materials and assessments to predict performance.
- **Natural Language Processing (NLP):** A branch of AI that enables computers to understand, interpret, and generate human language, used in assessment for tasks like automated essay scoring and feedback generation.
- **Personalized Feedback:** Tailored comments and guidance provided to students, often by AI systems, based on their specific responses and learning patterns to support individual improvement.
- **Summative Assessment:** Evaluation conducted at the end of an instructional period (e.g., unit, course) to measure overall student achievement and assign grades.

INTRODUCTION: THE SYNERGISTIC POTENTIAL OF AI IN EDUCATIONAL ASSESSMENT

Assessment is a cornerstone of education, fundamental for gauging student progress and instructional effectiveness. Traditional methods like tests and assignments are designed to evaluate knowledge, skills, and abilities. These methods often culminate in summative evaluations at the end of a learning period to aggregate what a student has learned, though some argue they may not fully capture critical thinking or creative problem-solving (Astin & Antonio, 2012).

The emergence of Artificial Intelligence (AI) as a powerful technology is impacting numerous sectors, including education (Al-Zahrani & Alasmari, 2024). This has led to a growing interest in, and adoption of, AI-powered tools designed to enhance both formative and summative assessment. AI's potential includes significantly reshaping assessment practices, offering new possibilities for evaluating student understanding and progress (González-Calatayud et al., 2021). AI-driven systems can analyze vast student data, offer real-time feedback, and personalize learning (González-Calatayud et al., 2021), holding the potential to significantly improve the efficiency, personalization, and data-driven insights within the assessment process (Owan et al., 2023).

However, the proliferation of sophisticated AI, particularly large language models (LLMs), presents not only opportunities but also significant challenges. AI's increasing ability to perform tasks used to evaluate learning, including essay writing and problem-solving, necessitates a fundamental re-evaluation of assessment approaches. This re-evaluation must promote authentic student work and responsible AI use (Dockens, 2023), as AI's sophisticated mimicry of human work challenges traditional pre-AI assessment validity. AI's disruption requires a thoughtful and innovative response that prioritizes relevant and effective learning experiences in an AI-augmented world. This chapter, while exploring the synergistic potential of AI, will address this call for a deeper re-evaluation, moving beyond operational benefits to consider how educational assessment itself must evolve. To fully understand this evolution, it is essential to first define how AI is reshaping formative and summative assessment.

The Promise and Concerns of AI in Assessment

Formative assessment, the ongoing evaluation of learning, is being redefined by AI, which offers more dynamic and responsive assessment through real-time analysis, immediate, personalized feedback, and continuous progress monitoring (Hooda et al., 2022; Kim, 2023). This provides a more tailored learning experience, addressing learning gaps as they arise (Baker, 2021). Summative assessment, which evaluates overall achievement, is also being transformed. AI offers opportunities for automated grading of various assessment types using Natural Language Processing (NLP) (Mizumoto & Eguchi, 2023), can contribute to consistent grading rubrics, and offers scalable efficiency for large-scale testing (Tang et al., 2024). While still in its early stages, AI also shows promise in creating personalized summative tasks (Merino-Campos, 2025).

Given this potential, it is imperative to consider how these advancements can be strategically integrated. A balanced approach that combines the strengths of AI-driven methods with human expertise is needed (Agrawal et al., 2025). This chapter advocates for a thoughtful and ethical integration that complements, rather than replaces, human judgment and educators' nuanced understanding.

Early AI integration in assessment began with intelligent tutoring systems in the 1960s (Shute & Psotka, 1996; The Grainger College of Engineering, 2025), with research interest surging as machine learning advanced in the 1990s (Guo et al., 2021). More recently, models like ChatGPT have significantly increased AI's application in educational assessment (Adıgüzel et al., 2023; İpek et al., 2023). These advancements position AI as a tool to address the limitations of traditional assessments, achieving a balance between personalization and efficiency that previous methods struggled to attain (Akavova et al., 2023). However, the ethical implications, particularly concerning academic integrity and data privacy, must be addressed to guide responsible use (Chan, 2023; Dockens, 2023; Dockens & Shelton, 2025). The ongoing evolution of AI in assessment suggests that while the technology offers significant advantages, careful consideration of its ethical implications is essential for fostering a responsible and equitable learning environment (Fu & Weng, 2024). For a clear summary of how these different assessment paradigms compare, see Table 1.

Table 1. Comparing Traditional and Modern Assessment Approaches

Characteristic	Traditional Assessment	Modern/Alternative Assessment
Focus	Recall of facts, memorization	Application of knowledge, problem-solving, creativity
Timing	Primarily summative, end of learning period	Formative and summative, ongoing and end of period
Personalization	Low, often a "one-size-fits-all" approach	High, aims to cater to individual learning styles and needs
Feedback	Delayed, often limited to grades	Timely, descriptive, and actionable
Skills Assessed	Narrow, primarily cognitive knowledge and skills	Broad, encompasses cognitive, socio-emotional, practical skills

continued on following page

Table 1. Continued

Characteristic	Traditional Assessment	Modern/Alternative Assessment
Objectivity	Aims for high objectivity through standardization	Can vary, may involve more subjective human judgment
Efficiency	Often high for administration and grading	Can vary, some methods may be more time-consuming

TRANSFORMING LEARNING: AI IN FORMATIVE ASSESSMENT PRACTICES

Formative assessment is crucial for effective teaching, continuously monitoring understanding, and guiding instruction (Hattie & Timperley, 2007; Irons & Elkington, 2021). Its primary goal is to improve learning by identifying struggles and informing teaching adjustments (Miranda & Hermann, 2015), for which timely, specific feedback is crucial (Irons & Elkington, 2021).

AI-Powered Personalized Feedback and Adaptive Learning

AI can revolutionize formative assessment by providing instant, personalized feedback (Trajkovski & Hayes, 2025). AI tools analyze student responses to identify strengths and weaknesses, such as by recognizing error patterns and offering tailored resources (Owan et al., 2023). This immediate feedback can engage students and foster a growth mindset (Jeffs et al., 2021).

Furthermore, AI can be seamlessly integrated into adaptive learning platforms that adjust content difficulty in real-time based on performance (Strielkowski et al., 2025). These systems use algorithms to dynamically adjust content, tailoring the learning pathway. As students progress, AI identifies strengths and weaknesses, offering customized pathways for appropriate levels of challenge, thus improving motivation and outcomes. This framework facilitates mastery of difficult concepts and accelerates progress through easier ones (Naseer et al., 2024). Adaptive platforms like *DreamBox* (DreamBox, Inc., 2025) and *Smart Sparrow* (Pearson, 2020) use AI to create differentiated pathways, adapting problems in real-time for optimal challenge and support (Palakurti et al., 2025).

AI-Enhanced Monitoring and Gamification

AI applications can support the monitoring of student learning through various approaches. Data gathered can be instrumental in identifying learning trends, tracking individual progress, and facilitating timely interventions (Lourenço et al., 2025). Educators can use this data, based on analysis of digital interactions like time spent and error types, to adjust instructional strategies (Yao et al., 2025). Platforms like *Formative* track student progress against learning standards, providing valuable data for informed decisions (Formative, 2025).

Integrating gamification and AI also powerfully enhances student engagement (Kassenkhan et al., 2025). AI can gamify formative assessments, making learning more engaging by adding game elements like points and rewards to encourage active learning (Deabanico & Caballes, 2023). AI analyzes student behavior in these environments to adapt game mechanics and challenges for optimal engagement, such as by providing more practice on struggling concepts (Kassenkhan et al., 2025). Platforms like Kahoot! and Quizizz use AI to gamify learning with interactive quizzes and real-time feedback (Kahoot!, 2025; Quizizz, 2025).

Formative Assessment for AI Literacy

Beyond personalized feedback, formative assessment is a potential tool for developing AI literacy. As AI integrates into academic and professional life, students must learn to use it effectively, ethically, and critically–an "AI-integrative" approach (Maphalala & Ajani, 2025; Walter, 2024). Formative activities can develop essential skills such as crafting effective prompts, critically evaluating AI-generated content for bias and inaccuracies, understanding AI's limitations, and reflecting on its influence on learning. By embedding such activities, educators can help students become active, critical, and ethical AI users, preparing them for a future of AI collaboration (Walter, 2024). For a list of AI-powered tools for formative assessment, see Table 2.

Table 2. Examples of AI-Powered Tools for Formative Assessment

Tool Name	Overview
Grammarly	An AI-powered writing assistant that provides feedback on grammar, spelling, punctuation, clarity, and writing style (Grammarly, Inc., 2025).
DreamBox	An adaptive learning platform for mathematics that uses AI algorithms to adjust problems in real-time based on student performance (DreamBox Learning, Inc., 2025).
Smart Sparrow by Pearson	An adaptive learning platform for science that uses AI algorithms to adjust problems and simulations in real-time based on student performance. *Acquired by Pearson (Pearson, 2020).

continued on following page

Table 2. Continued

Tool Name	Overview
Formative	An interactive instructional platform that supports live assignments and assessments with real-time progress tracking and immediate teacher feedback (Formative, 2025).
Socrative	A student response system that engages learners through interactive quizzes, polls, and exit tickets with real-time data visualization (Showbie, 2025).
Quizizz	A gamified learning platform that offers interactive quizzes and games with features like an adaptive question bank and instant feedback (Quizizz, 2025).
Eduaide	An AI-powered assistant that helps educators generate lesson plans, teaching resources, and assessments to streamline content creation (Eduaide, 2025).

Navigating the Challenges: Ethical Considerations in AI-Driven Formative Assessment

While the integration of AI promises significant advancements in formative assessment, it is crucial to address potential challenges and ethical considerations to ensure equitable and responsible implementation.

- ***Data Privacy and Security*:** AI-powered formative assessment tools often collect and analyze vast amounts of student data, raising critical concerns about privacy and security. Ensuring the secure storage and ethical use of this sensitive information is paramount. Educational institutions must establish clear guidelines and robust security measures to protect student data from unauthorized access or misuse. Transparency regarding data collection practices and how AI algorithms utilize student information is also essential to build trust among students, parents, and educators (Huang, 2023).
- ***Algorithmic Bias and Fairness*:** AI algorithms are trained on data, and if this data reflects existing societal biases, the AI systems can perpetuate or even amplify these biases in their feedback and adaptive learning pathways. In formative assessment, this could lead to certain student groups receiving less effective feedback or being placed on less challenging learning trajectories based on biased algorithms. Careful attention must be paid to the design, training data, and ongoing monitoring of AI algorithms to mitigate bias and ensure fairness across all student populations. Regular audits and evaluations of AI systems for potential bias are necessary to promote equitable learning opportunities (Baker & Hawn, 2022).
- ***Over-Reliance on AI and the Diminished Role of Human Educators*:** While AI can automate certain aspects of formative assessment, it is crucial to avoid over-reliance on these tools to the detriment of human interaction and ped-

agogical expertise. The nuanced understanding, empathy, and contextual awareness that human educators bring to the assessment process are irreplaceable. AI should serve as a tool to augment, not replace, the role of teachers in providing meaningful feedback and fostering student growth (Chen et al., 2020; Zhai et al., 2024). Maintaining a balance between AI-driven insights and human judgment is essential for a holistic and effective formative assessment approach.

- ***The "Black Box" Problem and Explainability***: Some AI algorithms, particularly complex deep learning models, can operate as "black boxes," making it difficult to understand how they arrive at specific feedback or adaptive adjustments (Popenici & Kerr, 2017). This lack of transparency can be problematic in an educational context, where understanding the rationale behind feedback is crucial for learning. Efforts to develop more explainable AI (XAI) is underway (Gunning, 2019) and may prove necessary for educational to provide insights into how AI systems function and to build educators' and students' trust in their recommendations.
- ***The Potential for Deskilling and Over-Standardization***: If AI-driven formative assessment tools become too prescriptive, they could potentially lead to a deskilling of educators, limiting their autonomy in designing and implementing assessment strategies (Selwyn, 2019). Furthermore, an over-emphasis on standardized AI-driven feedback might neglect the importance of diverse pedagogical approaches and the unique needs of individual learners. It is important to ensure that AI tools are flexible and adaptable enough to support a variety of teaching styles and learning contexts. Addressing these ethical considerations proactively is essential for harnessing the transformative potential of AI in formative assessment responsibly and equitably (Popenici & Kerr, 2017). Open dialogue, collaboration between AI developers and educators, and the establishment of ethical guidelines and best practices are crucial steps in navigating these challenges.
- ***The Importance of the Teacher-Student Relationship***: While AI can enhance assessment practices, it is important to remember that assessment is not solely about data collection and grading; it is also a deeply human endeavor (Noddings, 2005; Selwyn, 2019). Teachers play a vital role in interpreting assessment results within the context of their students' individual circumstances, providing nuanced feedback that goes beyond what algorithms can offer, and supporting students' social and emotional development (Noddings, 2005; Selwyn, 2019). AI should be used to augment and complement these human elements of assessment, rather than replace them (Selwyn, 2019). The empathy, understanding, and personalized guidance that human teachers provide are essential for fostering a positive and supportive learning environment,

and the integration of AI should not diminish the importance of this critical teacher-student relationship (Noddings, 2005).

EVALUATING ACHIEVEMENT: THE IMPACT OF AI ON SUMMATIVE ASSESSMENT

Summative assessment critically evaluates overall student achievement at the end of an instructional period (National Research Council, 2001). Concerns about academic integrity in this context are exacerbated by sophisticated AI, as students may rely on these technologies instead of authentic learning (Cotton et al., 2023; Kizilcec et al., 2024). Current plagiarism detection often fails with AI-generated material (Cotton et al., 2023; Walters, 2023), suggesting a need to focus on broader educational reform rather than solely on detection or policing AI use (Cotton et al., 2023; Kasneci et al., 2023; Lo, 2023). The complexities of AI necessitate a reevaluation of assessment strategies (Kizilcec et al., 2024), as simply banning AI is unsustainable (Lo, 2023). There is an urgent need to fundamentally rethink and redesign summative assessment (Cotton et al., 2023; Rudolph et al., 2023).

Automated Grading: Enhancing Efficiency with Human Oversight

Automated grading systems use Natural Language Processing (NLP) to analyze and score student work (Xu et al., 2024). These systems offer significant efficiency benefits, providing "instant feedback" and addressing time-consuming assessment challenges, particularly in large educational contexts (Zribi & Smaoui, 2021). Automated systems can process hundreds of submissions in minutes, a task that could take hours for a human grader (Kumar & Boulanger, 2020; Vittorini et al., 2020). This allows instructors to dedicate more time to individualized feedback and instructional support.

However, research on reliability presents mixed findings. While some studies show promising results, with moderate to substantial agreement between automated and human scoring (Gabon et al., 2025; Vittorini et al., 2020), others indicate performance variations where automated systems assign significantly different scores (Zribi & Smaoui, 2021). Key challenges remain in achieving consistent accuracy across diverse assignments and topics (Xu et al., 2024). Therefore, it is crucial to apply human oversight before finalizing grades. A "human-AI fusion" model, where AI lessens workload but humans maintain final quality control, is recommended (Kumar & Boulanger, 2020). Current evidence suggests these systems are best used as supplementary tools rather than replacements for human judgment, particularly in high-stakes contexts (Zribi & Smaoui, 2021).

Redesigning Assessment: "AI-Immune" and "AI-Integrative" Frameworks

Given the challenges AI poses to traditional methods, educators are developing strategic responses through two distinct yet potentially complementary frameworks: "AI-immune" and "AI-integrative" approaches. Both aim to maintain assessment integrity while addressing the realities of AI in education. Course learning objectives will lead faculty to determine which approach is more appropriate. Both approaches may be applied within the same course. For this reason, it is recommended that educators share assignment- or assessment-specific guidance on the allowable or unallowable use of AI rather than a "blanket" AI statement.

The "AI-Immune" Approach

The "AI-immune" approach centers on designing assessments that prioritize and evaluate uniquely human capabilities that are beyond the current scope of AI. This framework emphasizes creativity, critical thinking in novel situations, nuanced ethical reasoning, and sophisticated communication (Alkouk & Khlaif, 2024). While AI excels at data analysis, it struggles with empathy, creativity, and ethical judgment—distinctly human traits (Pavone et al., 2024). The goal is to create assessments where using AI to generate the core of the work provides little advantage or proves difficult to complete.

Examples of "AI-immune" assessment methods include:

Process-Oriented Assessments

These focus on the learning process, requiring multiple iterations, reflection, and documentation of thinking (Alkouk & Khlaif, 2024). Process-oriented assessments require students to focus on the process of learning itself, a method that inherently resists AI intervention by design (Teo & Chew, 2025). These tasks require multiple iterations in development, along with reflection and the documentation of learning processes and thinking over time. For instance, a research portfolio assessment might obligate a student to document their intellectual development throughout a semester. Instead of a single final product, the student provides evidence of evolving thought through submissions such as initial research questions, drafts incorporating instructor feedback, and revised versions with tracked changes.

Critical reflection is a key component; assignments like reflective journals and personal narratives require students to connect course material to their unique experiences (Chan & Lee, 2021), a task that may be more difficult for AI to replicate. This comprehensive documentation of an iterative and personal learning journey creates an assessment environment where outsourcing the work to artificial intelligence is significantly more challenging. By focusing on the demonstration of thinking processes and reasoning, these methods provide a more valid measure of student learning. This emphasis on metacognitive awareness and process documentation not only helps to deter academic dishonesty but also enhances learning outcomes by requiring students to become more aware and articulate about their own intellectual growth.

Interactive and Collaborative Assessments

These require students to demonstrate knowledge in real time through in-class discussions, debates, oral presentations, and defenses where they must think critically and respond spontaneously (Dockens, 2023). Interactive and collaborative assessments require students to demonstrate knowledge through real-time engagement, a method that inherently resists AI substitution through its demand for immediate human cognitive processes (Teo & Chew, 2025). These approaches necessitate spontaneous critical thinking, active listening, and adaptive response generation that cannot be pre-scripted or outsourced to artificial intelligence. For instance, a Socratic seminar assessment (Delić & Bećirović, 2016) might require students to engage in structured discussions where they assume rotating roles such as "devil's advocate", "synthesizer", or "evidence analyzer", with role changes occurring without preparation time. Instead of relying on predetermined responses, students must demonstrate their understanding through impromptu defenses of their positions, synthesis of multiple viewpoints, and navigation of unexpected challenges from peers and instructors.

The collaborative dimension is equally significant; students must engage in real-time problem-solving within groups, negotiate conflicting interpretations, and build seamlessly upon each other's contributions without prior coordination. This dynamic interaction creates an assessment environment where the unpredictable nature of human discourse, combined with the need for emotional intelligence and social awareness, makes AI intervention practically impossible. By emphasizing live demonstration of knowledge through discussion, debate, and collaborative reasoning, these methods provide authentic measures of student comprehension and critical thinking skills (Vlachopoulos & Makri, 2024). This focus on spontaneous intellectual engagement not only deters academic dishonesty but also cultivates essential communication and collaboration skills that reflect genuine learning and prepare students for professional environments where such capabilities are paramount.

Authentic Assessments

These challenge students to apply learning in realistic, complex situations that mirror real-world demands, such as simulations or performance tasks in controlled environments (Dockens, 2023). Authentic assessments require students to apply their learning within realistic, complex situations that mirror the demands and constraints of their future professional environments or real-world scenarios (Alkouk & Khlaif, 2024), a method that inherently resists AI intervention through its emphasis on contextual problem-solving and application. These tasks necessitate the integration of multiple competencies, practical judgment, and adaptive decision-making within controlled yet dynamic scenarios that cannot be adequately addressed through pre-generated responses. For instance, a business simulation assessment might require students to manage a "company" over several weeks, making strategic decisions based on changing market conditions, resource limitations, and stakeholder demands. Instead of theoretical knowledge demonstration, students must navigate ambiguous situations, respond to unexpected crises, and justify their decisions based on real-time feedback and evolving circumstances.

The complexity of authentic tasks lies in their multifaceted nature; students must synthesize knowledge from various domains, consider ethical implications, and demonstrate professional competencies such as communication, leadership, and critical analysis within realistic constraints (Darling-Hammond & Snyder, 2000; Vlachopoulos & Makri, 2024). Performance-based assessments in controlled environments, such as clinical simulations for healthcare students or mock trials for law students, create scenarios where theoretical knowledge must be translated into practical action under pressure. This application-focused approach creates an assessment environment where the nuanced understanding required for real-world performance, combined with the need for contextual adaptation and professional judgment (Lateef, 2010), makes AI substitution highly impractical. By emphasizing authentic demonstration of competency through realistic application, these methods provide valid measures of student readiness for professional practice while simultaneously deterring academic dishonesty through their inherently complex and contextual nature.

Context-Specific and Personal Assignments

Tasks that require interaction with specific local, niche, or individual experiences, such as reflective journals and personal narratives, are more difficult for AI to replicate authentically (Alkouk & Khlaif, 2024; Dockens, 2023). Context-specific and personal assignments require students to draw upon their unique lived experiences and local contexts, a method that inherently resists AI intervention through its reliance on individual history, cultural background, and personal meaning-making processes (Teo & Chew, 2025). These tasks necessitate the integration of course material with deeply personal reflections, specific community knowledge, and individual experiential learning that cannot be authentically generated by artificial intelligence systems lacking personal biography or local embeddedness. For instance, a reflective journal assignment might require students to connect theoretical concepts from their coursework to specific experiences within their own community, workplace, or family context, documenting how abstract principles manifest in their particular cultural or geographic setting. Instead of generic analysis, students must demonstrate understanding through personal narrative that reveals their individual journey of learning and growth within specific situational constraints.

The personal dimension of these assignments lies in their requirement for authentic voice and genuine introspection; students must articulate how course content intersects with their own values, challenges, and aspirations while drawing upon memories, relationships, and cultural knowledge that are uniquely their own (Darling-Hammond & Snyder, 2000). Context-specific tasks, such as analyzing local policy issues, interviewing community members, or reflecting on workplace dynamics, demand intimate familiarity with specific environments and social networks that extend beyond readily available information sources. This personalized approach creates an assessment environment where the authentic integration of individual experience with academic content, combined with the need for genuine self-reflection and contextual knowledge, makes AI replication highly improbable. By emphasizing personal meaning-making and context-specific application, these methods provide valid measures of individual learning while simultaneously deterring academic dishonesty through their inherently personal and experientially grounded nature.

Complex Case Studies

Assessments involving ill-defined parameters or complex ethical implications often fall outside AI's current capabilities (Alkouk & Khlaif, 2024; Dockens, 2023). Complex case studies require students to navigate ill-defined parameters and multifaceted ethical dilemmas, a method that inherently resists AI intervention through its demand for nuanced judgment, moral reasoning, and tolerance for ambiguity that extends beyond algorithmic capabilities. These assessments necessitate the integration of competing perspectives, consideration of unquantifiable human factors, and decision-making within scenarios where multiple valid solutions may exist, challenging students to demonstrate sophisticated analytical thinking that cannot be reduced to pattern recognition or template responses. For instance, a healthcare ethics case study (Seshan et al., 2021) might present students with a scenario involving conflicting patient autonomy, family wishes, cultural considerations, resource limitations, and professional obligations, requiring them to weigh competing moral frameworks while acknowledging the inherent uncertainty and emotional complexity of real-world ethical decision-making. Instead of seeking predetermined correct answers, students must articulate their reasoning process, defend their position while acknowledging alternative viewpoints, and demonstrate understanding of the contextual factors that complicate straightforward application of theoretical principles.

The complexity of these assessments lies in their resistance to formulaic approaches; students must grapple with incomplete information, competing stakeholder interests, and situations where ethical principles may conflict with practical constraints or cultural norms. Case studies involving organizational dilemmas, controversial policy decisions, or social justice issues might demand sophisticated understanding of systemic factors, power dynamics, and long-term consequences that require human judgment and experiential wisdom. This multidimensional analytical approach creates an assessment environment where the nuanced reasoning required for ethical decision-making, combined with the need for empathetic understanding and moral imagination, exceeds current AI capabilities. By emphasizing complex problem-solving within ambiguous contexts, these methods provide authentic measures of critical thinking and ethical reasoning while simultaneously deterring academic dishonesty through their inherently sophisticated and judgment-dependent nature.

The "AI-Integrative" Approach

In contrast, the "AI-integrative" approach strategically embraces AI as a tool to enhance learning and develop essential skills for working effectively and ethically with AI technologies (Dockens, 2023). This perspective views AI not as a threat, but as a partner in the learning process. This approach advocates for developing students' abilities to understand and utilize AI critically. Research indicates AI's utility in fostering critical thinking and analytical skills through practices like prompt engineering (Heston & Khun, 2023; Hu & Lee, 2024), and its integration in collaborative learning also shows promise.

Assessments within the AI-Integrative framework might include:

AI-Assisted Research Projects

The focus is on the critical evaluation of AI output and synthesis of information (Martin et al., 2025). AI-assisted research projects require students to strategically utilize artificial intelligence tools while developing critical evaluation skills and synthesis capabilities, a method that intentionally embraces AI as a collaborative partner in the learning process rather than viewing it as a threat to academic integrity. These assignments necessitate sophisticated understanding of AI capabilities and limitations, requiring students to design effective prompts, critically assess generated outputs, and synthesize AI-provided information with traditional research sources to create original scholarly work. For instance, a comparative literature research project might encourage students to use AI tools to generate initial bibliographies, summarize complex theoretical frameworks, or identify thematic patterns across large corpora of texts, while requiring them to verify sources, evaluate the accuracy of AI interpretations, and develop original arguments that extend beyond AI-generated insights. Instead of prohibiting AI use, students must demonstrate their ability to leverage these tools effectively while maintaining scholarly rigor and intellectual honesty.

The pedagogical value of this approach lies in its emphasis on developing essential 21st-century skills; students must learn to craft precise queries, recognize AI biases and limitations, cross-reference generated content with authoritative sources, and articulate the reasoning behind their synthesis decisions. Research projects incorporating AI assistance require explicit documentation of AI tool usage, critical reflection on the quality and reliability of generated content, and demonstration of how human judgment enhanced or corrected AI outputs. This integrative methodology creates an assessment environment where students develop both technological literacy and critical thinking skills essential for professional environments where AI collaboration is increasingly prevalent. By emphasizing strategic AI utilization alongside critical evaluation and original synthesis, these methods prepare students for future academic and professional contexts while fostering responsible and effective human-AI collaboration skills that reflect the evolving nature of research and knowledge creation.

Critique of AI-Generated Content

Students analyze AI-produced essays, code, or solutions to identify strengths, weaknesses, biases, and ethical concerns (Martin et al., 2025). Critique of AI-generated content requires students to develop sophisticated analytical skills for evaluating artificial intelligence outputs, a method that strategically positions AI as a subject for critical examination rather than a tool to be avoided or uncritically accepted (Zhai et al., 2024). These assignments necessitate deep understanding of both disciplinary standards and AI capabilities, requiring students to systematically assess the accuracy, logic, bias, and ethical implications of machine-generated work while developing expertise in identifying the subtle ways AI systems may perpetuate problematic assumptions or produce plausible but flawed reasoning. For instance, students might receive AI-generated policy briefs, scientific explanations, or literary analyses and be tasked with conducting comprehensive evaluations that examine factual accuracy, logical coherence, source reliability, cultural sensitivity, and adherence to disciplinary conventions. Instead of simply accepting or rejecting AI outputs, students must demonstrate their ability to articulate specific strengths and weaknesses while providing evidence-based justifications for their assessments.

The educational value of this approach lies in its development of critical literacy skills essential for navigating an AI-saturated information environment; students must learn to recognize algorithmic biases, identify gaps in reasoning, evaluate the appropriateness of AI recommendations for specific contexts, and understand how training data limitations may influence generated content (Almatrafi, Johri, & Lee, 2024). Critique assignments require students to apply disciplinary knowledge rigorously, as they must possess sufficient expertise to identify errors, omissions, or inappropriate generalizations that may not be immediately apparent to novice learners. This analytical methodology creates an assessment environment where students strengthen their own subject matter expertise while developing the evaluative skills necessary for responsible AI interaction in professional contexts. By emphasizing systematic critique and evidence-based evaluation, these methods cultivate both domain-specific knowledge and technological literacy, preparing students to serve as informed intermediaries between AI capabilities and human decision-making in their future careers (Naamati-Schneider, 2024).

Prompt Engineering Tasks

Assessments evaluate students' ability to guide AI tools toward specific learning objectives (Martin et al., 2025). Prompt engineering tasks require students to develop sophisticated communication skills for directing artificial intelligence systems toward specific learning objectives, a method that strategically positions students as architects of AI interaction while fostering deep understanding of both subject matter and technological capabilities (Walter, 2024). These assignments necessitate mastery of disciplinary knowledge alongside technical skill development, requiring students to craft precise queries that elicit accurate, relevant, and ethically appropriate responses from AI systems while demonstrating their ability to iteratively refine their approach based on output quality and learning goals. For instance, students might be tasked with designing prompt sequences that guide an AI system through complex problem-solving processes in fields such as data analysis, creative writing, or scientific reasoning, requiring them to anticipate potential misunderstandings, specify desired formats, and incorporate appropriate constraints that align with disciplinary standards. Instead of passively consuming AI-generated content, students must demonstrate their ability to serve as informed directors of AI capabilities while maintaining responsibility for final outcomes.

The educational significance of this approach lies in its development of metacognitive awareness and strategic thinking skills; students must understand their learning objectives clearly enough to translate them into effective AI instructions while recognizing when generated responses meet, exceed, or fall short of their intended goals. Prompt engineering assessments require students to document their iterative design process, explain their reasoning for specific prompt choices, and reflect on how different approaches yield varying results, thereby developing both technical proficiency and critical evaluation skills – necessary in the modern age (Федерякин et al., 2024). This collaborative methodology creates an assessment environment where students must possess sufficient domain expertise to recognize quality outputs while simultaneously developing the communication precision necessary for effective human-AI collaboration. By emphasizing strategic AI guidance and reflective practice, these methods prepare students to leverage AI tools productively in professional contexts while maintaining intellectual ownership and responsibility for their work outcomes.

Collaborative Projects Using AI

Students ethically integrate AI into their workflow, with their ability to use the tool effectively being part of the assessment (Elshall & Badir, 2025). Collaborative projects using AI require students to ethically integrate artificial intelligence tools into their workflow while developing professional competencies in human-AI collaboration, a method that strategically positions AI as a legitimate partner in knowledge creation while emphasizing student responsibility for ethical usage and quality outcomes. These assignments necessitate sophisticated understanding of both course principles and AI capabilities, requiring students to make strategic decisions about when, how, and why to incorporate AI-generated elements while maintaining transparency about their usage and demonstrating that AI enhancement amplifies rather than replaces their creative vision and technical skills (Ruiz-Rojas et al., 2024). For instance, art students might collaborate on multimedia art projects where they utilize AI image generators to create base visual elements that they then manipulate through digital editing, physical painting techniques, or sculptural transformation, or employ AI recommendation systems to suggest color palettes and compositional arrangements that they critically evaluate and selectively incorporate into their original artistic vision while documenting their integration decisions, evaluating AI contributions critically, and demonstrating how their human expertise shaped, refined, and validated the collaborative output. Instead of concealing AI usage, students must articulate their workflow decisions and demonstrate effective partnership management between human creativity and artificial intelligence capabilities.

The educational value of this approach lies in its development of professional skills increasingly essential in contemporary work environments; students must learn to allocate tasks appropriately between human and artificial intelligence capabilities, maintain quality control over AI contributions, and navigate ethical considerations surrounding attribution, originality, and intellectual honesty. Students will likely learn more about AI, which may reduce fear of a technology that they will encounter in their professions (Marrone et al., 2022). Collaborative AI projects require explicit documentation of integration strategies, critical reflection on the effectiveness of human-AI partnerships, and demonstration of how students leveraged AI tools to achieve learning objectives that would have been difficult to accomplish independently (Atchley et al., 2024). This partnership methodology creates an assessment environment where students develop both technological fluency and ethical reasoning skills necessary for responsible AI collaboration in professional contexts. By emphasizing transparent integration and reflective practice, these methods prepare students to work effectively with AI systems while maintaining intellectual integrity and professional accountability in environments where human-AI collaboration represents the emerging standard for knowledge work.

Ethical deliberation and impact analysis

Students analyze the ethical implications of AI use in various professional and social contexts. Ethical deliberation and impact analysis require students to examine the moral implications and societal consequences of artificial intelligence deployment across various professional and social contexts, a method that strategically positions ethical reasoning as fundamental to responsible AI integration while developing critical thinking skills essential for navigating complex technological landscapes. These assignments necessitate sophisticated understanding of both ethical frameworks and AI capabilities, requiring students to analyze how artificial intelligence systems may perpetuate biases, disrupt established practices, or create unintended consequences (Hanna et al., 2025) while demonstrating their ability to weigh competing values and stakeholder interests in morally complex scenarios. For instance, students might examine case studies involving AI implementation in healthcare diagnostics, criminal justice algorithms, or educational assessment systems, requiring them to identify potential benefits and harms, analyze power dynamics, and propose ethical guidelines that balance innovation with social responsibility.

Instead of accepting technological progress uncritically, students must demonstrate their capacity to anticipate ethical challenges and articulate principled approaches to AI governance and implementation.

The educational significance of this approach lies in its development of moral reasoning and systemic thinking skills essential for responsible leadership in an AI-integrated society (The How Institute for Society, 2024); students must learn to consider multiple perspectives, anticipate long-term consequences, and navigate tensions between efficiency and equity, privacy and transparency, or individual autonomy and collective benefit. Ethical deliberation assignments require students to engage with various philosophical traditions, analyze real-world case studies, and develop nuanced positions that acknowledge the complexity of moral decision-making in technological contexts. This analytical methodology creates an assessment environment where students cultivate both ethical sensitivity and practical wisdom necessary for making responsible decisions about AI deployment in their future professional roles. By emphasizing principled reasoning and stakeholder consideration, these methods prepare students to serve as ethical leaders who can guide AI integration in ways that promote human flourishing while mitigating potential harms, fostering a generation of professionals equipped to navigate the moral complexities of our increasingly automated world.

These complementary assessment approaches collectively emphasize the development of metacognitive skills and critical thinking abilities essential for navigating an increasingly AI-integrated professional landscape. The AI-immune framework preserves the authenticity of human learning by focusing on processes, interactions, and experiences that resist artificial replication, while the AI-integrative approach strategically harnesses AI capabilities to develop technological literacy and ethical reasoning skills. Together, these frameworks provide educators with a comprehensive assessment toolkit that helps educators maintain academic integrity while preparing students for future contexts where effective human-AI collaboration will be paramount. Rather than viewing AI as merely a challenge to overcome or a tool to exploit, this dual approach recognizes that educational excellence requires both the preservation of distinctly human capabilities and the cultivation of skills necessary for responsible AI partnership. This balanced methodology ensures that students develop both the critical thinking skills that distinguish human intelligence and the technological fluency required for professional success in an AI-enhanced world, ultimately fostering graduates who can contribute meaningfully to society while maintaining ethical standards and intellectual integrity.

BROADER IMPLICATIONS: RETHINKING LEARNING CURRENCY

The rise of AI necessitates a reevaluation of traditional evaluative metrics. The reliance on grades faces pressure when AI can assist in achieving them, potentially without deep learning. Some have termed this era where individuals use AI ubiquitously, changing how we view integrity (Eaton, 2023). In this, there is a risk that AI could inflate grades without genuine skill mastery, diminishing the reliability of traditional metrics (Stankov, 2024). This context is shifting the dialogue towards alternative assessment strategies, including:

- **Comprehensive ePortfolios:** These showcase complex projects and reflections, providing a more nuanced perspective on student abilities and can positively influence learning (Eynon & Gambino, 2017).
- **Digital Badges and Micro-credentials:** These recognize specific skills and provide granular, detailed evidence of learning, particularly in disciplines requiring mastery of discrete skills (Felton et al., 2022).
- **Authentic Assessment Products:** These emphasize creating tangible outputs that require applying knowledge in real-world contexts, which nurtures critical thinking and promotes deeper learning (Alkouk & Khlaif, 2024).

The "currency" of learning may need to evolve to encompass demonstrable skills, innovation, and the capacity to navigate AI effectively. Educational assessment frameworks need to innovate beyond conventional metrics to maintain rigor and accurately reflect the multifaceted skill sets vital for contemporary learners (Hutson & Ceballos, 2023).

NAVIGATING THE CHALLENGES: ETHICAL AND PRACTICAL CONSIDERATIONS OF AI IN ASSESSMENT

The integration of AI into assessment is accompanied by significant ethical and practical challenges that demand careful navigation, spanning issues of bias, data privacy, the teacher-student relationship, over-reliance on technology, transparency, and equitable access.

Bias, Fairness, and the Unreliability of AI Content Detection

A critical challenge is the potential for bias in AI algorithms (Angwin et al., 2016; Floridi et al., 2018; Sadasivan et al., 2025). AI systems trained on biased data can perpetuate inequities, a significant issue for AI content detection tools, which have been shown to be both unreliable and biased (Barton, 2024; Hirsch, 2024). Research reveals inconsistent accuracy rates, often below vendor claims (Weber-Wulff et al., 2023). Even the best detection performance is not consistently achieved; under paraphrasing attacks, many detectors perform poorly—sometimes no better than chance (Sadasivan et al., 2025).

The issue of false positives—where human work is incorrectly flagged—poses a severe threat to student well-being (Sadasivan et al., 2025). Even OpenAI's former classifier incorrectly identified human text as AI-generated in 9% of cases (OpenAI, 2023). Conversely, false negatives—where AI text is missed—undermine the tools' purpose (Barton, 2024; Weber-Wulff et al., 2023). For example, Turnitin's checker can miss approximately 15% of AI text (Barton, 2024), and OpenAI's former classifier correctly identified AI text only 26% of the time (OpenAI, 2023).

Importantly, these tools show significant bias against certain student subgroups.

- **Non-Native English Speakers (NNES):** Studies show NNES text is much more likely to be misclassified as AI-generated (Liang et al., 2023). One analysis indicated over 61% of TOEFL essays were flagged by at least one detector, with over 19% unanimously misclassified by seven different detectors (Liang et al., 2023).
- **Neurodivergent Students:** Emerging research suggests students with autism, ADHD, or dyslexia may be at a higher risk of being falsely flagged due to unique writing styles or reliance on legitimate assistive technologies (Hirsch, 2024).
- **Other Biases:** Human biases can also be amplified by these tools, with reports indicating Black students are more likely to be accused of AI plagiarism by teachers (Common Sense Media as cited in Hirsch, 2024).

Such biases can transform detection tools into instruments of systemic inequity. It is essential that AI systems undergo regular audits to mitigate bias and ensure fairness across all student populations.

Data Privacy, Security, and the Teacher-Student Relationship

AI-powered assessment tools collect and analyze vast amounts of student data, raising critical concerns about privacy and security. Educational institutions must establish clear guidelines and robust security measures to protect this sensitive information from misuse. Transparency regarding data collection practices is essential to build trust (Al-Zahrani & Alasmari, 2024).

Furthermore, the nuances of the teacher-student relationship risk being undermined. Assessment is a deeply human endeavor (Noddings, 2005; Selwyn, 2019). The empathy, understanding, and contextual awareness that human educators bring to the process are irreplaceable (Chen et al., 2020; Zhai et al., 2024). AI should be used to augment and complement these human elements, not replace them (Selwyn, 2019).

Over-Reliance, Transparency, and Equitable Access

There is a risk of fostering an environment of over-reliance on AI, which could undermine the development of critical thinking and independent judgment (Zhai et al., 2024) and potentially lead to a deskilling of educators (Stacey et al., 2023). A balanced approach is crucial, where AI supports and enhances, rather than supplants, human expertise.

Transparency in AI decision-making, often referred to as the "black box" problem, is also paramount (Popenici & Kerr, 2017). Understanding how AI systems arrive at conclusions is critical for educators and students to trust and effectively utilize them (Popenici & Kerr, 2017). Efforts to develop more explainable AI (XAI) are necessary to provide this insight and build trust (Gunning, 2019).

Finally, the issue of equitable access cannot be overlooked. Disparities in access to technology could exacerbate the existing digital divide, creating new forms of educational inequality (Deng & El Hag, 2024). Coordinated efforts are required to make AI-based tools accessible to all students, regardless of their socioeconomic background (Abrahamson, 2025).

The Institutional and Faculty Imperative for the AI Era

The challenges presented by AI place a significant imperative on both faculty and institutions to take an active role in redesigning courses and assessment strategies (Dockens, 2023). This is a pedagogical necessity to ensure the continued value and integrity of education.

Institutions must develop clear, flexible, and forward-thinking policies to guide the ethical and sound use of AI. Key recommendations include:

- **Define Acceptable Use and Collaboration Parameters:** Institutions should establish guidelines clarifying the acceptable use of AI in coursework and assessment. These should address distinctions between assistance and misconduct, articulating when and how students may use generative AI tools (e.g., brainstorming, editing, citation formatting) and when their use is prohibited. Faculty should retain discretion to set stricter or more permissive standards within their courses – provided expectations are clearly communicated.
- **Promote Transparency and Disclosure:** Policies should encourage or require students to disclose the use of AI tools when submitting assignments, much like source citations. Standardized AI-use statements (e.g., "AI tools were used to generate an outline") can foster a culture of transparency and accountability, while also allowing instructors to better interpret and evaluate student work.
- **Invest in Faculty and Staff Training:** Provide ongoing professional development to help faculty understand AI tools, ethics, educational implication, and design appropriate assessments. Workshops, resource hubs, and instructional design consultations can empower educators to integrate policy and pedagogy coherently.
- **Develop a Multi-Stakeholder AI Review Body**: Establishing a standing committee—composed of faculty, students, instructional designers, IT professionals, and legal advisors—can help ensure policies evolve alongside AI technologies. This body should regularly review AI-related cases, audit detection tool efficacy, and make recommendations for updates based on pedagogical, ethical, and technological developments.
- **Ensure Equity and Fair Grievance Processes:** As AI detectors can yield false positives or inconsistently flag student work, institutions must provide a clear, equitable pathway for students to appeal decisions. Policies should protect students from unjust penalties and require instructors to provide evidence beyond AI detection alone when alleging misconduct.
- **Emphasize Guidelines Over Rigid Policies to Support and Promote Innovation:** Given the rapid pace of change in AI technology, institutions should favor living guidelines over fixed policies. Guidelines allow space for experimentation and innovation, encouraging faculty to try emerging tools and assess their pedagogical value. Instead of prescribing one-size-fits-all mandates, institutions should cultivate a culture of reflective practice and professional autonomy, supporting educators in responsibly testing and adapting AI-integrated approaches. Flexibility enables institutions to evolve alongside the tools they regulate and better serve a diverse and dynamic learning environment.

Faculty must lead this charge by proactively redesigning learning experiences where the use of AI for superficial completion does not diminish the inherent learning value (Grubaugh & Levitt, 2023).

CONCLUSION: FOSTERING A BALANCED AND ETHICAL INTEGRATION

The integration of Artificial Intelligence into educational assessment presents a transformative opportunity to enhance learning, yet it must be balanced with careful attention to significant ethical challenges (Popenici & Kerr, 2017). AI offers the potential for profound benefits, including the ability to provide personalized, real-time feedback, create adaptive learning experiences, and increase the efficiency of grading processes (Owan et al., 2023; Trajkovski & Hayes, 2025). These advancements promise to equip educators with powerful, data-driven insights to support student growth (Lourenço et al., 2025). However, these opportunities are accompanied by critical risks that demand proactive solutions, such as the potential for algorithmic bias (Baker & Hawn, 2022), the need to protect student data privacy (Huang, 2023), and the necessity of preserving the irreplaceable teacher-student relationship (Noddings, 2005; Selwyn, 2019).

The path forward requires a fundamental paradigm shift, moving beyond simply augmenting old methods to actively redesigning assessment for an AI-augmented world (Cotton et al., 2023; Rudolph et al., 2023). Faculty and institutional leadership are essential in this transition (Dockens, 2023). By strategically implementing frameworks like "AI-immune" assessments—which cultivate uniquely human skills such as critical thinking and creativity (Alkouk & Khlaif, 2024)—and "AI-integrative" approaches that teach students to use these tools effectively and ethically (Dockens, 2023; Walter, 2024), educators can maintain academic integrity while preparing students for their professional futures.

Ultimately, the future of assessment is a collaborative and resilient one that depends on proactive innovation from educators (Dockens, 2023; Grubaugh & Levitt, 2023). This is not merely a technological challenge but a pedagogical imperative. By fostering a culture of experimentation, prioritizing ethical guidelines (Chan, 2023), and engaging in open dialogue, the educational community can ensure AI serves as a powerful and responsible tool that enhances learning and empowers students to thrive in a world where human-AI collaboration is the new standard (Atchley et al., 2024).

REFERENCES

Abrahamson, E. (2025, March 10). *AI in higher education: Bridging the divide between access, equality, and opportunity*. International Center for Academic Integrity. https://www.academicintegrity.org/aws/ICAI/pt/sd/news_article/587198/_PARENT/layout_details/false

Adıgüzel, T., Kaya, M., & Cansu, F. (2023). Revolutionizing education with AI: Exploring the transformative potential of ChatGPT. *Contemporary Educational Technology*, *15*(3), ep429. DOI: 10.30935/cedtech/13152

Agrawal, A., Bhadhouriya, S., Pandey, A. K., Bhadoriya, S., Shrivastava, D., Dubey, G., Dubey, M., Sengar, H., Shakywar, K., & Shrivastava, V. (2025). Transforming student assessment in higher education: The role of artificial intelligence tools. In Moreira, F., & Teles, R. (Eds.), *Improving student assessment with emerging AI tools* (pp. 363–386). IGI Global., DOI: 10.4018/979-8-3693-6170-2.ch013

Akavova, A., Temirkhanova, Z., & Lorsanova, Z. (2023, November 20). Adaptive learning and artificial intelligence in the educational space. *E3S Web of Conferences*, *451*, 06011. DOI: 10.1051/e3sconf/202345106011

Al-Zahrani, A. M., & Alasmari, T. M. (2024). Exploring the impact of artificial intelligence on higher education: The dynamics of ethical, social, and educational implications. *Humanities & Social Sciences Communications*, *11*(1), 912. DOI: 10.1057/s41599-024-03432-4

Alkouk, W. A., & Khlaif, Z. N. (2024). AI-resistant assessments in higher education: Practical insights from faculty training workshops. *Frontiers in Education*, *9*, 1499495. DOI: 10.3389/feduc.2024.1499495

Almatrafi, O., Johri, A., & Lee, H. (2024). A systematic review of AI literacy conceptualization, constructs, and implementation and assessment efforts (2019–2023). *Computers and Education Open*, *6*, 100173. DOI: 10.1016/j.caeo.2024.100173

Angwin, J., Larson, J., Mattu, S., & Kirchner, L. (2016, May 23). *Machine bias*. ProPublica. https://www.propublica.org/article/machine-bias-risk-assessments-in-criminal-sentencing

Astin, A. W., & Antonio, A. L. (2012). *Assessment for excellence: The philosophy and practice of assessment and evaluation in higher education*. Bloomsbury Publishing PLC.

Atchley, P., Pannell, H., Wofford, K., Hopkins, M. M., & Atchley, R. A. (2024). Human and AI collaboration in the higher education environment: Opportunities and concerns. *Cognitive Research: Principles and Implications*, *9*(1), 38. DOI: 10.1186/s41235-024-00547-9 PMID: 38589710

Baker, R. S. (2021). Artificial intelligence in education: Bringing it all together. In *OECD Digital Education Outlook 2021: Pushing the frontiers with AI, Blockchain, and robotics* (pp. 43–56). OECD Publishing., DOI: 10.1787/589b283f-en

Baker, R. S., & Hawn, A. (2022). Algorithmic bias in education. *International Journal of Artificial Intelligence in Education*, *32*(4), 1052–1092. DOI: 10.1007/s40593-021-00285-9

Barton, R. (2024, January 9). *Turnitin adding AI writing detection, but instructors should use it with caution*. Purdue University Online. https://www.purdue.edu/online/turnitin-adding-ai-writing-detection-but-instructors-should-use-it-with-caution/

Chan, C. K. Y. (2023). A comprehensive AI policy education framework for university teaching and learning. *International Journal of Educational Technology in Higher Education*, *20*(1), 38. DOI: 10.1186/s41239-023-00408-3

Chan, C. K. Y., & Lee, K. (2021). Reflection literacy: A multilevel perspective on the challenges of using reflections in higher education through a comprehensive literature review. *Educational Research Review*, *32*, 100376. DOI: 10.1016/j.edurev.2020.100376

Chen, L., Chen, P., & Lin, Z. (2020). Artificial intelligence in education: A review. *IEEE Access : Practical Innovations, Open Solutions*, *8*, 75463–75488. DOI: 10.1109/ACCESS.2020.2988510

Cotton, D. R. E., Cotton, P. A., & Shipway, J. R. (2024). Chatting and cheating: Ensuring academic integrity in the era of ChatGPT. *Innovations in Education and Teaching International*, *61*(2), 228–239. DOI: 10.1080/14703297.2023.2190148

Darling-Hammond, L., & Snyder, J. (2000). Authentic assessment of teaching in context. *Teaching and Teacher Education*, *16*(5-6), 523–545. DOI: 10.1016/S0742-051X(00)00015-9

Deabanico, G., & Caballes, D. (2023). Revolutionizing learning: How eGamification assessment is changing teaching? *Psychology and Education: A Multidisciplinary Journal*, *10*(4), 1030–1034. https://ssrn.com/abstract=4516247

Delić, H., & Bećirović, S. (2016). Socratic method as an approach to teaching. *European Researcher*, *110*(10), 511–517. DOI: 10.13187/er.2016.110.511

Deng, X., & Hag, S. E. (2024). Digital inequality and two levels of the digital divide in online learning: A mixed methods study of underserved college students. *Journal of Information Systems Education, 35*(3), 377–389. DOI: 10.62273/SSIF6302

Dockens, A., & Shelton, K. (2025). The AI scholar: AI in higher education research and writing. In Wang, V. (Ed.), *AI integration into andragogical education* (pp. 109–136). IGI Global., DOI: 10.4018/979-8-3373-0502-8.ch005

Dockens, A. L. (2023). *Promoting authenticity of student work in the age of artificial intelligence: A faculty guide*. Lamar University Center for Teaching and Learning Enhancement. https://www.lamar.edu/lu-online/_files/documents/blog/ai-faculty-guide.pdf

DreamBox Learning, Inc. (2025). *DreamBox*. https://www.dreambox.com

Eaton, S. E. (2023). Postplagiarism: Transdisciplinary ethics and integrity in the age of artificial intelligence and neurotechnology. *International Journal for Educational Integrity, 19*(1), 14. DOI: 10.1007/s40979-023-00144-1

Eduaide. (2025). *Eduaide*. https://www.eduaide.ai

Elshall, A. S., & Badir, A. (2025). Balancing AI-assisted learning and traditional assessment: The FACT assessment in environmental data science education. *Frontiers in Education, 10*, 1596462. DOI: 10.3389/feduc.2025.1596462

Eynon, B., & Gambino, L. M. (2017). *High-impact ePortfolio practice: A catalyst for student, faculty, and institutional learning* (1st ed.). Routledge.

Federyakin, D., Molerov, D., Zlatkin-Troitschanskaia, O., & Maur, A. (2024). Prompt engineering as a new 21st century skill. *Frontiers in Education, 9*, 1366434. DOI: 10.3389/feduc.2024.1366434

Felton, S. D., Whitehouse, G., Motley, C., Jaeger, D., & Timur, A. (2023). How I stopped fearing micro-credentials and began to love digital badging – a pilot project. *Industry and Higher Education, 37*(2), 309–317. DOI: 10.1177/09504222221117951

Floridi, L., Cowls, J., Beltrametti, M., Chatila, R., Chazerand, P., Dignum, V., Luetge, C., Madelin, R., Pagallo, U., Rossi, F., Schafer, B., Valcke, P., & Vayena, E. (2018). AI4People—an ethical framework for a good AI society: Opportunities, risks, principles, and recommendations. *Minds and Machines, 28*(4), 689–707. DOI: 10.1007/s11023-018-9482-5 PMID: 30930541

Formative. (2025). *Formative*. https://www.formative.com

Fu, Y., & Weng, Z. (2024). Navigating the ethical terrain of AI in education: A systematic review on framing responsible human-centered AI practices. *Computers and Education: Artificial Intelligence*, *7*, 100306. DOI: 10.1016/j.caeai.2024.100306

Gabon, D. C., Vinluan, A. A., & Carpio, J. T.Dennis C. Gabon. (2025). Automated grading of essay using natural language processing: A comparative analysis with human raters across multiple essay types. *Journal of Information Systems Engineering & Management*, *10*(6s), 67–72. Advance online publication. DOI: 10.52783/jisem.v10i6s.700

Gikandi, J. W., Morrow, D., & Davis, N. E. (2011). Online formative assessment in higher education: A review of the literature. *Computers & Education*, *57*(4), 2333–2351. DOI: 10.1016/j.compedu.2011.06.004

González-Calatayud, V., Prendes-Espinosa, P., & Roig-Vila, R. (2021). Artificial intelligence for student assessment: A systematic review. *Applied Sciences (Basel, Switzerland)*, *11*(12), 5467. DOI: 10.3390/app11125467

Grammarly, Inc. (2025). *Grammarly*. https://www.grammarly.com

Grubaugh, S., & Levitt, G. (2023). Artificial intelligence and the paradigm shift: Reshaping education to equip students for future careers. *International Journal of Social Sciences and Humanities Invention*, *10*(6), 7931–7941. DOI: 10.18535/ijsshi/v10i06.02

Gunning, D., & Aha, D. W. (2019). DARPA's explainable artificial intelligence (XAI) program. *AI Magazine*, *40*(2), 44–58. DOI: 10.1609/aimag.v40i2.2850

Guo, L., Wang, D., Gu, F., Li, Y., Wang, Y., & Zhou, R. (2021). Evolution and trends in intelligent tutoring systems research: A multidisciplinary and scientometric view. *Asia Pacific Education Review*, *22*(3), 441–461. DOI: 10.1007/s12564-021-09697-7

Hanna, M. G., Pantanowitz, L., Jackson, B., Palmer, O. M. P., Visweswaran, S., Pantanowitz, J., Deebajah, M., & Rashidi, H. H. (2025). Ethical and bias considerations in artificial intelligence/machine learning. *Modern Pathology*, *38*(3), 100686. DOI: 10.1016/j.modpat.2024.100686 PMID: 39694331

Hattie, J., & Timperley, H. (2007). The power of feedback. *Review of Educational Research*, *77*(1), 81–112. DOI: 10.3102/003465430298487

Heston, T. F., & Khun, C. (2023). The good, the bad, and the ugly of ChatGPT in medical education [Preprint]. *SSRN*. https://doi.org/DOI: 10.2139/ssrn.4532671

Hirsch, A. (2024, December 12). *AI detectors: An ethical minefield.* Center for Innovative Teaching and Learning, Northern Illinois University. https://citl.news.niu.edu/2024/12/12/ai-detectors-an-ethical-minefield/

Hooda, M., Rana, C., Dahiya, O., Rizwan, A., & Hossain, M. S. (2022). Artificial intelligence for assessment and feedback to enhance student success in higher education. *Mathematical Problems in Engineering, 2022*, 5215722. Advance online publication. DOI: 10.1155/2022/5215722

Hu, L.-K., & Lee, D. C. (2024). Prompt engineering for critical thinking and equity in general education. *American Research Journal of Humanities and Social Sciences, 10*(1). Advance online publication. DOI: 10.21694/2378-7031.24019

Huang, L. (2023). Ethics of artificial intelligence in education: Student privacy and data protection. *Science Insights Education Frontiers, 16*(2), 2577–2587. DOI: 10.15354/sief.23.re202

Hutson, J., & Ceballos, J. (2023). Rethinking education in the age of AI: The importance of developing durable skills in the Industry 4.0. *Journal of Information Economics, 1*(2), 26–35. DOI: 10.58567/jie01020002

İpek, Z. H., Gözüm, A. İ. C., Papadakis, S., & Kallogiannakis, M. (2023). Educational applications of the ChatGPT AI system: A systematic review research. *Educational Process: International Journal, 12*(3), 26–55. DOI: 10.22521/edupij.2023.123.2

Irons, A., & Elkington, S. (2021). *Enhancing learning through formative assessment and feedback* (2nd ed.). Routledge., DOI: 10.4324/9781138610514

Jeffs, C., Nelson, N., Grant, K. A., Parb, N., & Viceer, N. (2023). Feedback for teaching development: Moving from a fixed to growth mindset. *Professional Development in Education, 49*(5), 842–855. DOI: 10.1080/19415257.2021.1876149

Kahoot! (2025). *Kahoot!* https://kahoot.com/

Kasneci, E., Seßler, K., Küchemann, S., Bannert, M., Dementieva, D., Fischer, F., Gasser, U., Groh, G., Günnemann, S., Hüllermeier, E., Krusche, S., Lall, G., Nerdel, C., Nolda, G., Rivot, H., Röhl, T., Schelling, S., Stadler, M., Szekely, E., & Wirsing, M. (2023). ChatGPT for good? On opportunities and challenges of large language models for education. *Learning and Individual Differences, 103*, 102274. DOI: 10.1016/j.lindif.2023.102274

Kassenkhan, A. M., Moldagulova, A. N., & Serbin, V. V. (2025). Gamification and artificial intelligence in education: A review of innovative approaches to fostering critical thinking. *IEEE Access : Practical Innovations, Open Solutions, 13*, 98699–98728. DOI: 10.1109/ACCESS.2025.3576147

Kim, T. W. (2023). Application of artificial intelligence chatbots, including ChatGPT, in education, scholarly work, programming, and content generation and its prospects: A narrative review. *Journal of Educational Evaluation for Health Professions, 20*, 38. DOI: 10.3352/jeehp.2023.20.38 PMID: 38148495

Kizilcec, R. F., Huber, E., Papanastasiou, E. C., Cram, A., Makridis, C. A., Smolansky, A., Zeivots, S., & Raduescu, C. (2024). Perceived impact of generative AI on assessments: Comparing educator and student perspectives in Australia, Cyprus, and the United States. *Computers and Education: Artificial Intelligence*, *7*, 100269. DOI: 10.1016/j.caeai.2024.100269

Kumar, V., & Boulanger, D. (2020). Explainable automated essay scoring: Deep learning really has pedagogical value. *Frontiers in Education*, *5*, 572367. DOI: 10.3389/feduc.2020.572367

Lateef, F. (2010). Simulation-based learning: Just like the real thing. *Journal of Emergencies, Trauma and Shock*, *3*(4), 348. DOI: 10.4103/0974-2700.70743 PMID: 21063557

Liang, W., Yuksekgonul, M., Mao, Y., Wu, E., & Zou, J. (2023). GPT detectors are biased against non-native English writers. *Patterns (New York, N.Y.)*, *4*(7), 100779. DOI: 10.1016/j.patter.2023.100779 PMID: 37521038

Lo, C. K. (2023). What is the impact of ChatGPT on education? A rapid review of the literature. *Education Sciences*, *13*(4), 410. DOI: 10.3390/educsci13040410

Lourenço, J., Pereira de Morais, J. C., Paulo, J. B., & Lucas, C. (2025). Artificial intelligence as a diagnostic tool in education: Enhancing personalization and learning outcomes. In *EDULEARN25 Proceedings* (pp. 9354–9361). IATED., https://library.iated.org/view/LOURENCO2025ART DOI: 10.21125/edulearn.2025.2410

Maphalala, M. C., & Ajani, O. A. (2025). Leveraging artificial intelligence as a learning tool in higher education. *Interdisciplinary Journal of Education Research*, *7*(1), a01. DOI: 10.38140/ijer-2025.vol7.1.01

Marrone, R., Taddeo, V., & Hill, G. (2022). Creativity and artificial intelligence—A student perspective. *Journal of Intelligence*, *10*(3), 65. DOI: 10.3390/jintelligence10030065 PMID: 36135606

Martin, A. F., Tubaltseva, S., Harrison, A., & Rubin, G. J. (2025). Participatory co-design and evaluation of a novel approach to generative AI-integrated coursework assessment in higher education. *Behavioral Sciences (Basel, Switzerland)*, *15*(6), 808. DOI: 10.3390/bs15060808 PMID: 40564589

Mena-Guacas, A. F., Urueña Rodríguez, J. A., Santana Trujillo, D. M., Gómez-Galán, J., & López-Meneses, E. (2023). Collaborative learning and skill development for educational growth of artificial intelligence: A systematic review. *Contemporary Educational Technology*, *15*(3), ep428. DOI: 10.30935/cedtech/13123

Merino-Campos, C. (2025). The impact of artificial intelligence on personalized learning in higher education: A systematic review. *Trends in Higher Education*, *4*(2), 17. DOI: 10.3390/higheredu4020017

Miranda, R. J., & Hermann, R. S. (2015). Teaching in real time: Integrating continuous formative assessment into inquiry-based classroom instruction. *Science and Children*, *53*(1), 80–85. DOI: 10.2505/4/sc15_053_01_80

Mizumoto, A., & Eguchi, M. (2023). Exploring the potential of using an AI language model for automated essay scoring. *Research Methods in Applied Linguistics*, *2*(2), 100050. DOI: 10.1016/j.rmal.2023.100050

Naamati-Schneider, L. (2024). Enhancing AI competence in health management: Students' experiences with ChatGPT as a learning tool. *BMC Medical Education*, *24*(1), 595. DOI: 10.1186/s12909-024-05595-9 PMID: 38816721

Naseer, F., Khan, M. N., Tahir, M., Addas, A., & Aejaz, S. M. H. (2024). Integrating deep learning techniques for personalized learning pathways in higher education. *Heliyon*, *10*(11), e32628. DOI: 10.1016/j.heliyon.2024.e32628 PMID: 38961899

National Research Council. (2001). *Knowing what students know: The science and design of educational assessment*. National Academies Press.

Nazaretsky, T., Ariely, M., Cukurova, M., & Alexandron, G. (2022). Teachers' trust in AI-powered educational technology and a professional development program to improve it. *British Journal of Educational Technology*, *53*(4), 914–931. DOI: 10.1111/bjet.13232

Noddings, N. (2005). *The challenge of care in schools: An alternative approach to education* (2nd ed.). Teachers College Press.

Open, A. I. (2023, January 31). *New AI classifier for indicating AI-written text*. https://openai.com/index/new-ai-classifier-for-indicating-ai-written-text/

Owan, V. J., Abang, K. B., Idika, D. O., Etta, E. O., & Bassey, B. A. (2023). Exploring the potential of artificial intelligence tools in educational measurement and assessment. *Eurasia Journal of Mathematics, Science and Technology Education*, *19*(8), em2307. Advance online publication. DOI: 10.29333/ejmste/13428

Palakurti, N. R. (2025). Comparative study of adaptive learning platforms: A machine learning perspective. *International Journal of Advanced Research in Education and Technology*, *12*(1), 17. DOI: 10.15680/IJARETY.2025.1201002

Pavone, G., Meyer-Waarden, L., & Munzel, A. (2024). From analytics to empathy and creativity: Charting the AI revolution in marketing practice and education. [English Edition]. *Recherche et Applications en Marketing*, *40*(1), 92–120. DOI: 10.1177/20515707241283311

Pearson. (2020, January 16). *Pearson acquires interactive learning technology from Smart Sparrow* [Press release]. PR Newswire. https://www.prnewswire.com/news-releases/pearson-acquires-interactive-learning-technology-from-smart-sparrow-300987673.html

Popenici, S. A. D., & Kerr, S. (2017). Exploring the impact of artificial intelligence on teaching and learning in higher education. *Research and Practice in Technology Enhanced Learning*, *12*(1), 22. DOI: 10.1186/s41039-017-0062-8 PMID: 30595727

Quizizz. (2025). *Quizizz*. https://quizizz.com/

Rudolph, J., Tan, S., & Tan, S. (2023). ChatGPT: Bullshit spewer or the end of traditional assessments in higher education? *Journal of Applied Learning & Teaching*, *6*(1), 1–7. DOI: 10.37074/jalt.2023.6.1.9

Ruiz-Rojas, L. I., Salvador-Ullauri, L., & Acosta-Vargas, P. (2024). Collaborative working and critical thinking: Adoption of generative artificial intelligence tools in higher education. *Sustainability (Basel)*, *16*(13), 5367. DOI: 10.3390/su16135367

Sadasivan, V. S., Kumar, A., Balasubramanian, S., Wang, W., & Feizi, S. (2023). *Can AI-generated text be reliably detected?* [Preprint]. arXiv. https://doi.org//arxiv.2303.11156DOI: 10.48550

Sambell, K., McDowell, L., & Montgomery, C. (2013). *Assessment for learning in higher education*. Routledge.

Selwyn, N. (2019). *Should robots replace teachers? AI and the future of education*. Routledge.

Seshan, V., Matua, G. A., Raghavan, D., Arulappan, J., Hashmi, I. A., Roach, E. J., & Prince, E. J. (2021). Case study analysis as an effective teaching strategy: Perceptions of undergraduate nursing students from a Middle Eastern country. *SAGE Open Nursing*, *7*, 23779608211059265. Advance online publication. DOI: 10.1177/23779608211059265 PMID: 34869864

Showbie Inc. (2025). *Socrative*. https://www.socrative.com

Shute, V. J., & Psotka, J. (1996). Intelligent tutoring systems: Past, present, and future. In Jonassen, D. (Ed.), *Handbook of research on educational communications and technology* (pp. 570–600). Macmillan.

Stacey, M., Gavin, M., Fitzgerald, S., McGrath-Champ, S., & Wilson, R. (2024). Reducing teachers' workload or deskilling 'core' work? Analysis of a policy response to teacher workload demands. *Discourse (Abingdon), 45*(2), 187–199. DOI: 10.1080/01596306.2023.2271856

Stankov, P. (2024). The death of exams? Grade inflation and student satisfaction when coursework replaces exams. *International Review of Economics Education, 46*, 100289. DOI: 10.1016/j.iree.2024.100289

Strielkowski, W., Grebennikova, V., Lisovskiy, A., Rakhimova, G., & Vasileva, T. (2025). AI-driven adaptive learning for sustainable educational transformation. *Sustainable Development (Bradford), 33*(2), 1921–1947. DOI: 10.1002/sd.3221

Tang, X., Chen, H., Lin, D., & Li, K. (2024). Harnessing LLMs for multi-dimensional writing assessment: Reliability and alignment with human judgments. *Heliyon, 10*(14), e34262. DOI: 10.1016/j.heliyon.2024.e34262 PMID: 39113951

Teo, T. H., & Chew, D. (2025, June 18). A comprehensive review of strategies and policies toward AI-resistant education [Preprint]. *SSRN*. DOI: 10.2139/ssrn.5355928

The Grainger College of Engineering. (2025). *PLATO*. University of Illinois. Retrieved July 26, 2025, from https://grainger.illinois.edu/news/magazine/plato

The How Institute for Society. (2024, August). *AI and moral reasoning in leadership: Examining the role generative AI can play in navigating moral leadership challenges.* https://thehowinstitute.org/wp-content/uploads/2024/08/How_AiandMoralReasoning_070224.pdf

Trajkovski, G., & Hayes, H. (2025). AI-assisted formative assessment and feedback. In Thomas, M. (Ed.), *AI-assisted assessment in education* (pp. 283–312). Springer Nature., DOI: 10.1007/978-3-031-88252-4_7

Vittorini, P., Menini, S., & Tonelli, S. (2021). An AI-based system for formative and summative assessment in data science courses. *International Journal of Artificial Intelligence in Education, 31*(2), 159–185. DOI: 10.1007/s40593-020-00230-2

Vlachopoulos, D., & Makri, A. (2024). A systematic literature review on authentic assessment in higher education: Best practices for the development of 21st century skills, and policy considerations. *Studies in Educational Evaluation, 83*, 101425. DOI: 10.1016/j.stueduc.2024.101425

Walter, Y. (2024). Embracing the future of artificial intelligence in the classroom: The relevance of AI literacy, prompt engineering, and critical thinking in modern education. *International Journal of Educational Technology in Higher Education*, *21*(1), 15. DOI: 10.1186/s41239-024-00448-3

Walters, W. H. (2023). The effectiveness of software designed to detect AI-generated writing: A comparison of 16 AI text detectors. *Open Information Science*, *7*(1), 158–181. DOI: 10.1515/opis-2022-0158

Weber-Wulff, D., Anohina-Naumeca, A., Bjelobaba, S., Foltýnek, T., Guerrero-Dib, J., Popoola, O., Šigut, P., & Waddington, L. (2023). Testing of detection tools for AI-generated text. *International Journal for Educational Integrity*, *19*(1), 13. DOI: 10.1007/s40979-023-00146-z

Xu, W., Mahmud, R., & Hoo, W. L. (2024). A systematic literature review: Are automated essay scoring systems competent in real-life education scenarios? *IEEE Access : Practical Innovations, Open Solutions*, *12*, 77639–77657. DOI: 10.1109/ACCESS.2024.3399163

Yao, X., Zhong, Y., & Cao, W. (2025). The analysis of generative artificial intelligence technology for innovative thinking and strategies in animation teaching. *Scientific Reports*, *15*(1), 18618. DOI: 10.1038/s41598-025-03805-y PMID: 40436985

Zhai, X., Wibowo, S., & Li, L. (2024). The effects of over-reliance on AI dialogue systems on students' cognitive abilities: A systematic review. *Smart Learning Environments*, *11*(1), 16. DOI: 10.1186/s40561-024-00316-7

Zribi, R., & Smaoui, C. (2021). Automated versus human essay scoring: A comparative study. *International Journal of Information Technology and Language Studies*, *5*(1), 62–71.

Chapter 14
Artificial Intelligence in Education:
Supporting Diverse Learning Styles and Addressing Ethical Considerations

Pi-Chi Han
https://orcid.org/0000-0001-9429-4967
National Kaohsiung Normal University, Taiwan

ABSTRACT

This chapter explores the transformative potential of artificial intelligence (AI) in education, focusing on how AI technologies support diverse learning styles and foster inclusive pedagogy. Drawing on theories such as Gardner's multiple intelligences and Vygotsky's social constructivism, it examines the role of intelligent tutoring systems, adaptive learning platforms, and natural language processing tools in personalizing instruction and promoting learner autonomy. The chapter also addresses critical ethical concerns, including data privacy, algorithmic bias, and the evolving role of educators. Emphasizing alignment with Universal Design for Learning (UDL) and global AI ethics frameworks, it advocates for responsible integration of AI to enhance accessibility and equity in education while reaffirming the indispensable human dimension of teaching.

DOI: 10.4018/979-8-3373-5102-5.ch014

INTRODUCTION

The integration of AI into educational ecosystems has ushered in a transformative shift in how learners with diverse cognitive needs and learning preferences engage with instructional content. Through AI-powered tools and platforms, educators gain unprecedented capabilities to design and implement personalized, inclusive, and dynamic learning experiences. These technologies address a wide spectrum of learning styles—including visual, auditory, reading/writing, and kinesthetic modalities—thereby supporting differentiated instruction and enhancing educational equity (Saffari & Khodayar, 2024).

AI's adaptive capabilities allow it to tailor instruction to individual learners by analyzing their behavior, performance, and preferences, thereby offering nuanced, real-time pedagogical support. This personalization is particularly impactful for students who may not thrive in traditional instructional environments, as it enables them to receive guidance aligned with their unique strengths and challenges (Saffari & Khodayar, 2024). In parallel, AI-driven educational technologies hold great promise for addressing educational disparities—especially in underserved communities—by democratizing access to high-quality resources and individualized feedback (Leon Jr, 2024; Roshanaei et al., 2023).

The convergence of AI with education is multifaceted. AI facilitates customized learning trajectories, streamlines assessment processes, and supports intelligent tutoring systems that evolve in tandem with each learner's development (Bulut et al., 2024). These innovations have the potential to create engaging, equitable, and effective educational experiences regardless of students' socioeconomic status or cultural background (Dey, 2024). However, alongside these benefits, AI introduces a range of ethical complexities. Chief among these are issues of data privacy, algorithmic bias, and the evolving role of educators. A thoughtful examination of these implications is vital for the responsible deployment of AI in education (Gligorea et al., 2023).

This chapter explores the dual promise and challenge of AI in education. It examines how AI aligns with contemporary pedagogical theories, its capacity to support a wide range of learning styles, and its potential to foster inclusivity—while also confronting the ethical questions that arise from AI's integration. Through an interdisciplinary lens, the chapter provides a critical overview of how AI-driven technologies are reshaping teaching and learning, and it outlines what educators and policymakers must consider to ensure equitable, ethical, and effective implementation.

THEORETICAL FRAMEWORK

The role of AI in supporting diverse learning styles is firmly grounded in established educational theories, notably Howard Gardner's Theory of Multiple Intelligences and Lev Vygotsky's Social Constructivism. These frameworks provide a foundation for understanding how AI applications can align with pedagogical best practices to optimize learning outcomes and enhance inclusivity.

Gardner's Theory of Multiple Intelligences posits that individuals have varied cognitive strengths and that intelligence is not a singular attribute but a multifaceted construct encompassing linguistic, logical-mathematical, spatial, bodily-kinesthetic, musical, interpersonal, intrapersonal, and naturalistic intelligences. AI technologies can be harnessed to support this diversity by customizing instructional strategies and content delivery to cater to different forms of intelligence. For example, visual learners benefit from AI-generated data visualizations and simulations, whereas linguistic learners engage more deeply with AI-supported reading and writing tools. This capacity to individualize instruction underscores AI's potential to honor and respond to learners' cognitive diversity (Kamalov et al., 2023).

Vygotsky's Social Constructivism emphasizes the central role of social interaction, cultural tools, and collaborative learning in the construction of knowledge. AI-powered platforms can facilitate such socially grounded experiences by enabling peer collaboration, providing virtual tutors, and mediating scaffolded learning tasks that align with each learner's zone of proximal development. These platforms analyze student performance in real time and adjust their instructional scaffolding accordingly, acting as responsive mediators that reflect the interactive principles of constructivist learning (Kamalov et al., 2023).

AI tools also excel at curating customized learning pathways by analyzing vast amounts of student data—such as prior knowledge, engagement patterns, and performance metrics—and dynamically adapting content and strategies to meet learners' evolving needs. Guided by machine learning algorithms and predictive modeling, this process enables educators to craft targeted interventions that are both timely and effective. By integrating AI with the pedagogical principles of Gardner and Vygotsky, educators can design learning environments that are not only cognitively responsive but also socially meaningful. This dual alignment is crucial in contemporary classrooms where learner diversity is the norm rather than the exception. Rooting AI-enhanced learning systems in sound theory helps guard against technology-driven determinism, wherein tools might be adopted for efficiency rather than genuine educational efficacy (Kamalov et al., 2023).

Moreover, aligning AI with these theoretical paradigms ensures that educational technology augments human-centered teaching instead of replacing pedagogical wisdom and interpersonal engagement. As Kamalov and Gurrib (2023) argue, AI deployment in education should be guided by a principled understanding of how students learn best, recognizing that technological innovation must support—not supplant—the human elements of teaching and learning. Accordingly, educators and policymakers must approach AI integration with a comprehensive understanding of its theoretical foundations, ethical implications, and practical constraints. This integrative approach is essential for fostering inclusive, effective, and equitable learning environments that not only accommodate, but also celebrate, learner variability.

AI-DRIVEN PERSONALIZATION IN EDUCATION

AI-driven personalization represents a paradigm shift away from the conventional "one-size-fits-all" educational model toward an approach that embraces learner diversity through differentiated, data-informed instruction. By adapting to individual students' needs, learning preferences, and cognitive pace, AI technologies offer educators a robust toolkit for cultivating inclusive and responsive pedagogical environments (Jian, 2023).

Intelligent tutoring systems provide a prime illustration of AI's potential in this realm. Such systems continuously monitor student interactions, diagnose individual strengths and weaknesses, and deliver immediate, personalized feedback and scaffolding (Jian, 2023; Bayly-Castaneda et al., 2024). This real-time adaptive support empowers students to master learning objectives at a pace and in a format that align with their cognitive styles. By observing students' past learning behaviors and synthesizing performance data, AI algorithms can recommend tailored content, guide curriculum design, and even facilitate peer-to-peer learning matches—maximizing learning efficacy and engagement. In this way, AI systems do more than merely respond to learners' needs—they proactively shape the trajectory of each learner's educational journey. These technologies dynamically calibrate the complexity of tasks and the modality of content delivery based on performance metrics, ensuring that learners are neither overburdened nor under-stimulated. This approach maintains an optimal level of cognitive challenge and fosters academic growth for each student.

Natural language processing (NLP) technologies and AI-driven chatbots are also revolutionizing student support systems. These tools can offer instant explanations, summarize complex concepts, and assist learners who experience reading or writing difficulties (Jian, 2023; Mahmoud & Sørensen, 2024). Functioning as conversational agents, chatbots engage students in natural dialogue, clarify misunderstandings, and help them navigate challenging content in a non-threatening environment. For students hesitant to seek help from instructors or peers, such AI tools foster self-directed inquiry and sustained engagement. Beyond on-demand support, NLP tools can analyze student writing to provide feedback on grammar, syntax, style, and clarity. These technologies promote writing fluency and literacy development while also enhancing students' metacognitive awareness. Their ability to provide context-sensitive feedback—tailored to each student's proficiency and learning history—encourages independent learning and greater academic ownership (Mahmoud & Sørensen, 2024).

Adaptive learning platforms further extend personalization by continuously tailoring each learner's path based on real-time performance. These platforms leverage analytics to monitor student input, identify misconceptions, and deliver precise corrective feedback (Mahmoud & Sørensen, 2024). The dynamic nature of adaptive systems ensures that instruction is always calibrated to an appropriate level of challenge, optimizing student engagement and knowledge retention (Zhai et al., 2021). Such systems also generate actionable insights for educators, offering visibility into student learning patterns and enabling evidence-based pedagogical decisions (Ayeni et al., 2024). By responding to students' cognitive progress in real time, adaptive platforms enhance instructional quality and foster learner autonomy. Indeed, these tools have become indispensable for promoting educational equity—especially in heterogeneous classrooms with diverse abilities, backgrounds, and pacing needs (Dey, 2024; Gligorea et al., 2023).

Learning analytics and predictive modeling, integral components of AI-enhanced education, enable educators to identify each learner's strengths and weaknesses through systematic analysis of engagement data and performance metrics (Global Educational Studies Review, 2020). These data-driven insights inform timely instructional interventions and support differentiated teaching. For example, predictive algorithms can flag students who are at risk of underperformance, dropping out, or experiencing socio-emotional difficulties, thereby prompting preemptive support from educators (Demartini et al., 2024). AI systems can even analyze affective states—such as frustration or confusion—by interpreting students' facial expressions and other behavioral cues, providing a nuanced understanding of learner engagement (Strielkowski et al., 2023; Zawacki-Richter et al., 2019). Such fine-grained diagnostics allow for precision teaching and comprehensive learner support. Notably, similar analytics techniques have been used in business to forecast customer behavior; in an educational context, these models can drive student success and retention through informed, data-driven decision-making (Strielkowski et al., 2023).

Moreover, AI has a transformative impact on educational administration and operations. By automating routine tasks such as grading, record-keeping, scheduling, and resource allocation, AI systems enhance institutional efficiency and free up educators' time for personalized instruction and mentoring (Onesi-Ozigagun et al., 2024). This operational optimization contributes to a more learner-centered educational environment, allowing teachers to focus on high-impact pedagogical activities rather than administrative burdens.

AI APPLICATIONS FOR SPECIFIC LEARNING STYLES

Artificial intelligence technologies offer tremendous potential to tailor educational experiences to the diverse learning styles recognized in contemporary pedagogy. By providing customized content and instructional strategies, AI enables learners to engage with material in ways that align with their cognitive preferences—whether visual, auditory, reading/writing, or kinesthetic. These AI-driven customizations create a more inclusive and responsive learning environment that promotes learner agency and educational equity (Demartini et al., 2024; Zhai et al., 2021).

For visual learners, AI-powered platforms can generate rich, interactive visual content—such as charts, graphs, infographics, and simulations—to facilitate conceptual understanding. Tools that support data visualization, virtual field trips, and immersive multimedia presentations provide students with engaging spatial representations of complex concepts (Ma et al., 2024). AI-enhanced visuals help learners explore abstract ideas through concrete imagery, and they are especially effective in subjects like science, mathematics, and geography.

AI supports auditory learners through text-to-speech systems that convert written text into spoken words. This functionality allows students to absorb information aurally, reinforcing comprehension through listening (Tonbuloğlu, 2023). Additionally, AI can generate audio summaries of key topics, which helps students review and retain content over time. These tools benefit not only those who prefer auditory learning but also students with reading challenges or visual impairments by providing alternative pathways to access information.

For learners who favor reading and writing, AI-driven educational platforms can provide personalized reading lists, adaptive comprehension quizzes, and intelligent writing prompts tailored to individual interests and ability levels. NLP-powered tools further support this group by analyzing written assignments for grammar, coherence, vocabulary, and clarity, then offering constructive feedback to help students refine their writing skills (Akgün & Greenhow, 2022; AlTwijri & Alghizzi, 2024). Such systems promote iterative learning and scaffold the development of academic literacy, allowing learners to improve through guided practice and revision.

Kinesthetic learners—those who learn best through movement, manipulation, and hands-on experimentation—benefit from AI applications that gamify learning and offer interactive simulations. For example, AI can power 3D virtual environments and labs that allow students to perform simulated science experiments, explore historical settings, or construct digital prototypes. These environments provide safe, controlled spaces for experiential learning, making abstract content tangible and engaging (Egunjobi & Adeyeye, 2024). Through gamified challenges and virtual reality scenarios, kinesthetic learners can interact physically or virtually with educational material, helping to sustain their attention and deepen their understanding.

Across all modalities, AI personalizes learning by offering tailored support and feedback. Intelligent systems continuously monitor learners' progress, adapt content in real time, and provide just-in-time assistance aligned with each student's pace and preferences (Rakya, 2023). These dynamic adjustments foster mastery while also sustaining learner motivation and engagement. AI-powered technologies are likewise pivotal in supporting students with disabilities and special learning needs. For example, text-to-speech, speech-to-text, and screen-reader tools enable students with visual or motor impairments to access digital learning materials more equitably (Lin et al., 2023). Such tools break down barriers to participation and reflect Universal Design for Learning (UDL) principles by making content accessible to all learners. AI-based systems can even adapt content in real time to ensure it remains accessible, thereby promoting inclusion at both individual and classroom levels (Woo & Choi, 2021; Zhai et al., 2021).

Facial recognition and emotion-detection technologies represent another layer of personalization in AI-mediated learning. Educators can use these tools to analyze student engagement and attitudes based on facial expressions and other cues, helping to identify when learners are confused, disengaged, or in need of support (Saputra et al., 2023). Such insights allow instructors to intervene proactively and adjust their instruction to maintain an optimal level of challenge, ensuring that students are both supported and appropriately stretched to reach their potential. Similarly, AI-driven translation tools facilitate communication in multilingual classrooms, fostering linguistic inclusivity. Real-time translation enables students from different language backgrounds to collaborate and engage meaningfully with course content, improving accessibility and affirming cultural diversity as an asset in the classroom.

Despite AI's technological sophistication, it cannot replace the nuanced pedagogical judgment of teachers. As Klímová et al. (2023) and Gentile et al. (2023) emphasize, while AI can enhance instructional delivery, it lacks the capacity to discern the relational, emotional, and ethical dimensions of teaching. Teachers must therefore remain central to the design and facilitation of AI-rich learning experiences, adapting the use of AI tools to the specific needs and contexts of their learners. Ultimately, AI-driven personalization should be framed as a means to empower learners and educators alike—not as a substitute for human interaction, but as a complement to it. In this role, teachers serve as interpreters and mediators of AI outputs, ensuring that technological interventions are pedagogically sound, contextually appropriate, and ethically grounded (Chaudhry & Kazim, 2022; Kamalov et al., 2023; Kalniņa et al., 2024).

SUPPORTING NEURODIVERSE LEARNERS WITH AI

AI offers transformative potential for addressing the unique needs of neurodiverse learners, including those with autism spectrum disorder (ASD), attention-deficit/hyperactivity disorder (ADHD), dyslexia, and other cognitive or developmental differences. By implementing intelligent, responsive, and inclusive technologies, educators can create highly personalized learning environments that accommodate individual cognitive styles, processing preferences, and behavioral patterns (Romero et al., 2023).

AI-driven tools can design customized learning plans that adjust instructional content, sequence, and modality based on real-time feedback. These systems streamline lesson delivery and provide immediate, actionable feedback tailored to each learner's needs and pacing. This responsiveness enables neurodiverse students to process information in ways that align with their cognitive profiles, fostering deeper understanding and reducing the frustration often associated with standardized instruction (Romero et al., 2023; Vincent-Lancrin & Van der Vlies, 2020). For example, adaptive learning systems can break complex information into manageable segments, present content in multiple modalities, and repeat or reinforce concepts as needed—all while continuously monitoring learner progress and adjusting instruction dynamically (Chan & Tsi, 2023). Such features make AI an effective tool for supporting students who require more flexible or differentiated approaches to learning.

By facilitating individualized educational pathways, AI allows students to exert greater control over their learning journeys. Instructors, in turn, play a critical role in guiding students' interactions with AI tools—helping them harness these technologies in ways that enhance rather than overwhelm the learning process. For instance, AI platforms can recommend reading materials, suggest relevant activities, or provide personalized prompts based on a student's past performance, interests, and identified needs (Zhai et al., 2021). Teachers then help students interpret and apply these AI-generated suggestions, ensuring that they are integrated meaningfully into the learning experience.

AI tools that offer interactive simulations and virtual laboratories are particularly advantageous for neurodiverse learners. These platforms provide hands-on, experiential learning environments where students can explore abstract concepts safely and at their own pace. For example, a student with ADHD might benefit from engaging, gamified learning modules that help maintain attention and motivation, whereas a learner on the autism spectrum might prefer structured, predictable digital environments that reduce cognitive overload (Lin et al., 2023).

Real-time performance prediction and behavior-monitoring features further enhance instruction for neurodiverse students. AI can assess learners' progress, engagement patterns, and potential obstacles, alerting educators when timely interventions are needed. Such tools enable a responsive pedagogical approach aligned with each student's emotional and academic readiness (Saputra et al., 2023; Qiu et al., 2022). Likewise, AI systems can adapt content delivery on the fly, allowing students to access material at a pace suited to their processing capacity. This level of customization helps reduce the anxiety that neurodiverse learners might experience in rigid classroom settings, facilitating a mastery-based learning approach (Vincent-Lancrin & Van der Vlies, 2020).

While AI can greatly enhance learning for students with special needs, it cannot replicate the empathetic understanding and pedagogical intuition of skilled human educators. Teachers remain essential for interpreting learners' affective and contextual cues—particularly for neurodiverse students whose needs often extend beyond what algorithms can detect (Chan & Tsi, 2023). The personalization provided by AI must therefore be integrated within human-centered frameworks that emphasize trust, respect, and mutual understanding. AI can also assist neurodiverse learners through accessibility technologies. Tools like text-to-speech, speech-to-text, and screen readers improve access for those with reading difficulties or motor impairments, eliminating many structural barriers and enabling greater learner independence (Lin et al., 2023). When paired with UDL principles, these applications promote inclusion at both individual and systemic levels, ensuring that curricula are accessible to a broad range of learners. Furthermore, AI-driven organizational tools (such as smart planners or AI-based reminders) help students with executive functioning challenges or working-memory limitations stay organized and focused (Hidayat et al., 2022).

As emphasized by Akgün and Greenhow (2022), AI-powered tools support differentiated instruction by addressing varied learning modalities and offering immediate feedback that promotes self-regulated learning. The integration of AI not only boosts academic achievement but also cultivates learners' self-confidence and autonomy, especially when educational experiences are tailored to individual strengths and needs. Nonetheless, the effectiveness of AI in supporting neurodiverse learners is contingent upon thoughtful implementation, inclusive design, and appropriate ethical safeguards. As with any educational intervention, care must be taken to ensure that AI applications respect student dignity, privacy, and agency. Moreover, instructors must be adequately trained to integrate AI meaningfully into their pedagogy, understanding both its capabilities and its limitations.

ETHICAL CONSIDERATIONS AND CHALLENGES

While AI offers substantial promise for enhancing educational equity, personalization, and inclusivity, its integration into learning environments raises urgent ethical considerations. These concerns—ranging from data privacy and algorithmic bias to transparency, explainability, and the evolving role of educators—must be critically addressed to ensure that AI systems are implemented responsibly and equitably across educational contexts (Akgün & Greenhow, 2022; Bulut et al., 2024).

Central to the ethical discourse is the issue of data privacy and security. AI systems often rely on collecting and analyzing vast amounts of student data—including demographic information, academic performance records, engagement behaviors, and even emotional indicators—to generate predictive insights and deliver personalized learning experiences (Karpouzis, 2024). However, this reliance introduces significant risks if such data are mishandled, breached, or used without informed consent. Students and parents may be unaware of the nature and extent of the data being collected, raising concerns about surveillance and the erosion of digital autonomy (Klímová et al., 2023).

To mitigate these risks, educational institutions must adopt robust data governance frameworks that ensure encryption, secure storage, strict access controls, and compliance with relevant privacy regulations. Transparent policies regarding data use, anonymization, retention, and sharing should be established. Informed consent should be obtained from students (and their guardians, where appropriate), ensuring they understand how their data will be used and the implications of algorithmic decision-making (Gouseti et al., 2025; Huang, 2023).

Another pressing concern is algorithmic bias, which can emerge when AI systems—trained on incomplete, unbalanced, or historically biased datasets—reinforce or amplify existing inequities. If training data reflect societal disparities, AI models may inadvertently deliver unequal or unfair outcomes to marginalized groups of students, such as those from minority backgrounds, low-income communities, or with atypical learning profiles (Thelma et al., 2024; Roshanaei et al., 2023). For instance, an AI-powered assessment tool trained primarily on data from high-performing students in well-resourced schools might misjudge or undervalue students from under-resourced schools, leading to misclassification or inappropriate academic tracking (Chinta et al., 2024). Ensuring algorithmic fairness is therefore imperative. Datasets used to train AI models should be comprehensive, representative, and regularly audited for bias. Developers must engage in bias detection, validation, and correction throughout the model lifecycle (İlikhan et al., 2024). Inclusive design practices—inviting diverse stakeholders (students, educators, ethicists, policymakers) into the development process—can help identify blind spots and promote more equitable AI systems (Harry, 2023).

Transparency and explainability are equally crucial ethical pillars in AI implementation. Many AI systems operate as "black boxes," producing outputs or recommendations without revealing the logic behind them. This opacity can undermine trust and accountability, particularly in high-stakes contexts such as student assessment or behavioral monitoring (Neji et al., 2023). Educators and learners should be able to interrogate how AI decisions are made and understand the factors influencing those decisions. Promoting explainable AI (XAI) involves developing models that not only generate accurate predictions but also provide clear rationales for their outputs. Techniques such as saliency maps, feature importance analyses, attention mechanism visualizations, SHAP (Shapley Additive Explanations), and LIME (Local Interpretable Model-Agnostic Explanations) allow educators to see which input factors influence an AI's conclusions (Saffari & Khodayar, 2024; Khodayar & Regan, 2023). These methods enable practitioners to evaluate the reliability, fairness, and pedagogical appropriateness of AI-driven recommendations (Adams et al., 2023; Holmes et al., 2022).

In response to growing ethical concerns, policy bodies have begun issuing guidelines for AI in education. The European Commission, for example, published comprehensive ethical guidelines in late 2022 for integrating AI into primary and secondary schools, aligning with UNESCO's global standards for AI ethics (endorsed by 193 countries in 2021) (Klímová et al., 2023; Nguyen et al., 2023). These documents advocate for AI systems that uphold core values such as human agency, fairness, and human-centric design in educational contexts. They emphasize that teachers and school leaders must be equipped with ethical, digital, pedagogical, and data-literacy competencies to navigate the complexities of AI-enhanced education effectively (Kalniņa et al., 2024).

The role of teachers is particularly significant in this ethical landscape. While AI can automate routine tasks and augment instruction, it cannot replicate the human insight, empathy, or professional judgment essential for holistic education. Teachers serve as critical gatekeepers of AI implementation, interpreting AI outputs, contextualizing algorithmic recommendations, and adapting practices to fit learners' emotional and cultural contexts (Gentile et al., 2023; Chaudhry & Kazim, 2022). As Kamalov et al. (2023) stress, AI should be viewed as a complement—not a substitute—for teachers' pedagogical expertise. Consequently, teacher preparation programs must evolve to include training on the responsible and ethical use of AI. Educators need to understand how AI functions, recognize its limitations, and identify potential ethical red flags. They must also develop the capacity to integrate AI into student-centered pedagogy in ways that are inclusive, reflective, and empowering (Kalniņa et al., 2024).

The proliferation of facial recognition and emotion-detection technologies in education likewise warrants ethical scrutiny. While these tools can provide real-time feedback on student engagement, they may also infringe on privacy or contribute to a sense of surveillance in the classroom. Schools should tread carefully, balancing the benefits of real-time analytics with the imperative to preserve student dignity and autonomy (Roshanaei et al., 2023; Gentile et al., 2023). In sum, the ethical challenges posed by AI in education are multifaceted and evolving. They demand proactive strategies that prioritize transparency, equity, inclusivity, and human dignity. Stakeholders—including developers, educators, institutions, and policymakers—must engage in continuous dialogue, ethical foresight, and collaborative policymaking to ensure that AI serves as a force for good in education.

FUTURE DIRECTIONS AND IMPLICATIONS FOR EDUCATORS

As AI technologies continue to advance, their integration into educational systems presents both profound opportunities and complex challenges. The potential for AI to personalize learning, improve access, and support differentiated instruction is significant. However, these benefits can only be fully realized if educators are adequately prepared, ethical considerations are addressed, and institutional infrastructures are aligned for equitable implementation (Akgün & Greenhow, 2022; Kalniņa et al., 2024).

A key imperative moving forward is the professional development of educators to ensure they can understand, evaluate, and implement AI tools effectively. Teachers must be trained not only in the technical operation of AI technologies but also in how to interpret the data these systems generate and use those insights to inform pedagogical decisions (Mello et al., 2023). This includes the ability to judge when and how AI tools can support diverse learning needs, and when human judgment and contextual sensitivity must prevail. As Bulathwela et al. (2024) emphasize, AI tools should be used to support—not replace—the relational and reflective aspects of teaching.

Another important consideration is the standardization of data practices in AI-supported learning environments. Inconsistent or poor-quality data can lead to erroneous predictions, misdiagnoses of learning needs, or biased outcomes. Thus, developing clear protocols for data collection, data governance, model training, and performance evaluation is critical to maintaining the reliability and fairness of AI applications (Ma et al., 2024). Future research should also focus on expanding the empirical evidence base for AI's effectiveness across different educational levels and contexts. Many existing studies are limited by small sample sizes or short-term evaluations, making it difficult to generalize findings (Strielkowski et al., 2023).

Longitudinal and cross-contextual studies are needed to explore the long-term impacts of AI on learning outcomes, student well-being, and educational equity.

To support effective AI integration, educational institutions must prioritize infrastructure development and resource allocation. This includes investing in secure digital environments, ensuring equitable access to devices and high-speed internet, and providing ongoing technical support for both students and teachers. Schools and districts should also develop policies to ensure transparency in AI-driven decision-making (for instance, clearly communicating when an AI is influencing a student's learning path) and to protect student data privacy (Han et al., 2025; Global Educational Studies Review, 2020).

Teacher training and professional development initiatives should incorporate AI ethics, data literacy, and algorithmic awareness as core components (Azzam & Charles, 2024). Teachers must be equipped to recognize biases in AI systems, respond to ethical dilemmas, and foster student awareness of how AI technologies shape learning experiences. Such training is essential to ensure that AI-enhanced instruction aligns with democratic values, cultural sensitivity, and the rights of learners (Bulut et al., 2024). Policy frameworks must evolve in tandem with AI adoption as well. National and local education policies should provide guidelines on AI integration, enforce compliance with ethical standards, and support innovation that aligns with educational equity goals. Strategic policy planning is crucial to bridge the gap between rapid technological advancement and pedagogical practice (Chetry, 2024; Leon Jr, 2024).

In parallel, student AI literacy is becoming increasingly important. As Rizvi et al. (2023) and Otero et al. (2023) argue, students must develop the ability to critically engage with AI systems, understand their underlying logic, and question the implications of algorithmic outputs. AI literacy for students should encompass not only basic technical competencies but also ethical reasoning, digital citizenship, and critical thinking skills—attributes that are essential for navigating an AI-driven world. Moreover, integrating AI topics into humanities and liberal arts education is vital. Scholars have stressed that technical competence must be accompanied by moral imagination, intercultural awareness, and philosophical inquiry (George, 1992; Leon Jr, 2024). By combining technical and humanistic education, institutions can prepare students to lead ethically in AI-influenced societies. AI also holds promise for specific domains such as language learning; for example, AI-powered tools in English as a Foreign Language classes can support pronunciation practice and cultural immersion (AlTwijri & Alghizzi, 2024), opening new avenues for global engagement.

National governments are beginning to integrate AI education into primary and secondary curricula as part of broader digital strategies (Sanusi et al., 2024). The rationale is clear: many future jobs will be AI-related or will require AI literacy as a basic skill. As Gligorea et al. (2023) and Otero et al. (2023) note, AI education is rapidly becoming as essential as reading and writing. However, to ensure equity, the digital divide must be addressed. AI-enhanced education risks exacerbating inequalities if access to high-quality AI tools and internet connectivity remains concentrated in affluent or technologically advanced communities. Public investment in infrastructure, teacher capacity-building, and inclusive curriculum design is critical to ensure that all students can benefit from AI, regardless of socioeconomic background (Bulathwela et al., 2024).

Finally, AI should be integrated with Universal Design for Learning (UDL) principles, which advocate flexible, accessible, and inclusive instructional design. As Kohnke and Zaugg (2025) argue, when aligned with UDL, AI can help close achievement gaps by personalizing learning, improving accessibility, and supporting a diversity of learners. In essence, AI is not just a technological tool—it can be a catalyst for educational transformation aligned with sustainable development goals (Ibrahim et al., 2023; Avurakoghene & Oredein, 2023).

CONCLUSION

The integration of AI into educational settings represents a transformative development with far-reaching implications for teaching, learning, and institutional practice. AI offers significant potential to support personalized instruction, enhance accessibility, and foster inclusivity across diverse learner populations. By enabling customized learning trajectories, providing real-time feedback, and automating routine administrative functions, AI tools empower educators to focus on pedagogical creativity and relational engagement (Pahi et al., 2024; Walter, 2024). At the core of AI's promise is its ability to accommodate diverse learning styles and needs. Through technologies such as intelligent tutoring systems, natural language processing, adaptive platforms, and analytics, AI facilitates responsive instruction that meets learners where they are—cognitively, emotionally, and developmentally. These tools not only improve learning outcomes but also cultivate learner agency, resilience, and engagement (Dey, 2024). AI's capacity to support students with disabilities and neurodiverse learners further affirms its potential to transform education into a more inclusive and equitable domain.

Nevertheless, realizing this potential depends on addressing the significant ethical challenges that accompany AI implementation. Issues such as data privacy, algorithmic bias, lack of transparency, and unequal access must be systematically addressed through comprehensive policies, stakeholder engagement, and ethical oversight (Karpouzis, 2024; Thelma et al., 2024). Educators need to be equipped not only with technical skills but also with ethical literacy, enabling them to navigate the complex interplay between AI and pedagogy with integrity and discernment (Al-Zahrani, 2024; Akgün & Greenhow, 2022). As AI continues to evolve, the role of educators must be redefined—not diminished. Teachers remain at the center of educational innovation, interpreting AI-generated insights, designing meaningful learning experiences, and fostering the human relationships essential for student development. AI must be framed as a tool to support, not supplant, educators' professional judgment and pedagogical expertise (Klímová et al., 2023; Kamalov et al., 2023).

Educational institutions should also prioritize the development of AI policies that ensure responsible implementation. These include protocols for ethical data use, clear communication about AI systems' functions and limitations, investment in digital infrastructure, and a commitment to including all learners regardless of socioeconomic status (Chetry, 2024; Han et al., 2025). Moreover, AI should be aligned with UDL principles to ensure that personalization enhances—rather than limits—accessibility and inclusion (Kohnke & Zaugg, 2025).

Preparing learners for a future shaped by AI will require incorporating AI literacy into curricula at all levels. This entails not only a technical understanding of AI but also critical reflection on its ethical, social, and political dimensions. As countries integrate AI into national education strategies, it is crucial to ensure that students acquire the skills to engage with AI responsibly and creatively (Rizvi et al., 2023; Otero et al., 2023; Sanusi et al., 2024). Looking forward, cross-sector collaboration among educators, technologists, policymakers, researchers, and communities is essential to fulfill AI's promise in education. Stakeholders must collectively imagine and implement AI applications that are not only effective but also just, transparent, and humane (Ojha et al., 2023).

As emerging tools such as speech-to-text, emotion recognition, and adaptive feedback systems continue to develop, educators should be prepared to harness these innovations while safeguarding learners' rights, well-being, and futures (Zaman, 2023). The field of educational measurement is already witnessing rapid advancements through automated scoring, natural language processing, and machine learning models, which further personalize feedback and enhance assessment accuracy (Bulut et al., 2024).

Ultimately, the success of AI in education will depend not only on technological progress but also on our collective commitment to ethical stewardship, inclusive practice, and the enduring human values that guide educational excellence. If thoughtfully implemented, AI can become a powerful catalyst for realizing the vision of education as a public good—responsive to individual needs, grounded in equity, and driven by the pursuit of human flourishing (Abbas et al., 2023; Lin et al., 2023; Ibrahim et al., 2023).

REFERENCES

Abbas, N., Ali, I., Manzoor, R., Hussain, T., & Hussaini, M. H. A. (2023). Role of artificial intelligence tools in enhancing students' educational performance at higher levels. Journal of Artificial Intelligence [JAIMLNN]. *Machine Learning and Neural Network, 3*(5), 36–49. DOI: 10.55529/jaimlnn.35.36.49

Adams, C., Pente, P., Lemermeyer, G., & Rockwell, G. (2023). Ethical principles for artificial intelligence in K-12 education. *Computers and Education: Artificial Intelligence, 4*, 100131. DOI: 10.1016/j.caeai.2023.100131

Akgun, S., & Greenhow, C. (2022). Artificial intelligence in education: Addressing ethical challenges in K-12 settings. *AI and Ethics, 2*(3), 431–440. DOI: 10.1007/s43681-021-00096-7 PMID: 34790956

Al-Zahrani, A. M. (2024). Unveiling the shadows: Beyond the hype of AI in education. *Heliyon, 10*(9). Advance online publication. DOI: 10.1016/j.heliyon.2024.e30696 PMID: 38737255

AlTwijri, L., & Alghizzi, T. M. (2024). Investigating the integration of artificial intelligence in English as foreign language classes for enhancing learners' affective factors: A systematic review. *Heliyon, 10*(10). Elsevier BV. https://doi.org/DOI: 10.1016/j.heliyon.2024.e31053

Avurakoghene, O. P., & Oredein, A. (2023). Educational leadership and artificial intelligence for sustainable development. OP Avurakoghene & AO Oredein, Educational Leadership and Artificial Intelligence for Sustainable Development. *Shodh Sari-An International Multidisciplinary Journal, 2*(3). DOI: 10.59231/sari7600

Ayeni, O. O., Al Hamad, N. M., Chisom, O. N., Osawaru, B., & Adewusi, O. E. (2024). AI in education: A review of personalized learning and educational technology. *GSC Advanced Research and Reviews, 18*(2), 261–271. DOI: 10.30574/gscarr.2024.18.2.0062

Azzam, A., & Charles, T. (2024). A Review of Artificial Intelligence in K-12 Education. *Open Journal of Applied Sciences, 14*(8), 2088–2100. DOI: 10.4236/ojapps.2024.148137

Balta, N. (2023). Ethical considerations in using AI in educational research. *Journal of Research in Didactical Sciences, 2*(1), 14205. DOI: 10.51853/jorids/14205

Bayly-Castaneda, K., Ramirez-Montoya, M. S., & Morita-Alexander, A. (2024, August). Crafting personalized learning paths with AI for lifelong learning: a systematic literature review. *In Frontiers in Education* (Vol. 9, p. 1424386). Frontiers Media SA. DOI: 10.3389/feduc.2024.1424386

bin Mohamed, M. Z., Hidayat, R., binti Suhaizi, N. N., bin Mahmud, M. K. H., & binti Baharuddin, S. N. (2022). Artificial intelligence in mathematics education: A systematic literature review. *International Electronic Journal of Mathematics Education, 17*(3), em0694. DOI: 10.29333/iejme/12132

Bulathwela, S., Pérez-Ortiz, M., Holloway, C., Cukurova, M., & Shawe-Taylor, J. (2024). Artificial intelligence alone will not democratise education: On educational inequality, techno-solutionism and inclusive tools. *Sustainability*, *16*(2), 781. DOI: 10.3390/su16020781

Bulut, O., Beiting-Parrish, M., Casabianca, J. M., Slater, S. C., Jiao, H., Song, D., & Morilova, P. (2024). The rise of artificial intelligence in educational measurement: Opportunities and ethical challenges. *arXiv preprint arXiv:2406.18900*. https://doi.org//arxiv.2406.18900DOI: 10.48550

Casal-Otero, L., Catala, A., Fernández-Morante, C., Taboada, M., Cebreiro, B., & Barro, S. (2023). AI literacy in K-12: A systematic literature review. *International Journal of STEM Education*, *10*(1), 29. DOI: 10.1186/s40594-023-00418-7

Chan, C. K. Y., & Tsi, L. H. (2023). The AI revolution in education: will AI replace or assist teachers in higher education? *arXiv preprint arXiv:2305.01185*. https://doi.org//arxiv.2305.01185DOI: 10.48550

Chaudhry, M. A., & Kazim, E. (2022). Artificial Intelligence in Education (AIEd): A high-level academic and industry note 2021. *AI and Ethics*, *2*(1), 157–165. DOI: 10.1007/s43681-021-00074-z PMID: 34790953

Chetry, K. K. (2024). Transforming education: How AI is revolutionizing the learning experience. *International Journal of Research Publication and Reviews*, *5*(5), 6352–6356. DOI: 10.55248/gengpi.5.0524.1277

Chinta, S. V., Wang, Z., Yin, Z., Hoang, N., Gonzalez, M., Quy, T. L., & Zhang, W. (2024). FairAIED: Navigating fairness, bias, and ethics in educational AI applications. *arXiv preprint arXiv:2407.18745*. https://doi.org//arxiv.2407.18745DOI: 10.48550

Cordero, J., Torres-Zambrano, J., & Cordero-Castillo, A. (2024). Integration of Generative Artificial Intelligence in Higher Education: Best Practices. *Education Sciences*, *15*(1), 32. DOI: 10.3390/educsci15010032

Demartini, C. G., Sciascia, L., Bosso, A., & Manuri, F. (2024). Artificial intelligence bringing improvements to adaptive learning in education: A case study. *Sustainability, 16*(3), 1347. DOI: 10.3390/su16031347

Dey, D. N. C. (2024). Enhancing Educational Tools Through Artificial Intelligence in Perspective of Need of AI. *Available at SSRN* 5031275. DOI: 10.2139/ssrn.5031275

Egunjobi, D., & Adeyeye, O. J. (2024). Revolutionizing Learning: The Impact of Augmented Reality (AR) and Artificial Intelligence (AI on Education). *Research-Gate*, (Oct). Advance online publication. DOI: 10.55248/gengpi.5.1024.2734

Gentile, M., Città, G., Perna, S., & Allegra, M. (2023, March). Do we still need teachers? Navigating the paradigm shift of the teacher's role in the AI era. *In Frontiers in Education* (Vol. 8, p. 1161777). Frontiers Media SA. DOI: 10.3389/feduc.2023.1161777

Gligorea, I., Cioca, M., Oancea, R., Gorski, A. T., Gorski, H., & Tudorache, P. (2023). Adaptive learning using artificial intelligence in e-learning: A literature review. *Education Sciences, 13*(12), 1216.Publishing Institute. DOI: 10.3390/educsci13121216

Global Educational Studies Review. (2020). In Global Educational. *Studies and Reviews (General Fisheries Commission for the Mediterranean)*. DOI: 10.31703/gesr

Gouseti, A., James, F., Fallin, L., & Burden, K. (2025). The ethics of using AI in K-12 education: A systematic literature review. *Technology, Pedagogy and Education, 34*(2), 161–182. DOI: 10.1080/1475939x.2024.2428601

Gr, G. (1992). One moment, please. *PubMed, 82*(1), 37. https://pubmed.ncbi.nlm.nih.gov/1499783

Han, B., Coghlan, S., Buchanan, G., & McKay, D. (2025). Who is Helping Whom? Student Concerns about AI-Teacher Collaboration in Higher Education Classrooms. *Proceedings of the ACM on Human-Computer Interaction, 9*(2), 1–32. DOI: 10.48550/arxiv.2412.14469

Harry, A. (2023). Role of AI in Education. [INJURITY]. *Interdisciplinary Journal & Humanity, 2*(3). DOI: 10.58631/injurity.v2i3.52

Holmes, W., Porayska-Pomsta, K., Holstein, K., Sutherland, E., Baker, T., Shum, S. B., & Koedinger, K. R. (2022). Ethics of AI in education: Towards a community-wide framework. *International Journal of Artificial Intelligence in Education*, 1–23.

Huang, L. (2023). Ethics of artificial intelligence in education: Student privacy and data protection. *Science Insights Education Frontiers, 16*(2), 2577–2587.

Ibrahim, H., Asim, R., Zaffar, F., Rahwan, T., & Zaki, Y. (2023). Rethinking homework in the age of artificial intelligence. *IEEE Intelligent Systems*, *38*(2), 24–27.

Jian, M. J. K. O. (2023). Personalized learning through AI. *Advances in Engineering Innovation*, *5*, 16–19.

Kalniņa, D., Nīmante, D., & Baranova, S. (2024). Artificial intelligence for higher education: Benefits and challenges for pre-service teachers. *Frontiers in Education*, *9*, 1501819. DOI: 10.3389/feduc.2024.1501819

Kamalov, F., Santandreu Calonge, D., & Gurrib, I. (2023). New era of artificial intelligence in education: Towards a sustainable multifaceted revolution. *Sustainability*, *15*(16), 12451.

Karpouzis, K. (2024, September). Artificial Intelligence in Education: Ethical Considerations and Insights from Ancient Greek Philosophy. In *Proceedings of the 13th Hellenic Conference on Artificial Intelligence (pp.* 1-7*)*. DOI: 10.1145/3688671.3688772

Khodayar, M., & Regan, J. (2023). Deep neural networks in power systems: A review. *Energies*, *16*(12), 4773. DOI: 10.3390/en16124773

Klimova, B., Pikhart, M., & Kacetl, J. (2023). Ethical issues of the use of AI-driven mobile apps for education. *Frontiers in Public Health*, *10*, 1118116. DOI: 10.3389/fpubh.2022.1118116 PMID: 36711343

Kohnke, S., & Zaugg, T. (2025). Artificial Intelligence: An Untapped Opportunity for Equity and Access in STEM Education. *Education Sciences*, *15*(1), 68. DOI: 10.3390/educsci15010068

Leon, C. D.Jr. (2024). Education and Artificial Intelligence: Revolutionizing Learning as a Unique Tandem. *Available at SSRN* 4721768. https://doi.org/DOI: 10.2139/ssrn.4721768

Lin, C. C., Huang, A. Y., & Lu, O. H. (2023). Artificial intelligence in intelligent tutoring systems toward sustainable education: A systematic review. *Smart Learning Environments*, *10*(1), 41. DOI: 10.1186/s40561-023-00260-y

Ma, K., Zhang, Y., & Hui, B. (2024). How Does AI Affect College? The Impact of AI Usage in College Teaching on Students' Innovative Behavior and Well-Being. *Behavioral Sciences (Basel, Switzerland)*, *14*(12), 1223. DOI: 10.3390/bs14121223 PMID: 39767364

Mahmoud, C. F., & Sørensen, J. T. (2024). Artificial Intelligence in Personalized Learning with a Focus on Current Developments and Future Prospects. *Research and Advances in Education*, *3*(8), 25–31. DOI: 10.56397/rae.2024.08.04

Mello, R. F., Freitas, E., Pereira, F. D., Cabral, L., Tedesco, P., & Ramalho, G. (2023). Education in the age of Generative AI: Context and Recent Developments. *arXiv preprint arXiv:2309.12332*. https://doi.org//arxiv.2309.12332DOI: 10.48550

Neji, W., Boughattas, N., & Ziadi, F. (2023). EXPLORING NEW AI-BASED TECHNOLOGIES TO ENHANCE STUDENTS' MOTIVATION. *Issues in Informing Science & Information Technology*, *20*. DOI: 10.28945/5149

Nguyen, A., Ngo, H. N., Hong, Y., Dang, B., & Nguyen, B. P. T. (2023). Ethical principles for artificial intelligence in education. *Education and Information Technologies*, *28*(4), 4221–4241. DOI: 10.1007/s10639-022-11316-w PMID: 36254344

Ojha, S., Mohapatra, S., Narendra, A., & Misra, I. (2023, October). From robots to books: An introduction to smart applications of AI in education (AIEd). In *The International Conference on Recent Innovations in Computing* (pp. 311-322). Singapore: Springer Nature Singapore. DOI: 10.48550/arxiv.2301.10026

Onesi-Ozigagun, O., Ololade, Y. J., Eyo-Udo, N. L., & Ogundipe, D. O. (2024). Revolutionizing education through AI: A comprehensive review of enhancing learning experiences. *International Journal of Applied Research in Social Sciences*, *6*(4), 589–607. DOI: 10.51594/ijarss.v6i4.1011

Pahi, K., Hawlader, S., Hicks, E., Zaman, A., & Phan, V. (2024). Enhancing active learning through collaboration between human teachers and generative AI. *Computers and Education Open*, *6*, 100183. DOI: 10.1016/j.caeo.2024.100183

Qiu, Y., Pan, J., & Ishak, N. A. (2022). [Retracted] Effectiveness of Artificial Intelligence (AI) in Improving Pupils' Deep Learning in Primary School Mathematics Teaching in Fujian Province. *Computational Intelligence and Neuroscience*, *2022*(1), 1362996. DOI: 10.1155/2022/1362996 PMID: 36193186

Rakya, Z. H. (2023). Exploring the impact of artificial intelligence (AI) on learner-instructor interaction in online learning (literature review). *International Journal of Emerging Multidisciplinary: Computer Science & Artificial Intelligence*, *2*(1), 1–14. DOI: 10.54938/ijemdcsai.2023.02.1.236

Rizvi, S., Waite, J., & Sentance, S. (2023). Artificial Intelligence teaching and learning in K-12 from 2019 to 2022: A systematic literature review. *Computers and Education: Artificial Intelligence*, *4*, 100145. DOI: 10.1016/j.caeai.2023.100145

Robert, A., Potter, K., & Frank, L. (2024). The impact of artificial intelligence on students' learning experience. *Wiley Interdisciplinary Reviews: Computational Statistics*, *2*(01). DOI: 10.2139/ssrn.4716747

Romero, M., Heiser, L., Lepage, A., Gagnebien, A., Bonjour, A., Lagarrigue, A., . . . Borgne, Y. A. L. (2023). Teaching and learning in the age of artificial intelligence. *arXiv preprint arXiv:2303.06956.*

Roshanaei, M., Olivares, H., & Lopez, R. R. (2023). Harnessing AI to foster equity in education: Opportunities, challenges, and emerging strategies. *Journal of Intelligent Learning Systems andApplications*, *15*(4), 123–143. DOI: 10.4236/jilsa.2023.154009

Saffari, M., & Khodayar, M. (2024). *Spatiotemporal deep learning for power system applications: a survey*. IEEE., DOI: 10.1109/access.2024.3424854

Sanusi, I. T., Martin, F., Ma, R., Gonzales, J. E., Mahipal, V., Oyelere, S. S., & Tukiainen, M. (2024). AI MyData: Fostering Middle School Students' Engagement with Machine Learning through an Ethics-Infused AI Curriculum. *ACM Transactions on Computing Education*, *24*(4), 1–37. DOI: 10.1145/3702242

Saputra, I., Astuti, M., Sayuti, M., & Kusumastuti, D. (2023). Integration of Artificial Intelligence in Education: Opportunities, Challenges, Threats and Obstacles. A Literature Review. *The Indonesian journal of computer science, 12*(4). DOI: 10.33022/ijcs.v12i4.3266

Strielkowski, W., Vlasov, A., Selivanov, K., Muraviev, K., & Shakhnov, V. (2023). Prospects and challenges of the machine learning and data-driven methods for the predictive analysis of power systems: A review. *Energies*, *16*(10), 4025. DOI: 10.3390/en16104025

Tanjga, M. (2023). E-learning and the Use of AI: A Review of Current Practices and Future Directions. DOI: 10.32388/ap0208

Thelma, C. C., Sain, Z. H., Shogbesan, Y. O., Phiri, E. V., & Akpan, W. M. (2024). Ethical Implications of AI and Machine Learning in Education: A Systematic Analysis. *International Journal of Instructional Technology*, *3*(1), 1–13. DOI: 10.33650/ijit.v3i1.9364

Tonbuloğlu, B. (2023). An evaluation of the use of artificial intelligence applications in online education. *Journal of Educational Technology and Online Learning*, *6*(4), 866–884. DOI: 10.31681/jetol.1335906

Uygun İlikhan, S., Özer, M., Tanberkan, H., & Bozkurt, V. (2024). How to mitigate the risks of deployment of artificial intelligence in medicine? *Turkish Journal of Medical Sciences*, *54*(3), 483–492. PMID: 39050000

Vincent-Lancrin, S., & van der Vlies, R. (2020). Trustworthy Artificial Intelligence (AI) in Education: Promises and Challenges. OECD Education Working Papers, No. 218. *OECD Publishing*. DOI: 10.1787/a6c90fa9-en

Vistorte, A. O. R., Deroncele-Acosta, A., Ayala, J. L. M., Barrasa, A., López-Granero, C., & Martí-González, M. (2024). Integrating artificial intelligence to assess emotions in learning environments: A systematic literature review. *Frontiers in Psychology*, *15*, 1387089. DOI: 10.3389/fpsyg.2024.1387089 PMID: 38966729

Walter, Y. (2024). Embracing the future of Artificial Intelligence in the classroom: The relevance of AI literacy, prompt engineering, and critical thinking in modern education. *International Journal of Educational Technology in Higher Education*, *21*(1), 15. DOI: 10.1186/s41239-024-00448-3

Woo, J. H., & Choi, H. (2021). Systematic Review for AI-based Language Learning Tools. *Journal of Digital Contents Society*, *22*(11), 1783. DOI: 10.9728/dcs.2021.22.11.1783

Zaman, B. U. (2023). Transforming education through ai, benefits, risks, and ethical considerations. *Authorea Preprints, 1*, 1-26. DOI: 10.36227/techrxiv.24231583

Zawacki-Richter, O., Marín, V. I., Bond, M., & Gouverneur, F. (2019). Systematic review of research on artificial intelligence applications in higher education–where are the educators? *Internationa journal of educational technology in higher education, 16*(1), 1-27. DOI: 10.1186/s41239-019-0171-0

Zhai, X., Chu, X., Chai, C. S., Jong, M. S. Y., Istenic, A., Spector, M., & Li, Y. (2021). A Review of Artificial Intelligence (AI) in Education from 2010 to 2020. *Complexity*, *2021*(1), 8812542. DOI: 10.1155/2021/8812542

Compilation of References

Abbas, N., Ali, I., Manzoor, R., Hussain, T., & Hussain, M. (2023). Role of artificial intelligence tools in enhancing students' educational performance at higher levels. *Journal of Artificial Intelligence, Machine Learning, and Neural Network*, (35), 36–49. DOI: 10.55529/jaimlnn.35.36.49

Abbasnejad, B., Soltani, S., & Wong, P. (2023). A systematic review of online learning and teaching strategies during the COVID-19 pandemic: Implications for the construction management sector. *Smart and Sustainable Built Environment*, *13*(4), 934–959. DOI: 10.1108/sasbe-08-2022-0174

Abbes, F., Bennani, S., & Maalel, A. (2024). Generative AI and gamification for personalized learning: *Literature review and future challenges. SN Computer Science*, *5*(8), 1–12. DOI: 10.1007/s42979-024-03491-z

Abdullayeva, M., & Musayeva, Z. M. (2023). The impact of chat Gpt on students' writing skills: An exploration of AI-assisted writing tools. *Int. Conf. Educ. Res. Innov.*, *4*, 61–66.

Abubakar, U., Falade, A., & Ibrahim, H. (2024). Redefining student assessment in Nigerian tertiary institutions: The impact of AI technologies on academic performance and developing countermeasures. *Advances in Mobile Learning Educational Research*, *4*(2), 1149–1159. DOI: 10.25082/amler.2024.02.009

Abykanova, B., Nugumanova, S., Yelezhanova, S., Kabylkhamit, Z., & Sabirova, Z. (2023). The use of interactive learning technology in institutions of higher learning. *International Journal of Environmental and Science Education*, *11*(18), 12528–12539.

Adams, C., Pente, P., Lemermeyer, G., & Rockwell, G. (2023). Ethical principles for artificial intelligence in K-12 education. *Computers and Education: Artificial Intelligence*, *4*, 100131. DOI: 10.1016/j.caeai.2023.100131

Adams, D., & Thompson, P. (2025). Transforming School Leadership with Artificial Intelligence: Applications, Implications, and Future Directions. *Leadership and Policy in Schools*, *24*(1), 77–89. DOI: 10.1080/15700763.2024.2411295

Adekanmbi, F., & Ukpere, W. I. (2021). Stimulating creative behaviors in the work environment: Influences of employee engagement, authentic leadership, and human capital factors on employee creativity. *EUREKA: Social and Humanities*, (5), 24–33. DOI: 10.21303/2504-5571.2021.001995

Adıgüzel, T., Kaya, M., & Cansu, F. (2023). Revolutionizing education with AI: Exploring the transformative potential of ChatGPT. *Contemporary Educational Technology*, *15*(3), ep429. DOI: 10.30935/cedtech/13152

Adjei, Y., Osei-Himah, V., Duku, P., & Siaw, W. N. (2023). The Impact of performance-based assessment strategies on pre-service teachers' self-efficacy and academic achievement in general physics. *Pedagogical Research*, *8*(4), em0168. Advance online publication. DOI: 10.29333/pr/13388

Afzal, S., Dempsey, B., D'Helon, C., Mukhi, N. K., Pribic, M., Sickler, A., Strong, P., Vanchiswar, M., & Wilde, L. (2019). The personality of AI systems in education: Experiences with the Watson Tutor, a one-on-one virtual tutoring system. *Childhood Education*, 95.

Agarwal, V. (2018). Sustainable fashion education in changing world scenario. *European Journal of Sustainable Development*, *7*(1), 365–365.

Aguiar-Castillo, L., Clavijo-Rodriguez, A., Hernández-López, L., De Saa-Pérez, P., & Pérez-Jiménez, R. (2021). Gamification and deep learning approaches in higher education. *Journal of Hospitality, Leisure, Sport and Tourism Education*, *29*, 100290. DOI: 10.1016/j.jhlste.2020.100290

Ahanotu, A., DeVore, E. K., Carroll, T. L., Edelen, M., Morcos, M., Willard, E., Zhao, N. W., Belafsky, P., & Shin, J. J. (2023). Can EAT-10 become EAT-5? Improving measurement efficiency of dysphagia with item response theory. *The Laryngoscope*, *133*(12), 3327–3333. DOI: 10.1002/lary.30732 PMID: 37166087

Ahmady, S., Mirmoghtadaie, Z., Zarifsanaiey, N., & Thor, J. (2021). Designing e-learning in medical education: Toward a comprehensive model. *Turkish Online Journal of Distance Education*, *22*(2), 254–271. DOI: 10.17718/tojde.907351

AI4VET4AI. (n.d.). Transforming vocational training: The essential role of AI in employee skill development. https://www.ai4vet4ai.eu/news/transforming-vocational-training-the-essential-role-of-ai-in-employee-skill-development/

Akella, D. (2010). Learning together: Kolb's experiential theory and its application. *Journal of Management & Organization, 16*(1), 100–112. DOI: 10.5172/jmo.16.1.100

Akgün, S., & Greenhow, C. (2021). Artificial intelligence in education: Addressing ethical challenges in K-12 settings. *AI and Ethics, 2*(3), 431–440. DOI: 10.1007/s43681-021-00096-7 PMID: 34790956

Akpan, V. I., Igwe, U. A., Mpamah, I. B. I., & Okoro, C. O. (2020). Social constructivism: Implications on teaching and learning. *Brock Journal of Education, 8*(8), 49–56.

Akpen, C. N., Asaolu, S., Atobatele, S., Okagbue, H., & Sampson, S. (2024). Impact of online learning on student's performance and engagement: A systematic review. *Discover Education, 3*(1), 1–15. DOI: 10.1007/s44217-024-00253-0

Akram, S. V., Malik, P. K., Singh, R., Gehlot, A., Juyal, A., Ghafoor, K. Z., & Shrestha, S. (2022). Implementation of Digitalized Technologies for Fashion Industry 4.0: Opportunities and Challenges. *Scientific Programming, 2022*, 1–17. DOI: 10.1155/2022/7523246

Al Hazaa, K., Abdel-Salam, A. S. G., Ismail, R., Johnson, C., Al-Tameemi, R. A. N., Romanowski, M. H., & Elatawneh, A. (2021). The effects of attendance and high school GPA on student performance in first-year undergraduate courses. *Cogent Education, 8*(1), 1956857.

Alabi, M. (2024). Data-Driven Product Strategy: Leveraging AI to Forecast Market Trends and Identify Emerging Opportunities.

Alagar, A. (2024, November 14). *How AI is transforming the creative process for artists*. IABAC. https://iabac.org/blog/how-ai-is-transforming-the-creative-process-for-artists

Alam, S., Kumar, M., Khursheed, S., Mahato, Z., Bashar, H. K., & Suman, A. (2024). Designing an AI driven intelligent tutorial system. *5th International Conference on Recent Trends in Computer Science and Technology (ICRTCST)*, 585-588.

Al-Balushi, S. M., Ambusaidi, A., Al-Balushi, K., Al-Hajri, F. H., & Al-Sinani, M. S. (2020). Student-centered and teacher-centered science classrooms as visualized by science teachers and their supervisors. *Teaching and Teacher Education, 89*, 103014. DOI: 10.1016/j.tate.2019.103014

Alenezi, M. (2023). Digital Learning and Digital Institution in Higher Education. *Education in Science*, 13.

Alibasic, H., Atkinson, C. L., & Pelcher, J. (2024). The liminal state of academic freedom: Navigating corporatization in higher education. *Discover Education*.

Ali, K., Barhom, N., & Duggal, M. (2022). Online assessment platforms: What is on offer? *European Journal of Dental Education*, *27*(2), 320–324. DOI: 10.1111/eje.12807 PMID: 35445509

Alizadehsalehi, S., Hadavi, A., & Huang, J. C. (2021). Assessment of AEC students' performance using BIM-into-VR. *Applied Sciences (Basel, Switzerland)*, *11*(7), 3225.

Almarzouki, A. F., Alqahtani, A. I., Baessa, J. K., Badaood, D. K., Nujoom, R. R., Malibari, R. W., Aljared, E. M., & Alghamdi, R. S. (2025). Neuroscience literacy and academic outcomes: Insights from a university student population. *Brain Sciences*, *15*(1), 44. DOI: 10.3390/brainsci15010044 PMID: 39851411

Alotaibi, B. S., Shema, A. I., Ibrahim, A. U., Abuhussain, M. A., Abdulmalik, H., Dodo, Y. A., & Atakara, C. (2024). Assimilation of 3D printing, Artificial Intelligence (AI) and Internet of Things (IoT) for the construction of eco-friendly intelligent homes: An explorative review. *Heliyon*. PMID: 39286162

Alotaibi, N. S. (2024). The Impact of AI and LMS Integration on the Future of Higher Education: Opportunities, Challenges, and Strategies for Transformation. *Sustainability*, *16*(23), 10357.

Alotaibi, S. (2021). A novel framework of success using of e-assessment during corona pandemic. *International Journal of Emerging Technologies in Learning*, *16*(12), 215–232. DOI: 10.3991/ijet.v16i12.22063

Al-Rawi, O. Y. M., Elfezzani, W., Edwar, M. E., Al-Rawi, B. O., & Rashed, A. N. (2025). Challenges and Recent Developments in Smart Education Post-COVID-19 Pandemic. Business Sustainability with Artificial Intelligence (AI). *Challenges and Opportunities*, *1*, 857–870. DOI: 10.1007/978-3-031-71526-6_77

Alsbou, M. K. K., & Alsaraireh, R. E. A. I. (2024, April). Data-driven decision-making in education: leveraging AI for school improvement. In *2024 International Conference on Knowledge Engineering and Communication Systems (ICKECS)* (Vol. 1, pp. 1-6). IEEE.

Alshahrani, B., Pileggi, S., & Karimi, F. (2024). A social perspective on ai in the higher education system: A semi-systematic literature review. *Electronics (Basel)*, *13*(8), 1572. DOI: 10.3390/electronics13081572

Altbach, P. G. (2015). The deteriorating guru: The crisis of the professoriate. *International Higher Education*.

Alt, D., Naamati-Schneider, L., & Weishut, D. J. (2023). Competency-based learning and formative assessment feedback as precursors of college students' soft skills acquisition. *Studies in Higher Education, 48*(12), 1901–1917. DOI: 10.1080/03075079.2023.2217203

AlTwijri, L., & Alghizzi, T. M. (2024). Investigating the integration of artificial intelligence in English as foreign language classes for enhancing learners' affective factors: A systematic review. *Heliyon, 10*(10). Elsevier BV. https://doi.org/DOI: 10.1016/j.heliyon.2024.e31053

Alwaqdani, M. (2024). Investigating teachers' perceptions of artificial intelligence tools in education: Potential and difficulties. *Education and Information Technologies*, 1–19.

Alyaz, Y. (2003). Yabancı il öğretim yazılımlarında yapay zekaya dayalı etkileşim. *Dil Dergisi*, (121), 22–35.

Al-Zahrani, A. M. (2024). Unveiling the shadows: Beyond the hype of AI in education. *Heliyon, 10*(9). Advance online publication. DOI: 10.1016/j.heliyon.2024.e30696 PMID: 38737255

Al-Zahrani, A. M., & Alasmari, T. M. (2024). Exploring the impact of artificial intelligence on higher education: The dynamics of ethical, social, and educational implications. *Humanities & Social Sciences Communications, 11*, 912. DOI: 10.1057/s41599-024-03432-4

Amzil, I., Aammou, S., & Tagdimi, Z. (2023). Enhance students' learning by providing personalized study pathways. *Conhecimento & Diversidade Journal, 15.*

Anderson, L. W. (Ed.). Krathwohl, D. R. (Ed.), Airasian, P. W., Cruikshank, K. A., Mayer, R. E., Pintrich, P.R., Raths, J., & Wittrock, M.C. (2001). *A taxonomy for learning, teaching, and assessing: A revision of Bloom's taxonomy of educational objectives*. Longman.

Andrisano, A. O., Leali, F., Pellicciari, M., Pini, F., & Vergnano, A. (2012). Hybrid Reconfigurable System design and optimization through virtual prototyping and digital manufacturing tools. [IJIDeM]. *International Journal on Interactive Design and Manufacturing, 6*(1), 17–27. DOI: 10.1007/s12008-011-0133-9

Angwin, J., Larson, J., Mattu, S., & Kirchner, L. (2016). Machine bias. *ProPublica.* https://www.propublica.org/article/machine-bias-risk-assessments-in-criminal-sentencing

Antony, J. I. P. J., & Khalid, P., Z., M. (2024). Integrating artificial intelligence (AI) in teaching and learning. *International Journal for Multidisciplinary Research, 6*(2). DOI: 10.36948/ijfmr.2024.v06i02.14064

Arora, C., Tubino, L., Cain, A., Lee, K., & Malhotra, V. (2023, May). Persona-based assessment of software engineering student research projects: An experience report. *In 2023 IEEE/ACM 45th International Conference on Software Engineering: Software Engineering Education and Training (ICSE-SEET)* (pp. 198-209). IEEE. DOI: 10.48550/arXiv.2302.05618

Ashraf, S. R. (2024). The Role of Artificial Intelligence in Enhancing Managerial Decision-Making in Education. *International Journal of Advanced Social Sciences Research, 1*(1), 10–20.

Atalay, S. (2018). When students become customers; The changing relationship between the student and the academic: A case study from social sciences in Turkey. *Journal of Higher Education and Science, 8*(3), 512–521.

Attai, L. (2019). *Protecting student data privacy: Classroom fundamentals*. Rowman & Littlefield.

Attard, C., & Holmes, K. (2022). An exploration of teacher and student perceptions of blended learning in four secondary mathematics classrooms. *Mathematics Education Research Journal, 34*(4), 719–740.

Avădanei, M., Blaga, M., & Kazlacheva, Z. (2021). Best Practices of Sustainable Product Development through 3D-Design and Visualization. In *International Symposium Technical Textiles-Present and Future* (pp. 227-235).

Avdiu, V., & Ahmedi, V. (2024). Alternative Assessment Strategies to Enhance Learning for Students with Special Needs. *Journal of Social Studies Education Research, 15*(5), 1–25.

Avram, M., Lazăr, D., Maris, M., & Olariu, S. (2023). Artificial intelligence in improving the outcome of surgical treatment in colorectal cancer. *Frontiers in Oncology, 13*. DOI: 10.3389/fonc.2023.1116761 PMID: 36733307

Avurakoghene, O. P., & Oredein, A. (2023). Educational leadership and artificial intelligence for sustainable development. OP Avurakoghene & AO Oredein, Educational Leadership and Artificial Intelligence for Sustainable Development. *Shodh Sari-An International Multidisciplinary Journal, 2*(3). DOI: 10.59231/sari7600

Ayeni, O. O., Al Hamad, N. M., Chisom, O. N., Osawaru, B., & Adewusi, O. E. (2024). AI in education: A review of personalized learning and educational technology. *GSC Advanced Research and Reviews, 18*(2), 261–271. DOI: 10.30574/gscarr.2024.18.2.0062

Aytaç, T., & Kula, S. S. (2020). The effect of student-centered approaches on Students' creative thinking skills: A meta-analysis study. *International Journal of Contemporary Educational Research, 7*(2), 62–80. DOI: 10.33200/ijcer.723894

Azzam, A., & Charles, T. (2024). A Review of Artificial Intelligence in K-12 Education. *Open Journal of Applied Sciences, 14*(8), 2088–2100. DOI: 10.4236/ojapps.2024.148137

Badke, W. (2021). *Research strategies: Finding your way through the information fog*. iUniverse.

Baeza, C., & Jushchyshyn, N. (2024). BRIDGING THE GAP BETWEEN THE FASHION INDUSTRY AND DIGITAL MEDIA: AN INTERDISCIPLINARY COURSE ON ETHICS, SUSTAINABILITY, AND IMMERSIVE TECHNOLOGY. In ICERI2024 Proceedings (pp. 9762-9767). IATED.

Bajaj, M. (2024). THE ROLE OF DIGITAL LEARNING PLATFORMS IN ENHANCING STUDENT ENGAGEMENT. *UNIFIED VISIONS, 1*. DOI: 10.70088/xq3gy756

Baker, R. S. J. D. (2010). Data mining for education. In McGaw, B., Peterson, P., & Baker, E. (Eds.), *International Encyclopedia of Education* (3rd ed., Vol. 7, pp. 112–118). Elsevier.

Baker, R. S., & Hawn, A. (2022). Algorithmic Bias in Education. *International Journal of Artificial Intelligence in Education, 32*, 1052–1092. DOI: 10.1007/s40593-021-00285-9

Baker, R. S., & Inventado, P. S. (2014). Educational Data Mining and Learning Analytics. In Larusson, J. A., & White, B. (Eds.), *Learning Analytics: From Research to Practice* (pp. 61–75). Springer.

Baker, R. S., McLaren, B. M., Hutt, S., Richey, J. E., Rowe, E., Almeda, M. V., & Andres, J. M. A. (2021, June). Towards sharing student models across learning systems. In *International conference on artificial intelligence in education* (pp. 60-65). Cham: Springer International Publishing.

Balen, E., Haverman, L., Hassan, S., Taal, E., Smit, C., Driessens, M., Beckers, E. A. M., Coppens, M., Eikenboom, J., Hooimeijer, H., Leebeek, F. W. G., van Vulpen, L. F. D., Schols, S. E. M., Terwee, C. B., Rosendaal, F. R., van der Bom, J. G., & Gouw, S. (2021). Validation of promis profile-29 in adults with hemophilia in the Netherlands. *Journal of Thrombosis and Haemostasis*, *19*(11), 2687–2701. DOI: 10.1111/jth.15454 PMID: 34245088

Balta, N. (2023). Ethical considerations in using AI in educational research. *Journal of Research in Didactical Sciences*, *2*(1), 14205. DOI: 10.51853/jorids/14205

Bandura, A. (1986). Social foundations of thought and action. *Englewood Cliffs*, NJ, 1986(23-28), 2.

Bao, H. (2024). Learning evaluation method based on artificial intelligence technology and its application in education. *Journal of Electrical Systems*, *20*(3s), 1833–1842. DOI: 10.52783/jes.1722

Barocas, S., Hardt, M., & Narayanan, A. (2023). *Fairness and machine learning: Limitations and Opportunities*. MIT Press.

Barton, R. (2024, January 9). Turnitin adding AI writing detection, but instructors should use it with caution. Purdue University Online. https://www.purdue.edu/online/turnitin-adding-ai-writing-detection-but-instructors-should-use-it-with-caution/

Bauer, J. M. (2022). Toward new guardrails for the information society. *Telecommunications Policy*.

Bayly-Castaneda, K., Ramirez-Montoya, M. S., & Morita-Alexander, A. (2024, August). Crafting personalized learning paths with AI for lifelong learning: a systematic literature review. *In Frontiers in Education* (Vol. 9, p. 1424386). Frontiers Media SA. DOI: 10.3389/feduc.2024.1424386

Baysal, Y. E., Mutlu, F., & Nacaroglu, O. (2023). The Effectiveness of Student-Centered Teaching Applications Used in Determining Motivation toward Science Learning: A Meta-Analysis Study. *International Journal of Psychology and Educational Studies*, *10*(1), 1–21.

Belda-Medina, J., & Calvo-Ferrer, J. R. (2022). Using chatbots as AI conversational partners in language learning. *Applied Sciences (Basel, Switzerland)*, *12*(17), 8427.

Belwalkar, B. B., & Maki, B. (2023). Role of Artificial Intelligence in Workforce Development. *American Institutes for Research*, 2023-11.

Benitta, G., Asha, H. J., & Josephine, J. A. (2024). An Integrated (Hybrid Based) Besuited Education System Design for the Better Models. *2024 4th International Conference on Advance Computing and Innovative Technologies in Engineering (ICACITE)*, 561-565.

Berame, J., Bulay, M., Mercado, R., Ybanez, A., Aloyon, G., Dayupay, A. M., Hunahunan, R. D., & Jalop, N. (2022). Improving grade 8 students' academic performance and attitude in teaching science through augmented reality. *American Journal of Education and Technology*, *1*(3), 62–72. DOI: 10.54536/ajet.v1i3.840

Bernacki, M. L., Greene, M. J., & Lobczowski, N. G. (2021). A systematic review of research on personalized learning: Personalized by whom, to what, how, and for what purpose (s)? *Educational Psychology Review*, *33*(4), 1675–1715. DOI: 10.1007/s10648-021-09615-8

Bernacki, M. L., & Walkington, C. (2018). The role of situational interest in personalized learning. *Journal of Educational Psychology*, *110*(6), 864–881. DOI: 10.1037/edu0000250

Bernardus, D., Murwani, F. D., Aji, I. D. K., Radianto, W. E. D., Padmawidjaja, L., Jatiperwira, S. Y., & Jacob, G. H. (2023). Do entrepreneurial characteristics moderate the relationship between experiential learning and entrepreneurial mindset? *Journal of Educational and Social Research*, *13*(1), 106–122. DOI: 10.36941/jesr-2023-0010

Bertola, P., & Colombi, C. (2021). Reflecting on the future of fashion design education: New education models and emerging topics in fashion design. The Routledge companion to fashion studies, 90-98.

Bhandari, A., Liong, R., Koppen, J., Murthy, S., & Lasocki, A. (2020). Noninvasive determination of IDH and 1p19q status of lower-grade gliomas using MRI radiomics: A systematic review. *AJNR. American Journal of Neuroradiology*, *42*(1), 94–101. DOI: 10.3174/ajnr.a6875 PMID: 33243896

Bhardwaj, V., Zhang, S., Tan, Y. Q., & Pandey, V. (2025, February). Redefining learning: Student-centered strategies for academic and personal growth. [). Frontiers Media SA.]. *Frontiers in Education*, *10*, 1518602.

Bhat, R. A. (2023). The Impact of technology integration on student learning outcomes: A comparative study. *International Journal of Social Science, Educational, Economics* [IJSET]. *Agricultural Research & Technology: Open Access Journal*, *2*(9), 592–596.

bin Mohamed, M. Z., Hidayat, R., binti Suhaizi, N. N., bin Mahmud, M. K. H., & binti Baharuddin, S. N. (2022). Artificial intelligence in mathematics education: A systematic literature review. *International Electronic Journal of Mathematics Education, 17*(3), em0694. DOI: 10.29333/iejme/12132

Black, P., & Wiliam, D. (1998). Assessment and Classroom Learning. *Assessment in Education: Principles, Policy & Practice*, *5*(1), 7–74.

Black, P., & Wiliam, D. (1998). Assessment and classroom learning. *Assessment in Education: Principles, Policy & Practice*, *5*(1), 7–74. DOI: 10.1080/0969595980050102

Bloom, B. S. (1956). *Taxonomy of Educational Objectives, Handbook: The Cognitive Domain*. David McKay.

Bloom, B. S. (1984). The 2-sigma problem: The search for methods of group instruction as effective as one-to-one tutoring. *Educational Researcher*, *13*(6), 4–16.

Bonini, T., & Magaudda, P. (2023). Artificial Intelligence: Where the Music of the Future Is Heading. In *Platformed! How Streaming, Algorithms and Artificial Intelligence are Shaping Music Cultures* (pp. 121–148). Springer Nature Switzerland.

Borenstein, J., & Howard, A. (2021). Emerging challenges in AI and the need for AI ethics education. *AI and Ethics*, *1*(1), 61–65. PMID: 38624388

Borhan, M., Saleh, S., Li, A., & Ong, E. (2020). Readiness in Implementing Student-centred Learning (SCL): An Insight to Developing a Problem-based Learning (PBL), Module *Universal. The Journal of Educational Research*, *8*(1), 119–126. http://www.hrpub.org. DOI: 10.13189/ujer.2020.080114

Boussakuk, M. (2020). A fully individualized adaptive and intelligent educational hypermedia system: Details of CleverUniversity. *International Journal of Emerging Trends in Engineering Research*, *8*(5), 1497–1502. DOI: 10.30534/ijeter/2020/04852020

Bozzi, M., Raffaghelli, J. E., & Zani, M. (2021). Peer learning as a key component of an integrated teaching method: Overcoming the complexities of physics teaching in large size classes. *Education Sciences, 11*(2), 67. 11020067DOI: 10.3390/educsci

Bray, B., & McClaskey, K. (2014). *Make learning personal: The what, who, wow, where, and why* (1st ed., Vol. 1). Corwin Press.

Brenner, L., Betthauser, L., Penzenik, M., Germain, A., Li, J. J., Chattopadhyay, I., Frank, E., Kupner, D. J., & Gibbons, R. (2021). Development and validation of computerized adaptive assessment tools for the measurement of posttraumatic stress disorder among us military veterans. *JAMA Network Open*, *4*(7), e2115707. DOI: 10.1001/jamanetworkopen.2021.15707 PMID: 34236411

Brightwood, S., Olusegun, J., Oluwaseyi, J., & Temitope, O. M. (2024). INTELLIGENT ASSESSMENT SYSTEMS: USING AI FOR FORMATIVE AND SUMMATIVE EVALUATIONS.

Bringula, R. (2024). Chatgpt in a programming course: Benefits and limitations. *Frontiers in Education*, *9*. Advance online publication. DOI: 10.3389/feduc.2024.1248705

Brint, S. F. (2018). *The Ends of Knowledge*. Two Cheers for Higher Education.

Brookhart, S. M., & Nitko, A. J. (2019). *Educational Assessment of Students*. Pearson.

Bruggeman, B., Tondeur, J., Struyven, K., Pynoo, B., Garone, A., & Vanslambrouck, S. (2021). Experts speaking: Crucial teacher attributes for implementing blended learning in higher education. *The Internet and Higher Education*, *48*, 100772. DOI: 10.1016/j.iheduc.2020.100772

Brunese, M. C., Fantozzi, M. R., Fusco, R., De Muzio, F., Gabelloni, M., Danti, G., Borgheresi, A., Palumbo, P., Bruno, F., Gandolfo, N., Giovagnoni, A., Miele, V., Barile, A., & Granata, V. (2023). Update on the applications of Radiomics in diagnosis, staging, and recurrence of Intrahepatic Cholangiocarcinoma. *Diagnostics (Basel)*, *13*(8), 1488. DOI: 10.3390/diagnostics13081488 PMID: 37189589

Bruno, C., & Canina, M. (2019). CREATIVITY 4.0. EMPOWERING CREATIVITY IN THE DIGITAL ERA. In *DS 95: Proceedings of the 21st International Conference on Engineering and Product Design Education (E&PDE 2019), University of Strathclyde, Glasgow. 12th-13th September 2019.*

Bruno, C., & Canina, M. (2020). Developing a Method for Understanding How to Empower Creativity Through Digital Technologies: The Case of AI. In *Advances in Creativity, Innovation, Entrepreneurship and Communication of Design: Proceedings of the AHFE 2020 Virtual Conferences on Creativity, Innovation and Entrepreneurship, and Human Factors in Communication of Design, July 16-20, 2020, USA* (pp. 113-120). Springer International Publishing.

Brusilovsky, P., & Peylo, C. (2003). Adaptive and intelligent web-based educational systems. *International Journal of Artificial Intelligence in Education*, *13*, 156–169.

Bulathwela, S., Perez-Ortiz, M., Holloway, C., Cukurova, M., & Shawe-Taylor, J. (2024). Artificial Intelligence Alone Will Not Democratise Education: On Educational Inequality, Techno-Solutionism and Inclusive Tools. *Sustainability*. DOI: 10.3390/su16020781

Buldu, E., & Buldu, M. (2021). Investigating pre-service early childhood teachers' cPCK and pPCK on the knowledge used in scientific process through core. *SAGE Open, 11*(2). DOI: 10.1177/21582440211025564

Bunce, L. (2020). A degree of studying - students who treat education as a commodity perform worse than their intrinsically motivated peers. *Active Learning in Higher Education*.

Burawoy, M. (2016). The neoliberal university: Ascent of the spiralists. *Critical Sociology*, *42*(7/8), 941–942.

Burke, H. B., Hoang, A., Lopreiato, J. O., King, H., Hemmer, P., Montgomery, M., & Gagarin, V. (2023). Assessing the ability of a large language model to score free text medical student notes: Quantitative study. *JMIR Medical Education*, *10*(e56342). DOI: 10.2196/56342 PMID: 39118469

Burns, R. (2020). *The adult learner at work*. Routledge.

Busch, L. (2017). *Knowledge for Sale: The Neoliberal Takeover of Higher Education. Publication*. MIT Press.

Büyük, K., Uğur, S., Saykılı, A., & Şahin, V. (2018). Using games with gamification elements in open and distance learning: Sorukūp application example. *Journal of Open Education Applications and Research*, *4*(2), 211–234.

Bygrave, L. A. (2014). *Data privacy law: An international perspective*. Oxford University Press., DOI: 10.1093/acprof:oso/9780199675555.001.0001

Cai, J., & Qian, X. (2021). Effect of New ICTs on Vocational Education in China: A Case Study of Wuxi Vocational Institute of Commerce. In Kosaka, M., Wu, J., Xing, K., & Zhang, S. (Eds.), *Business Innovation with New ICT in the Asia-Pacific: Case Studies*. Springer., DOI: 10.1007/978-981-15-7658-4_11

Cao, C.C., Ding, Z., Lin, J., & Hopfgartner, F. (2023). AI chatbots as multi-role pedagogical agents: Transforming engagement in CS education. *ArXiv, abs/2308.03992*

Capone, R. (2022). Blended learning and student-centered active learning environment: A case study with STEM undergraduate students. *Canadian Journal of Science, Mathematics and Technology Education = Revue Canadienne de l'Enseignement des Sciences, des Mathématiques et de la Technologie, 22*(1), 210–236. DOI: 10.1007/s42330-022-00195-5

Casal-Otero, L., Catala, A., Fernández-Morante, C., Taboada, M., Cebreiro, B., & Barro, S. (2023). AI literacy in K-12: A systematic literature review. *International Journal of STEM Education, 10*(1), 29. DOI: 10.1186/s40594-023-00418-7

Casciani, D., & D'Itria, E. (2024). Fostering Directions for Digital Technology Adoption in Sustainable and Circular Fashion: Toward the Circular Fashion-Tech Lab. *Systems, 12*(6), 190.

Çela, E., Vajjhala, N. R., Eappen, P., & Vedishchev, A. (2025). Artificial Intelligence in Vocational Education and Training. In Transforming Vocational Education and Training Using AI (pp. 1-16). IGI Global Scientific Publishing.

Cerruti, C., & Valeri, A. (2022). *AI-Powered Platforms: automated transactions in digital marketplaces* (Doctoral dissertation, Dissertation, Master of Science in Business Administration, Università degli Studi di Roma" Tor Vergata" Department of Management and Law).

Chan, C. K. (2023). A comprehensive AI policy education framework for university teaching and learning. *International Journal of Educational Technology in Higher Education.*

Chan, C. K. Y., & Tsi, L. H. (2024). Will generative AI replace teachers in higher education? A study of teacher and student perceptions. *Studies in Educational Evaluation, 83*, 101395.

Chang-Tik, C. (2022). Student Collaboration Through Assessment, Feedback, and Peer Instruction. In Chang-Tik, C., Kidman, G., & Tee, M. Y. (Eds.), *Collaborative Active Learning*. Palgrave Macmillan., DOI: 10.1007/978-981-19-4383-6_3

Chang, W., Hsu, K., & Su, Y. (2022). Association between early sonographic findings and acetabular index at the age of 6 months: A prospective observational study. *BMC Pediatrics, 22*(1). Advance online publication. DOI: 10.1186/s12887-022-03268-4 PMID: 35473514

Chaudhary, S. (2024). Challenges in Student-Centered Learning. *International Journal for Research in Applied Science and Engineering Technology, 12*(7), 983–986. DOI: 10.22214/ijraset.2024.63702

Chaudhry, M. A., & Kazim, E. (2022). Artificial Intelligence in Education (AIEd): A high-level academic and industry note 2021. *AI and Ethics*, *2*(1), 157–165. DOI: 10.1007/s43681-021-00074-z PMID: 34790953

Chemnad, K., & Othman, A. (2024). Digital accessibility in the era of artificial intelligence—Bibliometric analysis and systematic review. *Frontiers in Artificial Intelligence*, *7*. Advance online publication. DOI: 10.3389/frai.2024.1349668 PMID: 38435800

Chen, A., Liu, H., Li, K.-C., & Jia, J. (2023). For educational inclusiveness: Design and implementation of an intelligent tutoring system for student-athletes based on self-determination theory. *Sustainability*, *15*(20). Advance online publication. DOI: 10.3390/su152014709

Chen, E., Jiang, J., Su, R., Gao, M., Zhu, S., Zhou, J., & Huo, Y. (2020). A new smart wristband equipped with an artificial intelligence algorithm to detect atrial fibrillation. *Heart Rhythm*, *17*(5), 847–853. DOI: 10.1016/j.hrthm.2020.01.034 PMID: 32354449

Chen, J., & Zhang, M. (2022). Exploration and research on industry-education integration of vocational education in AI era. *Advances in Vocational and Technical Education*, *4*, 41–47. DOI: 10.23977/avte.2022.040306

Chen, K., Stotter, C., Klestil, T., & Nehrer, S. (2022). Artificial intelligence in orthopedic radiography analysis: A narrative review. *Diagnostics (Basel)*, *12*(9), 2235. DOI: 10.3390/diagnostics12092235 PMID: 36140636

Chen, L., Chen, P., & Lin, Z. (2020). *Artificial Intelligence in Education: A Review* (Vol. 8). IEEE Access. [Online], DOI: 10.1109/ACCESS.2020.2988510

Chen, L., Chen, P., & Lin, Z. (2020). Artificial intelligence in education: A review. *IEEE Access : Practical Innovations, Open Solutions*, *8*, 75264–75278.

Chen, L., Chen, P., & Lin, Z. (2020). Artificial Intelligence in Education: A Review. *IEEE Access : Practical Innovations, Open Solutions*, *8*, 75264–75278.

Chetry, K. K. (2024). Transforming education: How AI is revolutionizing the learning experience. *International Journal of Research Publication and Reviews*, *5*(5), 6352–6356. DOI: 10.55248/gengpi.5.0524.1277

Chiang, F.-K., Shang, X., & Qiao, L. (2021). Augmented reality in vocational training: A systematic review of research and applications. *Computers in Human Behavior*, *129*, 107125. DOI: 10.1016/j.chb.2021.107125

Childs, E., Mohammad, F., Stevens, L., Burbelo, H., Awoke, A., Rewkowski, N., & Manocha, D. (2023). An overview of enhancing distance learning through emerging augmented and virtual reality technologies. *IEEE Transactions on Visualization and Computer Graphics*. PMID: 37037228

Chimbunde, P., & Moreeng, B. B. (2024). The Sustainability of Curriculum Reform and Implementation Through Teacher Participation. *Evidence from Social Studies Teachers*, *6*(1), 83–98.

China National Academy of Educational Sciences. (2024). Practical Cases of Smart Education in China: Data-Driven Curriculum and Research Innovation in Higher Education and Vocational Education. In *Report on China Smart Education 2023. Research in Chinese Education*. Springer., DOI: 10.1007/978-981-97-5090-0_5

Chinta, S. V., Wang, Z., Yin, Z., Hoang, N., Gonzalez, M., Quy, T. L., & Zhang, W. (2024). FairAIED: Navigating fairness, bias, and ethics in educational AI applications. arXiv preprint arXiv:2407.18745.

Chiu, T. K., Moorhouse, B. L., Chai, C. S., & Ismailov, M. (2023). Teacher support and student motivation to learn with Artificial Intelligence (AI) based chatbot. *Interactive Learning Environments*.

Choffin, B., Popineau, F., Bourda, Y., & Vie, J. J. (2019). DAS3H: Modeling student learning and forgetting for optimally scheduling distributed practice of skills. *arXiv preprint arXiv:1905.06873*. https://doi.org//arXiv.1905.06873DOI: 10.48550

Chounta, I. A. (2020). Collaborative learning and patterns of practice. In *Encyclopedia of Education and Information Technologies* (pp. 310–323). Springer International Publishing., DOI: 10.1007/978-3-030-10576-1_83

Chun, M., Choi, J., Kim, S., Ahn, C., & Kim, J. (2022). Fully automated image quality evaluation on patient CT: Multi-vendor and multi-reconstruction study. *PLoS One*, *17*(7), e0271724. DOI: 10.1371/journal.pone.0271724 PMID: 35857804

Chu, Y., Huang, R., Chen, T., Lin, W., Tang, J. T., Lin, C.-W., Huang, C.-H., Lin, C.-Y., Chen, J.-S., Kurtz-Rossi, S., & Sørensen, K. (2022). Effect of health literacy and shared decision-making on choice of weight-loss plan among overweight or obese participants receiving a prototype artificial intelligence robot intervention facilitating weight-loss management decisions. *Digital Health*, *8*, 205520762211363. DOI: 10.1177/20552076221136372 PMID: 36353693

Çıldır, M. (2023). Collaborating with ChatGPT: An exploratory study on german language teaching. *Journal of German Language and Culture Studies*, *5*(2).

Çınar Yağcı, Ş., & Aydın Yıldız, T. (2023). Is ChatGPT a reliable artificial intelligence chat buddy of a foreign language learner? *RumeliDE Journal of Language and Literature Studies*, (37), 1315–1333. DOI: 10.29000/rumelide.1407539

Clauser, B. E., Yaneva, V., Baldwin, P., An Ha, L., & Mee, J. (2024). Automated Scoring of Short-Answer Questions: A Progress Report. *Applied Measurement in Education, 37*(3), 209–224. DOI: 10.1080/08957347.2024.2386945

Cojorn, K., & Sonsupap, K. (2024). A collaborative professional development and its impact on teachers' ability to foster higher-order thinking. [EduLearn]. *Journal of Education and Learning, 18*(2), 561–569. DOI: 10.11591/edulearn.v18i2.21182

Collegenp. (2025). The future of vocational education: Emerging trends and technologies. https://www.collegenp.com/article/the-future-of-vocational-education-emerging-trends-and-technologies

Collins, A., & Halverson, R. (2018). *Rethinking education in the age of technology: The digital revolution and school in America*. Teachers College Press.

Collinson, V., Kozina, E., Lin, Y.-H. K., Ling, L., Matheson, I., Newcombe, L., & Zogla, I. (2009). Professional development for teachers: A world of change. *European Journal of Teacher Education, 32*(1), 3–19.

Colombi, C., & Casciani, D. (2021). Fashion-Tech Alliance: Innovating professional digital competences and skills in the Fashion Industry. In INTED2021 Proceedings (pp. 7842-7852). IATED.

Columbia Center for Teaching and Learning. (2020). Creating Assignments and Grading Online with Gradescope. Columbia University. https://ctl.columbia.edu/resources-and-technology/teaching-with-technology/teaching-online/gradescope/

Conlon, J., & Gallery, C. (2024). Developing digital skills: A fashion business masterclass in virtual 3D prototyping with Style3D. *International Journal of Fashion Design, Technology and Education, 17*(1), 76–85.

Connell, R. (2019). *The good university: What universities actually do and why it's time for radical change*. Bloomsbury Publishing.

Connery, A. K., Raghunathan, R. S., Colbert, A. M., Erdodi, L., Warschausky, S., Huth-Bocks, A., Gerry Taylor, H., Raghunathan, T., Berglund, P., Staples, A. D., Lukomski, A., Kirkland, J., Cano, J., & Lajiness-O'Neill, R. (2023). The influence of sociodemographic factors and response style on caregiver report of infant developmental status. *Frontiers in Pediatrics, 10*(2022). DOI: 10.3389/fped.2022.1080163

Cooperman, S. R., & Brandão, R. A. (2024). AI tools vs AI text: Detecting AI-generated writing in foot and ankle surgery. *Foot & Ankle Surgery: Techniques, Reports, &. Cases*, *4*(1). DOI: 10.1016/j.fastrc.2024.100367

Cope, B., Kalantzis, M., & Searsmith, D. (2021). Artificial intelligence for education: Knowledge and its assessment in AI-enabled learning ecologies. *Educational Philosophy and Theory*, *53*(12), 1229–1245.

Cordero, J., Torres-Zambrano, J., & Cordero-Castillo, A. (2024). Integration of Generative Artificial Intelligence in Higher Education: Best Practices. *Education Sciences*, *15*(1), 32. DOI: 10.3390/educsci15010032

Crabtree-Ireland, D. (2025, January 21). *Labour leaders: Artificial intelligence must serve human creativity, not replace it*. World Economic Forum. https://www.weforum.org/stories/2025/01/artificial-intelligence-must-serve-human-creativity-not-replace-it/

Cuban, L. (1986). *Teachers and Machines: The Classroom Use of Technology Since 1920*. Teachers College Press. [ISBN: 9780807727928]

Cugini, U., Bordegoni, M., & Mana, R. (2008). The role of virtual prototyping and simulation in the fashion sector. [IJIDeM]. *International Journal on Interactive Design and Manufacturing*, *2*, 33–38.

Cummings, C., Mason, D., Shelton, K., & Bauer, K. (2014). Active learning assessment strategies for online and blended learning environments. In Keengwe, S., & Agamba, J. J. (Eds.), *Models for improving and optimizing online and blended learning in higher education* (pp. 58–82). IGI-Global Publishing., DOI: 10.4018/978-1-4666-6280-3.ch004

D'Amico, S., Giustiniano, L., Nenni, M. E., & Pirolo, L. (2013). Product Lifecycle Management as a tool to create value in the fashion system. *International Journal of Engineering Business Management*, *5*, 33.

Dai, L. (2011, July). The 3D digital technology of fashion design. In 2011 international symposium on computer science and society (pp. 178-180). IEEE.

Daish, P., Micallef, N., Lorenzo-Dus, N., Paiement, A., & Sahoo, D.R. (2024). Towards co-designing a continuous-learning human-AI interface: A case study in online grooming detection. *SYNERGY@AVI*.

Dakka, S. M. (2015, September). Using Socrative to enhance in-class student engagement and collaboration. *International Journal of Integrating Technology in Education*, *4*(3), 13–19.

Damaševičius, R. (2024). Commentary: ChatGPT-supported student assessment – Can we rely on it? *Journal of Research in Innovative Teaching & Learning*, *17*(2), 414–416. DOI: 10.1108/JRIT-09-2024-195

Damaševičius, R., & Sidekerskiene, T. (2024). AI as a teacher: A new educational dynamic for modern classrooms for personalized learning support. In Ahmed, Z., Hassan, A., & Saeed, R. (Eds.), *AI-enhanced teaching methods* (pp. 1–24). IGI Global Scientific Publishing., DOI: 10.4018/979-8-3693-2728-9.ch001

Das, S., Mutsuddi, I., & Ray, N. (2025). *Artificial Intelligence in Adaptive Education.*, DOI: 10.4018/979-8-3693-8227-1.ch002

Daviet, B. (2016). Revisiting the Principle of Education as a Public Good. *United Nations Educational, Scientific and Cultural Organization (UNESCO), 17.*

Davoodi, A. (2024). EQUAL AI: A Framework for Enhancing Equity, Quality, Understanding and Accessibility in Liberal Arts through AI for Multilingual Learners. *Language, Technology, and Social Media*, *2*(2), 178–203.

De la Vall, R. R. F., & Araya, F. G. (2023). Exploring the benefits and challenges of AI-language learning tools. *International Journal of Social Sciences and Humanities Invention*, *10*(01), 7569–7576.

Deci, E. L., & Ryan, R. M. (2000). The" what" and" why" of goal pursuits: Human needs and the self-determination of behavior. *Psychological Inquiry*, *11*(4), 227–268. DOI: 10.1207/S15327965PLI1104_01

DeCoito, I., & Estaiteyeh, M. (2022). Online teaching during the covid-19 pandemic: Exploring science/stem teachers' curriculum and assessment practices in Canada. *Disciplinary and Interdisciplinary Science Education Research*, *4*(8). DOI: 10.1186/s43031-022-00048-z PMID: 37520635

Deep, S., Athimoolam, K., & Enoch, T. (2024). Optimizing administrative efficiency and student engagement in education: The impact of ai. *International Journal of Current Science Research and Review*, *7*(10), 7792–7804. DOI: 10.47191/ijcsrr/v7-i10-34

Degago, A. T., & Kaino, L. M. (2015). Towards student-centered conceptions of teaching: The case of four Ethiopian universities. *Teaching in Higher Education*, *20*, 493–505. DOI: 10.1080/13562517.2015.1020779

Delello, J. A., Watters, J. B., & Garcia-Lopez, A. (2024). *Artificial Intelligence in Education.*, DOI: 10.4018/979-8-3693-3003-6.ch001

Deloitte. (n.d.). Development of AI-based education in China. Retrieved January 18, 2025, from https://www2.deloitte.com/cn/en/pages/technology-media-and-telecommunications/articles/development-of-ai-based-education-in-china.htm

Demartini, C. G., Sciascia, L., Bosso, A., & Manuri, F. (2024). Artificial intelligence bringing improvements to adaptive learning in education: A case study. *Sustainability*, *16*(3), 1347. DOI: 10.3390/su16031347

Deterding, S., Dixon, D., Khaled, R., & Nacke, L. (2011, September). From game design elements to gamefulness: defining" gamification". In *Proceedings of the 15th international academic MindTrek conference: Envisioning future media environments* (pp. 9-15).

Dey, D. N. C. (2024). Enhancing Educational Tools Through Artificial Intelligence in Perspective of Need of AI. *Available at SSRN* 5031275. DOI: 10.2139/ssrn.5031275

Dilobarkhon, K. (2019). The importance of modern innovation in education. *European Journal of Research and Reflection in Educational Sciences Vol, 7*(12).

Dimitriadou, E., & Lanitis, A. (2023). A critical evaluation, challenges, and future perspectives of using artificial intelligence and emerging technologies in smart classrooms. *Smart Learn. Environ., 10*, 12. DOI: 10.1186/s40561-023-00231-3 PMID: 40478141

Dockens, A. L. (2023). Promoting authenticity of student work in the age of artificial intelligence: A faculty guide. Lamar University Center for Teaching and Learning Enhancement. https://www.lamar.edu/lu-online/_files/documents/blog/ai-faculty-guide.pdf

Dockens, A., & Shelton, K. (2025). The AI Scholar: AI in Higher Education Research and Writing. In Wang, V. (Ed.), *AI integration into andragogical education* (pp. 109–136). IGI Global., https://www.igi-global.com/book/integration-into-andragogical-education/359630, DOI: 10.4018/979-8-3373-0502-8

Donoghue, F. (2018). *The Last Professors: The Corporate University and the Fate of the Humanities*. Fordham University Press.

Drakou, A., Papachristou, E., Tarnanidis, T., & Bilalis, N. (2024). Transforming Fashion Education: The Impact of AI-Driven 3D Design on Learning, Creativity, and Sustainability. *Proceedings of the 13th Hellenic Conference on Artificial Intelligence*, 1–6. https://doi.org/DOI: 10.1145/3688671.3688794

DreamBox Learning. (2023). [https://www.dreambox.com/] About DreamBox Learning.

Dumbuya, E. (2024). Personalized learning through artificial intelligence: Revolutionizing education. *International Journal of Science and Research Archive*.

Dunbar, K., & Yadav, A. (2022). Shifting to student-centered learning: Influences of teaching a summer service learning program. *Teaching and Teacher Education, 110*, 103578. DOI: 10.1016/j.tate.2021.103578

Duterte, J. P. (2024). The Impact of Educational Gamification on Student Learning Outcomes. *International Journal of Research and Innovation in Social Science, 8*(10), 477–487. DOI: 10.47772/IJRISS.2024.8100040

Dutta, S., He, M., & Tsang, D. C. (2023). Reflection and peer assessment to promote self-directed learning in higher education. *Journal of Educational Research and Reviews, 11*(3), 35–46. DOI: 10.33495/jerrv11i3.23.111

Dweck, C. S. (2006). *Mindset: The new psychology of success*. Random House.

Dwivedi, Y. K., Hughes, L., Ismagilova, E., Aarts, G., Coombs, C., Crick, T., & Williams, M. D. (2021). Artificial Intelligence (AI): Multidisciplinary perspectives on emerging challenges, opportunities, and agenda for research, practice and policy. *International Journal of Information Management, 57*, 101994.

Eden, C. A., Chisom, O. N., & Adeniyi, I. S. (2024). Integrating AI in education: Opportunities, challenges, and ethical considerations. *Magna Scientia Advanced Research and Reviews, 10*(2). Advance online publication. DOI: 10.30574/msarr.2024.10.2.0039

Egunjobi, D., & Adeyeye, O. J. (2024). Revolutionizing Learning: The Impact of Augmented Reality (AR) and Artificial Intelligence (AI on Education). *ResearchGate*, (Oct). Advance online publication. DOI: 10.55248/gengpi.5.1024.2734

Ejjami, R. (2024). AI's impact on vocational training and employability: Innovation, challenges, and perspectives. [IJFMR]. *International Journal for Multidisciplinary Research, 6*(4), 1–16.

El Hajj, M., & Harb, H. (2023). Rethinking Education: An In-Depth Examination of Modern Technologies and Pedagogic Recommendations. *IAFOR Journal of Education, 11*(2), 97–113.

Elaiess, R. (2024). Academic integrity in the age of artificial intelligence: Exploring ethical challenges in a digital era. *International Journal of Academic Multidisciplinary Research, 8*(11), 12–15. http://www.ijeais.org/ijamr/

Ellikkal, A., & Rajamohan, S. (2024). AI-enabled personalized learning: Empowering management students for improving engagement and academic performance. *Vilakshan - XIMB. Journal of Management.* DOI: 10.1108/XJM-02-2024-0023

Ellikkal, A., & Rajamohan, S. (2024). *AI-enabled personalized learning: empowering management students for improving engagement and academic performance.* Vilakshan-XIMB Journal of Management.

English, R., & Maguire, J. (2020). Experiences of assessment in data and security courses using personal response systems. *Proceedings of the 2020 9th International Conference on Educational and Information Technology*, 38-43. DOI: 10.1145/3383923.3383963

Erişti, S. D. B., & Freedman, K. (2024). Integrating Digital Technologies and AI in Art Education: Pedagogical Competencies and the Evolution of Digital Visual Culture. *Participatory Educational Research, 11*(Prof. Dr. H. Ferhan Odabaşı Gift Issue), 57-79.

Ermer, C. (2018). Implementing sustainable thinking and acting into design-and textile education—A holistic and interdisciplinary learning model. Trends in Textile Engineering, 1(2).

Esomonu, N. P. M. (2025) Utilizing AI and Big Data for Predictive Insights on Institutional Performance and Student Success: A Data-Driven Approach to Quality Assurance. *AI and Ethics, Academic Integrity and the Future of Quality Assurance in Higher Education*, 29.

ETS. (2023). Education and tech leaders come together to offer guidance on integrating AI safely into classrooms worldwide. https://www.ets.org/news/press-releases/education-and-tech-leaders-come-together-to-offer-guidance-on-integrating-ai-safely-into-classrooms-worldwide.html

Eugene, M., Montes-Rivera, J., & White, B. (2023). Education research: Perspectives and experiences of clinical neurology faculty regarding the end-of-rotation assessment: A qualitative study. *Neurology. Education*, *2*(4). DOI: 10.1212/ne9.0000000000200104 PMID: 39359322

European Commission. (2021). AI and education: Guidance for policymakers. https://school-education.ec.europa.eu/en/discover/publications/ai-and-education-guidance-policymakers

Evangelidis, V., Theodoropoulou, H. G., Katsouros, V., & Kiourt, C. (2024). AI-Enabled Art Education: Unleashing Creative Potential and Exploring Co-Creation Frontiers. In *CSEDU (2)* (pp. 294-301).

Faculty of Computing and Information Technology. King Abdulaziz University, Jeddah, Saudi Arabia, Alshahrani, K., & Jameel Qureshi, R. (2024). Review the Prospects and Obstacles of AIEnhanced Learning Environments: The Role ofChatGPT in Education. *International Journal of Modern Education and Computer Science, 16*(4), 71–86. https://doi.org/DOI: 10.5815/ijmecs.2024.04.06

Faerm, S. (2012). Towards a future pedagogy: The evolution of fashion design education. *International Journal of Humanities and Social Science*, *2*(23), 210–219.

Faerm, S. (2014). From classroom to design room: The transitional experience of the fashion design graduate. *Cuadernos del Centro de Estudios en Diseño y Comunicación. Ensayos*, (48), 129–152.

Fahyuni, E., Taurusta, C., Hariastuti, R., & Arifin, M. (2022). Improving students learning strategy trough mobile counselling online application. *Journal of Educational and Social Research*, *12*(5), 185. DOI: 10.36941/jesr-2022-0133

Fahyuni, E., Taurusta, C., Hariastuti, R., Bandono, A., & Muhid, A. (2021). Mobile counselling online an alternative counselling guidance system for millennial era student. *Journal of Education Technology*, *5*(3), 425–433. DOI: 10.23887/jet.v5i3.36191

Falasi, M. (2024). Innovative pedagogies: A comparative analysis of traditional and modern teaching methods. *Academy of Educational Leadership Journal*, *28*(1), 1–2.

Familoni, B. T., & Onyebuchi, N. C. (2024). Augmented and virtual reality in our education: a review: analyzing the Impact, effectiveness, and future prospects of ar/vr tools in enhancing learning experiences. *International Journal of Applied Research in Social Sciences*, *6*(4), 642–663. DOI: 10.51594/ijarss.v6i4.1043

Fan, Y., Tang, L., Le, H., Shen, K., Tan, S., Zhao, Y., Shen, Y., Li, X., & Gašević, D. (2025). Beware of metacognitive laziness: Effects of generative artificial intelligence on learning motivation, processes, and performance. *British Journal of Educational Technology*, *56*, 489–530. DOI: 10.1111/bjet.13544

Farahani, M. S., & Ghasmi, G. (2024). *Artificial intelligence in education: A comprehensive study*. Forum for Education Studies.

Feng, L., Close, E. W., Luxford, C. J., Pierson, J. A., Olmstead, A., Shim, J., & Galloway, H. C. (2025). Transforming Undergraduate STEM Education: The Learning Assistant Model and Student Retention and Graduation Rates. *Research in Higher Education*, *66*(1), 1–26.

Ferguson, K., & Aitken, R. (2019). A large-scale project to develop personalized learning pathways at a university. *Online Journal of Distance Learning Administration*, 22.

Ferguson, R. (2012). Learning Analytics: Drivers, Developments and Challenges. *International Journal of Technology Enhanced Learning*, *4*(5-6), 304–317.

Feroz, H. M. B., Zulfiqar, S., Noor, S., & Huo, C. (2022). Examining multiple engagements and their Impact on students' knowledge acquisition: The moderating role of information overload. *Journal of Applied Research in Higher Education*, *14*(1), 366–393. DOI: 10.1108/JARHE-11-2020-0422

Figaredo, D. D., & Stoyanovich, J. (2023). Responsible AI literacy: A stakeholder-first approach. *Big Data & Society*, •••, 1.

Flodén, J. (2024). Grading exams using large language models: A comparison between human and ai grading of exams in higher education using Chatgpt. *British Educational Research Journal*, *51*(1), 201–224. DOI: 10.1002/berj.4069

Flores-Viva, J. M., & García-Peñalvo, F. J. (2023). Reflections on the Ethics, Potential, and Challenges of Artificial Intelligence in the Framework of Quality Education (SDG4). *Comunicar: Media Education Research Journal*, *31*(74), 35–44.

Fortino, A. (2023, November 2). *Embracing creativity: How AI can enhance the creative process*. NYU School of Professional Studies. https://www.sps.nyu.edu/homepage/emerging-technologies-collaborative/blog/2023/embracing-creativity-how-ai-can-enhance-the-creative-process.html

Fox, J. (2016). Using Portfolios for Assessment/Alternative Assessment. In Shohamy, E., Or, I., & May, S. (Eds.), *Language Testing and Assessment. Encyclopedia of Language and Education*. Springer., DOI: 10.1007/978-3-319-02326-7_9-1

Freedman, K., & Hernández-Hernández, F. (Eds.). (2024). *Curriculum, culture, and art education: Comparative perspectives*. Suny Press.

Fryer, L., & Carpenter, R. (2006). Bots as anguage learning tools. *Language Learning & Technology*, *10*(3), 8–14.

Gade, K. R. (2021). Data-driven decision making in a complex world. *Journal of Computational Innovation*, *1*(1).

Gaftandzhieva, S., Hussain, S., Hilcenko, S., Doneva, R., & Boykova, K. (2023). Data-driven decision making in higher education institutions: State-of-play. *International Journal of Advanced Computer Science and Applications*, *14*(6).

Galli, G., Carabotti, M., Pilozzi, E., Lahner, E., Annibale, B., & Conti, L. (2021). Relationship between persistent gastrointestinal symptoms and duodenal histological findings after adequate gluten-free diet: A gray area of celiac disease management in adult patients. *Nutrients*, *13*(2), 600. DOI: 10.3390/nu13020600 PMID: 33673062

Gandhi, S., Ahmed, M. S., Huang, L., Behl, A., & Manrai, A. K. (2025). AI's Impact on academic research integrity: Guidelines from the editors of Journal of Global Marketing. *Journal of Global Marketing, 1-4*. Advance online publication. DOI: 10.1080/08911762.2025.2488060

Gan, Z., An, Z., & Liu, F. (2021). Teacher feedback practices, student feedback motivation, and feedback behavior: How are they associated with learning outcomes? *Frontiers in Psychology*, *12*, 697045. DOI: 10.3389/fpsyg.2021.697045 PMID: 34234729

García, F. P., Cánovas, Ó., & Clemente, F. J. G. (2024). Exploring AI Techniques for Generalizable Teaching Practice Identification. *IEEE Access, PP*, (99), 1–1.

Garcia, R., Treude, C., & Valentine, A. (2024, March). Application of Collaborative Learning Paradigms within Software Engineering Education: A Systematic Mapping Study. *In Proceedings of the 55th ACM Technical Symposium on Computer Science Education* V. 1 (pp. 366-372).DOI: 10.1145/3626252.3630780

Gardner, H. (1983). *Frames of Mind: The Theory of Multiple Intelligences.,* Published by Basic Books, A Member of the Perseus Books Group.

Gardner, P. (2024). Loosening the straps on the neoliberal strait-jacket subjugating educational research. *Issues in Educational Research*, *34*(1), xi–xiv.

Garg, A., Babu, B. V., & Balas, V. E. (2024). *Advances in Technological Innovations in Higher Education*. CRC Press., DOI: 10.1201/9781003376699

Gasser, R.B. (2024). Neoliberalism in academia: Reflections from a parasitologist. *Gasser Parasites & Vectors, 17.*

Gentile, M., Città, G., Perna, S., & Allegra, M. (2023, March). Do we still need teachers? Navigating the paradigm shift of the teacher's role in the AI era. *In Frontiers in Education* (Vol. 8, p. 1161777). Frontiers Media SA. DOI: 10.3389/feduc.2023.1161777

Georgia State University. (2023). Pounce Chatbot. [https://news.gsu.edu/2022/03/21/classroom-chatbot-improves-student-performance-study-says/],

Giray, M., & Kim, V. (2023). Spiral progression approach in teaching science in the k-12 curriculum. *International Journal of Research Publication and Reviews, 4*(8), 1363–1378. DOI: 10.55248/gengpi.4.823.50813

Giroux, H. A. (2019). *Public Scholarship, Public Intellectuals, and the Role of Higher Education in a Time of Crisis*. The Oxford Handbook of Methods for Public Scholarship.

Glerup, C., Davies, S. R., & Horst, M. (2017). Nothing really responsible goes on here: Scientists' experience and practice responsibility. *Journal of Responsible Innovation*, *4*(3), 319–336.

Gligorea, I., Cioca, M., Oancea, R., Gorski, A., Gorski, H., & Tudorache, P. (2023). Adaptive learning using artificial intelligence in e-learning: A literature review. *Education Sciences*, *13*(12), 1216. DOI: 10.3390/educsci13121216

Gligorea, I., Yaseen, M., Cioca, M., Gorski, H., & Oancea, R. (2022). An interpretable framework for an efficient analysis of students' academic performance. *Sustainability*, *14*(14), 8885. DOI: 10.3390/su14148885

Global Educational Studies Review. (2020). In Global Educational. *Studies and Reviews (General Fisheries Commission for the Mediterranean)*. DOI: 10.31703/gesr

Goel, A. K., & Joyner, D. A. (2017). Using AI to teach AI: Lessons from an online AI class. *AI Magazine*, *38*(2), 48–59.

González-Calatayud, V., Prendes-Espinosa, P., & Roig-Vila, R. (2021). Artificial intelligence for student assessment: A systematic review. *Applied Sciences (Basel, Switzerland)*, *11*(12), 5467.

Gonzalez-Nucamendi, A., Noguez, J., Neri, L., Robledo-Rella, V., & García-Castelán, R. M. G. (2023, October). Predictive analytics study to determine undergraduate students at risk of dropout. *In Frontiers in Education (Vol. 8*, p. 1244686). Frontiers Media SA. DOI: 10.3389/feduc.2023.1244686

Gouseti, A., James, F., Fallin, L., & Burden, K. (2025). The ethics of using AI in K-12 education: A systematic literature review. *Technology, Pedagogy and Education*, *34*(2), 161–182. DOI: 10.1080/1475939x.2024.2428601

Goyal, P., Minz, N. K., & Sha, A. (2023). *Chatbots and virtual assistants in education: Enhancing student support and engagement.*

Gr, G. (1992). One moment, please. *PubMed*, *82*(1), 37. https://pubmed.ncbi.nlm.nih.gov/1499783

Grenander, M., Belfer, R., Kochmar, E., Serban, I. V., St-Hilaire, F., & Cheung, J. C. (2021, May). Deep discourse analysis for generating personalized feedback in intelligent tutor systems. *In Proceedings of the AAAI Conference on Artificial Intelligence* (Vol. 35, No. 17, pp. 15534-15544). DOI: 10.48550/arXiv.2103.07785

Grimes, D. A., & Schulz, K. F. (2002). Descriptive studies: What they can and cannot do. *Lancet, 359*(9301), 145–149. PMID: 11809274

Grit Daily. (2025). The role of AI education in global workforce development. https://gritdaily.com/role-of-ai-education-in-global-workforce-development/

Grubaugh, S., & Levitt, G. (2023). Artificial intelligence and the paradigm shift: Reshaping education to equip students for future careers. *International Journal of Social Sciences and Humanities Invention, 10*(6), 7931–7941. DOI: 10.18535/ijsshi/v10i06.02

Gumport, P. J. (2019). *Academic fault lines: The rise of industry logic in public higher education*. Johns Hopkins University Press.

Gupta, P., Sreelatha, C., Latha, A., Raj, S., & Singh, A. (2024). Navigating the future of education: The impact of artificial intelligence on teacher-student dynamics. *EATP, 30*(4), 6006–6013. DOI: 10.53555/kuey.v30i4.2332

Gupta, R. K., & Gadikar, A. (2024). *Evaluating and enhancing user interaction in AI-driven educational tools: A comparative study of machine learning algorithms and design principles*. Computer Science, Engineering and Technology.

Gupta, Y. (2024). Innovation In Education: Traditional To Modern. [IJCRT]. *International Journal of Creative Research Thoughts., 12*(1), d792–d796.

Guzmán, E., & Millan, E. (2024). Evaluating the performance of copula-based item response theory models for interpretable assessment. *Proceedings of the ICCE 2024: The 32nd International Conference on Computers in Education*. https://doi.org/DOI: 10.58459/icce.2024.4811

Hakimi, M., Shahidzay, A., Fazi, A., & Qarizada, A. (2024). Empirical assessment of ICT impact on teaching and learning in high schools: A study in the context of Balkh, Afghanistan. *Eiki Journal of Effective Teaching Methods, 2*(1). DOI: 10.59652/jetm.v2i1.96

Halaweh, M. (2023). Chatgpt in education: Strategies for responsible implementation. *Contemporary Educational Technology, 15*(2), ep421. DOI: 10.30935/cedtech/13036

Hamdi, M. (2024). How AI is Transforming and Shaping the Future of Education. *2024 IEEE 28th International Conference on Intelligent Engineering Systems (INES)*, 000115-000116.

Han, B., Coghlan, S., Buchanan, G., & McKay, D. (2025). Who is Helping Whom? Student Concerns about AI-Teacher Collaboration in Higher Education Classrooms. *Proceedings of the ACM on Human-Computer Interaction*, *9*(2), 1–32. DOI: 10.48550/arxiv.2412.14469

Hardaker, G., & Glenn, L. E. (2025a). Artificial intelligence for personalized learning: A systematic literature review. *The International Journal of Information and Learning Technology*, *42*(1), 1–14. DOI: 10.1108/IJILT-07-2024-0160

Hardiyanti, E., Fitriani, V., & Ashari, W. (2023). The Influence of Digital Tools on Student Engagement and Academic Outcomes Across Educational Levels. *Education Journal*, *1*(2), 59–68.

Haristiani, N. (2019, November). Artificial Intelligence (AI) chatbot as language learning medium: An inquiry. [). IOP Publishing.]. *Journal of Physics: Conference Series*, *1387*(1), 012020.

Harlen, W. (2007). *Assessment of Learning*. SAGE Publications.

Harris, D. (2022). Promoting Critical Thinking Skills through Inquiry-Based Learning. *Frontiers of Educational Review*, *4*(1), 28. DOI: 10.69610/j.fer.20220413

Harry, A. (2023). Role of AI in Education. [INJURITY]. *Interdisciplinary Journal & Humanity*, *2*(3). DOI: 10.58631/injurity.v2i3.52

Hattie, J., & Timperley, H. (2007). The Power of Feedback. *Review of Educational Research*, *77*(1), 81–112.

Hattie, J., & Timperley, H. (2007). The power of feedback. *Review of Educational Research*, *77*(1), 81–112. DOI: 10.3102/003465430298487

Heritage, M. (2007). Formative assessment: What do teachers need to know and do? *Phi Delta Kappan*, *89*(2), 140–145. DOI: 10.1177/003172170708900210

Herod, L. (2012). "Adult learning: from theory to practice," available at: http://en.copian.ca/library/learning/adult_learning/adult_learning.pdf

Heston, T., & Khun, C. (2023). Prompt engineering in medical education. *International Medical Education*, *2*(3), 198–205. DOI: 10.3390/ime2030019

Hillman, D. C. A., Willis, D. J., & Gunawardena, C. N. (1994). Learner-interface interaction in distance education: An extension of contemporary models and strategies for practitioners. *American Journal of Distance Education*, *8*(2), 30–42.

Hirsch, A. (2024, December 12). AI detectors: An ethical minefield. Center for Innovative Teaching and Learning - Northern Illinois University. https://citl.news.niu.edu/2024/12/12/ai-detectors-an-ethical-minefield/

Hirschberg, J., & Manning, C. D. (2015). Advances in Natural Language Processing. *Science*, *349*(6245), 261–266. PMID: 26185244

Hockly, N. (2023). Artificial intelligence in English language teaching: The good, the bad and the ugly. *RELC Journal*, *54*(2), 445–451.

Hogenhout, L. (2021). A framework for ethical AI at the United Nations. *ArXiv, abs/2104.12547.*

Holdsworth, S., Turner, M., & Scott-Young, C. M. (2019). Developing the resilient learner: A resilience framework for universities. In *Transformations in Tertiary Education: The Scholarship of Engagement at RMIT University* (pp. 27–42). Springer Singapore., DOI: 10.1007/978-981-13-9957-2_3

Holeman, I., & Kane, D. (2020). Human-centered design for global health equity. *Information Technology for Development*, *26*(3). DOI: 10.1080/02681102.2019.1667289 PMID: 32982007

Hollingsworth, H. (2023). *Conservatives take aim at tenure for university professors*. AP NEWS. https://apnews.com/article/politics-colleges-and universities-florida-state-government-texas-education-4f0fe0c5c18ed227fabae3744e8ff51d.

Holloway, K., & Herder, M. (2019). A responsibility to commercialize? Tracing academic researchers' evolving engagement with the commercialization of biomedical research. *Journal of Responsible Innovation*, *6*(3), 263–283.

Holmes, W., Porayska-Pomsta, K., Holstein, K., Sutherland, E., Baker, T., Shum, S. B., & Koedinger, K. R. (2022). Ethics of AI in education: Towards a community-wide framework. *International Journal of Artificial Intelligence in Education*, 1–23.

Holstei, K., Wortman Vaughan, J., Friedler, S. A., & Wallach, H. (2019). Improving fairness in machine learning systems: What do industry practitioners need? In *Proceedings of the 2019 ACM CHI Conference on Human Factors in Computing Systems*. 1-16. https://doi.org/DOI: 10.48550/arXiv.1812.05239

Holstein, K., McLaren, B. M., & Aleven, V. (2018). Student learning benefits of a mixed-reality teacher awareness tool in AI-enhanced classrooms. In Artificial Intelligence in Education: 19th International Conference, AIED 2018, London, UK, June 27–30, 2018 [Springer International Publishing.]. *Proceedings, 19*(Part I), 154–168.

Hooda, M., Rana, C., Dahiya, O., Rizwan, A., & Hossain, M. S. (2022). Artificial intelligence for assessment and feedback to enhance student success in higher education. *Mathematical Problems in Engineering, 2022*(1), 5215722.

Hossain, M., Anglin, M., Safi, A., Ahmed, T., & Khan, S. (2024). Adapting to the digital age: An evaluation of online learning strategies in public health and social care education. *Education Research International, 5079882*. DOI: 10.1155/2024/5079882

Huang, A. Y., Lu, O. H., & Yang, S. J. (2023). Effects of Artificial Intelligence—Enabled personalized recommendations on learners' learning engagement, motivation, and outcomes in a flipped classroom. *Computers & Education, 194*, 104684. DOI: 10.1016/j.compedu.2022.104684

Huang, L. (2023). Ethics of artificial intelligence in education: Student privacy and data protection. *Science Insights Education Frontiers, 16*(2), 2577–2587.

Huang, W., Hew, K. F., & Fryer, L. K. (2022). Chatbots for language learning-are they really useful? A systematic review of chatbot-supported language learning. *Journal of Computer Assisted Learning, 38*(1), 237–257.

Huong, X. V. (2024). The implications of artificial intelligence for educational systems: Challenges, opportunities, and transformative potential. *The American Journal of Social Science and Education Innovations, 6*(3). DOI: 10.37547/tajssei/Volume06Issue03-17

Hurix. (2024). Data privacy in education through FERPA and GDPR adherence. https://www.hurix.com/data-privacy-in-education-through-ferpa-and-gdpr-adherence/

Hussain, S. A. (2024). The integration of artificial intelligence in web accessibility: Enhancing inclusivity. *International Journal for Research in Applied Science and Engineering Technology, 12*(4).

Hutson, J. (2024). Integrating art and AI: Evaluating the educational impact of AI tools in digital art history learning. *Faculty Scholarship, 578*. Lindenwood University. https://digitalcommons.lindenwood.edu/faculty-research-papers/578

Hutson, J., & Cotroneo, P. (2023). Generative AI tools in art education: Exploring prompt engineering and iterative processes for enhanced creativity. *Metaverse, 4*(1), 14.

Hyun, J., Ediger, R., & Lee, D. (2017). Students' Satisfaction with Their Learning Process in Active Learning and Traditional Classrooms. *International Journal on Teaching and Learning in Higher Education*, *29*(1), 108–118.

Ibrahim, H., Asim, R., Zaffar, F., Rahwan, T., & Zaki, Y. (2023). Rethinking homework in the age of artificial intelligence. *IEEE Intelligent Systems*, *38*(2), 24–27.

Igbokwe, I. C. (2023). Application of artificial intelligence (AI) in educational management. *International Journal of Scientific and Research Publications*, *13*(3), 300.

Ikwuanusi, U. F., Azubuike, C. H. I. M. A., Odionu, C. S., & Sule, A. K. (2022). Leveraging AI to address resource allocation challenges in academic and research libraries. *Iconic Research and Engineering Journals*, *5*(10), 311.

Imran, M. C., Amaliah, N., Syam, N. I., Room, F., & Sage, M. S. D. (2023). The Feasibility of Artificial Intelligences (AI) In Speaking Skill: Lecturers' Perceptions. *IJOLEH: International Journal of Education and Humanities*, *2*(2), 135–144.

Indroes, G.M., Noviandy, T.R., Maulana, A., Irvanizam, I., Jalil, Z., Lensoni, L., Lala, A., Abas, A., Tallei, T., & Idroes, R. (2023). Student Perspectives on the Role of Artificial Intelligence in Education: A Survey-Based Analysis. *Journal of Educational Management and Learning*. DOI: .DOI: 10.60084/jeml.v1i1.58

Jain, N. (2025). AI as a catalyst for educational equity: Addressing global teacher shortages and learning disparities. *International Journal of Scientific Research in Computer Science*, *11*(1), 69–76. DOI: 10.32628/CSEIT25111200

Jali, V., Zhang, Q., Chong, J. R., Wong, D., Tan, B., Garhöfer, G., Hilal, S., Lai, M. K. P., Schmetterer, L., Chen, C. L.-H., & Chua, J. (2024). Diagnosis of cognitive impairment and dementia: Blood plasma and optical coherence tomography. *Brain Communications*, *7*(1), fcae472. Advance online publication. DOI: 10.1093/braincomms/fcae472 PMID: 39749011

Janah, K., & Anam, S. (2021). Investigating the implementation of classroom assessment by novice English teachers. *Jo-Elt (Journal of English Language Teaching). Fakultas Pendidikan Bahasa & Seni Prodi Pendidikan Bahasa Inggris Ikip*, *8*(2), 99. DOI: 10.33394/jo-elt.v8i2.3883

Jantanukul, W. (2024). AI and human synergy: Utilizing AI to enhance teaching and learning. *Journal of Education and Learning Reviews*.

Javvaji, V. R., & Raghavulu, P. V. (2024). The Transformative Impact of Artificial Intelligence on Education. *International Journal for Multidisciplinary Research*, *6*(4). Advance online publication. DOI: 10.36948/ijfmr.2024.v06i04.24987

Jeon, J. (2021). Exploring AI chatbot affordances in the EFL classroom: Young learners' experiences and perspectives. *Computer Assisted Language Learning*, 1–26.

Jeon, J., Lee, S., & Choe, H. (2022). Enhancing EFL pre-service teachers' affordance noticing and utilizing with the Synthesis of Qualitative Evidence strategies: An exploratory study of a customizable virtual environment platform. *Computers & Education*, *190*, 104620.

Jeon, M. J., & Kim, J. (2021). A Study on the Production of Real-Time Algorithmic Composition System Using the VQ-VAE Algorithm of OpenAI Jukebox. *Journal of Digital Contents Society*, *22*(3), 375–381.

Jeon, Y., Jin, S., Shih, P. C., & Han, K. (2021, May). FashionQ: an ai-driven creativity support tool for facilitating ideation in fashion design. In *Proceedings of the 2021 CHI Conference on Human Factors in Computing Systems* (pp. 1-18).

Jiang, H. (2023). Research on Innovation and Reform Strategy of Fine Arts Education in Colleges and Universities. *Journal of Humanities, Arts and Social Science, 7*(4).

Jian, M. J. K. O. (2023). Personalized learning through AI. *Advances in Engineering Innovation*, *5*, 16–19.

Ji, Y., Luo, X., & Chen, J. (2024). Operation and exploration of the international top talent innovation training program. *Communications in Humanities Research*, *63*(1), 95–102. DOI: 10.54254/2753-7064/63/20242532

Jonas, R., Earls, J., Marques, H., Chang, H.-J., Choi, J. H., Doh, J.-H., Her, A.-Y., Koo, B. K., Nam, C.-W., Park, H.-B., Shin, S., Cole, J., Gimelli, A., Khan, M. A., Lu, B., Gao, Y., Nabi, F., Nakazato, R., Schoepf, U. J., & Choi, A. D. (2021). Relationship of age, atherosclerosis and angiographic stenosis using artificial intelligence. *Open Heart*, *8*(2), e001832. DOI: 10.1136/openhrt-2021-001832 PMID: 34785589

Jony, M. S. (2016). Student-Centered Instruction for Interactive and Effective Teaching Learning: Perceptions of Teachers in Bangladesh. *Online Submission*, *3*(3), 172–178.

Jurafsky, D., & Martin, J. H. (2025). *Speech and language processing: An introduction to natural language processing, computational linguistics, and speech recognition with language models* (3rd ed.). Online manuscript released January 12, 2025. https://web.stanford.edu/~jurafsky/slp3

Jütte, L., González-Villà, S., Quintana, J., Steven, M., García, R., & Roth, B. (2024). Integrating generative ai with abcde rule analysis for enhanced skin cancer diagnosis, dermatologist training and patient education. *Frontiers in Medicine*, *11*. DOI: 10.3389/fmed.2024.1445318 PMID: 39421873

Kablitz, D., Conrad, M., & Schumann, S. (2023). Immersive VR-based instruction in vocational schools: Effects on domain-specific knowledge and wellbeing of retail trainees. *Empirical Research in Vocational Education and Training*, *15*, 9. DOI: 10.1186/s40461-023-00148-8

Kahoot! (n.d.). *Kahoot!* https://kahoot.com/

Kakungulu, S. J. (2024). The role of artificial intelligence in educational assessment. [EEJSAR]. *Eurasian Experiment Journal of Scientific and Applied Research*, *5*(2), 44–47.

Kalniņa, D., Nīmante, D., & Baranova, S. (2024). Artificial intelligence for higher education: Benefits and challenges for pre-service teachers. *Frontiers in Education*, *9*, 1501819. DOI: 10.3389/feduc.2024.1501819

Kamalov, F., Santandreu Calonge, D., & Gurrib, I. (2023). New era of artificial intelligence in education: Towards a sustainable multifaceted revolution. *Sustainability*, *15*(16), 12451.

Kaminskienė, L., Järvelä, S., & Lehtinen, E. (2022). How does technology challenge teacher education? *International Journal of Educational Technology in Higher Education*, *19*(1), 64. DOI: 10.1186/s41239-022-00375-1 PMID: 36591440

Kamysheva, E., Kulamikhina, I., & Samylova, O. (2021). Open innovation model of improving critical thinking competence in university students. In O. Kolmakova, O. Boginskaya, & S. Grichin (Eds.), *Language and technology in the interdisciplinary paradigm: Vol 118. European proceedings of social and behavioural sciences* (pp. 9-16). European Publisher. https://doi.org/DOI: 10.15405/epsbs.2021.12.2

Kannan, J., & Munday, P. (2018). New trends in second language learning and teaching through the lens of ICT, networked learning, and artificial intelligence. In Fernández Juncal, C., & Hernández Muñoz, N. (Eds.), *Vías de transformación en la enseñanza de lenguas con mediación tecnológica. Círculo de Lingüística Aplicada a la Comunicación, 76, 13-30.*, DOI: 10.5209/CLAC.62495

Kapp, K. (2012). *The gamification of learning and instruction: Game-based methods and strategies for training and education*. John Wiley & Sons.

Karadağ, Y., & Yalçın, S. (2023). The Impact of peer feedback on collaborative problem-solving skills in the online environment. *International Journal of Assessment Tools in Education*, *10*(3), 563–579. DOI: 10.21449/ijate.1290901

Karpouzis, K. (2024, September). Artificial Intelligence in Education: Ethical Considerations and Insights from Ancient Greek Philosophy. In *Proceedings of the 13th Hellenic Conference on Artificial Intelligence (pp.* 1-7*).* DOI: 10.1145/3688671.3688772

Karpov, N. (2020). *Artificial Intelligence for Music Composing: Future Scenario Analysis*. Can be accessed at https://urn.fi/URN:NBN:fi:amk-2020052012578

Katawazai, R. (2021). Implementing outcome-based education and student-centered learning in Afghan public universities: The current practices and challenges. *Heliyon*, *7*(5), e07076. DOI: 10.1016/j.heliyon.2021.e07076 PMID: 34095574

Katayama, A., Toss, M. S., Parkin, M., Sano, T., Oyama, T., Quinn, C. M., Ellis, I. O., & Rakha, E. A. (2021). Nuclear morphology in breast lesions: Refining its assessment to improve diagnostic concordance. *Histopathology*, *80*(3), 515–528. DOI: 10.1111/his.14577 PMID: 34605058

Kavitha, R. K., Krupa, C. R., & Kaarthiekheyan, V. (2025). AI-Powered Digital Solutions for Smart Learning: Revolutionizing Education. In *Cybersecurity and Data Science Innovations for Sustainable Development of HEICC* (pp. 213-227). CRC Press.

Kazimova, D., Tazhigulova, G., Shraimanova, G., Zatyneyko, A., & Sharzadin, A. (2025). Transforming university education with AI: A systematic review of technologies, applications, and implications. *International Journal of Engineering Pedagogy*, *15*, 4–24.

Kazlacheva, Z., Stoykova, V., Georgieva, K., & Ilieva, J. (2018, December). Application of innovative technologies in fashion design education. [). IOP Publishing.]. *IOP Conference Series. Materials Science and Engineering*, *459*(1), 012080.

Kazu, I. Y., Kazu, H., & Kuvvetli, M. (2022). Evaluation of language skill areas in digital game-based foreign language learning. *SSD Journal*, *7*(29), 117–127.

Ke, Z., & Ng, V. (2019). Automated essay scoring: A survey of the state of the art. *Proceedings of the Twenty-Eighth International Joint Conference on Artificial Intelligence*. https://www.ijcai.org/proceedings/2019/0879.pdf

Kerimbayev, N., Umirzakova, Z., Shadiev, R., & Jotsov, V. (2023). A student-centered approach using modern technologies in distance learning: A systematic review of the literature. *Smart Learning Environments*, *10*(1), 61. DOI: 10.1186/s40561-023-00280-8

Kerry, M., Volken, T., Biller-Andorno, N., Gläßel, A., & Melloh, M. (2023). A Swiss digital Delphi study on patient-reported outcomes. *Swiss Medical Weekly*, *153*(11), 40125. DOI: 10.57187/smw.2023.40125 PMID: 37988458

Khaldi, A., Bouzidi, R., & Nader, F. (2023). Gamification of e-learning in higher education: A systematic literature review. *Smart Learning Environments*, *10*(1), 10. PMID: 40478066

Khalid, M., Bashir, S., & Amin, H. (2020). Relationship between Self-Directed Learning (SDL) and Academic Achievement of University Students: A Case of Online Distance Learning and Traditional Universities. *Bulletin of Education and Research*, *42*(2), 131–148.

Khan Academy. [https://www.khanacademy.org/about]. [Accessed on 10th November, 2024]

Khare, K., Stewart, B., & Khare, A. (2018). *Artificial intelligence and the student experience: An institutional perspective.* IAFOR Journal of Education.

Khodayar, M., & Regan, J. (2023). Deep neural networks in power systems: A review. *Energies*, *16*(12), 4773. DOI: 10.3390/en16124773

Khoury, O. (2022). Perceptions of student-centered learning in online translator training: Findings from Jordan. *Heliyon*, *8*(6), e09644. DOI: 10.1016/j.heliyon.2022.e09644 PMID: 35756111

Kilag, O. K. (2024). Innovative Practices for 21st Century Education: The Future of Education Through Technology and Inclusivity. *International Multidisciplinary Journal of Research for Innovation, Sustainability, and Excellence (IMJRISE), 1*(12), 91-99. https://risejournals.org/index.php/imjrise/article/view/883

Kilkauer T. & Young M. (2021). Academentia: the organization insanity of the modern university. *Counterpunch, 28.*

Kim, B., Suh, H., Heo, J., & Choi, Y. (2020). AI-driven interface design for intelligent tutoring system improves student engagement. *ArXiv, abs/2009.08976.*

Kim, H. Y., Lampertico, P., Nam, J. Y., Lee, H. C., Kim, S. U., Sinn, D. H., & Lee, J. H. (2022). An artificial intelligence model to predict hepatocellular carcinoma risk in Korean and Caucasian patients with chronic hepatitis B. *Journal of Hepatology*, *76*(2), 311–318. PMID: 34606915

Kim, J., Lee, H., & Cho, Y. H. (2022). Learning design to support student-AI collaboration: Perspectives of leading teachers for AI in education. *Education and Information Technologies*, *27*(5), 6069–6104.

Kim, S., Park, K., Yoon, S., Choi, Y., Lee, S., & Choi, K. (2021). A brief online and offline (paper-and-pencil) screening tool for generalized anxiety disorder: The final phase in the development and validation of the mental health screening tool for anxiety disorders (MHS: A). *Frontiers in Psychology*, *12*. Advance online publication. DOI: 10.3389/fpsyg.2021.639366 PMID: 33692730

Kim, Y., & Lee, H. (2022). Falling in love with virtual reality art: A new perspective on 3D immersive virtual reality for future sustaining art consumption. *International Journal of Human-Computer Interaction, 38*(4), 371–382.

Kinnula, M., Iivari, N., Sharma, S., Eden, G., Turunen, M., Achuthan, K., Nedungadi, P., Avellan, T., Thankachan, B., & Tulaskar, R. (2021). Researchers' toolbox for the future: Understanding and designing accessible and inclusive artificial intelligence (AIAI). *Proceedings of the 24th International Academic Mindtrek Conference.*

Kiven, S., Wang, Y., Aich, A., Argueta, D. A., Lei, J., Sagi, V., Tennakoon, M., Bedros, S. J., Lambrecht, N., & Gupta, K. (2020). Spatiotemporal alterations in gait in humanized transgenic sickle mice. *Frontiers in Immunology, 11*. DOI: 10.3389/fimmu.2020.561947 PMID: 33178189

Klimova, B., Pikhart, M., & Kacetl, J. (2023). Ethical issues of the use of AI-driven mobile apps for education. *Frontiers in Public Health, 10*, 1118116. DOI: 10.3389/fpubh.2022.1118116 PMID: 36711343

Klinck-van der Merwe, R., & Goosen, L. (2024). *Artificial Intelligence Algorithms as a Precursor for Personalized Learning and Education.*, DOI: 10.4018/979-8-3693-4252-7.ch009

Kocaballi, A. B. (2023). *Conversational ai-powered design: Chatgpt as designer, user, and product.* arXiv preprint arXiv:2302.07406.

Köhler, T., & Drummer, J. (2018). Recent technological challenges in (vocational) education. Vocational Teacher Education in Central Asia: Developing Skills and Facilitating Success, 3-14.

Kohli, J. K. (2024). Impact of Artificial Intelligence on Fashion Education for Future Jobs. *Higher Education for the Future*, 23476311241284860.

Kohnke, S., & Zaugg, T. (2025). Artificial Intelligence: An Untapped Opportunity for Equity and Access in STEM Education. *Education Sciences, 15*(1), 68. DOI: 10.3390/educsci15010068

Kokku, R., Sundararajan, S. C., Dey, P., Sindhgatta, R., Nitta, S. V., & Sengupta, B. (2018). Augmenting classrooms with AI for personalized education. *2018 IEEE International Conference on Acoustics, Speech and Signal Processing (ICASSP).*

Kolb, A. Y., & Kolb, D. A. (2017). Experiential Learning Theory as a Guide for Experiential Educators in Higher Education. *Experiential Learning & Teaching in Higher Education, 1*(1), 1-38. Available at: https://nsuworks.nova.edu/elthe/vol1/iss1/7

Kolb, D., Boyatzis, R. E., & Mainemelis, C. (1999). "Experiential learning theory: previous research and new directions", available at: http://learningfromexperience.com/media/2010/08/experiential- learning-theory.pdf.

Kolb, D. (1984). *Experiential Learning Theory: Experience as a Source of Learning and Development*. Prentice-Hall.

Komalavalli, K., Hemalatha, R., & Dhanalakshmi, S. (2020). A survey of artificial intelligence in smart phones and its applications among the students of higher education in and around chennai city. *Shanlax International Journal of Education, 8*(3), 89–95.

Komatsu, H., Rappleye, J., & Silova, I. (2021). Student-centered learning and sustainability: Solution or problem? *Comparative Education Review, 65*(1), 6–33. DOI: 10.1086/711829

Kovalchuk, V., Maslich, S. V., Tkachenko, N., Shevchuk, S. S., & Shchypska, T. P. (2022). Vocational education in the context of modern problems and challenges. *Journal of Curriculum and Teaching, 8*(11), 329–338.

Kraiem, D. I. (2015). The Cost of Opportunity: Student Debt and Social Mobility. *Suffolk, 689.*

Kraszewski, S., Szczurek, W., Szymczak, J., Reguła, M., & Neubauer, K. (2021). Machine learning prediction model for inflammatory bowel disease based on laboratory markers. working model in a discovery cohort study. *Journal of Clinical Medicine, 10*(20), 4745. DOI: 10.3390/jcm10204745 PMID: 34682868

Kuleto, V., & Ilić, M., ManeaTonis, R., Živanović, Z., & Păun, D. (2022). K-12 modern schools in Serbia: Exploratory research regarding teachers' genuine knowledge and perception of ai-based opportunities and challenges in education. *Journal of Economic Development Environment and People, 11*(2), 5–15. DOI: 10.26458/jedep.v11i2.762

Kumar, M. K. (2016). Challenges of implementing student-centered strategies in classrooms. *International Research Journal of Engineering and Technology, 3*(2), 1224–1227.

Kushmar, L. V., Vornachev, A. O., Korobova, I. O., & Kaida, N. O. (2022). Artificial intelligence in language learning: What are we afraid of. *Arab World English Journal (AWEJ). Special Issue on CALL*, (8), 262–273.

Kwon, Y. M., Lee, Y. A., & Kim, S. J. (2017). Case study on 3D printing education in fashion design coursework. *Fashion and Textiles, 4*, 1–20.

Labidi, L., & Barhoumi, W. (2023). *The Evolving Role of the University Professor Navigating the Past and the Present*. Information Sciences Letters.

Lane, S. (2010). *Performance assessment: The state of the art. (SCOPE Student Performance Assessment Series)*. Stanford University, Stanford Center for Opportunity Policy in Education.

Lange, J. (2015). Rise of the digitized public intellectual: Death of the professor in the network neutral internet age. *Interchange*, *46*, 95–112.

Lantada, A. D. (2020). Engineering education 5.0: Continuously evolving engineering education.

Lata, P. (2024). Beyond Algorithms: Humanizing Artificial Intelligence for Personalized and Adaptive Learning. *International Journal of Innovative Research in Engineering and Management, 11*(5), 10-55524. Available at *SSRN*: https://ssrn.com/abstract=4987208

Latif, G., Alghazo, R., Pilotti, M. A., & Brahim, G. B. (2022). Identifying "at-risk" students: An AI-based prediction approach. *International Journal of Computing and Digital Systems*, *11*(1).

Latifi, S., Noroozi, O., & Talaee, E. (2023). Worked example or scripting? Fostering students' online argumentative peer feedback, essay writing and learning. *Interactive Learning Environments*, *31*(2), 655–669. DOI: 10.1080/10494820.2020.1799032

Le Glaz, A., Haralambous, Y., Kim-Dufor, D.-H., Lenca, P., Billot, R., Ryan, T. C., Marsh, J., DeVylder, J., Walter, M., Berrouiguet, S., & Lemey, C. (2021). Machine learning and natural language processing in mental health: Systematic review. *Journal of Medical Internet Research*, *23*(5), e15708. DOI: 10.2196/15708 PMID: 33944788

Leavy, S., O'Sullivan, B., & Siapera, E. (2020). Data, power and bias in artificial intelligence. *ArXiv, abs/2008.07341*.

Lee, D. C., & Chang, C. Y. (2024). Evaluating self-directed learning competencies in digital learning environments: A meta-analysis. *Education and Information Technologies*, 1–22. DOI: 10.1007/s10639-024-13083-2

Lee, J. (2022). Toward Sustainable Fashion Product Development: The use of 3D Virtual Prototyping Technologies in the Synchronous Remote Learning Classroom. *Journal of Educational Technology Systems*, *51*(2), 215–235. DOI: 10.1177/00472395221132305

Lee, J. L., Kim, R. J., & Park, S.-Y. (2020). Using technologies to prevent cheating in remote assessments during Covid-19 pandemic. *Journal of Dental Education, 85*(1), 1015–1017. DOI: 10.1002/jdd.12350 PMID: 32717106

Lee, N., & Suh, S. (2024). How Does Digital Technology Inspire Global Fashion Design Trends? Big Data Analysis on Design Elements. *Applied Sciences (Basel, Switzerland), 14*(13), 5693.

Lee, Y. K. (2021). Transformation of the innovative and sustainable supply chain with upcoming real-time fashion systems. *Sustainability, 13*(3), 1081.

Leiker, D., Gyllen, A. R., Eldesouky, I., & Cukurova, M. (2023). Generative AI for learning: Investigating the potential of learning videos with synthetic virtual Instructors. In N. Wang, G. Rebolledo-Mendez, & V. Dimitrova, (Eds.), *International Conference on Artificial Intelligence in Education*, Springer Nature Switzerland. https://arxiv.org/abs/2304.03784

Lemoine, P., Jenkins, W., & Richardson, M. (2017). Global higher education: Development and implications. *J Educ Dev., 1*, 58. DOI: 10. 20849/ jed.v1i1.253

Leon, C. D.Jr. (2024). Education and Artificial Intelligence: Revolutionizing Learning as a Unique Tandem. *Available at SSRN* 4721768. https://doi.org/DOI: 10.2139/ssrn.4721768

Leong, W. Y., Leong, Y. Z., & Leong, W. S. (2023). Virtual reality in education: Case studies and applications. *IET International Conference on Engineering Technologies and Applications (ICETA 2023)*, 186–187. https://doi.org/DOI: 10.1049/icp.2023.3332

Lewis, K., & Kuhfeld, M. (2024). *Recovery Still Elusive: 2023-24 Student Achievement Highlights Persistent Achievement Gaps and a Long Road Ahead. Brief.* NWEA.

Liando, N. V. F., & Tatipang, D. P. (2024). *Enlightened Minds: Navigating The Nexus Of Artificial Intelligence And Educational Modernization*. Penerbit Tahta Media.

Liang, W., Yuksekgonul, M., Mao, Y., Wu, E., & Zou, J. (2023). GPT detectors are biased against non-native English writers. *Patterns (New York, N.Y.), 4*(7), 100779. DOI: 10.1016/j.patter.2023.100779 PMID: 37521038

Lim, T., Gottipati, S., & Cheong, M. L. (2023). Ethical considerations for artificial intelligence in educational assessments. In Keengwe, J. (Ed.), *Creative AI tools and ethical implications in teaching and learning* (pp. 32–79). IGI Global Scientific Publishing., DOI: 10.4018/979-8-3693-0205-7.ch003

Lin, C. C., Huang, A. Y., & Lu, O. H. (2023). Artificial intelligence in intelligent tutoring systems toward sustainable education: A systematic review. *Smart Learning Environments*, *10*(1), 41. DOI: 10.1186/s40561-023-00260-y

Linnenbrink-Garcia; Patall, E.A., & Pekrun, R. (2016). Policy insights from the behavioral and brain sciences. *Sage (Atlanta, Ga.)*, *3*(2).

Liow, M. L. S. (2025). Artificial Intelligence Shaping the Future of Vocational Education and Training: Roles, Impacts, and Insights. In Transforming Vocational Education and Training Using AI (pp. 183-210). IGI Global Scientific Publishing.

Li, S. (2025). The impact of AI-driven music production software on the economics of the music industry. *Information Development*, 02666669241312170.

Litman, D., Strik, H., & Lim, G. S. (2018). Speech technologies and the assessment of second language speaking: Approaches, challenges, and opportunities. *Language Assessment Quarterly*, *15*(3), 294–309.

Liu, C., Hou, J., Tu, Y. F., Wang, Y., & Hwang, G. J. (2021). Incorporating a reflective thinking promoting mechanism into artificial intelligence-supported English writing environments. *Interactive Learning Environments*, *31*, 3340–3359. DOI: 10.1080/10494820.2021.1927115

Liu, X., Wang, X., Chen, D., & Zhang, H. (2023). Automatic quantitative coronary analysis based on deep learning. *Applied Sciences (Basel, Switzerland)*, *13*(5), 2975. DOI: 10.3390/app13052975

Liu, Y., & Sra, M. (2024, July). DanceGen: Supporting Choreography Ideation and Prototyping with Generative AI. In *Proceedings of the 2024 ACM Designing Interactive Systems Conference* (pp. 920-938).

Loewen, S., Isbell, D. R., & Sporn, Z. (2020). The effectiveness of app-based language instruction for developing receptive linguistic knowledge and oral communicative ability. *Foreign Language Annals*, *53*(2), 209–233.

Long, Y., Zhang, X., & Zeng, X. (2024). Application and effect analysis of virtual reality technology in vocational education practical training. *Education and Information Technologies*. DOI: 10.1007/s10639-024-13197-7

Lötsch, J., Kringel, D., & Ultsch, A. (2021). Explainable artificial intelligence (XAI) in biomedicine: Making ai decisions trustworthy for physicians and patients. *BioMedInformatics*, *2*(1), 1–17. DOI: 10.3390/biomedinformatics2010001

Lottu, O.A., Jacks, B. S., Aala, O. Ab., & Okafor, E.S. (2024). Towards a conceptual framework for ethical AI development in IT systems. *World Journal of Advanced Research and Reviews*.

Loyens, S. M., Van Meerten, J. E., Schaap, L., & Wijnia, L. (2023). Situating higher-order, critical, and critical-analytic thinking in problem-and project-based learning environments: A systematic review. *Educational Psychology Review*, *35*(2), 39. DOI: 10.1007/s10648-023-09757-x

Luckin, R., Holmes, W., Griffiths, M., & Forcier, L. B. (2016). *Intelligence unleashed: An argument for AI in education*. Pearson.

Luştrea, A., Dincă, M., Berge, T., Oniţiu, A., Thomassen, M., Craşovan, M., & Lucheş, D. (2024). The Digital Reflective Journal: A Self-Assessment Tool for Higher Education Students. In *Digital Assessment in Higher Education: Navigating and Researching Challenges and Opportunities* (pp. 259–283). Springer Nature Singapore., Singapore., DOI: 10.1007/978-981-97-6136-4_12

Ma, X. (2018). Towards human-engaged AI. *Proceedings of the Twenty-Seventh International Joint Conference on Artificial Intelligence* (IJCAI-18).

Madaio, M.A., Blodgett, S., Mayfield, E., & Dixon-Rom'an, E. (2021). Confronting structural inequities in AI for education. *ArXiv, abs/2105.08847*.

Madhavan, R., Kerr, J. A., Corcos, A. R., & Isaacoff, B. (2020). Toward trustworthy and responsible artificial intelligence policy development. *IEEE Intelligent Systems*, •••, 35.

Maemichi, T., Matsumoto, M., Meguriya, S., Furusho, A., Yamashita, T., Tsutsui, T., & Kumai, T. (2024). Effect of low-frequency acupuncture on muscle and fascia stiffness: Examination with or without intervention. *Frontiers in Rehabilitation Sciences*, *5*. DOI: 10.3389/fresc.2024.1324000 PMID: 39726565

Magallanes, E. (2023). Construction and validation of outcomes-based work text in calculus. *International Journal for Multidisciplinary Research*, *5*(5). DOI: 10.36948/ijfmr.2023.v05i05.5875

Mahdi, H., & Alkhateeb, A. (2025). Revolutionising essay evaluation. *International Journal of Computer-Assisted Language Learning and Teaching*, *15*(1), 1–19. DOI: 10.4018/ijcallt.368226

Mahmoud, C. F., & Sørensen, J. T. (2024). Artificial Intelligence in Personalized Learning with a Focus on Current Developments and Future Prospects. *Research and Advances in Education*, *3*(8), 25–31. DOI: 10.56397/rae.2024.08.04

Maisano, D. A., Carrera, G., Mastrogiacomo, L., & Franceschini, F. (2024). Remote STEM education in the post-pandemic period: Challenges from the perspective of students and faculty. *International Journal of Educational Technology in Higher Education, 21*(1), 64. DOI: 10.1186/s41239-024-00497-8

Ma, K., Zhang, Y., & Hui, B. (2024). How Does AI Affect College? The Impact of AI Usage in College Teaching on Students' Innovative Behavior and Well-Being. *Behavioral Sciences (Basel, Switzerland), 14*(12), 1223. DOI: 10.3390/bs14121223 PMID: 39767364

Malik, Z., Munir, A., & Lestari, L. A. (2024). Integrating Alternative Assessment with Differentiated Instruction: Insights from a University-Level Setting. *Loquen: English Studies Journal, 17*(2), 65–77.

Mambile, C., & Mwogosi, A. (2024). Transforming higher education in Tanzania: Unleashing the true potential of ai as a transformative learning tool. *Technological Sustainability, 4*(1), 51–76. DOI: 10.1108/techs-03-2024-0014

Mann, P. (2015). Market Logic in Higher Education: Rethinking with Sociological Imagination. *International Journal of Research in Finance and Marketing, 5*, 1–7.

Manu, A. (2024). *Transcending Imagination: Artificial Intelligence and the Future of Creativity*. CRC Press.

Manzo, D. S. H., Jiang, Y., Elyan, E., & Isaacs, J. (2024). Artificial Intelligence-Based Conversational Agents Used for Sustainable Fashion: Systematic Literature Review. *International Journal of Human-Computer Interaction*, 1–13.

Maphalala, M. C., & Ajani, O. A. (2025). Leveraging artificial intelligence as a learning tool in higher education. *Interdisciplinary Journal of Education Research, 7*(1), a01. DOI: 10.38140/ijer-2025.vol7.1.01

Mardiana, H. (2020). Lecturers' adaptability to technological change and its Impact on the teaching process. [Jurnal Pendidikan Indonesia]. *JPI, 9*(2), 275–289.

Marginson, S. (2016). *Higher education and the common good*. Melbourne University Publishing.

Marinko, I., Baužienė, Z., Daniels, N., Gołębiowski, A., Hughes, J., Kairienė, V., Knyviene, I., Krawczak, M., Maj, G. P., Marcinkiewicz-Marszałek, K., Marinko, J., Perkumienė, D., & Rees, A. (2022). Empowering teachers for a student-centered approach. Retrieved from https://ec.europa.eu/programmes/erasmus-plus/project-result-content/c55c65b9-7799-482e-b941cfe94b3f3924/2%20SCL%20RESEARCH%20IN%20ENGLISH.pdf

Markauskaite, L., Marrone, R.L., Poquet, O., Knight, S., Martínez-Maldonado, R., Howard, S., Tondeur, J., de Laat, M., Shum, S.B., Gašević, D., & Siemens, G. (2022). Rethinking the entwinement between artificial intelligence and human learning: What capabilities do learners need for a world with AI? *Computer and Education: Artificial Intelligence Journal, 3.*

Marku, E. (2023). *AI-Artifcial Intelligence and the Growth of the Creative Potential of Designers in the Fashion Industry.* INTERDISCIPLINARY JOURNAL OF ARCHITECTURE AND BUILT ENVIRONMENT.

Marmoah, S., Murwaningsih, T., Nurhasanah, F., Saddhono, K., Sutomo, A. D., & Legowo, B. (2024). An Integration of AI and Traditional Methodology in the Education Field in Order to transform the trends. *2024 4th International Conference on Advance Computing and Innovative Technologies in Engineering (ICACITE)*, 884-889.

Márquez, J., Lazcano, L., Bada, C., & Arroyo-Barrigüete, J. L. (2023). Class participation and feedback as enablers of student academic performance. *SAGE Open, 13*(2), 21582440231177298. DOI: 10.1177/21582440231177298

Martins, J., Cunha, J., Lopes, S., Moreira, T., & Rosário, P. (2022). School engagement in elementary school: A systematic review of 35 years of research. *Educational Psychology Review, 34*(2), 793–849.

Ma, T., Li, Y., Yuan, H., Li, F., Yang, S., Zhan, Y., & Mu, D. (2023). Reflection on the teaching of student-centered formative assessment in medical curricula: An investigation from the perspective of medical students. *BMC Medical Education, 23*(1), 141. DOI: 10.1186/s12909-023-04110-w PMID: 36864421

Mateo-Berganza Díaz, M. M., Lim, J. R., Cárdenas-Navia, I., & Elzey, K. (2022). *A World of Transformation: Moving from Degrees to Skills-Based Alternative Credentials.* IDB Publication.

Matias, A., & Zipitria, I. (2023). Promoting ethical uses in artificial intelligence applied to education. *International Conference on Intelligent Tutoring Systems.*

McFarlane, B. (2016). *Freedom to learn.* Routledge.

McGrath, C., Cerratto P., T., Juth, N., & Palmgren, P.J. (2023). University teachers' perceptions of responsibility and artificial intelligence in higher education - An experimental philosophical study. *Computer Educational Artificial Intelligence, 4.*

McHaney, R. (2023). *The new digital shoreline.* Routledge.

McLaren, B. M. (2003). Extensionally Defining Principles and Cases in Ethics: An AI Model. *Artificial Intelligence*, *150*(1–2), 145–181.

McLaren, B. M. (2006). Computational Models of Ethical Reasoning: Challenges, Initial Steps, and Future Directions. *IEEE Intelligent Systems*, *21*(4), 29–37.

McLaren, B. M., Adams, D. M., & Mayer, R. E. (2015). Delayed Learning Effects with Erroneous Examples: A Study of Learning Decimals with a Web-Based Tutor. *International Journal of Artificial Intelligence in Education*, *25*(4), 520–542.

McLaren, B. M., Adams, D. M., Mayer, R. E., & Forlizzi, J. (2017). A Computer-Based Game That Promotes Mathematics Learning More Than a Conventional Approach. *International Journal of Game-Based Learning*, *7*(1), 36–56.

McLaren, B. M., Scheuer, O., & Mikšátko, J. (2010). Supporting Collaborative Learning and E-Discussions Using Artificial Intelligence Techniques. *International Journal of Artificial Intelligence in Education*, *20*(1), 1–46.

McLaren, B. M., van Gog, T., Ganoe, C., Yaron, D., & Karabinos, M. (2015). Worked examples are more efficient for learning than high-assistance instructional software. In Artificial Intelligence in Education: 17th International Conference, AIED 2015, Madrid, Spain, June 22-26, 2015. [Springer International Publishing.]. *Proceedings*, *17*, 710–713.

McQuillan, H. (2020). Digital 3D design as a tool for augmenting zero-waste fashion design practice. *International Journal of Fashion Design, Technology and Education*, *13*(1), 89–100.

Mehdaoui, A. (2024). Unveiling Barriers and Challenges of AI Technology Integration in Education: Assessing Teachers' Perceptions, Readiness and Anticipated Resistance. *Futurity Education*, *4*(4), 95–108.

Mena-Guacas, A., Rodríguez, J., Trujillo, D., Galán, J., & Meneses, E. (2023). Collaborative learning and skill development for educational growth of artificial intelligence: A systematic review. *Contemporary Educational Technology*, *15*(3), ep428. DOI: 10.30935/cedtech/13123

Mendez, G., Ochoa, X., Chiluiza, K., & De Wever, B. (2014). Curricular design analysis: A data-driven perspective. *Journal of Learning Analytics*, *1*(3), 84–119.

Miller, W. (2024). Adapting to AI: Reimagining the Role of Assessment Professionals. Intersection: A Journal at the Intersection of Assessment and Learning, 5(4), 99-113.

Mimbus. (n.d.). Enhancing education: VR use cases for vocational training. https://blog.mimbus.com/en/enhancing-education-vr-use-cases-for-vocational-training

Mimoudi, A. (2024). AI, personalized education, and challenges. *International Conference on AI Research, 4*(1). https://doi.org/DOI: 10.34190/icair.4.1.3133

Mintz, B. (2021). Neoliberalism and the crisis in higher education: The cost of ideology. *American Journal of Economics and Sociology, 80*(1), 79–112.

Mishra, N., Ramanathan, M., Tulsulkar, G., & Magnenat-Thalmann, N. (2022). Uncanny valley for interactive social agents: An experimental study. *Virtual Real. Intell. Hardw., 4.*

Mitre, X., & Zeneli, M. (2024). Using AI to improve accessibility and inclusivity in higher education for students with disabilities. *21st International Conference on Information Technology Based Higher Education and Training (ITHET).*

Mladenović, R., Kalevski, K., Davidović, B., Janković, S., Todorović, V., & Vasovic, M. (2023). The role of artificial intelligence in the accurate diagnosis and treatment planning of non-syndromic supernumerary teeth: A case report in a six-year-old boy. *Children (Basel, Switzerland), 10*(5), 839. DOI: 10.3390/children10050839 PMID: 37238387

Mohammadi, Y., Malik, S., & Shibani, A. (2024). Students as collaborative partners. *ASCILITE 2024 Conference Companion Materials*, 125-126.DOI: 10.14742/apubs.2024.1196

Mohitha, M., Terlapu, P., Anusrilekha, B., Narendra, R., Shekar, P., Chaitanya, P., & Kumar, T. (2024). Streamlining text generation with ai powered prompt simplification strategies. In *Proceedings of the International Conference on Computational Innovations and Emerging Trends (ICCIET- 2024)* (pp. 160-169). Atlantis Press International BV. https://doi.org/DOI: 10.2991/978-94-6463-471-6_16

Mohiuddin Babu, M., Akter, S., Rahman, M., Billah, M. M., & Hack-Polay, D. (2024). The role of artificial intelligence in shaping the future of Agile fashion industry. *Production Planning and Control, 35*(15), 2084–2098.

Molina-Torres, G., Sandoval-Hernández, I., Ropero-Padilla, C., Rodriguez-Arrastia, M., Martínez-Cal, J., & Gónzalez-Sánchez, M. (2021). Escape room vs. traditional assessment in physiotherapy students' anxiety, stress and gaming experience: A comparative study. *International Journal of Environmental Research and Public Health, 18*(23), 12778. DOI: 10.3390/ijerph182312778 PMID: 34886502

Monib, W., Karimi, A., & Nijat, N. (2020). Effects of alternative assessment in EFL classroom: A systematic review. *American International Journal of Education and Linguistics Research, 3*(2), 7–18. DOI: 10.46545/aijelr.v3i2.195

Moore, M. G., & Kearsley, G. (2012). Distance Education: A Systems View of Online

Moore, M. (1973). Toward a theory of independent learning and teaching. *The Journal of Higher Education, 44*, 661–679.

Moore, M. G. (1983). The individual adult learner. In Tight, M. (Ed.), *Adult Learning and Education* (pp. 153–168). Croom Helm.

Moore, M. G. (1989). Editorial: Three types of interaction. *American Journal of Distance Education, 3*(2), 1–6.

Moore, M. G. (1993). Theory of transactional distance. In Keegan, D. (Ed.), *Theoretical principle of distance education* (pp. 22–38). Routledge.

Morris, E. M., & Bilich-Eric, L. (2017). A framework to support experiential learning and psychological flexibility in supervision: SHAPE. *Australian Psychologist, 52*(2), 104–113. DOI: 10.1111/ap.12267

Moskal, B. M., & Leydens, J. A. (2000). Scoring rubric development: Validity and reliability. *Practical Assessment, Research & Evaluation, 7*, 71–81.

Muganga, L., & Ssenkusu, P. (2019). Teacher-centered vs. student-centered: An examination of student teachers' perceptions about pedagogical practices at Uganda's Makerere University. *Cultural and Pedagogical Inquiry, 11*(2), 16–40.

Mukwada, G., Mazibuko, S., Moeletsi, M., & Robinson, G. (2021). Can famine be averted? A spatiotemporal assessment of the impact of climate change on food security in the Luvuvhu river catchment of South Africa. *Land (Basel), 10*(5), 527. DOI: 10.3390/land10050527

Mula-Falcón, J., Moya-Roselo, I., & Ruiz-Ariza, A. (2022). The active methodology of gamification to improve motivation and academic performance in an educational context: A meta-analysis. *Review of European Studies, 14*, 32. DOI: 10.5539/res.v14n2p32

Mulenga, R., & Shilongo, H. (2024). Hybrid and Blended Learning Models: Innovations, Challenges and Future Directions in Education. *Acta Pedagogia Asiana, 4*(1), 1–13. DOI: 10.53623/apga.v4i1.495

Munna, A. S., Alharahsheh, H., Ferrazza, A., & Pius, A. (Eds.). (2024). *Transforming Education for Personalized Learning*. IGI Global., DOI: 10.4018/979-8-3693-0868-4

Mutsuddi, I. (2024). *Ethical Considerations in the Intersection of AI and Environmental Science*., DOI: 10.4018/979-8-3693-6336-2.ch011

Myers, A. (2023). *AI-detectors biased against non-native English writers*. Stanford University: Human-Centered Artificial Intelligence. https://hai.stanford.edu/news/ai-detectors-biased-against-non-native-english-writers

Najar, A. S., Mitrovic, A., & McLaren, B. M. (2014). Adaptive support versus alternating worked examples and tutored problems: which leads to better learning? In User Modeling, Adaptation, and Personalization: 22nd International Conference, UMAP 2014, Aalborg, Denmark, July 7-11, 2014. [Springer International Publishing.]. *Proceedings*, *22*, 171–182.

Nakao, Y., Nishihara, T., Sasaki, R., Fukushima, M., Miuma, S., Miyaaki, H., Akazawa, Y., & Nakao, K. (2024). Investigation of deep learning model for predicting immune checkpoint inhibitor treatment efficacy on contrast-enhanced computed tomography images of hepatocellular carcinoma. *Scientific Reports*, *14*(1), 6576. DOI: 10.1038/s41598-024-57078-y PMID: 38503827

Narciss, S. (2008). Feedback strategies for adaptive tutoring systems. In Jonassen, D., Spector, M. J., Driscoll, M., Merrill, M. D., van Merrienboer, J., & Driscoll, M. P. (Eds.), *Handbook of research on educational communications and technology* (3rd ed., pp. 125–144). Taylor & Francis., DOI: 10.4324/9780203880869

Narne, S., Adedoja, T., Mohan, M., & Ayyalasomayajula, T. (2024). AI-Driven Decision Support Systems in Management: Enhancing Strategic Planning and Execution. *International Journal on Recent and Innovation Trends in Computing and Communication*, *12*(1), 268–276.

National Education Association. (2024, April). *Report of the NEA Task Force on Artificial Intelligence in Education.*

Nazaretsky, T., Ariely, M., Cukurova, M., & Alexandron, G. (2022). Teachers' trust in ai-powered educational technology and a professional development program to improve it. *British Journal of Educational Technology*, *53*(4), 914–931. DOI: 10.1111/bjet.13232

Nazaretsky, T., Cukurova, M., & Alexandron, G. (2021). An instrument for measuring teachers' trust in ai-based educational technology. Center for Open Science. https://doi.org/DOI: 10.35542/osf.io/bcjme

Nazim, M., Alzubi, A. A. F., & Fakih, A. (2024). Teachers' employment for student-centered pedagogy and assessment practices in the EFL classroom from students' perspective. [IJEMST]. *International Journal of Education in Mathematics, Science, and Technology*, *12*(3), 605–620. DOI: 10.46328/ijemst.4089

Negi, S., Mathur, A., Tripathy, S., Mehta, V., Snigdha, N. T., Adil, A. H., & Karobari, M. I. (2024). Artificial intelligence in dental caries diagnosis and detection: An umbrella review. *Clinical and Experimental Dental Research*, *10*(4). DOI: 10.1002/cre2.70004 PMID: 39206581

Neji, W., Boughattas, N., & Ziadi, F. (2023). EXPLORING NEW AI-BASED TECHNOLOGIES TO ENHANCE STUDENTS' MOTIVATION. *Issues in Informing Science & Information Technology*, *20*. DOI: 10.28945/5149

Newsela. (n.d.). *Formative*. https://www.formative.com/

Nguyen, A., Ngo, H. N., Hong, Y., Dang, B., & Nguyen, B. P. T. (2023). Ethical principles for artificial intelligence in education. *Education and Information Technologies*, *28*(4), 4221–4241. DOI: 10.1007/s10639-022-11316-w PMID: 36254344

Nguyen, T., Nguy n, M., & Tran, H. (2023). Artificial intelligent based teaching and learning approaches: A comprehensive review. *International Journal of Evaluation and Research in Education*, *12*(4), 2387. DOI: 10.11591/ijere.v12i4.26623

Niles, L. L., Sullivan, V., & Amiri, A. (2024). Emergency management simulation of an unexpected opioid overdose in a rural setting: An innovative use of drone technologies. *Simulation & Gaming*, *56*(1), 137–147. DOI: 10.1177/10468781241287852

Nishio, M., Ota, E., Matsuo, H., Matsunaga, T., Miyazaki, A., & Murakami, T. (2023). Usefulness of Pystan and Numpyro in Bayesian item response theory. Cold Spring Harbor Laboratory. DOI: 10.1101/2023.03.29.23287903

Nithideechaiwarachok, B., & Chano, J. (2024). Socio-Cultural and Social Constructivist Theories and Its Application in EFL Classroom for Thai Pre-Service Teachers: A Review for Further Research. *International Journal of Language Education*, *8*(3), 564–572. DOI: 10.26858/ijole.v8i3.66499

Noddings, N. (2005). 'Caring in education. The encyclopedia of pedagogy and informal education. https://infed.org/mobi/caring-in-education

Noia, E., Silvia, P. B., Mazzucotelli Salice, S., Carini, L., & Angeles, B. P. M. (2024). Digital, international, interdisciplinary learning: enhancing competences and changing mindsets about sustainability in fashion and food. Ciencias sociales en abierto, 1-14.

Norori, N., Hu, Q., Aellen, F., Faraci, F., & Tzovara, A. (2021). Addressing bias in big data and ai for health care: A call for open science. *Patterns (New York, N.Y.)*, *2*(10), 100347. DOI: 10.1016/j.patter.2021.100347 PMID: 34693373

Nwachukwu, B., Beck, E., Chapman, R., Chahla, J., Okoroha, K., & Nho, S. (2019). Preoperative performance of the PROMIS in patients undergoing hip arthroscopic surgery for Femoroacetabular Impingement Syndrome. *Orthopaedic Journal of Sports Medicine*, *7*(7). DOI: 10.1177/2325967119860079 PMID: 31384620

Nwaimo, C. S., Adegbola, A. E., & Adegbola, M. D. (2024). Data-driven strategies for enhancing user engagement in digital platforms. *International Journal of Management & Entrepreneurship Research, 6*(6). DOI: 10.51594/ijmer.v6i6.1170

O'Brien, W. D., Persinger, R., & Sahami, H. (2015). Integrating student-centered learning to promote critical thinking skills in the 21st-century classroom: A collaborative action research study thesis.

O'Neil, C. (2016). *Weapons of math destruction: How big data increases inequality and threatens democracy*. Crown.

Obermeyer, Z., Powers, B., Vogeli, C., & Mullainathan, S. (2019). Dissecting racial bias in an algorithm used to manage the health of populations. *Science, 366*, 447–453. DOI: 10.1126/science.aax2342 PMID: 31649194

Observer. (2024, September). How generative AI is transforming workforce development and corporate training.https://observer.com/2024/09/how-generative-ai-is-transforming-workforce-development-corporate-training/

OECD. (2019). *Artificial intelligence in society*. OECD Publishing., DOI: 10.1787/eedfee77-

Ojha, S., Mohapatra, S., Narendra, A., & Misra, I. (2023, October). From robots to books: An introduction to smart applications of AI in education (AIEd). In *The International Conference on Recent Innovations in Computing* (pp. 311-322). Singapore: Springer Nature Singapore. DOI: 10.48550/arxiv.2301.10026

Okeleke, P. A., Ajiga, D., Folorunsho, S. O., & Ezeigweneme, C. (2024). Predictive analytics for market trends using AI: A study in consumer behavior. *International Journal of Engineering Research Updates, 7*(1), 36–49.

Okokoyo, I. E., Nwaham, C. O., & Nwachukwu, O. G. (2024). Leveraging artificial intelligence for enhanced administrators decision making in educational institutions: A comprehensive exploration of applications, challenges, and opportunities. *NIU Journal of Educational Research, 10*(1), 63–72.

Okongo, R. B., Ngao, G., Rop, N. K., & Nyongesa, W. J. (2015). Effect of availability of teaching and learning resources on the implementation of inclusive education in pre-school centers in Nyamira North Sub-County, Nyamira County, Kenya. *Journal of Education and Practice, 6*(35), 132–141.

Omughelli, D., Gordon, N., & Al Jaber, T. (2024). Fairness, Bias, and Ethics in AI: Exploring the Factors Affecting Student Performance. *Journal of International Communication, 3*(2), 100–110.

Onesi-Ozigagun, O., Ololade, Y. J., Eyo-Udo, N. L., & Ogundipe, D. O. (2024). Revolutionizing education through AI: A comprehensive review of enhancing learning experiences. *International Journal of Applied Research in Social Sciences, 6*(4), 589–607. DOI: 10.51594/ijarss.v6i4.1011

Ong, M., Yasin, N., & Ibrahim, N. (2021). Immersive experience during covid-19: The mediator role of alternative assessment in online learning environment. *International Journal of Interactive Mobile Technologies, 15*(18), 16–32. DOI: 10.3991/ijim.v15i18.24541

OnlineEducation. (2024). Opportunities and guidelines for AI in education: Statistics.https://www.onlineeducation.com/features/opportunities-and-guidelines-for-ai-in-education-statistics

Open, A. I. (2023, January 31). New AI classifier for indicating AI-written text. OpenAI. https://openai.com/index/new-ai-classifier-for-indicating-ai-written-text/

Osborne, G., & Wilton, S. (2017). Professing in the Local Press: Professors and Public Responsibilities. *Journal of Community Engagement and Scholarship, 10*(1), 67–80. DOI: 10.54656/VGBZ5148

Owan, V., Abang, K., Idika, D., Etta, E., & Bassey, B. (2023). Exploring the potential of artificial intelligence tools in educational measurement and assessment. *Eurasia Journal of Mathematics, Science and Technology Education, 19*(8), em2307. DOI: 10.29333/ejmste/13428

Özdamlı, F., & Karagözlü, D. (2022). Online education during the pandemic: A systematic literature review. *International Journal of Emerging Technologies in Learning, 17*(16), 167–193. DOI: 10.3991/ijet.v17i16.32287

Page, E. B. (2003). Technology and the future of testing. *Educational Measurement: Issues and Practice, 22*(4), 23–29.

Pahi, K., Hawlader, S., Hicks, E., Zaman, A., & Phan, V. (2024). Enhancing active learning through collaboration between human teachers and generative AI. *Computers and Education Open, 6*, 100183. DOI: 10.1016/j.caeo.2024.100183

Paiva, J. C., Leal, J. P., & Figueira, Á. (2022). Automated assessment in computer science education: A state-of-the-art review. [TOCE]. *ACM Transactions on Computing Education, 22*(3), 1–40.

Panadero, E., Jonsson, A., Pinedo, L., & Fernández-Castilla, B. (2023). Effects of rubrics on academic performance, self-regulated learning, and self-efficacy: A meta-analytic review. *Educational Psychology Review, 35*(4), 113. DOI: 10.1007/s10648-023-09823-4

Pane, J. F., Steiner, E. D., Baird, M. D., Hamilton, L. S., & Pane, J. D. (2017). *Informing progress: Insights on personalized learning implementation and effects.* RAND Corporation. https://www.rand.org/pubs/research_reports/RR2042.html

Papahristou, E., & Bilalis, N. (2017). 3D virtual prototyping traces new avenues for fashion design and product development: A qualitative study. *Journal of Textile Science & Engineering*, *7*(2), 1–6.

Papamitsiou, Z. K., Pappas, I. O., Sharma, K., & Giannakos, M. N. (2020). Utilizing multimodal data through fsQCA to explain engagement in adaptive learning. *IEEE Transactions on Learning Technologies*, 13.

Pappalardo, G., Mineo, S., Caliò, D., & Bognandi, A. (2022). Evaluation of natural stone weathering in heritage building by infrared thermography. *Heritage*, *5*(3), 2594–2614. DOI: 10.3390/heritage5030135

Patel, S. (2025). 21 Ways AI in Education is Reshaping the Industry. https://vlinkinfo.com/blog/ai-in-education-industry/

Pedro, F., Subosa, M., Rivas, A., & Valverde, P. (2019). Artificial intelligence in education: Challenges and opportunities for sustainable development.

Pente, P., Adams, C., & Yuen, C. (2022). Artificial Intelligence, ethics, and art education in a posthuman world. In *Global media arts education: Mapping global perspectives of media arts in education* (pp. 197–211). Springer International Publishing.

Perkins, M., Furze, L., Roe, J., & MacVaugh, J. (2024). The Artificial Intelligence Assessment Scale (AIAS): A framework for ethical integration of generative AI in educational assessment. *Journal of University Teaching & Learning Practice*, *21*(6), 49–66. DOI: 10.53761/q3azde36

Petrovic, J. E. (2024). Toward a non-economistic understanding of higher education as a public and private good for the public good. *Educational Philosophy and Theory*. Advance online publication. DOI: 10.1080/00131857.2024.2412755

Phakamach, P., Senarith, P., & Wachirawongpaisarn, S. (2022). The metaverse in education: The future of immersive teaching & learning. *RICE Journal of Creative Entrepreneurship and Management* www. ricejournal. net, *3*(2), 75-88.

Phillips, P., Hahn, C., Fontana, P., Yates, A., Greene, K., Broniatowski, D., & Przybocki, M. (2021). *Four principles of explainable artificial intelligence.* National Institute of Standards and Technology, U.S. Department of Commerce., DOI: 10.6028/nist.ir.8312

Pitta, J. P. (2023). AI in Art & Creativity. *The Spicerian*, *72*(2), 3–7.

Platonova, R. I., Orekhovskaya, N. A., Dautova, S. B., Martynenko, E. V., Kryukova, N. I., & Demir, S. (2022, July). Blended learning in higher education: Diversifying models and practical recommendations for researchers. *In Frontiers in education* (Vol. 7, p. 957199). Frontiers Media SA. https://doi.org/DOI: 10.3389/feduc.2022.957199

Poleneni, S., & Chandrupatla, M. (2023). Importance of online self-assisted assessments for medical students in knowledge acquisition. *Journal of Education and Health Promotion*, *12*(1). Advance online publication. DOI: 10.4103/jehp.jehp_342_22 PMID: 37288417

Ponomarioviené, J., Jakavonytė-Staškuvienė, D., & Torterat, F. (2025). Implementing Competency-Based Education Through the Personalized Monitoring of Primary Students' Progress and Assessment. *Education Sciences*, *15*(2), 252. DOI: 10.3390/educsci15020252

Poonpon, K., Manorom, P., & Chansanam, W. (2023). Exploring effective methods for automated essay scoring of non-native speakers. *Contemporary Educational Technology*, *15*(4), ep475.

Popenici, S. A., & Kerr, S. (2017). Exploring the impact of artificial intelligence on teaching and learning in higher education. *Research and Practice in Technology Enhanced Learning*. PMID: 30595727

Pratama, M. P., Sampelolo, R., & Lura, H. (2023). Revolutionizing education: harnessing the power of artificial intelligence for personalized learning. Klasikal: Journal of education, language teaching and science, 5(2), 350-357.

Pratomo, A., Santoso, J., Nugroho, A., Fildansyah, R., & Vandika, A. (2024). Analysis of data privacy policy, data processing ethics, and technology ethics awareness on user privacy protection in west java. *West Science Social and Humanities Studies*, *2*(03), 412–422. DOI: 10.58812/wsshs.v2i03.715

PRO EDU. (2024, November 22). *Collaborating with AI: Co-creative processes in art revolutionize artistic expression*. PRO EDU. https://proedu.com/blogs/photoshop-skills/collaborating-with-ai-co-creative-processes-in-art-revolutionize-artistic-expression

Qiu, Y., Pan, J., & Ishak, N. A. (2022). [Retracted] Effectiveness of Artificial Intelligence (AI) in Improving Pupils' Deep Learning in Primary School Mathematics Teaching in Fujian Province. *Computational Intelligence and Neuroscience*, *2022*(1), 1362996. DOI: 10.1155/2022/1362996 PMID: 36193186

Qorbani, M. (2020). *Humanity in the Age of AI: How to Thrive in a Post-Human World*. Bloomsberry.

Qu, H., Tang, H., Gao, D., Li, Y., Zhao, Y., Ban, Q., Chen, Y.-C., Lu, L., & Wang, W. (2024). Target-based deep learning network surveillance of non-contrast computed tomography for small infarct core of acute ischemic stroke. *Frontiers in Neurology, 15*. DOI: 10.3389/fneur.2024.1477811 PMID: 39364421

Quizizz. (n.d.). *Quizizz*. https://quizizz.com/

Ragolane, M., Patel, S., & Salikram, P. (2024). Ai versus human graders: Assessing the role of large language models in higher education. *Asian Journal of Education and Social Studies*, *50*(10), 244–263. DOI: 10.9734/ajess/2024/v50i101616

Rahiman, H. U., & Kodikal, R. (2024). Revolutionizing education: Artificial intelligence empowered learning in higher education. *Cogent Education, 11*(1). Advance online publication. DOI: 10.1080/2331186X.2023.2293431

Rajiani, I., Arisanty, D., & Riana, I. (2024). Social media: The new frontier for human resource management in Asia. *Human Behavior and Emerging Technologies, 2024*, 1–13. DOI: 10.1155/2024/6664626

Rajkumar, A., & Sindhu, H. (2024). Reimagining education – exploring the factors influencing perception towards artificial intelligence and its educational outcome. *Journal of Informatics Education and Research*, *4*(1). DOI: 10.52783/jier.v4i1.579

Rakya, Z. H. (2023). Exploring the impact of artificial intelligence (AI) on learner-instructor interaction in online learning (literature review). *International Journal of Emerging Multidisciplinary: Computer Science & Artificial Intelligence*, *2*(1), 1–14. DOI: 10.54938/ijemdcsai.2023.02.1.236

Ram, D., & Bhandari (2023). CHATGPT and AI Tools: A Paradigm Shift in Education and Other Domains. *Pravaha*.

Ramdhani, A. W. F., & Susanti, A. (2024). Pemanfaatan Teknologi Openai Dall-E 2 dalam Meningkatkan Kreativitas Desainer Grafis pada Komunitas Desain Grafis Indonesia. *Jurnal Bisnis Dan Komunikasi Digital*, *1*(2), 8–8.

Ramesh, D., & Sanampudi, S. (2021). An automated essay scoring systems: A systematic literature review. *Artificial Intelligence Review*, *55*(3), 2495–2527. DOI: 10.1007/s10462-021-10068-2 PMID: 34584325

Rane, N. L., Choudhary, S. P., & Rane, J. (2023). Education 4.0 and 5.0: Integrating artificial intelligence (AI) for personalized and adaptive learning. *Social Science Research Network (*SSRN*) Electronic Journal.*

Rangavittal, B. P. (2024). Transforming Higher Education with Artificial Intelligence - Benefits, Challenges, and Future Directions. [IJSR]. *International Journal of Scientific Research.*

Rattanayium, F., Asrori, A., & Rusman, R. (2023). Critical incident strategy: Improving motivation and learning outcomes of Islamic education students in Pattanakarnsuksa school Songkhla Thailand. *Al-Ulum Jurnal Pemikiran Dan Penelitian Ke Islaman, 10*(2), 140–153. DOI: 10.31102/alulum.10.2.2023.140-153

Ravaglia, R. (2024, December 26). AI agents will shape every aspect of education in 2025. Forbes. https://www.forbes.com/sites/rayravaglia/2024/12/26/ai-agents-will-shape-every-aspect-of-education-in-2025/

Ravindran, A., Killingsworth, M., & Bhaskar, S. (2020). Cerebral collaterals in acute ischaemia: Implications for acute ischaemic stroke patients receiving reperfusion therapy. *The European Journal of Neuroscience*, *53*(4), 1238–1261. DOI: 10.1111/ejn.14955 PMID: 32871623

Reekie, M., de Bosch Kemper, N., Epp, S., Denison, J., Willson, M., & Moralejo, L. (2023). Learning pathways: Levelling, scaffolding & mapping curriculum. *Journal of Professional Nursing*, 46. PMID: 37188406

Renkema, M., & Tursunbayeva, A. (2024). The future of work of academics in the age of Artificial Intelligence: State-of-the-art and a research roadmap. *Futures*, *163*, 103453.

Richardson, J. W., & Khawaja, S. (2025, February). Meta-synthesis of school leadership competencies to support learner-centered, personalized education. *In Frontiers in Education* (Vol. 10, p. 1537055). Frontiers Media SA. https://doi.org/ DOI: 10.3389/feduc.2025.1537055

Ridler, S. J. (2020). The designer perspective: Opportunities and Obstacles toward circular fashion.

Rincon-Flores, E. G., Santos-Guevara, B. N., Martinez-Cardiel, L., Rodriguez-Rodriguez, N. K., Quintana-Cruz, H. A., & Matsuura-Sonoda, A. (2023). Gamit! Icing on the Cake for Mathematics Gamification. *Sustainability*, *15*(3), 2334. DOI: 10.3390/su15032334

Rissanen, T. (2017). Possibility in fashion design education—A manifesto. *Utopian Studies*, *28*(3), 528–546.

Ritzhaupt, A. D., Huang, R., Sommer, M., Zhu, J., Stephen, A., Valle, N., & Li, J. (2021). A meta-analysis on the influence of gamification in formal educational settings on affective and behavioral outcomes. *Educational Technology Research and Development, 69*(5), 2493–2522. DOI: 10.1007/s11423-021-10036-1

Rizvi, S., Waite, J., & Sentance, S. (2023). Artificial Intelligence teaching and learning in K-12 from 2019 to 2022: A systematic literature review. *Computers and Education: Artificial Intelligence, 4*, 100145. DOI: 10.1016/j.caeai.2023.100145

Rizzi, G., & Vandi, A. (2023). ARTIFICIAL INTELLIGENCE IN FASHION DESIGN EDUCATION: REDEFINING CREATIVE PROCESSES TOWARDS DESIGNER-AI CO-CREATION. In ICERI2023 Proceedings (pp. 3905-3912). IATED.

Robert, A. (2024a). *Your ai tutor: Personalized learning paths and 24/7 support.* EasyC-hair. Sanal lise öğretmeni 3d—Google Play'de Uygulamalar.

Robert, A. (2024b). *Investigating the Effectiveness of AI Tutors in Developing Personalized Learning Paths for Students* (No. 13031). EasyChair.

Robert, A., Potter, K., & Frank, L. (2024). The impact of artificial intelligence on students' learning experience. *Wiley Interdisciplinary Reviews: Computational Statistics, 2*(01). DOI: 10.2139/ssrn.4716747

Robert, P. (2019). *Performativity, Big Data and Higher Education: The Death of the Professor?* Beijing International Review of Education.

Rocky Mountain College of Art + Design. (2024, December 23). *The future of art education: Exciting possibilities for teaching art with technology*. RMCAD. https://www.rmcad.edu/blog/the-future-of-art-education-exciting-possibilities-for-teaching-art-with-technology/

Rodríguez-Gómez, F., Monferrer, D., Penon, O., & Gil, P. (2025). Regulatory pathways and guidelines for nanotechnology-enabled health products: A comparative review of EUand US frameworks. *Frontiers in Medicine, 12*. DOI: 10.3389/fmed.2025.1544393 PMID: 40109724

Rodriguez, H. C., Rust, B., Hansen, P. Y., Maffulli, N., Gupta, M., Potty, A. G., & Gupta, A. (2023). Artificial intelligence and machine learning in rotator cuff tears. *Sports Medicine and Arthroscopy Review, 31*(3), 67–72. DOI: 10.1097/jsa.0000000000000371 PMID: 37976127

Rodriguez, N. M., Burleson, G., Linnes, J. C., & Sienko, K. H. (2023). Thinking beyond the device: An overview of human and equity-centered approaches for health technology design. *Annual Review of Biomedical Engineering*. DOI: 10.1146/annurev-bioeng-081922-024834 PMID: 37068765

Romero, M., Heiser, L., Lepage, A., Gagnebien, A., Bonjour, A., Lagarrigue, A., . . . Borgne, Y. A. L. (2023). Teaching and learning in the age of artificial intelligence. *arXiv preprint arXiv:2303.06956.*

Rona-Tas, A. (2020). Predicting the future: Art and algorithms. *Socio-economic Review, 18*(3), 893–911.

Rosenberg, R. (2023). The impact of artificial intelligence on society. *International Research Journal of Modernization in Engineering Technology and Science, 5*(10), 3120–3125. DOI: 10.56726/irjmets45708

Roshanaei, M., Olivares, H., & Lopez, R. R. (2023). Harnessing AI to Foster Equity in Education: Opportunities, Challenges, and Emerging Strategies. *Journal of Intelligent Learning Systems and Applications, 15*, 123–143.

Roshanaei, M., Olivares, H., & Lopez, R. R. (2023). Harnessing AI to foster equity in education: Opportunities, challenges, and emerging strategies. *Journal of Intelligent Learning Systems and Applications, 15*, 123–143. DOI: 10.4236/jilsa.2023.154009

Rosunally, Y. Z. (2024). Harnessing generative AI for educational gamification: A framework and practical guide for educators. 2024 21st International Conference on Information Technology Based Higher Education and Training (ITHET), 1–8. DOI: 10.1109/ITHET61869.2024.10837655

Rudolph, J., Tan, S., & Tan, S. (2023). ChatGPT: Bullshit spewer or the end of traditional assessments in higher education? *Ed-tech Reviews, 6*(1). DOI: 10.37074/jalt.2023.6.1.9

Ruijuan, L., Srikhoa, S., & Jantharajit, N. (2023). Blending of Collaborative and Active Learning Instructional Methods to Improve Academic Performance and Self-Motivation of Vocational Students. *Asian journal of education and training, 9*(4), 130-135. DOI: 10.20448/edu.v9i4.5211

Rutner, S. M., & Scott, R. A. (2022). Use of artificial intelligence to grade student discussion boards: An exploratory study. *Information Systems Education Journal, 20*(4), 4–13.

Saaida, M. B. E. (2023). AI-driven transformations in higher education: Opportunities and challenges. *International Journal of Educational Research and Studies, 5*(1), 29–36.

Sadler, D. R. (1998). Formative assessment: Revisiting the territory. *Assessment in Education: Principles, Policy & Practice*, *5*(1), 77–84.

Sadri, H., & Fraser, N. (2023). The role of innovative technologies in reducing health system inequity. *Healthcare Management Forum*, *37*(2), 101–107. DOI: 10.1177/08404704231207509 PMID: 37861228

Sáez-Velasco, S., Alaguero-Rodríguez, M., Delgado-Benito, V., & Rodríguez-Cano, S. (2024). Analysing the Impact of Generative AI in Arts Education: A Cross-Disciplinary Perspective of Educators and Students in Higher Education. *Informatics (MDPI)*, *11*(2), 37. DOI: 10.3390/informatics11020037

Safdar, D. S., Kamran, D. F., & Anis, D. F. (2024). *Beyond accommodation artificial intelligence's role in reimagining inclusive classrooms*. Indus Journal of Social Sciences.

Saffari, M., & Khodayar, M. (2024). *Spatiotemporal deep learning for power system applications: a survey*. IEEE., DOI: 10.1109/access.2024.3424854

Sailer, M., Hense, J. U., Mayr, S. K., & Mandl, H. (2017). How gamification motivates: An experimental study of the effects of specific game design elements on psychological need satisfaction. *Computers in Human Behavior*, *69*, 371–380.

Sa, K., Lang, D., Wang, C., & Bai, Y. (2020). Specific emitter identification techniques for the internet of things. *IEEE Access : Practical Innovations, Open Solutions*, *8*, 1644–1652. DOI: 10.1109/access.2019.2962626

Salendab, F. A. (2023). Proposed Instructional Scheme in the New Normal Education: Basis for Pedagogical Strategies/Practices. *Psychology and Education: A Multidisciplinary Journal*, *6*(8), 1-1.

Salendab, F. A., & Dapitan, Y. C. (2021). Performance of Private Higher Education Institutions and the School Heads' Supervision in South Central Mindanao. *Psychology and Education*, *58*(3), 3980–3997.

Sallam, M. (2023). ChatGPT utility in healthcare education, research, and practice: Systematic review on the promising perspectives and valid concerns. *Health Care*, *11*(6), 887. DOI: 10.3390/healthcare11060887 PMID: 36981544

Samala, A. D., Rawas, S., Criollo-C, S., Bojic, L., Prasetya, F., Ranuharja, F., & Marta, R. (2024). Emerging technologies for global education: A comprehensive exploration of trends, innovations, challenges, and future horizons. *SN Computer Science*, *5*(8), 1–24. DOI: 10.1007/s42979-024-03538-1

Sánchez-López, I., Bonilla-del-Río, M., & Soares, I. D. O. (2021). Digital Creativity to Transform Learning: Empowerment from a Com-Educational Approach. *Comunicar: Media Education Research Journal*, *29*(69), 105–114.

Sánchez-López, M., Violero-Mellado, J., Martínez-Vizcaíno, V., Laukkanen, A., Sääkslahti, A., & Visier-Alfonso, M. E. (2025). Impact and Perceptions of Active Learning Classrooms on reducing sedentary behavior and improving physical and mental Health and Academic indicators in children and Adolescents: A scoping Review. *PLoS One*, *20*(2), e0317973. DOI: 10.1371/journal.pone.0317973 PMID: 39908255

Sandhu, D. S. (1994). Cultural Diversity in Classrooms: What Teachers Need To Know.

Sandipa, B., Mitratne, D., Isurika, M., Kandanaarachchi, D., Rathnayaka, S., & Tissera, W. (2023). Artificial intelligence and machine learning based approach to motivate and assist primary school ADHD children. *International Research Journal of Innovations in Engineering and Technology*, *07*(09), 89–96. DOI: 10.47001/irjiet/2023.709010

Santos, L., & Cai, J. (2016). Curriculum and assessment. In *The second handbook of research on the Psychology of Mathematics Education* (pp. 151–185). Brill.

Sanusi, I. T., Martin, F., Ma, R., Gonzales, J. E., Mahipal, V., Oyelere, S. S., & Tukiainen, M. (2024). AI MyData: Fostering Middle School Students' Engagement with Machine Learning through an Ethics-Infused AI Curriculum. *ACM Transactions on Computing Education*, *24*(4), 1–37. DOI: 10.1145/3702242

Saputra, I., Astuti, M., Sayuti, M., & Kusumastuti, D. (2023). Integration of Artificial Intelligence in Education: Opportunities, Challenges, Threats and Obstacles. A Literature Review. *The Indonesian journal of computer science, 12*(4). DOI: 10.33022/ijcs.v12i4.3266

Saracostti, M., Toro, X., Rossi, A., Lara, L., & Barros, M. (2022). Implementation of a web-based system to measure, monitor, and promote school engagement strategies. A Chilean experience. *Frontiers in Psychology*, *13*. DOI: 10.3389/fpsyg.2022.980902 PMID: 36204741

Särmäkari, N. (2023). Digital 3D fashion designers: Cases of atacac and the fabricant. *Fashion Theory*, *27*(1), 85–114.

Sasson, I., Yehuda, I., & Miedijensky, S. (2022). Innovative learning spaces: Class management and universal design for learning. *Learning Environments Research*, *25*(3), 725–739. DOI: 10.1007/s10984-021-09393-8

Schmand, B. (2019). Why are neuropsychologists so reluctant to embrace modern assessment techniques? *The Clinical Neuropsychologist*, *33*(2), 209–219. DOI: 10.1080/13854046.2018.1523468 PMID: 30882285

Schöni, W. (2022). Continuing education as value creation. *European Journal for Research on the Education and Learning of Adults*, *13*(3), 261–283. DOI: 10.3384/rela.2000-7426.3694

Scott, J. W. (2019). *Knowledge, power, and academic freedom*. Columbia University Press.

Scriven, M. (1967). The methodology of evaluation. In Tyler, R. W., Gagne, R. M., & Scriven, M. (Eds.), *Perspectives of Curriculum Evaluation Chicago* (pp. 39–83). Rand McNally.

Sedlacek, Q., Lemmi, C., Feldman, K., Ortiz, N., & León, M. (2024). African American language in science education: A translanguaging perspective. *Journal of Research in Science Teaching*, *62*(1), 228–269. DOI: 10.1002/tea.22011

Sehnem, S., Troiani, L., Lara, A. C., Guerreiro Crizel, M., Carvalho, L., & Rodrigues, V. P. (2024). Sustainable fashion: Challenges and barriers for advancing the circular economy. *Environment, Development and Sustainability*, *26*(2), 4097–4118.

Selwyn, N. (2016). *Is technology good for education?* Polity Press.

Selwyn, N., & Facer, K. (2014). The sociology of education and digital technology: Past, present and future. *Oxford Review of Education*, *40*(4), 482–496.

Şenel, S., Şenel, H., & Günaydın, S. (2019). Herkes için mobil öğrenme: Mobil uygulamaların evrensel tasarım ilkelerine göre incelenmesi. *Ankara Üniversitesi Eğitim Bilimleri Fakültesi Özel Eğitim Dergisi*, *20*(1), 73–92.

Sewagegn, A. A., & Diale, B. (2019). Empowering learners using active learning in higher education institutions. Manuel Brito, S. (Ed.). *Active Learning - Beyond the Future*. IntechOpen. https://doi.org/ DOI: 10.5772/intechopen.73460

Sghir, N., Adadi, A., & Lahmer, M. (2023). Recent advances in Predictive Learning Analytics: A decade systematic review (2012–2022). *Education and Information Technologies*, *28*, 8299–8333. DOI: 10.1007/s10639-022-11536-0 PMID: 36571084

Shao, J. (2024). *Personalized Learning for Art Major Students Based on Learner Characteristics*. [Doctoral dissertation, Chapman University]. Chapman University Digital Commons. https://doi.org/DOI: 10.36837/chapman.000560

Shehata, B., Tlili, A., Huang, R., Hodges, C. B., & Kanwar, A. (2025). Implications and Challenges of Technology Adoption in Education: A 20-Year Analysis of Horizon Reports. *TechTrends*, *69*(1), 162–175. DOI: 10.1007/s11528-024-01027-z

Shemileva, M., Alikhadzhiev, C., & Budnikov, D. (2023). The use of modern innovative technologies. *SHS Web of Conferences, 172*, 01003. DOI: 10.1051/shsconf/202317201003

Shen, Y., Liu, Q., Zhang, K., & Zou, R. (2024). The Application of Artificial Intelligence Technology in Vocational College Training. In Paas, F., Patnaik, S., & Wang, T. (Eds.), *Recent Trends in Educational Technology and Administration. EduTA 2023. Learning and Analytics in Intelligent Systems* (Vol. 38). Springer., DOI: 10.1007/978-3-031-60777-6_11

Shepard, L. A. (2017). Formative assessment: Caveat emptor. In Dwyer, C. A. (Ed.), *The future of assessment* (pp. 279–303). Routledge., https://www.taylorfrancis.com/chapters/edit/10.4324/9781315086545-12/formative-assessment-caveat-emptor-lorrie-shepard

Shermis, M. D., & Burstein, J. (Eds.). (2013). *Handbook of automated essay evaluation: Current applications and new directions*. Routledge/Taylor & Francis Group.

Shevat, A. (2017). Designing bots: Creating conversational experiences. " O'Reilly Media, Inc.". Shawar, B. A. (2017). Integrating CALL systems with chatbots as conversational partners. *Computación y Sistemas*, *21*(4), 615–626.

Shiva, K., Etikani, P., Bhaskar, V. V. S. R., Nuguri, S., & Dave, A. (2024). Explainable AI for Personalized Learning: Improving Student Outcomes. *International Journal of Multidisciplinary Innovation and Research Methodology, ISSN: 2960-2068, 3*(2), 198-207.

Shneiderman, B. (2022). *Human-Centered AI*. Oxford University Press., DOI: 10.1093/oso/9780192845290.001.0001

Shute, V. J. (2011). Stealth assessment in computer-based games to support learning. *Computer games and instruction, 55*(2), 503-524.

Siemens, G. (2013). Learning analytics: The emergence of a discipline. *The American Behavioral Scientist*, *57*(10), 1380–1400.

Silva, A. de O., & Janes, D. dos S. (2020). Exploring the role of artificial intelligence in education: A comprehensive perspective. *Review of Artificial Intelligence in Education, 1*. Advance online publication. DOI: 10.37497/rev.artif.intell.education.v1i00.5

Silva, R., Farias, C., & Mesquita, I. (2024). "It is Good to Have a Voice": What Do Students Think about the Impact of a Flexible Curricular Implementation of Student-Centered Pedagogies on Their Own Learning Experiences? *Education Sciences, 14*(10), 1074. DOI: 10.3390/educsci14101074

Škiljić, A. (2021). When art meets technology or vice versa: Key challenges at the crossroads of AI-generated artworks and copyright law. *IIC-International Review of Intellectual Property and Competition Law, 52*(10), 1338–1369.

Smart Sparrow. (2023). [https://www.smartsparrow.com/] Adaptive Elearning Platform. [Accessed on 11th November, 2024].

Song, C., Shin, S.-Y., & Shin, K.-S. (2024). Implementing the Dynamic Feedback-Driven Learning Optimization Framework: A Machine Learning Approach to Personalize Educational Pathways. *Applied Sciences (Basel, Switzerland), 14*(2), 916. DOI: 10.3390/app14020916

Spivakovsky, O., Omelchuk, S., Kobets, V., Valko, N., & Malchykova, D. (2023). Institutional policies on artificial intelligence in university learning, teaching and research. *Information Technologies and Learning Tools, 97*(5), 181–202. DOI: 10.33407/itlt.v97i5.5395

Sridharan, B., McKay, J., & Boud, D. (2023). The four pillars of peer assessment for collaborative teamwork in higher education. In *The Power of Peer Learning: Fostering Students' Learning Processes and Outcomes* (pp. 3–24). Springer International Publishing., DOI: 10.1007/978-3-031-29411-2_1

Srinivasan, M., Venugopal, A., Venkatesan, L., & Kumar, R. (2024). Navigating the pedagogical landscape: Exploring the implications of ai and chatbots in nursing education. *JMIR Nursing, 7*, e52105. DOI: 10.2196/52105 PMID: 38870516

Stamate, A., Denis, P., & Sauvé, G. (2024). How cognitive ability shapes personality differentiation in real job candidates: Insights from a large-scale study. *Journal of Intelligence, 12*(3), 34. DOI: 10.3390/jintelligence12030034 PMID: 38535168

Stanley, E., Wilms, M., Mouchès, P., & Forkert, N. (2022). Fairness-related performance and explainability effects in deep learning models for brain image analysis. *Journal of Medical Imaging (Bellingham, Wash.), 9*(06). DOI: 10.1117/1.jmi.9.6.061102 PMID: 36046104

Steinert, S., Avila, K. E., Ruzika, S., Kuhn, J., & Küchemann, S. (2023). Harnessing large language models to enhance self-regulated learning via formative feedback. *arXiv preprint arXiv:2311.13984*. DOI: 10.1186/s40561-024-00354-1

Stevanović, K. (2024). Regulating artificial intelligence for higher education. *10th International Scientific Conference Technics, Informatic, and Education.*

Stewart, C., Kumaravel, B., O'Dowd, J., McKeown, A., & Harris, J. (2021). The ROSCE: A remote clinical examination during COVID lockdown and beyond. *MedEdPublish, 10*(1). Advance online publication. DOI: 10.15694/mep.2021.000011.1 PMID: 38486571

Stotter, C., Klestil, T., Chen, K., Hummer, A., Salzlechner, C., Angele, P., & Nehrer, S. (2023). Artificial intelligence-based analyses of varus leg alignment and after high tibial osteotomy show high accuracy and reproducibility. *Knee Surgery, Sports Traumatology, Arthroscopy : Official Journal of the ESSKA, 31*(12), 5885–5895. DOI: 10.1007/s00167-023-07644-0 PMID: 37975938

Strielkowski, W., Grebennikova, V., Lisovskiy, A., Rakhimova, G., & Vasileva, T. (2025). AI-driven adaptive learning for sustainable educational transformation. *Sustainable Development, 33*(2), 1921–1947. DOI: 10.1002/sd.3221

Strielkowski, W., Vlasov, A., Selivanov, K., Muraviev, K., & Shakhnov, V. (2023). Prospects and challenges of the machine learning and data-driven methods for the predictive analysis of power systems: A review. *Energies, 16*(10), 4025. DOI: 10.3390/en16104025

Subaveerapandiyan, A., Paladhi, M., & Maruthaveeran, V. (2023). Evaluating ai literacy proficiency among LIS researchers in ASEAN. *Library Hi Tech News, 41*(4), 6–8. DOI: 10.1108/lhtn-07-2023-0121

Sumbera, B. G. (2025). The Ethical Use of AI in Education. In *Integrating AI Into Pedagogical Education* (pp. 175–210). IGI Global Scientific Publishing.

Sun, J. C. Y., Ye, S. L., Yu, S. J., & Chiu, T. K. (2023). Effects of wearable hybrid AR/VR learning material on high school students' situational interest, engagement, and learning performance: The case of a physics laboratory learning environment. *Journal of Science Education and Technology, 32*(1), 1–12.

Supramaniam, J. K., Baharudin, S. M., Halid, N. M., Abbas, M. S., Amin, M., Ghani, A., Affendy, K., Halim, A., & Nordin, M. N. (2024). Leveraging AI to bridge educational inequities: A global perspective. *Nanotechnology Perceptions.*

Supramaniam, J. K., Baharudin, S. M., Halid, N. M., Abbas, M. S., Amin, M., Ghani, A., Affendy, K., Halim, A., & Nordin, M. N. (2024). Leveraging AI To Bridge Educational Inequities: A Global Perspective. *Nanotechnology Perceptions.*

Suraworachet, W., Zhou, Q., & Cukurova, M. (2023). The Impact of combining human and analytics feedback on students' engagement with and performance in reflective writing tasks. *International Journal of Educational Technology in Higher Education, 20*(1), 1–24. DOI: 10.48550/arXiv.2211.08222

Svantesson, E., Senorski, E., Webster, K., Karlsson, J., Diermeier, T., Rothrauff, B., & Zheng, M. (2020). Clinical outcomes after anterior cruciate ligament injury: Panther symposium ACL injury clinical outcomes consensus group. *Orthopaedic Journal of Sports Medicine, 8*(7). DOI: 10.1177/2325967120934751 PMID: 32754624

Swargiary, K. (2024). *Exploring The Impact Of Artificial Intelligence On Visual Arts: Technological Advancements, Market Dynamics, Ethical Considerations, And Human Creativity*. GOOGLE.

Swiecki, Z., Khosravi, H., Chen, G., Martinez-Maldonado, R., Lodge, J. M., Milligan, S., Selwyn, L., & Gašević, D. (2022). Assessment in the age of artificial intelligence. *Computers and Education: Artificial Intelligence, 3*, 100075.

Sywelem, M. M., & Mahklouf, A. M. (2024). Ethical considerations in the integration of artificial intelligence in education. *Education and Information Technologies.*

Takeda, H., Akatsuka, J., Kiriyama, T., Toyama, Y., Numata, Y., Morikawa, H., Tsutsumi, K., Takadate, M., Hasegawa, H., Mikami, H., Obayashi, K., Endo, Y., Takahashi, T., Fukumoto, M., Ohashi, R., Shimizu, A., Kimura, G., Kondo, Y., & Yamamoto, Y. (2024). Clinically significant prostate cancer prediction using multimodal deep learning with prostate-specific antigen restriction. *Current Oncology (Toronto, Ont.), 31*(11), 7180–7189. DOI: 10.3390/curroncol31110530 PMID: 39590160

Tamrin, S., Omar, N., Kamaruzaman, K., Zaghlol, A., & Aziz, M. (2024). Evaluating the impact of ai dependency on cognitive ability among Generation Z in higher educational institutions: A conceptual framework. *Information Management and Business Review, 16*(3S(I)a), 1027-1033. DOI: 10.22610/imbr.v16i3s(i)a.4191

Tang, K. H. D. (2023). Student-centered Approach in Teaching and Learning: What Does It Really Mean? *Acta Pedagogia Asiana, 2*(2), 72–83. DOI: 10.53623/apga.v2i2.218

Tang, Y., Liang, J., Hare, R., & Wang, F. Y. (2020). A personalized learning system for parallel intelligent education. *IEEE Transactions on Computational Social Systems, 7*(2), 352–361.

Tanjga, M. (2023). E-learning and the Use of AI: A Review of Current Practices and Future Directions. DOI: 10.32388/ap0208

Tan, Y., Xu, W., Li, S., & Chen, K. (2022). Augmented and virtual reality (AR/VR) for education and training in the AEC industry: A systematic review of research and applications. *Buildings (Basel, Switzerland)*, *12*(10), 1529.

Tao, W., Zhao, D., Yue, H., Horton, I., Tian, X., Xu, Z., & Sun, H. J. (2022). The influence of growth mindset on the mental health and life events of college students. *Frontiers in Psychology*, *13*, 821206. DOI: 10.3389/fpsyg.2022.821206 PMID: 35496212

Tariq, U. (2024). Challenges in AI-Powered Educational Technologies: Teacher Perspectives and Resistance. *Journal of AI Integration in Education*, *1*(3), 1–10.

Taylor, R.C., Liang, X., Laubichler, M.D., West, G.B., Kempes, C.P., & Dumas, M. (2019). The Scalability, Efficiency and Complexity of Universities and Colleges: A New Lens for Assessing the Higher Educational System. *ArXiv, abs/1910.05470.*

Tejeswar. (n.d.). Understanding GDPR and data privacy in AI educational tools. Medium. Retrieved January 18, 2025, from https://medium.com/@tejeswar_79802/understanding-gdpr-and-data-privacy-in-ai-educational-tools-6e576eaa6d16

Terra, A. C. W. (2021). Blockchain as a tool to improving work condition in the fashion supply chain. *Master's dissertation, COPPEAD Graduate School of Business, Universidade Federal do Rio de Janeiro.*

Teunissen, J., Hovius, S., Ulrich, D., Issa, F., Rodrigues, J., & Harrison, C. (2023). Computerized adaptive testing for the patient evaluation measure (PEM) in patients undergoing cubital tunnel syndrome surgery. *The Journal of Hand Surgery, European Volume*, *48*(10), 1042–1047. DOI: 10.1177/17531934231164959 PMID: 37066610

Thakur, G. S. M., Banerjee, A., & Sarkar, P. (2025). AI in Vocational Education and Training: Technologies and Applications. In Transforming Vocational Education and Training Using AI (pp. 49-72). IGI Global Scientific Publishing.

Thelma, C. C., Sain, Z. H., Shogbesan, Y. O., Phiri, E. V., & Akpan, W. M. (2024). Ethical Implications of AI and Machine Learning in Education: A Systematic Analysis. *International Journal of Instructional Technology*, *3*(1), 1–13. DOI: 10.33650/ijit.v3i1.9364

Thinh, N. T., Hai, N. D. X., & Tho, T. P. (2020). The influential role of robot in second language classes based on artificial intelligence. *International Journal of Mechanical Engineering and Robotics Research*, *9*(9), 1306–1311.

Tılıç, G. (2016). Yabancı dil öğreniminde kullanılan etkileşimli mobil uygulamalar: Duolingo örneği. *Journal of Research in Education and Teaching*, *5*, 34.

Tomaskinova, J., & Tomaskin, J. (2024). UNLOCKING THE FUTURE OF EDUCATION: EMPOWERING EDUCATORS WITH AI BY OVERCOMING PROFESSIONAL DEVELOPMENT CHALLENGES. In *ICERI2024 Proceedings* (pp. 10633-10642). IATED.

Tomlinson, C. A. (2001). *How to Differentiate Instruction in Mixed-Ability Classrooms*. ASCD.

Tonbuloğlu, B. (2023). An evaluation of the use of artificial intelligence applications in online education. *Journal of Educational Technology and Online Learning*, *6*(4), 866–884. DOI: 10.31681/jetol.1335906

Torres Carceller, A. (2024). The ARTificial revolution: Challenges for redefining art education. *Digital Education Review*, *45*, 84–90. DOI: 10.1344/der.2024.45.84-90

Tosun, N., Özgür, H., & Şahin, İ. (2009, October). Student-content interaction in e-learning environments. *In 3rd International Computer&Instructional Technologies Symposium* (pp. 327- 331).

Tsidylo, I. M., & Sena, C. E. (2023). Artificial intelligence as a methodological innovation in the training of future designers: Midjourney tools. *Information Technologies and Learning Tools*, *97*(5), 203.

Turing, A. (1950). Computing machinery and intelligence. *Mind*, *49*(236), 433–460.

Twilt, J., Leeuwen, K., Huisman, H., Fütterer, J., & Rooij, M. (2021). Artificial intelligence-based algorithms for prostate cancer classification and detection on magnetic resonance imaging: A narrative review. *Diagnostics (Basel)*, *11*(6), 959. DOI: 10.3390/diagnostics11060959 PMID: 34073627

Tyen, G., Brenchley, M., Caines, A., & Buttery, P. (2022). Towards an open-domain chatbot for language practice. In *Proceedings of the 17th Workshop on Innovative Use of NLP For Building Educational Applivations* (pp. 234-249), Association for Computational Linguistics.

Tyler, R. (2021). *Basic Principles of Curriculum and Instruction*. University of Chicago Press.

U.S. Department of Education, Office of Educational Technology. (2023). *Artificial intelligence and the future of teaching and learning: Insights and recommendations*. U.S. Department of Education.

U.S. Department of Education. (2000). Family Educational Rights and Privacy Act (FERPA) [20 U.S.C. § 1232g; 34 CFR Part 99].

U.S. Department of Education. (2016). *Future Ready Learning: Reimagining the Role of Technology in Education*. Http://Tech.Ed.Gov/Files/2015/12/NETP16.Pdf

Uğur, S., & Okur, M. R. (2016). The use of interactive video in open and distance learning. *Journal of Open Education Applications and Research, 2*(4), 104–126.

Underwood, J. (2017). Exploring AI language assistants with primary EFL students. *CALL in a climate of change: adapting to turbulent global conditions–short papers from EUROCALL, 2017*, 317-321. https://doi.org/DOI: 10.14705/rpnet.2017.eurocall2017.733

University of Illinois. (2023). [https://online.illinois.edu/] Illinois Compass.

University of Southern California. (2023). [https://viterbigrad.usc.edu/] USC Hybrid Learning [Accessed on 11th November, 2024].

Usca, N., Samaniego, M., Yerbabuena, C., & Pérez, I. (2024). Arts and Humanities Education: A Systematic Review of Emerging Technologies and Their Contribution to Social Well-Being. *Social Sciences, 13*(5), 269.

Uygun İlikhan, S., Özer, M., Tanberkan, H., & Bozkurt, V. (2024). How to mitigate the risks of deployment of artificial intelligence in medicine? *Turkish Journal of Medical Sciences, 54*(3), 483–492. PMID: 39050000

Üzmez, A., & Kavakli Ulutaş, N. (2024). An inquiry on the psychological well-being of the university students during emergency remote teaching: Application of the EMPATHICS model. *Smart Learning Environments, 11*(1), 17. DOI: 10.1186/s40561-024-00302-z

Valero Haro, A., Noroozi, O., Biemans, H. J. A., & Mulder, M. (2022). Argumentation Competence: Students' argumentation knowledge, behavior, attitude, and relationships with domain-specific knowledge acquisition. *Journal of Constructivist Psychology, 35*(1), 123–145. DOI: 10.1080/10720537.2020.1734995

Vallée, A., Blacher, J., Cariou, A., & Sorbets, E. (2020). Blended learning compared to traditional learning in medical education: Systematic review and meta-analysis. *Journal of Medical Internet Research, 22*(8), e16504. DOI: 10.2196/16504 PMID: 32773378

VanLehn, K. (2011). The relative effectiveness of human tutoring, intelligent tutoring systems, and other tutoring systems. *Educational Psychologist, 46*(4), 197–221. DOI: 10.1080/00461520.2011.611369

Vartak, A., Khot, A., Rane, S., Naik, P., & Mundye, G. (2024, May). Virtual Stylist Using IOT. In *2024 3rd International Conference on Artificial Intelligence For Internet of Things (AIIoT)* (pp. 1-4). IEEE.

Vasquez, J. A., Marcotte, K., & Gruppen, L. D. (2021). The parallel evolution of competency-based education in medical and higher education. *The Journal of Competency-Based Education*, *6*(2), e1234. DOI: 10.1002/cbe2.1234

Vaza, R. N., Parmar, A. B., Mishra, P. S., Abdullah, I., & Velu, C. M. (2024). Security And Privacy Concerns In AI-Enabled Iot Educational Frameworks: An In-Depth Analysis. *Educational Administration: Theory and Practice*, *30*(4), 8436–8445.

Vertemati, M., Zuccotti, G., & Porrini, M. (2024). Enhancing anatomy education through flipped classroom and adaptive learning a pilot project on liver anatomy. *Journal of Medical Education and Curricular Development*, *11*. DOI: 10.1177/23821205241248023 PMID: 38854913

Vican, S., Friedman, A., & Andreasen, R. (2019). Metrics, Money, and Managerialism: Faculty Experiences of Competing Logics in Higher Education. *The Journal of Higher Education*, *91*(1), 139–164.

Vincent-Lancrin, S., & van der Vlies, R. (2020). Trustworthy Artificial Intelligence (AI) in Education: Promises and Challenges. OECD Education Working Papers, No. 218. *OECD Publishing*. DOI: 10.1787/a6c90fa9-en

Vinokur, E., Yomtovian, A., Marom, M. S., Itzchakov, G., & Baron, L. (2024). Social-based learning and leadership in school: Conflict management training for holistic, relational conflict resolution. *Frontiers in Social Psychology*, *2*, 1412968. DOI: 10.3389/frsps.2024.1412968

Vishwakarma, A., Mehrotra, D., Agrahari, R., Kharub, M., Gupta, S., & Jagtap, S. (2024). Breaking barriers: paving the path to sustainable fashion–insights for a greener apparel and textile sector. *Journal of Advances in Management Research*.

Vistorte, A. O. R., Deroncele-Acosta, A., Ayala, J. L. M., Barrasa, A., López-Granero, C., & Martí-González, M. (2024). Integrating artificial intelligence to assess emotions in learning environments: A systematic literature review. *Frontiers in Psychology*, *15*, 1387089. DOI: 10.3389/fpsyg.2024.1387089 PMID: 38966729

Vistorte, E. T., Caballes, A. B., Genelza, J. B., & Gonzaga, R. A. (2024). Gamification in formative assessment: Effects on student engagement and academic performance. *Education and Information Technologies*, *29*(1), 103–123.

Vlasova, E. Z., Avksentieva, E. Y., Goncharova, S. V., & Aksyutin, P. A. (2019). Artificial intelligence-The space for the new possibilities to train teachers. *Espacios*, *40*(9), 17.

Volino, P., Cordier, F., & Magnenat-Thalmann, N. (2005). From early virtual garment simulation to interactive fashion design. *Computer Aided Design*, *37*(6), 593–608.

Wagner, C., & Liu, L. (2021). Creating immersive learning experiences: A pedagogical design perspective. In *Creative and collaborative learning through immersion: Interdisciplinary and international perspectives* (pp. 71–87). Springer International Publishing., DOI: 10.1007/978-3-030-72216-6_5

Wainer, H., Dorans, N. J., Flaugher, R., Green, B., & Mislevy, R. J. (2000). *Computerized Adaptive Testing*. Routledge., DOI: 10.4324/9781410605931

Walkington, C., & Bernacki, M. L. (2020). Appraising research on personalized learning: Definitions, theoretical alignment, advancements, and future directions. *Journal of Research on Technology in Education*, *52*(3), 235–252. DOI: 10.1080/15391523.2020.1747757

Walter, Y. (2024). Embracing the future of Artificial Intelligence in the classroom: The relevance of AI literacy, prompt engineering, and critical thinking in modern education. *International Journal of Educational Technology in Higher Education*, *21*(1), 15. DOI: 10.1186/s41239-024-00448-3

Wang, L. (2023). The Impact of student-centered learning on academic motivation and achievement: A comparative research between traditional instruction and student-centered approach. *Journal of Education. Humanities and Social Sciences*, *22*, 346–353.

Wang, Q. (2023). Computer aided teaching system for football teaching and training based on video image. *International Journal of Sports Technology*, *4*(1). DOI: 10.38007/ijst.2023.040103

Wang, Q., Yuan, L., Ding, X., & Zhou, Z. (2021). Prediction and diagnosis of venous thromboembolism using artificial intelligence approaches: A systematic review and meta-analysis. *Clinical and Applied Thrombosis/Hemostasis : Official Journal of the International Academy of Clinical and Applied Thrombosis/Hemostasis, 27*. DOI: 10.1177/10760296211021162 PMID: 34184560

Warshaw, J. B., & Upton, S. (2020). Hybrid logics in the resource strategies of US public research universities. *Journal of Further and Higher Education*, *44*, 1289–1303.

Watiktinnakorn, C., Seesai, J., & Kerdvibulvech, C. (2023). Blurring the lines: How AI is redefining artistic ownership and copyright. *Discover Artificial Intelligence*, *3*(1), 37.

Weber, A. S. (2020). Ethics concerns in artificial intelligence use in education. *14th International Technology, Education and Development Conference.*

Weber-Wulff, D., Anohina-Naumeca, A., Bjelobaba, S., Foltýnek, T., Guerrero-Dib, J., Popoola, O., Šigut, P., & Waddington, L. (2023). Testing of detection tools for AI-generated text. *International Journal for Educational Integrity*, *19*(1), 26. DOI: 10.1007/s40979-023-00146-z

White, J. D. (2023, November 6). Academic integrity in the age of AI. *Educause Review*. https://er.educause.edu/articles/sponsored/2023/11/academic-integrity-in-the-age-of-ai

Wijnia, L., Noordzij, G., Arends, L. R., Rikers, R. M., & Loyens, S. M. (2024). The effects of problem-based, project-based, and case-based learning on students' motivation: A meta-analysis. *Educational Psychology Review*, *36*(1), 29. DOI: 10.1007/s10648-024-09864-3

Wilhoit, G. E. N. E., Pittenger, L. I. N. D. A., & Rickabaugh, J. (2016). *Leadership for learning: What is leadership's role in supporting success for every student?* Center for Innovation in Education.

Willis, J. E., & Strunk, V. A. (2015). *Ethical Responsibilities of Preserving Academicians in an Age of Mechanized Learning: Balancing the Demands of Educating at Capacity and Preserving Human Interactivity*. IGI Global.

Willkomm, A. (2024). Ai literacy and ethical responsibility: Gaining faculty buy-in by using it for assessment. *Intersection: A Journal at the Intersection of Assessment and Learning, 5*(4), 127-144. https://doi.org/DOI: 10.61669/001c.124829

Wisniewski, B., Zierer, K., & Hattie, J. (2020). The power of feedback revisited: A meta-analysis of educational feedback research. *Frontiers in Psychology*, *10*, 487662. DOI: 10.3389/fpsyg.2019.03087 PMID: 32038429

Wiyaka, W. (2022). The practice of classroom assessments during curriculum change: A study of inservice teachers. *KnE Social Sciences*, *7*(19), 776–788. DOI: 10.18502/kss.v7i19.12497

Wong, L., & Meeker, J. (2022). The promise of computer adaptive testing in collection of orthopaedic outcomes: An evaluation of PROMIS utilization. *Journal of Patient-Reported Outcomes*, *6*(23). DOI: 10.1186/s41687-021-00407-w PMID: 34982280

Woo, J. H., & Choi, H. (2021). Systematic Review for AI-based Language Learning Tools. *Journal of Digital Contents Society*, *22*(11), 1783. DOI: 10.9728/dcs.2021.22.11.1783

Woo, L. J., & Choi, H. (2021). Systematic review for AI-based language learning tools. *Journal of Digital Contents Society*, *22*(11), 1783–1792.

World of TVET. (2024). TVET and AI. https://www.worldoftvet.com/blog/tvet-and-ai

Wu, Z., Li, Y., Ji, D., Wu, D., Shidujaman, M., Zhang, Y., & Zhang, C. (2022, December). Human-AI co-creation of art based on the personalization of collective memory. In 2022 *6th Asian Conference on Artificial Intelligence Technology (ACAIT)* (pp. 1-6). IEEE.

Wylder, J. (2022). *An Illustrated Guide to AI Prompt Mastery: for MidJourney, DALL-E, NightCafe, Deep Dream Generator, and More*. Baen Books.

Xie, H., Tao, L., & Xie, L. (2024, February 21). Research on prospective scope and approaches of artificial intelligence education in vocational college of China. In *Proceedings of the 3rd International Conference on Education, Language and Art (ICELA 2023)* (pp. 484–492). Atlantis Press. https://doi.org/DOI: 10.2991/978-2-38476-214-9_59

Xie, K. (2020). Projecting learner engagement in remote contexts using empathic design. *Educational Technology Research and Development*, 69. PMID: 33223779

Xiong, J., Ding, S., Fen, L., & Luo, Z. (2020). Online calibration of polytomous items under the graded response model. *Frontiers in Psychology*, *10*. DOI: 10.3389/fpsyg.2019.03085 PMID: 32038427

Xuto, P., Prasitwattanaseree, P., Chaiboonruang, T., Chaiwuth, S., Khwanngern, P., Nuntakwang, C., Nimarangkul, K., Suwansin, W., Khiaokham, L., & Bressington, D. (2025). Development and Evaluation of an AI-Assisted Answer Assessment (4A) for Cognitive Assessments in Nursing Education. *Nursing Reports*, *15*(3), 80. DOI: 10.3390/nursrep15030080 PMID: 40137653

Xu, Z. (2024). AI in education: Enhancing learning experiences and student outcomes. *Appl. Comput. Eng*, *51*, 104–111.

Yadav, D. S. (2024). *Navigating the landscape of AI integration in education: Opportunities, challenges, and ethical considerations for harnessing the potential of artificial intelligence*. BSSS Journal of Computer., DOI: 10.51767/jc1503

Yağcı, M. (2022). Educational data mining: Prediction of students' academic performance using machine learning algorithms. *Smart Learning Environments*, *9*(1), 11.

Yakubu, M. A., Sain, Z. H., Lawal, U. S., & Budiman, S. A. (2024). Application of Artificial Intelligence [AI] for Automated Essay Grading in Nigerian Schools. [IJoEd]. *Indonesian Journal on Education, 1*(2), 93–103.

Yaman, I. (2016). The potential benefits of podcasts for language learning. *Journal of educational and instructional studies in the world, 6*(1), 60-66.

Yang, C., Luo, L., Vadillo, M., Yu, R., & Shanks, D. (2021). Testing (quizzing) boosts classroom learning: A systematic and meta-analytic review. *Psychological Bulletin, 147*(4), 399–435. DOI: 10.1037/bul0000309 PMID: 33683913

Yang, E., & Beil, C. (2024). Ensuring data privacy in AI/ML implementation. *New Directions for Higher Education, 2024*(207), 63–78.

Yang, T.-C., Hwang, G.-J., & Yang, S. J.-H. (2013). Development of an adaptive learning system with multiple perspectives based on students' learning styles and cognitive styles. *Journal of Educational Technology & Society, 16*(4), 185–200.

Yang, T., Zhang, Q., Sun, Z., & Hou, Y. (2024). Automatic assessment of divergent thinking in Chinese language with TransDis: A transformer-based language model approach. *Behavior Research Methods, 56*(6), 5798–5819. DOI: 10.3758/s13428-023-02313-z PMID: 38129737

Yang, Y., Emmen, R., Bruijn, Y., & Mesman, J. (2023). Crisis and bias: Exploring ethnic prejudice among Chinese Dutch children before and during the covid-19 pandemic. *Infant and Child Development, 32*(6). DOI: 10.1002/icd.2462

Yang, Y., Yuan, Y., Zhang, G., Wang, H., Chen, Y.-C., Liu, Y., Tarolli, C. G., Crepeau, D., Bukartyk, J., Junna, M. R., Videnovic, A., Ellis, T. D., Lipford, M. C., Dorsey, R., & Katabi, D. (2022). Artificial intelligence-enabled detection and assessment of Parkinson's disease using nocturnal breathing signals. *Nature Medicine, 28*(10), 2207–2215. DOI: 10.1038/s41591-022-01932-x PMID: 35995955

Yaseen, H., Mohammad, A. S., Ashal, N., Abusaimeh, H., Ali, A., & Sharabati, A.-A. A. (2025). The Impact of Adaptive Learning Technologies, Personalized Feedback, and Interactive AI Tools on Student Engagement: The Moderating Role of Digital Literacy. *Sustainability, 17*(3), 1133. DOI: 10.3390/su17031133

Yaseen, M. (2023). Scriptwriting in the Age of AI: Revolutionizing Storytelling with Artificial Intelligence. [JMC]. *Journal of Media & Communication, 4*(1).

Yavuz, F., Çelik, Ö., & Çelik, G. (2024). Utilizing large language models for EFL essay grading: An examination of reliability and validity in rubric-based assessments. *British Journal of Educational Technology, 56*(1), 150–166. DOI: 10.1111/bjet.13494

Yazici, H. (2020). Project-based learning for teaching business analytics in the undergraduate curriculum. *Decision Sciences Journal of Innovative Education, 18*(4), 589–611. DOI: 10.1111/dsji.12219

Yee, N. (2006). Motivations for play in online games. *Cyberpsychology & Behavior, 9*(6), 772–775. DOI: 10.1089/cpb.2006.9.772 PMID: 17201605

Yekollu, R. K., Bhimraj Ghuge, T., Sunil Biradar, S., Haldikar, S. V., & Farook Mohideen Abdul Kader, O. (2024). *AI-Driven Personalized Learning Paths: Enhancing Education Through Adaptive Systems* (pp. 507–517). DOI: 10.1007/978-981-97-3191-6_38

Yezhova, O., Pashkevich, K., & Manoilenko, N. V. (2018). Comparative analysis of foreign models of fashion education. Revista Românească pentru Educaţie Multidimensională.

Yıldırım, Ö. (2012). A Study on a Group of Indian English as a Second Language Learners' Perceptions of Autonomous Learning. *Turkish Online Journal of Qualitative Inquiry, 3*(2).

Yildirim, Y., Camci, F., & Aygar, E. (2023). Advancing Self-Directed Learning Through Artificial Intelligence. In Mncube, D. W., & Maphalala, M. C. (Eds.), (pp. 146–157). Advances in Higher Education and Professional Development. IGI Global., DOI: 10.4018/978-1-6684-6772-5.ch009

Yilmaz, M., Buchanan, M., & Martin, J. (2022). Disrupting majoritarian narratives in high stakes testing: A critical race theory analysis of assessment. *Equity in Education & Society*, *2*(1), 28–42. DOI: 10.1177/27526461221141903

Zainuddin, Z., Chu, S. K. W., Shujahat, M., & Perera, C. J. (2020). The Impact of gamification on learning and instruction: A systematic review of empirical evidence. *Educational Research Review*, *30*, 100326. DOI: 10.1016/j.edurev.2020.100326

Zajda, J. (Ed.). (2020). *Globalisation, ideology and neo-liberal higher education reforms*. Springer.

Zaman, B. U. (2023). Transforming education through ai, benefits, risks, and ethical considerations. *Authorea Preprints, 1*, 1-26. DOI: 10.36227/techrxiv.24231583

Zaman, B. U. (2023). Transforming education through AI, benefits, risks, and ethical considerations. Institute of Electrical and Electronics Engineers (IEEE). Retrieved from Institute of Electrical and Electronics Engineers (IEEE) website:DOI: 10.36227/techrxiv.24231583.v1

Zawacki-Richter, O., Marin, V. I., Bond, M., & Gouverneur, F. (2019). Systematic review of research on artificial intelligence applications in higher education – where are the educators? *International Journal of Educational Technology in Higher Education, 16*(39). DOI: 10.1186/s41239-019-0171-0

Zeide, E. (2017). The Structural Consequences of Big Data-Driven Education. *Big Data, 5*(2). DOI: 10.1089/big.2016.0061 PMID: 28632444

Zhai, X., Chu, X., Chai, C. S., Jong, M. S. Y., Istenic, A., Spector, M., & Li, Y. (2021). A Review of Artificial Intelligence (AI) in Education from 2010 to 2020. *Complexity, 2021*(1), 8812542. DOI: 10.1155/2021/8812542

Zhaı, X., Haudek, K., Shi, L., Nehm, R., & Urban-Lurain, M. (2020). From substitution to redefinition: A framework of machine learning-based science assessment. *Journal of Research in Science Teaching, 57*(9), 1430–1459. DOI: 10.1002/tea.21658

Zhai, X., & Nehm, R. H. (2023). AI and formative assessment: The train has left the station. *Journal of Research in Science Teaching, 60*(6), 1390–1398.

Zhang a, H., & Galaup ab, M. (2023). Reflection on the construction and Impact of an adaptive learning ecosystem. *Revue internationale des technologies en pédagogie universitaire, 20*(2), 125-138. DOI: 10.18162/ritpu-2023-v20n2-10

Zhang, H., & Lee, Y. (2020). Variations and types of high-tech fashion. *Journal of the Korea Fashion and Costume Design Association, 22*(2), 117–136.

Zhang, Q., Gong, D., Li, K., Dang, K., Wang, Y., Pan, C., Yan, Z., & Yang, W. (2024). From inception to innovation: Bibliometric analysis of the evolution, hotspots, and trends in implantable collamer lens surgery research. *Frontiers in Medicine, 11*. DOI: 10.3389/fmed.2024.1432780 PMID: 39224608

Zhang, T., Lu, X., Zhu, X., & Zhang, J. (2023). The contributions of ai in the development of ideological and political perspectives in education. *Heliyon, 9*(3), e13403. DOI: 10.1016/j.heliyon.2023.e13403 PMID: 36879973

Zhao, L., Zhao, B., & Li, C. (2023). Alignment analysis of teaching–learning-assessment within the classroom: How teachers implement project-based learning under the curriculum standards. *Disciplinary and Interdisciplinary Science Education Research, 5*(1), 13. DOI: 10.1186/s43031-023-00078-1

Zhao, S., Hai, G., & Ma, H. (2024). Adaptive learning systems: Exploring personalized paths in vocational education. *Curriculum Learning and Exploration, 2*(2). Advance online publication. DOI: 10.18686/cle.v2i2.3720

Zhao, T. (2023). AI in educational technology. *Preprints*. DOI: 10.20944/preprints202311.0106.v1

Zhao, X., Guo, Z., & Liu, S. (2021). Exploring key competencies and professional development of music teachers in primary schools in the era of artificial intelligence. *Scientific Programming*, *2021*(1), 5097003.

Zhaoyan, & Renli. (2011). Interdisciplinary Education Model of Fashion Marketing and E-Commerce. In Communication Systems and Information Technology: Selected Papers from the 2011 International Conference on Electric and Electronics (EEIC 2011) in Nanchang, China on June 20-22, 2011, Volume 4 (pp. 789-793). Springer Berlin Heidelberg.

Zhen, H., & Yahaya, W. A. J. W. (2024). *Use of Generative AI Tools to Facilitate Personalized Learning in the Flipped Classroom.*, DOI: 10.4018/979-8-3693-1351-0.ch016

Zhou, H., & Zhou, D. (2024). Transformation of vocational education based on generative artificial intelligence: Impact, opportunity, and countermeasures. *Proceedings of the 3rd International Conference on Internet Technology and Educational Informatization (ITEI 2023)*, November 24–26, 2023, Zhengzhou, China. EAI. https://doi.org/DOI: 10.4108/eai.24-11-2023.2343636

Zileli, E. N. (2023). ChatGPT Example in Turkish learning as a foreign language. *International Karamanoğlu Mehmetbey Journal of Educational Research*, *5*(1), 42–51. DOI: 10.47770/ukmead.1296013

Zylich, B., & Lan, A. (2021, April). Linguistic skill modeling for second language acquisition. *In LAK21: 11th International Learning Analytics and Knowledge Conference* (pp. 141-150).

About the Contributors

Viktor Wang is a globally recognized professor and leader in the field of Education in the Department of Educational Leadership and Technology at California State University, San Bernardino. His distinguished career is marked by innovation, scholarship, and mentorship. With more than 240 peer-reviewed publications, Dr. Wang has made transformative contributions to academic research and thought leadership. His work has inspired over 200 scholarly articles and more than 1,500 book chapters contributed to his edited volumes and journals by scholars around the world. His publications are widely respected and housed in top-tier institutions, including Stanford University Libraries and other globally renowned academic collections. Dr. Wang has received numerous prestigious honors, including the 2016 Presidential Award for Exceptional and Innovative Leadership from the American Association for Adult and Continuing Education (AAACE), as well as institutional recognition such as the Distinguished Faculty and Scholarly Achievement Award from CSULB. A dedicated mentor, Dr. Wang has successfully guided more than 80 doctoral students through dissertation completion. His leadership has also driven measurable institutional outcomes, including enrollment growth, the launch of innovative academic programs, and the establishment of international educational partnerships.

***

Nurul Ajleaa binti Abdul Rahman is a Head Centre of Studies at the Academy of Language Studies, Universiti Teknologi MARA (Terengganu, Malaysia). She received the Ph.D degree in TESL from Universiti Kebangsaan Malaysia (UKM), in 2017. She has more than 15 years of teaching experience. She is currently teaching several English language proficiency courses. Her interests are Technology Innovations in Education, ESL Writing Skills, ESL Oral Communication Skills, Education, Social Sciences and Innovative Teaching and Learning.

Güzin Başdemir graduated from Ondokuz Mayıs University. I am doing my master's degree in English Language Teaching at Anadolu University and I am currently working as a research assistant at the same university.

Yiming Chen, With nearly 20 years of experience in innovation and entrepreneurship education, I has dedicated their career to empowering students to adapt to the rapid evolution of science and technology. A key focus of their work has been integrating emerging technologies and efficiency tools into educational practices, enabling students to excel academically and acquire the practical skills necessary for employment. Their research and efforts consistently center on enhancing students' learning experiences by leveraging new tools and methodologies to equip them for the challenges of the modern workforce.

Nurul Ain Chua Binti Abdullah is a Senior Lecturer at Universiti Malaysia Terengganu (UMT), where she focuses on teaching Mandarin as a foreign language to non-native learners. She is actively involved in research related to Mandarin language acquisition and educational technology in language learning. Dr. Nurul Ain has over 30 years of experience in education and has taught at various levels, from primary to tertiary. She has presented her research at numerous national and international conferences. Her research interests include technology-enhanced language learning, language pedagogy, and differentiated instruction.

Sandip Dey was an Associate Professor and the HOD with the Department of Computer Science and Engineering, Global Institute of Management and Technology, India. He worked as an Assistant Professor in OmDayal Group of Institution and Camellia Institute of Technology for several years. Before that he worked as a Lecturer in Narula Institute of Technology. He is currently an Assistant Professor in the Department of Computer Science, Sukanta Mahavidyalaya, Jalpaiguri. He has coauthored one book titled "Quantum-Inspired Metaheuristics for Image Analysis"; Publisher: John Wiley & Sons, UK, coedited three books, and authored or coauthored about 70 research publications in international journals, book chapters, and conference proceedings. His research interests include soft computing, hybrid intelligence, quantum computing, and image analysis. Dey reviewed several international peer-reviewed journals like Applied Soft Computing, Swarm and Evolutionary Computation, Information Sciences, Journal of Computational Science, Engineering Applications of Artificial Intelligence, Expert Systems With Applications, Advanced Engineering Informatics, IEEE Transactions on Signal Processing and so on.

Ashley L. Dockens, PhD, AuD, CCC-A, is a dynamic academic leader serving at Lamar University as the Associate Provost of Academic Innovation and Digital

Learning, Office of Academic Affairs, and the Associate Dean of Policy and Procedure, College of Graduate Studies. In these roles, she shapes and implements policies to drive academic excellence and compliance. Having previously served as the Director of the Center for Teaching and Learning Enhancement, Dr. Dockens is dedicated to promoting innovative teaching practices and leading all university AI initiatives, ensuring ethical and effective integration into academic programs. As an Associate Professor of Audiology, she shares her passion for the field, having previously directed the Doctor of Audiology program. In higher education, she serves as a regular speaker on the topic of generative AI at state, national, and international venues. Since March 2024, Dr. Dockens has served as Chair of the AI Taskforce for the Council of Academic Programs in Communication Sciences and Disorders, an international accreditor for the field. Dr. Dockens' diverse roles reflect her commitment to higher education through leadership, contributing to the overall success of the academic community.

Linda Ellington, after working at IBM for 23 years, Linda is a Professor of Business at Southern New Hampshire University, where she has taught since 2014. She conducted her doctoral research at the University of Oxford and the University of Warwick in the United Kingdom. Her research focus is on the intersection of leadership and organizational change, uncovering strategies that explore how effective leaders navigate complex challenges to make impactful strategic choices. Dr. Ellington has published extensively in top-tier journals, scholarly books, and is a member of several university doctoral dissertations, such as at the University of Johannesburg, South Africa. Beyond academia, she has published eight children's books in the genres of bullying and environmental care. She collaborates with community leaders to read stories to local children, fostering a love of literacy and inspiring the next generation of readers. She lives with her three coolest four-legged friends, Max, Riley, and Bandit.

Pi-Chi Han works as an associate professor at National Kaohsiung Normal University in Taiwan. Formerly, she was an assistant professor in the Division of Educational Leadership and Policy Studies at the University of Missouri-St. Louis (UMSL) and also a visiting scholar at the Chinese Academy of Social Science in China. Currently, she serves as a senior advisor to Asia-Pacific Economic Cooperation (APEC) in the HRD Working Group and Policy Partnership on Women and the Economy. She is a scholar-practitioner in the field of intercultural HRD, an adult educator of global workforce development, and a consultant of global talent development. Her research and publications have focused on intercultural effectiveness (ICE) competencies, cross-cultural mentoring, global leadership development, Confucian leadership, and women's leadership development. She has been certified as a Trainer of Trainers for the Developing Diversity Training for the Workplace and Global Art Markets Collecting and Connoisseurship by Sotheby's Institute of Art. She conducted intercultural workshops in Spain, China, and Taiwan.

Dayna Mitchell, Ed.D., (She/Her) has served PK-12 public education for 30 years as a High School Teacher and Administrator, Middle School Principal, Director of Curriculum, Instruction, and Assessment, and Assistant Superintendent. Using an equity lens, Dr. Mitchell developed a district-wide professional learning system focused on continuous cycles of improvement designed to increase student achievement, equity, and engagement in order to close opportunity gaps and accelerate learning for all students, with an emphasis on multilingual learners. Dr. Mitchell is an Assistant Professor, Educational Leadership, CSU Pomona

Indranil Mutsuddi is PhD in Management Studies from Amity University Uttar Pradesh. He is presently associated with the Faculty of Management, JIS University, Kolkata as HOD and Associate Professor in HR. Dr. Indranil has more than 21+ years of teaching experience as a faculty member in Human Resources Management, Organizational Behaviour and Behavioural Sciences. He had published 62 research papers, authored 3 textbooks in Human Resource Management and contributed 16 chapters in edited books.

Jyoti Rani, Assistant professor, school of fashion design and technology. Research and Academic experience. 2 year experience in academics and research. Research area: fashion, textile, natural dyeing, consumer behaviour, AI, merchandising. she has published 28 research paper in refered journal and 5 book chapters.

Rukuan Wei is currently a PhD candidate in Education at Teesside University (UK) and a lecturer at Zhujiang College, Guangzhou. He holds master's degrees in Musicology and Applied Music Arts from Saint Petersburg State University of Culture and Arts (Russia) and in Economics from Sumy National Agrarian University (Ukraine). His research interests span across arts research, business administration, and economic development in the Guangdong-Hong Kong-Macao Greater Bay Area. He has published several papers in international journals focusing on cultural heritage preservation, regional economic integration, and management. Mr. Wei is a member of the Western Returned Scholars Association, Chinese Folk Orchestra Society, and serves as a researcher at Beijing Folk Arts Intangible Cultural Heritage Research Institute. He is also an accomplished musician and has received multiple awards in international music competitions.

S. Deepa is currently working as Assistant Professor in the Department of Computer Science and Engineering in SRM Institute of Science and Technology (Ramapuram Campus). She received her BE (CSE) from Sri Venkateswara College of Engineering and Technology, Madras University, ME (CSE) from Jaya Engineering College, Anna University and PhD from College of Engineering, Anna University. She has 16 years of teaching experience, and she has published more than 30 papers in reputed journals and conferences. She has 2 patents. She is an active member in ISTE. She has published 2 books in her discipline. Her research interest includes Image processing and Pattern Recognition. She also hosted many FDP, workshop and seminar and key role in accreditation activities.

Fahad Salendab is a scholar and leader in the field of higher education, holding a Ph.D. in Educational Administration. As a Licensed Professional Teacher and Associate Professor, he has dedicated his career to advancing the quality of education through research, teaching, and leadership. A multi-awarded faculty member, Dr. Salendab is recognized for his outstanding contributions to education, research, and institutional development. He is a registered author with the National Book Development Board (NBDB). His commitment to research is further reflected in his role as an Associate Member of the DOST–National Research Council of the Philippines, where he collaborates on initiatives that address critical issues in education and development. He also serves as an editorial board member for various national and international research journals, contributing to the advancement of scholarly publishing and peer-reviewed academic discourse. As an active participant in accreditation processes, Dr. Salendab ensures the continuous improvement of academic programs, demonstrating his dedication to quality assurance and institutional growth.

Kaye Shelton is a University Professor of Educational Leadership at Lamar University in the Center for Doctoral Studies. In this role, she teaches doctoral courses and chairs dissertation studies. She has chaired more than 100 completed dissertation studies since 2011. Previously, as Dean of Online Education for Dallas Baptist University, she led the development and ongoing operations of online programs with over 55 majors and degrees offered fully online. She is a certified online instructor and has taught online since 1999. In addition, Dr. Shelton works nationally and internationally with the OLC Quality Scorecard for the Administration of Online Programs. She is also an Online Learning Consortium Quality Scorecard program evaluator and teaches workshops regarding its implementation. Dr. Shelton has been involved with research in online education since 1997 and has advised peer institutions regarding the creation of online learning programs and best practices for teaching online and faculty support. An inductee of the Texas

Distance Learning Hall of Fame, an Online Learning Consortium Fellow, and winner of both the Blackboard and eLearning exemplary online course awards, she has published articles and book chapters along with An Administrator's Guide to Online Education. Dr. Shelton was awarded a Sloan-C Effective Practice award for her research regarding the Quality Scorecard for the Administration of Online Education Programs and the John R. Bourne award for Outstanding Achievement in Online Education.

Serap Uğur graduated from an undergraduate program in "Computer Education and Instructional Technology" at Anadolu University and the master degree of the same program and doctorate degree of the Distance Education. She worked as a lecturer at the Distance Education Department of Open Education Faculty. She currently works as a Asst. Prof. at the Education Faculty. Sisman-Ugur works research and development activities&projects in fields such as e-learning content types, digital storytelling, animation, game-based learning, gamification, instructional design, crosscultural aspects, artificial intelligence, individual differences and human-computer interaction. She interested in technological singularity and transhumanism. She was Social Media Coordinator of Anadolu University Open Education System, Social Media Unit Manager of Anadolu University and Vice of Corporate Communication Coordinator of Anadolu University, Vice Coordinator Internship and Practice Courses, Coordinator of the Social Media and Digital Security Education, Research and Application Center. Uğur is currently working as Assistant Professor at Anadolu University Education Faculty.

Kendatu L. Tago is a Licensed Professional Teacher and a seasoned academic with a strong background in education, currently serving as an Associate Professor V at Sultan Kudarat State University. With an extensive career in education, he has steadily advanced through various academic ranks, demonstrating expertise in teaching, research, and mentorship. He holds a Bachelor of Secondary Education from Mindanao State University and a Master of Arts in Social Studies from Sultan Kudarat State University. He has also completed the academic requirements (CAR) for a Ph.D. in Peace and Development at Notre Dame University-Cotabato City. His professional qualifications include passing the Professional Board Examination for Teachers, solidifying his credentials as an educator. Beyond academia, Professor Tago also holds a National Certificate II in Building and Wiring Installation, showcasing his diverse technical skills. His career is marked by dedication to education, leadership in higher learning, and a commitment to community development.

Liu Wenpang, male, Chinese, professional leader of Liaocheng Infant Normal School, Deputy director of the Entrepreneur Committee of Shandong Provincial Committee of Zhigong Party, member of Zhigong Party of China, senior engineer, senior technician, education doctoral student of Teesside University, Registered Information Security Engineer (CISO), with National Computer Rank Examination Level II certificate, High-level talents of Hainan Province.

Goh Ying Soon is a senior lecturer, and he currently teaches Mandarin as the third language to non-native learners in MARA University of Technology, Malaysia. He is a member of the International Society for Chinese Language Teaching. He has experiences in teaching Mandarin at primary, secondary and tertiary level for more than 25 years. He has been actively presenting papers in national and international conferences. His research interests are on the use of educational technology in Mandarin teaching and learning, web-based instruction, translation, and etc. Updated resume: click here (dropbox). Google Scholar record. researchgate, academia.edu, cnki, scopus (Author ID: 25925392000), book publication, http://www.researcherid .com/rid/U-7238-2017, http://myrid.gov.my/2014-1221-3221

Index

Symbols

A

C

D

E

N

P

R

S

T

V

W

www.ingramcontent.com/pod-product-compliance
Lightning Source LLC
LaVergne TN
LVHW060007031026
849161LV00025B/2245
9798337351025